Lecture Notes in Computer Science 14043

Founding Editors

Gerhard Goos
Juris Hartmanis

Editorial Board Members

The series Lecture Notes in Computer Science (LNCS), including its subseries Lecture Notes in Artificial Intelligence (LNAI) and Lecture Notes in Bioinformatics (LNBI), has established itself as a medium for the publication of new developments in computer science and information technology research, teaching, and education.

LNCS enjoys close cooperation with the computer science R & D community, the series counts many renowned academics among its volume editors and paper authors, and collaborates with prestigious societies. Its mission is to serve this international community by providing an invaluable service, mainly focused on the publication of conference and workshop proceedings and postproceedings. LNCS commenced publication in 1973.

Qin Gao · Jia Zhou
Editors

Human Aspects of IT for the Aged Population

9th International Conference, ITAP 2023
Held as Part of the 25th HCI International Conference, HCII 2023
Copenhagen, Denmark, July 23–28, 2023
Proceedings, Part II

 Springer

Editors
Qin Gao
Tsinghua University
Beijing, China

Jia Zhou
Chongqing University
Chongqing, China

ISSN 0302-9743 ISSN 1611-3349 (electronic)
Lecture Notes in Computer Science
ISBN 978-3-031-34916-4 ISBN 978-3-031-34917-1 (eBook)
https://doi.org/10.1007/978-3-031-34917-1

This Springer imprint is published by the registered company Springer Nature Switzerland AG
The registered company address is: Gewerbestrasse 11, 6330 Cham, Switzerland

Foreword

Human-computer interaction (HCI) is acquiring an ever-increasing scientific and industrial importance, as well as having more impact on people's everyday lives, as an ever-growing number of human activities are progressively moving from the physical to the digital world. This process, which has been ongoing for some time now, was further accelerated during the acute period of the COVID-19 pandemic. The HCI International (HCII) conference series, held annually, aims to respond to the compelling need to advance the exchange of knowledge and research and development efforts on the human aspects of design and use of computing systems.

The 25th International Conference on Human-Computer Interaction, HCI International 2023 (HCII 2023), was held in the emerging post-pandemic era as a 'hybrid' event at the AC Bella Sky Hotel and Bella Center, Copenhagen, Denmark, during July 23–28, 2023. It incorporated the 21 thematic areas and affiliated conferences listed below.

A total of 7472 individuals from academia, research institutes, industry, and government agencies from 85 countries submitted contributions, and 1578 papers and 396 posters were included in the volumes of the proceedings that were published just before the start of the conference, these are listed below. The contributions thoroughly cover the entire field of human-computer interaction, addressing major advances in knowledge and effective use of computers in a variety of application areas. These papers provide academics, researchers, engineers, scientists, practitioners and students with state-of-the-art information on the most recent advances in HCI.

The HCI International (HCII) conference also offers the option of presenting 'Late Breaking Work', and this applies both for papers and posters, with corresponding volumes of proceedings that will be published after the conference. Full papers will be included in the 'HCII 2023 - Late Breaking Work - Papers' volumes of the proceedings to be published in the Springer LNCS series, while 'Poster Extended Abstracts' will be included as short research papers in the 'HCII 2023 - Late Breaking Work - Posters' volumes to be published in the Springer CCIS series.

I would like to thank the Program Board Chairs and the members of the Program Boards of all thematic areas and affiliated conferences for their contribution towards the high scientific quality and overall success of the HCI International 2023 conference. Their manifold support in terms of paper reviewing (single-blind review process, with a minimum of two reviews per submission), session organization and their willingness to act as goodwill ambassadors for the conference is most highly appreciated.

This conference would not have been possible without the continuous and unwavering support and advice of Gavriel Salvendy, founder, General Chair Emeritus, and Scientific Advisor. For his outstanding efforts, I would like to express my sincere appreciation to Abbas Moallem, Communications Chair and Editor of HCI International News.

July 2023   Constantine Stephanidis

HCI International 2023 Thematic Areas and Affiliated Conferences

Thematic Areas

- HCI: Human-Computer Interaction
- HIMI: Human Interface and the Management of Information

Affiliated Conferences

- EPCE: 20th International Conference on Engineering Psychology and Cognitive Ergonomics
- AC: 17th International Conference on Augmented Cognition
- UAHCI: 17th International Conference on Universal Access in Human-Computer Interaction
- CCD: 15th International Conference on Cross-Cultural Design
- SCSM: 15th International Conference on Social Computing and Social Media
- VAMR: 15th International Conference on Virtual, Augmented and Mixed Reality
- DHM: 14th International Conference on Digital Human Modeling and Applications in Health, Safety, Ergonomics and Risk Management
- DUXU: 12th International Conference on Design, User Experience and Usability
- C&C: 11th International Conference on Culture and Computing
- DAPI: 11th International Conference on Distributed, Ambient and Pervasive Interactions
- HCIBGO: 10th International Conference on HCI in Business, Government and Organizations
- LCT: 10th International Conference on Learning and Collaboration Technologies
- ITAP: 9th International Conference on Human Aspects of IT for the Aged Population
- AIS: 5th International Conference on Adaptive Instructional Systems
- HCI-CPT: 5th International Conference on HCI for Cybersecurity, Privacy and Trust
- HCI-Games: 5th International Conference on HCI in Games
- MobiTAS: 5th International Conference on HCI in Mobility, Transport and Automotive Systems
- AI-HCI: 4th International Conference on Artificial Intelligence in HCI
- MOBILE: 4th International Conference on Design, Operation and Evaluation of Mobile Communications

List of Conference Proceedings Volumes Appearing Before the Conference

47. CCIS 1836, HCI International 2023 Posters - Part V, edited by Constantine Stephanidis, Margherita Antona, Stavroula Ntoa and Gavriel Salvendy

https://2023.hci.international/proceedings

Preface

The 9th International Conference on Human Aspects of IT for the Aged Population (ITAP 2023) was part of HCI International 2023. The ITAP conference addresses the design, adaptation, and use of IT technologies targeted for the use of older people in order to counterbalance ability changes due to age, support cognitive, physical, and social activities, and maintain independent living and quality of life.

This year's proceedings address a variety of topics. Researchers from all over the world shared their findings on how older people accept and use new technologies to stay informed and connected, how they develop ICT competencies and skills, and how such understanding informs the design and development of technologies to support and empower older people. In particular, a research theme that attracts much attention in this year's proceedings is how to design immersive and playful experience–through the use of XR technologies and game design–to provide supportive functions for older people, such as promoting physical activity and maintaining cognitive functions, in addition to its entertainment value. Furthermore, an emerging theme of this year is the design of IT support for both formal and informal caregivers for older people. These changes highlight the importance of making IT applications and services an enjoyable, engaging, and integral part of older people's lives.

Two volumes of the HCII 2023 proceedings are dedicated to this year's edition of the ITAP conference. The first part focuses on topics related to designing and assessing the older user's experience, older people's use of social media and its impact, design of voice assistants and chatbots, games and exergames for older people, as well as research on XR experiences for older people. The second part focuses on topics related to smart homes and other technologies supporting aging in place, eHealth applications for older people and their health literacy, IT support for caregivers, as well as socioeconomic views on ICT use and digital literacy of older people.

Papers of these volumes are included for publication after a minimum of two single-blind reviews from the members of the ITAP Program Board or, in some cases, from members of the Program Boards of other affiliated conferences. We would like to thank all of them for their invaluable contribution, support, and efforts.

July 2023

Qin Gao
Jia Zhou

9th International Conference on Human Aspects of IT for the Aged Population (ITAP 2023)

The full list with the Program Board Chairs and the members of the Program Boards of all thematic areas and affiliated conferences of HCII2023 is available online at:

http://www.hci.international/board-members-2023.php

HCI International 2024 Conference

The 26th International Conference on Human-Computer Interaction, HCI International 2024, will be held jointly with the affiliated conferences at the Washington Hilton Hotel, Washington, DC, USA, June 29 – July 4, 2024. It will cover a broad spectrum of themes related to Human-Computer Interaction, including theoretical issues, methods, tools, processes, and case studies in HCI design, as well as novel interaction techniques, interfaces, and applications. The proceedings will be published by Springer. More information will be made available on the conference website: http://2024.hci.international/.

General Chair
Prof. Constantine Stephanidis
University of Crete and ICS-FORTH
Heraklion, Crete, Greece
Email: general_chair@hcii2024.org

https://2024.hci.international/

Contents – Part II

IT Support for Caregivers

Aging, ICT Use and Digital Literacy

Contents – Part I

Aging and Social Media

Voice Assistants and Chatbots

Games and Exergames for Older People

XR Experiences and Aging

Smart Homes and Aging in Place

Smart Homes and Aging in Place

An Iterative Approach to User-Centered Design of Smart Home Systems

Lauren C. Cerino[✉], Chaiwoo Lee, Sheng-Hung Lee, Shabnam Fakhr-Hosseini, Heesuk Son, Shen Shen, and Joseph F. Coughlin

Massachusetts Institute of Technology, AgeLab, Cambridge, MA 02142, USA
lcerino@mit.edu

Abstract. Recent technological advances have brought smart homes to the forefront of innovation, transforming the home into a platform that can support residents' connectivity and care. Smart home systems promise a more convenient and comfortable lifestyle for people across ages and of different living arrangements, for example improving older adults' ability to safely age in place. The present study aims to illustrate how an iterative design process with user involvement and evaluation in real-world settings could be used to inform and facilitate the development of an integrated, remotely-deployed smart home technology system. An experimental smart home prototype was developed to demonstrate a secure, scalable service model addressing future home service needs. The process was informed by user-centered design methods and iteratively refined based on feedback from target users. This study demonstrates key considerations for design researchers and practitioners in designing user studies that can provide a comprehensive, holistic understanding of the user experience and, in turn, most effectively inform future design decisions.

Keywords: Iterative Design · User-Centered Design · Smart Home Systems · Aging in Place · Field Study

1 Introduction

Recent technological advances have brought smart homes to the forefront of innovation, transforming the home into a platform that can support residents. As of 2020, the smart home market was expected to reach USD 317 billion by 2026, up 5% from pre-COVID-19 forecasts [1].

User-centered design is a framework for a design process that optimizes the usability and acceptance of a system by involving users in the development of a product [2, 3]. According to Gulliksen et al. [4] and Buurman [5], when using a user-centered design approach, products should be developed based on an interdisciplinary design team; knowledge of users' needs, abilities, attitudes, and characteristics; and an iterative approach to design with active user involvement. Iterative design is defined by the World Design Organization [6] as "a design methodology based on a cyclic process of

© The Author(s), under exclusive license to Springer Nature Switzerland AG 2023
Q. Gao and J. Zhou (Eds.): HCII 2023, LNCS 14043, pp. 3–16, 2023.
https://doi.org/10.1007/978-3-031-34917-1_1

prototyping, testing, analyzing, and refining a product or process. Based on the results of testing the most recent iteration of a design, changes and refinements are made."

Another important factor in user-centered design is the involvement of a diverse range of users in the iterative design and evaluation process. Some demographic groups, such as older adults, have historically been underrepresented in user research. Older adults can benefit greatly from adopting smart home technologies [7]. Various smart home technologies have the potential to fulfill common needs of older adults including everyday tasks such as personal care and housework, social connectedness and companionship, health monitoring, home security and maintenance, and more [8]. Technology-enabled support for these tasks can facilitate aging in place, allowing older adults to remain independently in their homes for longer [9]. Thus, older adults have the potential to be key users of smart home technologies, but their exclusion from user research results in products that may not meet their unique needs and abilities.

Past research has explored the benefits and challenges of user-centered design, demonstrating the value of participatory and iterative approaches to designing smart home systems for older adults [10–12]. Wilson et al. [13] evaluated the usability of a robot system designed to provide in-home support for individuals requiring assistance with basic and instrumental activities of daily living (ADLs) in the smart home environment. The system was tested with target users in a smart home testbed environment and then collecting and analyzing feedback. Other research has explored the co-creation approach, e.g., leveraging additional stakeholders; Ghods et al. [14] described the iterative design of an interactive graphical interface for remote in-home monitoring of aging patients, as informed by feedback from an experienced set of health professionals who used the system in a real-world setting. Results indicated that this approach resulted in improved usability over iterations.

In order to most effectively assess products, user feedback is most valuable when research takes place in real-world environments. For example, in Wilson et al. [13], the system was tested in a testbed environment and the procedure was reliant on "scripted activities." Although participants provided valuable feedback that informed a better understanding of target user needs, researchers outlined the needs to test smart home systems in more realistic settings (e.g., the home) over longer periods of time such that the aptitude of the system to meet real-world user needs could be more accurately assessed.

Smart home research involving user testing in in-home settings has traditionally required researchers to make in-person visits for installation, participant training, ongoing support and maintenance, data collection, and study closure [15]. However, the COVID-19 pandemic has rendered these in-person visits less feasible. Thus, new approaches to system deployment for user testing that allow for self-installation and remote deployment have been required. Although potentially complicated in a technical sense, the need for new approaches presents an opportunity to design procedures that more closely reflect a realistic smart home experience.

The present study aims to illustrate how an iterative design process with user involvement and evaluation in real-world settings could be used to inform and facilitate the development of an integrated, remotely-deployed smart home technology system.

2 The Iterative Design Process

To inform the selection of components and the design of features, implementation, and development for a first prototype, key user needs were identified based on a review of past literature, user interviews, and a large-scale online survey [16]. The initial prototype was built with these user needs in mind then refined based on user feedback from an in-home pilot study. With the refined version 1 prototype, an in-home field study was completed to collect insights to inform future design. A second version of the prototype implemented new design considerations based on feedback from the main field study and researcher learnings. In the future, the second version will be piloted and fielded.

The overall design process, which can be conceptualized as an ongoing cycle of human-centered and iterative design principles, extends upon the design thinking approach described by IDEO [3] and Nielsen Norman Group [17]. The process is depicted in Fig. 1.

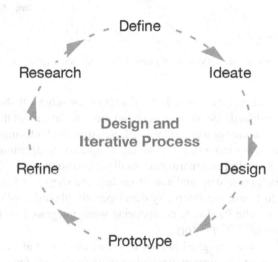

Fig. 1. Overall depiction of the cyclical design and iterative process.

2.1 Development of the First Prototype

Initial Ideation and Concept Development
The prototype was built with the goal of providing users with useful information about themselves and their home, as well as companionship. Logistically, the system would be low-cost and efficient, with advanced data analytics capabilities. It would also be scalable for future research and possible to deploy remotely.

In addition to considerations regarding remote deployment, one key goal was to achieve system versatility for supporting various smart home use cases. Due to the vastness of possible use cases and user needs, a targeted set of use cases and related user needs was required. A large set of use cases was identified based upon a set of user interviews, a large-scale online survey [16, 18], and a review of past studies [15]. Then, eleven diverse participants were interviewed about their routines, pain points, and expectations for smart homes. Ten key needs and concerns related to safety, convenience, self-care, and family care were identified and analyzed alongside the earlier findings. Finally, with feedback from industry experts, three of the most practical and feasible use cases were selected. The final set of use cases was safety and security, caregiving needs, and home energy and environment control. The overall process of identifying user needs is depicted in Fig. 2.

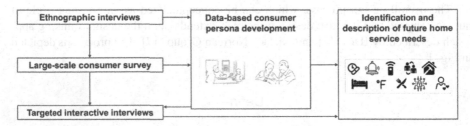

Fig. 2. Process of identifying user needs before condensing to a set of three.

The initial physical prototype consisted of a set of low-cost, off-the-shelf hardware components that could facilitate awareness of and provide data about the home environment. An internet-connected power strip was selected to collect information about power usage. Sensors addressing motion, light, sound, air quality, temperature, and humidity were affixed on a wooden frame, creating a centralized "sensor module" for easy shipping and installation. The power strip and sensor module are shown in Fig. 3. An Android tablet was chosen to house the internally-developed dashboard application and serve as the user interface. The hardware components were integrated with the dashboard application using the IFTTT[1] platform.

The user interface was designed to provide information that allows users to understand in-home activity and to support the final set of use cases. Six features were selected and developed for the dashboard application: Today, Climate, Activity, Energy Use, Alerts, and Wellness. As depicted in Fig. 4, these features leverage data from the hardware (e.g., sensor module and power strip) in addition to user input on the dashboard.

An iterative process was used to design the dashboard interface, during which mockups were drawn (see Fig. 5) and evaluated based on the identified user needs. The finalized dashboard application interface, as shown in Fig. 6, summarizes information about each of the features and relevant data. A menu bar is static on the left side of the interface, and users can use these buttons to seek more information about each of the features and navigate between pages at any time.

As depicted in Fig. 7, back-end dashboard support was implemented via AWS EC2 server optimization and stabilization for concurrent data transactions, and HTTPS-based secure data transmission.

---

[1] If This Then That – An online digital automation platform for integration of devices, apps, and services using conditional statements. https://ifttt.com/.

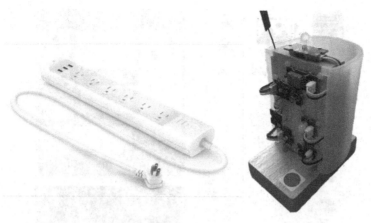

Fig. 3. The power strip on the left and finalized sensor module on the right.

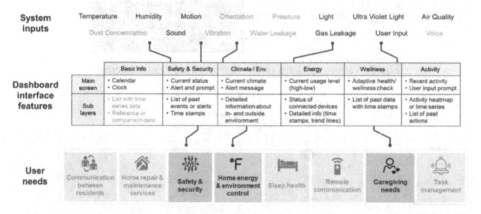

Fig. 4. Depiction of relationships between user needs, system inputs, and interface features.

The prototypes were accompanied by a comprehensive user instruction document to guide participants through the installation and usage of the prototype in an accessible, user-friendly manner. The document consisted of plain-language, step-by-step instructions and troubleshooting advice for potential obstacles, as well as helpful illustrations and screenshots. The document was designed based on a full walkthrough of the installation process and relevant user preferences as identified in earlier interviews and surveys.

Refining the First Prototype based on User Feedback
The first prototype was refined based on feedback from two small pilot studies. The main intent of the first pilot study was to gather insights and feedback that could inform modifications to the installation and operation processes before piloting the larger-scale field study. The prototypes were packaged and delivered directly to a convenience sample of 8 participants' homes. The goal was to determine whether participants were able to install the kit themselves without onsite support from researchers. After some minor

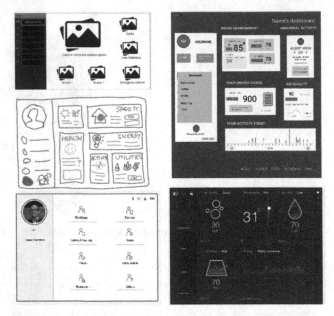

Fig. 5. Various mockups for the dashboard application interface.

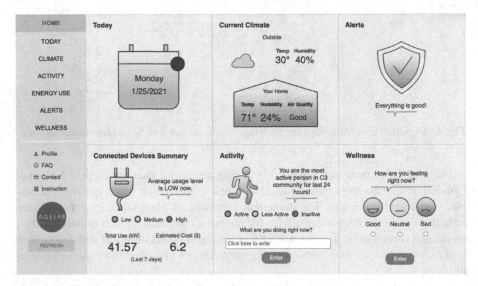

Fig. 6. The finalized Homepage for the dashboard application interface.

refinements to the self-installation process based on the initial feedback, 5 externally recruited participants completed the second pilot study in accordance with the field study procedure as depicted in Fig. 8. These pilot study participants' characteristics are described in Table 1.

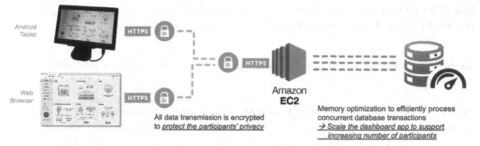

Fig. 7. Back-end implementation.

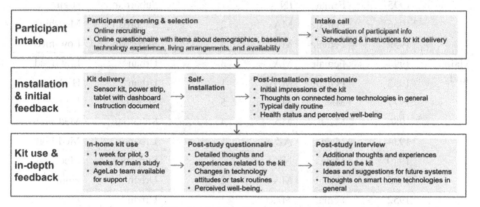

Fig. 8. Field study procedure.

Survey results indicated that, although participants found the self-installation process to be quite easy, older participants found the self-installation process to be more challenging than younger participants did. Many participants cited particular issues with installing the sensor module. Because the camera on the included Android tablet was low-resolution, the participants who used the tablet reported challenges with the QR-code-based pairing of the sensor module. As a result of this unforeseen challenge, researchers made the decision to complete this pairing prior to shipping to participants such that participants would only need to reconnect the paired system to their WiFi upon its arrival. Nonetheless, ongoing challenges and failures with this portion of the process resulted in frustration and made the overall installation process considerably more time-consuming, indicating a need for more detailed instructions and troubleshooting guidance in the instruction manual.

Aside from challenges with the sensor module, survey ratings and interview feedback suggested that the manual was successful in facilitating a seamless installation process. One participant said: "My compliments on the instructions. Nicely done, step by step, clear and photos were awesome. Nice touch putting the email login info at the top right corner. This is all thinking out loud, but it may reflect some elements of what the public might be thinking too." Minor improvements were suggested to indicate where components should most ideally be placed in the home. In addition, survey results showed that older participants had difficulties in using small hardware components, suggesting the need to improve the design and interface of the sensor module.

Table 1. Demographic information for participants of the field study; both the pilot study and the main study.

Study category	Birth year	Gender	Location[a]	Household size	Residential environment	Technology savviness[b]
Pilot study	1997	Female	MA	2	Urban	High
	1953	Female	MA	1	Suburban	Med-high
	1995	Female	IN	1	Suburban	High
	1966	Female	MA	2	Suburban	Med-high
	1959	Female	MA	3	Suburban	Low-med
Main study	1994	Female	MA	3	Urban	Low-med
	1953	Female	MA	1	Urban	High
	1977	Male	MA	5	Suburban	High
	1986	Male	MA	4	Suburban	Med-high
	1934	Male	AZ	1	Urban	Med-high
	1940	Male	NY	2	Suburban	Med-high
	1995	Female	MA	2	Urban	High
	1952	Female	MA	1	Urban	Low
	1990	Female	CA	3	Suburban	High
	1974	Female	OH	2	Suburban	Med
	1977	Female	GA	3	Suburban	Med-high
	1934	Male	WA	2	Urban	High
	1950	Male	FL	2	Urban	Med-high
	1984	Female	NC	5	Suburban	Med-high

[a] State name abbreviation. All participants lived in the United States
[b] Assessed using three questions regarding technology experience and attitudes: 1) How would you rate your overall level of trust in technology? (Answer options ranging from "very low trust" to "very high trust"); 2) How interested are you in learning about new technologies? (Answer options ranging from "not interested at all" to "very interested"); and 3) In general, how would you rate yourself as being an avoider or an early adopter of new technology? (Answer options ranging from "avoid as long as possible" to "try as soon as possible")

Finalizing the Prototype and Gathering User Evaluations
Based on user feedback received during the pilot, various changes were made to finalize the prototype before beginning the field study. The sensor module frame was modified to add a plastic covering over the sensors. This alleviated some of the dexterity-related challenges experienced by older participants and added a layer of physical protection

to the individual sensors, some of which had been damaged in shipment. To address the possibility of future changes to data privacy-related requirements, the architecture of the prototype was refined to more easily accommodate new changes. The Google Home voice assistant was excluded; first, it was solely an extra mode of interaction without supporting any use cases, and second, it presented some privacy concerns. The instruction document was updated to provide more examples and clarity, with specific attention to the section focused on installing the sensor module. The dashboard features remained the same.

A total of 14 technologically- and demographically-diverse participants received the newly-updated prototype and went through the field study procedure (as depicted in Fig. 8). Participants provided feedback via surveys and an interview.

Although the exposure to the kit resulted in significantly greater willingness to adopt new technologies, the dashboard features did not offer high practical value to participants [19]. Participants rated the climate, energy use, and menu bar features as most useful; they rated participant support, alerts, and wellness the least useful. Participants rated the kit highly for ease-of-use and the self-installation process was generally successful for most participants.

2.2 Making Revisions for the Second Prototype

Design Implications and Recommendations Identified from the Previous Version
In designing the second version of the prototype, design implications were largely informed by participant feedback from the field study as well as limitations identified by researchers throughout fielding. Some general qualities of the prototype were demonstrated with version 1, but desired to be improved for version 2. These qualities included interactivity, privacy, scalability in development and deployment, and ease of use. New priorities for version 2 included customizability in features and interface, additional convenience and information features for health and housework support, and additional security features.

Design implications for the second prototype were largely informed by the results of the field study. An updated set of features and functionalities for the dashboard application was required. An effort was made to maintain and improve the features from version 1 that participants liked and found useful (e.g., indoor and outdoor environment information, device use monitoring, and activity level indicator). Possible additional features suggested by participants involved needs related to task management (e.g., calendar, shopping list), device management, wellbeing monitoring, health statistics, and multi-room activity recording. Participants also expressed a desire to be able to interact with a more advanced set of data collection and analysis capabilities (e.g., to view both real-time and historical data displays). Participants also suggested implementing the ability to personalize the dashboard according to their preferences; for example, to hide a feature that is not relevant to their needs.

Researchers also identified some potential technical design changes throughout the field study. Limitations in the development of the prototype included limited and static sensing capability and data stream, reliance on a central server in the cloud, and unopti-mized software implementation and hardware build. Updates to the display of informa-tion were done infrequently. There were also logistical restrictions in the deployment and management of the prototype throughout the field study. Between participants, manual code babysitting and resetting of the kit was required, which resulted in a long turnaround time (e.g., kits needed to be shipped back and manually reset before being shipped to the next participant).

Selection and Integration of Components and Features
A small collection of individual, off-the-shelf sensors were selected to replace the orig-inal sensor module. Using separate sensors allows participants to place them as desired throughout their home. The off-the-shelf sensors also reduce the need for manual techni-cal maintenance, facilitating a more streamlined integration process from a development and installation standpoint. The same power strip and tablet were kept based on mini-mal issues from a user and research standpoint. The main peripherals, power strip and sensors, are shown in Fig. 9.

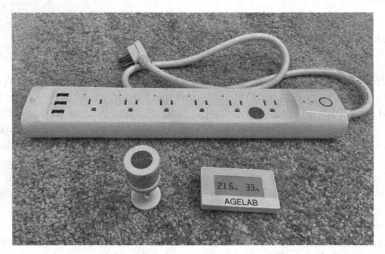

Fig. 9. Selected hardware for version 2 of the kit. Wifi-enabled power strip (top), Zigbee-enabled motion sensor (bottom left), and Zigbee-enabled air quality monitor (bottom right).

To address various needs identified by both users and researchers, and to test and evaluate how an alternative system may impact users' experiences, a decision was made to create a new dashboard application and implement a new system of integration for the second version of the kit. The new dashboard application was developed and integrated with the hardware using Home Assistant, an open source software for home automation, and a Raspberry Pi and Zigbee hub host the instance of Home Assistant.

The Home Assistant platform is designed for easily connecting to a large variety of off-the-shelf devices and systems and supports increased scalability compared to the previous dashboard, which was optimized to fit selected components. The change to this system may address needs identified by researchers around optimization of the software implementation, deployment, and management; for example, there is no longer a need for manual code babysitting and resetting throughout deployment. Additionally, for users, the change may reduce the complexity of and avoid problems with the setup process by allowing off-the-shelf components to be paired to the interface by researchers prior to shipment.

The system also addresses concerns expressed by many field study participants regarding privacy and data security. Some had concerns related directly to the kit, and others had concerns related to smart home technology in general. The new implementation may mitigate these user privacy concerns by utilizing a more familiar platform with an emphasis on local control and privacy, and by storing user data locally rather than on a cloud-based central server.

Updates to the dashboard addressed many of the preferences and recommendations expressed by participants during the first field study. On the new interface, summaries of each feature are displayed across four categorized columns, or "panels," on a homepage. The panels are Home Environment, which consists of blocks for externally-sourced weather, indoor humidity and temperature, light brightness, and motion; Energy Usage, which consists of blocks for powerstrip outlets, total energy consumption, and outlet-specific consumption; Health and Wellbeing, which consists of externally-sourced, widespread health data, a wellbeing index with symbols for reporting, and externally-sourced modules for leisure such as Wordle and Cute Animals; and Task Assistance, which consists of an interactive functional calendar and a shopping list. Users can efficiently view further information, such as historical data about energy consumption, by tapping on the feature. The finalized interface is shown in Fig. 10.

Fig. 10. The user interface for the version 2 dashboard with all features visible.

To address user feedback around a desire to personalize the system, the new dashboard application includes features that support greater user customizability. The dashboard allows users to simplify the layout of the full main interface (as shown in Fig. 10) based on their priorities; for example, users may choose to hide or minimize panels that they are not interested in or move higher-priority features to the top. Users may also personalize within panels. Labels and icons can be designated for each of the powerstrip outlets within the Energy Usage panel, and an interactive calendar—which additionally supports identified needs around task management—was added. All personalizations are optional such that there is no negative impact or change to the overall functionality for users who prefer not to customize.

Researchers identified the potential to incorporate externally-sourced information and interactivity. Thus, the updated system leverages third-party integrations offered by Home Assistant that may support the user experience and enhance engagement, such as broad public health data from the CDC and widgets for playing a word game (Wordle) and displaying uplifting photos (Cute Animals).

3 Conclusion

3.1 Implications

The pilot and field studies demonstrated key considerations for design researchers and practitioners in designing user studies that can provide a holistic understanding of the user experience and, in turn, most effectively inform future design decisions.

When recruiting participants, researchers and practitioners should make an effort to include users that represent all aspects of the target group in terms of both demographics and technology experience. For example, the field study found that evaluations of usefulness varied between participants of different demographic characteristics and technology experience. Involving a diverse group of individuals results in a better understanding of needs and experiences that people of different characteristics may have, and generates insights for addressing requirements that may vary across target user segments.

When seeking insights that will hold true in a real-world setting, a user's experience with a product should reflect their real-world experience as closely as possible. Thus, when possible, users testing a product in their natural environment (e.g., in users' own homes for smart home products) is most ideal. Field study participants were able to share valuable insights on things that would likely not be observed in a typical lab setting, such as how the prototype affected their everyday routine, usage dynamics with other members of their household, and variations in usage by housing type. In addition to the environmental dimension, a longer-term study can result in more meaningful insights than a short-term engagement. Placing the product in participants' homes for a longer period of time allows a more comprehensive observation of changes in usage behavior beyond initial interactions and the learning phase.

When evaluating and analyzing users' experiences, utilizing various methods appropriate for gathering multidimensional feedback is crucial. For example, the design process for the prototype was informed by both quantitative insights from ongoing surveys and qualitative insights from interviews. The more structured, quantitative method allowed trends to be plotted and to do comparisons, whereas the less-structured, qualitative method allowed for variation between participants and provided an opportunity to follow up and ask in-depth questions tailored to participants' individual situations and experiences. Thus, the combination of these two methods for gathering feedback resulted in a significantly more comprehensive understanding of the user experience.

3.2 Future Work

For future iterations of the prototype design and development, the cycle of iteratively refining the prototype based on feedback from real-world user testing will continue. The immediate next step will be to repeat the field study with the finalized second version of the prototype.

Through all cycles of testing and evaluation, insights from participants will be leveraged to learn about how new changes and features, such as the newly-added customizability in the second version, may impact the user experience and acceptance. In general, gathering feedback from a larger and more diverse pool of participants in future iterations of the field study could improve the validity and generalizability of findings and allow for more in-depth comparisons of preferences between users of different characteristics.

Acknowledgment. Support for this study was provided by the MIT AgeLab C3 Connected Home Logistics Consortium.

References

1. Smart Home. Technical Report MD-HAS-117. ABI research (2020). https://www.abiresearch.com/market-research/product/7778940-smart-home/?src=svcrecent
2. Brown, T., Katz, B.: Change by design: how design thinking transforms organizations and inspires innovation. Harper Business, New York (2009)
3. IDEO: The Field Guide to Human Centered Design. Ideo Org (2015)
4. Gulliksen, J., Lantz, A., Boivie, I.: User Centered Design in Practice - Problems and Possibilities (1999)
5. Buurman, R.D.: User-centred design of smart products. Ergonomics **40**, 1159–1169 (1997)
6. WDO Glossary. https://wdo.org/glossary/iterative-design/. Accessed 10 Dec 2022
7. Lee, C.: Technology and aging: the jigsaw puzzle of design, development and distribution. Nat. Aging (2022). https://doi.org/10.1038/s43587-022-00325-6
8. Choi, Y., Lazar, A., Demiris, G., Thompson, H.: Emerging smart home technologies to facilitate engaging with aging. J. Gerontol. Nurs. **45**(12), 41–48 (2019)
9. Wiles, J.L., Leibing, A., Guberman, N., Reeve, J., Allen, R.E.: The meaning of "aging in place" to older people. Gerontologist **52**(3), 357–366 (2012)
10. Ferreira, F., et al.: Elderly centered design for interaction – the case of the s4s medication assistant. Procedia Comput. Sci. **27**, 398–408 (2014). 5th Int. Conf. on Software Development and Technologies for Enhancing Accessibility and Fighting Info-exclusion, DSAI 2013
11. Kanis, M., Robben, S., Hagen, J., Bimmerman, A., Wagelaar, N., Krose, B.: Sensor monitoring in the home: giving voice to elderly people. In: Proceedings of ICTs for improving Patients Rehabilitation Research Techniques, pp. 2–5 (2013)

12. Iacono, I., Marti, P.: Engaging older people with participatory design. In: Proceedings 8th Nordic Conference on Human-Computer Interaction: Fun, Fast, Foundational (NordiCHI 2014), pp. 859–864. ACM, New York (2014)
13. Wilson, G., et al.: Robot-enabled support of daily activities in smart home environments. Cogn. Syst. Res. **54**, 258–272 (2019)
14. Ghods, A., et al.: Iterative design of visual analytics for a clinician-in-the-loop smart home. IEEE J. Biomed. Health Inform. **23**(4), 1742–1748 (2019)
15. Son, H., Lee, C., FakhrHosseini, S., Lee, S., Coughlin, J., Rudnik, J.: Reshaping the smart home research and development in the pandemic era: considerations around scalable and easy-to-install design. Proc. ACM Hum.-Computer Interact. **6**(CSCW1), Article 114 (2022)
16. FakhrHosseini, S., Lee, S.H., Rudnik, J., Son, H., Lee, C., Coughlin, J.: User needs of smart home services. In: Proceedings of the Human Factors and Ergonomics Society Annual Meeting, vol. 65, no. 1, pp. 457–461. SAGE Publications, Los Angeles (2021)
17. Nielson Norman Group Design Thinking 101. https://www.nngroup.com/articles/design-thinking/. Accessed 10 Dec 2022
18. Lee, C., Rudnik, J., Fakhrhosseini, S., Lee, S., Coughlin, J.: Development of data-based personas for user-centered design of the connected home. In: 22nd DMI: Academic Design Management Conference Impact the Future by Design (2020)
19. Cerino, L., FakhrHosseini, S., Lee, C., Lee, S.H., Son, H., Coughlin, J.: Towards a more connected home: user attitudes and perceptions after an integrated home technology exposure. In: Proceedings of the Human Factors and Ergonomics Society Annual Meeting, vol. 66, no. 1, pp. 1917–1921. SAGE Publications, Los Angeles (2022)

Research on Influencing Factors of Elderly User Experience of Smart Home Social Software Based on Grounded Theory

Ke Ma[1]([✉]) [iD], Meng Gao[1], Francesco Ermanno Guida[2], and Renke He[1]

[1] School of Design, Hunan University, Yuelu Area, Changsha 410082, China
{make,meng_gao}@hnu.edu.cn
[2] Dipartimento di Design, Politecnico di Milano, Bovisa, 20158 Milan, Italy
francesco.guida@polimi.it

Abstract. As a new generation of essential terminals for future homes environment, smart home has become one of the important media for smart home care, which has the potential to improve the social participation of the elderly at home, but the utilization rate is not high, and the user experience is not good. It mainly explores the influencing factors of user experience design of young elderly people on the use of smart home for social interaction, abstracts and refines layer by layer from the empathy and understanding of young elderly people from bottom to top through the research method of grounded theory and constructs the user experience design influencing factor model of young elderly based on smart home social software through open coding, spindle coding and selective coding. The results show that the model mainly includes user interface quality, interaction quality, content quality and service quality. This study aims to provide theoretical reference and practical guidance for designers and product managers to design smart home-related social software from the perspective of design.

Keywords: Smart-home smart screen · Social media · Chinese younger older adults · User experience design · Grounded Theory · Design influences

1 Introduction

China is in the midst of an aging and digitalized society. On the one hand, China's aging problem is very serious. The seventh national census data released in May 2021 showed that 18.7% of the total population, or 264 million people, are aged 60 and above [1]. At the same time, the director of the National Bureau of Statistics (NBS) stated that the proportion of the lower-aged elderly population aged 60 to 69 reached 55.83%, or about 10.44% of the total population [2]. To solve the problem of aging, the first thing is to solve the problem of old-age care, because China adopts the "90-7-3" pattern of old-age care at home, that is, more than 90% of the old-age care at home in China. The first issue confronting a large number of elderly people living alone and empty nesters is how to meet their social participation needs. According to the continuity theory [3], these personal and social factors can cause a lack of social interaction with the rest of society,

Q. Gao and J. Zhou (Eds.): HCII 2023, LNCS 14043, pp. 17–30, 2023.
https://doi.org/10.1007/978-3-031-34917-1_2

resulting in social isolation of the elderly, due to declines in physical function, mobility, retirement from work, a shrinking social circle, and the post-epidemic era. They may feel lonely and emotionally unavailable, which can be psychologically damaging. Cacioppo et al. [4] noted that loneliness is associated with and synergistic with depression, which in turn reduces the well-being of older adults. As a result, how to socially engage empty nesters and older adults living alone who are aging at home has emerged as a critical practical issue.

On the other hand, technological progress has made the digital and intelligent era come, accelerating the wisdom and innovation of the family unit system. The smart-home smart screen series is a class of smart-home products that has only started to emerge in recent years. As a new media platform, the smart home smart screen retains the functions of smart speakers, such as voice control and control of the smart home, but also carries out human-computer interaction with users through a large touchable screen, which can carry out operations such as video calling, online chatting, listening to songs and catching up with dramas, and life assistants. Alibaba officially launched its first new smart home wisdom screen - Tmall Genie CC in April 2019, followed by Baidu, Amazon, Google, Xiaomi, Huawei, and other brands, which have also made efforts to release their own smart home products equipped with large wisdom screens. Smart home products are becoming more popular, and their relative ease of access, low cost, and application in home scenarios make them one of the most important products for smart aging. Intelligence and digitization play a big role in helping older people live better. Using smart-home smart screens could help older people be more involved in their communities and give them the chance to take an active role in smart wellness at home. But older adults have trouble taking advantage of the convenience of new technologies and products because their physical and mental differences make them hesitant to try new things. The digital divide makes the adoption of using smart-home smart screens for social behavior relatively low among the elderly population and causes poor user stickiness, mainly because of the poor elderly user experience of smart-home social software. And providing better design for the elderly to have a better user experience can provide inspiration to effectively address the digital divide among the elderly, thus realizing smart aging for the elderly, practicing active aging, and improving the well-being of the aging population. However, few studies have investigated the factors influencing the user experience design of socialization among older adults adopting smart homes.

Therefore, it is an important topic to accurately grasp the user experience design factors that affect the use of smart home social software by the elderly. However, it is currently unclear which design factors influence the aging user experience of smart home social. Due to the different usage contexts, application areas, and target groups, it is not possible to directly adopt the existing information system's user experience influencing factors to improve the aging user experience based on smart home social, which is not only unscientific but also may not be effective. In light of this, this paper uses smart home social software as a point of contact for design intervention and conducts an exploratory nature study on the design influence factors of aging user experience based on smart home social software and its mechanism of action from the perspective of design in order to provide theoretical support and practical guidance for smart home social software developers and designers in order to improve aging user experience.

2 Literature Review

2.1 Information Behavior of Elderly Users Based on Social Interaction

At present, the academic community has focused on psychology, ergonomics, management, information management, and gerontology in the study of social-based information behavior of aging users, focusing on four categories of aging user behavior: adoption/actual use, use motivation/behavioral motivation/motivation, acceptability, and willingness to continue using. Chen et al. (2021) [5] called 57 older adults in Hong Kong, China, to investigate their acceptance of using platform computer technology, and found through questionnaires and focus groups that the influential factors affecting acceptance were personal usage intention and convenience, and that platform computers were perceived to be beneficial for social relationships and communication. In terms of wearable products, Talukder et al. (2020) [6] investigated the predictors of wearable product adoption among 325 Chinese older adults aged 60 years or older, and an empirical study based on the UTAUT2 model found that social influence, performance expectations, functional consistency, self-actualization, and hedonic motivation were positively related to wearable product adoption. In the context of computers, Yu (2020) [7] investigated the antecedent influences of older adults over 60 years of age on Facebook use on computers in Taiwan, China, through questionnaires and interviews, and empirically found that the influences of aging socially included technology use and social force. In terms of social bots, Chen et al. (2020) [8] explored the acceptance of social robots among 103 Hong Kong older adults aged 60 years and older through a questionnaire and an ABAB withdrawal experimental design.

From the above studies, it can be seen that although many scholars have conducted research on the social-based information behavior of aging users, the relevant research at this stage has the following problems: 1. Most of the target groups are all elderly people, while the first-age group, as a special category of people, is very important to study. However, scholars have given limited attention to this group. 2. The research on the social behavior of aging users mainly focuses on computers, smartphones, social robots, wearable products, tablets, and other technical devices, but there is no research on smart homes, which should be due to the fact that smart home wisdom screens belong to a relatively new type of home product.

2.2 Elderly User Experience

American user experience designer and cognitive psychologist Donald Norman and others introduced the concept of user experience (UE or UX) in the mid-1990s [9]. UX is a cross-cutting concept that spans many fields and involves many disciplines, such as psychology, sociology, computer science, and ergonomics. Because of its interdisciplinary nature, there is no unified definition of UE in academic circles. The International Organization for Standardization (ISO) defines "user experience" as the subjective feelings and reactions generated by users when they plan to use or are using a product, service, or system. Tsai et al. (2017) [10] investigated how user interface design affects the user experience of older adults by developing TreeIt, a social application designed for older adults. Through a survey of 111 older adults, the empirical study showed that the main elements of social-based aging user experience influence include system support, user interface design, and navigation. Alzahrani et al. (2021) [11] explored the factors that influence the user experience of using smart home technology, remote monitoring, and telemedicine systems to support healthcare for older adults, using semi-structured interviews with older adults (65 years and older, N = 17), and showed that lack of technology, usability, cost, platform management, infrastructure, and privacy management influence the user experience of using smart homes for older adults. Kalimullah and Sushmitha (2017) [12] In order to investigate how to increase the use of mobile health apps by older adults, a research hypothesis was proposed to implement this idea by examining the factors that influence the user experience of user interface design elements in older adults. They verified through an experiment that the user experience of the elderly changes with the user interface design elements and proposed the influencing factors that affect the user experience of the elderly, i.e., iconic factors, textual factors, and color factors.

From the foregoing, it is clear that although there are more research results on the influencing factors of the user experience, fewer of them are related to the prime-age population, and those focusing on using smart homes for socialization are also not common, and the existing research results do not provide effective explanations for similar behaviors in the smart home environment. Therefore, it is important to conduct research on the factors influencing the design of the user experience of the first-aged population based on smart home socialization to improve their user experience and explore the internal mechanisms of information behavior in the first-aged population. Secondly, most of the types of external variables in the existing studies are the variables in personal factors and social factors of the user experience as independent variables, and there are few design studies conducted with variables in user experience design factors as external variables of the study; therefore, the existing studies are negligent about the design variables of the user experience, which is a blank spot.

Therefore, based on the smart home application context, this paper explores the factors influencing the user experience design of smart home social software with the first-time elderly population as the target population and the emerging medium of the smart-home smart screen from the perspective of design, using the method of programmed rooting theory.

3 Methodology

3.1 Grounded Theory

The rooted theory research method was developed by Anselm Strauss and Barney Glaser (1967) of Columbia University [13]. A research method jointly developed by two scholars, it is a qualitative research method that uses a systematic procedure to collect data on a phenomenon and extracts theories from the empirical data. In 1990, Strauss and Corbin [14] developed a procedural development of grounded theory, where they conceptualized and categorized the survey data in a step-by-step manner and divided the coding into open coding, spindle coding, and selective coding. The three steps are to distill the original data (speech, text, etc.) into initial concepts and initial categories, further excavate the connections between the initial categories to inductively deduce the main categories, and finally analyze the relationships between the main categories and form a relevant theory rooted in the real data.

3.2 Data Collection and Study Subjects

The interview outline is based on desktop research data and will be properly fine-tuned according to the interview content. It contains two major parts: basic information and interview question content. The interview content mainly focuses on four aspects: a basic view on smart home socialization, design dimensions, perception dimensions, and other dimensions. The user group for data collection is mainly the prime-age population, aged 50–65, with experience in using smart home products and who have used smart home products equipped with smart big screens for socializing and entertainment activities. The interviewees were selected by the snowball sampling method, using the semi-structured interview method and contextualized experiment as the two main forms. 24 interviewees were interviewed, 14 of whom conducted online video interviews through WeChat and 10 conducted offline interviews. First, the respondents were introduced to the background, purpose, process, and related terms and concepts of this interview. They signed a user-informed consent form, which promised them that the content of this study was limited to academic use and all data about the users would be kept strictly confidential, and the consent of the respondents was obtained to make audio recordings. Finally, 24 transcripts were made, including 11 males and 13 females, and the voice data were textualized with the help of "Xunfei Hearing," a speech-to-text assistant, resulting in a total of 73,637 words of interview text, or nearly 80,000 words, for post-coding purposes.

4   Research Process

4.1   Open Coding

Open coding is a process of refinement and abstraction in order to implement concepts as well as scope the collected primary interview materials. The researcher must follow a systematic and rigorous normative procedure to gradually extract and condense the large amount of information gathered from the bottom up when using open coding. Open coding entails categorizing the raw material, assigning concepts to the raw statements, and naming them, and further analyzing and comparing them to merge similar concepts to form more generalized subcategories.

Coding Process. In this study, the collected textual materials were processed, and the interview data were analyzed using NVivo, a qualitative analysis software aid developed by QSR. The main processes used by NVivo to process the interview textual materials: selecting materials, writing codes, filing, and establishing a coding system, coding consistency reliability test, and theory construction. To ensure systematic coding, the coding researchers were screened, and two interaction designers were finally identified as coders for the coding phase of this study. Both coders had more than 1 year of experience in using smart home terminals. To ensure that both could strictly follow the process and procedure coding during the coding process, they were given basic training based on NVivo software. The open coding randomly selected 2/3 of the interview text materials, a total of 16, and first carried out the text normalization process, i.e., some repetition, speech-to-text errors, etc. were manually proofread, and then two coders separately imported the normalized interview text materials into NVivo 20.0 software in the form of word documents and conceptualized and categorized the text of the materials. The main process was as follows: by analyzing the interview text sentence by sentence, the statements that did not answer the substantive content were eliminated, and the substantive original statements were distilled into an initial concept and named. In the process of conceptualizing the entire interview text in this way, the newly created initial concept is repeatedly compared with the established initial concept, and if the newly created concept is not consistent with the meaning of any existing concept, then a new concept is created. In this way, the initial conceptualization of the interview text material was achieved.

Reliability Test for Coding Consistency. To ensure the accuracy of the coding, the coding consistency reliability (inter-rater reliability) was tested on the coding results of the open coding generation of the initial concepts and subcategories by the two coders. This computational evaluation process was continuously adjusted and repeated through the computational results until the confidence level reached an acceptable level. The formula for calculating the inter-rater reliability between two coders is shown in Eq. (1) [15]:

$$R = (n \times K)/(1 + (n - 1) \times K) \tag{1}$$

In Eq. (1), the n denotes the number of coders, and K denotes the average agreement between the two coders, and the interaction discriminant reliability between the two coders is obtained by calculating.

To get R the first requirement is K value. Calculate K of the equation as shown in Eq. (2).

$$K_{ab} = \frac{2S}{N_a + N_b} \tag{2}$$

In Eq. (2), the S denotes the number of categorically consistent codes for the two coders, the N_a, and N_b denote the number of codes for each of the two coders, respectively.

Ultimately, the interaction discriminant confidence between the two coders was calculated based on Eqs. (1) and (2).

After initial conceptualization of the interview text by the two coders, coder a obtained 131 initial concepts and coder b obtained 136 initial concepts. After repeated discussions, a total of 109 initial concepts were obtained by synthesis and generalization. As a result, applying Eqs. (1) and (2), the interaction discriminant reliability between the two coders for the initial conceptualization was 0.898. R is 0.898. Normally, if this value is lower than 0.5, then the data needs to be recoded; if the value is lower than 0.8, then the coding result needs to be further revised until it reaches an acceptable level of 0.8 or higher [16]. After adjustment, the interaction discriminant reliability of the initial conceptualization R was 0.898, indicating that the open coding initial conceptualization stage is highly reliable.

On this basis, the two coders used the node (initial concept) combination function of NVivo 20.0 to further refine and cluster the 109 initial concepts based on causality and similarity, and finally coder a abstracted 12 subcategories and coder b abstracted 14 subcategories. After repeated discussions, 10 subcategories, numbered B1-B10, were synthesized and summarized, and after applying formulas (1) and (2), the number of codes S, the total number of codes, and the interaction discriminant reliability R of the two coders for each subcategory were calculated, adjusted, and evaluated during the abstraction and refinement of each subcategory by the two coders, as shown in Table 1. It can be seen that the interaction discriminant reliability of the open-ended coding of the subcategories was greater than 0.8, and more than half of them reached the excellent level of 0.9 or higher, so it can be said that the coding results passed the reliability test.

Table 1. Open coding interaction discriminant reliability

Sub-categories	S	$N_a + N_b$	R
B1 Graphic Features (GF)	9	26	0.818
B2 Information Architecture (IA)	10	24	0.909
B3 Human-Computer Interaction (HCI)	8	20	0.889
B4 Interpersonal Interaction (HI)	11	25	0.936
B5 Intelligence (INT)	9	23	0.878
B6 Socialization (SOC)	11	27	0.898
B7 Shareability (SHA)	10	22	0.952
B8 User Generated Content (UGC)	8	18	0.941
B9 Social Security (SE)	10	27	0.851
B10 Empathy (EMP)	11	26	0.917

Coding Results. In the open coding stage, two coders synthesized and abstracted 109 initial concepts to form 28 initial concepts, numbered a1-a28. The original interview representative statements, corresponding initial concepts, and subcategories obtained from the open coding are shown in Table 2 below. Due to space limitations, only one original interview statement and initial concept are listed for each subcategory formation.

4.2 Spindle Coding

Coding Process. On the basis of the open coding, the spindle coding was further developed by considering and comparing the initial concept with the sub-categories in order to make a generalization. To ensure that the results of the spindle coding are scientific

Table 2. Open coding categorizations (partial)

Original statement	Categorizations
Our eyesight is not particularly good; I have farsightedness, and my partner is a bit nearsighted, so we both can't see the words on the screen very clearly. I believe the smart home screen text is still much larger than the phone, especially for our poor eyesight. Especially the lyrics, which I can see very clearly. (Text features)	B1 Graphic Features (GF)
The interface shows a lot of content, so if you see something you like, you can just click on it and find the features you're looking for all at once. (Function layout)	B2 Information Architecture (IA)
For example, if I like to listen to some opera and comic shows, I will call out my name directly to it, and it will respond to me, after which we can have a conversation, and then I will say whose comic I want to listen to, whose story I want to listen to, and which channel I want to watch, and it will be able to execute it immediately. (Naturalness)	B3 Human-Computer Interaction (HCI)
Because I have trouble with my legs, I keep my Xiaodu smart screen on my bed, and it has made me better able to communicate with my family because it has a convenient watcher function, and I can interact and video chat with my family when I tap on it. I think it is good for maintaining my relationships with my friends and with my family. (Family Connection)	B4 Interpersonal Interaction (HI)
For example, sometimes I forget to take my medication, or some things that I do daily, such as taking my blood pressure, I may forget, so it would be best if it could remind me. I think overall it is still very smart and very easy to operate. (Intelligent monitoring)	B5 Intelligence (INT)
Sometimes, we like to organize some programs and some activities, such as some community volunteer activities or some old friends in the community, and we go to plant trees, go fishing, or walk in the park together. We organize activities, we go to such a group activity together, and we share information through some such social platform. (Collective behavior)	B6 Socialization (SOC)

(continued)

Table 2. (*continued*)

Original statement	Categorizations
I usually just also go shopping; that is to say, we shop inside the group to buy food or whatever, which is very convenient. Some of my friends, for example, will frequently share with me if he has some good things—good cheap food, suitable clothes. I also like to buy some brands of clothes that my friends share with me, which are quite good. (Disseminate information)	B7 Shareability (SHA)
I generally like to post some of my own pictures and words to record some snippets of my own life. After all, most of my life I have been working; now I finally have some time for myself, and while I still have energy, I want to express it through social platforms. (Self-recording)	B8 User Generated Content (UGC)
Above and beyond the social function of the app, I believe some smart homes have some strangers on them who do not feel safe and are afraid of being cheated. (Social risk)	B9 Social Security (SE)
The Xiaoai smart screen is more like the other half of my life; I can't live without it. I feel that it gives me a sense of belonging, that it understands me, and that I am connected to it. (Sense of Belonging)	B10 Empathy (EMP)

and rigorous, one design expert is invited to participate in the spindle coding, and the two coders have a real-time discussion to confirm the main scope.

Coding Results. By combining the expert opinions and exploring the relationship between the above 10 sub-categories, the four main categories—interface quality, interaction quality, content quality, and service quality—were further consolidated and merged as shown in Table 3.

4.3 Selective Coding

The stage of extracting the core categories from the main categories is called selective coding. In this stage, we need to summarize and refine the main categories again, discover the core categories that can cover other main categories by organizing the related relationships among them, maximize the unification, and build a model to establish the relationship between the core categories and the main categories and determine the meaningful relationship between the core categories and the main categories. In this paper, through repeated research, comparison, and analysis of the four main categories, we finally extracted the core category of "the influencing factors of user experience design and its mechanism based on smart home socialization for first-time seniors". This core

Table 3. Main categories and their connotations

Main Category	Sub-categories	The connotation of the main category
C1 User Interface Quality (UIQ)	B1 Graphic Features (GF)	Images, text, logos, icons, color blocks and some buttons for smart home social interface
	B2 Information Architecture (IA)	Smart home social interface layout, hierarchy, navigation, search, etc.
C2 Interaction Quality (IQ)	B3 Human-Computer Interaction (HCI)	The social interaction between the elderly and the smart home should be more natural, such as using voice interaction, and it should be easier to wake up and respond to the elderly instantly
	B4 Interpersonal Interaction (HI)	Communication and interaction between people in the process of using smart home socialization for the first age group
	B5 Intelligence (INT)	The degree of intelligence in the use of smart-home social processes for the first-time elderly population
C3 Content Quality (CQ)	B6 Socialization (SOC)	Group interaction and linkage behaviors of the first-time seniors using smart home social processes
	B7 Shareability (SHA)	First-time seniors can share interesting and useful information in the process of using smart homes socially
	B8 User Generated Content (UGC)	The beginning elderly can generate content for self-expression and to please others in the process of using smart home social
C4 Service Quality (SQ)	B9 Social Security (SE)	The security enjoyed by the younger population in using smart home social processes, such as privacy security, payment security, etc.

(*continued*)

category includes four main categories: interface quality, interaction quality, content

Table 3. (*continued*)

Main Category	Sub-categories	The connotation of the main category
	B10 Empathy (EMP)	The companionship, care, and personalized service that first-time seniors feel during the use of smart home socialization

quality, and service quality. The typical relationship structure and the connotation of the relationship structure are shown in Table 4 below.

5 Results and Discussions

5.1 Model Construction

Through the three-level coding, 28 initial concepts, 10 sub-categories, and 4 main categories were obtained to build the model of the Senior User Experience Design of the Smart-home Social System. The model is shown in Fig. 1 below.

5.2 User Interface Quality

In the model, the user interface quality factor is one of the external user experience design influences that affects the user experience of the first-age smart home social group, which is mainly reflected in the influence of the graphic features and information architecture of the smart home social interface on the user experience. Therefore, designers, product managers, and administrators should consider how to design the graphic features and information architecture of the smart home social interface according to the specific initial physiological and psychological decline of the first-age population to help the first-age users use smart home social better and thus give them a better experience.

5.3 Interaction Quality

In the model, the interaction quality factor directly affects the information behavior of the first-aged people using smart homes for socializing and is one of the external user experience design influencing factors, which is mainly reflected in three dimensions: human-computer interaction, interpersonal interaction, and intelligence. Therefore, to improve user experience and enhance user stickiness, designers, product managers, and administrators should strengthen the intelligent design and construction of voice interaction and design a more natural voice interaction mode according to the human-computer communication mode and habits of the first-aged people so that the first-aged users can also enjoy a more convenient and rapid response interaction service experience.

Table 4. Selective coding

Typical relationship structure	Nature of relationship	Relationship structure connotation
User Interface quality → User Experience	External factors (cause and effect)	Interface quality factors such as graphic features and information architecture are external design factors that affect the user experience during the use of smart homes for socialization by the aging population
Interaction quality → User Experience	External factors (cause and effect)	Human-computer interaction, interpersonal interaction and intelligence and other interaction quality factors are external design factors that affect the user experience in the process of using smart home socialization for the first-time seniors
Content quality → User Experience	External factors (cause and effect)	Content quality factors such as socialization, shareability and user-generated content are external design factors that influence the user experience during the use of smart home socialization by the aging population
Service Quality → User Experience	External factors (cause and effect)	Quality of service factors such as social security and empathy are external design factors that influence the user experience during the use of smart home socialization by the first-time seniors

5.4 Content Quality

In the model, the content quality factor is one of the external user experience design influences that affect the social information behavior of first-time home users, mainly in the three dimensions of community, shareability, and user-generated content. Therefore, designers, product managers, and administrators should take advantage of the large screen in smart home social software to design specific community groups and other functions to help the elderly people show themselves and express their emotions more conveniently, and at the same time, design according to their specific needs so that

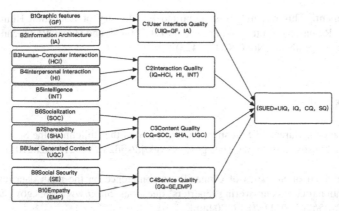

Fig. 1. User Experience Design Influencing Factors Model for First Agers Based on Smart Home Social software

they can share information with others in the group more conveniently, helping them to gain attention more easily, eliminate loneliness, and improve their health. It helps them get attention more easily, eliminate the feeling of loneliness, and improve their user experience of using smart home social networking at home.

5.5 Service Quality

In the model, the service quality factor directly affects the social information behavior of the first-time home users and is one of the external user experience design influencing factors, which is mainly reflected in the two dimensions of social security and empathy. In view of this, to increase the perception of service quality and improve the user's viscosity, designers, product managers, and administrators should provide more care and support for the first-time users through specific service design elements from the design perspective, so as to help the first-time users improve their social experience.

6 Conclusion

In general, although this paper strictly abides by the analytical research process of rooted theory, it is still more or less disturbed by the subjective influence of thinking, which is the shortcoming of the study. Meanwhile, since the research method is qualitative and the interview sample size is 24 first-time and old users, statistical tests of reliability and validity of large samples should be conducted in the future in conjunction with empirical evidence, and the exogenous user experience design variables in the model should also be operationally defined and multidimensional scales should be developed. Based on this, structural equation modeling and quantitative verification of the internal mechanism of the factors influencing the user experience design of smart homes for people in their prime years are combined with pertinent theories, and they further suggest an ageing-friendly design method for smart homes for people in their prime years based on the verified causality. This provides theoretical guidance for future smart homes for people in their prime years of design and research, with high-quality results.

Acknowledgement. This research was supported by Ministry of Education Humanities and Social Sciences Research - Youth Fund Project (19YJC760075) and Hunan Provincial Innovation Foundation for Postgraduate (No. CX20200425).

References

1. China's National Bureau of Statistics: interpretation of the Bulletin of the Seventh National population Census. http://www.stats.gov.cn/xxgk/jd/sjjd2020/202105/t20210512_1817342.html
2. National Bureau of Statistics of China: Press conference on the main data results of the seventh national census answering reporters' questions. http://www.stats.gov.cn/xxgk/jd/sjjd2020/202105/t20210511_1817280.html
3. Robert, C.A.: Continuity and Adaptation in Aging: Creating Positive Experiences. Johns Hopkins University Press, Baltimore (1999)
4. Cacioppo, J.T., Hughes, M.E., Waite, L.J., Hawkley, L.C., Thisted, R.A.: Loneliness as a specific risk factor for depressive symptoms: cross-sectional and longitudinal analyses. Psychol. Aging **21**, 140–151 (2006)
5. Chen, K., Lou, V.W.Q., Lo, S.S.C.: Exploring the acceptance of tablets usage for cognitive training among older people with cognitive impairments: a mixed-methods study. Appl. Ergon. **93**, 103381 (2021)
6. Talukder, M., Sorwar, G., Bao, Y., Ahmed, J.U., Palash, M.: Predicting antecedents of wearable healthcare technology acceptance by elderly: a combined SEM-neural network approach. Technol. Forecast. Soc. Chang. **150**, 119793 (2020)
7. Yu, R.P.: Use of messaging apps and social network sites among older adults: a mixed-method study. Int. J. Commun. **14**, 4453–4473 (2020)
8. Chen, K., Lou, V.W., Tan, K.C., Wai, M.Y., Chan, L.L.: Changes in technology acceptance among older people with dementia: the role of social robot engagement. Int. J. Med. Inform. **141**, 104241 (2020)
9. Donald, N., Jim, M., Austin, H.: What you see, some of what's in the future, and how we go about doing it: hi at apple computer. Presented at the Conference Companion on Human Factors in Computing Systems (1995)
10. Tsai, T.-H., Chang, H.-T., Chen, Y.-J., Chang, Y.-S.: Determinants of user acceptance of a specific social platform for older adults: an empirical examination of user interface characteristics and behavioral intention. PLoS ONE **12**, e0180102 (2017)
11. Alzahrani, T., Hunt, M., Whiddett, D.: Barriers and facilitators to using smart home technologies to support older adults: perspectives of three stakeholder groups. Int. J. Healthc. Inf. Syst. Inf. **16**, 22 (2021)
12. Kalimullah, K., Sushmitha, D.: Influence of design elements in mobile applications on user experience of elderly people. Procedia Comput. Sci. **113**, 352–359 (2017)
13. Glaser,B., Anselm, S.: Discovery of grounded theory: strategies for qualitative research. Nursing Research (1967)
14. Juliet, C., Anselm, S.: Basics of Qualitative Research: Techniques and Procedures for Developing Grounded Theory. Sage Publications Inc., Thousand Oaks (1990)
15. Holsti, O.R.: Content analysis for the social sciences and humanities. Addison-Wesley, Reading (content analysis) (1969)
16. Kassarjian, H.H.: Content analysis in consumer research. J. Consum. Res. **4**, 8–18 (1977)

My Iliad: A Ludic Interface Using Ambient Assistive Technology to Promote Aging in Place

Hubert Ngankam[1]([✉])(iD), Célia Lignon[1], Maxime Lussier[2](iD),
Aline Aboujaoudé[2](iD), Renée-pier Filiou[2], Hélène Pigot[1](iD),
Sébastien Gaboury[3](iD), Kevin Bouchard[3](iD), Guy Paré[6](iD), Carolina Bottari[5](iD),
Mélanie Couture[4](iD), Nathalie Bier[2](iD), and Sylvain Giroux[1](iD)

[1] Laboratoire DOMUS, Département d'informatique, Université de Sherbrooke,
Sherbrooke, Canada
{hubert.ngankam,helene.pigot,sylvain.giroux}@usherbrooke.ca
[2] Centre de recherche de l'Institut universitaire de gériatrie de Montréal -
CIUSSS-CSMTL, Université de Montréal, Montréal, Canada
{aline.aboujaoude,renee-pier.filiou,nathalie.bier}@umontreal.ca
[3] LIARA Lab, Université du Québec à Chicoutimi, Chicoutimi, Canada
{Sebastien_Gaboury,Kevin_Bouchard}@uqac.ca
[4] Faculté des lettres et sciences humaines, Université de Sherbrooke, Sherbrooke,
Canada
Melanie.Couture@usherbrooke.ca
[5] Centre de recherche interdisciplinaire en réadaptation du Montréal métropolitain,
Université de Montréal, Montréal, Canada
carolina.bottari@umontreal.ca
[6] Département de Technologies de l'information, HEC Montréal, Montréal, Canada
guy.pare@hec.ca

Abstract. Remote monitoring uses smart home features to promote aging in place by preventing emergencies and increasing the quality of life of older adults. However, traditional reports, data, and graphs produced by remote monitoring technologies are not well suited to older adults' needs. Thus, the complexity for older adults to use and interpret reports can lead to usability and adoption issues. The goals of this study were 1) to incorporate ludic-based design principles into an application that provides older adults with an alternative way to interact with information about their Activities of Daily Living (ADL), and 2) involve older adults in creating new ludic interfaces that address usability and reduce adoption issues. This ambient assistive technology offers older adults the opportunity, through its interface, to promote curiosity and exploration, the pursuit of non-external goals, and openness about the user's routine and lifestyle. By using an iterative, Human-Centered, co-design approach in 4 workshops with older adults ($N = 7$), we combine older adults' needs with ludic elements to propose a new user experience.

Q. Gao and J. Zhou (Eds.): HCII 2023, LNCS 14043, pp. 31–46, 2023.
https://doi.org/10.1007/978-3-031-34917-1_3

Keywords: Assistive Technology · Human-Centered Design · Ludic Design · Human-Computer Interaction · Participatory Design · User-centered Design

1 Introduction

Assistive technology (AT) is seen as facilitating independence and quality of life for people, including those with dementia [18]. First and foremost, AT aims to support people to live as long as possible at home [18]. The applications of AT are many and varied, including supporting informal caregivers [3,15] or assisting with meal preparation [22]. AT can also be used for health monitoring, for assisting people with dementia while they engage in activities of daily living (ADL), for maintaining social contacts, or for remote monitoring of activities of daily living.

Ambient Assisted Living (AAL) is a type of assistive technology that uses the Internet of Things (IoT) to assist older adults. The goal of Ambient Assisted Living systems is to help older adults stay at home longer by increasing their autonomy and assisting them with activities of daily living [4]. AAL uses intelligent products, the context of the user, and the provision of remote services, including care services, to support aging [20]. Most efforts to build AAL systems for older adults are based on developing pervasive devices and using ambient intelligence to integrate these devices to create a safe environment. Ambient Intelligence intends to provide services in a way that is sensitive and responsive to the presence of older adults and is unobtrusively integrated into the daily environment [5].

If some of AAL solutions require interaction with users, most of them are poorly suited for human-machine interaction [21], resulting in a risk for non-adoption of the technology. Especially for older adults, these technologies might not be unsuitably designed for their daily use. One way to ensure that new technologies are usable, acceptable, and tailored to the users they are intended to support, is to ensure that users themselves are central to the design and development process [1,21]. Co-design offers a way to ensure that new technologies and interventions are tailored to users' needs.

In the context of AAL, co-design can be defined as a process based on the shared creativity of software developers, caregivers, clinicians, and other stakeholders working together towards the same goal [13]. To achieve this goal, special attention is paid to involving end users and ensuring that their contribution as experience experts is at the heart of the design process and that their specific needs are understood and met [13].

An aging population has led researchers to focus on developing assistive technologies to address the health problems of the elderly population. Blackman et al. [4] explored how using assisted living solutions could promote aging in place. Much research is being done to create intelligent environments around people. This research in AAL has improved the independence of older adults and has helped individuals to maintain and continue with their current activities of daily living. Acceptance of a product or service depends in large part on its ability to solve a particular problem [21]. It also depends on how well it fits into the lives of older adults [1]. Therefore, design for older people requires that they be at the center of the design process. However, several barriers related to usability and lack of experience exist despite the motivation of older people to use digital technologies [14].

1.1 Promoting Adoption of Technology by Older Adults

Recently, researchers have been exploring ways to increase the adoption of ambient assistance. Among the various solutions proposed, gamification seems to be an interesting option [10,26]. Gamification refers to a design approach that aims to improve a service or system with the possibility of an experience that is similar to the one created by a game [16]. In other words, gamification is the use of the mechanics and elements of video games in a non-gaming context to encourage and engage the user by making the experience rewarding and enjoyable. In AAL systems, the main function of gamification is to reinforce positive behaviors in older adults. In AAL systems, gamification can be used to reinforce positive behaviors and engagement in performing ADLs [23].

However, most gamification-based systems are conceptualized for a younger audience and do not account for age-specific changes in motivation to continue using the system or perception of gamification elements [1,2]. Overall, a systematic review of gamification initiatives for older people found weak indications of positive effects [16]. Altmeyer et al. (2018) investigated what affected positively 75+ years old adults while playing and their attitudes toward common game elements. They found that badges and points put the user under pressure but are also considered meaningless. They see no value in them, especially for tasks that are not necessarily worthy of praise. One participant said: "I don't have the feeling of having reached something that has value. I don't see the benefit of collecting points". Kappen et al. [14] reported that older adults are keen to receive feedback from peers or professionals, but are apprehensive to accept feedback from technology (e.g., fitness applications). Steinert and colleagues [25], noted that the older adults were more motivated by the tangible information provided by the activity monitors than by more abstract gameful feedback. Finally, adaptive or increasing difficulty elements are prevalent in gamification (i.e. the feedback pushed you to surpass yourself) [17], which may be detrimental to one's motivation and self-image, especially in the context of aging with increasing cognitive, motor and/or sensory challenges.

Building on a shared element from gamification, ludic design might be a better approach for inclusion and accessibility in aging. Ludic design is defined by Sengers as belonging to design exploration [24]. Huizinga describes ludic activities as playful experiences that are not organized as goal-oriented tasks, where people optimize [11]. The focus is not on the task, but on the global aesthetic experience and how people make sense of it through gestures and comments [19]. To build a ludic design is to: 1) promote curiosity, exploration, and reflection;

2) de-emphasize the pursuit of external goals; 3) maintain openness and ambiguity [9].

In a recent study, participants used an eHealth service focusing on fall prevention, for 4 weeks [12]. The service used elements of ludic design and gamification. Analyses showed that enjoyment affected perceived usefulness and aesthetics affected perceived ease of use.

1.2 Objective

In this work, through co-designing with older adults, we aimed to develop a ludic interface presenting the user with feedback on their daily routine that they would feel curious to explore, and this, without measuring their accomplishment or pressuring them into accomplishing something. We believe this approach would benefit acceptability, usability, and motivation. We will call this technology My Iliad.

My Iliad is an application and assistive technology that aims to help people perform their activities of daily living. The objective is to promote their autonomy by displaying visual prompts aware of the person's context. My Iliad is an ecosystem that allows one to: (1) Follow one's routine (sleep, meal preparation, outings, hygiene...); (2) Schedule appointments or reminders; (3) Federate certain smart home technologies within the same ecosystem; (4) Offer personalized suggestions and advice according to the time and activities; (5) Provide a companion that accompanies the older adult in his daily life.

My Iliad aims at being a simple, pleasant, welcoming, caring, intuitive, motivating, and reassuring user interface. The purpose of this research is to show how the different elements of ludic design are integrated into My Iliad. Through numerous iterations developed in co-design workshops, this article explains how the important criteria of ludic design were merged with the needs of older adults.

2   Co-design Process of My Iliad

The proposed methodological approach aimed to offer active participation that goes beyond consultation or receiving information. The proposed approach includes participation in decision-making and giving participants a degree of control and responsibility over the research results. Working with older adults requires an adapted approach to ensure active participation in co-design [7,14]. A balance must be found between meaningful active participation and consideration of the users' ability to abstract. To do this, we adopted the Human-Centered Design (HCD) process. This is a methodology for creating effective design solutions.

In this methodology, the research team focuses on end users from the beginning of product development and asks users to test each iteration of a product. As a result, it is expected that end users will get a product that meets their needs [8]. Specifically, we have organized this approach into a rapid prototyping process divided into two iterations: (1) a Participatory Design (PD) iteration and (2) a User-Centered Design (UCD) iteration. Each iteration consisted of 4 steps. Figure 1 shows how we adapted the Human-Centered methodology to our context. The project was approved by the Ethical Review Board of Aging-Neuroimaging of the CIUSSS Centre-sud-de-l'île-de-Montréal.

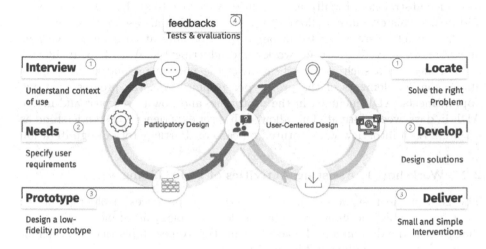

Fig. 1. Adaptive design process based on the Human-centered design process used to co-design My Iliad.

2.1 Participatory Design Iteration

Participatory design is a co-design approach that places end-user participants at the heart of the design process. Participants are considered on an equal footing with other stakeholders in the co-creation process [8]. We chose the participatory design approach because it allows us to start from the premise that design engagements should not begin in the laboratory, but in the practices, environments, and developmental trajectories of the people who will become the users. In the co-design of My Iliad, this practice was used in the first and second workshops. In Fig. 1, this corresponds to the first iteration.

Participants were recruited from a private residence for independent and semi-independent older adults. The participants consisted of 6 women and 1 man, aged between 70 and 91 years. As far as we know, none of the participants suffered from health problems at the time of the study. Inclusion criteria were that the older adults were in good health, had some ability for abstract thinking, had little knowledge of IT, and had no cognitive or physical impairments that would prevent them from understanding instructions or participating in videoconferencing sessions. The participants took part in all the co-design workshops. In collaboration with the older adults, a Housing Unit Manager, and the research project team, a total of 4 co-design workshops were organized. Two (2) workshops took place in person with the older adults at the residence. One (1) workshop was held virtually online, and One (1) workshop was organized with the managers and Housing Unit Manager of the residents. In each workshop, the 4 steps: Interview, Needs, Prototypes, and Evaluation were applied. Based on the interviews, the needs were clarified. Then, rapid prototypes were built to avoid too much abstraction. Finally, an evaluation was done to see how the needs were addressed. This evaluation allowed for a new iteration in case of unmet needs.

Participants were asked to fill out a questionnaire at each interview. This questionnaire served as a framework for conducting the Workshop. It allowed us to collect data such as identification of the participant and their opinions about specific elements of the prototype: graphic style, the progress of time, appointments, ADL included in the prototype, and how to see past and future ADL in days/weeks format. This allowed the user experience to be understood as a whole. Each interview was captured on camera. Participatory design iteration

2.2 Workshop 1: Assisting Activities of Daily Living

The goal of the first workshop was to use the experiences of older adults to identify favorable and unfavorable factors for technology assistance applications that present the data in a dashboard format. Due to health restrictions, the first workshop was held online and lasted 1 h.

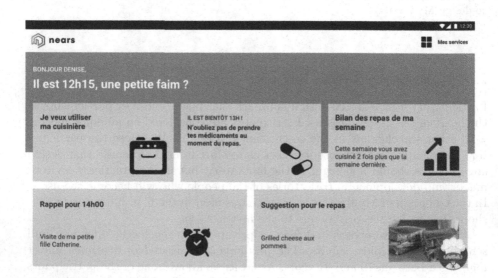

Fig. 2. Example of a daily life activities visualization dashboard presented to older adults during the workshop.

During this workshop, older adults' opinions on the presentation and accessibility of information related to their daily routine were collected. Two members of the research team met each participant individually. Since the older adults all spoke French, we left the material (photos) in the language used during the workshop.

Prior to the workshop, the participants had received paper copies of the various activities of daily living (sleep, meal preparation, outings, hygiene...) and a classic GUI dashboard presentation of these activities, as shown in Fig. 2. Among other things, they were asked questions such as: What aspects do you like best about this type of GUI? What aspects do you find less interesting? What would you like to see on your screen? Do you have any suggestions? Other accessibility questions such as: How comfortable are you interacting with your dashboard screen while standing? After how long would you be uncomfortable? If the screen is fixed, what room is it in? If your screen offers a service to help you cook, do you choose the same room? Would you like to be able to move the screen with you?

2.3   Workshop 2: Think Outside the Box

To address some of the barriers identified in workshop 1. The objective of this workshop was to let the elders build, with visual components, a low-fidelity prototype of an interface to display the content of an activity. The second workshop lasted two hours, and the participants were met individually.

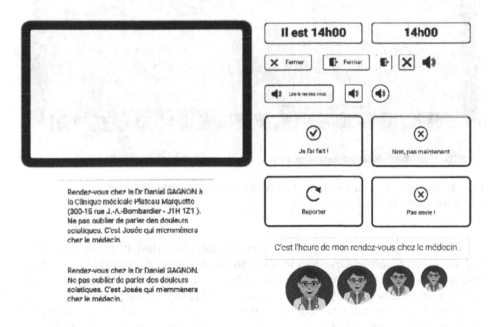

Fig. 3. Bank of elements in the form of Lego bricks for the graphic interface design workshop.

While one member of the team took notes, the other accompanied the participant by presenting the elements useful for the construction of a graphic interface in Lego mode. Initially, a whiteboard was placed on the table. Around the board, several pieces of paper were cut out indicating: the time, the page title, buttons, screen boxes, an alarm, a volume, useful information... Figure 3. Each piece of information was presented in different ways (shapes, sizes, and stylistic tones) to accommodate the participants' requirements. Additional blank post-it notes were present if the person was looking for or wanted something they could not find among the bank of items.

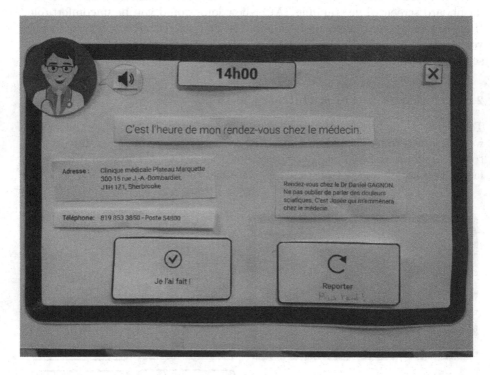

Fig. 4. Example of a model built by an older adult. Graphical interface built with a set of free tools in the form of Lego.

Then, the person was asked to build an interface that displays a medical appointment. Complete freedom was left to the participants' creativity on where and how to place the elements on the whiteboard. Sketches of the models used during the workshop were presented on paper and tablets. This prototype made it possible to quickly validate how the different sketches interacted and depended on each other. Figure 4 shows an example of a participant's proposal. Taking advantage of this workshop to manipulate graphic elements, we asked them to choose three appointment titles out of 6 and to position them in order of preference on the whiteboard. Each title announced the same information, but differently, with a different tone. The purpose of the exercise was to address accessibility issues regarding the size and format of the items to be displayed.

2.4 User-Centered Design Iteration

User-centered design is an iterative design process in which project design teams focus on users and their needs at each phase of the design process [8]. Design teams engage users throughout the design process through a variety of research and design techniques to create highly usable and accessible products for them. In Fig. 1, this represents the second part of the co-design process.

In the My Iliad co-design process, each iteration of the User-centered design approach has four distinct phases. First, we try to understand the context in which users may use a system to solve the right problem. Next, we identify and specify the user requirements. A design phase follows, during which the design team develops solutions. Then we perform a small, simple intervention and learn from it one by one. The team then moves into an evaluation phase, to prototype, test, and continually refine the proposals to ensure that the small solutions actually meet the needs of the participant we are focusing on. This practice was used in the third and fourth workshops.

2.5 Workshop 3: Ludic Interface for Assistive Technology

The objective of this workshop was to respond to the concerns of the older adults in workshops 1 and 2. Among other things, to design the different prototypes made by older adults, and to facilitate the acceptability of the assistive technologies. As far as the older adults were concerned, none of them participated in this workshop, which was spread over 3 months with about 4 h of work per day. We wanted to avoid exhausting our older adults with meetings and the use of specialized software development tools. The research team worked on some occasions with housing unit managers and residence administrators to clarify needs and identify techniques to address them.

Feedback from each previous workshop was reviewed and discussed by the project team. The project team prioritized the changes based on the effort required to implement them and their impact on the end user's daily routine. The project team's goal was to empower older adults to accept and adopt AT while reflecting end-user acceptance and without creating new biases such as infantilization. To achieve this, the team tried several user-centered solutions. Ultimately, a ludic design was chosen.

In this workshop, we wanted to introduce the concept of a ludic interface to older adults. The goal was to offer them the opportunity to be the heroes of their day. Heroes with missions, goals, rewards, and a quest through the achievement of ADLs. Strong iconography and illustrations were prioritized to promote accessibility (Recommendation from Workshop 2). Since the users wanted a companion and not an application that told them what to do, we addressed this issue by designing My Iliad as an odyssey and not as a dashboard.

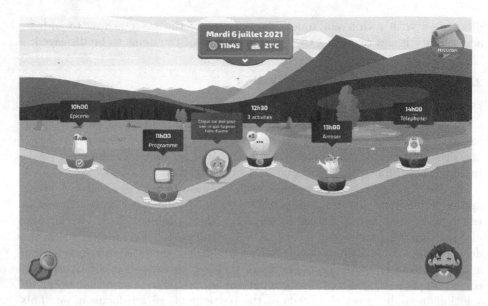

Fig. 5. My Iliad main screen.

The main screen of My Iliad is shown in Fig. 5. In this figure, 5 ADLs are placed along the path and follow the context of the older adult... The rest of this section shows how older adult needs and feedback were merged with the 3 principles of ludic design (1) curiosity, exploration, and reflection; (2) de-emphasizing the pursuit of external goals; (3) maintaining openness and ambiguity. The intention of the approach is to offer an application that acts more like a companion than a dashboard.

Curiosity, Exploration and Reflection. In video games, user engagement is a widely used strategy in gamification to keep user attention, improve retention rates, and increases interaction with the game [23]. This can potentially lead to addiction [14]. With My Iliad, we did wish to enforce regular interaction with the service. The goal of My Iliad was to allow older adults to live their day. No interaction with the application is required. In other words, it is enough for the person to carry out their activities of daily living without pressure to interact regularly with the interface. The user is always in control.

Instead, through the ambient sensor, activities performed within the day will be presented on the screen as part of their avatar odyssey. Interactions with the system are almost automatic and everything happens in real-time thanks to the existing ecosystem of sensor networks [20]. Several activities performed by the user are passively recognized and displayed on the interface, without judgment on quality or quantity. In My Iliad, the achievements are presented in a quick and accurate vision of three elements: the past, the present, and the future. With this view available at all times, the user knows his level, the distance he has covered, and the distance he still has to cover to reach his goal. Using this implicit progression mechanic helps users understand how far they've come in their odyssey.

Users are curious, they can simply look at the screen to see what has already been accomplished, a visual projection of the activities ahead, and what remains to be done with the possibility of zooming in or out to calibrate one's appreciation. If they wish to further explore, they can interact with the interface to go back in time to see what has been accomplished. Depending on the person's profile, it is possible to go back or forward one or more weeks. This view allows for the creation of a sense of accomplishment that links My Iliad to the sense of pleasure and creates a strong link between ADL performance and cognitive support. This can also be used to refresh the user's memory. Ultimately, the users can use this to reflect and make an intrinsic choice about his lifestyle (i.e., I see that I have not spent much time outside this month. I will try to change that for next month). A partial view of the user's week is shown in Fig. 6. In this view, it is possible to evaluate and see all the activities that have been performed during the whole week.

Fig. 6. View by week in My Iliad, allowing to visualize achievements.

De-emphasize the Pursuit of External Goals. Gamified software often requires users to perform some task or activity to achieve some milestone or mission [6]. Typically, the number of activities to be completed for the achievement of a clear goal is specified, and the next milestone is clearly stated. While My Iliad aims to promote a better lifestyle, the quality of a lifestyle is objective and cannot be simply operationalized and reinforced. It should be self-determined by the user. Some individuals might benefit from going for a walk, while some might expose themselves to a greater risk of falls or be annoyed by a service telling them to perform an activity they do not enjoy. Therefore, the only objectives and milestones used in My Iliad are those set by the users. Each older adult chooses the activities that they want to do, and they choose the activities that will appear in their journey Specifically, it is a to-do list of ADLs that the person set to do at his own pace and without constraints. The reward is not a score or a badge, but simply a visually pleasing summary of all the goals accomplished by the user so far. By creating their journey, their odyssey in My Iliad, users decide how to proceed and how to interact. They are therefore more likely to enjoy the experience. And once again, the implicit progression mechanic helps users understand how close there are to some objectives they made for themselves and how many objectives they have cleared so far.

Fig. 7. Example of context awareness in My Iliad to reflect the real world.

Maintaining Openness and Ambiguity. Finally, while My Iliad mainly focuses on self-determined goals, it can also use all the contextual information collected by the sensor network to offer activity suggestions and recommendations. This scarce notification can be ignored or embraced by users. They are meant to break the routine and promote openness to change and novelty. The theory of flow suggests that if a task is too easy, too difficult, or too repetitive, it will cause the user to quickly abandon the current activity [25]. These notifications also create a sense of two-way interaction with the service, which can increase motivation and adoption. Suggestions are always phrased as questions and not orders. They are inviting users to reflect on themselves and decide whether this recommendation is for them or not, without guilt. To promote a sense of connection between the real-world and the interface, My Iliad can follow contextual cues such as day/night cycle, seasons, and weather. Figure 7 shows the application during the night. Also, during the night, the level of brightness as well as the amount of information presented is reduced in order to lower cognitive load and anxiety. Positive thoughts are also displayed. To improve accessibility and greater acceptance among participants, the interface can be customized to reduce the amount of information displayed, and some aesthetic distractors can be removed. This can be relevant for older adults with visual or attentional deficits.

2.6   Workshop 4: An Odyssey, Not Just an App

The purpose of this workshop was to go back and get feedback from the older adults on the first results of the My Iliad project. Again, the older adults were met individually. The workshop lasted 1 h. We used a tablet computer to present the deliverables in addition to paper printouts of the screens.

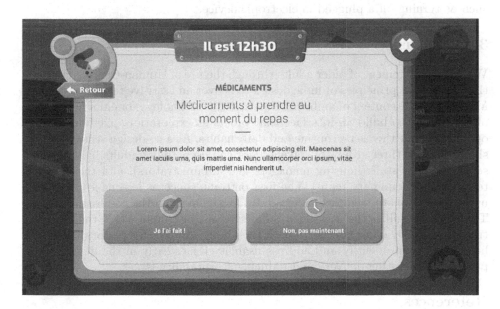

Fig. 8. Design of an interface prototyped by an older adult during workshop 2 see Fig. 4.

Some of the developed features were demonstrated. In particular, the start screen, which shows the timeline of the journey. It was explained to them as follows: "The timeline represents in an imaginary way the path of your day. It accompanies you to remind you of important appointments, activities, or tasks. The character on the timeline is customizable". We then asked: How do you find the timeline path? Do you find it clear/understandable? Effective or ineffective in representing your day? What action do you think you can take from this timeline? Where can you click? Several versions of this timeline were created. Three, five, and eight appointments in the day were presented in different versions. We asked them what they would prefer and how many items they would like to see at the same time.

Then we showed them a version of an appointment that had been designed based on the prototype they had suggested. See Fig. 8. They were told, "When you click on an event, you will see a description of the event on your tablet. In addition, you should know that the description will also be able to appear automatically on your screen when the time comes". The next question they were asked was, How do you like the presentation of the events? Can you explain what you like and/or dislike?

The fact that My Iliad is an odyssey, or a quest offered several possibilities for the representation of the quests or the odyssey (travel, fishing, walking in the forest, gardening...). As the quests evolved, so did the AT. There was talk of evolving the AT so that what you see in the outside world is reflected in the AT. Some of the things you do in My Iliad are reflected in the outside world, such as turning off a plugged-in electronic device.

3   Conclusion

With the engagement of older adults through the use of Human-Centered design, this study used principles of ludic design to deliver an assistive technology called My Iliad. In the context of ambient home assistive technology for older adults, the objective was to build an interface that promotes exploration, playfulness, and openness about the user's routine and daily habits. As a co-design study, 4 workshops involved three groups of stakeholders: end users (older adults living alone), senior housing staff (housing managers and administrators), and the research team (multidisciplinary team). The first outcome concerns lessons learned from using basic tools to facilitate older adults' engagement in the co-design process. The second result is the identification of several constraints where the information provided by older adults through their daily routines for performing ADLs helped our team identify and address usability issues early in the development process, accelerating delivery and reducing acceptability issues.

References

1. Ahmad, A., Mozelius, P.: Critical factors for human computer interaction of ehealth for older adults, pp. 58–62. ACM Press (2019). https://doi.org/10.1145/3312714. 3312730. http://dl.acm.org/citation.cfm?doid=3312714.3312730

2. Altmeyer, M., Lessel, P., Krüger, A.: Investigating gamification for seniors aged 75+, pp. 453–458. ACM (2018). https://doi.org/10.1145/3196709.3196799. https://dl.acm.org/doi/10.1145/3196709.3196799

3. Amirabdollahian, F., et al.: Assistive technology design and development for acceptable robotics companions for ageing years. Paladyn **4**, 94–112 (2013). https://doi.org/10.2478/PJBR-2013-0007/MACHINEREADABLECITATION/ RIS. https://www.degruyter.com/document/doi/10.2478/pjbr-2013-0007/html

4. Blackman, S., et al.: Ambient assisted living technologies for aging well: a scoping review. J. Intell. Syst. **25**, 55–69 (2016). https://doi.org/10.1515/jisys-2014-0136. https://www.degruyter.com/document/doi/10.1515/jisys-2014-0136/html

5. Cook, D.J., Augusto, J.C., Jakkula, V.R.: Ambient intelligence: technologies, applications, and opportunities. Pervasive Mob. Comput. **5**, 277–298 (2009). https:// doi.org/10.1016/j.pmcj.2009.04.001

6. Floryan, M.R., Ritterband, L.M., Chow, P.I.: Principles of gamification for internet interventions. Transl. Behav. Med. **9**, 1131–1138 (2019). https://doi.org/10.1093/ tbm/ibz041. https://academic.oup.com/tbm/article/9/6/1131/5427116

7. Fox, S., et al.: Co-design of a smartphone app for people living with dementia by applying agile, iterative co-design principles: development and usability study. JMIR mHealth uHealth **10**, e24483 (2022). https://doi.org/10.2196/24483. https://mhealth.jmir.org/2022/1/e24483

8. Gasson, S.: Human-centered vs. user-centered approaches to information system design. J. Inf. Technol. Theory Appl. (JITTA) **5**(2), 5 (2003)

9. Gaver, W.W., et al.: The drift table, pp. 885–900. ACM (2004). https://doi.org/ 10.1145/985921.985947. https://dl.acm.org/doi/10.1145/985921.985947

10. Guo, Y., Yuan, T., Yue, S.: Designing personalized persuasive game elements for older adults in health apps. Appl. Sci. **12**, 6271 (2022). https://doi.org/10.3390/ app12126271

11. Huizinga, J.: Homo Ludens: A Study of the Play-Element in Culture. Routledge, Milton Park (2014)

12. Hurmuz, M.Z., Jansen-Kosterink, S.M., Hermens, H.J., van Velsen, L.: Game not over: explaining older adults' use and intention to continue using a gamified ehealth service. Health Inf. J. **28**, 146045822211060 (2022). https://doi.org/ 10.1177/14604582221106008

13. Hwang, A.S., et al.: Co-designing ambient assisted living (AAL) environments: unravelling the situated context of informal dementia care. Biomed. Res. Int. **2015**, 1–12 (2015). https://doi.org/10.1155/2015/720483

14. Kappen, D.L., Nacke, L.E., Gerling, K.M., Tsotsos, L.E.: Design strategies for gamified physical activity applications for older adults, pp. 1309–1318. IEEE (2016). https://doi.org/10.1109/HICSS.2016.166. http://ieeexplore. ieee.org/document/7427345/

15. Khakhar, J., Madhvanath, S.: Jollymate: assistive technology for young children with dyslexia, pp. 576–580. IEEE (2010). https://doi.org/10.1109/ICFHR.2010.95. http://ieeexplore.ieee.org/document/5693625/

16. Koivisto, J., Hamari, J.: The rise of motivational information systems: a review of gamification research. Int. J. Inf. Manag. **45**, 191–210 (2019). https://doi.org/10. 1016/j.ijinfomgt.2018.10.013

17. Koivisto, J., Malik, A.: Gamification for older adults: a systematic literature review. Gerontologist **61**, e360–e372 (2021). https://doi.org/10.1093/geront/ gnaa047. https://academic.oup.com/gerontologist/article/61/7/e360/5856423

18. Martinez-Martin, E., Costa, A.: Assistive technology for elderly care: an overview. IEEE Access **9**, 92420–92430 (2021). https://doi.org/10.1109/ACCESS.2021. 3092407. https://ieeexplore.ieee.org/document/9465105/

19. Mivielle, C.: What is ludic about ludic design? A back and forth between theory and practice (2015)

20. Ngankam, H., et al.: Sapa technology: an AAL architecture for telemonitoring, pp. 892–898. SciTePress (2022)

21. Nunes, F., Silva, P.A., Abrantes, F.: Human-computer interaction and the older adult, pp. 1–8. ACM (2010). https://doi.org/10.1145/1839294.1839353. https://dl. acm.org/doi/10.1145/1839294.1839353

22. Pinard, S., et al.: Design and usability evaluation of cook, an assistive technology for meal preparation for persons with severe TBI. Disabil. Rehabil. Assist. Technol. **16**, 687–701 (2021). https://doi.org/10.1080/17483107.2019.1696898. https:// www.tandfonline.com/doi/full/10.1080/17483107.2019.1696898

23. Santos, L.H.D.O., et al.: Effects of social interaction mechanics in pervasive games on the physical activity levels of older adults: quasi-experimental study. JMIR Serious Games **7**, e13962 (2019). https://doi.org/10.2196/13962. http://games.jmir. org/2019/3/e13962/

24. Sengers, P., Boehner, K., David, S., Kaye, J.J.: Reflective design, pp. 49–58. ACM (2005). https://doi.org/10.1145/1094562.1094569

25. Steinert, A., Buchem, I., Merceron, A., Kreutel, J., Haesner, M.: A wearable-enhanced fitness program for older adults, combining fitness trackers and gamification elements: the pilot study fmooc@ home. Sport Sci. Health **14**, 275–282 (2018)

26. Suh, A., Wagner, C., Liu, L.: Enhancing user engagement through gamification. J. Comput. Inf. Syst. **58**, 204–213 (2018). https://doi.org/10.1080/08874417.2016. 1229143

Visual Ambient Assisted Living Technologies for Different Daily Activities: Users' Requirements and Data Handling Preferences

Julia Offermann[(✉)] [iD], Caterina Maidhof[iD], and Martina Ziefle[iD]

Chair of Communication Science, RWTH Aachen University, Aachen, Germany
{offermann,maidhof,ziefle}@comm.rwth-aachen.de

Abstract. Ambient Assisted Living technologies (AAL) represent an opportunity to meet the high demands of support in care due to demographic change and enable older people to live autonomously and as long as possible in their own home environments. Despite their potential, AAL technologies and in particular visual-based systems have hardly been used neither in home care nor professional care due to a lack of user acceptance. Therefore, the present study investigates future users' privacy and data handling needs contrasting the usage of video-based AAL technologies (VAAL) for three different types of daily activities: household, social, and intimate activities. Applying an online survey, a sample of N = 122 participants took part and evaluated three contrasting activities in which VAAL technologies were used by assessing different conditions of technology usage, different entities getting access to recorded data, different storage options as well as different storage durations. The results showed some significant differences regarding the evaluation of the conditions of using VAAL technologies and the entities being allowed to have access to recorded data differentiating between the three activity types. In contrast, storage options and storage durations were not evaluated differently. Overall, the results indicate a rather generic attitude towards VAAL technologies being only slightly affected by different activity types. Beyond that, the results showed that privacy and data handling preferences are closely related to the perception and acceptance of VAAL technology. These insights enable to derive recommendations and information strategies to enable a targeted and user-centered technology development.

Keywords: Video-based AAL technology · data handling · privacy · technology acceptance · user preferences · quantitative study

1 Introduction

To meet the growing challenges of demographic change, innovative approaches such as Ambient Assisted Living (AAL) technologies have been developed to

Q. Gao and J. Zhou (Eds.): HCII 2023, LNCS 14043, pp. 47–65, 2023.
https://doi.org/10.1007/978-3-031-34917-1_4

support and care for the elderly and those in need of long-term care [1–3]. Besides sensor- and audio-based technologies, video-based devices, e.g., RGB cameras, RGB-D devices, or thermal cameras have been increasingly used in recent years enabling continuous monitoring of events and environments and providing detailed visual information [4,5]. Advances in computer vision and underlying algorithms have paved the way for the development of intelligent visual systems being used in various fields, but being particularly promising in the field of health care [4–7]. Such systems are not only capable of transmitting video in real-time but are also able to extract useful and relevant information from the visual data and make this information available to specific target groups. Typical examples of applications of visual technologies in health care are predominantly the detection and prevention of emergencies such as falls, but also physiological monitoring, detection of activities of daily living, or analyses of gait, human behavior and corresponding changes [4,8,9].

Although such visual AAL approaches (short: VAAL) have a great potential to support people in their daily lives by increasing their safety and independence in older age, there are also barriers and concerns, especially regarding privacy and data security violations, being able to impact the acceptance and adoption of such technical innovations [10–12]. In more detail, concerns about data security and resulting feelings of an invasion of the own privacy play a more relevant role within the assessments of cameras and VAAL technologies compared to non-visual approaches, such as audio- or sensor-based systems [13,14]. Beyond this knowledge, a detailed understanding of users' specific preferences regarding privacy and data handling and their role in the perception and acceptance of VAAL technologies is so far missing. However, identified preferences and relationships between privacy requirements, data handling preferences, and the acceptance of VAAL technology enable to derive concrete recommendations for more targeted and user-centred technology development.

Therefore, this study aimed at an investigation of privacy and data handling preferences related to the usage of VAAL technologies for different activities of daily living. Thereby, three different exemplary types of activities were focused on in order to analyze whether the context of using VAAL technologies influenced the preferences with regard to privacy and data handling. Beyond that, it was of interest to identify whether privacy and data handling preferences played a relevant role in the perception and acceptance of VAAL technologies. In the following, the research state regarding VAAL technologies, technology acceptance, and the role of perceptions related to privacy and data handling is summarized. Subsequently, the empirical approach of the study is introduced, describing the concept, the structure of the online survey, methods of data analysis as well as the characteristics of the sample. Then, the results of the study are presented. Finally, we discuss the insights, derive implications and recommendations, and outline limitations as well as ideas for future research.

1.1   VAAL Technologies

Despite their diversity in functions and design, all AAL technologies have a common aim in terms of providing support and assistance in older age. In this regard, literature reviews (e.g., by Rashidi and Mihailidis [1] or Blackman et al. [2]) provide an overview of relevant approaches, functions, and application areas, e.g., detection of emergencies, reminding functions, or relief in everyday life.

Addressing not only older people in need of care themselves but also their (in)formal caregivers, the application of AAL technologies has the potential to enable a longer and more autonomous life within their own home environments and to provide support by analyzing health-related data [1,2]. In this context, the shape and design of the technical applications are extremely diverse, ranging from small, wearable sensors to systems that are installed in the environment and integrate different types of sensors. In addition, the application contexts are quite diverse, aiming at support and assistance in private environments and professional care settings, such as hospitals, rehabilitation and specific care facilities, or nursing homes. Thereby, the functional spectrum of the systems and technologies is also very broad: more generic functions aim at the detection of individual activities and movements for health monitoring [17], of social activities [15], or health parameters to motivate physical activity [16], while specific functions address the identification of symptoms of dementia, e.g., detect and analyze typical and changes in patterns of movements and behaviors [18] or providing early notification of physicians and caregivers based on the detection of falls and specific dangerous situations (e.g., [19,20]).

Aiming at support and assistance in older age at home, the integration of video-based applications within the own home environments has been focused in different research areas [4,21]. Such approaches enable the extraction of useful information from the video data based on intelligent systems and underlying algorithms [5,6] enabling the previously described functions, e.g., detailed analyses of gait patterns or human behavior as well as the detection of emergencies, falls, and other dangerous situations. Thanks to visual capturing by one or just a few sensors information-rich data output can be obtained and can be easily interpreted by humans [4]. This makes video-based technology (VAAL) a highly effective and efficient health-monitoring technology given also the decreasing prices for camera sensors and constant improvements in computer vision [4].

In summary, a large number of applications are aimed at supporting and assisting people in their private home environment based on intelligent monitoring and analysis using computer vision. Beyond the potential and the advantages of these applications, future users' acceptance and willingness to use them are necessary.

1.2   Technology Perception and Acceptance

In the last decades, technology acceptance has frequently been analyzed by applying well-established models, namely, the Technology Acceptance Model [22] and the Unified Theory of Acceptance and Use of Technology [23], as well as their extensions and adaptions [24]. These models provided the basis for numerous studies and enabled an understanding of acceptance patterns and processes for new technologies. In addition to model-related parameters such as perceived usefulness and ease of use, research has shown that individual user characteristics (e.g., age, gender, experience) play a decisive role indicating that technology acceptance differs among different user groups (e.g., [23]). Besides the user as an acceptance subject, acceptance also differs depending on the specific type of technology (acceptance object) and the respective application context. Therefore, the perception and acceptance of a specific technology have to be examined separately taking specific technology- and context-dependent parameters into account.

In this regard, previous research has shown that context-related perceptions of benefits and concerns play a decisive role in its acceptance and sustainable adoption [10,25]. Enabling an autonomous life, support within the activities of daily living, relief for caring relatives, and increased safety represent major motives to use and advantages of using AAL technologies [10,12,25]. On the opposite, concerns regarding data security, a lack of human interaction, loneliness, and predominantly concerns regarding the intrusion of one's own privacy (i.e., perceived surveillance, unauthorized access to sensible health data) represent the most relevant barriers associated with the usage of AAL technologies [10,12,26]. The latter is becoming of utmost importance for the specific case of VAAL technologies such as cameras: here, previous research identified a comparably low acceptance and reluctant willingness to use camera-based AAL technologies to capture health-related data within the own home environment indicating high assessments of privacy concerns (e.g., [14,27]).

Due to its meaning for the acceptance of VAAL technologies, the multifaceted phenomenon of privacy is addressed in more detail in the following.

1.3 Privacy and Data Handling

Understanding privacy as a state of mind or an assertion of control (e.g., [28]), there are different approaches to describe and differentiate between diverse facets and dimensions of privacy (e.g., [28–30]). For instance, Burgoon [30] distinguishes four dimensions of privacy (informational, social, psychological, and physical privacy) and highlights the ability to control the specific aspects of privacy within the dimensions as relevant for the perception of whether privacy is high or low. Furthermore, privacy is defined as a regulation process that depends on personal and situational factors and is, therefore, contextual [31,32]. Focusing on digital environments and technologies, the regulation process is even more challenging, as it easily leads to perceptions of loss of control over personal information and people focus more on protecting against privacy threats than on meeting their actual needs [33] which among other, are contemplation, autonomy and confiding [34,45]. In this regard, digital (health) technologies enabling ubiquitous surveillance, storing of high amounts of data, and allowing rapid and global dissemination of information represent major threats to privacy [32].

Considering VAAL technologies, privacy is predominantly focused as a concern in terms of fears of access and misuse of personal information and feelings of permanent surveillance, having the potential to decrease acceptance and finally hinder the adoption of such systems [10,11,35]. While the digital environment and especially the specific visual technology are responsible for major privacy threats and concerns, these perceived dangers may be partly diminished by technological features itself such as image filters [4], limited timeslots for monitoring [36] or the restriction of data access and storage duration [37,38]. Indeed, especially when visual-based technologies are applied and with the definitions of privacy mentioned above in mind, privacy can be understood to be multi-faceted and context-dependent. Regarding aspects of context, previous research identified the performed activity as a relevant impacting factor for the comfortableness of being monitored with a camera-based technology [39] indicating that sensitive activities (e.g., hygiene care) were perceived as most uncomfortable. Of course, performed activities depend on situational factors which may play an important role in privacy perception. In this regard, findings showed that the acceptance of medical camera monitoring declines the more private the monitored spaces are [40] and the more skin is shown [41]. Taking personal factors into account, previous research showed that perceptions of safety and security [42] as well as the need for care [43] and the degree of disability [44] may impact the acceptance of VAAL technology. To sum up, these insights show that privacy is malleable and - under certain situational and personal circumstances - can be governed by a trade-off with various benefits associated with visual monitoring, e.g., increased security and helpfulness [42,43].

Beyond the insights of previous research, it is so far not well known which technical requirements are relevant and which ways of data handling are preferred (data access and data storage) focusing on the usage of VAAL technologies being applied for different activities of daily living.

2 Methods

Within this section, the methodological approach of the study is described, starting with the research aim and the underlying empirical concept. Subsequently, the structure of the online survey, the data analysis, and the characteristics of the sample are described.

2.1 Empirical Concept

The present study aimed at a detailed investigation of future users' preferences regarding technological requirements, different ways of data access, and different options of data storage within the context of applying VAAL technologies for different activities of daily living. For that purpose and based on a literature review and a preceding qualitative study, relevant parameters regarding technological requirements, data access, and data storage were selected.

Enabling a comparison of diverse activities of daily living, three different activity types were selected covering a broad range of possible activities: 1) household activity, 2) social activity, and 3) intimate activity. For each of the three activity types, a short scenario was presented to the participants in randomized order to control for order effects. For the scenario of a household activity, it was described that during cooking, cleaning, and tidying up a fire was caused as detected by the monitoring camera. The scenario of a social activity focused on longer interactions (i.e., playing and chatting) with friends or (grand)children and described that forgotten medicine was detected by the video-based system due to deviations from normal behavior. The last scenario described an intimate activity in terms of showering and changing clothes during which a fall was happening (due to physical decline in older age) and was also detected by the video-based AAL system. Following each scenario, the participants assessed their preferred ways of data access and data storage as well as technical requirements and technology acceptance.

The empirical concept was designed to answer the following research questions related to the usage of VAAL technologies:

1. RQ1: What are the most and least important aspects of technical requirements, data access, and data storage?
2. RQ2: To what extent does the activity type affect the evaluation of technical requirements, data access, and data storage?
3. RQ3: Which privacy and data handling preferences (requirements, access, storage) are relevant for the acceptance of VAAL technology?

2.2   Online Survey

An online survey was conceptualized and consisted of two main parts. Within the first part, the participants were asked for demographic information, such as their age, gender, educational level, and living situation. Following that, the participants indicated health-related information by stating if they suffer from a chronic illness and if they needed assistance and care in their everyday life (answer options: yes/no). In addition, they indicated if they had previous experiences in caring for other persons, i.e. professional ad private care experience (answer options: yes/no). Addressing attitudinal factors, the participants' technical understanding, psychometrics, and their general attitude towards privacy were assessed.

At the beginning of the second part of the survey, the participants were introduced to VAAL technologies. The participants were then asked to evaluate three different types of activities of daily living imagining themselves living with a VAAL system being installed in their home environment. Three specific activities (see Sect. 2.1) of daily living were described within scenarios in a randomized order. For each scenario, the participants assessed different technical requirements (6 items), different ways of data handling (6 items), and two different options for data storage. All items are illustrated in Fig. 1. Storage duration was evaluated by selecting the preferred option out of 5 options: not stored at all, max. 1 week, max. 1 month, max. 1 year, unlimited (see Fig. 3). Furthermore, the participants evaluated their acceptance, perceived benefits, and perceived barriers of using the visual-based AAL system for the respective type of activity. If not described otherwise, all items were rated on six-point Likert scales (1 = I completely disagree, 6 = I completely agree).

At the end of the survey, the participants could write their comments, feedback, and critiques regarding the survey or the topic in an open field.

2.3 Data Analysis

We report descriptive statistics for the evaluations indicating means (M) and standard deviations (SD). To investigate potential differences between the three activity types one-way repeated measure ANOVAs were applied. To examine potential relationships between the analysed constructs, correlation analyses were performed. Spearman's ρ was used for bivariate correlations and Pillai's V was stated for the omnibus test of ANOVAs. Linear regression analyses were calculated to analyze the relevance of the data handling preferences for technology acceptance. The level of statistical significance (p) was set at 5%.

2.4 Participants

N = 122 participants completed the online survey, and passed the data cleaning procedure (i.e., control for speeders, quality fails etc.) and their data sets were used for further statistical analyses. The participants were on average 38.39 years old (SD = 16.69; min = 17; max = 81) and almost two-thirds of the participants were female (63.9%, n = 78). The educational level of the sample was comparably high with the majority (61.5%, n = 75) holding a university degree, 3.3% (n = 4) a PhD, and 29.5% (n = 36) an university entrance qualification. Only 5.7% (n = 7) indicated lower educational levels.

Asked for their health status, almost a quarter of the participants indicated suffering from a chronic illness (24.6%, n = 30) and only 6.6% (n = 8) reported being in need of assistance and care. Beyond that, 13.1% (n = 16) reported having professional experience in care, while more than a third of the participants (36.9%, n = 45) reported having private experience in care by indicating that they have already cared for a person in need of care in their personal environment.

3 Results

In this section, the results of the empirical study are described, starting with an overview of the assessments of technical requirements and data handling preferences overall. In the second step, the results are shown differentiated between the three activity types. In the last step, relationships between technical requirements, data handling preferences, and technology acceptance are communicated.

3.1   Evaluation of Requirements and Data Handling (RQ1)

The descriptive overall results (independent from the three activity types) of the evaluated technical requirements and data handling preferences are visualized in Fig. 1. Starting with the **technical requirements**, it was evaluated as most important that *Technology must be controllable and checkable at all times* (M = 5.01; SD = .88). *Technology must be able to be switched on and off at any time* (M = 4.82; SD = .92) received the second highest agreement. Further, the participants slightly agreed with the requirement that *Technology must only be used when alone* (M = 3.96; SD = 1.17). Referring to specific requirements regarding what is allowed to be recorded, the participants showed indistinct evaluations. They slightly agreed with the requirement that *No video recordings are allowed* (M = 3.70; SD = 1.15) and they showed neutral evaluations of the statement that *Technology may record all activities* (M = 3.48; SD = 1.21). However, the requirement that *Only audio recordings are allowed to be made* was in tendency slightly rejected (M = 3.35; SD = 1.12).

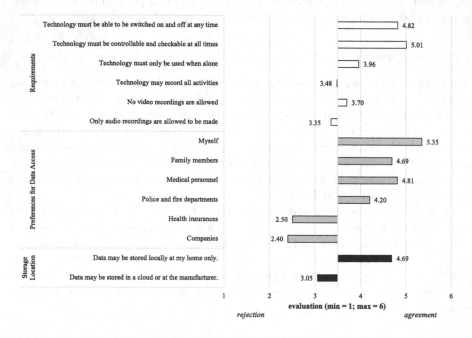

Fig. 1. Descriptive results of data handling preferences.

Asked for different entities being allowed to **access the recorded data**, the participants showed very distinct evaluation patterns. Data access was most desired for the respective persons themselves: *Myself* (M = 5.35; SD = .88). *Medical personnel* (M = 4.81; SD = .90) and *Family members* (M = 4.69; SD = 1.03) were also clearly allowed to have access to the recorded data. For *Police and* *fire departments* (M = 4.20; SD = 1.08), the results showed a lower, but still clear agreement for data access. In contrast, data access was unequivocally rejected for *Health Insurances* (M = 2.50; SD = 1.27) and *Companies* (M = 2.40; SD = 1.33).

Considering the **storage options**, it was clearly preferred that *Data may be stored locally at my own home only* (M = 4.69; SD = 1.04), while the option that *Data may be stored in a cloud or at the manufacturer* was rather rejected (M = 3.05; SD = 1.38).

The results of the evaluation of **storage duration** options showed that overall 21.30% (n = 26) of the participants selected the option that *Data may be stored unlimitedly*. Further, 25.4% (n = 31) preferred that *Data may be stored for max. 1 week.*, while 23.8% (n = 29) of the participants desired the option *Data may be stored for max. 1 month.*. Finally, 29.5% (n = 36) selected the option *Data may be stored for max. 1 year*. The option that *Data may not be stored at all* was not selected averaged over all three activity types. However, differences dependent on the three activity types are described in the next subsection.

3.2 Preferences for Different Activities (RQ2)

The descriptive results of the evaluated data handling preferences depending on the three activity types are visualized in Fig. 2. The results of one-way repeated measure analyses revealed overall rather similar evaluation patterns with significant differences only in single aspects.

Starting with the **technical requirements**, the most relevant requirements that technology must be *able to be switched on and off at any time* ($F(2,118) = 2.67$; $p = .07$, n.s.), *controllable and checkable at all times* ($F(2,117) = .31$; $p = .74$, n.s.), and *only be used when alone* ($F(2,117) = 1.51$; $p = .23$, n.s.) were all not evaluated significantly differently. Further, also the requirement that *Technology may record all activities* ($F(2,118) = 2.11$; $p = .13$, n.s.) did not reveal significant differences for the three activity types. Instead, the last two requirements were evaluated significantly differently indicating a higher relevance of these aspects for intimate compared to social and household activities: first, the requirement *No video recordings are allowed* ($F(2,117) = 3.87$; $p < .05$) received the highest agreement for intimate activities (M = 3.86; SD = 1.44), followed by social (M = 3.73; SD = 1.44) and lastly household activities (M = 3.48; SD = 1.44); second, that *Only audio recordings are allowed to be made* ($F(2,115) = 4.43$; $p < .05$) received a slight agreement for intimate activities (M = 3.60; SD = 1.38), while it was slightly rejected for social (M = 3.28; SD = 1.29) and household activities (M = 3.26; SD = 1.35).

Moving to the different options of **data access**, allowing data access for *Myself* ($F(2,118) = .16$; $p = .85$, n.s.) and *Medical personnel* ($F(2,117) = .17$; $p = .85$, n.s.) were not evaluated significantly different. In line with this, also the both rejected alternatives of providing data access for *Health insurances* ($F(2,115) = 2.11$; $p = .11$, n.s.) and *Companies* ($F(2,116) = .62$; $p = .54$, n.s.) was assessed equally. In contrast, the participants showed different evaluation patterns for two of the data access options: allowing data access for *Family members* ($F(2,117) = 5.95$ (HF); $p < .01$) received higher agreements for household

(M = 4.86; SD = 1.10) compared to social (M = 4.69; SD = 1.16) and intimate activities (M = 4.56; SD = 1.23); in accordance with that, data access for *Police and fire departments* (F(2,115) = 8.79 (HF); $p < .01$) was also significantly higher related to household activities (M = 4.49; SD = 1.39) compared to social (M = 4.15; SD = 1.44) and intimate activities (M = 4.08; SD = 1.48).

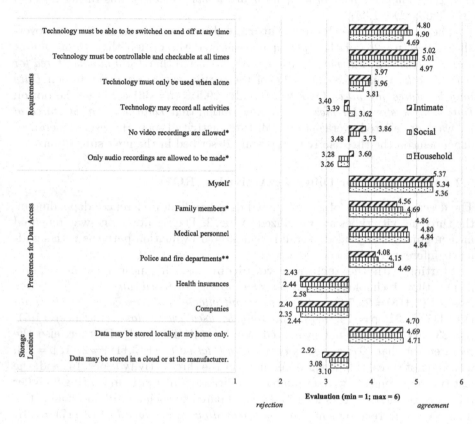

Fig. 2. Data handling preferences for different activities (* = $p < .05$; ** = $p < .01$).

Related to the different **storage options**, neither *locally at my own home* (F(2,114) = .02; p = .98, n.s.) nor *stored in a cloud* (F(2,115) = 1.96; p = .15, n.s.) received significantly different evaluations depending from the three activity types.

The results of the evaluated **storage duration** preferences depending on the three activity types are shown in Fig. 3. Overall, the results of a two-way Friedman ANOVA analysis showed that the evaluation pattern of the storage duration was not equal for the three activities (F(2,120) = 12.67; $p < .01$). Pairwise comparisons revealed effects between the three activity types, but not on a significant level. Nevertheless, looking at the descriptive results in Fig. 3, it can be seen that the evaluation patterns between household and social activities were

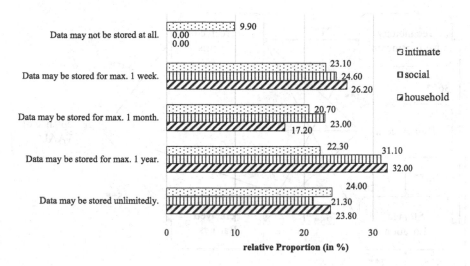

Fig. 3. Storage Duration preferences for different activities.

rather similar. In contrast, intimate activities represented the only activity type for which the option *Data may not be stored at all* was chosen (9.90%, n = 12).

Overall, the results regarding the three activity types showed a rather generic evaluation of VAAL technologies as only isolated differences between the three activity types were identified.

3.3 Relationships with Technology Perception and Acceptance (RQ3)

On the basis of the previous results, we conducted correlation analyses independent from the three activity types in order to identify relevant relationships between the preferences with regard to technical requirements and data handling on the one hand, and the perception and acceptance of VAAL technology on the other hand. The respective results are illustrated in Fig. 4.

First of all, the results revealed a significant relationship between the perceived benefits and the acceptance of VAAL technologies ($\rho = .58$; $p < .01$) as well as between the perceived barriers and acceptance ($\rho = -.35$; $p < .01$). Beyond that, the technology requirements correlated with the perceived benefits ($\rho = .21$; $p < .05$) and the perceived barriers ($\rho = .33$; $p < .01$), but not directly with the acceptance of VAAL technologies. Data access showed a slight correlation with the perceived barriers ($\rho = -.18$; $p < .05$) and a stronger correlation with the perceived benefits ($\rho = .34$; $p < .01$) and even directly with the acceptance of VAAL technology ($\rho = .41$; $p < .01$). For the storage location, the results revealed relationships with the perceived benefits ($\rho = .28$; $p < .01$) and the acceptance of VAAL technology ($\rho = .25$; $p < .05$). In contrast, the storage duration did neither correlate with the perceived benefits and barriers nor with the acceptance of VAAL technology. Among the preferences, technology

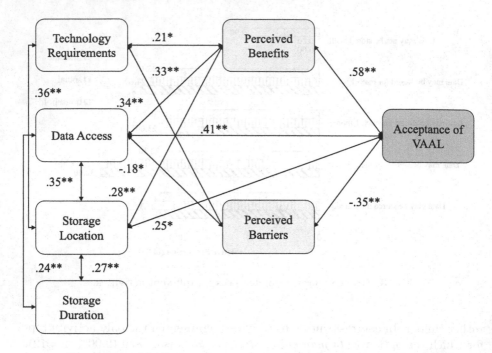

Fig. 4. Data handling preferences related to technology acceptance.

requirements showed a correlation with the storage location ($\rho = .36$; $p < .01$). In addition, the storage location was related to data access ($\rho = .35$; $p < .01$) and the storage duration ($\rho = .27$; $p < .01$). Lastly, data access correlated also with storage duration ($\rho = .24$; $p < .01$).

In order to assess the relevance of the requirements and data handling preferences for the acceptance of VAAL technology, a linear (forward) regression analysis was conducted in the last step. The final regression model explained 48.4% (adj. $r^2 = .484$) of the variance of the acceptance of VAAL technology ($F(3,121) = 38.82$; $p < .01$) based on the constructs perceived benefits ($\beta = .51$; $p < .01$) and perceived barriers ($\beta = -.24$; $p < .01$) as well as data access ($\beta = .18$; $p < .05$). All other constructs (requirements, storage location, and storage duration) were excluded from analyses and did therefore not represent explaining predictors for the acceptance of VAAL technology.

4   Discussion

In this section, the results of the empirical study are discussed, starting with the key insights and answering the underlying research questions. Afterwards, we derive implications for technology development and design, describe the limitations of the conducted approach, and highlight recommendations for future work in this research area.

4.1   Social Implications of Empirical Findings

The present study investigated technology requirements and data handling preferences of potential future users of video-based AAL technology for three different activities of daily living. Therefore, study participants were introduced to safety-critical scenarios with a household activity, a social activity and an intimate activity respectively. For each activity, technology acceptance, several conditions of technology usage (e.g., on/off switching, controllability, video/audio recordings), data access, and data storage location and duration were assessed. The aim was to understand the least and most important aspects of technology requirements and data handling (RQ1), to examine the influence of activity type on the single evaluations (RQ2) and lastly, to investigate the relevance of these preferences for the acceptance of video-based AAL (RQ3).

Concerning the evaluation of the requirements, controlling and checking the technology and being able to switch it on and off resulted in the most important prerequisites. These findings are completely in line with literature assessing AAL in general (e.g., [37,45,46]). Previous studies report that older adults (i.e., AAL users) consider it as part of autonomy preservation wanting to control technology and deliberately switching devices on and off is one way of exercising this control [37,46]. Furthermore, there was no clear trend for or against monitoring all activities, which underlines the importance of assessing requirements for single activity types to obtain valuable information. Indeed, monitoring all household activities is slightly accepted but not the recording of all social and intimate activities. This reflects current literature about camera monitoring, reporting more private rooms as less acceptable to be filmed [13,49] and intimate activities as more critical and uncomfortable to be captured [39,41,47,48]. Similarly, evaluations for audio and video recordings did not reveal any overall positioning. Clear patterns as well as significantly different positioning emerged when zooming into the specific activities. No video recordings were slightly favoured for intimate activity but not for social and household activity. Only audio recording was an acceptable option for intimate activity but not for social and household activity. Considering these nuanced findings across activities, the low acceptance rates for video-based monitoring in the own home documented in the literature [13,40,49] may mostly refer to the monitoring of these intimate moments and not towards the entire home.

Another important aspect for potential users of VAAL is the question of who accesses the data. In the evaluation of data access, a clear pattern could be observed that people with whom one can have a direct relationship and contact are more likely to be granted access. In contrast, health insurance and companies which are rather collective and anonymous identities with potential economical interests are strictly rejected. This rejection did not differ across the three activities and is in line with previous findings (e.g., [27,38,50]). Besides access for oneself, medical personnel is the most accepted person group, who have an interest in one's health and well-being. The fact that health matters independently from activity, may be one reason why there is no significant difference for medical personnel among the activities assessed - health matters in any scenario equally. The willingness to share data with medical personnel is partly in line with [27,50]. However, for family members, as well as police and fire departments the data access allowance was rated differently for the three activities. For the intimate activity scenario, data access was least granted whereas providing family members and police and fire corps access to data from the household activity was rather accepted. This result suggests differing privacy and intimacy implications for each activity being filmed which may explain these different evaluations among the scenarios. As already known from previous studies, the comfortableness and showing of skin are highly sensitive and monitoring is critical or rejected [39,41]. Furthermore, the scenario of the household activity described a fire incident which may have further impacted the decision to let police and fire corps access the data. Independent from activity, local storage was strongly favoured whereas cloud/external storage was slightly rejected. This may be partly explained by the main concerns of VAAL which are fear of data hacking, data misuse and unauthorized data access [10,11,35]. Naturally, the more public the storage location, the less control over it and the higher the potential risk that these concerns become reality. In addition, the preference for local storage is in line with previous investigations [38]. Interestingly, regarding storage duration, participants did not decide with the same logic - the longer the data exists, the more possibilities of hacking and misusing it. Indeed, for household and social activity participants preferred relatively long storage of one year the most. If looking at the relative proportion of the most favoured storage duration of intimate activities the most selected one was unlimited storage. At first sight, this might seem very disruptive but when considering the remaining evaluations, a relatively short duration of one-week storage was the second most selected option and, different from the other two activities, some participants even selected no storage at all for the data from the intimate activity. The fact that the evaluation patterns for storage duration differed across activities is further evidence that technical preferences for VAAL usage are strongly dependent on what activity is monitored. The overall trend towards a rather long storage duration suggests that participants may have considered the informational value of past data to allow for a better understanding of their own health. Indeed, one of the benefits of lifelogging and continuous monitoring and data storage is that it enables the detection of abnormalities and deviations from normal behaviour and usual routines [4,51].

Furthermore, as part of the third research question, relationships between technological requirements, data handling and technology acceptance together with benefits and barriers were looked at. As logical, benefits had a positive relationship with acceptance whereas barriers had a negative one, which just confirms them as concepts. Technological requirements affect perceptions of benefits and barriers but not directly the technology acceptance. It may be that several technological requirements or the lacking thereof may even be perceived as either benefits or barriers respectively. Frequently framed under data handling, data access, storage location, and storage duration are all connected with each other. When looking at their relationships with VAAL acceptance and perceived benefits and barriers, storage duration seems to be irrelevant and storage location is only slightly relevant for perceived benefits and to a lesser extent for acceptance. In turn, data access was revealed to be the most relevant facet of data handling preferences impacting perceptions of benefits and barriers as well as acceptance. Linear regression analysis further confirmed data access as the only facet of data handling which serves as a predictor of acceptance of VAAL. This makes sense, considering that people strongly protect themselves from the disclosure of harmful and/or sensitive information about themselves to preserve privacy [33, 34] and protecting data is one of the most important factors for users of pervasive health-monitoring systems [45]. Related to the study result that among data handling only data access predicts acceptance, this means that disclosure happens of course through data access no matter where data is stored and how long it is stored there.

4.2 Managerial Recommendations, Limitations and Future Work

The insights of this study enable us to derive some recommendations and implications for future technology development and design in order to enable the consideration of users' needs and requirements.

Focusing on technical requirements, future users should be able to control the technology at any time (e.g., switching on/off) as it represents a central prerequisite for sustainable usage and adoption. Further, access to recorded data should be controlled by the users themselves. It is of utmost importance that data access for third parties, such as companies and health insurance, serves as a "No Go" and represents central obstacles to the acceptance and adoption of VAAL technologies in the everyday life. These recommendations are even more important in case the technology is aimed to be used to record potentially intimate activities and thus sensitive information. The differences in evaluations between the three activities highlight that there is not one customized technological solution. One single user may want to customize each area in his or her home differently or different activities detected should be visualized differently and access allowances should vary. These variances among one single (potential) user mean that the system and the single devices should account for that and make this detailed customization possible. Taking the storage options into account, local storage is preferred, however, storage options played a minor role in perceptions and acceptance of VAAL technology. Overall, it should be aimed at providing transparent and comprehensible information about functions, requirements, and data handling of using VAAL technology in order to enable a trustworthy and sustainable usage of VAAL technology.

Besides novel insights and derived implications, there are also limitations of this study that should be considered for future research enabling to derive some ideas for future work in the field.

Starting with sample-related aspects, the sample of our study was comparably small and not perfectly balanced regarding age, gender, and educational level. In particular, future studies should try to reach larger samples, including higher proportions of older people and people with lower educational levels. In addition, it has to be mentioned that the participants from this study originated from Germany and Bulgaria. Country- and culture-related comparisons were not part of this investigation, but should be focused on in future analyses. Beyond that, more detailed country- and culture-specific analyses would be useful to gain more insights into value- and culture-based differences in data handling preferences, technology acceptance, and perception.

The applied methodological approach was useful to investigate whether activity types affect the preferences of requirements and data handling. However, only three rather generic types of daily activities were considered disregarding specific activities, such as care-related aspects or severe health situations, e.g., falls or emergencies. Future studies should therefore also consider more specific activities and situations to investigate potential changes within the evaluation patterns of data handling and preferences. Beyond that, the conducted survey and analyses enabled only absolute evaluations of the technical requirements and data handling. For future research, it would be useful to analyze the relative importance of the different aspects (e.g., by applying conjoint analysis approaches). As a last idea for future research, future users' knowledge, information, and mental models can be decisive for the adoption of innovative technologies. Here, it would be interesting to analyze and investigate potential influences of the users' perceived and real knowledge about the specific technology and data handling on the evaluations of using VAAL technology in the everyday life.

5 Conclusion

The conducted quantitative study applied an online survey to identify potential users' most relevant requirements and data handling preferences for using VAAL technology. The results revealed a rather generic evaluation of VAAL (being only sporadically influenced by specific activity types) and identified data access to be a relevant predictor for technology acceptance in addition to technology-related perceived benefits and barriers. The insights are used to derive implications for user-centred technology development and design by considering user-relevant requirements and data handling preferences.

Acknowledgements. The authors thank all participants for sharing their opinions and needs in the context of privacy and acceptance of VAAL technologies. We also thank Ivanina Buchkova for her research support. This work resulted from the project VisuAAL "Privacy-Aware and Acceptable Video-Based Technologies and Services for Active and Assisted Living" and was funded by the European Union's Horizon 2020 research and innovation programme under the Marie Skłodowska-Curie grant agreement No 861091.

References

1. Rashidi, P., Mihailidis, A.: A survey on ambient-assisted living tools for older adults. IEEE J. Biomed. Health Inform. **7**, 579–590 (2013)
2. Blackman, S., et al.: Ambient assisted living technologies for aging well: a scoping review. J. Intell. Syst. **25**, 55–69 (2016)

3. Calvaresi, D., Cesarini, D., Sernani, P., Marinoni, M., Dragoni, A.F., Sturm, A.: Exploring the ambient assisted living domain: a systematic review. J. Ambient Intell. Hum. Comput. **8**, 239–257 (2017)
4. Climent-Pérez, P., Spinsante, S., Mihailidis, A., Flórez-Revuelta, F.: A review on video-based active and assisted living technologies for automated lifelogging. Exp. Syst. Appl. **139**, 112847 (2020)
5. Ćirić, I.T., et al.: Thermal vision based intelligent system for human detection and tracking in mobile robot control system. Therm. Sci. **20**, 1553–1559 (2016)
6. Chen, L., Yang, H., Liu, P.: Intelligent robot arm: vision-based dynamic measurement system for industrial applications. In: Yu, H., Liu, J., Liu, L., Ju, Z., Liu, Y., Zhou, D. (eds.) ICIRA 2019. LNCS (LNAI), vol. 11744, pp. 120–130. Springer, Cham (2019). https://doi.org/10.1007/978-3-030-27541-9_11
7. Sefat, M.S., Khan, A.A.M., Shahjahan, M.: Implementation of vision based intelligent home automation and security system. In: Proceedings of the International Conference on Informatics, Electronics & Vision (ICIEV), Dhaka, Bangladesh, pp. 1–6 (2014)
8. Mubashir, M., Shao, L., Seed, L.: A survey on fall detection: principles and approaches. Neurocomputing **100**, 144–152 (2013)
9. Sathyanarayana, S., Satzoda, R.K., Sathyanarayana, S., Thambipillai, S.: Vision-based patient monitoring: a comprehensive review of algorithms and technologies. J. Ambient. Intell. Hum. Comput. **9**, 225–251 (2018)
10. Peek, S.T., Wouters, E.J., Van Hoof, J., Luijkx, K.G., Boeije, H.R., Vrijhoef, H.J.: Factors influencing acceptance of technology for aging in place: a systematic review. Int. J. Med. Inform. **83**, 235–248 (2014)
11. Lorenzen-Huber, L., Boutain, M., Camp, L.J., Shankar, K., Connelly, K.H.: Privacy, technology, and aging: a proposed framework. Ageing Int. **36**, 232–252 (2011)
12. Jaschinski, C.: Independent aging with the help of smart technology: investigating the acceptance of ambient assisted living technologies. Ph.D. Thesis, University of Twente, Twente (2018)
13. Himmel, S., Ziefle, M.: Smart home medical technologies: users' requirements for conditional acceptance. i-com. **15**, 39–50 (2016)
14. Offermann-van Heek, J., Schomakers, E.M., Ziefle, M.: Bare necessities? How the need for care modulates the acceptance of ambient assisted living technologies. Int. J. Med. Inform. **127**, 147–156 (2019)
15. Wang, L., Gu, T., Tao, X., Lu, J.: Sensor-based human activity recognition in a multi-user scenario. In: Tscheligi, M., et al. (eds.) AmI 2009. LNCS, vol. 5859, pp. 78–87. Springer, Heidelberg (2009). https://doi.org/10.1007/978-3-642-05408-2_10
16. Schoeppe, S., et al.: Efficacy of interventions that use apps to improve diet, physical activity and sedentary behaviour: a systematic review. Int. J. Behav. Nut. Phys. Act. **13**, 127 (2016)
17. Nambu, M., Nakajima, K., Noshiro, M., Tamura, T.: An algorithm for the automatic detection of health conditions. IEEE Eng. Med. Bio. Mag. **24**, 38–42 (2005)
18. Meditskos, G., Plans, P.M., Stavropoulos, T.G., Benois-Pineau, J., Buso, V., Kompatsiaris, I.: Multi-modal activity recognition from egocentric vision, semantic enrichment and lifelogging applications for the care of dementia. J. Vis. Comm. Image Repres. **51**, 169–190 (2018)
19. Shi, G., Chan, C.S., Li, W.J., Leung, K.-S., Zou, Y., Jin, Y.: Mobile human airbag system for fall protection using mems sensors and embedded SVM classifier. IEEE Sens. J. **9**, 495–503 (2008)

20. Postawka, A., Rudy, J.: Lifelogging system based on averaged hidden Markov models: dangerous activities recognition for caregiver support. Comput. Sci. **19**, 257–278 (2018)
21. Jalal, A., Kamal, S., Kim, D.: A depth video sensor-based lifelogging human activity recognition system for elderly care in smart indoor environments. Sensors. **14**, 11735–11759 (2014)
22. Davis, F.D.: Perceived usefulness, perceived ease of use, and user acceptance of information technology. MIS Q. **13**, 319–340 (1989)
23. Venkatesh, V., Morris, M.G., Davis, G.B., Davis, F.D.: User acceptance of information technology: toward a unified view. MIS Q. **27**, 425–478 (2003)
24. Rahimi, B., Nadri, H., Afshar, H.L., Timpka, T.: A systematic review of the technology acceptance model in health informatics. Appl. Clin. Inform. **9**(3), 604–634 (2018)
25. Jaschinski, C., Ben Allouch, S.: Why should i use this? Identifying incentives for using AAL technologies. In: De Ruyter, B., Kameas, A., Chatzimisios, P., Mavrommati, I. (eds.) AmI 2015. LNCS, vol. 9425, pp. 155–170. Springer, Cham (2015). https://doi.org/10.1007/978-3-319-26005-1_11
26. Wilkowska, W.: Acceptance of eHealth Technology in Home Environments: Advanced Studies on User Diversity in Ambient Assisted Living. Apprimus Verlag, Aachen, Germany (2015)
27. Wilkowska, W., Offermann-van Heek, J., Florez-Revuelta, F., Ziefle, M.: Video cameras for lifelogging at home: preferred visualization modes, acceptance, and privacy perceptions among German and Turkish participants. Int. J. Hum.-Comput. Inter. **37**, 1436–1454 (2021)
28. Westin, A.F.: Privacy and Freedom. Atheneum, New York (1967)
29. Marshall, N.J.: Dimensions of privacy preferences. Multivar. Behav. Res. **9**, 255–271 (1974)
30. Burgoon, J.K.: Privacy and communication. Ann. Int. Commun. Assoc. **6**, 206–249 (1982)
31. Altman, I.: Privacy: a conceptual analysis. In: Carson, D.H. (ed.) Man-Environment Interactions: Evaluations and Applications: Part 2, pp. 3–28. Environmental Design Research Association: Washington, DC (1974)
32. Nissenbaum, H.: Privacy in Context. Stanford University Press, Stanford (2009)
33. Lombardi, D.B., Ciceri, M.R.: More than defense in daily experience of privacy: the functions of privacy in digital and physical environments. Eur. J. Psychol. **12**, 115–136 (2016)
34. Pedersen, D.M.: Psychological functions of privacy. J. Environ. Psychol. **17**(2), 147–156 (1997)
35. Demiris, G., et al.: Older adults' attitudes towards and perceptions of 'smart home' technologies: a pilot study. Med. Inform. Internet Med. **29**, 87–94 (2004)
36. Lapierre, N., et al.: Older women's perceptions of a programmable video monitoring system at home: a pilot study. Gerontechnology 4(17), 245–254 (2018)
37. Maidhof, C., Ziefle, M., Offermann, J.: Exploring privacy: mental models of potential users of AAL technology. In: ICT4AWE 2022 - Proceedings of the 8th International Conference on Information and Communication Technologies for Ageing Well and e-Health (2022)
38. Wilkowska, W., Offermann-van Heek, J., Colonna, L., Ziefle, M.: Two faces of privacy: legal and human-centered perspectives of lifelogging applications in home environments. In: Gao, Q., Zhou, J. (eds.) HCII 2020. LNCS, vol. 12208, pp. 545–564. Springer, Cham (2020). https://doi.org/10.1007/978-3-030-50249-2_39

39. Caine, K., Šabanovic, S., Carter, M.: The effect of monitoring by cameras and robots on the privacy enhancing behaviors of older adults. In: Proceedings of the Seventh Annual ACM/IEEE International Conference on Human-Robot Interaction, Boston, MA, USA, pp. 343–350 (2012)

40. Arning, K., Ziefle, M.: "Get that camera out of my house!" conjoint measurement of preferences for video-based healthcare monitoring systems in private and public places. In: Geissbühler, A., Demongeot, J., Mokhtari, M., Abdulrazak, B., Aloulou, H. (eds.) ICOST 2015. LNCS, vol. 9102, pp. 152–164. Springer, Cham (2015). https://doi.org/10.1007/978-3-319-19312-0_13

41. Maidhof, C., Hashemifard, K., Offermann, J., Ziefle, M., Florez-Revuelta, F.: Underneath your clothes: a social and technological perspective on nudity in the context of AAL technology. In: Proceedings of the 15th International Conference on PErvasive Technologies Related to Assistive Environments, Crete, Greece, July 2022, pp. 439–445 (2022)

42. Londei, S.T., et al.: An intelligent video monitoring system for fall detection at home: perceptions of elderly people. J. Telemed. Telecare 15, 383–390 (2009)

43. Offermann-van Heek, J., Ziefle, M.: Nothing else matters! Trade-offs between perceived benefits and barriers of AAL technology usage. Front. Public Health 7, 134 (2019)

44. Beach, S., Schulz, R., Downs, J., Matthews, J., Barron, B., Seelman, K.: Disability, age, and informational privacy attitudes in quality of life technology applications: results from a national web survey. ACM Trans. Access. Comput. 2, 1–21 (2009)

45. McNeill, A., Briggs, P., Pywell, J., Coventry, L.: Functional privacy concerns of older adults about pervasive health-monitoring systems. In: Proceedings of the 10th International Conference on Pervasive Technologies Related to Assistive Environments, pp. 96–102 (2017)

46. Berridge, C., et al.: Control matters in elder care technology: evidence and direction for designing it in. In: Designing Interactive Systems Conference, pp. 1831–1848 (2022)

47. Choe, E.K., Consolvo, S., Jung, J., Harrison, B., Kientz, J.A.: Living in a glass house: a survey of private moments in the home. In: Proceedings of the 13th International Conference on Ubiquitous Computing, pp. 41–44. Springer, Heidelberg (2011)

48. Offermann, J., Wilkowska, W., Maidhof, C., Ziefle, M.: Shapes of you? Investigating the acceptance of video-based AAL technologies applying different visualization modes. Sensors 23(3), 1143 (2023)

49. Ziefle, M., Himmel, S., Wilkowska, W.: When your living space knows what you do: acceptance of medical home monitoring by different technologies. In: Holzinger, A., Simonic, K.-M. (eds.) USAB 2011. LNCS, vol. 7058, pp. 607–624. Springer, Heidelberg (2011). https://doi.org/10.1007/978-3-642-25364-5_43

50. Boise, L., Wild, K., Mattek, N., Ruhl, M., Dodge, H.H., Kaye, J.: Willingness of older adults to share data and privacy concerns after exposure to unobtrusive in-home monitoring. Gerontechnology: Int. J. Fund. Aspects Technol. Serve Ageing Soc. 11(3), 428 (2013)

51. Selke, S. (ed.): Lifelogging: Digital Self-tracking and Lifelogging-Between Disruptive Technology and Cultural Transformation. Springer, Wiesbaden (2016). https://doi.org/10.1007/978-3-658-13137-1

Smart Home for the Elderly - A Comparative Study on Interaction Techniques

Monika Schak[⊠], Isabell Bürkner, Rainer Blum, and Birgit Bomsdorf

Fulda University of Applied Sciences, Fulda, Germany
{monika.schak,isabell-mechthild.buerkner,rainer.blum,
birgit.bomsdorf}@cs.hs-fulda.de

Abstract. We present the findings of a study to determine which inter-action technique (touch control, voice control, gesture control, or activity control) is preferred by the elderly to control smart home devices. We conducted a workshop with eight senior citizens during which they were introduced to smart home devices in a smart living laboratory and learned how to control them. After experiencing the interaction techniques, they were asked about their experience, what they liked and disliked and which was their most and least favorite interaction technique for a specific scenario. We compared the results to their previous opinion gained from a postal survey conducted a year before the workshop to validate our assumption that senior citizens, when asked about which interaction technique they like most, will pick the technique they know best, i.e. touch control, instead of what would actually be the easiest and most intuitive way to control a smart home device. In the postal survey, most participants selected touch control as their favorite interaction technique. During the workshop it became apparent that many of them would prefer voice control or gesture control as it is close to how they would interact with a human being and they experienced it as a very natural, thus intuitive, form of communication.

Keywords: Human Aspects of IT for the Aged Population · Accommodations for aging-in-place · Daily living activity support · Generational differences in IT use · Smart home and IoT

1 Introduction

Research has found that senior citizens can benefit from using smart home devices to allow them to live a self-determined life at home instead of moving to a nursing home or assisted living facility. Such devices have to be easy to use for the elderly, among other factors, in order to unfold their benefits. If the devices require extensive training, senior citizens are often discouraged from using them [5].

Therefore, we conducted a study to answer the following question: Which interaction technique is preferred by the elderly when controlling smart home

© The Author(s), under exclusive license to Springer Nature Switzerland AG 2023
Q. Gao and J. Zhou (Eds.): HCII 2023, LNCS 14043, pp. 66–79, 2023.
https://doi.org/10.1007/978-3-031-34917-1_5

devices? The study was organized in the form of what we call a workshop. It followed a postal survey [13] with 87 participants, that we conducted in 2021, where we asked about experiences and knowledge about technical devices - especially smart home devices - and opinions about the four interaction techniques touch control, voice control, free-hand gesture control, and activity control (recognizing activities to trigger actions respectively). In the follow-up study, we invited eight of the senior citizens - four males and four females with an average age of 77 years - who previously had participated in the postal survey, to our smart living laboratory.

In the postal survey, many participants ranked touch control as their favorite interaction technique. Our assumption is that they often pick what they know best. Since touch control is readily available in many situations, e.g. in smartphones, tablet computers, cash points or ticket machines, it is an interaction technique the elderly are familiar with and thus prefer to something they have not experienced yet. We also believe that senior citizens can benefit from smart home devices but are scared to use them. Intuitive and natural interaction techniques could help lower the barriers and even enable senior citizens with impairments or disabilities to use smart home devices.

2 Related Work

This work examines four different interaction techniques: touch control, voice control, gesture control, and activity, all of which are common in recent research for human-machine interaction.

Touch control means interacting with a technical device by touching the display with one or more fingers. Predefined graphical control elements or gestures on the screen lead to distinct behavior. Touch control is very common in smartphones or tablet computers, but is also used for e.g. ticket machines. A lot of research regarding human-computer interaction for the elderly has focused on touch control. Kobayashi et al. [10] conducted studies to find common problems senior citizens face when interacting with touch devices. They conclude that basic gestures (tapping, dragging, and pinching motions) are easy to use for most of the elderly, but experience and training is needed for them to feel comfortable. Bara et al. [4] also take into consideration that the elderly often struggle with impairments, such as limitations in vision and motion. Those difficulties can lead to a reduced acceptance of touch devices. Their research rather focuses on how the user can be notified in case of an event instead of addressing the special requirements of users with impairments. This is where our research ties in.

The second interaction technique in our research is voice control. Voice control means interacting with a device by spoken commands, it is commonly used in voice assistants like Siri, or smart speakers like Amazon Echo. Voice control is also extensively researched in the scope of technical devices for the elderly. The difficulties senior citizens may face when using touch devices, as stated above, lead to over one third of the elderly who refuse to use touch devices [9]. Sahlab et al. [12] used this fact as the starting point for their research and suggest using speech to interact with smart devices as it is more natural and familiar for senior citizens. At the same time, they find that the elderly have reservations about using voice-controlled devices, e.g. due to missing known benefit, safety and security concerns, and insecurities how to use such devices, which is also something we want to address in our study.

Gesture control means using freehand gestures to interact with a technical device without direct physical contact. It is already used in cars to allow the driver to interact with the infotainment system without being distracted by locating a button or a graphical area on the screen, e.g. BMW Gesture Control [1]. Most research on gesture control for senior citizens focuses on the technical aspect. Vorwerg et al. [17] as well as Ayubi et al. [3] suggest an intuitive gesture-controlled device to control smart home devices for senior citizens with and without impairments in mobility. Another contribution of their work is the proof that it is technically possible to develop technical devices with gesture control interfaces for people with mobility impairments without a disadvantage in the user experience. A similar result has been achieved by Wang et al. [18], who present a gesture-controlled smart home system operable by senior citizens with impairments in motion, hearing, or speaking.

The fourth interaction technique we used for our study is activity control, which is a system that monitors daily living activities, classifies and predicts them in order to be able to trigger actions accordingly. It could, for example, turn the lights on if the resident is going to read, or lock the door if the resident is going to sleep. Such a system is not yet available on the market, but still focused on in research. The functionality can be compared to what is already available in smartwatches, that are able to recognize and record activities, e.g. when the user is sleeping or working out. Lentzas and Vrakas [11] showed that activity control – also called human activity recognition or abnormal behavior detection – are of increasing interest in the scientific community. Thakur and Han [16] propose a system that can analyse and predict human behavior and thus can improve the daily life of senior citizens by anticipating the users' activities and assist with everyday tasks without the need for the user to consciously interact with the system. A major use case of activity control is fall detection for the elderly, e.g. as presented by Alazrai et al. [2]. Sucerquia et al. [15] conducted real-life validations of their system for effective fall detection for the elderly to provide immediate support by alerting relatives or health care services in case of a fall. Chernbumroong et al. [7] follow a different approach as their system constantly monitors the users' activity pattern to detect behavioral changes that can be an early sign of long-term health detriment.

Our assumption that the elderly would rather prefer something they are familiar with is based on the "Status Quo Bias" [19]. The same was noted by Bejanaro et al. [6], who state that "as long as mobile devices are required [...], they will continue to be the preferred interface by many users". This is the starting point for our research as we intend to prove this hypothesis to be correct and that senior citizens would rather adopt other forms of interaction if they were broadly available.

3   Methodology

We conducted a study in the form of a workshop with eight participants in our smart living laboratory to answer the research question mentioned before: Which interaction technique is preferred by the elderly when controlling smart home devices? The postal survey showed that many of the elderly did not seem to completely understand all questions, especially not the ones regarding unfamiliar interaction techniques such as gesture control or activity control. Therefore, we developed a human-centered workshop format with distinct materials tailored to the elderly to support them and minimize problems that occurred during the postal survey.

Our assumption was that they would rather prefer something they are familiar with (i.e. touch control) instead of something they have not tried before, even if the new interaction technique might be easier to use and learn for the senior citizens [19]. Therefore, we conducted a workshop in which all four interaction techniques were thoroughly introduced, the senior citizens were able to control smart home devices with all four interaction techniques and thus experience them. Finally, we asked them to rank the interaction techniques from the one they would prefer the most to the one they would rather not use. We then compared those results with their answers from the postal survey a year ago when they did not experience the smart home devices yet.

(a) Living room area.   (b) Dining room area.

Fig. 1. Setting in our smart living laboratory: (a) living room area and (b) dining room area.

The smart living laboratory is built to look like a small apartment. It consists of a living room area (shown in Fig. 1a) and a dining room area (see Fig. 1b). It is equipped with several smart home devices, such as smart lights, a smart door lock, and a smart roller shutter, as well as multiple video cameras (360-degree cameras) and a microphone.

3.1 Participants

All participants of our workshop already participated in the preceding postal survey [13]. During the questionnaire the respondents were asked whether or not they would be interested to participate in continuative studies. Out of the 87 respondents, 61 showed their interest and all of these were invited to the workshop.

We were only able to conduct workshops with a limited number of participants due to time and personnel restrictions. Therefore, we invited eight senior citizens – four females and four males. The four males were aged between 71 and 83 years – with an average age of 76.8 years –, the four females were between 65 and 90 years old – with an average age of 76.3 years. Neither mentioned any major impairments in their vision, hearing, or mobility, but some require glasses or a hearing aid device.

In their postal survey, two of the participants mentioned they have not heard of smart home before, three of them have heard about it but have not tried it yet, two have already watched someone else using it, and one owns smart home devices but barely uses them. This shows that the previous knowledge about smart home devices differs a lot, which had to be addressed during the workshop to ensure that all participants had the same knowledge base and were able to understand their tasks.

(a) Screen from the video explaining touch control.

(b) Screen from the video explaining voice control.

(c) Screen from the video explaining gesture control.

(d) Screen from the video explaining activity control.

Fig. 2. Screens from the explanatory videos that show a senior citizen amateur actress in the smart living laboratory controlling the smart door look using the four interaction techniques (a–d).

3.2   Workshop Procedure

Each workshop was conducted with only one participant at a time – due to Covid19 restrictions and to better compare the respondents' opinions with their answers during the postal survey. A *moderator* led the participant through the workshop, answered questions, and made sure formal restrictions were followed. Another member of our team fulfilled a "less formal" role (here called *peer*) by acting as informal conversational partner for our participants. The workshop consisted of five parts:

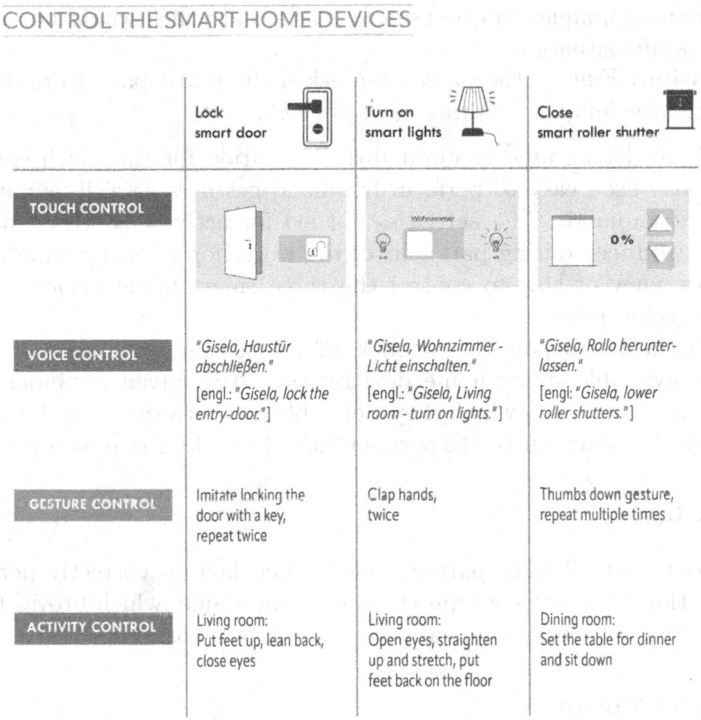

CONTROL THE SMART HOME DEVICES			
	Lock smart door	Turn on smart lights	Close smart roller shutter
TOUCH CONTROL		Wohnzimmer	0%
VOICE CONTROL	"Gisela, Haustür abschließen." [engl.: "Gisela, lock the entry-door."]	"Gisela, Wohnzimmer - Licht einschalten." [engl.: "Gisela, Living room - turn on lights."]	"Gisela, Rollo herunter- lassen." [engl.: "Gisela, lower roller shutters."]
GESTURE CONTROL	Imitate locking the door with a key, repeat twice	Clap hands, twice	Thumbs down gesture, repeat multiple times
ACTIVITY CONTROL	Living room: Put feet up, lean back, close eyes	Living room: Open eyes, straighten up and stretch, put feet back on the floor	Dining room: Set the table for dinner and sit down

Fig. 3. Overview of how to control the three smart home devices using the four interaction techniques.

1. **Welcome:** The *peer* and the participant met in a separate area outside the smart living laboratory and got to know each other. This allowed them to build a foundation for the conversation that followed later in the workshop and also allowed the participant to relax and accommodate to the new situation [8, 14].
2. **Introduction:** The *moderator* welcomed the participant into the smart living laboratory. After completing formalities, the *moderator* showed a presentation about smart home and the four interaction techniques in general. This served to establish a comparable degree of knowledge among the group.

3. **Experimentation:** In this part, the participant got to watch four didactic explanatory videos (cf. Figure 2), one per interaction technique, that showed a senior citizen amateur actress in the smart living laboratory controlling the available smart home devices (smart door lock, smart lights, smart roller shutter). Afterwards, the participants experimented how to control the smart home devices in the smart living laboratory according to what they observed in the videos.
4. **Conversation:** In this step, the *peer* joined the participant again. The *moderator* gave both of them the task to talk about three scenarios (locking the door, turning on the lights and lowering the roller shutters), how the four interaction techniques can be used for each, and which would be best suited in the specific situation.
5. **Conclusion:** Finally, the *moderator* asked the participant to rank the four interaction techniques and rate each of them.

For this study, we used a minimalist application for the touch control scenario. We also used easy to perform free-hand gestures as well as natural and short voice commands. The activities needed for activity control followed the scenarios introduced during part four of the workshop (Conversation). Figure 3 gives an overview of how to control the three smart home devices with each interaction technique.

To help the participants remember all interaction techniques and how to control the available smart home devices, they were given reminder cards as shown in Figs. 4 (a) to (d) which they were able to use throughout the workshop, especially during parts three (Experimentation) and four (Conversation).

4   Findings

It turned out that all eight participants learned how to correctly perform the four interaction techniques within the short time frame, which proves that they were easy enough to learn to be able to work in our workshop.

4.1   Touch Control

All participants mentioned that they are familiar with touch control as they regularly use smartphones or tablet computers. Although the participants found touch control to be easy to use and neither of them had problems controlling the smart home devices with it, they criticized that the touch device has to be close to them at all times to have the functionality available. This is seen as inconvenient because they are looking for their smartphones often. Also, the device has to be charged and turned on. They also would have to carry it around which most of them are not willing to do and find rather inconvenient.

One participant also mentioned that some conditions that often come with age make using a touch device more difficult, e.g. neuropathy. It was also mentioned that using a touch device can be difficult under certain circumstances, e.g. trying to turn the light on when the room is dark, because it would require the light to be turned on to locate the touch device.

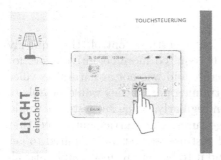

(a) Reminder card to turn on the lights using touch control.

(b) Reminder card to turn on the lights using voice control.

(c) Reminder card to turn on the lights using gesture control.

(d) Reminder card to turn on the lights using activity control.

Fig. 4. Reminder cards that were given to the participants to help them remember how to control the smart home devices.

4.2 Voice Control

Only one of the participants was familiar with voice assistants before our workshop. Regardless, all participants were able to control the smart home devices by voice commands and found this to be a very intuitive form of interaction. The fact that a voice assistant listens to all private conversations was reflected on by the participants but did not seem to be a main concern. It was important to most participants that the permitted voice commands are variable so they can speak naturally as if talking to another human.

Voice control was found to be a very fast and practical solution since it does not require the resident to carry a device with them at all times, it can be performed fast and easily in almost all situations they could imagine, and they deemed it to be a practical solution. However, it was mentioned that the voice commands have to be short and concise and the system has to give some form of feedback so that the user knows they were understood. Only one participant mentioned that he felt "odd" talking to inanimate objects.

4.3   Gesture Control

Although all participants were unfamiliar with gesture control, they quickly learned to correctly perform the gestures. It required more cognitive effort for them to learn and remember the correct gesture and was not as natural as voice control. But, they agreed that after a short training period they would be able to memorize the correct gestures and use them regularly. Some suggested it would be helpful if they could choose their own gestures. One participant noted that it did not feel natural to perform free-hand gestures at first and required to get accustomed to it, although most others found it to be very intuitive and natural.

One of the elderly pointed out that they felt uneasy because they were aware that it requires a camera to record everything they are doing to be able to recognize gestures. Another feared that gestures they unknowingly performed while talking to someone else or doing tasks would accidentally lead to actions in their smart home they did not intend.

4.4   Activity Control

Activity control was too complex for most participants to understand its implications. They do not want to rely on a system that promises to learn their daily living activities and to automatically control smart home devices accordingly. They also do not believe that it is possible for a system to learn their daily routines and adjust to each individual. Also, some participants mentioned an alarming lack of privacy, because they understood that it requires multiple cameras and other sensors to observe their daily living activities to control the smart home accordingly.

Therefore, most participants agreed that if this actually works it would be very easy to use since most would happen automatically according to their wishes and there would be very little they would have to do themselves, however, they would not feel comfortable with the amount of sensors and observation needed to make this possible. And even then, one participant mentioned that life is never the same and it cannot be possible to program and plan every contingency. Only one participant was very enthusiastic about activity control.

4.5   Combination

To summarize, the participants suggested a combination of voice control and gesture control, while using touch control to remotely control the smart home devices when being away from home. Most participants want to keep manual control (e.g. a light switch) in case of an emergency or for visitors.

They agreed that a combination of voice control and gesture control would be best. That way they could select what suits the current situation, e.g. voice commands when hands are not free to perform gestures and gesture control when talking to someone, so there is no interruption in the conversation. The participants want to be able to choose which interaction technique better fits the current situation since they learned that every form of interaction has advantages and disadvantages. One participant also noted that needs and desires can change as the senior citizens' condition changes and it needs to be possible for the system to adapt to these changes, e.g. if impairments in mobility occur. Another remark was that if there is more than one resident being able to choose from more than one interaction technique is even more important.

Most of them liked the idea of remotely accessing their smart home devices when they are not at home, e.g. to check if the door is locked, and if not, correct it via their smartphone.

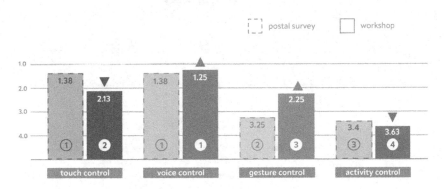

Fig. 5. Comparison of the rankings of touch control, voice control, gesture control, and activity control during the postal survey and the workshop.

4.6   Ranking

The participants had already ranked the four interaction techniques as part of the postal survey and did it again after they had experienced the four interaction techniques during the workshop. A comparison showed that touch control was ranked first during the postal survey because the participants were familiar with it and presumably did not fully understand the other interaction techniques. Gesture control and voice control were ranked higher after the participants got acquainted with them. As a major factor, we assume that they perceived how intuitive and easy to use these forms of interaction are. Activity control was ranked last in both studies, presumably because most participants agreed they did not trust the system enough and they had privacy concerns. It also needs to be taken into consideration that activity control could only be imitated since such a system is not yet available and it also would require learning the users' daily routines to function properly.

During the postal survey, the eight participants ranked touch control first with an average rank of 1.38. After the workshop, the average rank dropped to 2.13. Voice control was ranked second with an average rank of 1.38. Afterward, it was ranked first with an average rank of 1.25. The average rank of gesture control changed from 3.25 during the postal survey to 2.25. Activity control was ranked last during the postal survey with an average rank of 3.4 and also again after the workshop with an average rank of 3.63.

Figure 5 shows a comparison of the rankings during the postal survey and the workshop.

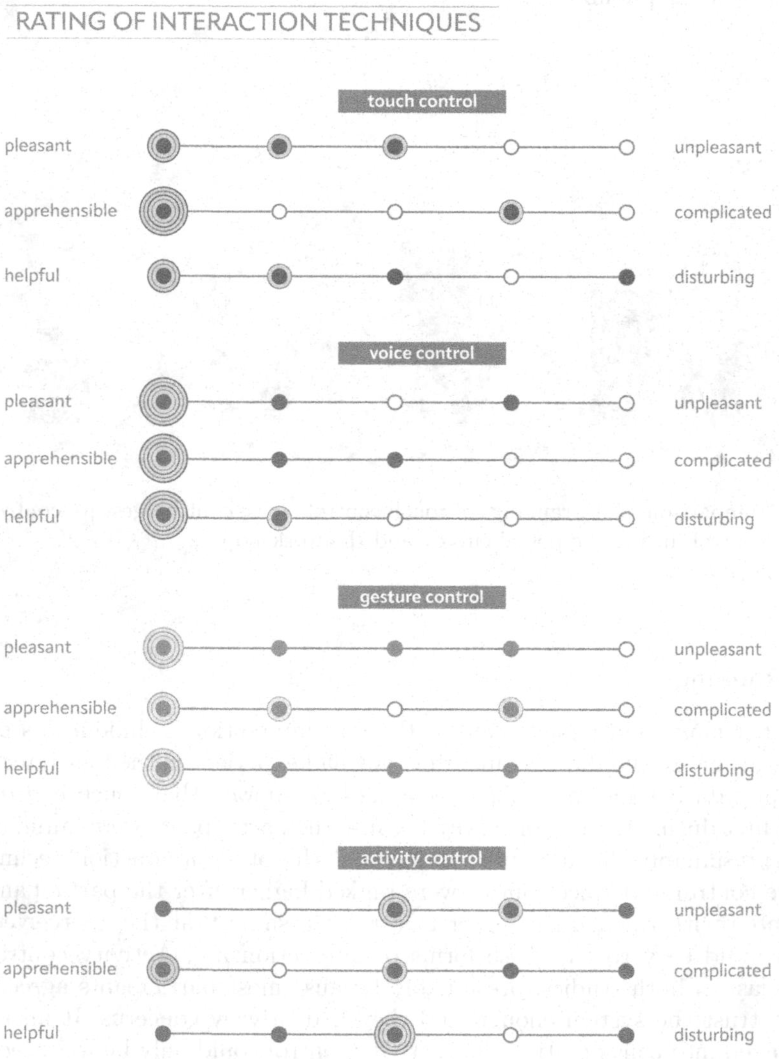

Fig. 6. Ratings of touch control, voice control, gesture control, and activity control in the three categories. Only 7 responses available, as one participant was not able to conduct the rating due to time limitations.

We also asked the participants to rate all four interaction techniques in three categories:

- Was the interaction technique very **pleasant**, rather pleasant, neither pleasant nor unpleasant, rather unpleasant, or very **unpleasant** to use?
- Was the interaction technique very **apprehensible**, rather apprehensible, neither apprehensible nor complicated, rather complicated, or very **complicated**?
- Was the interaction technique very **helpful**, rather helpful, neither helpful nor disturbing, rather disturbing, or very **disturbing**?

Figure 6 shows how the participants have rated the interaction techniques at the end of the workshop.

5   Conclusion and Future Work

To conclude, the workshop showed that our assumption that senior citizens would rather pick a familiar interaction technique instead of something they have not tried before, even if the new interaction technique is easier and more intuitive to use, was correct. It turned out that touch control – which was the most preferred form of interaction during the postal survey – actually holds many disadvantages, e.g. the device has to be turned on and carried around at all times.

The participants noted that there is not the one perfect form of interaction. However, they agreed that a combination of touch control, voice control, and gesture control would be their preferred solution. That way, they can pick the easiest and most intuitive form of control for the current situation. Also, when there is more than one resident, everyone should be able to pick their own preferred form of interaction, especially when health conditions and impairments lead to difficulties with one or more interaction techniques.

Future work should focus on how to design smart home devices that allow multiple interaction techniques, as well as what kind of touch applications, voice commands, and gestures (and combinations thereof) are suitable for senior citizens, especially if they are affected by impairments or deteriorating health conditions. Also, another interesting aspect is how to convey smart home devices and their interaction techniques to senior citizens.

In general, we find that senior citizens are very interested in this topic and are eager to participate in research projects that focus on how technical devices can benefit the elderly. They have shown to ask critical questions, voice concerns, and make valuable suggestion that can help researchers as well as developers of such technical devices to adjust their product to a new, growing target group.

Acknowledgement. The authors acknowledge the financial support by the Federal Ministry of Education and Research of Germany (BMBF) in the framework of "Innovative Hochschule" (project number 03IHS052, Regionales Innovationszentrum Gesundheit und Lebensqualität Fulda (RIGL), Umsetzungsprojekt GetAll - Gesundheitstechnik für die Alltagsbewältigung).

References

1. Dorofte, A.: OPINION: BMW Gesture Control really improves in-car operation. https://www.bmwblog.com/2019/11/08/opinion-bmw-gesture-control-really-improves-in-car-operation/. Accessed 07 Feb 2022
2. Alazrai, R., Zmily, A., Mowafi, Y.: Fall detection for elderly using anatomical-plane-based representation. In: 2014 36th Annual International Conference of the IEEE Engineering in Medicine and Biology Society, pp. 5916–5919 (2014). https://doi.org/10.1109/EMBC.2014.6944975
3. Ayubi, S.A., Sudiharto, D.W., Jadied, E.M., Aryanto, E.: The prototype of hand gesture recognition for elderly people to control connected home devices. J. Phys. Conf. Ser. **1201**(1), 012042 (2019). https://doi.org/10.1088/1742-6596/1201/1/012042
4. Bara, C.-D., Cabrita, M., op den Akker, H., Hermens, H.J.: User interaction concepts in smart caring homes for elderly with chronic conditions. In: Geissbühler, A., Demongeot, J., Mokhtari, M., Abdulrazak, B., Aloulou, H. (eds.) ICOST 2015. LNCS, vol. 9102, pp. 38–49. Springer, Cham (2015). https://doi.org/10.1007/978-3-319-19312-0_4
5. Barnard, Y., Bradley, M.D., Hodgson, F., Lloyd, A.D.: Learning to use new technologies by older adults: perceived difficulties, experimentation behaviour and usability. Comput. Hum. Behav. **29**(4), 1715–1724 (2013). https://doi.org/10.1016/j.chb.2013.02.006. https://www.sciencedirect.com/science/article/pii/S0747563213000721
6. Bejarano, A., Fernández, A., Jimeno, M., Salazar, A., Wightman, P.: Towards the evolution of smart home environments: a survey. Int. J. Autom. Smart Technol. **6**, 105–136 (2016). https://doi.org/10.5875/ausmt.v6i3.1039
7. Chernbumroong, S., Cang, S., Atkins, A., Yu, H.: Elderly activities recognition and classification for applications in assisted living. Expert Syst. Appl. **40**(5), 1662–1674 (2013). https://doi.org/10.1016/j.eswa.2012.09.004
8. Dickinson, A., Arnott, J., Prior, S.: Methods for human - computer interaction research with older people. Behav. Inf. Technol. **26**(4), 343–352 (2007). https://doi.org/10.1080/01449290601176948
9. Jakob, D., Wilhelm, S., Gerl, A., Ahrens, D.: A quantitative study on awareness, usage and reservations of voice control interfaces by elderly people. In: Stephanidis, C., et al. (eds.) HCII 2021. LNCS, vol. 13096, pp. 237–257. Springer, Cham (2021). https://doi.org/10.1007/978-3-030-90328-2_15
10. Kobayashi, M., Hiyama, A., Miura, T., Asakawa, C., Hirose, M., Ifukube, T.: Elderly user evaluation of mobile touchscreen interactions. In: Campos, P., Graham, N., Jorge, J., Nunes, N., Palanque, P., Winckler, M. (eds.) INTERACT 2011. LNCS, vol. 6946, pp. 83–99. Springer, Heidelberg (2011). https://doi.org/10.1007/978-3-642-23774-4_9
11. Lentzas, A., Vrakas, D.: Non-intrusive human activity recognition and abnormal behavior detection on elderly people: a review. Artif. Intell. Rev. **53**(3), 1975–2021 (2019). https://doi.org/10.1007/s10462-019-09724-5
12. Sahlab, N., Sailer, C., Jazdi, N., Weyrich, M.: Designing an elderly-appropriate voice control for a pill dispenser (2020). https://doi.org/10.18416/AUTOMED.2020
13. Schak, M., Blum, R., Bomsdorf, B.: Smart home for the elderly - a survey of desires, needs, and problems. In: Gao, Q., Zhou, J. (eds.) HCII 2022. LNCS, pp. 107–121. Springer, Cham (2022). https://doi.org/10.1007/978-3-031-05654-3_7

14. Silva, P.A., Nunes, F.: 3 x 7 usability testing guidelines for older adults. In: MexIHC 2010 (2010)
15. Sucerquia, A., López, J.D., Vargas-Bonilla, J.F.: Real-life/real-time elderly fall detection with a triaxial accelerometer. Sensors **18**(4) (2018). https://doi.org/10. 3390/s18041101
16. Thakur, N., Han, C.Y.: Framework for an intelligent affect aware smart home environment for elderly people. CoRR abs/2106.15599 (2021). https://arxiv.org/ abs/2106.15599
17. Vorwerg, S., Eicher, C., Ruser, H., Piela, F., Obée, F., Kaltenbach, A., Mechold, L.: Requirements for gesture-controlled remote operation to facilitate human-technology interaction in the living environment of elderly people. In: Zhou, J., Salvendy, G. (eds.) HCII 2019. LNCS, vol. 11592, pp. 551–569. Springer, Cham (2019). https://doi.org/10.1007/978-3-030-22012-9_39
18. Wang, R.J., Lai, S.C., Jhuang, J.Y., Ho, M.C., Shiau, Y.C.: Development of smart home gesture-based control system. Sens. Mater. **33**, 3459 (2021). https://doi.org/ 10.18494/SAM.2021.3522
19. Zeckhauser, R., Samuelson, W.: Status quo bias in decision-making. J. Risk Uncertain. **1**, 7–59 (1988). https://doi.org/10.1007/BF00055564

Living in a Networked Home: Older Adults' Expectations and Attitudes

Yash Trivedi, Shabnam Fakhr-Hosseini[(⊠)], Chaiwoo Lee, Sheng-Hung Lee, Lauren C. Cerino, and Joseph F. Coughlin

AgeLab, Massachusetts Institute of Technology, Cambridge, MA 02142, USA
{ashtriv,shabnam1,shdesign,lcerino,coughlin}@mit.edu

Abstract. A challenge facing our rapidly aging population is the need to age independently, preferably at home. Smart home technologies promise to provide older adults with better health, safety, and peace of mind. However, their adoption remains low, and identifying the potential barriers remains an open question. This study investigated older adults' opinions and attitudes toward various smart home technologies and their integration in a connected environment. Seven older adults participated in an in-lab study to interact with two types of simulated smart home environments varying in degrees of task automation and technology integration. Results suggest that older adults perceive smart home technologies to be beneficial for supporting aging-in-place, and for maintaining health, safety, and convenience, and are open to living in a connected and automated environment. Discussions also took place around barriers and potential risks – including costs, privacy, reliability and learning curve – as well as future design implications.

Keywords: Networked Home · Smart Home · Older Adults · Home Automation · Aging in Place

1 Introduction

The longevity revolution is sweeping the globe, with some societies at the forefront and others further along. In countries with the highest life expectancy, the likelihood of living to 65 years old is more than 90% today (United Nations, 2019) . Consequently, the number of persons aged 65 and older has been projected to increase from approximately 35 million in 2000 to an estimated 71 million in 2030, and the number of persons aged 80 years and older is expected to increase from 9.3 million in 2000 to 19.5 million in 2030 in the United States (Centers for Disease Control and Prevention [CDC], 2022).

The aging of the population is one of the most important policy issues facing the United States today, with its consequences for health status, costs, and service provision. Nearly 90% of seniors want to age in their own homes. "Aging in place" is "the ability to live in one's own home and community safely, independently, and comfortably, regardless of age, income, or ability level" (CDC, 2017) . However, decline in physical and cognitive health often makes it necessary for older adults to get assistance in completing daily household tasks. Researchers have been investigating how equipping homes with smart home technologies can improve people's lifestyles and reduce the physical and cognitive burdens associated with aging. Home automation has the potential to improve a person's quality of life, particularly when used in combination with other forms of technology. For example, smart home technologies are being developed to support home-based health management: medication management and remote monitoring; facilitation of long-distance caregiving, including family caregiving coordination; fighting loneliness; and home safety, including fall detection and security.

However, there are barriers to adoption of smart home technologies by older adults. Accessibility, stigma, lack of perceived need, affordability and privacy are some of the factors found by previous studies (Coughlin, D'Ambrosio, Reimer, Pratt, 2007; Demiris, Oliver, Dickey, Skubic, Rantz, 2008; 2004; FakhrHosseini, Lee, Rudnik, Son, Lee, & Coughlin, 2021; Pal, Funilkul, Vanijja, & Papasratorn, 2018). In order to overcome these limitations, various studies have been conducted to come up with a set of principles and recommendations that design professionals can use when designing home environments (Ayala & Susana, 2019; Kim, Cho, & Jun, 2020). For example, FakhrHosseini et al. (2021) suggested that newer and smarter devices should be able to facilitate remote communication and cohabitation among residents. They also recommended that new devices should be compatible with existing in-home devices and external services (outside of the home; e.g., safety departments, transportation, and energy management) and be designed to facilitate a connected living space. Additional recommendations were made for new devices to be able to support multiple tasks, and to have measures in place to securely manage data and protect privacy.

Although the existing studies provide a great background and perspective on user needs and design considerations of smart devices, little is known about the design of a connected home, especially through the lens of older adults. The core focus of this study is to design and validate a simulated study platform to gain insights regarding the perception of connected home space among older adults. Therefore, a simulated smart home space was built to generate rich insights through an exploratory approach to derive design considerations of more connected homes for older adults.

2 Method

This section presents the study's approaches to designing and building a simulated living experience, recruiting participants, and evaluating the impacts of the experience.

2.1 Defining the Smart Home

For technology selection and simulation in the simulated smart home, there is a need for a standardized framework (FakhrHosseini, Lee, Coughlin, 2019). In a recent effort, MIT AgeLab (2022) suggested a taxonomy to explain various degrees of home automation and different types of integrated and connected homes. Based on their definition, homes with technologies that integrate user-programmed connected devices are called "Networked Homes". Similar to Sovacool & Del Rio's (2020) descriptions "bundled" homes, Networked Homes provide a richer connectivity among different devices, also known a "connected" home (e.g., Bugeja, Jacobsson, & Davidsson, 2020). This connectivity is accomplished based on interoperability solutions supporting seamless primitive data communications. Users in these Networked Homes can set rules for their devices through a central home gateway according to their needs (e.g., turn on lights upon arrival, turn on coffee machine when waking up). As more devices are integrated, users can define more sophisticated home automation logic. Networked Homes are characterized by the degree of technological integration and task automation that is more advanced than most devices and services currently available. However, while existing discussions focused on smart home systems that are widely available, little is known about the role of user and the design of Networked Homes, especially for older users.

Table 1. Demographic information of participants.

| | Participant Number | | | | | | |
	P1	P2	P3	P4	P5	P6	P7
Gender	Female	Female	Female	Male	Female	Female	Female
Age	70	76	66	73	69	73	70
Occupation	Retired	Retired	Employed full-time	Retired	Employed full-time	Retired	Employed part-time
Self-rated health	Excellent	Excellent	Good	Average	Good	Excellent	Excellent
Home type	Condo, townhouse, or duplex	Condo, townhouse, or duplex	Single-family home	Single-family home	Single-family home	Single-family home	Single-family home
Number of years in current home	More than 10 years	More than 10 years	5 or more but less than 10	2 or more but less than 5	More than 10 years	More than 10 years	More than 10 years
Living with	Spouse or romantic partner	Living alone	Living alone	Spouse or romantic partner	Spouse or romantic partner	Child(ren) above 18	Living alone
Self-rated technology experience*	Somewhat experienced	Somewhat experienced	Quite experienced	Somewhat experienced	Somewhat experienced	Somewhat experienced	Quite experienced

* Self-rated technology experience was asked with question "How would you rate your overall level of experience with technology?". Answer options included "Not experienced at all," "A little experienced," "Somewhat experienced," "Quite experienced," and "Very experienced."

In this study, a space was built to simulate key features and capabilities of Networked Homes to provide study participants with examples of how higher levels of smart home technology integration and automation may be experienced. The space also enabled a simulation of a basic level home, "Traditional Home" (MIT AgeLab, 2022), in which devices and appliances function without environmental awareness or inter-system connections e.g., to better demonstrate the differences between these types of homes and what types of technologies, and automations may be present.

Table 2. Sample schedule and durations calculated to fit within reduced simulation time.

Start time	End time	Task	Simulated duration
6:00 AM	10:00 AM	Early morning routine: getting up, opening blinds, drinking coffee, and checking vitals	4 min
10:00 AM	12:30 PM	Late morning routine: adjusting blinds, reading, working, browsing the internet or doing other miscellaneous things	2.5 min
12:30 PM	1:30 PM	Lunch	1 min
1:30 PM	2:30 PM	Afternoon nap	2 min
2:30 PM	5:30 PM	Afternoon routine: folding sheets, adjusting blinds, reading, working, browsing the internet or doing other miscellaneous things	3 min
5:30 PM	7:00 PM	Dinner	1.5 min
7:00 PM	9:00 PM	Evening routine: watching TV or doing other leisurely activities	2 min
9:00 PM	10:00 PM	Bedtime routine: closing blinds, setting an alarm, adjusting temperature, and turning lights off	1 min
10:00 PM	–	Sleep	–

2.2 Participants

Inclusion criteria for this study included older adults in the range of 65 to 76 years old. Prospective participants were provided with descriptions about the study, including its in-person nature. In this study, seven local participants were recruited from MIT AgeLab volunteer database that includes people across the United States to represent a range of demographic characteristics, living arrangements, and levels of experience with technology. The participants ranged in age from 66 to 76 years. Four participants were retired, two worked full-time, and one worked part-time. As for living arrangements, five lived in single-family homes, and two lived in condominium, townhouse, or duplex. All participants had lived in their current homes for at least two years, and five had lived in their current homes for at least ten years. Three participants were living with a spouse or partner, three were living alone, and one lived with adult child(ren). Table 1 summarizes demographic information of each participant.

2.3 Building the Simulation

Physical Foundation of the Simulated Living Space. As shown in Fig. 1, the simulated living space was built in an existing demonstration room with 190 sq. Feet of space. The space was modeled after a small studio apartment and contained furnishings and decorations typical of a living space to evoke the feeling of being in one's own home. To make the most of the small space, some areas were designed to serve multiple purposes; for example, the living room and bedroom areas were combined by having the couch serve as both a bed and a seating area.

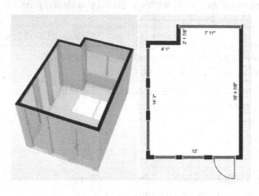

Fig. 1. Renderings of layout and dimensions for space (left) and aerial photo of the space with furnishings (right).

Conceptualizing the Simulation Experience. The goal of the simulation is to assess how individuals might experience a typical day living in a Networked Home. In developing the simulation experience, three key factors were considered: temporal dimension, a simulated schedule, and technology. Each of these factors play a role in understanding participants' actual home experience and, in turn, in designing an experience that enables them to feel "at home" in the simulated environment.

Temporal dimension. Time is one of the key elements in replicating the experience that an individual has in their home. Thus, to simulate the experience of living in a smart home, an individual's typical daily routine should be observed and replicated. To enable the simulation of one's daily routine, the time spent completing tasks in the simulated environment should be representative of the actual tasks completed in the real-time environment to maintain consistency across tasks. The estimated time required to complete a real-time task is proportionately scaled to the simulated time scale:

$$\frac{\text{Time for Real Day}}{\text{Time for Simulated Day}} = \frac{\text{Time for Real Time Task}}{\text{Time for Simulated Task}}$$

Simulated schedule. Since an average healthy adult spends roughly eight hours of the day sleeping, the active routine is assumed to last only 16 h. To minimize participants' time commitment and potential discomfort with an unfamiliar environment, those 16 h were reduced to 16 min.

The simulated schedule serves to replicate the typical routine of an older adult. Individuals are assumed to wake up and begin their morning ritual and eat breakfast between 6:00AM and 7:30AM. Depending on individual preferences and personalities, they may engage in socialization, rest, volunteering, running errands, and other activities during the day. After 5:00PM, before and after preparing an evening meal, they may engage in some form of lounging and/or socialization. Lastly, they complete a sleep ritual before their bedtime around 10:00PM. Table 2 depicts a mock schedule created based on these four distinct stages and a broad idea of the activities older adults may include in their daily routine (Bayar & Türkoglu, 2021). While this serves as an example for creation of simulated schedules, participants' actual schedules were taken into account when creating the actual schedules used. This serves as an approximation of a schedule that an older person may follow.

Technology. The technology selection framework and degrees of home automation were informed by the user needs analysis illustrated by FakhrHosseini et al. and the smart home taxonomy by MIT AgeLab (2022), respectively. Based on an additional review of literature (Alhafidh & Allen, 2018; Deschamps-Sonsino, 2018; El Jaouhari, Palacios-Garcia, Anvari-Moghaddam, & Bouabdallah, 2019; Li, Yigitcanlar, Erol, & Liu, 2021), four key themes and examples of associated devices were identified:

- Energy management: smart thermostat, lights, and smart plug
- Health and wellness: HR monitoring and medication
- Appliances: coffee machine, window blinds, and smart TV
- Safety and security: security alarm and door lock

Implementation. Each participant experienced two types of simulations – Traditional Home and Networked Home – one after the other. Both experiences occurred in the same space and follow the same "routine;" the same physical setup and routine/schedule would be maintained across both levels. In general, the sole difference between the two experiences was the incorporation of varied functionalities to represent the differences in levels of automation, as described in Table 3.

Table 3. Participant actions and simulation implementation.

Task	Traditional Home implementation	Networked Home implementation
Early morning routine	Participant opens blinds manually, uses coffeemaker to make coffee, uses oximeter to check and record heart rate and blood oxygen level	Participant gets up and puts on smart watch Blinds open automatically as participant wakes up, coffeemaker starts running itself, vitals are checked and recorded by smart watch
Late morning routine	Participant closes blinds halfway, goes to the study/office area, turns desk lamp on, uses computer to pretend to do work, or reads provided reading materials	Participant goes to the study/office area, uses computer to pretend to do work, or reads provided reading materials Blinds automatically adjust to preferred setting, desk lamp turns on as participant approaches the area
Lunch	Participant turns desk lamp off, goes to the kitchen area, and prepares "lunch" with provided snack items	Participant goes to the kitchen area, and prepares "lunch" with provided snack items Desk lamp automatically turns off

(continued)

Table 3. (*continued*)

Task	Traditional Home implementation	Networked Home implementation
Afternoon nap	Participant closes blinds manually, then goes to the bedroom/couch area to pretend to rest or nap	Participant goes to the bedroom/couch area to pretend to rest or nap Blinds automatically close
Afternoon routine	Participant folds blanket on couch, opens blinds halfway, goes to the study/office area, turns desk lamp on, uses computer to pretend to do work, or reads provided reading materials	Participant folds blanket on couch, goes to the study/office area, uses computer to pretend to do work, or reads provided reading materials Blinds automatically adjust to preferred setting, desk lamp turns on as participant approaches the area
Dinner	Participant turns desk lamp off, then goes to the kitchen area to prepare "dinner" with provided snack items	Participant goes to the kitchen are to prepare "dinner" with provided snack items Desk lamp automatically turns off
Evening routine	Participants goes to the living room/couch area, turns living room lights on, and turns TV on using remote control	Participants goes to the living room/couch area Living room lights and TV turns on automatically as participant approaches the area
Bedtime routine	Participant closes blinds, sets alarm using provided clock, adjusts room temperature using knob control, and turns lights off	Participant rests or does other miscellaneous activities Blinds automatically close, alarm is automatically set, and room temperature automatically adjusts to preferred setting
Sleep	Participant goes to the bedroom/couch area	Participant goes to the bedroom/couch area Lights turn off automatically

From an implementation perspective, some devices – specifically in the Networked Home, were simulated with a "Wizard of Oz" method in which the supposed "automation" of the devices was emulated to create the perception of the Networked Home. The devices whose automation was emulated using a smart home controller in the Networked Home simulation were desk lamp, couch lamp, security camera, smart plug, and smart assistant. Although their functionalities appeared to participants to be automated, these devices were actually controlled with the input of the study conductor. Similarly, the smart assistant prompts were prerecorded with some flexibility to modify and accommodate unforeseen circumstances during the study. Other devices in the smart home were linked to a custom dashboard and customized according to the routine provided to the participants:

1. Time: Time was a simulated counter starting at 5:30 am displayed via an iPad as a digital clock synced with the central dashboard.
2. Thermostat: Since changes in temperature would not be evident or immediate enough for the brief simulation, the thermostat was simulated using an iPad with a touch screen input to set the temperature. The feedback for the participant was visual wherein the temperature starts to reach equilibrium with the target temperature by the participant at the rate of 5°F per simulated hour. This thermostat was synced with the central dashboard and enabled 2-way communication.
3. Smart band: The smart band data was simulated as well, with random fluctuations within a normal range of HR and SpO2.
4. Coffee maker: The coffee maker was a one button push coffee maker with a button pusher was attached to it and synced with the demo time and routine of the participant.

2.4 Procedure

Recruited participants were invited to the lab for the in-person study. At the beginning of each session, before being introduced to the simulation room, participants were informed about the study procedure and completed the consent forms, including an addendum related to COVID-19. Each participant granted permission to record the duration of their 120-min study session. Participants were then provided with the following general and simple definition of smart home: "A smart home is a home in which devices are connected to the internet and can be controlled and can be customized according to the user's needs. Some of the devices could be automated as well." Based on this definition, participants were asked to name any smart home devices that they owned and/or used and to discuss their decision-making and purchase process for each device.

Participants were then introduced to the simulation room and the procedure for each simulation. The moderator provided a tour of the layout and areas representing a living room/bedroom, office, and kitchen (see Fig. 1). After familiarizing each participant with the environment, moderators reviewed the two simulation scenarios and provided additional information where relevant. For example, participants learned how to interpret the simulated time; they would be experiencing the simulation beginning at a simulated time of 5:30 am and ending at a simulated time of 10:30 pm, with each minute representing one hour of simulation time (for a total of 17 min for each simulation). In addition to this comprehensive verbal overview, participants received a physical copy of the schedule for reference throughout the simulation. They were reminded that there was no rush to complete the tasks during each simulation, and that the study was not a test of their abilities.

Participants were then left alone to complete the simulations according to the schedule, beginning with the Traditional Home simulation. During each simulation, participants' interactions with devices and punctuality (according to the simulated "time" and schedule) were recorded and observed. Immediately following the completion of each simulation, participants answered questions regarding their experience. These questions were intended to understand variations in the user's actual interactions versus those physically observed by the researchers, as well as their perception of the Traditional and

Networked Homes simulation. After completing both simulations, participants were escorted to a separate room for a final interview regarding their overall experience, preference, and related attitudes. These provide insights on potential changes in preferences regarding the specific devices and functionalities used during the simulation, as well as understanding of how perceptions and attitudes regarding smart homes in general (i.e., beyond the simulated home that they had experienced) may have been affected. Questions covered in the study are shown in Table 4.

Table 4. Questions asked to gather initial feedback and to evaluate the simulation experience.

Question group	Questions
Traditional Home	How difficult/easy was it to follow the routine?
	Which of these items in the home would you describe as smart? It can be none as well
	Which tasks did you think would have been better if automated?
Networked Home	What did you think of your experience? What changes did you notice?
	How difficult/easy was it to follow the routine?
	Were the voice cues annoying or helpful? In what ways?
	How do you think these devices are suggesting you with those commands?
	Which of these automated tasks seemed helpful to you?
	Which of the two homes was closer to your current home? Which one is easier? Which one do you prefer? Which one is "smarter"? Why?
General questions after both simulations	What do you see as potential benefits of having a smart home? Follow-ups: Would this help you be independent? Impacts on health and safety? Convenience? Entertainment?
	What do you see as potential barriers to having a smart home?
	Would you have any privacy concerns regarding a smart home? Do you see any other possible risks or issues?

3 Results

3.1 Simulation Experience

During each simulation, participants' experiences, including their interactions with the technologies and adherence to the schedule, were observed and recorded by researchers. Participants were also interviewed about their experiences once they had completed each simulation.

Observations. Some differences related to participants' adherence to the schedule and completion of tasks were observed between the two simulations. In the Traditional Home simulation, although all seven participants were frequently seen glancing at the clock, none were able to follow the provided schedule punctually. During the work periods from 10AM-12:30PM and 2:30PM-5:30PM, six participants appeared to become distracted, causing them to diverge from the schedule and complete their tasks late. Despite these challenges with punctuality, six out of seven participants were able to complete all of the tasks successfully at some point; the seventh participant opted to skip tasks in an attempt to catch up with the schedule. In the Networked Home simulation, on the other hand, less challenges were observed overall; six of the seven participants were able to adhere closely to the schedule and completed all tasks on time.

During the Networked Home simulation, additional observations were made about the ways in which participants interacted with the increased automation within their environment. By the simulated time of 12:30 PM, five participants had stopped referring their printed schedule, instead relying solely on the voice prompts to keep track of their schedule and tasks. Two participants handled the coffee machine incorrectly and removed the mug before dispensing, leading to a potential spillage which the system averted by disabling the machine. Despite the voice prompts, participants did not appear to fully understand how the machine would operate. During free time, three participants explored the room, played with Legos, or checked their personal phones; two watched news on the television. After hearing an alert from the voice assistant that the settings for two devices (thermostat and coffee machine) had been updated, all seven participants responded verbally in some way. One participant also checked these devices to verify that they were functioning correctly following these updates.

Participant Descriptions and Perceptions. First, participants shared thoughts about their experiences with the schedule. Despite the schedule-related challenges observed during the Traditional Home simulation, six participants rated the schedule as easy to follow for both simulations; however, they also clarified that it was easier to follow during the Networked Home simulation. One participant experienced confusion with the voice prompts in the Networked Home simulation, citing that it was difficult to decide whether to follow the printed schedule or the voice prompts.

When asked to identify what types of smart devices they believed had been present within each simulation, participants appeared to have a more accurate understanding of those in the Networked Home simulation. For the Traditional Home simulation, participants identified the digital thermostat as smart (possibly due to its touch-based interface), one incorrectly described the coffee machine to be smart (despite it being manually operated), and one also incorrectly believed the oximeter to be smart. Two participants mentioned that devices not connected to the internet could still be categorized as smart.

For the Networked Home simulation, all participants identified lights, thermostat, blinds, voice assistant, and alarm clock as smart. Five participants mentioned the coffee machine as smart. (For the other two participants, the coffee machine had needed to be stopped remotely to prevent spillage of coffee during the simulation after they had incorrectly handled the machine. Upon hearing an explanation of this spill prevention mechanism, both participants remarked that the feature was "really useful.").

Participants also discussed their thoughts around some of the automated features that they had experienced during the Networked Home simulation, and many discussed the voice assistant and notification features. Six participants had found the voice assistant to be "helpful." Five participants found the voice assistant non-intrusive and felt cared for by a virtual entity. Two participants mentioned that they did not want AI "dictating" their daily routine, preferring to input their preferences manually. Some participants expressed hesitation surrounding voice notifications. Two noted their preferences for a more subtle form of notification, such as vibration on a wearable. One reported that they did not want any notifications in their daily life besides in emergency situations. One thought that, although the notifications were during the simulation, they would be annoying in real life.

As for perceptions of how the automated features worked in the Networked Home simulation, five participants believed that most of the automation was time-based and had pre-set timings according to the schedule. Two participants perceived lights and some alerts from the voice assistant to be proactive and adjust according to the participants' real-time actions. Two participants identified the interconnectivity between wearable and lights for turning the lights on and off depending on user movement.

3.2 Post-study Interview

Simulation Preference. As depicted in Fig. 2, nearly all participants considered the home depicted in the Traditional Home simulation to be more similar to their current homes. However, all participants considered the home depicted in the Networked Home simulation to be smarter and easier to live in. The majority of the participants expressed a preference to live in a Networked Home, with the exception of two participants; one reported that they preferred a more "zen" lifestyle and would not want to disrupt their current routine and lifestyle with technology, and the other reported that, although they generally preferred a smarter home, they would prefer less automation to ensure they are doing some physical movement (e.g., by manually completing household chores).

Anticipated smart home benefits. For all participants, the most important benefit of smart homes was the ability to support independent living and aging in place. One participant reported that "elder housing and living in a group freak me out" and that, after living alone for 30 years, it was hard to imagine another living arrangement. Participants also discussed benefits related to health, safety, convenience, and energy management:

Health. All participants emphasized the importance of smart home automation in the context of their health and independence. Due to physical and cognitive decline, many regularly require medical assistance and health monitoring. Medication reminders and fall detection were the most common benefits discussed. Some participants who lived alone shared personal stories of being in an emergency and not being able to receive

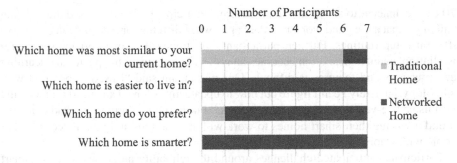

Fig. 2. Simulation preferences

timely help due to a lack of monitoring. Interestingly, half of participants mentioned their usage of some form of medical tracking device, some of which could be controlled remotely by their doctors.

Safety. Four participants reported that their existing home security systems provide a sense of safety to their loved ones and themselves. They conceptualized home security systems as going beyond just a burglar alarm system to include features like passive monitoring and alerts for environmental emergencies, such as gas leaks or fire hazards. Two participants described near-disaster situations in which they accidentally left their stoves on, and how these dangerous situations make them want a smart home to be notified of such potential hazards.

Convenience. Six participants referenced tasks such as turning the lights on and off and closing window blinds and said that they would benefit from automating these "inconvenient" household tasks. They noted that this automation would be convenient for all, regardless of aging-related factors. The automation would increase their productivity and creativity by saving time and effort for other, less mundane tasks. Participants also recalled moments during which they had wished to have smart lights and thermostats, particularly to avoid being interrupted from other more important tasks to make necessary adjustments.

Energy Management. While two participants already had government-installed energy management devices in their homes, a few others also mentioned the financial and energy savings benefits from energy management systems. According to participants, these systems could not only conserve energy, but also lead to significant financial savings. Participants also mentioned smart solar panels and other forms of energy storage that could help them to operate independently of the power grid.

3.3 Potential Barriers and Risks Regarding Smart Home Technologies

Participants also discussed why they may be reluctant to adopt smart home technologies. Commonly mentioned barriers included a steep learning curve, maintenance difficulties, associated costs, and poor reliability.

All participants anticipated challenges in setting up smart devices in their homes. One participant said "I have to either spend two hours on YouTube or call and pay

$70 to a technician to set up my smart device." Participants also discussed the learning challenges that arise - and worsen as they age - when different brands of devices involve different setup routines. Further, participants mentioned that, even after a successful installation, maintenance often becomes an issue. Keeping up with updates and learning new interfaces and features is difficult. One participant said "I used to be good with technology, but lately I can't figure out how to update my Adobe. I am an art director, and I still use a five-year-old version for my work." Furthermore, participants had concerns around adjusting their smart homes to work with the routines and preferences of other people with whom they live.

Participants anticipated challenges around the reliability and consistency of smart home technologies. Many expressed concerns around their limited ability to troubleshoot, and even simple issues would cause them discomfort if they were unable to resolve them. In general, participants believed that technology is not mature enough to be trusted to provide the levels of reliability and consistency that they would require and expect. Some participants also expressed worries regarding consequences of technologies failing to perform, especially when systems support safety-critical tasks. These concerns were particularly focused features such as alert systems for gas leaks, fire hazards, and home security.

Cost was also identified as a possible barrier, as participants perceived current smart home technology to be expensive. Beyond purchasing, costs associated with installation and maintenance was perceived as added financial burden, especially while retired without stable income.

Some participants perceived risks around privacy and data security. One participant remarked that "Internet is already a big experiment... someone out there can see and do something." During the simulation, multiple participants reacted to the voice prompts with remarks such as "She listens." Some participants also discussed privacy-related concerns held by other residents in their homes such as their spouses. Similarly, participants expressed concerns regarding storage of their financial and personal data. One participant had existing concerns around usage of her data by established websites like ancestry.com, and "monitoring" of in-home activities becomes even more concerning.

3.4 Differences Between Participants

While the study included a small group of older adults, some associations and trends were found between participants' baseline characteristics and study responses. Participants living alone seemed to be more interested in smart home technology and its potential to help them age independently. They found the voice prompts to be comforting, feeling cared for rather than monitored.

Participants closer to 65 years of age were more comfortable using technology as compared to participants near 75 years of age. Based on observations of the simulation experience, and participants' interactions with the technology in particular, digital literacy appeared to be higher in comparatively younger participants.

Participants who worked either full-time or part-time were more tech-savvy and were more easily able to envision their lives with smart home technology. As observed in the pre-study interview, working participants were more familiar with existing smart home technology as compared to those who had retired.

4   Conclusion and Future Work

The purpose of this study was to understand older adults' perceptions and attitudes around different levels of home automation by creating and presenting a simulated environment. In this study, a small laboratory space was designed as a home-like environment, and equipped with various devices and appliances needed for common everyday in-home tasks. The study schedule and incorporated devices were programmed to simulate two levels of automation: one in which devices had no situational awareness or automation features, similar to most of today's homes, or "Traditional Homes" as described in (MIT AgeLab, 2022), and one in which devices were more interconnected and highly automated based on environmental input or time of day (similarly to description of "Networked Homes" in (MIT AgeLab, 2022). Seven older adults participated in the study and experienced both simulations. All the participants were observed during their interaction with the two levels of home automation and interviewed before and after the study to explore future considerations and directions around designing smarter and more automated homes for older adults.

4.1   Practical Implications

Few design considerations were extracted from the findings of this study. While participants were able to mention some smart home devices known to them in the pre-study interview, they were able to much more easily envision smart home devices that could support their routines during the post-study interviews. Leveraging these findings, developers, retailers and distributors can benefit from creating a smart home experience or immersive space. The physical experience can convey how the technologies can benefit the lives and routines of older adults.

Furthermore, products should be bundled with installation support provided either remotely or in-person. Added customer support for troubleshooting issues would provide older adults with a sense of relief, security, and trust when purchasing a product.

Trust can be built among users by designing products which are "private by design" – in other words, which preserve the privacy of the users and do not export any identifiable data outside of the home local ecosystem. Smart home technology companies could adopt innovative methods to communicate to the users how their product works, and why it does not invade the privacy of its users.

4.2   Limitations

This study was limited to only seven participants, which is a relatively smaller participant pool as compared to traditional studies with focus groups and user interviews. We were able to provide a smart home experience for only Networked Homes as compared to the five-level framework discussed earlier. Nearly 50% of the simulation was a "Wizard of Oz" experiment and had some inconsistencies in terms of timely and accurate simulation of a responsive Networked Home as compared to the actual experience envisioned with a 100% automation. Due to the typical routine selected for the simulation, we would not be able to collect insights on how the participants would interact with the technology in their own home and their own routine.

4.3 Future Work

For future work, additional simulations can be created to incorporate other types of smart home implementation and more varied levels of automation. Furthermore, a larger-scale simulation with integration of the various technologies on a centralized platform across multiple in-home spaces could enhance the validity of the study design and findings. Additionally, the study setup and procedure can be improved by allowing personalization to better fit participants' actual routines. Lastly, gathering insights from a larger pool of participants would improve the generalizability of the findings, and utilizing a comparison group of younger participants could allow results and implications to be more effectively discussed in association with age-related characteristics.

Acknowledgment. Support for this study was provided by the MIT AgeLab C3 Connected Home Logistics Consortium. We thank Shen Shen and Manasi Atul Vaidya who provided technical and logistical support that greatly assisted the research.

References

Alhafidh, B.M., Allen, W.: Design and simulation of a smart home managed by an intelligent self-adaptive system. Int. J. Eng. Res. Appl. **6**(8), 64–90 (2016)

Bugeja, J., Jacobsson, A., Davidsson, P.: Is your home becoming a spy? A data-centered analysis and classification of smart connected home systems. In: Proceedings of the 10th International Conference on the Internet of Things, pp. 1–8, October 2020

Bayar, R., Türkoğlu, H.: The relationship between living environment and daily life routines of older adults. A/Z ITU J. Fac. Archit **18**, 29–43 (2021)

Benefield, L.E., Holtzclaw, B.J.: Aging in place: merging desire with reality. Nurs. Clin. **49**(2), 123–131 (2014)

CDC - Healthy Places, December 2017). Healthy Places Terminology. https://www.cdc.gov/hea lthyplaces/terminology.htm

Coughlin, J., D'Ambrosio, L.A., Reimer, B., Pratt, M.R.: Older adult perceptions of smart home technologies: implications for research, policy & market innovations in healthcare. In: Conference proceedings: Annual International Conference of the IEEE Engineering in Medicine and Biology Society. IEEE Engineering in Medicine and Biology Society. Annual Conference 2007, vol. 1810 (2007)

Demiris, G., Oliver, D.P., Dickey, G., Skubic, M., Rantz, M.: Findings from a participatory evaluation of a smart home application for older adults. Technol. Health Care **16**, 111–118 (2008)

Deschamps-Sonsino, A.: Smarter Homes: How Technology Will Change Your Home Life. Apress, New York (2018)

El Jaouhari, S., Jose Palacios-Garcia, E., Anvari-Moghaddam, A., Bouabdallah, A.: Integrated management of energy, wellbeing and health in the next generation of smart homes. Sensors **19**(3), 481 (2019)

FakhrHosseini, S., Lee, C., Coughlin, J.F.: Home as a platform: levels of automation for connected home services. In: Gao, Q., Zhou, J. (eds.) HCII 2020. LNCS, vol. 12208, pp. 451–462. Springer, Cham (2020). https://doi.org/10.1007/978-3-030-50249-2_32

FakhrHosseini, S., Lee, S. H., Rudnik, J., Son, H., Lee, C., Coughlin, J.: User needs of smart home services. In: Proceedings of the Human Factors and Ergonomics Society Annual Meeting, vol. 65, no. 1, pp. 457–461. Sage CA. SAGE Publications, Los Angeles, September 2021

Kim, M.J., Cho, M.E., Jun, H.J.: Developing design solutions for smart homes through user-centered scenarios. Front. Psychol. **11**, 335 (2020)

Li, W., Yigitcanlar, T., Erol, I., Liu, A.: Motivations, barriers and risks of smart home adoption: From systematic literature review to conceptual framework. Energy Res. Soc. Sci. **80**, 102211 (2021)

Marek, K.D., Rantz, M.J.: Aging in place: a new model for long-term care. Nurs. Adm. Q. **24**(3), 1–11 (2000)

MIT AgeLab (2022). Home Taxonomy. https://agelab.mit.edu/home-taxonomy

Pal, D., Funilkul, S., Vanijja, V., Papasratorn, B.: Analyzing the elderly users' adoption of smart-home services. IEEE access **6**, 51238–51252 (2018)

Tort Ayala, L.S.: Principles and recommendations to design aging-friendly homes (Master's thesis, Massachusetts Institute of Technology) (2019)

United Nations Department of Economic & Social Affairs. Annual Report on World Population Ageing (2019)

Data Privacy and Smart Home Technology Adoption: Older Adults' Attitudes and Beliefs

Manasi Vaidya$^{(\boxtimes)}$ ⓘ, Chaiwoo Lee ⓘ, Lisa D'Ambrosio ⓘ, Sophia Ashebir ⓘ, and Joseph F. Coughlin ⓘ

MIT AgeLab, Massachusetts Institute of Technology, Cambridge, MA 02139, USA
{manasiv,chaiwoo,dambrosi,sashebir,coughlin}@mit.edu

Abstract. This study investigates how older adults ages 85 and older view data privacy within smart home technologies and the impact of data privacy on their technology adoption. Privacy has been an important concern among older adults, and prior studies (Kang H.G. et al., 2010) have shown that it has a strong influence on whether they accept new technologies or not, hence it is important to understand their attitudes toward the privacy policies and user agreements of such smart technologies. This was a mixed methods study; our research included semi-structured focus groups and a 32-question survey conducted with 24 older adults 85 years of age and older. Findings suggest that multiple factors contributed to reluctance to adopt newer technologies, including ambiguity around data privacy, low accessibility standards, and unawareness of the most advanced technologies. In this study, we identified potential changes companies should be making around their data privacy practices according to the interviewed older adults to ensure their comfort using these devices and technologies. A privacy policy or user agreement must follow accessibility guidelines not just in terms of visual appeal, but also to allow comprehension, as the words and language used in these documents are hard to understand and are mostly intended for legal professionals. Understanding the content of these documents will make older adults feel more comfortable using the technology and better in control of their own data.

Keywords: Older adults · accessibility · data privacy · voice assistants · technology adoption · aging-in-place

1 Introduction

Smart home technologies use artificial intelligence (including natural language processing, deep learning, machine learning, etc.) to learn the user's habits and provide automated solutions. Some of the potential benefits of using smart home technology include remote health monitoring and remote control of various tasks in the house. A few tasks smart home technologies can do include automated opening and closing of blinds, having personal emergency alarms that alert the emergency numbers in the event of a fall, robots that remind a person to take their medications on time, remote control of the temperature in the home through smart thermostats, allowing certain people access through codes with the help of smart locks, and automated vacuuming of a home with the help of smart vacuum cleaners - to name a few. While certain serious conditions will require older adults to move out of their homes and into assisted living or independent living in communities, the technology available today can enable caregivers (family, friends, or formal caregivers) to remotely monitor the health of the older adults and allow them to age in place for as long as possible. Even though smart home technologies available today offer benefits as stated above, there are a few barriers to adoption including poor and complicated communications regarding data privacy.

Privacy, security, and reliability have proven to be some of the main reasons for older adults to shy away from adopting new and upcoming technologies. Within privacy there is a lot of uncertainty about who has access to the data, where the data collected from smart devices and technology is saved (Cahill et al., 2017), and whether the technology will function when they need it the most (e.g., fall detectors not responding or not being activated when and if an event occurs). Privacy policies and user agreements often make use of so-called dark patterns in user experience design to ensure the user signs and agrees to everything written in these documents. A dark pattern in user experience occurs when designs push and encourage the users to do things that are of benefit to the company rather than to the user (A. Narayanan et al. 2020).

In a previous study (T. Hui et al., 2017), seven key requirements were identified for building smart homes using Internet of Things (IoT) technologies: heterogeneity, self-configurability, extensibility, context awareness, usability, security and privacy protection, and intelligence. In smart homes, privacy and data security were chief concerns, as users were not fully confident in new and upcoming technology (S. FakhrHosseini et al., 2021). Studies focusing on technology adoption among older adults have not been as popular as studies that focus on the adoption of technology across the general population. Many people who design today's technology are younger adults, and as a result there are often some missing elements within technology that are designed and developed that fail to meet what older adults need and require (J. F. Coughlin and L. Yoquinto, 2018, B. Ostlund et al., 2020, Kim 2021, Köttl 2021).

The importance of privacy and ethics play in technology adoption among older adults has been highlighted in prior studies, but current products in the market tend to focus more on safety related concerns (Kang H. G. et al., 2010). Safety is equally important but is not the sole deciding factor that will influence older adults to adopt a particular technology. Our study attempts to look at how different companies making technology in the smart home space handle users' data and communicate with them about the ways in which their data is stored and used.

Various factors that influence older adults' adoption of technology have been examined in previous research (C. Lee, 2014). Lee concludes that there are multiple important factors such as trust and independence, in addition to existing factors like usability, usefulness of a technology, and the cost associated with it, that affect technology adoption. Another research study (C. Lee and J. Coughlin, 2015) discusses these various adoption factors in-depth and the implications they have for current products that are in the market.

The current study explores similar factors - i.e., accessibility, technical support, and support for independence, but through semi-structured interviews and survey questions from the perspective of data privacy. This research also considers potential changes smart home technology manufacturers could make to their data privacy practices supporting older adults' adoption of technology in an informed manner, and support continued use by making them feel comfortable and in control of the data that is collected.

2 Methods

2.1 Participants

We recruited participants for this study from MIT AgeLab's Lifestyle Leaders' Panel. The Lifestyle Leaders Panel is composed of older adults over the age of 85, some of whom have adopted technologies such as smartphones and smart home devices, and some of whom have not. This panel also has shown keen interest in contributing to research for the aging population to make the world a better place for older adults. The participants include members from the 85+ age group who are active in their community, for example, one participant arranged a weekly meeting with the fellow members of the care facility he lives in with an android expert who helps them all with any technology questions they might have with their phones.

To recruit participants for the study, an email was sent to this panel of approximately 60–65 active members, mentioning the topic of the study; members were asked to fill out a Google form if they were interested in participating. Twenty-nine older adults responded to the study invitation where 86.2% ($n = 25$) of the participants confirmed their participation in the study. The study invitation included three questions that helped place the participants into appropriate discussion groups based on their technology usage and concerns about data privacy.

For the in-person study, 5 participants over the age of 85 were contacted via phone and asked if they would be willing to take part in this study, and each one of them confirmed. They came to the MIT AgeLab in Cambridge, MA for 2 h to participate, and they were served lunch. A survey regarding data policy and smart home technology was sent to the Lifestyle Leaders' Panel two days prior to the virtual study. 37 members responded to the survey; and 94.59% of them volunteered to take the survey and 5.41% of them opted to not proceed. Out of the participants that took the survey, 40% ($n = 10$) lived in either senior independent living, an assisted living facility, or a nursing home.

Sample Demographics

Age: The oldest participant was 96 years old, while the youngest participant was 85 years old. There were 58.3% of the participants in the study were male (n = 14), while 41.7% of them were female (n = 10).

Technology Experience: Of all the participants that responded to the survey, 34.48% said they did not own any smart home technology devices. 51.72% said they own some kind of smart home technology, whereas 13.79% said they were unsure or didn't know if they did or did not own smart home technology. Out of the ones that were not sure, they were given a list of smart home technology devices and asked if they owned any particular ones from the list, where 21.43% of them said they did. Everyone who participated in the survey said that they had some level of experience with technology. No information related to their health was collected, however, in this questionnaire.

2.2 Data Collection

The RSVP form was constructed intentionally so that the questions would help us stratify participants into focus groups during the virtual discussion. (1) Do you own any smart home technology devices? The ones who answered no or unsure to these questions were assigned to one group. (2) Did you know that all users are required to sign user agreements/terms and conditions/privacy policies in return to be able to use the service a company provides? (3) Do you make a point to read the user agreement/terms and conditions/privacy policies of products and services you use? The ones who said they owned smart devices in the previous question and said that they were aware of signing these documents but did not read them were assigned to one group. This was a big group of around 10 participants, hence we split them into two groups with 5 in each for this particular category. Finally, the people who mentioned owning smart devices as well as said they read privacy policies and user agreements were assigned to one group.

We began the session with a 20-min presentation about data policy and smart home technology to ensure everyone was using the same definitions for what we meant by smart home technology, data, data privacy, user agreements, etc. (Table 1).

Table 1. The questionnaires used in this study

Questionnaire	Items and variables
1. Pre-workshop Survey	*Key questions:* – How would you rate the understandability of smart home devices' privacy policies and terms and conditions agreements? – How creepy do you think voice assistants are? (For example: Amazon Alexa, Google Assistant, Apple's Siri, etc.) – How fair is it to trade off your privacy for technology that helps you maintain your autonomy? – How comfortable are you with voice assistants (for example: Amazon Alexa, Google Assistant, Apple's Siri, etc.)?

(continued)

Table 1. (*continued*)

Questionnaire	Items and variables
2. Research questions (focus group discussions during the workshop	*Experience with voice assistants:* – What are your thoughts on voice assistants listening to your conversations? Do you believe that they listen to everything you might speak in your home? *Data privacy and fears:* – Tell us more about any fears or concerns you might have about smart technologies like voice assistants stealing your personal information – What kind of information do you fear they will steal? In other words, are you concerned that the company has access to details like your wake-up time, medication time, etc. or do you fear them having access to your credit card details that might allow the assistant to make unauthorized purchases? – Could you tell us about a time you might have changed the default privacy settings of a smart device you currently use or used in the past, how was the experience? Did you face any hurdles? – We noticed through the RSVP form that you generally don't read the privacy policies and user agreements that come with the smart devices. Could you elaborate on the reason why you chose not to read these documents? – What would motivate you to read these documents before you sign them? *Aging-in-place and technology adoption:* – What are your thoughts on the capability of technology today to allow you to live in your home for longer? In other words, do you think technology that would delay the move to a care facility or assisted living by allowing you to maintain the same level of autonomy exists today?
3. In-person study questions	*Key questions:* – What are your thoughts on the capability of technology today to allow you to live in your home for longer? In other words, do you think technology that would delay the move to a care facility or assisted living by allowing you to maintain the same level of autonomy exists today? – What would you consider if you were making a decision about whether to continue to live in your home independently by adopting additional smart home technology? – Do you generally read a physical printed paper that requires your signature? What are your thoughts on digital vs physical signatures? – Has there been an instance where you read a privacy policy or terms and conditions agreement and decided not to use that particular smart home device?

3 Results

3.1 Belief that Privacy is a Myth

Lack of Knowledge about Changing Settings
Throughout the focus group discussions, multiple themes were brought up indicating that participants did not believe privacy within smart home technology even existed. Data collection and privacy settings and their manipulation on the devices they used were very poorly understood by participants in the study. Smart home user agreements and privacy policies cram a lot of information into them, which contributes to this lack of knowledge as users don't read these long and intense documents before signing them.

> It did not even occur to me that I could change the privacy settings, and I don't know how I would do it (female older adult, smart phone user).

There was a strong sense of belief that voice assistants like Apple's Siri that accompanied iPads and iPhones were always listening to the users and rather than getting activated only when the wake word was heard. Siri and Alexa were very commonly used among the older adults that participated in the study, and there was no clarity among them about how the voice assistant could be deleted from the phone, and uncertainty regarding this even being a possibility. Majority of the participants believed that if they wanted to use any service provided by Apple, Siri would be present and remain activated on their phone or devices by default.

> Can we remove Siri from our iPhones or is she always there? Does anyone know how to deactivate her? She is obviously always there (female older adult, smart phone user).

Presentation of Privacy Policies
The length of the privacy policies and user agreements often contributed to why users don't end up reading the information present in these. Many participants highlighted that the language used in the privacy policies was meant for legal professions to understand, and not for older adults or anyone outside the legal space. If users decide to read these documents, they would probably need to look up meanings of multiple words as companies do not intend for regular people to read these and hence do not simplify the language enough for comprehension.

> I just can't deal with it. With forms and those contracts with minute print and hours of reading and interpretations, I have to look up some of the meanings (female older adult, smart phone user).

Some companies that own a big share of the smart home devices today, have extremely long privacy policies ranging from 9 pages (Amazon's privacy policy) to 49 pages (Philips' privacy policy). Some privacy policies have around 3505 words, while some have close to 11,950 words.

3.2 Concerns About Personal Information

There was a lot of uncertainty about when voice assistants wake up and start listening, and many participants in the study referred to voice assistants in the house as 'uninvited guests'. Users are unable to make informed decisions about consenting to anything involving their personal information due to the time it takes to read these documents and the multiple readability problems that come with it. Consent fatigue is developed due to the number of times a user is asked to make decisions regarding their personal information. Even if these policies and agreements are made shorter, more accessible, and easily comprehensible, the issue regarding the frequency to which a user needs to give this consent is still high. During the study, participants raised concerns about companies not making the intentions of collecting personal information clear, and the various purposes their personal information would be used for beyond the reason for which it was originally collected. In our study, older adults believed that they are being left behind by current document formats, where they are expected to read thousands of words before understanding how their personal information will be used.

Financial Information Being Leaked

Concerns over financial information being leaked was higher than any other concern with regard to personal information. While some users completely avoided using financial services online, some had a view that even if they end up paying an amount that they did not intend to due to not paying attention and signing an agreement, they can always dispute it with the bank and get their money back. A majority of users expressed that they are not comfortable sharing any credit card details with technology providers.

Privacy and Misuse of Medical Information

Another big concern within personal information was personal medical information being misused. Although most older adults in the study appreciated the benefits the medical field has seen with the rise in technology through remote physician visits and telehealth, some also raised concerns over medical information being misused and their families having to pay for it.

> I am concerned that some companies having access to my medical information might end up affecting my children and their children's insurance. Genetic information being in the reach of certain insurance companies might lead to some inference to be drawn (female older adult, smart phone user).

3.3 Eagerness to Learn About New Technologies

A majority of the participants in the group that did not use smart technology were comfortable using a personal computer and/or iPads. Even though they had been averse to using some technology due to data privacy concerns, they expressed keen interest in knowing more about the potential benefits of these new and advanced technologies and how their current ways of living might be enhanced if they adopted and started using these devices. Most of them were of the opinion that they are restricted to the minimal technology they use today only because it is enough for them, and that they are unaware of the upcoming technology that exists out in the world.

Am I missing something that could add value to my life and make this current moment in time better? Even if I was open to some kind of technology, I don't even know if something like this exists (female older adult, Siri and smart phone user).

Multiple participants expressed that technology education for older adults could be beneficial to them, as they find it hard to keep up with the current technology inventions. 26.9% of older adults said it was easy for them to learn new technologies, whereas 42.3% older adults said it was extremely or somewhat difficult for them to learn new technologies. Another 30.8% said it was neither easy nor difficult for them.

4 Discussion

Although participants (n = 24) in the study were divided into two groups based on their ownership of any smart devices, everyone demonstrated a strong interest and eagerness in learning more about the technology that is out there today that could better support their needs. A majority of the participants were open to adopting technology that would improve the quality of their life, and a primary reason that many had not yet done this is just because they aren't even aware that such technology exists. One participant (P12) who has owned a robot since 2018 mentioned that he enjoyed interacting with it, but it had stopped working for a year or so, and he had not found anyone to repair it. Many such conversations highlighted the need to expand efforts, either through families or companies, to help older adults maintain their technology (Trajkova and Martin-Hammond, 2020). Among those who were concerned about privacy and are not yet using any smart home devices except a smartphone, there was also a lot of emphasis throughout the in-person as well as virtual focus groups on the accessibility of smart home devices' privacy policies and user agreements. A lot of older adults expressed their frustration about not being able to access these documents because of the low visual and cognitive accessibility standards followed while presenting them. Technology companies having clearer and easily understandable privacy policies about how they use and store collected data will enable older adults to feel comfortable while using the devices without the fear of compromising their personal data.

4.1 Implications

Need for Technology Education
This need was highlighted as part of a question that asked older adults to elaborate on whether they see digital signatures and physical signatures differently. Many participants commented and took part in this discussion and mentioned that they preferred physical signatures, as people from their generation were more used to signing a document and being held accountable for it by using a pen and paper. They also pointed out that this might be the way their generation thinks, and these insights might be particular to the 85+ group, as a big percentage of them never really got acquainted with digital signature technology that well. Participants also expressed the comfort with signing using a pen

and paper, as there is a real person on the other end who asks for this signature, and any or every doubt that is there in the signer's mind can be clarified or discussed; often times the person seeking the signatures even explains the document briefly before expecting a signature - which is completely eliminated in digital signatures, particularly for privacy policies and user agreements.

Discussions around how the notion of signing a document digitally could be made similar to physically signing led to exploring if adding summaries of what the content is all about in the beginning would help comprehension. A number of the participants in the study owned a smartphone, specifically an iPhone, but did not use Siri (Apple's voice assistant) on it due to privacy concerns. Siri has its limitations, but at the same time the voice assistant can be useful to older adults as it requires only voice commands in order to operate. Statistics have shown that 20% of the seniors above the age of 85 suffer from permanent vision loss and other vision impairments like impaired acuity and. These data suggest the important support voice assistants could play in the lives of older adults in this age group, and hence if more older adults are comfortable with voice assistants, their social life and interaction with others could see an increase. Adding summaries that address concerns seniors might have and how these can be navigated when decisions about enabling/disabling certain technology that you could use on their existing devices will be valuable to help them make an informed decision.

Designing for Comprehension and Accessibility
The format of the documents as well as the language used to convey the material is not designed for comprehension. The various companies designing the smart home technologies could include older adults as one of their personas while designing the product, as this will help to ensure that they are included as a potential primary user of the device. Privacy guidelines that need to be signed digitally should also ensure that there is a summary of what the document contains. Transparency will help all users attempting to make a decision on whether or not to sign the policies and agreements, not just older adults. Clearer and upfront information regarding changing the default privacy settings of a device will also encourage users who currently don't use smart home devices due to privacy concerns to take a look and re-evaluate their decision by helping them understand who controls the data and how these settings can be monitored and changed (or not).

Need for Revamping the Current Presentation of Privacy Policies:
The above implications suggest that there is much information present in documents like privacy policies and user agreements that is useful for the users to enable them to manipulate privacy settings. If the users are able to change the privacy settings according to their preferences, they will be comfortable while using the devices they own. Consenting to personal data being collected, stored, and used by technology companies is mandatory these days if we want to use a particular service or product. A lingering question in the minds of many participants was the possibility of revoking this consent if they feel uncomfortable while using the service. Currently there is an absence of revoking consent given to technology companies. Privacy policies do not allow for a user to agree to or disagree with a select set of terms and conditions, all terms and conditions must be agreed to or disagreed with. A research study (S. Egelman et al., 2009) has also shown

that the timing and design of notices can influence how individuals respond to them in regard to their privacy.

5 Conclusions

The overall understanding from the study was that older adults perceive the documents published online that contain privacy related information are presented in a form that only lawyers or an individual from the law field will be able to comprehend. These documents are not designed for consumer understanding but rather for the companies to protect themselves from lawsuits (if filed). A summary of what the documents mean at the beginning will be very helpful in order to increase adoption of smart technology like voice assistants that are not easy to navigate for novice users and often require the user to decode what the perfect protocol of framing sentences and questions looks like. Even though older adults showed eagerness to learn more about the technologies that exist today, they need to overcome multiple hurdles like keeping up with the advancements in the technology, successfully adopting it, as well as maintaining the technology or device. Companies should try, for example, to adhere to accessibility standards published by the Web Content Accessibility Guidelines (WCAG). For older adults to fully utilize smart home technology, we need to make sure they are adopting it in an informed manner. They may also be able to use it in a sustained manner once they see its value and feel confident about being in control of their data collection and where it goes. It is important that companies build their trust ethically, and to ensure that older adults are not required to trade off their privacy for autonomy and security. Design of privacy policies plays an important role and if companies designing smart products make it easier for the older adult population to understand their privacy laws and make them feel comfortable using their devices, it is estimated that the number of older adults using smart home technologies will only increase.

6 Recommendations for Future Work

Future studies could focus on expanding the participant pool to get perspectives from a more demographically diverse set of people with varied levels of education. 76% of the participants came from highly educated backgrounds, with 70% of them having completed a graduate degree; those who are not as highly educated and fall in this age group of 85 and above might have different experiences and preferences. Another area for future work is fundamentally understanding how older adults interact with technology and interfaces is key, followed by developing design guidelines for privacy policies and user agreements with the aim of comprehension and understandability, focusing on clear communication. Further research studies could be conducted with older adults over the age of 64 to compare the behaviors and have a set of recommendations that take them into consideration as well.

Acknowledgements. This study was supported in part by the MIT AgeLab's C3 Connected Home Logistics Consortium. The virtual and in-person workshop was supported by Adam Felts, Alexa Balmuth, Lauren Cerino, Sophia Ashebir, Taylor Patskanick, and Thomas Smythe from MIT AgeLab.

References

Coughlin, J.F., Yoquinto, L.: Opinion | technology for older people doesn't have to be ugly. Wall Street J. (2018). https://www.wsj.com/articles/technology-for-older-people-doesnt-have-to-be-ugly-1539546423. Accessed 6 Jan 2023

Egelman, S., Tsai, J., Cranor, L.F., Acquisti, A.: Timing is everything? In: Proceedings of the SIGCHI Conference on Human Factors in Computing Systems (2009). https://doi.org/10.1145/1518701.1518752

Goettsche Partners. GP. Amazon (2011). https://www.amazon.com/gp/help/customer/display.html?nodeId=GX7NJQ4ZB8MHFRNJ. Accessed 6 Jan 2023

Google. Privacy policy – privacy & terms. Google. https://policies.google.com/privacy?hl=en-US. Accessed 6 Jan 2023

Kang, H.G., et al.: In situ monitoring of health in older adults: technologies and issues. University of Texas Southwestern Medical Center (2010). https://utsouthwestern.pure.elsevier.com/en/publications/in-situ-monitoring-of-health-in-older-adults-technologies-and-iss. Accessed 6 Jan 2023

Kim, S.: Exploring how older adults use a smart speaker–based voice assistant in their first interactions: qualitative study. JMIR MHealth UHealth 9(1) (2021). https://doi.org/10.2196/20427

Köttl, H., Gallistl, V., Rohner, R., Ayalon, L.: "But at the age of 85? forget it!": internalized ageism, a barrier to technology use. J. Aging Stud. (2021). https://pubmed.ncbi.nlm.nih.gov/34794716/. Accessed 6 Jan 2023

Lee, C., Coughlin, J.F.: Older adults' adoption of technology. J. Prod. Innov. Manag. 32, 747–759 (2015). https://doi.org/10.1111/jpim.12176

Narayanan, A., Mathur, A., Chetty, M., Kshirsagar, M.: Dark patterns: past, present, and future. Queue 18(2), 67–92 (2020). https://doi.org/10.1145/3400899.3400901

Östlund, B., et al.: Using academic work places to involve older people in the design of digital applications. presentation of a methodological framework to advance co-design in later life. In: Gao, Q., Zhou, J. (eds.) HCII 2020. LNCS, vol. 12207, pp. 45–58. Springer, Cham (2020). https://doi.org/10.1007/978-3-030-50252-2_4

Philips Global Privacy Page. Philips (2020). https://www.philips.com/a-w/privacy.html. Accessed 6 Jan 2023

Trajkova, M., Martin-Hammond, A.: "Alexa is a toy": exploring older adults' reasons for using, limiting, and abandoning echo. In: Proceedings of the 2020 CHI Conference on Human Factors in Computing Systems (2020). https://doi.org/10.1145/3313831.3376760

Cahill, J., Mc Loughlin, S., Blazek, D.: The design of new technologies addressing independence, social participation & wellness for older people domicile in residential homes. In: Proceedings 2017 International Conference on Computational Science and Computational Intelligence (CSCI), pp. 1672–1677. American Council Sci & Educ., Las Vegas, NV (2017). https://doi.org/10.1109/CSCI.2017.291

FakhrHosseini, S., Lee, S.-H., Rudnik, J., Son, H., Lee, C., Coughlin, J.: User needs of smart home services. Proc. Hum. Factors Ergon. Soc. Annu. Meet. 65(1), 457–461 (2021). https://doi.org/10.1177/1071181321651218

Hui, T.K.L., Sherratt, R.S., Diaz Sanchez, D.: Major requirements for building smart homes in smart cities based on internet of things technologies. Future Gener. Comput. Syst. 76, 358–369 (2017). ISSN 0167-739X. https://doi.org/10.1016/j.future.2016.10.026. Retrieved from https://centaur.reading.ac.uk/67947/

Lee, C.: Adoption of smart technology among older adults: challenges and issues. Public Policy Aging Rep. 24(1), 14–17 (2014). https://doi.org/10.1093/ppar/prt005

eHealth Applications for Older People
and Health Literacy

Health Education Mobile Applications: Evaluation of Persuasion Strategies and Impact on Older Users

Shushan Fan and Yongyan Guo[✉]

East China University of Science and Technology, No. 130 Meilong Road, Xuhui District, Shanghai, China
Shushan3131@163.com

Abstract. The current aging situation and health needs in China are becoming increasingly serious, but the attitudes and behaviors of the elderly towards health apps are still not positive enough. For this reason, persuasion strategies are widely used in health APP applications. However, the existing literature rarely investigates the differences in the application of persuasion strategies in different types of health apps. There are also few studies on the corresponding persuasion strategies for health education APPs for older adults. Therefore, this paper first analyzes the classification and problems of health education APPs at home and abroad. Secondly, 59 health APPs were reviewed, the persuasion design strategies in them were extracted, and the distribution of persuasion strategies in different categories of health APPs was analyzed. Finally, suggestions of persuasion strategies for designing health education APPs for the elderly were proposed based on the classification results. The study found that there are differences in the persuasion strategies used in the development of different types of health apps. It is suggested that the distribution of persuasion strategies in this type of health education APP developed for the elderly should be taken into account in order to design a more reasonable health education APP system.

Keywords: elderly · health education APP · persuasion strategy · persuasion design

1 First Section

1.1 Status of Aging and Health Needs in China

In recent years, China has faced a serious problem of population aging, and an aging population means that Chinese older adults face many health risks and a heavy medical burden [1]. As people's living conditions and life expectancy increase, the demand for health, companionship, and care for the elderly is also growing. Today's healthcare system faces serious challenges, digital health delivery systems can change the way health and care are delivered to elderly patients [2], and mobile health management applications can provide solutions for various health risks of older adults [3]. For example, Meng

Q. Gao and J. Zhou (Eds.): HCII 2023, LNCS 14043, pp. 109–120, 2023.
https://doi.org/10.1007/978-3-031-34917-1_8

et al. [4] found that health apps were beneficial in controlling blood pressure in older patients with hypertension, improving self-efficacy and providing medication adherence in older patients with hypertension. Thus, the use of mobile health management apps can come to meet the challenges of an aging population.

1.2 Older Adults' Attitudes and Behaviors Towards mHealth Education APP

Studies have shown that older adults use cell phones at a much higher rate than the Internet [5]. The development of mobile health education app services for older adults, who have a heavy reliance on cell phones and high cell phone penetration, is an excellent opportunity. Mobile health apps are considered beneficial for older adults because they can save patients' visit time and healthcare costs, provide personalized and customized health information and services, and more efficient health service processes [6, 7]. However, in China, the development of mHealth app services is still in its infancy, and the adoption rate of such services among older adults remains relatively low [8]. Therefore, it is important to investigate the attitudinal and behavioral factors of mobile health education app adoption among older adults.

Guo et al. [9] studied the negative effects of e-health service use among older adults in China, and they highlighted technology anxiety [10, 11] and dispositional resistance to change [12] as the main factors influencing older users' use of health services. The reason for the predisposition to resist change among older adults was their perception that these services were not useful. Similarly, in a study by Deng et al. [8], it was found that although older adults had technology anxiety, most of them indicated that they were willing and able to learn the services if they were taught how to use them, suggesting that service providers should take steps to reduce and eliminate technology anxiety among older users.

Fogg proposed persuasion techniques as techniques to change human will and behavior using non-coercive methods [13]. Oinas Kukkonen and Harjumaa proposed 28 PSD persuasion strategies applied to interactive systems in 2009 [14]. However, the existing literature has rarely investigated the differences in the application of persuasion strategies in different types of health APPs, and few studies have been conducted on the corresponding persuasion strategies for health education APPs for older adults. Therefore, to solve this problem, the research framework of this paper is to first analyze the classification and problems of health education APPs at home and abroad, secondly, count the distribution of persuasion strategies applied in each type of health APP, and finally propose suggestions for designing persuasion strategies for health education APPs for the elderly based on the classification results.

2 Domestic and Foreign Health APP Analysis

2.1 Status and Distribution of Existing Health APPs in the Market

As the market demand continues to expand, the mobile health management application market has developed and offered many applications to enhance healthcare services for patients. According to the report [15], there are now more than 350,000 health-related mobile apps in the global app stores, and in a recent market report it was estimated that the global mHealth market is worth more than USD 40 billion [16]. Market estimates predict that the mobile health care app market will continue to grow in the coming years and will reach $150 billion by 2028 [17]. Although mobile health apps can provide users with low-cost, high-quality health management information, most of the health information contained in these apps is not reviewed by regulatory agencies, which may endanger the health of users [18]. Therefore, it is important for developers and healthcare professionals to understand the existing health apps in both domestic and international markets to drive change in mobile health apps.

2.2 Status of Foreign Health APP

Currently, the vast majority of mobile health apps in foreign markets are designed for consumers [19]. Patients are the most affected population in mHealth apps today [20]. Apps are increasingly focused on health condition management rather than health management, with the former accounting for 47% of all apps in 2020 and almost half of apps related to mental health, diabetes and cardiovascular disease [19].

The report shows that [15] the top two health management apps at are health management (e.g., fitness, diet, stress, and sleep) and chronic disease management (predicting and responding to periods of deterioration, detecting medication management, maintaining physician-patient contact, etc.). Other types of health apps include self-diagnosis, medication reminders, and for healthcare providers. (See Fig. 1).

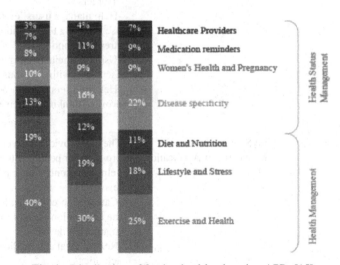

Fig. 1. Distribution of foreign health education APPs [15]

In addition, through the popular application of health education APPs abroad, the mobile medical model of "online appointment + online video diagnosis and treatment + drug purchase guidance + long-term patient data management" has been initially formed. Foreign health APPs can provide in-depth medical treatment and health monitoring for a single disease, which is still basically in a blank state in China [21]. Table 1 will analyze the examples of foreign mobile health apps in various categories.

Table 1. Examples of foreign health APPs by category

Category	Example applications	Description and functions
Health Management Class		
Sports & Fitness	MyFitnessPal fitness management application [22]	The app offers a weight loss program for obese patients to help them control their diet calories -Provides food database and records meals -Personalized user calorie intake goals -Allows generation of real-time reports showing personal user data -Social networking features to motivate users to progress
Wellness and Health	Wysa Mental Health Support Application	The application specializes in treating patients with depression, anxiety and other psychological disorders -Help manage users' emotions and use coaching tools to address users' stressful emotions -Using artificial intelligence to help users deal with emotions -Helping users relax through positive thinking exercises
Medical class		
Chronic Disease Management	mySugr Diabetes Management Application [23]	The app provides a coaching program for people with diabetes to help them control their blood sugar levels -Can be entered manually or into the application via a blood glucose monitoring device -Record meal and medication activities -Allows patients to share reports with physicians

(continued)

Table 1. (*continued*)

Category	Example applications	Description and functions
	AsthmaMD Asthma Management App [24]	The app allows asthma sufferers to track their peak flow measurements and symptoms and provides a plan during asthma attacks -Remind patients to use their inhalers on time -Allows patients to record periods of use
Medication Reminder	Medical safety drug management (MSDM) application [25]	The app reminds users to take their medication and provides a range of medication safety -Medication reminders for users -Measurement of physical condition data -Allows health reports to be shared with physicians -Allows one account to manage family member health information
For Healthcare Professionals	MyChart application [26]	The application can record all patient visits and hospitalizations -The medical team can view patient health information -Allows patients to send messages to the medical team regarding resolution of symptoms
Women's Health and Pregnancy	Spot On Period Tracker application	The application can record a woman's period time and remind the user to take the pill -Monitoring the user's menstrual cycle -Medication reminders for users

Through example analysis, health management apps were found to have intervention effects in diabetes, asthma, mental health, and weight management. Although mobile health apps can facilitate health management, there are still some problems. Wang et al. [27] found that one of the important problems faced by health apps is the lack of penetration among older patients.

2.3 Status of Domestic Health APP

Among domestic products, patient-side health education APPs occupy most of the market share. At present, the highest ranking of commonly used health medical APPs are the consultation and advice category (e.g. online consultation, online advice, etc.) and medical information category (medication assistant, medical science, etc.) [28], while the chronic disease management category (e.g. blood pressure monitoring, exercise reminder, etc.) has relatively low download volume.

Currently, the health category in the domestic market can be divided into two categories based on the function of health management and mobile medical category, Table 2 shows the classification of domestic health APPs.

Table 2. Domestic health APP classification

Function classification	APP type	Function
Health Management Class	Fitness Shape Up App	Sports and fitness, fat loss and shaping
	Wellness Management App	Diet records, nutrition science
Mobile Medical Class	Online Medical App	Appointment booking, consultation, handheld pharmacy, etc
	Health Monitoring App	Exercise tracking, sign monitoring, medication reminders, etc

According to the data of the China APP Client Registration Center, as of 2014, there have been 16,275 medical and health-related apps in the Apple Store, mainly focusing on exercise and health care, consultation platforms, and registered appointments. According to the report released by Ariadne Consulting, the registration and appointment category, consultation and advisory category, and medical information APPs account for 28.5%, 24.9% and 17.9% respectively, but these APPs have limited large functions and serious homogenization. Among them, the appointment registration APP is influenced by the distribution of domestic medical resources and is too concentrated in tertiary hospitals, which is only a platform to provide resources and lacks the ability to divert resources. Most of the consultation and consulting APPs only stay at the preliminary consultation stage due to the separation of online consultation and offline medical treatment, which makes it difficult to provide effective medical services [29].

2.4 Problems and Conclusion

The above analysis shows that the development of health APPs varies at home and abroad. In terms of health application types, health management and chronic disease management APPs are dominant in foreign countries, while the common types of health education APPs in China are mainly consultation and medical information APPs. The usage rate of chronic disease management APPs in China is relatively low, which may be due to the fact that chronic disease management APPs are in the initial exploration stage in general, and compared with other types of mobile health APPs, the operation process requires great effort and time, which is more difficult.

In addition, Zou et al. [30] study proved that using apps can provide health education. For example, the use of a diet education app by elderly users can provide them with knowledge about proper diet and support them to form healthy eating habits and control diseases such as hypertension. Although there have been some clinical trial papers on mobile health APPs for older adults, the use of health education APPs for older adults is still not popular in practice. Therefore, in addition to establishing standardized health management guidelines, it is important to consider the diverse characteristics of the population and to meet the actual needs of the elderly for mobile health education APPs, such as rehabilitation guidance and supervision reminders for chronic diseases in the elderly. Lee et al. [31] argue that simple intervention methods, such as directly telling elderly users what they need to do, are not effective. Therefore, if persuasive strategies are used in health education APPs to intervene in user behavior, is a valuable approach. In the following, we will analyze the distribution of persuasion strategies in health education APPs.

3   Analysis of Persuasion Strategies in Health Education APP

3.1   Introduction to the Experimental Procedure

To analyze the adoption of persuasion strategies in health education, we downloaded mainstream health apps and counted the persuasion strategies used in them. We first downloaded a sample app and used it for 10 days to ensure that no new strategies were found during use. After that, we downloaded and independently reviewed 59 health apps, including 59 Chinese versions. The list of extracted persuasion strategies was used to statistically analyze the persuasion strategies employed in the health apps. (1) Persuasion strategies were categorized according to the types of health management problems targeted by the apps. (2) The persuasion strategies that appeared in the health management APPs were extracted and statistically analyzed.

3.2   Review of the Mean Value of Persuasion Strategies Used in the Health Management Class of Applications

Among the 59 health management apps screened, 21 apps were about a combination of health management issues, 16 apps were about health and wellness issues, 27 apps were about the online consultation category, 6 apps were about online medicine buying, and 10 apps were about appointment registration. Therefore, the types of these apps were divided into four categories: health and wellness, online consultation, online medicine buying, and appointment registration. Figure 2 presents the sum of the persuasion strategies used for each type of health management app. We found 26 persuasive strategies among the health management apps reviewed. The number of persuasive strategies used by each app varied and ranged from 1 to 16. As shown in Fig. 2, the persuasion strategies used in the four categories of health management apps were counted, with the apps in the online consultation category using the most persuasion strategies, with a total of 26 persuasion strategies; the apps for health and wellness, online medicine buying, and appointment booking used 20, 19, and 10 persuasion strategies, respectively.

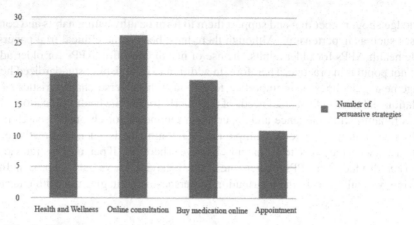

Fig. 2. Sum of persuasive strategies used by the health management apps reviewed

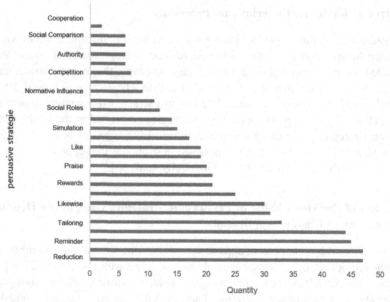

Fig. 3. Total number of occurrences of each persuasion strategy in the health management app

3.3 Statistics on the Application of Persuasion Strategies in Different Categories of Health APPs

To obtain the most frequently used persuasion strategies in health management apps, we counted the total number of occurrences of each persuasion strategy in the reviewed health management apps and the statistics are shown in Fig. 3. Comparing the total number of occurrences of each persuasion strategy in health management apps, the persuasion strategies with 10 or more occurrences were considered as the most frequently used persuasion strategies in health management apps. This resulted in the 18 most frequently used persuasion strategies in health management apps.

Figure 4 shows the distribution of the 18 most frequently used persuasion strategies in health management apps and the total number of occurrences of each persuasion strategy in all health management apps. The results show that the top five most commonly used persuasion strategies across all health management apps are "reduce," "personalize," "remind," "interface credibility" and "tailoring".

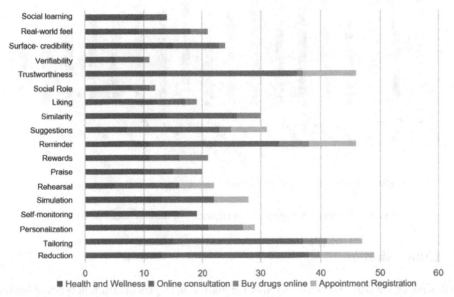

Fig. 4. Classification of persuasion strategies in the health management apps reviewed Distribution

3.4 Suggested Persuasion Strategies for Health Education APPs Designed for Older Adults

According to the user needs research, the main needs of the elderly for health education APPs are to get health and wellness information and online doctor consultation. Therefore, the persuasion strategies used in "health and wellness" and "online doctor consultation" should be used as a reference when choosing persuasion strategies. After the data analysis, we got the statistical results of the average of the persuasion strategies used by these two types of health apps (Fig. 5). Therefore, based on the ranking of the persuasion strategies, we suggest that the top five recommended persuasion strategies for health education app design for the elderly are as follows: reduce, cut, credibility, reminders, and similar.

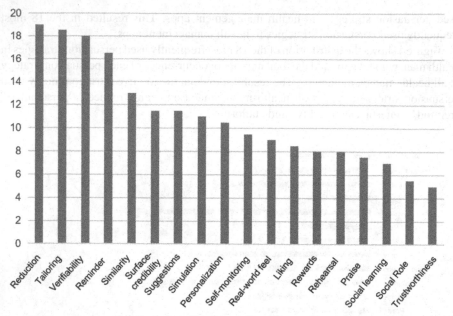

■ Average persuasion strategies of two types of health apps: "health and wellness" and "online consultation"

Fig. 5. Distribution of persuasion strategies of health education APPs

4 Conclusion

In this paper, we study the application of persuasion strategies in different types of health education APPs and suggest corresponding persuasion strategies for health education APPs for the elderly. We first analyze the classification and problems of health APPs at home and abroad. Secondly, we reviewed 59 Chinese health APPs, extracted the persuasion design strategies in them, and analyzed the distribution of persuasion strategies in different categories of health apps. Finally, according to the statistical results of the classification of health education APPs for the elderly, corresponding suggestions for persuasion strategies were proposed. The study found that there are differences in the persuasion strategies used in developing different types of health apps. The conclusion of this paper is to suggest that the distribution of persuasion strategies in health education APPs developed for older adults should be borrowed from this type, and the top five ranked persuasion strategies (reduction, clipping, credibility, reminder, and similarity) should be used in priority to design a more reasonable health education APP system.

The limitations of this paper are: in the process of screening health apps, we measured the effectiveness of apps based on mainstream health app malls, and only studied health apps in the Chinese category. In future work, we will expand the study to health apps in the English category; and expand the sample size to study the perceptions of elderly users on the persuasion strategies of health education apps in order to develop health education apps that are more suitable for the elderly.

Acknowledgement. This work was supported by the Ministry of Education Humanities and Social Sciences Foundation of China. (Grant number 17YJCZH055).

References

1. Jiang, Q., Yang, S., SánchezBarricarte, J.J.: Can China afford rapid aging? Springerplus **5**(1), 1–8 (2016). https://doi.org/10.1186/s40064-016-2778-0
2. Vicente, M.R.: ICT for healthy and active aging: The elderly as first and last movers. Telecommun. Policy. **46**, 102262 (2022)
3. Chen, Z., Qi, H., Wang, L.: Study on the types of elderly intelligent health management technology and the influencing factors of its adoption. Healthcare **9**(11), 1494 (2021). https://doi.org/10.3390/healthcare9111494
4. Xiao, M., et al.: Home blood pressure monitoring by a mobile-based model in Chongqing, China: a feasibility study. Int. J. Environ. Res. Public Health. **16** (2019)
5. AlRazgan, M.S., AlKhalifa, H.S., AlShahrani, M.D., AlAjmi, H.H.: Touch-based mobile phone interface guidelines and design recommendations for elderly people: a survey of the literature. In: Huang, T., Zeng, Z., Li, C., Leung, C.S. (eds.) Neural Information Processing. LNCS, vol. 7666, pp. 568–574. Springer, Heidelberg (2012). https://doi.org/10.1007/978-3-642-34478-7_69
6. Angst, C.M., Agarwal, R.: Adoption of electronic health records in the presence of privacy concerns: the elaboration likelihood model and individual persuasion. MIS Q. **33**, 339–370 (2009)
7. Mishra, A.N., Anderson, C., Angst, C.M., Agarwal, R.: Electronic health records assimilation and physician identity evolution: an identity theory perspective. Inf. Syst. Res. **23**, 738–760 (2012)
8. Deng, Z., Mo, X., Liu, S.: Comparison of the middle-aged and older users' adoption of mobile health services in China. Int. J. Med. Inform. **83**, 210–224 (2014)
9. Guo, X., Sun, Y., Wang, N., Peng, Z., Yan, Z.: The dark side of elderly acceptance of preventive mobile health services in China. Electron. Mark. **23**, 49–61 (2013)
10. Dyck, J.L., Gee, N.R., AlAwarSmither, J.: The changing construct of computer anxiety for younger and older adults. Comput. Hum. Behav. **14**, 61–77 (1998)
11. Laguna, K., Babcock, R.L.: Computer anxiety in young and older adults: implications for human-computer interactions in older populations. Comput. Hum. Behav. **13**, 317–326 (1997)
12. Oreg, S.: Personality, context, and resistance to organizational change. Eur. J. Work Organ. Psy. **15**, 73–101 (2006)
13. Fogg, B.J.: Chapter 7 - Credibility and the world wide web. In: Fogg, B.J. (ed.) Persuasive Technology, pp. 147–181. Morgan Kaufmann, San Francisco (2003)
14. Oinas-Kukkonen, H., Harjumaa, M.: Persuasive systems design: key issues, process model, and system features. Commun. Assoc. Inf. Syst. **24**, 28 (2009)
15. IQVIA Homepage. https://www.iqvia.com/insights/the-iqvia-institute/reports/digital-health-trends-2021
16. Nazir, S., et al.: A comprehensive analysis of healthcare big data management. Anal. Sci. Program. IEEE Access. **8**, 95714–95733 (2020)
17. Wang, C., Qi, H.: Influencing factors of acceptance and use behavior of mobile health application users: systematic review. Healthcare **9**(3), 357 (2021). https://doi.org/10.3390/healthcare9030357
18. Kao, C.-K., Liebovitz, D.M.: Consumer mobile health apps: current state, barriers, and future directions. PM&R. **9**, S106–S115 (2017)

19. IQVIA Homepage. https://www.iqvia.com/locations/france/library/white-papers/apps-and-connected-devices-in-healthcare
20. Research 2 Guidance Homepage. https://www.iqvia.com/locations/france/library/white-papers/apps-and-connected-devices-in-healthcare
21. Gao, Y., Ma, L., Shi, C., Yang, Y., Li, L.: Analysis of the application status and prospect of smart bracelets in the elderly. In: 2021 International Conference on Digital Society and Intelligent Systems (DSInS), pp. 95–101 (2021)
22. Laing, B.Y., et al.: Effectiveness of a smartphone application for weight loss compared with usual care in overweight primary care patients. Ann. Int. Med. **161**, S5–S12 (2014)
23. Debong, F., Mayer, H., Kober, J.: Real-world assessments of MySugr mobile health App. Diabetes Technol. Ther. **21**, S2-35 (2019)
24. AsthmaMD on the App Store. https://itunes.apple.com/us/app/asthmamd/id349343083. Accessed 14 Oct 2016
25. edisafe Pill Reminder & Medication Tracker on the App Store. https://itunes.apple.com/us/app/medisafe-pill-remindermedication/id573916946?m¼8. Accessed 21 Jan 2017
26. MyChart on the App Store. https://itunes.apple.com/us/app/mychart/id382952264?mt¼8. Accessed 21 Jan 2017
27. Wang, S.Y., Luo, R.: Research and analysis of the state of mobile medical health app applications in the United States. China Digital Med. **10**, 2–6 (2015)
28. Hsu, J., et al.: The top Chinese mobile health apps: a systematic investigation. J. Med. Internet Res. **18**, e222 (2016)
29. ElSappagh, S., Ali, F., ElMasri, S., Kim, K., Ali, A., Kwak, K.-S.: Mobile health technologies for diabetes mellitus: current state and future challenges. IEEE Access. **7**, 21917–21947 (2019)
30. Zou, P., Stinson, J., Parry, M., Dennis, C.-L., Yang, Y., Lu, Z.: A smartphone App (mDASHNa-CC) to support healthy diet and hypertension control for Chinese Canadian seniors: protocol for design, usability and feasibility testing. JMIR Res. Protoc. **9**, e15545 (2020)
31. Lee, D., Helal, S., Anton, S., De Deugd, S., Smith, A.: Participatory and persuasive telehealth. Gerontology **58**, 269–281 (2012)

Designing Intelligent Decision Assistants to Assist Seniors with Medicare Plan Decision-Making: An Application of Cognitive Response Theories

Ebenezer Nana Banyin Harrison[1,2]([email]) (iD), Wi-Suk Kwon[2] (iD), Xiao Huang[2] (iD), Nick McCormick[2] (iD), and Salisa Westrick[2] (iD)

[1] University of North Carolina Asheville, Asheville, NC 28804, USA
nharris5@unca.edu
[2] Auburn University, Auburn, AL 36849, USA

Abstract. Aging limits the capacity of one's working memory. Hence, in decision contexts where especially older people have to evaluate too many alternatives put a cognitive load on them, which impairs their decision-making process and their trust in their decisions. This study examined the effects of intelligent decision assistants on the perceived social support, perceived information load, and trust of seniors while using the Medicare Plan Finder website. A national sample of 420 seniors from the Qualtrics panel participated in this study. It was found that using an intelligent decision assistant on the Medicare Plan Finder website increased seniors' perceived social support, reduced their perceived information load, and increased their trust in the Medicare Plan Finder website especially when they are at the alternative evaluation stage of Medicare plan decision-making. Implications and suggestions for future research are discussed.

Keywords: Intelligent Decision Assistant · Decision-Making · Medicare Plan Finder

1 Introduction

The human brain can recall a maximum of seven to nine items of information at a given time [1], and this makes it difficult for people to make an in-depth evaluation of all available alternatives especially while shopping online [2]. The number of alternatives and attributes, attribute familiarity, the certainty of attribute values, and the number of shared attributes have been identified as the four factors that determine the level of complexity of consumers' choices [1]. Hence, the consumer decision-making process is impaired as decision options increase [3]. Cognitive functions such as attention, information processing speed, and multi-tasking performance have been found to decline with the normal aging process [4]. Therefore, older people will find it even more difficult to make the best choice when overloaded with various options and attributes.

Q. Gao and J. Zhou (Eds.): HCII 2023, LNCS 14043, pp. 121–130, 2023.
https://doi.org/10.1007/978-3-031-34917-1_9

Medicare is health insurance for seniors (65+ years old) in the U.S. Medicare Part D provides seniors with access to prescription drugs. A regular search for a Part D plan on Medicare Plan Finder (MPF), the official online Medicare marketplace run on the Medicare.gov website [5], returns about 30 plan options with varying attributes, suggesting a complex decision-making environment for any individual, especially for older users. We set out to design a conversational agent with artificial intelligence (AI), or an intelligent decision assistant (IDA), to assist older users of MPF with streamlining their decision strategies to select the most optimal Medicare Part D plan that meets their medication and financial needs.

Existing research found that IDAs effectively assist online shoppers in making efficient decisions with little effort [2]. IDAs, designed with the ability to verbally assist users in a specified decision context, have been used to assist with consumers' purchase decision-making both online [6, 8] and offline [9, 10]. Embedding IDAs that provide transactional assistance in an e-commerce site was found to increase aging users' perceived social support, trust, and patronage intentions as their lack of Internet competency often require significant assistance. Hence, a need exists for a broader integration of IDAs into crucial websites for decision-making relevant to seniors, such as MPF.

Social, cognitive, and trust barriers often hinder seniors' utilization of MPF and other e-healthcare tools [7]. Therefore, the purpose of this study is to examine the effects of an IDA embedded in an MPF interface on older users' perceived social support, perceived information load, and trust in MPF and how these effects are moderated by the decision-making stage (the need recognition stage vs. the alternative evaluation stage) in which the IDA assists. This study is innovative as no study thus far has integrated IDAs in MPF.

2 Theoretical Framework

The social response theory asserts that people apply social rules to their interactions with computers and hence treat computers as they would another human [11]. The computers as social actors (CASA) paradigm posits that people mindlessly apply similar social heuristics and expectations to computers because they bring to mind the social attributes of humans [12]. The CASA literature has consistently reported in both natural and lab settings that individuals exhibited anthropocentric reactions to computers [12]. According to CASA, the ability of computers to output words, interactivity, and performance of traditionally human tasks trigger scripts for human-human interaction, which makes people ignore the asocial nature of the computer [12]. Based on the CASA paradigm, we can predict that seniors would treat their interaction with IDAs as they would a human counselor and IDAs' assistance as a source of social support. We, therefore, hypothesize the following:

H1. Seniors perceive higher social support when the Medicare Part D decision-making is done with (vs. without) an IDA.

In a recent study [13], individuals' perception of the social support they received from an AI service agent positively influenced their trust in the agent. Specifically, it was found that the higher the perceived social support (PSS), the higher the trust in the agent. Similarly, another study [14] found that online shoppers' perception of the social support they received from a retailer positively influenced their trust in the retailer. Hence, the following is hypothesized:

H2. The higher the social support seniors perceive during the Medicare Part D decision-making using MPF, the higher their trust in MPF.

According to the cognitive load theory, the working memory which plays a pivotal role in an individual's learning has limited capacity, and is hence vulnerable to overload, particularly in complex problems [15]. Intrinsic cognitive load, which is the mental effort a task demands, or the inherent difficulty of a task, is governed by the number of attributes that must be processed simultaneously [16]. Tasks with a larger number of elements to be processed by an individual at a given time pose a higher intrinsic load on the working memory, and the inherent complexity of the task cannot be changed [16]. Presenting about 30 different Medicare part D plans, each with its own set of attributes carries a high level of complexity for seniors, and this will increase the load on their working memory. Having an IDA to assist them at different levels of the decision-making process, therefore, will potentially reduce the complexity of the decision-making process, freeing up cognitive resources to make an efficient decision. The following is, hence, hypothesized:

H3. Seniors perceive a lower information load when the Medicare Part D decision-making is done with (vs. without) an IDA.

Irrespective of where it originates, cognitive load has a detrimental effect on all types of tasks [17]. When under cognitive load, people are more likely to act impulsively and less analytically [18]; they are more likely to omit available data [19], use decision heuristics [20], and succumb to cognitive biases [21] under cognitive load. Cognitive load also reduces self-control [22] as a result of fewer resources available for reflection on a decision, making analytical processing more difficult and resulting in the use of cognitive shortcuts. Research has shown that cognitive load can have a significant negative impact on trust [23–25]. For example, cognitive load significantly reduced trust in a leader as well as individuals' confidence in their own decisions [25]. Hence, the following is hypothesized:

H4. The lower the information load seniors perceive during the Medicare Part D decision-making using MPF, the higher their trust in MPF.

The construal level theory proposes that the level of abstraction with which an individual conceptualizes a situation or event influences their decisions and behavior [26, 27]. Research has demonstrated that abstract or high-level construals can lead to more goal-directed behavior and improved decision-making [26, 28]. For instance, studies have shown that when individuals are presented with a problem at a more abstract level, they are more likely to consider the long-term consequences of their choices [28] and those abstract or high-level construals are associated with more positive outcomes, such as increased life satisfaction and reduced risk-taking behavior [27, 29]. Individuals who adopt an abstract or high-level construal of a situation are more likely to make decisions that are beneficial and lead to better outcomes in the long run [29]. Low-level construals, on the other hand, are characterized by a more concrete and detailed focus [27]. Research has found that low-level construals are associated with more present-oriented behavior, increased focus on immediate outcomes, and heightened motivation [27, 30].

According to the construal level theory, when people process concrete (psychologically close) objects, they pay attention to peripheral features; whereas when they process abstract (distant) ones, they omit peripheral features [31]. Consumer purchase decision-making usually begins with recognizing a need/problem, followed by evaluating alternatives available in the market before they make a purchase decision [32]. Compared to the need recognition stage, seniors will engage in more concrete information processing in the alternative evaluation stage where they have to make comparisons of specific Medicare Part D plan alternatives across specific plan attributes. Hence, users will experience a higher cognitive load in the alternative evaluation (vs. need recognition) stage [15], leading them to appreciate the IDA's support more. We, therefore, hypothesize the following:

H5. The effect of the IDA's assistance on perceived social support is stronger in the alternative evaluation stage than in the need recognition stage.

H6. The effect of the IDA's assistance on perceived information load is stronger in the alternative evaluation stage than in the need recognition stage.

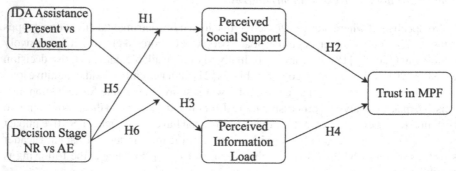

Fig. 1. Conceptual Model. NR = Need Recognition Stage. AE = Alternative Evaluation Stage

3   Method

An online experiment was conducted with a 2 (IDA Assistance: present vs. absent) × 2 (Decision Stage: need recognition vs. alternative evaluation) between-subjects design. The four conditions were manipulated by using simulation videos in which a male senior was using MPF either to identify his decision criteria (i.e., need recognition) or to compare different Medicare plans based on a set of criteria (i.e., alternative evaluation). In the videos, the male senior was performing these tasks either with or without the IDA's assistance. A national sample of 420 seniors (65 – 95 years old, $M_{age} = 72.45$, $SD_{age} = 5.329$, 210 men and 210 women) from the Qualtrics panel were randomly assigned to one of the four conditions and watched their assigned video, imagining themselves as the senior in the video. Following watching their assigned video, participants completed manipulation check measures for each of the two experimental factors, followed by dependent measures, including six items of perceived social support [33], four items for trust in MPF [34], and four items of perceived information load [35]. Figure 1 presents a screenshot of an MPF interface in the IDA present condition, while Table 1 presents sample IDA-user dialog scripts for each of the need recognition and alternative evaluation stages (Fig. 2).

Fig. 2. Screenshot of MPF with IDA appearing on the right upper corner

Table 1. Sample IDA-User Dialog Scripts for AE and NR Stages

Sample IDA-user dialog script for the alternative evaluation stage

AIDA: Hi, I am AIDA, your virtual Medicare counselor. Would you like my assistance?
USER: Yes please!
AIDA: How may I help you today?
User: There are too many plans to compare. Can you help me narrow them down?
AIDA: Sure. At the right upper corner of the screen, I see that the plans are already sorted according to drug + premium costs, so let's keep it as is
USER: Okay
AIDA: Since the quality of the plan is also important, let's screen out those plans with poor quality ratings. At the left side of the screen right above the first plan, please click the "Star Ratings" dropdown box by the text "Filter by." Because most plans' ratings fall between 3 and 4 stars, let's choose "3 stars & up" and click "Apply."
AIDA: Now in the plan list, you see only the plans with at least 3 stars, listed from the lowest to highest annual drug + premium costs. Do you have any specific dollar amount in your mind for monthly costs?
USER: Yes. I need to keep them below $300

Sample IDA-user dialog script for the need recognition stage

AIDA: Hi, I am IDA, your virtual Medicare counselor. Would you like my assistance?
User: Yes, please
AIDA: How may I help you today?
User: I am not sure which information on this website is relevant to my plan selection. Very confusing
AIDA: No problem. Most people think how much drugs and premiums would cost them monthly and for the entire year, as well as customer care of the plan as important plan attributes. Would you like to consider these attributes?
User: Yes. That sounds good!
AIDA: Great! Let's talk about what you need for each of these plan attributes. Shall we talk about the overall estimated annual costs first? These are how much you would pay the entire year combining the premiums you pay every month and the drug costs based on the list of prescriptions you entered when you searched for plans earlier. Do you have any specific criteria for annual costs?
User: I just want annual costs to be as low as possible
AIDA: Okay. Let's make sure your annual costs are as low as possible. This means we want a plan with low deductible, low premium, and low drug cost. By the way, do you have any specific dollar amount in your mind for monthly costs?
User: Yes. I need to keep it lower than $300 a month

4   Results and Discussion

The manipulation was successful; participants were able to indicate the decision stage of the user in their respective videos and whether or not IDA was present to assist the user in the video. Confirmatory factor analysis showed an acceptable model fit (CFI = .96, RMSEA = .091) with convergent and discriminant validity (AVE > .50; AVE > SVs) and internal consistency (α > .85) for all three dependent measures. Structural equation modeling results (CFI = .945, RMSEA = .073) showed that the main effect of IDA assistance was significant and positive for perceived social support ($\gamma = .20$, $p < .001$), supporting H1, but non-significant for perceived information load ($\gamma = -.11$, $p = .107$), rejecting H3. The effect of IDA assistance in reducing perceived information load was stronger for the alternative evaluation (vs. need recognition) stage, as indicated by the negative IDA $\times$ Stage interaction effect ($\gamma = -.35$, $p < .001$), supporting H6; whereas the IDA $\times$ Stage interaction effect on perceived social support ($\gamma = .089$, $p = .909$) was non-significant, rejecting H5. The structural equation modeling results also revealed that IDA assistance also had a significant indirect effect on MPF trust (IE = .19), and this indirect effect was mediated by perceived social support ($\beta = .64$, $p < .001$) and perceived information load ($\beta = -.52$, $p < .001$), supporting H2 and H4, respectively.

The results from the analysis showed that seniors perceived higher support with the assistance of the IDA than when the IDA was absent. This finding provides support for the social response theory that people treat computers as they would other humans. In this case, although the IDA was not human, being able to perform functions such as verbally interacting with the user as if a human Medicare counselor would trigger the perception of a human-human conversation [12]. This finding is again consistent with the previous finding that the presence of conversational agents has a significant positive effect on perceived social support [7].

On the other hand, the presence of IDA having no significant main effect on perceived information load suggests that seniors still felt overwhelmed with the information even with the IDA's assistance. However, this observation is qualified by the significant IDA $\times$ Stage interaction effect which shows that IDA assistance reduces seniors' cognitive load, particularly in the more complex decision stage where concrete alternatives and attributes have to be compared (i.e., alternative evaluation) although the IDA's role may be less prominent in a simpler and more abstract stage (i.e., need recognition). This significant moderating effect of the decision stage found in this study provides support for the construal level theory. Because the alternative evaluation stage is closer to the final decision-making, a low (concrete) construal is engaged which then increases the cognitive load. Hence, the assistance of the IDA at this is more impactful in reducing the perceived information load than at the need recognition stage which elicits a high construal level processing.

Yet, the decision stage did not moderate the effect of IDA assistance on perceived social support. This result, combined with the significant main effect of IDA assistance in enhancing perceived social support, suggests that the IDA's social presence is impactful regardless of the differences in the construal levels or the level of complexity of the decision stages.

Finally, the significant indirect effects found in this study imply that the IDA's role in increasing users' perceptions of social support and reducing information load helps older users form trust in MPF, which is likely to encourage them to reuse MPF, which is a critical e-healthcare decision tool for seniors, for future Medicare plan decision-making.

5 Implications and Future Research

The findings show that implementing an IDA on the MPF website would be beneficial to seniors by enhancing the social support they perceive and reducing the information overload they experience, particularly for a decision-making stage closer to the final decision where more cognitive load is required of the user. The findings further demonstrate that the use of an IDA on the MPF website can help to increase the trust of seniors in MPF and potentially, similar other e-healthcare decision tools. Our findings also provide empirical support for the theoretical reasonings (social response theory, cognitive load theory, and construal level theory) put forth for this study. This study offers critical recommendations for IDA designs that match the user's decision stage or cognitive load.

Although this research offers relevant insights, it also has some limitations. Generalizing the findings of this study to other demographics (particularly) younger people and also in contexts outside of MPF must be done with caution. Seniors (65 years and older) may have different characteristics and computer competencies from younger age groups. Future research should use different age groups and contexts outside of choosing Medicare plans, to compare the differences in outcomes.

Also, this study used scenarios based on simulation videos, rather than having participants directly experience the IDA, to test the IDA effects. This afforded the researchers better control over the consistency across participants' experiences by eliminating the possibility of participants randomly asking questions out of the role of the IDA, which can introduce confounding effects depending on how well that non-contextual conversation goes. However, the use of simulation videos may not attract participants' engagement as much as directly interacting with the AID would. Future research is recommended to replicate the findings when allowing participants to interact with the IDA by themselves in order to enhance the ecological validity of the findings.

Acknowledgments. This study was supported by the Auburn University Intramural Grant Program, the Alabama Agricultural Experiment Station, and the Hatch program of the National Institute of Food and Agriculture, U.S. Department of Agriculture.

References

1. Payne, J., Bettman, J. R., Johnson, E.J.: Consumer decision making. Handbook of Consumer Behaviour, pp. 50–84 (1991)
2. Häubl, G., Trifts, V.: Consumer decision making in online shopping environments: the effects of interactive decision aids. Mark. Sci. **19**(1), 4–21 (2000)
3. Maity, M., Dass, M.: Consumer decision-making across modern and traditional channels: E-commerce, m-commerce, in-store. Decis. Support Syst. **61**, 34–46 (2014)
4. Ebaid, D., Crewther, S.G.: Temporal aspects of memory: a comparison of memory performance, processing speed and time estimation between young and older adults. Front. Aging Neurosci. **10**, 352 (2018). https://doi.org/10.3389/fnagi.2018.00352
5. SingleCare. Medicare statistics 2022 (2022). https://www.singlecare.com/blog/news/medicare-statistics/

6. Kwon, W.-S., Chattaraman, V., Gilbert, J.E.: Effects of conversational agents in retail Web sites on aging consumers' interactivity and perceived benefits. In: Duh, H.B.-L., Do, E.Y.-L., Billinghust, M., Guek, F., Hsueh-Hua, V.C. (Eds.), Proceedings of the 28th ACM Conference on Human Factors in Computing Systems: CHI 2010 Workshop [Senior-Friendly Technologies: Interaction Design for the Elderly], pp. 40–43. Atlanta, GA (2010)

7. Chattaraman, V., Kwon, W.S., Gilbert, J.E.: Virtual agents in retail websites: benefits of simulated social interaction for older users. Comput. Hum. Behav. **28**(6), 2055–2066 (2012). https://doi.org/10.1016/j.chb.2012.06.009

8. Dean, T., Gurr, A.: What is conversational AI: A 2023 guide you'll actually use (2022). https://blog.hootsuite.com/conversational-ai/

9. Kwon, W.-S., Chattaraman, V., Ross, K., Alikhademi, K., Gilbert, J.E.: Modeling conversational flows for in-store mobile decision aids. In: Stephanidis, C. (ed.) HCI International 2018 – Posters' Extended Abstracts. CCIS, vol. 852, pp. 302–308. Springer, Cham (2018). https://doi.org/10.1007/978-3-319-92285-0_42

10. Alikhademi, K., et al.: Implementing MODA: a multi-strategy, mobile, conversational consumer decision-aid system. In the Proceedings of the CSCW 2018, 21st ACM Conference on Computer-Supported Cooperative Work and Social Computing, New York, NY (2018). https://accessiblevoice.files.wordpress.com/2018/10/2-alikhademi.pdf

11. Moon, Y.: Intimate exchanges: using computers to elicit self-disclosure from consumers. J. Consum. Res. **26**(4), 323–339 (2000). https://doi.org/10.1086/209566

12. Nass, C., Moon, Y.: Machines and mindlessness: social responses to computers. J. Soc. Issues **56**(1), 81–103 (2000). https://doi.org/10.1111/0022-4537.00153

13. Harrison, E.N.B.: Trust and distrust in conversational AI agents: The effects of agent interaction style and user information need. Doctoral Dissertation (2022). https://etd.auburn.edu/handle/10415/8427

14. Gupta, P., Yadav, M.S., Varadarajan, R.: How task-facilitative interactive tools foster buyers' trust in online retailers: a process view of trust development in the electronic marketplace. J. Retail. **85**(2), 159–176 (2009). https://doi.org/10.1016/j.jretai.2009.02.001

15. Sweller, J.: Cognitive load during problem solving: effects on learning. Cogn. Sci. **12**(2), 257–285 (1988). https://doi.org/10.1016/0364-0213(88)90023-7

16. Chandler, P., Sweller, J.: Cognitive load theory and the format of instruction. Cogn. Instr. **8**(4), 293 332 (1991). https://doi.org/10.1207/s1532690xci0804_2

17. Adcock, A.: Effects of cognitive load on processing performance (2000). https://citeseerx.ist.psu.edu/document?repid=rep1&type=pdf&doi=ef33266543649fbbc0c97ea4aad42ee6a5f2dbeb

18. Duffy, S., Smith, J.: Cognitive load in the multi-player prisoner's dilemma game: are there brains in games?. MPRA Paper no. 38825 (2012). http://mpra.ub.uni-muenchen.de/38825/

19. Gilbert, D.T., Pelham, B.W., Krull, D.S.: On cognitive busyness: when person perceivers meet persons perceived. J. Pers. Soc. Psychol. **54**(5), 733 (1988)

20. Bohner, G., Ruder, M., Erb, H.P.: When expertise backfires: contrast and assimilation effects in persuasion. Br. J. Soc. Psychol. **41**(4), 495–519 (2002)

21. Gilbert, D.T.: Thinking lightly about others: automatic components of the social inference process. In: Uleman, J.S., Bargh, J.A. (eds.) Unintended Thought, pp. 189–211. The Guilford Press (1989)

22. Ward, A., Mann, T.: Don't mind if I do: disinhibited eating under cognitive load. J. Pers. Soc. Psychol. **78**(4), 753 (2000)

23. Van Kleef, G.A., De Dreu, C.K.W., Manstead, A.S.R.: The interpersonal effects of emotions in negotiation: a motivated information processing approach. J. Pers. Soc. Psychol. **87**(5), 504–521 (2004)

24. Ito, T., Masuda, T., Nisbett, R.E.: Culture and the physical environment: holistic versus analytic perceivers in the perception of natural scenery. Pers. Soc. Psychol. Bull. **26**(4), 413–425 (2000)
25. Galinsky, A.D., Ku, G., Wang, C.S., Whitson, J.A.: Overworked and underleveraged: working memory capacity, attentional control, and executive decision-making. Organ. Behav. Hum. Decis. Process. **97**(2), 131–145 (2005)
26. Zhang, J., Monroe, K.B.: Construal-level theory and persuasion: the role of distance in advertising effectiveness. J. Consum. Res. **35**(3), 410–420 (2008)
27. Trope, Y., Liberman, N.: Temporal construal. Psychol. Rev. **110**(3), 403–421 (2003)
28. Pham, M.T.: The logic of feeling. J. Consum. Psychol. **14**(4), 360–369 (2004)
29. Williams, R.: The effects of construal level on health-related behavior. Soc. Pers. Psychol. Compass **7**(12), 922–935 (2013)
30. Trope, Y., Liberman, N., Wakslak, C.J.: Construal levels and psychological distance: effects on representation, prediction, evaluation, and behavior. J. Pers. Soc. Psychol. **79**(5), 876–889 (2000)
31. Trope, Y., Liberman, N.: Construal-level theory of psychological distance. Psychol. Rev. **117**(2), 440–463 (2010). https://doi.org/10.1037/a0018963
32. Chang, J.Y., Kwon, W.-S.: Social media information search behavior in consumption decisions: consumer segmentation and discriminant factors. In: International Textiles and Apparel Association Annual Conference Proceedings, No. 77 (2020). https://doi.org/10.31274/itaa.11978
33. Zimet, G.D., Dahlem, N.W., Zimet, S.G., Farley, G.K.: The multidimensional scale of perceived social support. J. Pers. Assess. **52**(1), 30–41 (1988)
34. Cyr, D., Hassanein, K., Head, M., Ivanov, A.: The role of social presence in establishing loyalty in e-service environments. Interact. Comput. **19**(1), 43–56 (2007)
35. Chen, Y.-C., Shang, R.-A., Kao, C.-Y.: The effects of information overload on consumers' subjective state towards buying decision in the internet shopping environment. Electron. Commer. Res. Appl. **8**(1), 48–58 (2009)

Aging in Place Virtual Care Technology from the User Experience Perspective

Irina Kondratova[1] (✉) ⓘ, Helene Fournier[2] ⓘ, and Fateme Rajabiyazdi[3] ⓘ

[1] Human Computer Interaction, Digital Technologies Research Centre, National Research Council Canada, Fredericton, NB, Canada
Irina.Kondratova@nrc-cnrc.gc.ca
[2] Human Computer Interaction, Digital Technologies Research Centre, National Research Council Canada, Moncton, NB, Canada
Helene.Fournier@nrc-cnrc.gc.ca
[3] Department of Systems and Computer Engineering, Carleton University, Ottawa, ON, Canada
FatemeRajabiyazdi@cunet.carleton.ca

Abstract. This paper reports on research being conducted under the National Research Council of Canada's Aging in Place Program. The objective of this program is to evaluate and assist in the adaptation of assistive technologies for older adults living at home. The aims are to produce guidelines and prototypes needed to design safe, usable, and affordable aging in place technology solutions for virtual care. In preparation for this initiative, relevant findings are presented from a scoping review of the literature. Additionally, we present the framework for surveying older adults' perspectives on their lived experiences with virtual care and digital technologies during the COVID-19 pandemic, which drove uptake of virtual care, particularly in critical areas such as cardiac rehabilitation. Here we discuss the target population for surveillance and describe the survey design, validation, and sampling approach that could achieve the widest range of perspectives; identify gaps, barriers, and challenges. Additionally, we explore remote usability assessment methods available for aging in place technology co-design and evaluation efforts.

Keywords: Remote Patient Monitoring · Telecare · Usability · Qualitative Research

1 Background

1.1 Virtual Care for Aging in Place

Considering the high prevalence of chronic disease among older Canadian adults [1], virtual care is important in the context of aging in place: to support home-based medical services, remote patient engagement or monitoring, digital integration with electronic health/medical records, and virtual access to healthcare practitioners. Access to healthcare is a priority and a responsibility of government in Canada, with healthcare continuing to be severely impacted by the COVID-19 pandemic due to associated physical distancing measures, moral injury to healthcare providers, burnout, and attenuated recruitment

Q. Gao and J. Zhou (Eds.): HCII 2023, LNCS 14043, pp. 131–144, 2023.
https://doi.org/10.1007/978-3-031-34917-1_10

and retention to a healthcare system resistant to change and innovation. Adoption of virtual care into routine care occurred rapidly in response to the pandemic in many jurisdictions, including Canada [2, 3]. This was most needed in Canada to augment delivery and access to virtual care in rural areas [4], with many senior adults living in rural areas that could potentially benefit the most from increased access to virtual care.

As virtual care accelerates forward to be integrated and hybridized with pre-pandemic practices, it is critical to include older Canadians as patient partners in the design and evaluation of virtual care services. An article on virtual care for older adults in Canada during COVID-19 pandemic [5] states that increased uptake of virtual care will be a positive healthcare system legacy of COVID-19. Canada must expedite its efforts to tackle equitable healthcare policies for older adults and learn from leading jurisdictions in the virtual care arena. The authors stated that only through purposeful engagement with end users and additional stakeholders, can Canada develop virtual care frameworks that embrace the needs of older adults, empower their engagement, and ultimately achieve the goal to optimize healthcare outcomes, improve patients, caregivers, and provider experience, and reduce or maintain costs.

Canada must improve how it translates pilot programs into standard of care practice supporting patients' access to virtual care in priority areas like cardiac rehabilitation and home health monitoring for the cognitively impaired (e.g., stroke, early dementia) or seniors living with a physical disability. There have been some demonstrated ongoing development and implementation challenges [5–8], that show significant usability and user experience problems with virtual care technologies, especially for older adults. Frequently reported challenges include difficulties with setting up digital devices for home health monitoring, not having full control of a device, problems with device synchronization, issues with technology reliability and stability, and lack of immediate technical support [9]. Additionally, older adults frequently express frustration in not having access to technology training and manuals or in home support during the installation phases of virtual care support systems.

1.2 Usability and User Acceptance Challenges

For older adult end users, barriers to adoption of virtual care systems may include a lack of instructions and guidance, a lack of knowledge and confidence, as well as feelings of inadequacy. Other barriers include age-related changes, such as vision and hearing loss and fine motor difficulties which correlate with physical competencies required to make full use of technologies within geriatric rehabilitation [10]. It has also been shown that older adults are at increasing risk of being digitally marginalized due to lower familiarity with technology, social isolation, and lack of resources, including peers who can provide the needed input [11].

Incorporating peer-to-peer support systems with "snowball" enrollment by seniors teaching seniors how to use technology can be a strategy that overcomes many of these issues. As well, within healthcare, onboarding protocols and human resources needed to plan for, remuneration policies adapted to virtual care and device prescribing should be integrated into coverage plans for older adults to maximize the benefit of virtual care utility and ensure good return on investment by government and insurers. This should be part of future discussions on policy-to-practice; role of bureaucracy and actuaries, cost-benefit analyses, and innovation adoption and change management.

At the design level for a virtual care tool, the focus should be on the value, design, and implementation process; not only addressing the older adults' needs and desires, but integrating with formal and informal caregivers' needs that intersect in supporting the older adult. More focus on caregivers' needs and their participation in the user-centric technology design process is needed. Empowering caregivers using virtual care systems should include training them on using the technology, training trainers, and training users; enabling active cooperative participation during virtual care conversations and the design process itself; providing clinical educational tools and parallel support services that augment caregiver efficiency and efficacy with reduced stress, and should include remote monitoring features, digital therapeutics, or peripheral devices that augment caregiver observations, treatment-to-effect, and health record keeping [5].

1.3 User Experience Perspective

There is a growing body of literature concerned with the design of technologies for older users [12–14] with an increasing number of participatory and co-design studies involving older adults as producers, rather than consumers of digital technologies [14]. Studies on digital technologies in healthcare have explored older users' interactions with different interfaces and their attitudes towards new technologies [15–18].

Ethnographic studies have been conducted to build a detailed picture of older participants' lives and lived experiences—including their illness experiences and use (or non-use) of technologies [13]. Still, there is a lack of emphasis on the heterogeneity of older adults as end users with diverse and unique needs, a gap between the current generation of so-called assisted living technologies and what older end users actually adopt and use (i.e., medical market-pull scenarios), as well as a lack of understanding around the factors that contribute to inappropriate or non-use of telehealth and virtual care [13].

Human Computer Interaction (HCI) researchers are calling for human-centered computing approaches in addressing the need for equal and equitable collaboration between older adults and designers of digital technologies [15]. The topic of equal and equitable design partnerships has been addressed in several studies with children, but very few studies have explored the dynamics of collaborations between designers and older adults [13, 15].

There is a need for frameworks that focus on life experiences, roles and ownership from the perspective of older end users as factors that contribute to balanced or unbalanced interactions during co-design activities and prototype development [15]. Our approach to co-designing prototypes for aging in place technologies in the context of virtual care will include the user experience perspective and participation from relevant users, in our case, patients, caregivers, and health professionals, in each stage of the design process. This should help to reduce user experience challenges and increase acceptance, leading to more effective digital health interventions. Core to addressing the current barriers and challenges to age tech adoption is appropriate and focused engagement with older adult end-user groups, caregivers, and health professionals.

1.4 Population Demographics and Survey Study

In Canada, heart disease is the second leading cause of death [19] and an increase in cardiovascular disease has been attributed to a rapidly aging population [20]. Population-based evidence from administrative health data across seven Canadian provinces shows that the Atlantic Provinces have the fastest aging population in Canada. The proportion of people aged 65 years and older in New Brunswick currently surpasses Canada's national average and is expected to reach 30.5% by 2043 [21]. The incidence of cardiovascular disease (CVD) in the province of New Brunswick (NB) is also above Canada's national average [1], and there is a lack of studies that explore regional variations in cardiovascular disease, risk factors, and broader determinants of health (e.g., unemployment) [22].

During the COVID-19 pandemic, the delivery of cardiac rehabilitation (CR) was impacted [3, 23] with programs closing completely or switching to fully virtual or hybrid delivery [24]. Barriers and facilitators to attending different CR models have been described in the literature [25–27], however, little is known about patients' journey through CR during the pandemic. We have designed a survey study to explore patients' lived experience with various CR delivery models, i.e., in-person, virtual and hybrid, the impact of the pandemic on CR completion, and changes in behaviors and habits following CR.

Our survey study aims to fill an important gap in the research around sociodemographic and clinical characteristics of participants who enroll in CR and those participants who successfully complete the program. Data from the New Brunswick Heart Centre shows a high numbers of eligible cardiac rehabilitation (CR) patients but low enrollment and participation rates. For example, 6,097 patients in New Brunswick were eligible for cardiac rehabilitation (2005–2006 fiscal year) but only 12% of patients were admitted to CR programs [28].

Furthermore, enrollment in CR programs varied from 0% to 20% in various health regions with the majority occurring in urban versus rural areas. Our current survey study targets patients who were eligible for CR between January 2020 and June 2022, a period marked by the COVID-19 pandemic. Given the aging population and increase in cardiovascular diseases, we expect that the number of eligible cardiac rehabilitation patients in New Brunswick will continue to climb, thus New Brunswick could serve as an ideal living laboratory to study and implement virtual or hybrid CR modalities for national use.

2 Survey Design, Validation and Sampling Method

A patient-centric survey is currently being designed by the Aging in Place (AIP) research project team, including clinical and translational medicine collaborators. Survey items include sociodemographic questions, clinical characteristics of patients, participation and experiences with CR models (i.e., in-person, virtual and hybrid), technology-related questions, health-related questions, as well as questions that explore the impact of COVID on CR participation and completion, and questions on long-term benefits such as changes in behaviors and habits following CR. Items include multiple choice options,

Likert-type scales, and open-ended response options with skip logic that allows for further exploration based on how respondents answer a question. Table 1 presents survey themes and sub-themes along with a description of the items.

Additional pilot testing and validation of questions are being conducted with experts by experience, that is, older adults who have lived experience with CR programs as cardiac care patients, and with subject-matter experts in cardiac rehabilitation and experimental methods. Interested parties in collaborating on this initiative or providing insightful input are welcome.

Table 1. Survey items by theme and sub-themes

Theme, sub-theme and number of items (questions)	Description of items
Sociodemographic (9)	Sex, gender, year of birth, ethnicity, province, level of education, household income, marital status, living arrangement
Clinical characteristics (9)	Disability and health: chronic health conditions, number of prescription medications, disabilities (cognitive, hearing, vision, mobility), current self-reported level of health
Cardiac rehabilitation (CR) general participation (2), Cardiac Support Groups (1), and mechanics/processes (3)	CR and CR non-participation, by region, referral, enrollment and intake experience, assessments, access to educational sessions and material
Models of CR delivery: in-person (2), virtual (9), or hybrid	In-person: technologies, devices, challenges and barriers Virtual: technologies, devices, data sharing, comfort level, challenges and barriers Hybrid: technologies, devices, comfort level, challenges and barriers
Preference for follow-up care, consultations, and coverage (2)	Preferences and choices, modality (in-person, virtual, or hybrid), confidence in accessing or continuing CR
Personal experiences (4)	All CR modalities (in-person, virtual, or hybrid): relationship with cardiac care team, CR instructors, comfort level, communication/contact with family physician, cardiologist or peers during CR program
Program completion (1), impact of COVID (2), post CR assessments and follow-up (1)	Completed (graduated) from CR program, Impact of COVID-19, Assessment and follow up after 3 months, 6 months
Health-related: long-term behavior change and benefits (4)	Change in behavior and habits: self-reporting on recovery, risk factor improvement, quality of life, overall satisfaction with CR program(s)

Maximum variation sampling will be used to identify key dimensions of variation and the widest range of perspectives possible to explore current gaps, barriers, and challenges experienced by older adults in adapting to virtual care delivery [29]. Sociodemographic and clinical characteristics will allow us to explore important subgroups, including older adults, women, and other higher risk and understudied groups [30–32]. Sex/gender differences in CR enrollment and outcomes, as well socio-economic factors need to be considered in more depth [25, 33–36] in order to inform efforts to produce guidelines and prototypes for aging in place technology solutions in virtual care.

3 Collaborative Design and Remote Evaluations

Historically, medical devices and virtual care technology were primarily tested in the laboratory and rarely tested in situ, e.g., in older adult homes [37, 38]. This testing limitation frequently results in inadequate usability of virtual care technology, when used at home by older adults and their caregivers, and results in poor user experience. Reduced usability and user experience could subsequently lead to low adoption of virtual care technology by older adults [11].

More research attention must be paid to deployment of appropriate design methodologies and remote usability tools to involve older adults in the collaborative design process and to capture everyday user experience and feedback. Research demonstrates that a deployment of a collaborative design process for aging in place technology that includes older adults in the design process from the start can improve virtual technology's usability and provide a better user experience [17].

In preparation for technology design and evaluation phases of our project, we conducted a literature review focusing on the limited number of studies conducted over the past three years of the COVID-19 pandemic that involved remote collaborative design and remote usability evaluation methodologies applied to assistive technologies and virtual care for older adults. Here we examine published research studies that deployed various remote design and usability evaluation methodologies to evaluate virtual care technologies during the pandemic, and assessed the benefits and shortcomings of various methodologies, and their potential fit for our project.

3.1 Literature Review

We targeted published research results about various aspects of remote usability evaluations for virtual care technology, including telehealth, although we did not limit the technology application area to a particular healthcare domain or only to older adults. We reviewed research papers published in scientific conferences and journals on the topic of remote design and usability evaluations for virtual care, telehealth and smart home technologies for aging in place, with publication dates from 2019 to 2022. The keywords we used to identify papers for evaluation are listed in Table 2. We used Google Scholar database to find research publications on topics such as collaborative design for virtual care technologies, remote usability evaluation, virtual care, and aging in place technology acceptance. The highlights of our findings are listed below.

Table 2. Keywords for Google Scholar database

Virtual care; older adults; collaborative design; remote usability evaluation; technology acceptance; usability; COVID-19.
Filters: published in the last three years (2020-2023), English language.

3.2 Literature Review Findings

We reviewed 54 research papers on the topics of remote usability evaluation for medical devices, smart home technologies, home monitoring, mobile health, telehealth, and aging in place, published between 2020 and 2023. Some papers we reviewed focused on virtual care technology evaluations conducted within a general population, or with healthcare professionals. While such papers were useful to inform our general understanding of the research field of remote evaluations, we mostly focused our analysis on research papers that targeted technology testing with older adults.

For example, a recent overview paper [2] presented a rapid literature review of practical approaches and findings for remote usability testing with a focus on older adults, although without a focus on virtual healthcare. The authors identified a current lack of remote usability testing methods, tools, and strategies for older adults, despite increased remote technology use and needs for older adults. They issued a call for the research community to invest more efforts in research in the area of remote usability evaluations [2].

Another in-depth research article on evaluating medical devices remotely [38] reviewed methods of remote evaluation for a wide range of medical devices, from testing labels and instruction to usability testing and simulated use, but without a focus on older adults aging in place. The authors developed a toolbox for evaluation of different remote usability methods and their application for medical device testing. They presented examples of how published usability studies of medical devices could be moved to remote data collection and suggested better ways to conduct targeted participant recruitment.

The authors of the review article on medical devices [38] concluded that while remote testing brings new opportunities and challenges to the field of medical devices, the majority of current remote usability methods are quite adequate for most purposes when testing medical devices, with the exception of Class III devices that are considered high risk, as they often sustain life, such as ventilators and pacemakers. We analyzed results presented by [2, 38] and other relevant research papers to narrow down on the most commonly used methods of remote usability testing in healthcare.

Synchronous Remote Usability Testing. A majority of research studies reviewed focused on synchronous remote usability testing normally conducted as a remote in-person testing that is supported by using video and audio transmissions, and remote desktop access. In the paper by [2], it was found that while results of synchronous remote testing are nearly identical to conventional in-person testing, some issues could impair the quality of remote testing results. These complicating issues for synchronous remote usability testing include things like missed indirect cues and context due to the remote nature of testing; participant's preference/familiarity for in-person testing that could introduce biases; and technology and experiment management challenges (e.g., network issues, remote troubleshooting, and set-up). It was also observed [2] that in remote synchronous testing scenarios users could take longer to complete tasks than during in-person testing, and users could make more errors than during in-person testing. Other issues observed with remote synchronous usability evaluations are difficulty with building trust with participants, and challenges with combating technological issues [39].

Other researchers used crowdsourcing for remote usability testing and found that crowdsourcing was a feasible and cost-effective solution to conduct synchronous remote usability testing with the Thinking Aloud (TA) method [40]. Researchers compared traditional TA protocol versus remote synchronous testing TA protocol and found that concurrent TA is more effective than retrospective TA, and synchronous remote TA is as effective as concurrent TA. Other researchers conducted synchronous Remote-Human Robot Interaction (R-HRI) studies to evaluate usability of human robot interaction (HRI) with older adults and found that remote synchronous studies could be a viable alternative to traditional face-to-face HRI studies [41].

Research demonstrates that remote collaborative design could be used for virtual technologies. For example, remote technology design sessions for the clinical virtual checklists were successfully deployed as a participatory design workshop with users using zoom video technology [39]. During the collaborative design workshop researchers used the screen share feature on Zoom and presented the PowerPoint slides about the checklist and past studies. Researchers observed some issues with user feedback via the virtual modality, but found ways to overcome these issues. For example, instead of having participants provide feedback about the checklist on Post-it notes, the researchers asked the users to describe issues with the checklist over the call.

Another useful suggestion from this study [39] was to ask users to sketch out their ideas for new checklist features and show them on video instead of using the traditional cardboard cut-outs for the co-design activity. In addition to design workshops, four remote near-live simulation sessions were deployed to evaluate potential new features for the digital checklist. Researchers successfully used near-live simulations, which imitate clinical workflows, with the users watching videos of actors simulating clinical cases, while using systems to evaluate their usability and effectiveness [39].

Asynchronous Remote Usability Testing. In several studies researchers deployed asynchronous remote testing to test usability of virtual care systems, where participants conducted testing without research moderation, and filled out web-based questionnaires as they completed tasks, or after the completion of tasks. For example [42] reported on a study with older adults where the goal was to remotely deliver and conduct usability testing for a mobile health technology intervention for older adult participants enrolled in a clinical trial of the technology. In this case, researchers developed a conceptual model for remote operations that combined the general requirements for spaceflight operations with agile project management processes to quickly respond to remote testing challenges. The study developed self-contained care packages that differed in their contents based on participants' needs. The packages were sent to study participants to deliver the medication management app and assess its usability. Usability data were collected using the System Usability Scale (SUS) along with a supplementary usability questionnaire to collect more in-depth data. In addition to spaceflight packages, one of the suggestions to improve the ease of use for the asynchronous remote testing process was, in addition to online instructions, to mail a printed copy of testing and set up instructions to the users, conduct web-based training prior to remote testing sessions, and send reminders to the participants [42].

For the asynchronous remote usability testing, some researchers utilized Amazon Mechanical Turk (Amazon MT) crowdsourcing marketplace that helped to recruit a large, heterogeneous population of participants [43]. In this study researchers concluded that remote crowdsourced usability testing is an effective method to simulate patients' real-life interaction with telehealth applications. However, others found that the quality of the feedback collected via the crowdsourcing approach was lower than the one from the laboratory sessions, since the participants were less focused in the remote testing approach [40].

For the unmoderated asynchronous remote usability testing researchers frequently deploy a System Usability Scale (SUS) post-questionnaire as a standardized method to evaluate usability of the application [42–44]. However, some noticed that the unmoderated test with a System Usability Scale (SUS) post-questionnaire can be a complex method to apply with older adults [44]. The SUS questionnaire could lead to mistakes and misinterpretation, with contradictory results that could be related to its complexity when deployed among older adults, and this could lead to a major negative impact on overall SUS scores. Other reported disadvantages of SUS in remote usability testing could surface when researchers apply negative and positive items in usability questionnaires which could lead to user confusion that cannot be rectified properly when using non-moderated remote tests. Additionally, since it is more difficult to correct possible mistakes participants could make in unmoderated testing, this could lead to a negative impact on overall SUS scores [44].

Mixed Methods Approach. Several research studies used a mixed methods approach to remote usability testing that combined several methods to improve usability testing procedure or results [37, 45–48]. For example, in-person testing is simulated by using video and audio transmissions at home with a remote moderator, plus in person studies in the lab are performed [37]. In other studies, researchers deployed both, User Experience Questionnaire (UEQ) after at home use, and laboratory usability testing via the Zoom application [45]. In this study, when the participants were given a task, an experimenter would wait until a participant completes a task and asked questions via Zoom [45]. Others successfully used the iterative convergent mixed methods design [46], that involved simultaneous qualitative and quantitative data collection and analysis that continued cyclically through rounds of mixed methods data collection and analysis, until the mobile health technology under evaluation was found to work to the agreed criteria.

Other researchers deployed a mixed-method approach to usability testing of telemedicine provider websites that involved content analysis, and both remote and empirical research such as traditional Think Aloud usability testing [47]. Remote usability testing in this case was performed using a large sample population of representative target users recruited via the Amazon MT online recruiting platform due to the rich availability of participants that resemble the heterogeneous population needed for testing the use case in the context of the USA. Researchers also utilized a survey designed to measure whether subjects were able to complete certain tasks and activities using the website, with task completion success used as a metric of usability [47].

Another mixed methods study [48] focused on feasibility, usability, and acceptability of a co-designed virtual reality exergame in community-dwelling older adults and tested assessment protocols for a future large-scale trial. A mixed methods evaluation included several weeks of technology use at home and post intervention focus groups, interviews and analysis of informal notes and reports from all participants to assess the feasibility of the study protocol. Importantly, researchers [48] developed a comprehensive strategy to introduce participants to technology use, with each participant meeting with the study staff for a remote introductory session via a videoconference platform. At the face-to-face session staff demonstrated how to use the system by sharing a computer screen. The participant could see instructor's interactions, become familiar with the visual information and the overall interaction with the system, learn about system calibration, play the game, and ask the questions. The participants were encouraged to interact with the system and try playing the game in the presence of the team member and speaking aloud about what they are seeing and experiencing, so that they could be guided if facing any difficulties.

The research team also made sure that the participants were able to contact the study staff and trainees to troubleshoot the system via email, phone, SMS text message, or video calls at any time as most appropriate for the situation and the participant's comfort. To facilitate troubleshooting video calls, the participants were offered screen-sharing options to help with the explanation and a view from the frontal camera of the computer to see how the team member is located and moving in the physical space [48].

Other Methods of Remote Usability Testing. Other methods of remote usability testing include web-based questionnaires or surveys, post-use interviews, user filled diaries and notes, and user-reported critical incidents [2]. These methods are frequently included as a part of the mixed methods evaluation strategies and have some shortcoming, such as they could be more time consuming to the users; deliver lower overall usability ratings than lab-based evaluations; identify less usability problems; and the validity of a self-reported approach could be problematic. However, there are some reported advantages in applying these methods, such as they could be more inclusive and beneficial for people with disabilities, and allow for data collection from a broader variety of users. It was also shown [2] that while quantitative data collected via remote usability testing are comparable to in-person testing data, the qualitative data could be less rich compared to in-person testing data, with in-person testing more suitable for formative testing, and remote testing more suitable for a summative evaluation.

3.3 Takeaway Lessons

Some takeaway lessons and approaches for our future remote usability testing are based on the current and the past literature reviews [9] related to remote usability monitoring, and on the overall guidelines for conducting usability evaluations with older adults [2, 9], including using a simplified version of the SUS questionnaire for older adults [49].

Participant Recruitment. We plan to recruit older adults as participants in collaboration with healthcare authorities, community support groups, and virtual care support programs, including cardiac rehabilitation. While social recruitment sites, like Amazon MT, could supply a broad range of participants for the remote usability testing, most of the Amazon MT workers do not fit into the category of older adults receiving virtual care. We are also aware of some specific challenges in recruiting a representative sample, especially among older adult populations that may be less comfortable with using digital technology, may have lower literacy skills, or may be mistrustful of research and not familiar with research studies [2, 9]. Additionally, some researchers observed problems with the quality of the feedback collected via the crowdsourcing approach [40]. When selecting usability testing participants, we will plan to strive for gender diversity, and incorporate caregivers into the collaborative technology design and evaluation process [50].

Methodology Choices. Our planned technology evaluation related to virtual care at home will include older adults interacting with mobile devices, wearables, medical devices, smart home technologies, and virtual care provider websites. Thus, it will be beneficial to conduct mixed methods remote usability evaluations that involve moderated synchronous and asynchronous remote testing, post-use surveys and interviews, user filled diaries and notes, and user-reported critical incidents. Special attention will be paid to technology delivery, set-up and training for the study participants and caregivers, incorporating lessons learned from creative and thorough remote testing approaches such as remote spaceflight methodology [2, 42], and virtual reality exergame remote evaluations with community living older adults [48, 50].

4 Conclusions and Future Work

The COVID-19 pandemic accelerated the deployment of digital technologies and their use for healthcare, however recent research studies highlighted some important gaps, barriers, and challenges still experienced by older adults, who in large part require the majority of healthcare services but are having trouble adapting to virtual care delivery. Amidst a rapidly aging population and high prevalence of chronic disease, the need for digital technologies to enable people to remain healthy and live independent lives, and to be able to age comfortably and safely at home, is urgent. Aging adults are the most likely beneficiaries of virtual care innovations and so critically need to be central to ongoing technology development and evaluation strategies.

Our survey study aims to shed light on current gaps, barriers, and challenges experienced by older adults in adapting to virtual care delivery, and on possible approaches to co-designing aging in place technologies that are more usable and effective for older adult populations, their caregivers, as well as their health care providers.

The review of the literature strongly suggests that more attention must be paid to the deployment of appropriate design methodologies and remote usability tools to involve older adults in the design and evaluation of aging in place technologies that they will actually adopt and use, based on their unique needs and requirements. The literature review also highlighted the need for the research community to invest more efforts in research in the area of remote usability evaluations. In our future research, we plan to conduct comparative evaluations of various approaches to remote usability testing with older adults including synchronous, asynchronous, and mixed methods remote usability testing with aging at home technology users and caregivers.

References

1. Canada, P.H.A.: Prevalence of Chronic Diseases and Risk Factors among Canadians aged 65 years and older. (2020)
2. Hill, J.R., Brown, J.C., Campbell, N.L., Holden, R.J.: Usability-in-place—remote usability testing methods for homebound older adults: rapid literature review. JMIR Format. Res. **5**(11), e26181 (2021). https://doi.org/10.2196/26181
3. Moulson, N., et al.: Cardiac rehabilitation during the COVID-19 era: guidance on implementing virtual care. Canadian J. Cardiol. **36**(8), 1317–1321 (2020). https://doi.org/10.1016/j.cjca.2020.06.006
4. Buyting, R., et al.: Virtual Care with Digital Technologies for Rural Canadians Living With Cardiovascular Disease. CJC Open (2021)
5. Pang, H.Y.M., Zhao, G., Kithulegoda, N., Agarwal, P., Ivers, N.M.: Aligning virtual care in Canada with the needs of older adults. Canadian J. Aging/La Revue canadienne du vieillissement **41**(4), 641–646 (2022). https://doi.org/10.1017/S0714980821000623
6. Danilewitz, M., Ainsworth, N.J., Bahji, A., Chan, P., Rabheru, K.: Virtual psychiatric care for older adults in the age of COVID-19: challenges and opportunities. Int. J. Geriatr. Psych. **35**, 1468 (2020)
7. Gosse, P.J., Kassardjian, C.D., Masellis, M., Mitchell, S.B.: Virtual care for patients with Alzheimer disease and related dementias during the COVID-19 era and beyond. CMAJ **193**, E371–E377 (2021)
8. Kondratova, I., Fournier, H.: Virtual Cardiac rehabilitation in a pandemic scenario: a review of HCI design features, user acceptance and barriers. In: Gao, Q., Zhou, J. (eds.) Human Aspects of IT for the Aged Population. Design, Interaction and Technology Acceptance: 8th International Conference, ITAP 2022, Held as Part of the 24th HCI International Conference, HCII 2022, Virtual Event, June 26–July 1, 2022, Proceedings, Part I, pp. 485–499. Springer, Cham (2022). https://doi.org/10.1007/978-3-031-05581-2_34
9. Kondratova, I., Fournier, H., Katsuragawa, K.: Review of remote usability methods for aging in place technologies. In: Gao, Q., Zhou, J. (eds.) Human Aspects of IT for the Aged Population. Technology Design and Acceptance. LNCS, vol. 12786, pp. 33–47. Springer, Cham (2021). https://doi.org/10.1007/978-3-030-78108-8_3
10. Mieronkoski, R., Azimi, I., Sequeira, L., Peltonen, L.-M.: Smart home technology for geriatric rehabilitation and the Internet of Things. In: Smart Home Technologies and Services for Geriatric Rehabilitation, pp. 25–42. Elsevier (2022). https://doi.org/10.1016/B978-0-323-85173-2.00006-0
11. Bitkina, O.V., Kim, H.K., Park, J.: Usability and user experience of medical devices: an overview of the current state, analysis methodologies, and future challenges. Int. J. Ind. Ergon. **76**, 102932 (2020)
12. Mannheim, Ittay, et al.: Inclusion of older adults in the research and design of digital technology. Int. J. Environ. Res. Public Health **16**(19), 3718 (2019). https://doi.org/10.3390/ijerph16193718
13. Greenhalgh, T., Wherton, J., Sugarhood, P., Hinder, S., Procter, R., Stones, R.: What matters to older people with assisted living needs? A phenomenological analysis of the use and non-use of telehealth and telecare. Soc Sci Med **93**, 86–94 (2013)
14. Waycott, J., et al.: Older adults as digital content producers. In: Proceedings of the SIGCHI conference on Human Factors in Computing Systems, pp. 39–48 (2015)

15. SakaguchiTang, D.K., Cunningham, J.L., Roldan, W., Yip, J., Kientz, J.A.: Co-design with older adults: examining and reflecting on collaboration with aging communities. Proc. ACM Human-Comput. Interact. **5**, 1–28 (2021)
16. Cole, A.C., Adapa, K., Khasawneh, A., Richardson, D.R., Mazur, L.: Codesign approaches involving older adults in the development of electronic healthcare tools: a systematic review. BMJ Open **12**, e058390 (2022)
17. Sumner, J., Chong, L.S., Bundele, A., Wei Lim, Y.: Co-designing technology for aging in place: a systematic review. Gerontologist **61**, E395–E409 (2021)
18. Tong, C., et al.: Lessons and reflections from an extended co-design process developing an mhealth app with and for older adults: multiphase, mixed methods study. JMIR Aging **5**, e39189 (2022)
19. Canada, P.H.A.: Heart Disease in Canada (2023)
20. Canada, P.H.A.: Report from the Canadian chronic disease surveillance system: heart disease in Canada, 2018. Public Health Agency of Canada (2018)
21. Canada, S.: Population Projections in Canada, Provinces and Territories. Interactive Dashboard (2022)
22. Filate, W.A., Johansen, H.L., Kennedy, C.C., Tu, J.V.: Regional variations in cardiovascular mortality in Canada. Can. J. Cardiol. **19**, 1241–1248 (2003)
23. Johnson, T., et al.: Building a hybrid virtual cardiac rehabilitation program to promote health equity: lessons learned. Cardiovasc. Digit. Health J. **3**, 158–160 (2022)
24. Ghisi, G.L.M., et al.: Impacts of the COVID-19 pandemic on cardiac rehabilitation delivery around the world. Glob. Heart **16**, 43 (2021)
25. Cotie, L.M., Ghisi, G.L.M., Vanzella, L.M., Aultman, C., Oh, P., Colella, T.J.F.: A social-ecological perspective of the perceived barriers and facilitators to virtual education in cardiac rehabilitation. J. Cardiopulm. Rehabil. Prev. **42**, 183–189 (2022)
26. Ganeshan, S., et al.: Clinical outcomes and qualitative perceptions of in-person, hybrid, and virtual cardiac rehabilitation. J. Cardiopulm. Rehabil. Prev. **42**, 338–346 (2022)
27. Tadas, S., Coyle, D.: barriers to and facilitators of technology in cardiac rehabilitation and self-management: systematic qualitative grounded theory review. J. Med. Internet Res. **22**, 1–17 (2020)
28. New Brunswick Cardiovascular News. New Brunswick Heart Centre Heart Beat (2019)
29. Benoot, C., Hannes, K., Bilsen, J.: The use of purposeful sampling in a qualitative evidence synthesis: a worked example on sexual adjustment to a cancer trajectory. BMC Med. Res. Methodol. **16**, 21 (2016)
30. Thomas, R.J., et al.: Home-based cardiac rehabilitation: a scientific statement from the American association of cardiovascular and pulmonary rehabilitation, the American heart association, and the American college of cardiology. J. Cardiopulm. Rehabil. Prev. **39**, 208–225 (2019)
31. Ades, P.A., Khadanga, S., Savage, P.D., Gaalema, D.E.: Enhancing participation in cardiac rehabilitation: focus on underserved populations. Prog. Cardiovasc. Dis. **70**, 102–110 (2022)
32. Vanzella, L.M., Oh, P., Pakosh, M., Ghisi, G.L.M.: Barriers and facilitators to virtual education in cardiac rehabilitation: a systematic review of qualitative studies. Eur. J. Cardiovasc. Nurs. **21**, 414–429 (2022)
33. Samayoa, L., Grace, S.L., Gravely, S., Scott, L.B., Marzolini, S., Colella, T.J.: Sex differences in cardiac rehabilitation enrollment: a meta-analysis. Can. J. Cardiol. **30**, 793–800 (2014)
34. Barth, J., et al.: Gender differences in cardiac rehabilitation outcomes: do women benefit equally in psychological health? J Womens Health (Larchmt) **18**, 2033–2039 (2009)
35. Molloy, G.J., Hamer, M., Randall, G., Chida, Y.: Marital status and cardiac rehabilitation attendance: a meta-analysis. Eur. J. Cardiovasc. Prev. Rehabil. **15**, 557–561 (2008)

36. Supervía, M., et al.: Cardiac rehabilitation for women: a systematic review of barriers and solutions. Mayo Clinic Proc. **92**(4), 565–577 (2017). https://doi.org/10.1016/j.mayocp.2017.01.002

37. Kumar, A.R., Cluff, K., McLeroy, T.: Is remote human factors testing an acceptable approach for human factors validation. Proc. Int. Symp. Human Factors Ergon. Health Care **10**, 152–156 (2021)

38. Mclaughlin, A.C., Drews, F.A.: Evaluating medical devices remotely: current methods and potential innovations. Hum. Factors **00**, 1041–1060 (2020)

39. Mastrianni, A., Kulp, L., Sarcevic, A.: Transitioning to remote user-centered design activities in the emergency medical field during a pandemic. Association for Computing Machinery (2021)

40. Gamboa, E., Galda, R., Mayas, C., Hirth, M.: The crowd thinks aloud: crowdsourcing usability testing with the thinking aloud method. In: Stephanidis, C., et al. (eds.) HCI International 2021 - Late Breaking Papers: Design and User Experience. LNCS, vol. 13094, pp. 24–39. Springer, Cham (2021). https://doi.org/10.1007/978-3-030-90238-4_3

41. Gittens, C.L.: Remote HRI: a methodology for maintaining COVID-19 physical distancing and human interaction requirements in HRI studies. Inf. Syst. Front. **2021**, 1–16 (2021). https://doi.org/10.1007/s10796-021-10162-4

42. Hill, J.R., Harrington, A.B., Adeoye, P., Campbell, N.L., Holden, R.J.: Going remote—demonstration and evaluation of remote technology delivery and usability assessment with older adults: survey study. JMIR mHealth uHealth **9**(3), e26702 (2021). https://doi.org/10.2196/26702

43. Campbell, J.L., Monkman, H.: The application of a novel, context specific, remote, usability assessment tool to conduct a pre-redesign and post-redesign usability comparison of a telemedicine website. Public Health Inform. Proc. MIE **2021**, 911–915 (2021)

44. da Silva, A.M., Ayanoglu, H., Silva, B.: Remote user testing for an age-friendly interface design for smart homes. In: Gao, Q., Zhou, J. (eds.) Human Aspects of IT for the Aged Population. Technology Design and Acceptance. LNCS, vol. 12786, pp. 168–182. Springer, Cham (2021). https://doi.org/10.1007/978-3-030-78108-8_13

45. Kushendriawan, M.A., Santoso, H.B., Putra, P.O.H., Schrepp, M.: Evaluating User Experience of a Mobile Health Application Halodoc using User Experience Questionnaire and Usability Testing (2021)

46. Lowe, C., Sing, H.H., Browne, M., Alwashmi, M.F., Marsh, W., Morrissey, D.: Usability testing of a digital assessment routing tool: Protocol for an iterative convergent mixed methods study. JMIR Res. Protocols. **10** (2021)

47. Lynn Campbell, J.: A mixed-methods approach to evaluating the usability of telemedicine communications. Association for Computing Machinery, Inc. (Year)

48. Mehrabi, S., et al.: Immersive virtual reality exergames to promote the well-being of community-dwelling older adults: protocol for a mixed methods pilot study. JMIR Res. Protocols **11**(6), e32955 (2022). https://doi.org/10.2196/32955

49. Holden, R.J.: A simplified system usability scale (SUS) for cognitively impaired and older adults. Proc. Int. Symp. Human Factors Ergon. Health Care **9**, 180–182 (2020)

50. Schöne, C., Große, U., Wölfel, A., Krömker, H.: Methods of usability testing for users with cognitive impairments. In: Antona, M., Stephanidis, C. (eds.) Universal Access in Human-Computer Interaction. Design Methods and User Experience. LNCS, vol. 12768, pp. 99–115. Springer, Cham (2021). https://doi.org/10.1007/978-3-030-78092-0_7

Privacy, Technology and Telehealth: Canadian Older Adults Voice Their Concerns

Constance Lafontaine[✉], Marie-Ève Ducharme, and Kim Sawchuk

Concordia University, 1455 Boul. De Maisonneuve W., QC H3G 1M8 Montréal, Canada
constance.lafontaine@concordia.ca

Abstract. This exploratory study examines older adults' perceptions of privacy within the Canadian healthcare system, a system that is increasingly reliant on digital flows of information and mediated communication. We present the results from in-depth interviews with ten older adults (aged 65–88) conducted in Canada between December 2022 and January 2023. These interviews are centered on how telehealth and the rapid digitization of healthcare have influenced their understandings of privacy. Although asked about privacy concerns in relation to telehealth, our findings indicate that these respondents conceive of privacy primarily outside of the digital realm. Privacy was initially discussed in personal terms. Participants conceived of privacy as relations of trust and intimacy with a small number of medical professionals. When they discussed risk in the context of telehealth, participants expressed concern in sharing specific information, such as credit card numbers, over digital networks. In follow-up interviews with three participants, where instances of the sharing of healthcare information were brought to their attention, attitudes shifted, and privacy was then discussed in relation to information flows. Drawing on Nissenbaum's approach to privacy as contextual integrity, we suggest that our older participants as "data subjects" have an understanding of privacy that is underpinned by expectations of integrity of the current healthcare system. Our findings also point to the need for more public discussion and debate on the sharing of healthcare information in Canada.

Keywords: Telehealth · Privacy · Canada · Older adults · Contextual integrity

1 Introduction

The COVID-19 pandemic accelerated the implementation of telehealth in many Western countries, including Canada [1]. Telehealth has been identified as a means to make healthcare more affordable and effective, as a 'solution' for increasing health costs tied to an aging population [2], and as a means of mitigating the challenges associated with older adults' mobility in providing them healthcare [3]. Even as statistics show a high rate of uptake among older adults [1, 4], there remain concerns about how to create conditions for building systems for engaging older adults in telehealth [3]. Concerns over privacy have been found to be among the many factors that could impede the use of telehealth for older adults [5–7]. Indeed, through the rapid implementation of telehealth, the literature identifies the need to engage thoroughly with questions of privacy broadly

© The Author(s), under exclusive license to Springer Nature Switzerland AG 2023
Q. Gao and J. Zhou (Eds.): HCII 2023, LNCS 14043, pp. 145–159, 2023.
https://doi.org/10.1007/978-3-031-34917-1_11

[8], and in particular in relation to specific concerns that may be held by older populations [5–7].

This exploratory study presents preliminary findings on how older adults (65+) perceive privacy within a Canadian healthcare landscape that is increasingly reliant on Information and Communications Technologies (ICTs) and networked communication. We conducted in-depth interviews with ten older adults who are users of digital technologies and who have recently become users of telehealth over the course of the COVID-19 pandemic. This engagement includes phone calls with doctors, consultations with medical professionals using platforms such as Zoom, and the use of online surveys. We seek to understand how the context of rapid digitization of healthcare has had an impact on the ways in which these older adults understand privacy. We investigate the following research question: How do Canadian older adults understand privacy in the context of increasing telehealth and reliance on digital flows of information?

2   Theory and Literature Review

2.1   Privacy as Contextual Integrity

In her book, *Privacy In Context: Technology, Policy, and the Integrity of Social Life,* Helen Nissenbaum explains that "a right to privacy is neither a right to secrecy nor a right to control but a right to appropriate flow of personal information" [9], p. 68]. Nissenbaum's approach emphasizes "contextual integrity" as a means of examining and evaluating appropriate patterns of data circulation. Contextual integrity entails an evaluation of practices in terms of their effects on the interests and preferences of the parties implicated in the exchange. Nissenbaum's approach to privacy as contextual integrity broadens the definition of privacy beyond personal relations of trust, encompassing an understanding of how privacy norms and practices sustain ethical, political and societal principles and values. Nissembaum highlights the importance of privacy not only for individuals, but for different social domains within a given culture. For instance, family, civil and political spheres will have their own norms of contextual integrity, as will the domains of health, finance and the marketplace. These informational norms are based on an analysis and awareness of five factors including: the data subject, the sender, the recipient, information type, and the mode of transmission. Norms established in a given context are based on ethical and social concerns, and they shift over time. The evolution and alteration of informational norms will also change in light of the affordances of sociotechnical systems, which are in constant flux. Contextual integrity provides a way to understand and evaluate privacy practices within a system that relies on the flow of information, such as the healthcare sector, where information systems which allow the electronic exchange of health data have intensified over the past decade [10].

2.2   Telehealth and Privacy

Several definitions for telehealth and telemedicine have been proposed. The World Health Organization (WHO) identifies telemedicine as:

"the delivery of healthcare services, where distance is a critical factor, by all healthcare professionals using information and communication technologies for the exchange of valid information for diagnosis, treatment and prevention of disease and injuries, research and evaluation, and for the continuing education of healthcare providers, all in the interests of advancing the health of individuals and their communities" [11, p. 10].

Although telemedicine and telehealth are often used interchangeably, telemedicine relates specifically to care provided by a doctor, while telehealth refers, more broadly, to all healthcare professions [8]. In the context of this paper, we favor the term telehealth to refer to the broad systems and practices within healthcare that are supported and enabled by ICTs. This includes, in Nissenbaum's parlance, the systems that are implemented to enable the digital capture, analysis and dissemination of information [9].

Research also has considered demographic differences in the disclosure and in perspectives on privacy. Although not specifically related to telehealth, a study of online disclosure found that "older adults made more rationally calculated decisions than younger adults, who made heuristic decisions based on app trust" [12, p. 1]. Older adults tended to weigh the risks and benefits of disclosure. These findings, the authors note, run counter to mainstream narratives suggesting older adults are less privacy-conscious than their younger counterparts [12]. Caine et al.'s [13] research suggests that "younger adults were less likely than older adults to intend to disclose sensitive information" while using computerized systems in their doctor's office [13, p. 1785], and that participants cited trust in their doctor as a motivation to disclose information *via* digital technologies [13, p. 1788]. Kang et al.'s research on the demographic factors associated with privacy awareness and risks show that individuals with more specialized computer knowledge had a better understanding of privacy risks associated with the Internet, even if they did not necessarily put in place practices to mitigate them [14].

Concerns over privacy have been identified as a factor that prevents older adults from "taking full advantage of the potential benefits of digital media" [15, p. 1089]. Similarly, concerns over privacy [5, 6] or perceived security [16] have been identified among the many factors that could impede the use of telehealth by older adults. This has included concern about whether video conference applications are secure [17]. A 2020 US-based national poll found that 24% of older adults (aged 50–80) were concerned about privacy in the context of telehealth. This figure is notable, but it is still less than other concerns about telehealth, such as the doctor's inability to conduct physical exams (75%) or the fear that older patients are receiving diminished care (63%) [18]. Research has identified the need to foster user-friendly approaches that are transparent in terms of security to allay concerns about privacy [19].

2.3 Context

Studies on telehealth and aging point to the importance of considering context, and not just age as a factor influencing telehealth usage. For example, Pool and colleagues [5] note that the realities for older adults living in their own dwellings using devices for communicating with their doctor will differ from those of older adults living in heavily monitored residences. In their review of the literature, they note that the most salient concerns when it comes to privacy and the care of older adults are related to telemonitoring and surveillance in home telecare. Teleconference appointments, conversely, elicited fewer concerns from older adults.

It also is worth outlining some contextual elements of the Canadian healthcare system. While Canada has a commitment to a public healthcare system, health is a domain of provincial and territorial governments. As such, thirteen decentralized provincial and territorial systems provide care to some 39 million Canadians [20]. Across the country, health systems are under pressure [21], and this includes a severe shortage of family doctors nationwide [22]. Among the provinces, the situation is particularly dire in Quebec, where most of our research participants live, and where one in five individuals does not have access to a family doctor [23].

Telehealth has greatly increased in the context of Quebec over the past three years. A recent report shows that the number of older adults (65+) who made appointments with doctors through online platforms grew from 18% in 2019 to 51% in 2022 in the province of Quebec [1, p. 14]. Moreover, in 2022, 12% of older adults in Quebec had carried out an online consultation with a health professional such as a doctor, pharmacist or psychologist [1, p. 14]. These statistics indicate a rapid social shift towards telehealth over the course of the pandemic, and the sorts of telehealth practices that have become increasingly prevalent in the provision of care.

3 Methodology and Analytical Approach

We undertook ten semi-directed in-depth interviews with Canadian older adults, with ages ranging from 67 to 88 in December 2022. The median range of our interviewees was 78.5 years old. Our interviews were conducted in French (6) and English (4) with individuals living in the Canadian provinces of Quebec (9) and Manitoba (1). We interviewed five women and five men, living in both rural (3) and urban or suburban areas (7). Most participants self-assessed their technology skills as moderate, wherein they can use a computer, answer emails, and conduct Internet searches, but might need some assistance to connect to a virtual meeting. Four participants attended university, while six attended high school. While most participants (9) are middle class, one (1) identified themselves as upper middle class. All our participants live in their own dwellings (renters or owners of houses or apartments). The bulk of their experience interacting with digital or remote systems of care has included virtual or phone appointments with their healthcare professionals.

We selected a purposive sampling approach, as our goal from the onset of the project was to focus on "information rich" cases [24]. We undertook these interviews at the end of December, as the Christmas holidays allowed us to hold many of our interviews in person (eight in person, two on Zoom). We undertook follow up interviews with three respondents in January 2023. As we discovered that our participants' understanding of privacy was narrower than we originally expected, we devised a strategy to further probe their perspectives. Specifically, we selected a series of media cases that each discuss an aspect of privacy in the context of digitized health system and used them as prompts for our follow-up discussions.

The decision to undertake purposive sampling was motivated by three reasons. First, the co-authors had pre-established relationships of trust through familial connections, which means that relations of trust were already in place, important when discussing sensitive medical information and issues of privacy. Second, as Seymour has argued [25], family interviews are useful for asking follow-up questions and providing prompts, which may unearth valuable supplementary information. In this case our relationships with the interviewees provided specific insight into their histories of engagement with digital technologies and telehealth. In many cases, the co-authors had served as "warm experts" [26] in the older adults' acquisition of digital skills over the years. The co-authors also played a supportive role in several of the interviewees' use of telehealth during the COVID-19 pandemic, including helping them set up and access telehealth appointments with healthcare professionals. Third, this approach gives us a vantage point to spot potential discrepancies between what participants said in interviews and our own recollection of past events. As Nash, O'Malley and Patterson's research on family ethnography shows, working within this context provides researchers a unique "ability to interrogate discrepancies between the two" [27] and reach a better mutual understanding of "what happened".

In terms of the analysis, the interviews were initially transcribed and coded by one of the co-authors. Attention was paid not only to what each participant said in response to each question, but which questions they did not answer, or where they did not identify concerns. These initial coded responses were then discussed by all three authors, who reviewed the transcripts and discussed emergent patterns. As many of the interviews were done in French, the authors translated some of the quotes in order to include them in English as part of this article.

4 Findings

4.1 Privacy and Disclosure in the Context of Telehealth

Our approach was designed to foreground the participants' understanding of both telehealth and privacy, to provide them with the space to define what they understood as telehealth and to elaborate what they saw as related privacy concerns. We asked participants to explain their concerns related to privacy in light of the expansion of the role of telehealth in their lives, in relation to their use of different media for communication, including the telephone, the computer or tablet, their engagement with online medical questionnaires, and their experiences with teleconferencing with medical personnel. At this early stage of the interview, seven of the ten participants did not express any overt unease or privacy concerns, with most individuals stating that they did not think about privacy in this setting or that they did not believe that it was a concern. Frequent comments were "I have no problem with it" (F-88, F-68), or "no problem" (M-88).

When digging deeper, it became clear that the lack of explicit concern about issues of privacy among our participants was tied to the context of their encounters with the health system. When participants were probed as to whether they would disclose health information online, the majority of the participants expressed no overt concerns about sharing personal information with healthcare providers. Some participants who expressed concern with their privacy in the context of other uses of digital technologies let down their guard when it came to telehealth. For instance, one participant explained at length his worries about "cookies" in web browsing but had few concerns about his engagement with the medical system through telehealth (M-67). Another participant stated that she was comfortable giving information online in the context of telehealth: "I like it, I'm in favor of it" (F-68).

4.2 Privacy as Trust

Through our interviews, it became clear that even while disclosing few overt concerns with privacy in a context of their experiences with telehealth, our interviewees had nuanced and diverse perspectives on why, how and to whom they disclosed health information. In their "privacy repertoires" [28], the language or terms used by participants to discuss privacy, questions of trust in one's doctor emerged as a key theme and contextual factor. Most of the participants expressed that their trust in their doctor, in particular, was enough to safeguard their privacy. "Obviously in the context where I'm with my doctor or with a healthcare specialist like a nurse, there is no problem" (M-88).

By the same token, participants were only comfortable sharing information with a limited number of individuals within the healthcare sector. Several participants mentioned that they would not share information and or their "boo boos" with their doctor's secretary, or with healthcare workers they do not know. One participant mentioned that "there is no problem" in sharing personal information with their regular doctor but with other healthcare providers "no" (F-78). Another explained: "if it's my regular healthcare professional, I don't have a problem with that. (…) If there are a multitude of healthcare professionals, I'd begin to question it more around privacy of information" (M-67). Along with this, there was an expectation that the doctor would treat the information ethically and only share information as it was required, for the benefit of the patient. A participant, who had a history of seeing multiple health professionals simultaneously in treating a cancer, explained: "I don't consider my health as much of a privacy issue (as others might). If my doctor says that I have cancer, then she should disclose it to other doctors (who are treating me). If my information is shared beyond that, then I would doubt how ethical my doctor is. I find that sharing data like that can only be helpful" (F-68).

When we asked about various forms of telehealth (like teleconference applications and the telephone), many of our participants stressed the importance of knowing the person "on the other end of the line". This was particularly important for six of our participants. In fact, having an established "real-world" connection with a medical professional served as a means of mitigating feelings of stress or anxiety associated with starting to use telehealth services. For eight of our participants, knowing the person or the healthcare provider on the other end of the line was reassuring: "I don't mind if I know the person, (…). Someone I never met, (…) would be less comfortable, simply because (…) there must be a kind of comfort level with the person" (M-72).

Compromises: When the Ends Justify the Means. Many of our interviewees have a keen awareness of the lack of resources available in the healthcare sector, and several have dealt first-hand with the aftermath of a system under acute pressure. For some, this had an impact on the ways in which they feel they can assert agency in the disclosure of information. In all, four of our participants explained that they were comfortable sharing personal information over the phone without being familiar with the person on the other end of the line. In the case of some of our participants, the ends justify the means. As one interviewee put it: "Well, anybody, like a nurse or a doctor or whoever, but someone who's a professional, I guess that would be okay if it's going to help you in the end" (F-84). Another one pointed out "I guess you have to go with the flow, you work with what you work with, the tools you have" (M-67).

Even if some people were in situations where they had to disclose their personal information for the sake of their health, it is notable that trust in doctors, as described by our participants, is often contingent on having a previous relationship. This was especially the case for participants with relationships with medical professionals from before the pandemic and prior to the generalized onset of telehealth. Those who expressed privacy in terms of trust in their doctor also had long periods of contact, including face-to-face encounters throughout their lives, with *their* doctor.

The importance of this contextual factor of a prior long-term relationship was brought home by one interviewee, who had no family doctor, amidst a nation-wide shortage of family doctors in Canada [22] and Quebec [23]. This participant relied on appointments with his local clinic for appointments with whichever doctor was available. When discussing a recent telephone appointment with a doctor, he explained the impact of the lack of a family doctor for him: "I don't have a very intimate relationship with him. There's no past understanding. He's very mechanical. He's very, you know, his computer is more important than his fingers to figure out what's wrong" (M-77). In this case, privacy is not only related to trust, but to a perceived lack of intimacy in their relationship. As this interviewee later added, given this lack of intimacy that the "experience by phone wasn't that different than the other experiences I've had with him" (M-77).

4.3 Privacy and Non-medical Information in the Context of Telehealth

As we noted above, seven of ten participants did not initially express concern with privacy in the context of telehealth. The three participants who initially expressed privacy concerns specifically raised the point that they are uncomfortable sharing specific information typically tied to financial fraud or identity theft in the context of telehealth: their credit card information, their social insurance number, and their health insurance number. For these respondents, the reluctance to share such information virtually or over the phone extended to the healthcare sphere. As one participant explained "I would not share it (…) sharing your name, address and health insurance number, I would say no because there is not enough trust in the digital systems" (M-72).

4.4 Probing Privacy Again: Considering Data-Sharing and Risk

Our initial interviews indicate that participants' understanding of telehealth and privacy focused primarily on the relationship between doctor and patient. Those who were most concerned about privacy in the context of telehealth focused on the disclosure of official documents and information that they surmised could most readily expose them to identity and financial fraud: sharing a credit card number, social insurance number or a health insurance number. Beyond these questions, our participants did not initially consider other implications of privacy and telehealth, including questions as to how, when and with whom their health data was shared, or how sharing health data could have positive or negative implications for them. In follow up interviews with three participants (M-67, F-68, M-77), we were able to delve more deeply in the theme of privacy and telehealth with three respondents.

In these conversations, we sought to understand the perspectives of participants on privacy beyond the immediate relationship with the medical professional, and the disclosure of information that could expose them to fraud and financial harm. We probed the implications of telehealth in the emergent context of the systems-wide integration of digital tools that includes an expansion of data-gathering and data-sharing practices. To do this we presented our participants with three recent and localized media cases that relate to some of the different ways in which health data circulates in society. This included an article about "Clic Santé" a provincial digital tool used during the pandemic that is being expanded into a broader health platform for making appointments and accessing medical information [29]. We also presented a recent news story explaining that medical professionals in Quebec would need to disclose the identity of all individuals with dementia to the provincial entity tasked with issuing drivers' licenses in Quebec, which would in turn automatically suspend their licenses [30]. This would replace the current system wherein healthcare professionals, at their discretion, would trigger a process where the individual would need to undertake a driving test. Finally, we shared an article about a cyberattack that targeted a Montreal health authority in 2020 [31].

The Risk of Disclosure. After being presented with three specific examples from the news, one of our participants expressed a more pointed concern about how his data was being shared and the risks that could be involved with the disclosure of medical information. This event prompted one participant to suggest that he might not share information on his health status, even with his doctor. In his words, "Every time you disclose something new there is a restriction elsewhere. (…) It just means that I'm going to go to the doctor and lie (M-67)".

When further prompted, he then disclosed that he had previously made decisions based on such a calculation of risks when he had given blood: "I went to give blood, and one of the questions was 'do you have high blood pressure?'. I thought of it, and I was going to say, 'sometimes it's a little high'. But it's like 'no, I don't have high blood pressure'. Because suddenly, you know what, it goes into your medical record that you have high blood pressure. Then you want to go for more insurance, and you can't. It'll cost more" (M- 67).

In other words, in this follow-up interview, when presented with these specific stories of the implications of data sharing, this participant began to consider how data presented in one context (health) might be used in another context (insurance). For this participant, it was not clear if there was an established systematic informational flow between Héma-Quebec (the NGO that collects blood in Quebec), the provincially governed healthcare system and his private insurance provider. Yet the fear of how they may be connected – now or in the future– impacted his decision to disclose. For this participant, the increased privatization of healthcare and the relationship with private insurance caused another layer of concern in relation to information sharing, that he did not share during the first interview.

Unclear Boundaries for Information Sharing. A second participant who was asked about the sharing of personal data did not feel as strongly, at least initially. She noted that she had never been in a position where she did not want to disclose information to a doctor because of a fear that the information would be shared without her knowledge. "I'm not that concerned about it," she said (F-68). However, when the interviewer presented with examples from the media about data being shared across sectors of society, her perceptions on disclosure changed. These news stories–which were revelations about the sharing of health data to this respondent–elicited a potential shift in perspective. The participant explained that she had a doctor's appointment that same day, and that what she had learned about privacy through our discussion of these specific cases discussed in the media would change the way she approached divulging information about mental health: "It's making me reconsider [disclosing the information]".

The participants with whom we conducted follow-up interviews were startled by news reports of data leaks in the healthcare sector and systematic information sharing on older adults that had emerged in the news and expressed a desire to know more. When presented with the same news stories, another participant immediately stated "I need to research that" (M-77). Participants expressed renewed concern and uncertainty about the way health information is being collected and shared, pointing to the importance of the public discussions of these issues in the news.

Other insights on how medical information might be shared emerged in these follow-up interviews. One participant expressed concern that information sharing could expose him to targeted advertising related to medical conditions or to new forms of discrimination. Two participants expressed concern over how mistakes in medical diagnoses and assessments by one medical professional could result in mistaken information about their health being circulated widely. There was a sense that, at one time, if one doctor made a mistake, it was possible to get a second opinion. The participants wondered if the increased sharing of information meant that one doctor's opinion–like a diagnosis of dementia–would automatically trigger a series of processes they would have no control over: "Shit could fall on your head because they interpreted the information a certain way, then you lose control over how the information is shared, it's out of your hands" (M-67). These follow-up conversations, though exploratory, shed light on the importance of media and news coverage of stories that discuss the implications of the opaque systems of data sharing between different sectors. They also indicate that when presented with specific examples of medical information sharing, participants became concerned with the risks associated with information flow and began to relate them to prior experiences with the healthcare system.

5 Discussion

5.1 Privacy Circumscribed by Human Relationships

In our initial round of interviews, there are two ways in which older adults discussed privacy when probed about their privacy concerns in relation to telehealth. Firstly, and present in most of our interviewees, there exists an explicit trust in medical professionals, most notably their doctor. This trust serves as a basis upon which they establish a belief that their privacy will be safeguarded in the context of telehealth. Privacy, in this instance, would be ensured by the individuals with whom they have an interpersonal intimate contact, who are assumed to exert control over a patient's health information. As one of our participants pointed out, they count on the medical professionals' sense of "ethics" to safeguard their privacy.

Digging deeper into this issue, the trust that was bestowed on the telehealth system was built through in-person relationships with individual medical professionals before the start of the COVID-19 pandemic. If participants did not know medical professionals well or if they have only become acquainted virtually over the course of the pandemic, then participants did not feel the same trust towards their doctor and saw little difference between an online consultation and an in-person visit. This begs the question on whether and how new relationships of trust will be formed and nurtured for our participants as more healthcare interactions become digitized or virtual.

Second, when individuals initially expressed concerns about their privacy, they often referenced discourses on privacy tied to issues of identity theft and finances, and not health in particular (*e.g.*, credit card numbers or social insurance numbers). What is feared in these circumstances is sharing sensitive information that could end up in the wrong hands; specifically, those of bad actors who could cause deliberate harm. These two conceptualizations of privacy, each in their own way, foreground that participants tended to emphasize the role of individuals in safeguarding information. However, when three participants were presented with specific news stories about the use of medical information for other purposes, such as retaining one's driver's license, participants expressed a concern of the privacy implications and risks of data flows from one sector in society to another.

5.2 Understanding the Telehealth Context

To return to Nissenbaum's approach, for these participants, privacy in digital systems is underpinned by the expectations associated with the contextual integrity of the health-care system. There was a general sense that information would be properly managed in the current healthcare system because of the association of that system with a trusted mediator: the doctor. It was only when confronted with specific instances of health infor-mation being used for decision-making in other sectors, that our participants began to engage in a discussion of how and when they had not fully disclosed medical information in their past, and to critically question information sharing between different contexts or sectors. This brings us to wonder how the "data subjects" of these systems, including our participants, understand and consent to the informational system within which they participate. As norms of appropriateness shift quickly with the expansion of telehealth, to what extent are patients –including older patients– keeping up with what is appropri-ate for systems to share or not share. How are their perspectives being factored in the establishment of norms, and what falls outside of their own privacy expectations in the healthcare context, given the expansion of telehealth?

The systems of information flow through which personal health information is shared in digital records, including across sectors of society, remained largely outside of our participants' initial framing of privacy until it was overtly presented to them. Our participants initially did not express concerns with the information flow that takes place within the healthcare context, and with who are the "senders", the "receivers" beyond the medical professionals they know. We found this to be even more pronounced in interviews with our participants with limited digital skills, a finding that is in line with the literature on privacy and digital expertise [32]. However, when probing the issue more deeply with participants and presenting them with media cases about concrete data leaks, privacy breaches and expanded medical data sharing across sectors in the participants' own locales, they then expressed concerns with other facets of their privacy rights. The interview itself became a way for participants to access new information about the workings of healthcare context and the norms of information flow. It also transformed their tacit knowledge and memories of prior experience with the disclosure or non-disclosure of health information into discourse [33]. The use of these stories as means to elicit conversation points to the usefulness of prompts in discussions of privacy with older adults, and to the need for more public discussions and news stories on privacy matters.

While our participants recognized the benefits of data sharing in their own healthcare trajectories, they also began to question the norms and the contextual integrity of the healthcare system when presented with specific instances that would potentially impact their lives. When speaking about these matters, they showed surprise and dismay, but quickly pivoted to recognizing that the rapid expansion of datafication and digitization of our health systems could impact them (and likely already had). This is when one of our participants expressed fear about "losing control" of his data as he ages and encounters more health issues. In a social context where older adults are frequently disempowered and are concerned with a loss of agency, avoiding the disclosure of potentially vital medical information like mental health wellness or high blood pressure emerged as the only solution that our participants envisaged to mitigate harm to themselves.

6 Conclusion

In this paper, we have tried to answer the question of how our older participants understand privacy in the context of telehealth. By conducting exploratory interviews with ten older adults on the topic of telehealth and privacy, we found that participants tended to equate privacy with a trust in their doctors, ignoring the scope of information flow that takes place in an increasingly digital healthcare context. Privacy was initially understood in interpersonal terms, as relationships of trust with a small number of medical professionals. The healthcare context was not initially defined as a sphere of concern, although participants initially identified risks in the act of sharing information like credit card numbers, social insurance numbers or health insurance numbers over digital networks. This changed when, in follow-up interviews, three participants were given specific examples of how health information might be deployed in future public policy, including policies that might automatically lead to revoking their driver's license. Understanding the participant responses in light of Nissenbaum's approach to privacy as contextual integrity highlights a broader concern in the present moment: participants did not have access to the regulations and norms that govern what is appropriate data sharing in the healthcare context. However, when presented with specific instances of data sharing that could affect other dimensions of their lives, they simultaneously became aware and concerned with the implications of information flow between different sectors that they assumed were distinct.

Older adults represent a segment of the population that is especially reliant on the healthcare sector. By the same token, they are disproportionately rendered into the "data subjects" of this system, whose health information gets collected, analyzed and disseminated at an unprecedented rate. Health data about older adults can be mobilized to make critical decisions about policy but also individual care pathways, including access to services and long-term care. If health data is shared across contexts, it can have a significant impact on other aspects of one's life, from one's ability to drive, to insurance cost. Within this context, older adults have an important stake in defining and preserving the contextual integrity of the boundaries of data sharing and privacy in the healthcare system.

The digitization of health records, the aggregating and sharing of data across healthcare institutions and different bureaucratic sectors of society and the implementation of automated decision-making through algorithms has been credited with improving efficiency and patient care. In light of the unprecedented expansion of information flows, researchers in the humanities and social sciences have pointed to the need to understand how automated systems can amplify existing means of social discrimination and bias or create new forms of inequality [34–36]. The digitization of health systems also has made these systems an important target of hacks or data breaches in recent years [37, 38], including in our home province of Quebec (e.g., [39, 40]). The circumstances around such breaches can often be clouded in secrecy and its implications for individuals often remain difficult to grasp. Our exploratory research suggests the need for greater public awareness and discussion of these issues, which are quickly being integrated into society.

7 Limitations

This exploratory study has several limitations. Our sample size is small and only covers two provinces. Further, even if their perspectives were varied, there are a number of similarities among our participants that are likely to have a bearing on the results gleaned: all but one live in the province of Quebec, most are middle-class, and all have a certain degree of digital proficiency. All of them have French or English (both official languages of Canada) as their first language and all are Caucasian. The general lack of diversity in our sample certainly limits the sorts of experiences with telehealth that we were able to capture in the context of this study. Further, we opted for a purposive sampling as a method of recruitment and thus consulted a narrow group of individuals, with whom the co-authors had pre-existing relationships. This was a means to build a conversation on healthcare upon established relationships of trust, but it can be a source of bias, from the perspective of the participants influencing what they opted to disclose, as well as from the perspective of the co-authors in how they analyzed data. Finally, we were only able to conduct follow-up interviews with three of our ten participants.

References

1. Académie de la transformation numérique: Les aînés connectés au Québec. NETendances 2022. **13**(6) (2022)
2. Dhillon, J. S., Wünsche, B. C., Lutteroth, C.: Designing and evaluating online telehealth systems for seniors. In: Hippe, Z. S., Kulikowski, J. L., Mroczek, T., Wtorek, J. (eds.) Human-Computer Systems Interaction: Backgrounds and Applications 3, pp.167–178. Springer International Publishing, Cham (2014). https://doi.org/10.1007/978-3-319-08491-6_14
3. Bernstein, P., et al.: Urgent and non-emergent telehealth care for seniors: findings from a multi-site impact study. J. Telemed. Telecare. 1357633X2110043 (2021)
4. Tan, L.F., Ho Wen Teng, V., Seetharaman, S.K., Yip, A.W.: Facilitating telehealth for older adults during the COVID-19 pandemic and beyond: strategies from a Singapore geriatric center. Geriatr. Gerontol. Int. **20**(10), 993–995 (2020)
5. Pool, J., Akhlaghpour, S., Fatehi, F., Gray, L.C.: Data privacy concerns and use of telehealth in the aged care context: an integrative review and research agenda. Int. J. Med. Informatics **160**, 104707 (2022)
6. Wardlow, L., et al.: Development of telehealth principles and guidelines for older adults: A modified Delphi approach. J. Am. Geriatrics Soc. 18123 (2022)
7. Kruse, C., Fohn, J., Wilson, N., Patlan, E.N., Zipp, S., Mileski, M.: Utilization barriers and medical outcomes commensurate with the use of telehealth among older adults: systematic review. JMIR Med. Inform. **8**(8), e20359 (2020)
8. Doraiswamy, S., Abraham, A., Mamtani, R., Cheema, S.: Use of telehealth during the COVID-19 pandemic: scoping review. J. Med. Internet Res. **22**(12), E24087 (2020)
9. Nissenbaum, H.: Privacy in context: Technology, Policy, and the Integrity of Social Life. Stanford University Press (2009).https://doi.org/10.1515/9780804772891
10. Motulsky, A., et al.: Usage and accuracy of medication data from nationwide health information exchange in Quebec, Canada. J. Am. Med. Inform. Assoc. **25**(6), 722–729 (2018)
11. WHO: A Health Telematics Policy. Report (1997)
12. Anaraky, R.G., Byrne, K.A., Wisniewski, P.J., Page, X., Knijnenburg, B.: To disclose or not to disclose: examining the privacy decision-making processes of older vs. younger adults. In: Proceedings of the 2021 CHI Conference on human factors in computing systems, pp. 1–14, Yokohama, Japan (2021)
13. Caine, K.E., Fisk, A.D., Rogers, W.A.: Benefits and privacy concerns of a home equipped with a visual sensing system: a perspective from older adults. Proc. Human Factors Ergon. Soc. Ann. Meet. **50**(2), 180–184 (2006). https://doi.org/10.1177/154193120605000203
14. Kang, R., Dabbish, L. Fruchter, N., Kiesler, S. 'My data just goes everywhere:' user mental models of the Internet and implications for privacy and security. In: Proceedings of the Eleventh USENIX Conference on Usable Privacy and Security (SOUPS 2015), pp. 39–52. USENIX Association, USA (2015)
15. QuanHaase, A., Ho, D.: Online privacy concerns and privacy protection strategies among older adults in East York, Canada. J. Am. Soc. Inf. Sci. **71**(9), 1089–1102 (2020)
16. Cimperman, M., Brenčič, M.M., Trkman, P., de Leonni Stanonik, M.: older adults' perceptions of home telehealth services. Telemed. J. E Health **19**(10), 786–790 (2013)
17. Goldberg, E.M., Lin, M.P., Burke, L.G., Jiménez, F.N., Davoodi, N.M., Merchant, R.C.: Perspectives on telehealth for older adults during the COVID-19 pandemic using the quadruple aim: interviews with 48 physicians. BMC Geriatrics. **22**(1), 188 (2022).
18. National Poll on Healthy Aging. Telehealth use among older adults before and during Covid-19 (2020)
19. Ray, H., Wolf, F., Kuber, R. Aviv, A. J.: Woe is me': examining older adults' perceptions of privacy. In: CHI Conference on Human Factors in Computing Systems. Glasgow Scotland UK, pp. 1–6 (2019)

20. Government of Canada, S. C.: Canada's population estimates, third quarter 2022. Statistics Canada (2022). https://www150.statcan.gc.ca/n1/daily-quotidien/221221/dq221221f-eng.htm. Accessed 14 Feb 2023

21. Paas-Lang, C.: With hospitals overwhelmed, can Canada overhaul health care for the long term?. CBC Radio (2022). https://www.cbc.ca/radio/thehouse/canada-health-care-long-term-reform-1.6316538. Accessed 15 Feb 2023

22. Hopper, T.: Why five million Canadians have no hope of getting a family doctor. National Post (2022). https://nationalpost.com/opinion/why-five-million-canadians-have-no-hope-of-getting-a-family-doctor. Accessed 15 Feb 2023

23. De Marcellis-Warin, N., Peignier, I.: Perception des risques au Québec. Baromètre Cirano (2021)

24. Patton, M.: Qualitative Research and Evaluation Methods, 3rd edn. SAGE Publications Ltd. (2002)

25. Seymour, J.: Keeping it in the family: conducting research interviews with your own family members (2011). https://hull-repository.worktribe.com/output/405228/keeping-it-in-the-family-conducting-research-interviews-with-your-own-family-members. Accessed 15 Feb 2023

26. Bakardjieva, M.: Internet society: The Internet in Everyday Life. Sage, London (2005)

27. Nash, C., O'Malley, L., Patterson, M.: Experiencing family ethnography: challenges, practicalities and reflections on practice. Qual. Market Res. Int. J. (2020)

28. Jacobs, L., Crow, B., Sawchuk, K.: Privacy rights mobilization among marginal groups in Canada. Final report. (2011)

29. The Canadian Press Staff.: You can now create an account, view past consultations on Quebec's Clic Santé health portal (2022). https://montreal.ctvnews.ca/you-can-now-create-an-account-view-past-consultations-on-quebec-s-clic-sante-health-portal-1.5976084. Accessed 15 Feb 2023

30. Robitaille, A.: Nouvelle règle de la SAAQ: des milliers de conducteurs aînés risquent de perdre leur permis. Le Journal de Montréal. (2022) https://www.journaldemontreal.com/2022/11/13/les-conducteurs-ages-dans-la-mire-de-la-saaq. Accessed 15 Feb 2023

31. Ha, T.T., Freeze, C.: Quebec health network targeted by cyberattack. the globe and mail. https://www.theglobeandmail.com/canada/article-quebec-health-network-targeted-by-cyberattack/. Accessed 15 Feb 2023

32. Kang, R., Dabbish, L., Fruchter, N., Kiesler, S.: 'My data just goes everywhere:' user mental models of the internet and implications for privacy and security. In: Eleventh Symposium on Usable Privacy and Security, pp. 39–52 (2015)

33. Tulloch, J.: Approaching the audience: the elderly., remote control: television, audiences and cultural power New York and London. Routledge (1989)

34. Lupton, D.: Digital Health: Critical and Cross-Disciplinary Perspectives. Routledge, Milton Park (2017). https://doi.org/10.4324/9781315648835

35. Panch, T., Mattie, H., Atun, R.: Artificial intelligence and algorithmic bias: implications for health systems. J. Glob. Health 9(2)

36. Eubanks, V.: Automating inequality. Macmillan (2018). https://us.macmillan.com/books/9781250074317/automatinginequality. Accessed 15 Feb 2023

37. Kamoun, F., Nicho, M.: Human and organizational factors of healthcare data breaches: the Swiss cheese model of data breach causation and prevention. IJHISI 9(1), 42–60 (2014)

38. Seh, A.H., et al.: Healthcare data breaches: Insights and implications. Healthcare 8(2), 133 (2020). https://doi.org/10.3390/healthcare8020133

39. CBC News. Cyberattack on Montreal's west end health agency leads it to unplug from internet. CBC News. https://www.cbc.ca/news/canada/montreal/cyber-security-west-island-health-agency-1.5781734. Accessed 14 Feb 2023

40. Radio-Canada. Le ministère de la santé du Québec responsable d'une fuite de données. Radio-Canada Info. Radio-Canada. https://ici.radio-canada.ca/info/videos/1-8451295/minist ere-sante-quebec-responsable-une-fuite-donnees. Accessed 15 Feb 2023

Paving the Way: Trust in Healthcare Systems as a Prerequisite for Technology Usage

Sophia Otten(✉) ⓘ, Julia Offermann ⓘ, and Martina Ziefle ⓘ

Human-Computer Interaction Centre, RWTH Aachen University, Campus-Boulevard 57, Aachen, Germany
{otten,offermann,ziefle}@comm.rwth-aachen.de

Abstract. Health changes in general, but especially in older age, inevitably lead interactions with different people and entities in the health care system. Particularly in the case of severe health decisions, trust in the healthcare system and the people involved is essential. This raises the question of which factors can promote or impede trust and how these can be influenced by individual or circumstantial parameters. Therefore, the current study aims to investigate how trust in healthcare systems is built and maintained in severe health decisions. Understanding trust-relevant factors in severe health decisions provides the basis for further investigations of trust in assistive technologies for people of older age and in need of care. Two semi-structured focus groups with each five participants were carried out and recorded (N = 10). The results showed that severe health decisions represent situations in which fundamental aspects of life change so that life is no longer comparable to what it was before. The analyses also identified multiple factors relevant in trust building and maintenance, e.g., competence, empathy, transparency, communication, and financing. By contributing to a greater understanding of the patients' needs, with the results of this study, recommendations for a more targeted and demand-oriented communication between the various stakeholders in health care systems can be derived.

Keywords: Trust · Healthcare Systems · Severe Health Decisions

1 Introduction

In Germany, roughly 2/3 of the population report being in good health. In Germans aged 65 and older, 1/3 is affected by chronic diseases [1]. During the span of life, people will come into contact with the healthcare system on multiple occasions. In individuals with chronic diseases however, this number increases substantially and the relationship with their primary care physician and the experiences in the healthcare system become all the more relevant [2]. The relationships between patients and their physicians have the potential to determine and affect the way patients decide [3–5], e.g., with regard to a recommended usage of assisting technologies in older age [6–8]. These relationships and interactions with physicians and other entities within the healthcare systems are based on patients' trust in specific stakeholders but also in the healthcare system itself.

Previous research has examined trust either for very specific phases (e.g., the COVID19 pandemic [9]) or quite generically (e.g., [10, 11]) disregarding underlying trust motives and factors being essential for paving the way to trust medical decisions and recommendations in severe health situations or in older age.

The present study aimed at an explorative identification of relevant parameters for trust in the healthcare system taking changing health conditions, i.e., severe health situations into account. For this purpose, a focus group study was conducted and the results enable to derive recommendations taking into account the requirements and needs of patients. In the following, an overview of previous research in the field of trust within the healthcare system is provided. Following that, the empirical procedure is presented and the results are described. Finally, the insights are discussed including the strengths and weaknesses of the study as well as derived implications.

1.1 Relationships of Trust Within the Healthcare System

There are many ways in which relationships of trust are exercised. One of the most direct and intuitive connection is the one between a patient and their treating physician. This relationship has been focused on in diverse research fields. Bell et al. [2] found that when patient's expectations about their primary care physician, such as medical information, new medications, medical tests, or a specialist referral, were not met, adherence to treatment plans was significantly lower than for patients whose expectation were met in the long run. Specifically in patients with chronic illnesses, patient-physician relationships are predictive of treatment adherence, patient activation, and overall satisfaction with their health plan [3–5].

While the patient-physician relationship is an important predictor for these variables, the construct of trust underlies almost all interactions and not only those with direct physician contact. In the bigger context of healthcare, this includes insurance companies, health care staff, availability of health information, emergency care, and political bodies functioning as sources of information. Studies have shown that trust in the healthcare system is linked to political trust and general trust in the government, as well as subjective health outcomes and the likelihood of seeking medical help [9–13]. In a meta-analysis by Birkhäuser et al. [10], the relationship of trust in healthcare professionals and health outcomes was analysed where they found moderate correlations of trust and health outcomes ($r = .24$). Moreover, they found a high correlation between trust and patient satisfaction ($r = .57$). While the correlation of trust and objective health outcomes was non-significant, it was significant for trust and subjective health outcomes ($r = .30$) and since subjective outcomes are predictive of objective outcomes, trust might have had an indirect effect [14]. The authors conclude that "patients' trust in the health care professional may best be conceptualized as a contextual factor of treatment effects" [10] which indicates that trust may have both direct and indirect relationships with other factors in the healthcare context.

Moreover, trust perceptions in the healthcare system differ across countries, with Germany showing low trust levels in a patient-focused treatment at their health institution [15]. Therefore, it is crucial to investigate how trust in the health care system is conceptualised in order to predict its underlying mechanism in the development and maintenance. Even more than that, it is important to investigate how trust conditions change across different medical decisions ranging from light to severe. There is an increasing shift from a *paternalistic view* (the healthcare provider being the sole decider of treatment plans, etc.) toward *shared decision making* (patient and provider come to a medical decision jointly) [16]. Research has shown that patient characteristics, such as affective states and previous experience, are influential in how they make decisions about their treatment plan, whether they adhere to medication, etc. [17]. This means that patients are increasingly questioning the information and options provided while they also have more options to choose from. At the same time, individual histories of patients, including their trust perceptions, shape their medical future and can be decisive [18].

1.2 Previous Concepts of Trust

Within the literature, trust is most often considered a belief and expectancy and is by definition an interdisciplinary concept, drawing from individual and social psychology, economics, sociology, and other disciplines [19]. Overall, there are three emerging types of trust, namely dispositional, structural, and interpersonal trust. Dispositional trust refers to the general attitude towards trust and decisions requiring some level of trust. It is considered to be a low-level personality trait. Structural (or sometimes called institutional) trust refers to the trust in situations and institutions, implying that there is a level of consistency expected in certain establishments and circumstanced. The interpersonal dimension refers to trust between two agents, a trustor and a trustee, and further divides into perceptual, intentional, and behavioural facets of trust. There are many definitions and conceptualisations focussing on different aspects, either from an agent perspective, i.e., the trustor and trustee's attributes, or from a context perspective, i.e., which situations elicit certain trust perceptions. Overall, there is no apparent consensus on the definition nor the approach on how to map trust [19]. It is, however, always assessed with a questionnaire when talking about quantitative approaches to the concept.

Within the context of healthcare, it becomes evident that all three distinctions of trust are highly relevant and need to be considered together. There are two literature reviews which capture the way trust has been operationalized in this field. Ozawa and Sripad [20] found that of $N = 45$ studies, most used an interpersonal measurement of trust (doctor/patient/nurse), and only some measured systems trust, i.e., institutional trust. Studies that investigated interpersonal trust did not consider institutional trust in their measurements whereas those measuring institutional trust did consider this domain. Moreover, they found that four domains, namely honesty, communication, confidence, and competence were stable across measurements. In their evaluation, the researchers also found that more than half of the studies employed one of more pre-study designs in the form of interviews, focus groups, literature searchers, etc. This indicates the importance of pre-testing the hypothesised questionnaire conceptualisation. LoCurto and Berg [21] also reviewed the literature ($N = 65$) on trust and its conceptualisation in the healthcare context. Similarly, the majority of studies investigated interpersonal trust, in this case doctors. Only few others investigated institutional trust relating to systems in healthcare. The researchers found as many as eight determinants of trust in the healthcare system, i.e., honesty, confidentiality, dependability, communication, competency, fiduciary responsibility, fidelity, and agency. On this basis, they recommend a methodological protocol of developing a scale, namely a review of the literature, interviews or focus groups, a pilot study, and an initial survey of the study, followed by a psychometric evaluation of the effectiveness of the scale. When comparing trust in healthcare with the general operationalisation, there are similarities signalling an underlying construct of trust with context-specific determinants of trust that needs to be outlined and investigated.

1.3 Aim of the Present Study

Taking these approaches together, it becomes evident that more work needs to be done in combining the conceptualisations of trust with regard to interpersonal and institutional trust but also the link to dispositional trust. More studies have focused on the interpersonal domain and as established above; this relationship is highly predictive of health behaviours. It does not however, capture the entirety of the healthcare system. In order to understand how trust in the healthcare system is developed, maintained and predictive of potential adherence to treatment plans, including the use of ambient assistive systems, a patient/user-centric view is needed. Therefore, the present study focuses on an explorative identification of motives and underlying parameters affecting trust in the healthcare system in general. In a second step, the perceptions are deliberately sharpened by defining severe health decisions and using them as an example to eventually adjust previously expressed trust criteria.

2 Methods

In the following, the empirical concept of the present study is described, starting with the procedure of the qualitative interview study. Subsequently, the conducted data analysis and the characteristics of the sample are presented.

2.1 Procedure

Two semi-structured focus groups were conceptualized and conducted in order to exploratively understand, examine and identify relevant factors for the formation and maintenance of trust in severe health decisions.

Both focus groups were held in German, lasted about an hour and were transcribed afterwards. Before beginning with the focus group process, the participants were welcomed and introduced to the intent of the focus group. Their rights were explained to them and informed consent as well as permission to record was obtained. Participants were firstly asked about demographic variables including age, gender, acute and chronic illnesses, profession, level of education, technical affinity, and experience with medical technology.

The focus group process consisted of two main parts: The first part focused on an exploration of relevant conditions and prerequisites for trust in the healthcare system. In more detail, the participants were asked to discuss several questions and form opinions about the relevance of various trust-building factors in the healthcare system, e.g., "What is important for you to trust in the healthcare system?" and "What defines a good functional/bad dysfunctional health care system for you?".

In the second part, the participants were asked to define what severe health decisions mean to them: i.e., "What do you describe as a severe health decision for you person-ally?". This was meant to explore the boundaries of severe as opposed to "regular" or less severe health decisions. Further, the participants were asked to outline and discuss specific scenarios in which trust could be put to the test, i.e. "If you had to imagine a specific situation in which a severe health decision had to be made and you had to trust the health care system, what would that look like for you?".

Lastly, and to combine the topics trust and severe health decisions, it was explored how and whether considerations for decision making would differ if the severity of their decisions differed: e.g., "When you think about these types of decisions, do you think differently about the health care system and relevant factors for trust?".

Finally, the participants were thanked for their participation, they were asked to provide feedback on the focus group and on an optional basis there was time to discuss about the topic and open questions in general.

2.2 Data Analysis

The focus groups were transcribed verbatim and in German language. The results were analysed according to the guidelines of qualitative content analysis by Mayring [22] with the software MAXQDA 2018 and compared to existing factors in the literature combing inductive and deductive analyses. The answers were also checked for group differences and groupings that are similar in answer patterns. Within the results section, the findings are structured following the main categories identified during data analysis.

2.3 Sample

Each focus group had five participants. Totally, five male and five female participants with a mean age of 30.2 *(SD = 12.39)* and a range of 22 to 55 years took part. Based on information about the sample, their evaluated technical affinity was rather good *(M = 4.6, SD = 1.48)*. The average level of education was vocational training, whereas two participants were currently enrolled as students. The majority had experience with medical technology. Some respondents stated to have chronic diseases, among others ulcerative colitis, Hashimoto disease, and chronic pain.

3 Results

In this section, the results of the qualitative focus group study are presented, starting with insights regarding relevant factors and conditions for trust in healthcare systems. An overview can be found in Fig. 1. Further, it is showed how the participants defined and discussed severe health decisions. In a last step, it is described if and how the relevance of trust conditions changed in the context of severe health decisions.

3.1 Trust Conditions in the Healthcare System

When discussing which aspects and factors are necessary for trusting the healthcare system in their interaction with it, participants agreed on three categories, namely **Competence & Efficiency**, **Cost Allocation & Fairness**, and **Communication & Empathy**. The respective results are now presented depending on these three categories.

Competence & Efficiency. This factor entailed both a correct diagnosis and treatment plan but also a good education of medical professionals in the first place.

"I would have no confidence in the system at all if I went to the doctor five times and five times I was given the wrong diagnosis and five times I was given the wrong treatment." [male, 26 years]

Moreover, participants agreed on the importance of sticking to appointment schedules, not being sent away as a patient, and also the guarantee the security of supply, i.e., that in an emergency, medical help was accessible. This point was heavily influenced by perceptions of the healthcare system during the Covid-19 pandemic. In both groups, it was unanimously agreed that this was the most important aspect for trust.

"Keeping promises, scheduling appointments, that when I say I need a referral that I get it and don't have to run after all the bureaucratic stuff in my already bad shape." [female, 24 years]

Cost Allocation & Fairness. This category was specific to the German healthcare insurance which distinguishes between public and private insurance. While everyone is provided with public insurance, some people can decide to switch to private insurance which typically covers more treatment options and offers other (time-efficient) benefits. Only relating to the aspect of cost allocation, participants agreed that nobody should have to worry about covering medical costs. They compared the German system to other countries, e.g., the US, and agreed that they would not trust or positively evaluate a system in which everyone is responsible for their own coverage.

"I believe that you shouldn't get into a process where you have to arrange something yourself, that all costs are covered [by the insurance company]." [male, 24 years]

In one focus group, they came to the conclusion that medical institutions, such as hospitals should not be allowed to be privatised, as is the case in both Germany and other countries. On that same note, they also would evaluate a hospital as less trustworthy if they knew that they administered unnecessary procedures to patients to earn more money.

"We also have many patients who stay much longer than they should. The treatment alone, if they get something intravenously, we get much more money than if we give it as tablets. I also have to wonder if I have to pump a 20-year-old full of it all the time. Or for a 90-year-old granny who can manage without pain and is always fiddling around with it, no. But it pays more money..." [female, 22 years]

With respect to the aspect of fairness, both groups agreed that they would define the healthcare system as being fair if everyone received the medical help they required, regardless of any other characteristics like socio-economic status, gender, race or else. Here, it was also relevant that where the funds go is transparently communicated to the patients by both the institutions themselves but also the insurance companies.

"For me, fairness is relatively easy to define, and that is that everyone should have access to the treatment options or the doctor they need for their condition." [male, 26 years]

However, both fairness and cost allocations as factors were put together because participant almost always referred to them in relation to one another. For them, being treated fairly is mostly decided by the cost allocation of the healthcare insurance companies and policies.

"It may be transparent what they are allowed to charge, but where a large part of the money disappears is not transparent at all." [male, 55 years]

Communication & Empathy. Participants described this category almost exclusively in relation to patient-physician communications. They mentioned that above all, a physician should have respect for the patient and a genuine interest to listen to them.

"Empathy [...] and that I am also taken seriously, so, also during the initial anamnesis, that the doctors do not dismiss me and take time to consider my concerns." [female, 24 years]

They also expected physician to consider the individual care plan of the patient and adapt it according to their needs. All participants also agreed that doctors should be taught how to deliver medical information in a way that is understandable and accessible patients who are non-experts.

"For me, it's the clarification, and sometimes you don't feel properly informed by the doctor and don't know what to do now, or you're sent to another doctor and referred, who suggests a completely different treatment. But both doctors can't explain exactly why this treatment and another doctor says something else, so you have to accept that, which I think is a shame because I want to know exactly why something is being done. And I would like to have that for the trust." [male, 26 years]

Above all, whether they perceived a physician to be transparent about why they chose a particular treatment was also indicative of whether or not they would trust them. These aspects were the second most important aspect for trust in the healthcare system and both groups quickly agreed on their qualities.

"Yes, the doctor should definitely communicate with his patient in a way that they understand. It's no use for him to beat you over the head with something and say everything will be fine, and then you don't know what's wrong with you." [male, 55 years]

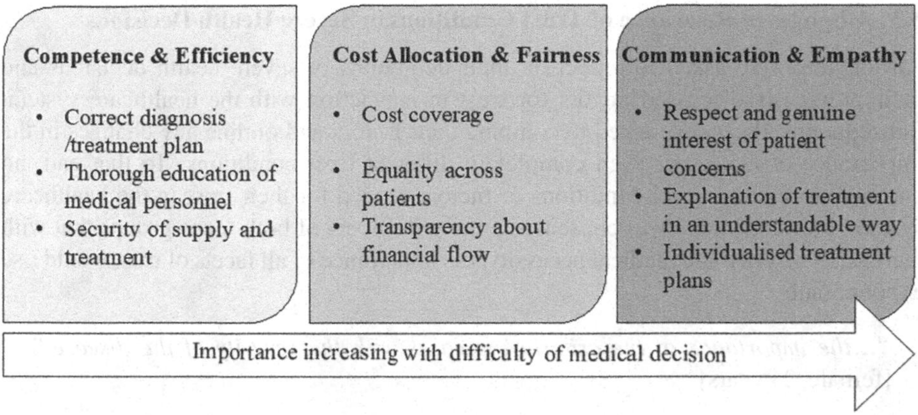

Competence & Efficiency	Cost Allocation & Fairness	Communication & Empathy
• Correct diagnosis /treatment plan • Thorough education of medical personnel • Security of supply and treatment	• Cost coverage • Equality across patients • Transparency about financial flow	• Respect and genuine interest of patient concerns • Explanation of treatment in an understandable way • Individualised treatment plans

Importance increasing with difficulty of medical decision

Fig. 1. Overview of Categories

3.2 Definitions of Severe Health Decisions

The strongest criterion of whether participants judged a medical decision to be severe or not was whether it would alter the course of their life. They agreed that when they had the choice to decide between contradicting treatments whereby one would alter the course of their life irreversibly, such as an amputation or a high-risk surgery to remove cancerous tissue, they would classify it as a severe health decision.

"Exactly, life-changing. An amputation or something. Of course, this builds up to a decision where it's really a matter of life and death. 'Do I do the surgery and live another 5 years or do I not do it and die in 2 weeks?'. So a severe medical decision for me starts when it really affects your life, where it will never be the same again [...]. If from a medical point of view it will be like before, I will be as healthy as before the illness or before the accident, whatever, it is not a difficult decision for me, because then the doctors will do what is right for me, [...] everything will be fine. But as soon as it has an impact on my life, it becomes a difficult decision for me." [male, 24 years].

"I would rather say when it comes to an operation or treatment where the consequences, depending on the outcome, are irreversible." [male, 26 years].

Meanwhile, if they were in a situation where medical help was necessary but the course of treatment would ensure them getting back to "normal", such as a broken leg that needed to be set straight in a cast, they agreed that this decision was hardly severe as there were no consequences that would inevitably change their life. One participant also mentioned that the simple decision of seeking medical help alone would be a severe one, as this meant admitting that they needed help in the first place. This concern however, was not shared by the majority of the group. For the most part, seeking help was not much of an issue but dealing with the consequences of deciding on and undergoing therapy was hard for them.

3.3 Changes in Relevance of Trust Conditions in Severe Health Decisions

Participants were asked to reflect on their definitions of severe health decisions and their previously discussed factors for trust in interaction with the healthcare system. Subsequently, they were asked to combine their factors and outline any changes in the importance of factors or even completely different trust conditions. To that end, no one mentioned any novel conditions or factors needed for their trust in the healthcare system. However, there was consensus among members of both focus groups that with increasing severity and medical necessity, the importance of all facets of trust would rise exponentially.

> *"...the importance of the criteria increases with the severity of the disease."*
> [female, 24 years]

They also argued that this was because they were forced to trust the system in a state of medical emergency as they only had limited resources to help themselves. Collectively, they agreed that if their health situation was not of critical status, they could spend more time evaluating and considering their needs and wants. In turn, this would give them more autonomy on the choice of medical help.

> *"If I had something serious, I think my trust would be greater, because I would want everything to work smoothly. Then my trust would necessarily have to grow because I would then voluntarily or involuntarily place myself in the care of other people and from then on I would no longer have any control over myself."* [male, 26 years]

In both groups, there were two participants each that argued about the relevance of empathy (of the treating physician) in relation to competence (of medical advice). One of them would argue that in a medical emergency, competence would have to take precedence over empathy, and they would renounce it if it added to the condition of competence.

> *"Empathy then is no longer an issue for me. I wouldn't care if he was empathic or not, I would just like to know how I would be treated best."* [female, 26 years]

The other participants would then argue the especially in times of a medical emergency, they would expect all the more empathy from their physician since they would want to be educated, taken seriously, and have their worries considered. To them, that was equally important when compared to the condition of competence.

> *"If I were to get a serious diagnosis and the doctor told me, but I don't have time now, I have to go to lunch, I think I would slap him in the face, that would make my worries even worse, so empathy for me would be just as important."* [female, 24 years]

3.4 Group Differences in Answers

When comparing participants demographic characteristics, the most recognisable difference was that between participants working in the medical field and those not working in the medical field. In both groups, there was one nurse and one health insurance employee, respectively. Overall, they had a bleaker perception of the healthcare system, focusing more on unfair insurance policies (specifically in relation to public and private insurance), inefficient processes, monetary interest over patient interest, and an overworked but under-appreciated system in general.

"I think that the healthcare system is not fundamentally bad, but it is simply far too overloaded, so people are simply broken, whether it's patients, doctors, or nurses. I just think they can't cope anymore and it's too much for everyone." [female, 22 years – nurse]

"It's really shocking to hear that from you [to the nurse], because as an outsider I would say that everything is working quite well so far, because I don't notice anything bad about it." [male, 26 years - engineer]

Participants that did not work in the medical field however, painted more optimistic pictures, e.g., that the German healthcare system is generally satisfactory, the medical treatment is very good, and the basis of it is fair and just towards every member of the community. Another aspect that emerged was that male participants stated that, when asked about what a severe medical decision meant to them, they had more issues with seeking medical help in the first place. Female participants on the other hand, did not share this concern but rather focused on the factual decision making outlined above.

"So for me, because I wouldn't like to go to hospital, I wouldn't like to admit to myself that I have to go there, it's the pride that makes it difficult for the decision. So putting myself in the care of other people to get better, I would say that's a bit of a threshold." [male, 26 years]

"If it's a serious illness, then I'd be more concerned with the "what therapies can you do". I'd find that more stressful than going to hospital or to a doctor at all." [female, 52 years]

4 Discussion

In this section, the findings of the focus group are discussed, starting with the key insights of the study. Afterwards, the strength and weaknesses of the approach are described and implications are derived.

4.1 Key Findings

This study employed a qualitative focus group design with the purpose of defining severe health decisions and establishing relevant trust conditions in such interactions with the healthcare system. In that respect, participants agreed on severe health decisions as life-altering, often irreversible choices of treatment. There were individual differences about the perceptions of when a severe decision begins, ranging from the decision to seek out medical help to actively making a decision to get a particular treatment which were mediated by gender. Moreover, participants working in the medical field had an overall worse impression of the current state of the healthcare system and met the trust conditions with more suspicion that participant that did not work in the medical field. This suggests that (previous) experience with the medical system severely impacts.

Based on the answers and discussions in the focus groups, relevant trust criteria included competence & efficiency, cost allocation & fairness, and communication & empathy. These factors increased in significance when participants imagined having to make a severe decision in the context of the healthcare system. While most participants agreed that all factors remained equally relevant but only increased in necessity, some argued about trading of empathy & communication for competence & efficiency. These findings corroborate previous research on trust conditions in the healthcare system [20, 21]. While some studies may have come to different groupings of dimensions, there are several common conditions, e.g., competence, empathy, communication, and transparency. In essence, these criteria are in line with the theoretical basis of trust with respect to structural and interpersonal trust [19]. What this means is that participants construe their trust heavily around the institutional and situational expectations and their interpersonal contact with medical personnel and most prominently, their treating physician. Connecting this back to the use of assistive technology, it becomes clear that trust is embedded in all of these situations and whether patients trust their healthcare provider, both on a macro- and micro-level, is essential for the integration of any such technology. The results also show that there are individual differences and trade-offs when it comes to the relevance of these factors.

4.2 Strengths and Weaknesses

As with any study, there are several strengths and weaknesses. First of all, the broad identification of relevant trust parameters in healthcare focusing not on specific entities or specific contexts (e.g., pandemic) can be considered helpful. It builds a basis for deepening and elaborating on the trust parameters needed in decision situations in the healthcare system. The results also show changes in the identified trust criteria: it relates and compares criteria within different situations of (severe) health decisions. These things serve as a first step that enables consecutive quantifications and experimental analyses.

However, subsequent (quantitative) studies are necessary to validate the findings while the influence of specific contexts and individual situations could be investigated in more detail. With regard to the sample, it is worth noting that it was relatively balanced with regard to gender and diverse professional backgrounds but still comparatively small and young. Therefore, perceptions of older people (aged 65 years and above) should be considered in future studies as they represent. Lastly, the sample was conducted in Germany on German participants which limits the generalisability of the definition of what the healthcare system constitutes. While some aspects can be interpreted as universal (e.g., communication & empathy), there are grave (inter)national differences in how the healthcare system is conceptualised. Adding to cultural implications, this needs to be taken into account and compared with other healthcare systems in other countries to derive robust results and trust criteria.

4.3 Implications and Conclusion

Although these findings are in line with existing literature on trust in general, they provide new insights into trust-relevant and trust-building factors related to severe health decisions. Moreover, looking at this topic from different perspectives, such as professional experience, has strong implications of the various requirements needed for different groups of people. The qualitative identification of relevant factors for trust in healthcare systems in severe health decisions opens up the possibility of validating the findings in subsequent quantitative studies. Furthermore, these results broaden the understanding of people's requirements for trust in healthcare within severe health decisions, paving the way for investigations of trust-relevant factors of using assisting technology in such severe health situations. In future studies, this interplay of variables should be broadened and other influences, such as health literacy and knowledge and expectations about the working of the medical system, could be taken into account as well. Globally, this study enables the identification of crucial requirements for patients to trust their respective healthcare provider. Moreover and by contributing to a greater understanding of the patients' needs, with the results of this study, recommendations for a more targeted and demand-oriented communication between the various stakeholders in health care systems can be derived.

References

1. OECD/European Observatory on Health Systems and Policies, Germany: Country Health Profile 2019, State of Health in the EU, OECD Publishing, Paris/European Observatory on Health Systems and Policies, Brussels (2019)
2. Bell, R.A., Kravitz, R.L., Thom, D., Krupat, E., Azari, R.: Unmet expectations for care and the patient-physician relationship. J. Gen. Intern. Med. **17**(11), 817–824 (2002)
3. Alexander, J.A., Hearld, L.R., Mittler, J.N., Harvey, J.: Patient–physician role relationships and patient activation among individuals with chronic illness. Health Serv. Res. **47**, 1201–1223 (2012)
4. Anderson, L.A., Zimmerman, M.A.: Patient and physician perceptions of their relationship and patient satisfaction: a study of chronic disease management. Patient Educ. Couns. **20**(1), 27–36 (1993)
5. Farin, E., Gramm, L., Schmidt, E.: The patient–physician relationship in patients with chronic low back pain as a predictor of outcomes after rehabilitation. J. Behav. Med. **36**(3), 246–258 (2013)
6. Copolillo, A., Teitelman, J.L.: Acquisition and integration of low vision assistive devices: understanding the decision-making process of older adults with low vision. Am. J. Occup. Ther. **59**(3), 305–313 (2005)
7. Aminzadeh, F., Edwards, N.: Exploring seniors' views on the use of assistive devices in fall prevention. Public Health Nurs. **15**(4), 297–304 (1998)
8. ZettelWatson, L., Tsukerman, D.: Adoption of online health management tools among healthy older adults: an exploratory study. Health Inform. J. **22**(2), 171–183 (2016)
9. Busemeyer, M.R.: Health care attitudes and institutional trust during the COVID-19 crisis: Evidence from the case of Germany (2021)
10. Birkhäuer, J., et al.: Trust in the health care professional and health outcome: a meta-analysis. PLoS ONE **12**(2), e0170988 (2017)

11. Rockers, P.C., Kruk, M.E., Laugesen, M.J.: Perceptions of the health system and public trust in government in low and middle-income countries: evidence from the world health surveys. J. Health Polit. Policy Law **37**(3), 405–437 (2012)
12. LaVeist, T.A., Isaac, L.A., Williams, K.P.: Mistrust of health care organizations is associated with underutilization of health services. Health Serv. Res. **44**(6), 2093–2105 (2009)
13. Mohseni, M., Lindstrom, M.: Social capital, trust in the health-care system and self-rated health: the role of access to health care in a population-based study. Soc. Sci. Med. **64**(7), 1373–1383 (2007)
14. Street, R.L., Jr., Makoul, G., Arora, N.K., Epstein, R.M.: How does communication heal? Pathways linking clinician–patient communication to health outcomes. Patient Educ. Couns. **74**(3), 295–301 (2009)
15. VanDer Schee, E., Braun, B., Calnan, M., Schnee, M., Groenewegen, P.P.: Public trust in health care: a comparison of Germany, the Netherlands, and England and Wales. Health Policy **81**(1), 56–67 (2007)
16. Stacey, D., Samant, R., Bennett, C.: Decision making in oncology: a review of patient decision aids to support patient participation. Cancer J. Clinic. **58**(5), 293–304 (2008)
17. Broadstock, M., Michie, S.: Processes of patient decision making: theoretical and methodological issues. Psychol. Health **15**(2), 191–204 (2000)
18. Lee, Y.Y., Lin, J.L.: How much does trust really matter? A study of the longitudinal effects of trust and decision-making preferences on diabetic patient outcomes. Patient Educ. Couns. **85**(3), 406–412 (2011)
19. HarrisonMcKnight, D., Chervany, N.L.: Trust and distrust definitions: One bite at a time. In: Falcone, R., Singh, M., Tan, Y.-H. (eds.) Trust in cyber-societies. LNCS (LNAI), vol. 2246, pp. 27–54. Springer, Heidelberg (2001). https://doi.org/10.1007/3-540-45547-7_3
20. Ozawa, S., Sripad, P.: How do you measure trust in the health system? A systematic review of the literature. Soc. Sci. Med. **91**, 10–14 (2013)
21. LoCurto, J., Berg, G.M.: Trust in healthcare settings: scale development, methods, and preliminary determinants. SAGE Open Med. **4**, 1–12 (2016)
22. Mayring, P.: Qualitative Inhaltsanalyse. Grundlagen und Techniken [Qualitative Content Analysis. Basics and Techniques], 12th Edn. Beltz, Weinheim (2015)

Trust in Health Information Among Older Adults in Iceland

Ágústa Pálsdóttir[✉]

School of Social Sciences, Information Science, University of Iceland, Oddi V/Sæmundargötu,
101 Reykjavík, Iceland
agustap@hi.is

Abstract. The aim of the study is to explore trust in health information among Icelanders´ who have reached the age of 56 years and older. In particular, it will examine their perceptions of factors that impact the evaluation of the quality of health information and their experience of false- and misinformation, as well as their media and information literacy in connection to it. The following research questions were asked: (1) What are older adults experience of false information and misinformation in relation to health? (2) How do they perceive their capabilities of critically evaluating and selecting quality health information? The data was gathered in April to June 2022 by a telephone survey and an internet survey from random samples of 214 people aged 56 years and older. Both datasets were merged, allowing answers from all individuals belonging to each set of data. The total response rate was 45%. The main findings are that the participants were rather confident about their ability to detect false- or misinformation about health and were not troubled by it. Information from health professionals was considered most reliable, and health information in social media the least. Nevertheless, it seems that during COVID-19 older adults have become more skeptical of health professionals. Furthermore, the findings indicate that the participants are more familiar with printed sources and that they find it easier to critically judge the quality of information in it rather than in digital sources. Thus, health information sources that they are more accustomed to use still seem to hold a higher value for them than digital sources.

Keywords: False information · Misinformation · Older adults · Trust in health information

1 Introduction

The study investigates older Icelanders´ trust in health information. In particular, it will examine older adult´s perceptions of factors that impact the evaluation of the quality of health information and their experience of false- or misinformation, as well as their media and information literacy in connection to it. False information is defined as information which is deliberately published or presented for the purpose of deception, while misinformation is not put forward with the intention to deceive the receiver although it is not in accordance with what the scientific world considers correct [1–3].

© The Author(s), under exclusive license to Springer Nature Switzerland AG 2023
Q. Gao and J. Zhou (Eds.): HCII 2023, LNCS 14043, pp. 173–185, 2023.
https://doi.org/10.1007/978-3-031-34917-1_13

The COVID-19 pandemic has drawn attention to the significance of quality health information and the serious harm that can be caused by the spread of false- or misinformation. Access to trustworthy health information, and the ability to select and use it, is of great value for people's health and wellbeing. The importance of making the right behavioral choices for maintaining health has been described as a joint responsibility of individuals and society [4, 5]. The society has an obligation to provide people with the means to obtain quality health information and individuals need to respond by taking advantage of it.

UNESCO and IFLA have put forward a joint definition of media and information literacy, recognizing it as a crucial factor for lifelong learning. Being media and information literate allows individuals ability to "…know when and what information is needed; where and how to obtain that information; how to evaluate it critically and organise it once it is found; and how to use it in an ethical way" [6]. At the core of it, and a prerequisite for people to be able to benefit from health information, is critical thinking and the capacity to use it to evaluate information quality. Furthermore, more research into how people evaluate digital health information is being called for [7].

Information and communication technology has rapidly transformed the possibilities to produce, disseminate, and access information, a progress that can be expected to continue in the coming years. Although older adults´ lag behind those who are younger there has been a substantial growth in their use of digital sources. This includes the use of the internet, as well as mobile technology such as smartphones and tablet computers [8–11], and the same goes for the use of social media [12]. Along with advances in digital technology and the growing amount of digital health information, new possibilities have been brought for people to manage their own health, practice better self-care, and improve their health behaviour [13]. For this to happen it is necessary that older people find the technology easy to use [14, 15], have confidence in the information sources and believe that they can trust the information found in them.

There are indications that health information on the internet is regarded as less reliable than information from other sources or channels [16–20] and that older adults prefer to rely on health professionals to guide them to reliable information [21]. Nevertheless, there are signs that trust in health scientists has decreased since the outbreak of COVID-19 [22]. In addition, it has been noted that older adults can find the amount of online health information to be confusing and difficult to choose from [23], and that it, together with lack of awareness about the sources providing the information, could explain their mistrust in online health information [24]. However, there are also indications that the perceived importance of online health information has been growing, particularly in countries that had high Internet usage [18, 25].

In particular, it has been warned that false- and misinformation is being spread widely on social media [26, 27]. A report from Iceland shows that the general public has very limited trust in social media as a sources of information about COVID-19 – [28]. Analysis of user profile characteristics revealed that those with the lowest and highest levels of user and membership levels were the most responsible for publishing misinformation [29]. Furthermore, it has been reported that although older adults were more confident than those who are younger that they can identify media sources that do original reporting they, nevertheless, were more uncertain when it came to distinguishing the origin of media news than younger people [30, 31].

People can obtain a wealth of health information in various forms and through different information channels, whether it is online or offline. However, this has also created a challenge, as to knowing what information is reliable, how to interpret it, and realizing how it can be used for maintaining health. The increase in false- and misinformation about health has been described as a complex issue that may create serious health risk. False- and misinformation is, however, not a novelty. For example, discussions about the possible side effects and even harmful effects of vaccines, with false- and misinformation being widely used, has regularly appeared over the years [32–35], and during the first years of the HIV epidemic false- and misinformation were spread which caused seriously harmful effects on people's lives [27]. It has been reported that people believe that false- or misleading information about COVID-19 have exacerbated problems in relation to the epidemic [36]. International organizations have warned that false- and misinformation, recently termed as "Infodemic", can cause serious harm during an international epidemic such as COVID-19 [37]. Furthermore, an identification of ways to counteract the situation has emphasized the importance of supporting people's media and information literacy [38].

In an ever more complex information landscape, the resources required to assess the contents and functions of health information have become increasingly more important. How people are able to handle the amount of health information by filtering accurate facts and come autonomously to their own conclusions is of great significance. Thus, there is an important societal demand in terms of empovering the people to think critically when they form an opinion on what health information is reliable, if it has been produced in a meaningful manner, and how health information can be utilized. This, however, cannot be achieved without knowledge about how people are able to evaluate the trustworthiness of health information. Leveraging media and information literacy skills could be of great value to help mitigate the harmful effects of false- or misinformation. Yet, studies assessing media and information literacy and trust in health information among older adults are scarce internationally [39], and in Iceland there is a great need to build up more knowledge about the topic.

Aim and Research Questions. The aim of the study is to explore trust in health information among older Iceland. The start of a retirement age is sometimes used to define "elderly" in Western countries [40]. Retirement age varies, however, between countries, it starts for example at 58 years in Lithuania, while in Iceland people can retire at the age of 65 [41, 42]. Thus, defining older age by retirement age is rather arbitrary. Considering that there is no clearly defined age when people become older adults it was decided to examine people who have reached the age of 56 years and older. In particular, it will examine their perceptions of factors that impact the evaluation of the quality of health information and their experience of false- and misinformation, as well as their media and information literacy in connection to it. The following research questions were asked: (1) What are older adults experience of false information and misinformation in relation to health? (2) How do they perceive their capabilities of critically evaluating and selecting quality health information? The project has both theoretical and applied value. It will address a gap in the existing literature both internationally and in Iceland and produce more knowledge on the matter. In addition, a better understanding of the factors that relate to older adults' media- and information literacy can have implications for health promotional activities and may be used to improve the outcome of health education.

2 Methods

2.1 Data Collection

Because the intention is to be able to generalize the results of the study to people aged 18 years and older in Iceland, a survey method was chosen. Data were gathered in from April to July 2022 from two samples using an internet and a telephone survey. The total sample for the survey consisted of 1.200 hundred people, 18 years and older. For the telephone survey, a sample of 300 people aged 60 years and older from the whole country, randomly selected from the National Register of Persons in Iceland, was used. For the internet survey a random sample of 900 people at the age of 18 to 59 years, from the Social Science Research Institute at the University of Iceland net panel, was used. The net panel is based on a random sample from the National Register of Persons in Iceland and consists of people aged 18 years or older from the whole country who has agreed to participate in online surveys organized by the organization. Both datasets were merged, allowing answers from all individuals belonging to each set of data. The total response rate was 45%.

Because of the response rate in the study, the data were weighted by gender (male, female), age in six categories, residence (within or outside the capital area) and education (primary, secondary, university) of participants so that they so that it corresponds with the distribution in the population. Reference figures for age, gender and place of residence were obtained from the National Registry of Iceland and for level of education from Statistics Iceland.

The current paper, however, focuses on a total of 214 participants who have reached the age of 56 years and older.

2.2 Measurements and Data Analysis

The measurements consisted of two sets of questions that are presented in Tables 1 and 2. Four questions examined the experience of false- and misinformation about health issues (e.g. about COVID-19 or any other health-related issue), see Table 1.

Six questions explored the participants beliefs about their ability to select reliable health information that they can trust, see Table 2.

The analysis of the data is descriptive. All analysis is based on weighed data.

Table 1. Experience of false information or misinformation

Questions	Response scale
How concerned are you about receiving false information or misinformation?	Five-point scale: very concerned – very small concern
How easy or difficult do you find it to recognize false information or misinformation?	Five-point scale: very difficult – very easy
Have you come across false information or misinformation about health (e.g. about Covid 19 or any other issue related to health)?	Two-point scale: yes – no
How often or selvdom have you come across false information or misinformation about health in the following places? A total of eight places were listed (see Fig. 2)	Five-point scale: very often – very selvdom

Table 2. Beliefs in ability to select reliable health information.

Questions	Responce scale
It is easy to select quality information that I can trust	Five-point scale: strongly disagree – strongly agree
If information is from sources whose background I do not know, it is difficult to know if it is reliable	Five-point scale: strongly disagree – strongly agree
It is easy to recognize reliable information on the Internet	Five-point scale: strongly disagree – strongly agree
The amount of nformation on the Internet makes it difficult to decide what is reliable	Five-point scale: strongly disagree – strongly agree
I always trust information from health professionals	Five-point scale: strongly disagree – strongly agree
Health experts don't always agree on what is best so I don't know what information I can trust	Five-point scale: strongly disagree – strongly agree

3   Results

The chapter starts by introducing results about the participants experience of false- and misinformation. After that, results about their perception of the ability to judge the quality of health information is presented.

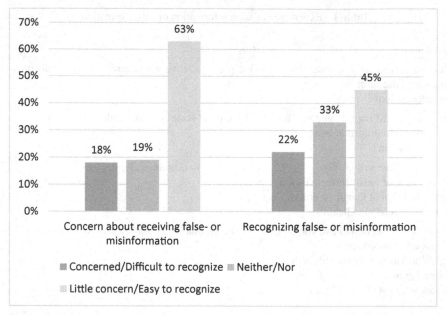

Fig. 1. Concern about false- or misinformation and ability to recognizing it

As can be seen in Fig. 1, the participants claimed not to be particularly worried about false- or misinformation. A total of 63% replied that they did not have concerns about receiving it. In addition, they had, in general, belief in their own information literacy, as 45% of them considered it either very or rather easy to recognise false- or misinformation while 22% found it difficult.

When asked if they had ever come across false- or misinformation the majority, or 69%, replied that they had not come across it, while 31% claimed that they had. However, when they were asked how often or selvdom they had come across the information in eight different sources, the results indicate that this is more common than so (see Fig. 2).

Figure 2 shows that social media was considered by far to be the most likely place for false- or misinformation. A total of 60% claimed that they had come across it very or rather often in social media and in addition to this 33% replied sometimes. After that come websites from others than health authorities, with 37% claiming to have come across it very or rather often and a further 37% sometimes. In addition, close to half of the respondents had sometimes come across this type of information in the media (47%), through conversations with relatives, friends or acquaintances (45%) or others (44%). The least likely sources for false- or misinformation were brochures and websites from the health system with 78% and 62%, rescpectively, claiming that they had never come across it there.

Resuts about the participants perception of their ability to judge the quality of health information is presented in Figs. 3, 4 and 5.

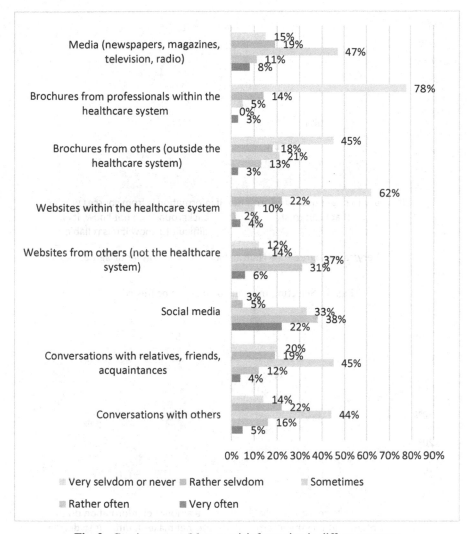

Fig. 2. Coming across false- or misinformation in different sources

As can be seen in Fig. 3. More than half of the participants consider it easy to select information that are trustworthy. Furthermore, the great majority of them is of the opinion that judging the reliability of information that come from unknown sources is difficult.

The results in Fig. 4. Show that there is a tendency to view the Internet as a rather dubious source of information. The percentage of those who disagree that it is easy to realize whether information on the Internet is reliable is only slightly higher than those who agree. However, when this is put into context with the amount of information that can be found on the internet more than half of the participants agree that it is difficult to decide what information is reliable.

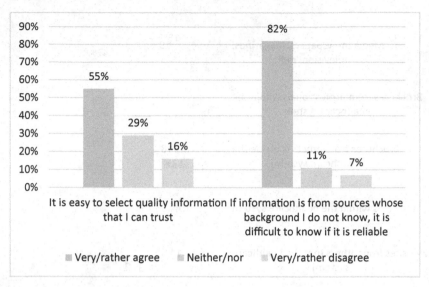

Fig. 3. Selecting information that can be trusted

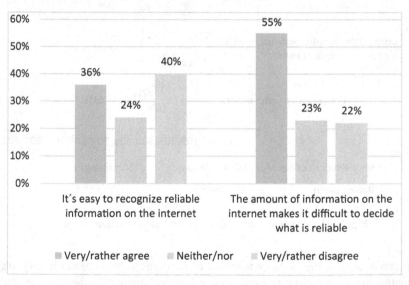

Fig. 4. Recognizing reliable information on the internet

As can be seen in Fig. 5., the participants expressed a lot of confidence in information from health professionals. The great majority claimed that they always trust information from them. However, when asked more specifically, almost half of them agreed that they did not know what information could be trusted if health specialists themselves do not agree on what is best for health protection.

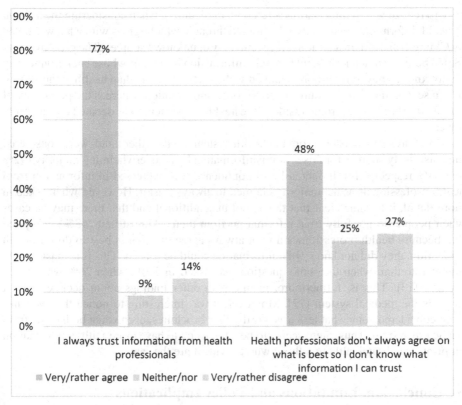

Fig. 5. Trust in information from health professionals

4   Discussion

Trust plays a central role in health information behaviour and can influence it in many ways. It can for example have impact on people's health information seeking, the sharing of it, as well as the acceptance of health information. The current study investigated factors that can connect to the evaluation of health information among people in Iceland who are 56 years and older in relation to their media and information literacy.

The study shows that the participants were not particularly concerned about false- or misinformation about health. Furthermore, they had in general belief in their own ability to recognise it, as well as being able to select quality health information. When asked where they had come across false- or misinformation, social media stood out as the most likely source and they expressed great mistrust towards health information found there. This corresponds with previous reports [26–28], as well as warnings that the features of social media mean that false- and misinformation is being spread faster and further than with other sources [29, 38]. Thus, it seems that the participants showed caution in relation to social media. Mistrust of information on social media can also be viewed in relation to attitudes towards health information in other internet sources. The participants were rather inclined to consider the internet as a suspicious source and believed that it is not easy to realize which information is reliable. Particularly, when considering the amount of health information that needs to be filtered through, which agrees with what was noted by Chung et al. [23]. In addition, they were wary of unknown sources. The great majority (82%) believed that it is difficult to assess information in sources whose background they do not know. They, furthermore, claimed websites from others than health authorities to be the second most likely source of false- or misinformation, whereas the possibility of finding it in brouchures from outside of the healthcare systems was deemed considerably lower.

Brochures and websites from the health system, on the other hand, were considered the least likely sources for false- or misinformation by an overwhelming majority (92% and 84% respectively). In fact, a lot of confidence was expressed in information from health professionals as the majority claimed to always trust it. However, when asked in more detail, it became clear that this is not unconditional and that there may be cases when people do not fully trust information from them. Almost half (48%) of replied that because health professionals do not always agree on what is best to do for health protection, they did not know what information could be trusted. This is a considerably higher rate than when the same question was asked in 2019, when 26% was of this opinion [13]. This is, furthermore, in line with other findings about decline in trust towards the medical system [22]. Moreover, it was interesting to notice that websites were considered somewhat less trustworthy than brochures, even when both came from the health system. Thus, there seems to be a tendency to have more faith in information on print than digital, although those who provide it are the same.

5   Conclusion, Limitations and Policy Implications

The study explore older adults´ trust in health information by examining their experience of false- and misinformation, as well as their perceptions of factors that impact the evaluation of the quality of health information. Answers were sought to two research questions. The first one asked about older adults experience of false information and misinformation in relation to health. The findings showed that the participants were not troubled by false- or misinformation about health and they seemed to be rather confident about their ability to detect it. Social media was considered to be most likely to spread false- or misinformation while health professionals were believed to be least likely to do so. The second question asked how they perceived their capabilities of critically evaluating and selecting quality health information? The findings indicate that the participants had faith in their ability to select quality health information. Although information from health professionals were regarded as trustworthy it nevertheless seems that during COVID-19 older adults have become more skeptical of health professionals, as trust in information from them has declined since 2019. Furthermore, the findings indicate that the partipants are more familiar with printed sources and that they find it easier to critically judge the quality of information in it rather than in digital sources. Thus, health information sources that they are more accustomed to use still seem to hold a higher value for them than digital sources.

The overall study is limited by a total response rate of 45%. Although his may be considered satisfactory in a survey it raises the question whether or not those who answered the survey are giving a biased picture of those who did not respond. To compensate for this bias, the data were weighed by sex, age, place of residence and education, so that it corresponds with the distribution in the population. Thus, the findings may provide valuable information.

There is an important societal demand in terms of empovering the general public to think critically when they form an opinion about the quality of health information. Without knowledge about how people evaluate the trustworthiness of health information this cannot be achieved. The policy implications of the study findings are that health authorities and professionals together need to find ways to enhance older adults' capacity to evaluate health information sources in different forms and sources.

Acknowledgments. The research project was supported by the University of Iceland Research Fund.

References

1. Ratzan, S.C, Sommariva, S., Rauh, L.: Enhancing global health communication during a crisis: lessons from the COVID-19 pandemic. Public Health Res. Pract. **30**(2), e3022010 (2020). https://doi.org/10.17061/phrp3022010
2. Vosoughi, S., Roy, D., Aral, S.: The spread of true and false news online. Science **359**(6380), 1146–1151 (2018). https://doi.org/10.1126/science.aap9559
3. Swire-Thompson, B., Lazer, D.: Public health and online misinformation: challenges and recommendations. Annu. Rev. Public Health **41**(1), 433–451 (2020)
4. Resnik, D.B.: Responsibility for health: personal, social, and environmental. J. Med. Health Ethics **33**(8), 444–445 (2007)
5. Wikler, D.: Personal and social responsibility for health. Ethics Int. Aff. **16**(2), 47–55 (2002)
6. IFLA (International Federation of Library Associations and Institutions): IFLA media and information literacy recommendations (2014).https://www.ifla.org/publications/ifla-media-and-information-literacy-recommendations
7. Diviani, N., Putte, B., Giani, S., Weert, J.: Low health literacy and evaluation of online health information: a systematic review of the literature. J. Med. Internet Res. **7**(5), e112 (2015)
8. Anderson, M., Perrin, A.: Tech adoption climbs among older adults: roughly two-thirds of those ages 65 and older go online and a record share now own smartphones: although many seniors remain relatively divorced from digital lifel. Pew Research Centre (2017). https://www.pewinternet.org/2017/05/17/tech-adoption-climbs-among-older-adults/
9. Statistics Iceland: Computer and internet usage in Iceland and other European countries 2013. Stat. Ser.: Tourism Transp. IT **99**(1) (2014). https://hagstofa.is/lisalib/getfile.aspx?ItemID=14251
10. Ivan, L., Loos, E.F., Bird, I: The impact of technology generations on older adults' media use: review of previous empirical research and a seven country comparison. Gerontechnology **19**(4) (2020)
11. Loos, E., Ivan, L.: Not only people are getting old, new media are too: Technology generations and the changes in new media use. New Media Soc. (2022)
12. Faverio, M.: Share of those 65 and older who are tech users has grown in the past decade (2022). https://www.pewresearch.org/fact-tank/2022/01/13/share-of-those-65-and-older-who-are-tech-users-has-grown-in-the-past-decade/

13. Pálsdóttir, Á.: The adoption of new health information and communication technology: perception of the abilities to use new technology and possibilities to get help at it. In: Well-Being in the Information Society. Fruits of Respect, WIS 2020. Communications in Computer and Information Science, vol. 1270, pp.226–237. Springer, Cham (2020).https://doi.org/10.1007/978-3-030-57847-3_16

14. Mendiola, M.F., Kalnicki, M., Lindenauer, S.: Valuable features in mobile health apps for patients and consumers: content analysis of apps and user ratings. JMIR Mhealth Uhealth 3(2), e40 (2015). https://www.ncbi.nlm.nih.gov/pmc/articles/PMC4446515/

15. Tsai, H.S., Taiwan, H., Shillair, R., Cotton, S.R., Winstead, V., Yost, E.: Getting grandma online: are tablets the answer for increasing digital inclusion for older adults in the U.S.? Educ. Gerontol. 41, 695–709 (2015)

16. Hesse, B.W., et al.: Trust and sources of health information the impact of the internet and its implications for health care providers: findings from the first health information national trends survey. JAMA Intern. Med. 165(22), 2618–2624 (2005)

17. Eriksson-Backa, K.: Finnish 'silfer surfers' and online health information. In: Eriksson-Backa, K., Luoma, A., Krook, E. (eds.) Exploring the Abyss of Inequalities, WIS 2012. Communications in Computer and Information Science, vol. 313, pp. 138–149. Springer, Heidelberg (2012). https://doi.org/10.1007/978-3-642-32850-3_13

18. Pálsdóttir, Á.: Icelanders´ and trust in the internet as a source of health and lifestyle information. Inf. Res. 16(1), paper 470 (2011). http://InformationR.net/ir/16-1/paper470.html

19. Soederberg Miller, L.M., Bell, R.A.: Online health information seeking: the influence of age, information trustworthiness, and search challenges. J. Aging Health 24(3), 525–541 (2012)

20. Pálsdóttir, Á.: Senior citizens, media and information literacy and health information. In: Kurbanoğlu, S., Boustany, J., Špiranec, S., Grassian, E., Mizrachi, D., Roy, L. (eds.) ECIL 2015. CCIS, vol. 552, pp. 233–240. Springer, Cham (2015). https://doi.org/10.1007/978-3-319-28197-1_24

21. Lee, K., Hoti, K., Hughes, J.D., Emmerton, L.: Dr Google is here to stay but health care professionals are still valued: an analysis of health care consumers' internet navigation support preferences. J. Med. Internet Res. 9(6), e210 (2017). https://doi.org/10.2196/jmir.7489

22. Kennedy, B., Tyson, A., Funk, C.: Americans' trust in scientists, other groups declines. Pew Research Centre (2022). https://www.pewresearch.org/science/2022/02/15/americans-trust-in-scientists-other-groups-declines/

23. Chung, J., Gassert, C.A., Kim, H.S.: Online health information use by participants in selected senior centres in Korea: current status of internet access and health information use by Korean older adults. Int. J. Older People Nurs. 6(4), 261–271 (2011)

24. Zulman, D.M., Kirch, M., Zheng, K., An, L.C.: Trust in the internet as a health resource among older adults: analysis of data from a nationally representative survey. J. Med. Internet Res. 13(1), e19 (2011). https://www.ncbi.nlm.nih.gov/pmc/articles/PMC3221340/

25. Kummervold, P.E., et al.: eHealth trends in Europe 2005–2007: a population-based survey. J. Med. Internet Res. 10(4), e42 (2008). http://www.ncbi.nlm.nih.gov/pmc/issues/175768/

26. Kouzy, R., et al.: Coronavirus goes viral: quantifying the COVID-19 misinformation epidemic on Twitter. Cureus 12(3), e7255 (2020). https://doi.org/10.7759/cureus.7255

27. Mian, A., Khan, S.: Coronavirus: the spread of misinformation. BMC Med 18, 89 (2020). https://doi.org/10.1186/s12916-020-01556-3

28. Stjórnarráð Ísland, þjóðaröryggisráð: Skýrsla vinnuhóps þjóðaröryggisráðs um upplýsingaóreiðu og COVID-19 (2020). https://www.stjornarradid.is/library/01--Frettatengt---myndir-og-skrar/FOR/Fylgiskjol-i-frett/Skyrsla_uppl.oreidacovid19_25.10.20.pdf

29. Zhao, Y., et al.: Understanding how and by whom COVID-19 misinformation is spread on social media: coding and network analyses. J. Med. Internet Res. 24(6), e37623 (2022). https://doi.org/10.2196/37623

30. Worden, K., Barthel, M.: Many Americans are unsure whether sources of news do their own reporting (2002). https://www.pewresearch.org/fact-tank/2020/12/08/many-americans-are-unsure-whether-sources-of-news-do-their-own-reporting/
31. Loos, E., Nijenhuis, J.: Consuming fake news: a matter of age? the perception of political fake news stories in Facebook ads. In: Gao, Q., Zhou, J. (eds.) Human Aspects of IT for the Aged Population. Technology and Society, HCII 2020, vol. 12209, pp. 69–88. Springer, Cham (2020). https://doi.org/10.1007/978-3-030-50232-4_6
32. Dube, E., Vivion, M., Macdonald, N.: Vaccine hesitancy, vaccine refusal and the antivaccine movement: influence, impact and implications. Expert Rev. Vaccines **14**(1), 99–117 (2015)
33. King, S.: Vaccination policies: individual rights v community health. BMJ **319**(7223), 1448–1449 (1999)
34. Omer, S.B., Richards, J.L., Ward, M., Bednarczyk, R.A.: Vaccination policies and rates of exemption from immunization. N. Engl. J. Med. **367**(12), 1170–1171 (2012)
35. Wakefield, A.J., et al.: Ileal lymphoid nodular hyperplasia, non-specific colitis, and pervasive developmental disorder in children. Lancet **351**, 637–641 (1998)
36. Funk, C., Tyson, A.: Lack of preparedness among top reactions Americans have to public health officials' COVID-19 response. Pew Research Centre (2022).https://www.pewresearch.org/science/2022/10/05/lack-of-preparedness-among-top-reactions-americans-have-to-public-health-officials-covid-19-response/
37. Dramé, D: The health crisis: fertile ground for disinformation. UNESCO Courier **3**, 24–26 (2020). https://en.unesco.org/courier/2020-3/health-crisis-fertile-ground-disinformation
38. WHO: Fighting misinformation in the time of CoVID-19, one click at the time (2020). https://www.who.int/news-room/feature-stories/detail/fighting-misinformation-in-the-time-of-covid-19-one-click-at-a-time
39. Griebel, L., Enwald, H., Gilstad, H., Pohl, A.-L., Moreland, J., Sedlmayr, M.: eHealth literacy research—quo vadis? Inform. Health Soc. Care **43**(4), 427–442 (2018)
40. Thane, P.: History and the sociology of ageing. Soc. Hist. Med. **2**(1), 93–96 (1989)
41. Social Insurance Administration: 65 years+. https://www.tr.is/en/65-years
42. OECD: OECD pensions at a glance 2021: OECD and G20 indicators. OECD Publishing, Paris (2021). https://doi.org/10.1787/ca401ebd-en

Tamamon: Designing a Gamified Medication Education Solution for Older Adults Patients

Tan Phat Pham[1(✉)], Yin-Leng Theng[1], Keng Teng Tan[2], Jie Chong Lim[2],
Su Qi Hong[1], Nur Atiqah Binte Mohamad[1], and Tng Shu Ting Valerie[1]

[1] Ageing Research Institute for Society and Education (ARISE), Nanyang Technological
University, Singapore, Singapore
{tppham,tyltheng,arise-sqhong,arise-nuratiqah,
arise-vsttng}@ntu.edu.sg
[2] Tan Tock Seng Hospital, Singapore, Singapore
{keng_teng_tan,jie_chong_lim}@ttsh.com.sg

Abstract. In this paper, we present the preliminary results of a pilot study with
older adult patients in the design and conceptualisation of a gamified medication
education. The study aimed to assess patients' level of understanding of their
health conditions, prescribed medications and gather their feedback for the game
design named '*Tamamon*'. Interviews were conducted with 10 older adult patients
aged between 53– 76 (M = 64.3, SD = 6.77). A range of proposed Tamamon game
concepts and mini games were used to elicit ideas. They allowed participants to
contribute their feedback and comments so that the research team could gain a
deeper understanding of older adult patients' desire to play. We gathered older
adults' feedback/comments on the proposed game mock-up, and their preferences
on the look-and-feel, game mechanism. Preliminary findings show older adults'
interests in gamified solutions for medication education. The paper concludes
with a discussion on recommendations to revise the game mock-up before further
development.

Keywords: gamification · medication education · medication adherence ·
mobile game

1 Introduction

The term "medication adherence" refers to patients consuming their prescribed medication at the proper time and in accurate dosages. According to the World Health Organization (WHO) [1], poor medication adherence among patients is a costly problem
in many countries. Non-adherence to medications can lead to readmissions and higher
use of healthcare resources. Patients in the recovery phase have been reported to feel
vulnerable and have the lack of motivation which leads to medication non-adherence
slowing the recovery process [2]. Even within developed countries, the WHO reported
that medication adherence among chronically ill patients averages only 50% with even
lower rates in developing countries [1]. Lack of medication adherence remains the primary cause of unnecessary disease progression, complications, reduced ability, lower
quality of life, and even avoidable mortality [3].

Reasons for non-adherence to medication may arise from lack of sufficient education about their medical conditions and medications, fears about potential and actual side effects of medications and polypharmacy. More education should be given to patients to address underlying reasons for potential non-adherence to medications, but healthcare workers are limited by manpower constraints and high workload. Medication counselling is often only given to patients on the day of discharge, which often leads to cognitive overload and insufficient information may be given to patients on what they can do if they experience problems with their medications.

In our Patient Alert Care Education (PACE) framework [4], we addressed medication adherence for patients with chronic conditions (tuberculosis) and provided theoretical underpinnings for the practice of holistic patient care in healthcare settings [4, 5]. PACE focuses on 3 areas (i) personalised communication support; (ii) patient generated media; and (iii) education [6].

In this study, we leveraged on the PACE framework in designing a gamified solution for medication education in older adult patients. Our solution was to provide a gamified educational platform that allowed patients to learn more about their medications during their hospital stay at their own time. This might in turn improve awareness of health conditions and medications.

2 Literature Review

2.1 Gamification

Gamification is defined as the application of typical elements of game playing (e.g., point scoring, competition with others, rules of play) to other areas of activity, typically as an online marketing technique to encourage engagement. According to a study done by Singapore General Hospital (SGH), it was found that 60% of older people surveyed did not take their medications as prescribed by their doctors, which is higher than the average 50% in international studies [7]. With the growth in elderly population in Singapore, the prevalence and predictor of medication non-adherence among older adult with at least one age-related chronic disease has been investigated [8], which is why non-medication adherence is a pertinent problem that contributes to the health issues of elderly. In this review, we examined the effectiveness of using gamification to improve medication adherence and the factors in improving the adherence to the games itself, which thereafter improved the adherence to mediation and information provided by the gameplay.

2.2 Adherence Motivation

One common theme seen across all studies is the importance of keeping motivation and enjoyment in games for older adults to adhere, therefore improving their medication adherence. Boot et al. (2016) agree that when designing digital game-based interventions, these games should not only be fun and enjoyable, but also allow for learning and furthering of the user's abilities [9]. Intrinsic motivation is an important factor in influencing people's learning performance and technology anxiety [10]. With increased motivations to continue utilising the games, there is retention thus habits and adherence towards the game. One of the most important functions of gamification is to offer older adults the experience of playing game, while subconsciously absorbing the learning points. In games, players' intrinsic motivation, such as doing an activity for its inherent satisfaction and pleasure rather than for some separable consequences, plays an important role in explaining players' engagement [10]. It is crucial for games to be challenging yet enjoyable for users to be both motivated yet learning when playing the games.

2.3 Effectiveness of Gamification Towards Medication Adherence

A study conducted by the National University of Singapore found that gamification is effective in increasing users' attention when engaging in mobile health applications and encouraging both healthy and unhealthy people to maintain their health status [11]. A review done by Pérez-Jover et al. in [12] also showed the rate of missed medications was lowered by 28% among app users who completed at least three "7 Day Challenges". This finding demonstrated a potential of such mobile solutions to improve medication adherence in the early postoperative period when patients may be at highest risk for medication non-adherence. A study done by Lurchenko in [13] has found a direct correlation between missed doses and level achieved in the game system. Overall, it shows a positive influence of the game element of the proposed solution to the medication adherence of the transplant patients.

Multiple sources have agreed that social interaction element in games allow the enhancement of well-being in older adults. Age-related visual decline, manual dexterity and usability issues of interface designs need to be considered carefully at the consideration for the older adults [14]. Studies have also found that social companions in gaming can keep users motivated in habitually utilising the games. With the addition of social interaction aspect, motivation in using the games by the users will increase. Not only that, research from Badawy in [15] also agrees that habit strength is strongly correlated with medication adherence, with stronger habit being associated with higher medication adherence rates. By collaborating habit to gamification, games can be designed for players to develop a habit in regularly playing the games, such as storylines and daily quest and rewards. With such formed habits, players are more familiar with the medication information taught in the game and thus increase the rate of medication adherence.

Though there are limited studies on the improvement of medication adherence through gamification, there may be a positive correlation that needs to be furthered observed and studied on how the habitual use of gamification is able to improve the rate of medication adherence. With the rising trends of older adults' non-adherence to medication in Singapore, it is crucial for interventions to not only be functional but also meaningful to ensure long-term application of gamification as well as overall improvement in medication adherence and quality of life.

3   Tamamon Application

Tamamon is a Tamagotchi-like mobile gamified solution designed to teach older adult patients about medical conditions, ways they can understand their medications, side effects, and tips on how to stay healthy.

Taking into consideration patients' gender and language barriers, the application includes a gender-specific (Male or Female) layout and a function to toggle between languages (English or Chinese). Notably, there will be no differences in content and customizations.

Players have a collection of Tamamon eggs (Egg Dex). The objective of the game is to take care of the Tamamon eggs, hatch them and evolve them. At the start, players will require to play mini games to fill up their hatching bar so that the Tamamon will hatch. Once hatched, players may continue playing mini games to fill up their Tamamon EXP (experience) bar to evolve them. Tamamon and their subsequent evolutions are diverse, and each represents a drug class for the treatment of diabetes and hypertension. Information related to the medication will be regularly displayed throughout the gameplay. Figures 1, 2, and 3 show examples of mock-ups of the Tamamon application.

To aid in knowledge transfer from the gameplay to real life, various authentic aspects of a patient's life were integrated into the gameplay. As an example, the application features a collection of mini games as shown in Fig. 4. These mini-games were designed to be educational, representative, and fun. In the case of "Puzzle Sliding" (mini game), the game aimed to provide tips on maintaining a normal blood glucose level. With the previously mentioned elements in mind, the game related to the patient by showcasing commonly eaten food and making the tips salient and easy to understand.

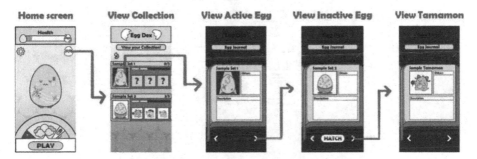

Fig. 1. Tamamon Gameplay Workflow.

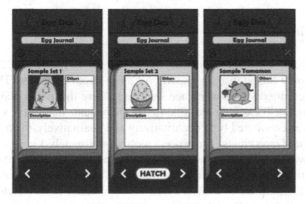

Fig. 2. Tamamon Index.

Fig. 3. Example of Mini Games.

Fig. 4. Collection of Mini Games.

4 Methodology

Older adult patients were recruited from Integrated Care Hub (ICH), Tan Tock Seng Hospital, a national hospital in Singapore, for an in-depth interview. The patient participants were recruited via convenience sampling where the team obtained assistance pharmacist from Tan Tock Seng Hospital to engage patients that fit the study criteria.

The study was conducted both quantitatively and qualitatively, via an online survey and semi-structured interviews. The process took approximately 1 h. Both online survey and interview were anonymous, and pseudonyms were used during the interview to protect the identity of the participants. The interview was audio recorded and recording transcribed for the purpose of analysis. The following data was collected: i) Patients' Belief about Medication (BMQ); ii) How patients manage medication; iii) Patients' health, and health progression; and iv) How patients look for information. The interview also consisted of open-ended questions that were crafted specially to draw out a wide range of responses about participants' management and understanding of their medical conditions and general attitude towards gamification of medicine education were asked. Table 1 lists the questions used in the interview. Paper mock-ups of the Tamamon concept and minigames were presented to the participants to aid in the visualization of the application.

Table 1. Questions used for interview.

Section	Questions
How they manage their medications and understanding about their medical conditions	**Q1.** Do you know what medical conditions you have? If patient is unsure, prompt them about high blood pressure and/or diabetes a. Do you know what you need to do to control these conditions? b. Do you know what will happen if these conditions are not well controlled? If unsure, prompt about heart attack, stroke, kidney damage, eye damage, poor healing wounds c. Would knowing these complications motivate you to have better control of your conditions?
How they look for information	**Q2.** Where do you usually find answers to your health-related questions? a. For example, if you feel unwell after taking a particular medication, what would you do? E.g., giddiness with blood pressure medication
Acceptability of a mobile game to educate the participants on their medications and medical conditions	**Q3.** Do you usually play games online or on your mobile devices? What kind of games do you play? a. Do you think adults can learn from games like how children can learn from the games that they play?
	Q4. What other things do you usually use your mobile phone to do? or what are the apps that you usually use? E.g., WhatsApp, online shopping, watch YouTube, internet banking
Perception and feedback on a mock-up version of the mobile game to be designed	**Q5.** If you were given a game that looks like this (referring to the mock up), would you be interested to play this game? a. Why are you interested or not interested? b. If not interested, what would interest you to try?

Note. Feedback includes how the participant will interact with the mobile game, ease of use and improvements required in the design.

The interviews were individually conducted in person. User information was anonymised and pseudonyms were used to protect the identity of the participants. The interview was audio recorded and recording transcribed for the purpose of analysis. The responses were extracted from the interviews, then coded and analysed using thematic analysis to get insights into patients' existing level of understanding of his/her health conditions and medications prescribed during ICH inpatient stay, on discharge, and post-discharge (i.e. pre- and post- interventions) as well as their attitudes towards the application.

A paper mock-up version of the mobile application was used. Participants were shown screenshots of the game to aid in their feedback on the interface design. For example, the factors that would interest participants to download the game to play. The paper mock-up version (see above) includes the gameplay (see Fig. 1), Tamamon Collection (see Fig. 2), and Mini Games (see Fig. 3).

5 Results and Findings

We recruited 10 older adult patients aged between 53–76 from Integrated Care Hub (ICH), Tan Tock Seng Hospital, a national hospital in Singapore, for an in-depth interview (5 males and 5 females) (M = 64.3, SD = 6.77). The participants were labelled as M1 to M5 for male participants, and F1 to F5 for female participants. A summary and findings of the main issues raised from the data collected are discussed in three main aspects: (i) *Health awareness and Lifestyle habits*; (ii) *Perception on games;* and (iii) *Response to the mock-up game*. Health Awareness and Lifestyle Habits.

Majority of participant patients, seven out of ten, had an understanding of what medical conditions they had. There is also a high level of understanding among the respondent on the consequences of not controlling their conditions well. 40% of respondents were not aware of the importance of having a healthy diet and medication adherence prior to being admitted. M1 mentioned his tendency to forget his medication on weekends as he left them on his office desk.

Respondents have also admitted that they did not exercise as much as they should be. Only 30% of respondents do physical activities often, be it intentional exercise or doing housework.

When respondents were asked on the resources most frequently used to find answers on health-related doubts, four male participants (M1, M3, M4 and M5) and one female participant (F1) (50%) mentioned the use of a search engine, specifically Google to clarify any of their doubts, while two male participants (M2, M4) and four female participants (F1, F2, F3 and F5) mentioned the consultation of doctors if they had any doubts to clarify, with also some (M1, M5) mentioned the consultation in friends and family.

5.1 Perception on Games

Majority of respondents, 60%, played some forms of games, whether it was on mobile devices and/or board games. Three male participants (M1, M2 & M3) were more frequent phone gamers, while the rest did not partake for various reasons. F1 and F5 mentioned the fear of phone gaming addiction while F3 and M5 commented a lack of interest, considering it as 'waste of time'. Overall, majority of the respondents agreed that games could be a possible way for adults to acquire medication knowledge..

5.2 Response to Mock-Up Game

Design and Graphics Feedback
Two male respondents (M1, M3) felt that the graphics were too child-like and suggested a more mature design that would appeal to them better. M1 preferred a less "cartoon-ish* design and noted that the design would appeal to a younger generation. M5 also mentioned his preference in having graphics that evoke nostalgia. 5 (M2, F1, F3, F4 & F5) out of 10 respondents, however, were receptive to the designs, mentioning that they were in favour of the eye-catching graphics and cute expressions, and approved of the idea of collecting different characters after hatching the egg. It is noted that among the 6 respondents who viewed the graphics positively, four were females (F1, F3, F4 & F5).

Minigames Feedback
Respondents had also pointed out on the importance for the games to be interesting and relatable for them to ensure continuous engagement. While F1, F2, F4 and M2 were more receptive and found most games quite interesting., F3 felt that she might not have the patience to complete the game, especially if it got too repetitive and time-consuming and reiterated the need to for the game to serve a purpose. M4 had also continuously voiced his disinterest in some of the games as it was not the type of game he would play, but rather his grandkids would.

Inclusion of Additional Features
Respondents mentioned the need to include additional aids in the game to improve positive experiences for users. M1 and F4 noted that the educational mini games needed to be designed simple enough to be easily understood, such as using simple layman's terms. F1 and F2 pointed out the importance of having a gameplay tutorial to ease players into the game. M3 also preferred less words in the information provided; suggested a more infographic style of presenting the information.

Respondents mentioned the need to cater to patients with varying disabilities as to allow inclusivity when playing the game. Respondents suggested less fast-moving graphics as F2 mentioned the issue of dizziness when playing phone games, while M1 and M2 replied they were not keen in fast-moving games. F3 and F4 also stated the need for text to be made available in larger fonts sizes for differing eyesight problems.

6   Discussion

Based on our findings, we recommend the following elements to be included in the future development of Tamamon:

a. **Customisation.** The heterogeneity of older adults must be considered as individuals have distinct personal preferences. This includes varying inclinations to different types of games, graphics, and difficulty levels. Gendered differences in preferences for the game graphics were found. Varying designs can be made available, including futuristic or endearing themes or styles to appeal to different likings. More age-appropriate designs, as well as brighter colours and motifs may be applied. Operating the games in 'Easy,' 'Moderate' and 'Challenging' mode is suggested to accommodate players of differing skill levels. Games with the ability to be played in fast and slow tempo will be beneficial to cater to those who enjoy high and low pace respectively. Therefore, players should be given the option of adjusting settings such as choosing their preferred graphics, difficulty levels and speed. Nostalgic elements can be integrated for relatability. This may come in the form of game features that allow players to relate to past experiences such as their previous occupations and encounters. Game components that can be tailored according to players' various wants and needs will successfully drive-up adoption, retention and satisfaction.

b. **Competition, progression, and incentives.** Older adults were driven by winning, high scores and levelling up. By infusing multi-player functions and leadership boards, Tamamon becomes more appealing as these game elements create a sense of satisfaction and achievement in players when they improve or achieve victory, motivating them to utilise the app more A daily or weekly quests system allows player retention in the game. Quests provide players with a task and an accompanying prize that acts as a motivator for them to advance in the game. Gamification reward provision stimulates positive reinforcement with the completion of quests. Examples of rewards include points, upgrades and unlocking of further content. Visualisation of the game progress as a path was also a feature that older adults were receptive to. However, while challenges enthuse them, at the same time, the games must be simple enough to get a hang of easily. In short, there should not be overly complicated rules. A balance of challenging and easy aspects must be achieved.

c. **Accessibility.** Although the games can help older adults with coordination, the physical constraints of players must be considered as some may have reduced function on one hand. Thus, the games should ideally be single-hand play. To further enhance inclusivity, games may be modified to accommodate those with other disabilities such as deafness by incorporating more visuals rather than audio. There should be the option of adjusting font size for those with sight issues to be able to see and navigate the app better. Information must be condensed to make it easier for older adults to read and understand. This includes using less words and utilising an infographic style of presenting the information (blend of images and text) as some people may not prefer to read heavy chunks of text. By improving accessibility of the gameplay elements, it would lower the barrier to play for the older adults and encourages them to continue using the games.

d. **General concerns:** Information in Tamamon ought to be backed by credible sources to allay older adults' anxiety. For those concerned about game addiction, there can be duration limits to set. To address the limited time due to personal commitments, the option of pausing the game and allowing players to resume later may be implemented.

Previous research focuses on the links between gamification and motivating users to engage in behavioural change. However, there is a research gap between motivation and behaviour change - providing users the capability to change in the first place. This study is in line with previous research on elements that enhances motivation in game

[14, 15]. The results provide a better understanding of the age-appropriate elements that can be incorporated into mobile application targeted at increasing medical adherence in older adults. Specifically, customisation, competition, progression and incentives, and accessibility were identified as elements that would increase older adults' intention to use the mobile application in the future. Furthermore, implications related to providing older adults the capability and opportunity to engage in behavioural change can be drawn. Using gamification, crucial healthcare knowledge is presented in an easy-to-understand and attention-capturing way. The mobile application also plays the role of an all-in-one healthcare resource; making it easily accessible and a reminder for older adults to take their medication. Hence, this study is the first to provide insights into how gamified behavioural change solutions on the mobile application can be used as an education tool. The implication of this solution extends beyond behavioural change per se, to broader questions of how such technology can be used to make healthcare simple and approachable to older adults.

Acknowledgments. This study was supported by Serious Game Grant from Games for Health Innovation Centre (ALIVE) (Project Reference Code: SGG20/SN05) and Ageing Research Institute for Society and Education (ARISE). The study was approved by National Healthcare Group (NHG) Domain Specific Review Board (DSRB). The NHG DSRB reference number is 2021/00964.

References

1. World Health Organisation : Adherence to long-term therapies: evidence for action. WHO, Geneva (2003). https://apps.who.int/iris/handle/10665/42682
2. Kardas, P., Lewek, P., Matyjaszczyk, M.: Determinants of patient adherence: a review of systematic reviews. Front. Pharmacol. 4(July), 91 (2013). https://doi.org/10.3389/fphar.2013.00091
3. National Council on Patient Information and Education: Enhancing Prescription Medicine Adherence: A National Action Plan (2007)
4. Theng, Y.L., Chandra, S., Goh, L.Y.Q., Lwin, M.O., Foo, S.: Exploratory qualitative study for community management and control of tuberculosis in India. Acta Trop. **132**, 98–105 (2014). https://doi.org/10.1016/j.actatropica.2013.12.01
5. Theng, Y.L., Lee, J.W.Y., Patinadan, P.V., Foo, S.: The use of videogames, gamification, and virtual environments in the self-management of diabetes: a systematic review of evidence. Games Health (2015). https://doi.org/10.1089/g4h.2014.0114
6. Theng, Y.L., et al.: CuePBox: an integrated physical and virtual pillbox for patient care. In: CHI 2013 Extended Abstracts on Human Factors in Computing Systems (CHI EA 2013), 2013, pp. 433–438 (2013)
7. Lim, S.: Taking your meds right. https://venus.wis.ntu.edu.sg/WSS2/Coord/MainJob.aspx
8. Chew, S.M., Lee, J.H., Lim, S.F., Liew, M.J., Xu, Y., Towle, R.M.: Prevalence and predictors of medication non-adherence among older community-dwelling people with chronic disease in Singapore. J. Adv. Nurs. **77**(10), 4069–4080 (2021). https://doi.org/10.1111/jan.14913
9. Boot, W.R., Souders, D., Charness, N., Blocker, K., Roque, N., Vitale, T.: The gamification of cognitive training: older adults' perceptions of and attitudes toward digital game-based interventions. In: Zhou, J., Salvendy, G. (eds.) ITAP 2016. LNCS, vol. 9754, pp. 290–300. Springer, Cham (2016). https://doi.org/10.1007/978-3-319-39943-0_28

10. Sun, K., Qiu, L., Zuo, M.: Gamification on senior citizen's information technology learning: the mediator role of intrinsic motivation. In: Zhou, J., Salvendy, G. (eds.) ITAP 2017. LNCS, vol. 10297, pp. 461–476. Springer, Cham (2017). https://doi.org/10.1007/978-3-319-58530-7_35

11. Lee, C., Lee, K., Lee, D.: Mobile healthcare applications and gamification for sustained health maintenance. Sustainability **9**, 772 (2017). https://doi.org/10.3390/su9050772

12. Pérez-Jover, V., Sala-González, M., Guilabert, M., Mira, J.J.: Mobile apps for increasing treatment adherence: systematic review. J Med Internet Res. **21**(6), e12505 (2019). https://doi.org/10.2196/12505

13. Lurchenko, A.: Medication non adherence: finding solutions through design thinking approach. ArXiv, abs/1708.02924 (2017)

14. Scase, M., Marandure, B., Hancox, J., Kreiner, K., Hanke, S., Kropf, J.: Development of and adherence to a computer-based gamified environment designed to promote health and wellbeing in older people with mild cognitive impairment. Stud. Health Technol. Inf. **236**, 348–355 (2017)

15. Badawy, S.M., Shah, R., Beg, U., Heneghan, M.B.: Habit strength, medication adherence, and habit-based mobile health interventions across chronic medical conditions: systematic review. J. Med. Internet Res. **22**(4), e17883 (2020)

The Age Factor and the Acceptance: A Rhetorical Study on the Older Audience of the COVID-19 Popular Science Animated Films

Yi Su[✉]

Tongji University, Siping Road 1239, Shanghai, China
Suyi2018@tongji.edu.cn

Abstract. In the age of the Internet, a large number of animated films are being used to disseminate information globally. The development of China's "Internet + Aging" model has shown us that the elderly will increasingly use animation to access medical and health information. As a group that is not noticed by the dominant animation producers, the acceptance of animation by the elderly audience and the essence and influence of the age factor are issues that the producers need to understand. Based on a rhetorical framework, this paper compares the acceptance of animated short films that convey serious information by older audiences over the age of 60 and younger audiences under the age of 40 through a one-on-one interview. The study summarizes the characteristics of older audiences' reception of serious information animation, points out the problem of unbalanced rhetorical stance among short films, authors and audiences, dissects the past experience factor as the essential of the age factor, highlights the shift in core values of animation creation and suggests creative suggestions.

Keywords: Animation · Rhetorical Stance · Age Factor

1 Introduction

China started to implement the "Internet+" strategy in 2015, combining traditional industries and Internet platforms into a new industrial ecosystem. With the rapid development of China's aging society, the "Internet + Nursing" model has become an important way to solve the imbalance between supply and demand of nursing care resources, which includes personal health data visualization, medical knowledge popularization and health guide services. China's "Internet + Aging" strategy is a microcosm of the global digital trend overlaid with the issue of aging - the lives of the over-60s are inevitably being integrated into the Internet and digital wave. Their difficulties in accepting digital products are also becoming increasingly evident. Scholars refer to the "digital divide" as a barrier to Internet awareness and adoption caused by the "old age" factor [2].

Animation is an important medium for presenting digital content on the Internet. Animation is increasingly used to convey serious information, such as knowledge, and guidelines, and we call such animated short films Serious Information Animation (SIA). Serious information animation can help viewers to get information, knowledge, and make the right decisions and improve their lives. The demand for medical and health information among the elderly is increasing daily. Much healthcare information is disseminated through online SIAs to the elder viewers. As a result, older people, who were not part of the target group of the animation film industry, have become the target audience for SIA. Therefrom I wonder whether there is a "digital divide" between the elderly audience and SIA. What factors affect the effectiveness of serious informative animation for the elderly audience? What are the individual factors behind age? The answers to these questions can help producers understand the characteristics of older audiences, guide the production of SIA and improve its effectiveness, and inspire the production of SIA for different groups.

Since 2020, the Covid-19 epidemic has swept the world. This unfamiliar and highly contagious disease has, on the one hand, created an urgent need for people to learn about it and, on the other hand, accelerated the digitization of people's lives and work in a short period of time, giving rise to online meetings, online consultations, etc. While medical expertise literature is difficult to understand, animation can explain disease principles and protection knowledge to a general audience in a visual and easy-to-understand way. Audience watch the Covid-19 films to gain knowledge, form a scientific understanding of the disease, and use it as a basis for taking effective protective measures. Younger audience forward online Covid-19 SIAs to older family members, and older audience receive such animated videos via mobile Internet devices. Studies targeting older audiences in relation to Covid-19 animations can help us reveal the influence of age factors on the acceptance of SIA.

In a previous study, we analyzed the literature on animation research in the field of Healthcare Service Science and found that SIA animation is essentially a tool for the creator to persuade the audience to make them understand and accept the subject matter and form a motivation for further action [3]. Reaching the audience's acceptance is the foundation of effective persuasion and the basis for effective SIA. Research on audience acceptance has been covered in studies of other subjects, such as studies of fan culture and studies of the aesthetics of film. However, the association between animation, serious information, and acceptance has not been studied systematically.

Rhetoric is the doctrine of the art of persuasion, exploring the relationship between the author (the producer of the animation), the argument (the subject of the SIA) and the audience (the user of the serious information). This structure provides a comprehensive perspective by shifting the focus from an author-centered text production process to an audience-centered acceptance process.

Based on the above, the research question is defined: Is there a barrier to the acceptance of SIA by older audiences? How does the age factor affect the acceptance of SIA? The research begins by explaining the terms: Serious Information Animation and Acceptance, and clarifying the difference between Artistic Animation and Useful Animation. The study designs a questionnaire with the help of New Rhetoric as the theoretical framework. A comparative analysis of young and older viewers' experiences of watching SIA is conducted in terms of Logos, Ethos, and Pathos to (1) explore whether there are barriers to accepting SIA by older people, (2) explore the association between acceptance and the age factor, (3) dissect the personal experience factor behind the age factor, and (4) reflect on the shift of the attributes of the audience of animated films to users.

Thus, the researcher conducted one-on-one interviews with two groups of viewers, older and younger, to collect their states after watching the case animations and analyze them against each other in a rhetorical framework.

2 Terminology Clarification

2.1 Serious Information Animation (SIA)

Serious Information Animation (SIA) refers to the creation of short films that use virtual images produced by animation technology as a medium to express rational information such as knowledge (e.g., scientific knowledge), information (e.g., news), regulations (e.g., laws), guidance (e.g., safety guidelines, medication instructions), etc. SIA is different from dramatic art animation films that aim to entertain; SIA aims to effectively, efficiently and accurately communicate rational information to its target audience. With the development of digital devices, the production of SIA animation is increasing. For example, an animation introducing the probability of colorectal cancer screening used to establish an effective risk information communication strategy [5], and an animation introducing information of dementia grief and the supporting social networks used to raise awareness of the carers and encourage them to access grief support [6], are all SIA.

In this paper, the short film [4] chosen for the experiment shows how the vaccine works in the human body through a microscopic view in order to persuade the audience to receive the Covid-19 vaccination ("Get vaccinated!"), whose content is a serious information. The film is well made, and the comments on the webpage show that the audience found the film "informative", "helpful", "great animation to understand", which can be regarded as a SIA case with good animation skills and clear information expression. Such a case can ensure that the audience reflect their own acceptance problems due to their own factors rather than the animation itself being difficult to understand.

2.2 Distinguish Between Artistic Animation and Useful Animation

The objective of SIA production is clear: to convey an argument to the audience so that the audience, with an accurate understanding, will form a point of view that agrees with the producer/communicator and will be guided by this point of view to take further action. The production of animated short films with the goal of conveying serious information is intended to achieve persuasion of the audience, so the audience's acceptance is the criterion for evaluating the success or failure of the creation, and therefore SIA are audience-centered. Animation as a tool of persuasion is not only expressible, it is useful animation.

In this respect, SIA distinguishes itself from the artistic animation. Artistic animation aims at expressiveness and intends to evoke diverse thinking. Artistic animation encourages unanimous, critical and opposing opinions, which is precisely the value of a work of art. Dramatical art are author-centered, attaching importance to the study of the production process of the image text and tending to place the audience in the position of passive viewing. Most of the animated movies, animated shorts and animated TV series that we are familiar with belong to the category of dramatic art animation, in addition, there are some experimental animations that emphasize visual art expression.

2.3 Acceptance

Acceptance means that the audience believes and forms an opinion that is consistent with the theme of the film based on a full understanding of the message conveyed in the film; Acceptance means not only the formation of the audience's perception, but also the motivation for subsequent action. The acceptance process of SIA begins when the audience watches the animated image and continues to act on the audience's thoughts and behaviors after the animated image has been shown. When audiences accept an animated film, it means they are persuaded. In digital production, the achievement of audience acceptance is the basis for the function of SIA.

Murray et al. showed that, computer animation can encourage physical activity among asthma patients, which lead to the conclusion that visual interventions (convinced with animation) is effective and acceptable [7]. The study by Meppelink et al. noted that animation combined with spoken message can significantly improve information recall and attitudes of low health literacy people [8]. These cases present the performance of the SIA audience's acceptance.

Some of the comments on the web page where the film case was selected questioned the scientific validity of the argument to encourage covid vaccination because the idea contradicted their prior knowledge [4]. Although the animation completes the information conveyed (the information is understood before it is questioned), the audience does not form an opinion that is consistent with the film's argument. This shows the opposite side of acceptance, where the failure of reaching acceptance leads to failure of persuasion. It precisely illustrates the complex personal factors of the audience that influence their acceptance of serious information.

3   Related Work

From the existing studies we can find that SIA is essentially a communication tool. Sometimes SIA applies creative methods of film and television art, such as story-based narrative [16], and sometimes animation is emphasized as part of a multimedia product, which is visual and interactive [13]. SIA can be viewed individually by audiences/users [14], e.g. used in self-administered mobile apps or web-based science videos; it can also be involved in communication between professionals and audience, e.g. used as a training tool. The animations have shown good acceptability [13] and good Cross-cultural validity [21]. Although animation is often studied as a part of digital products, it has been observed to be independently effective, for example, interviewees felt that 'animation was effective' [14], easy and comfortable to understand and learn [22], or animation videos are 'eye catching' [15], implying that the animation medium itself has good functional potential, such as a more visual representation.

Not only can animation be effective in improving knowledge, but also animation is effective when used as an emotional intervention for viewers, such as alleviating fear

[20]. Kayler and Majumder et al. showed that patients felt easy and comfortable when watching animated films related to their condition and treatment [22]. Baris's study showed that animation can increase the satisfaction of the viewers [23]. In Andraka's study, it is mentioned that an abstract visual style of animation can 'represent a range of students' [24], while Krieger's study reveals that animated virtual characters help to increase the willingness of audiences (seriously ill patients) to communicate with their doctors [25]. It is thus clear that when animation is rationally designed, it can provide positive emotional value to the audience while communicating information, thus providing some inclination for the audience's future actions.

The goal of SIA production is often to address issues that are closely related to the interests of the audience. The topics of SIA include personal health, safety-related issues such as discharge education that is used to improve self-management of post-surgery patients to reduce postoperative complications [15], promoting behavioral intentions to reduce sugar intake [16], educate older adults about unsafe medication harm [17], etc. It also includes the efficient reaching of information communication, such as information campaigns for the public [18], education [19], etc. Because of this, SIA has clear audience groups, defined by the application scenarios in which it is used, such as patient groups in healthcare scenarios, students in educational scenarios, passengers in public travel scenarios, etc.

The ability of SIA to deliver the desired effect depends on whether it is properly designed. The animation medium itself differs from other media only in terms of its properties and has no natural superiority. For example, in the experiments of Ghavami's study, there was no difference in the effectiveness of the animated model and the real model in presenting content [26], and in Shqaidef's experiments, no difference was shown in the effectiveness of animation versus booklets and textual media in conveying knowledge to patients [27]. And inappropriate design can lead to SIAs failing and the target audience not accepting specific arguments. Research by Essop states that animation can lead to high cognitive load, hindering deep learning [28]. This poses a challenge to the authors of SIAs, which are perhaps a co-creative group of professionals and animation artists. Not only that, but since the audience plays a decisive role in the author's decisions, the audience are in fact indirectly involved in the creation. Experiments have demonstrated that when members of the audience group are directly involved in the authoring, they perceive that their position is taken into account and are therefore more likely to accept SIA [29].

The above studies reveal that animation, when used for the communication of serious information, can not only perform a good function of conveying information, but also the beautiful image design can bring a pleasant viewing experience. In addition to sensory ease and comfort, animation, through virtual characters and storytelling, can also evoke emotional experiences in audiences, generating such things as trust and intimacy, all of which have a positive impact on viewers' acceptance of the content conveyed by SIA. The study reflects that the authorship of SIAs often includes traditional animation creators, the professionals who provide the serious information, and most importantly and easily overlooked, the target audience who are also directly involved or indirectly influence the creation - all three together constitute the authorship of SIAs. This places new demands on our understanding of the integrity of SIA's authorship. The self-interest of SIA's audience is closely related to the serious information, as shown in the above-mentioned studies. This correlation makes the acceptance of SIA's content by this audience group a more complex criterion, with significant influence of psychological factors. The influence of the characteristics of SIA's target audience group on the acceptance determines the direction of creation. The target audience group of SIA is clearly delineated and distinguished from the irrelevant people.

As reflected in the above studies, the association between the media characteristics of animation and usability has been observed in some studies but has not been analyzed in depth and systematically. As a result, all the tests can only correspond to the product under test, and there is a lack of summary of universal patterns. The barriers of the discipline have led to the fact that the study of pragmatic animation - that is, SIA - has always been initiated by the producers of serious information, and animation artists have always lacked dominance. The research in this paper attempts to explore the influence of individual factors behind the age of the audience on the acceptance of SIA, examining group characteristics on the one hand, and universal influences on the other.

4 Conceptual Framework and Experiment Design

4.1 The Conceptual Framework

The New Rhetoric

Aristotle's theory of rhetoric explains the art of persuasion, the skill of phrasing to make the listener agree with the speaker. Rhetoric was originally applied to the "speech situation" based on verbal language [9]. In the middle of the last century, rhetoricians revised the immorality of traditional rhetoric, which was "sophistry" without regard to truth, and proposed the New Rhetoric. According to the new rhetoricians, rhetoric is present in a wide range of human production, be it visual products, architecture, industrial design, etc. [10]. Richard Buchanan states that "Products are arguments about how we should lead our lives" [11]. In the new rhetorical perspective, artifacts can be seen as persuasive through their usability, suitable to the user, and unifying the user to identify the author [11]. According to the previous section, we believe that acceptance is the basis of successful persuasion, and therefore the theory of rhetoric provides us with the conditions for understanding the acceptance of the audience of SIA.

The Elements of Persuasion

In rhetoric, what influences persuasion is the result of three elements working together: Logos (the logical argument set out in the text), Ethos (the trustworthy character of the speaker), and Pathos (the emotional effect created by the speaker and text on the audience or reader) [9]. The questionnaire will be designed from the three aspects.

The Rhetorical Stance

Corresponding to the three effective elements of persuasion, Wayne Booth suggests that admirable writing relies on the balance status among the available argument, the (trustful) implied character of the speaker, and the interests and peculiarities of the audience. The three aspects constitute the rhetorical stance. Whether the rhetorical stance is balanced or not will be used as a criterion to evaluate the current status between SIA and the older audiences. Richard Buchanan proposed that Logos, Pathos and Ethos are translated into the attributes of useful, usable and desirable of products in the design field [11]. Therefore, in the analysis of the questionnaire, we argue that it is a balanced state of rhetorical stance when older viewers consider SIA useful, suable and desirable.

4.2 Questionnaire Design

The questionnaire (Table 1) first asks viewers about their overall impression of the film and their acceptance of the ideas. Question 1 begins with a scale of 1–5 for ease of understanding, enjoyment, trust, agreement, and willingness to take follow-up action, while Questions 2 ask the audience about the most memorable moments of the film. Question3 asks the audience about the state of being persuaded.

Question 4-Question12 asks the viewers about their post-viewing experience of the film in terms of logos, ethos and pathos, which are the elements that influence persuasiveness.

Logos is "the intelligent, rational argument of speech or a discourse", "technological reasoning or the intelligent structure of the subject" of design [11]. It means that the SIA provides reliable, logical reasoning for the argument that enables the audience to understand the knowledge. Question4 - Question7 asks how well the SIA argues for the argument (proposal).

Ethos, refers to the spiritual quality of the speaker in rhetoric, "leading to a special relationship with members of the intended audience". It creates identification between the manufacturer and the user via the products [11]. The authorship of SIA means the origin of serious informatio. The reliability and rigor of the author is closely related to the immediate interest and safety of the audience. Question 8-Quesetion10 asks about the characteristics of a trustworthy author for the audience.

Pathos, in rhetoric, refers to the fit of an argument with the audience's emotions and the audience's social environment. It is the affordance and suitability of a product to user community [11]. SIA's Pathos means that the film is adapted to a specific audience group. Question11-Question13 Ask about the association between acceptance and the audience's own characteristics.

Finally, the questionnaire set up questions for summative reflection.

4.3 Experiment Process

The study took the form of one-on-one interviews with 13 audience members over 60 years of age (aged 60–71 years) and 12 audience members under 40 years of age (aged 26–36 years). Among them, the pre-retirement occupations of the viewers in the 60 + group included newspaper retirees, financial officers, management staff, tax office leaders, workers, and clerks. The occupations of the audience in the under-40 group contained animators, comic book practitioners, teachers of drawing, psychology students, computer researchers, and doctoral students in engineering. Each interview was conducted individually, without any contact or communication between the interviewees.

First, a sample of the animated science video was transmitted to the interviewees via WeChat; subsequently, the researcher asked the designed questions one by one

Table 1. The rhetorical structure and design of the interview questions

Overall Impression	
1. What difficulties did you experience while watching it?	
2. What impressed you most in the film? Why?	
3. How did your willingness to get the Covid-19 vaccine change after watching the film? If not, why?	
The Logos	
4. Do you think the content expressed in the film is clear and easy to understand?	
5. Imagine that the content in this animated film is represented by text, static images, and live-action image. Which do you prefer? Why? What do you think are the advantages and disadvantages of animation?	
6. Do you think the cartoon shows real human cell tissue? What makes you think that what it shows is real/false?	
7. Do you think this is a useful short film? If so, how was it useful to you?	
The Ethos	
8. This film was produced by the Hungarian Academy of Sciences. Do you think that the identity of the author (not only the producer of the animation, but also the provider of the information) influences you to understand, believe, and agree with the content and views of the work?	
9. After watching this film, have you become interested in other works by the author of this short film (Hungarian Academy of Sciences)? Do you approve of the author's work and would recommend this film to others?	
10. If you had the opportunity to appoint the author of the short film (not only the producer of the animation, but also the provider of the information), who do you think you would prefer to have as the author of the proposal on vaccination? What qualities would your trusted author need to have?	
The Pathos	
11. How does the animation relate to you personally? Is your goal in watching this film to get pleasure or to get useful information?	
12. Did the animation stir up emotions in you? For example, joy, fear, sadness, etc.? Why were you triggered/not triggered emotionally? Did these emotions make it easier/more difficult for you to accept the suggestions made in the clip?	
13. What associations with real life did the animation evoke in you? Did these associations make you understand and agree more with the suggestions in the clip or vice versa?	

(continued)

Table 1. (*continued*)

Summarizing Reflections	
14. By watching this film, which of the following points do you think would most convince you to adopt the suggestions in a serious information animation for a animated film that disseminates serious information: A the clear explanation of the message, B the authority of the author's identity, C the fit of the work with your personal characteristics (such as habits, memories, occupation, life circumstances, social relationships, etc.) (multiple choices possible)?	
15. How do you think this short film could be improved to be more convincing to you?	

through recorded telephone interviews, with appropriate follow-up questions based on their responses. Each interview lasted from 15–30 min. Interview recordings were converted into text for further analysis using the Xun Fei Ting Jian platform at the end of the interviews. The results of the questionnaire for both groups were analyzed, compared and summarized.

The case clips were selected by the researcher after a lot of comparisons, and the Covid-19 vaccine knowledge science video produced by the Hungarian Academy of Sciences was finally selected [4]. Because the interviewees were Chinese, the researcher used Deepl translation software to translate the subtitles of the original video into Chinese, with Chinese narration and subtitles. The English narration and music in the original video were used as background sound with reduced volume and without disturbing the clarity of the Chinese narration. According to the feedback from several interviewees with good English skills, the Chinese part was accurate and fluent, with only one word translated differently from the Chinese idiom, but it did not affect comprehension.

5 Results

Overall Impression
When first asked what difficulties they encountered during viewing, the 60+ group expressed more "no difficulties", while an absolute majority of the under-40 group explicitly cited difficulties in understanding terminology. However, an overview of the entire interview process shows that difficulties in understanding the terminology in the Covid-19 vaccination video were repeatedly mentioned by respondents in both groups. Thus, the difficulty in understanding the terminology was the main difficulty faced by viewers in both groups.

Regarding the impressive segments, each interviewee gave different answers. Some were impressed by the fragment of the protective function of the vaccine, some were impressed by the introduction of the immune mechanism (e.g., antibodies wrapping the virus, the process by which infected cells are killed and repaired2 people, immune memory, etc.), some remembered new information (e.g., spike protein, the difference between mRNA vaccines and conventional vaccines), etc., and some said "(impressions) are pretty much the same ". In both groups, respectively, someone mentioned the color information in the film ("little blue feet", "the good side could be pink, the bad side could be green").

Several respondents over 60 years of age reported that they "do not have a habit of watching cartoons," indicating that the technological development stage of their era influenced their daily use of digital devices (Internet, digital TV, etc.). Compared to the under-40 group, more people in the over-60 group showed that when watching the sample animation, they focused on what they saw and heard ("shots", "cells were killed", "immune memory", etc.), and did not focus on the effects on the animation. etc.). They did not show observations that focused on the properties of the medium and design ideas (e.g., use of color), etc. For this, respondents in the under-40 group who had a background in art and design had concerns about color (e.g., the perception that green represents evil, the intent of the blue-green hues of the film's design confused her, etc.), shape (the unfamiliar shape of human tissue perhaps derived from real cellular structures), etc.

In response to the advice conveyed in the short film about getting the Covid-19 vaccine, most of the respondents in both groups said that their willingness to get the vaccine did not change as a result of watching the film. Only a few respondents indicated that their understanding of how the vaccine works had made them feel safer and more willing to get the vaccine. This shows that the persuasive effect of this film was limited and did not create significant acceptance or motivation to act on the part of the audience.

Logos

Most of the respondents in the 60+ group indicated that they found the content expressed in the sample films clear and easy to understand, and that it had the advantage of being intuitive and easy to watch ("I don't want to read text when I am older" and "it is much clearer than reading words"). It is clear that for viewers over 60 years old, animation is an easy and intuitive medium in comparison because it helps them to reduce the difficulty of reading due to their physical functions (difficulty in reading text).

Half of the respondents under the age of 40 thought that the content of the film was "not clear enough" and "not easy to understand", mainly because the film did not explain the professional information sufficiently ("say it once with professional terms The main reason is that the film does not explain the professional information sufficiently ("say it once with professional terms, then explain it in easy-to-understand language"). The design of the colors caused some confusion. This group of viewers has more experience watching films (based on the average viewing time), is physically able to watch without burden, and has a relevant professional background themselves. They showed higher demands on the professionalism of animation production and more refined evaluations (e.g., suggesting that text and images match each other, or that using still images is more convenient for repeated viewing, etc.).

Among respondents over 60 and under 40 years old, animated images were commonly mentioned as being good for visualizing evolutionary processes and microscopic scenes, but lacking in detail and realism. For example, "real cells are not in this shape and color", "after watching it, I feel that the jostling is not realistic", and suggested "using real cell microscopic images with animation to enhance understanding".

Both groups of interviewees jointly mentioned that the forced, uninterrupted playing of the animation compressed their time to understand the information, e.g., "I want to read it again, I'll have to go through this again from the beginning...... it's fixed there, you might not be in as much of a hurry in terms of mood".

A majority of respondents in each of the two groups said that they would not recognize the content in the animated images as real information when their own knowledge was insufficient. The vast majority of viewers in both groups (12/13, 10/12) felt that the short films had improved their understanding of how vaccines work or added new knowledge to some extent, and thus the films were useful to them.

Pathos

When asked about the relevance of the animation to themselves, respondents said that the content of the film was related to their own health and safety during the epidemic, and they formed thoughts such as "not taking it lightly," "telling friends and relatives," and being concerned about future outbreaks and new vaccines. One respondent recalled a middle school lesson that had "intellectual resonance," and another was reminded of preventive and control measures during an epidemic. Most of the respondents said that the main purpose of watching the cases was to obtain information, and the purpose of having fun was secondary.

Most respondents said they were "relatively calm" and "not emotionally aroused" when watching the case films because the films were mainly rational messages. One respondent under the age of 40 said they were initially "turned off" by the preachy content of such videos. A small number of respondents expressed their joy at getting the information. One respondent felt that the video evoked her feelings of sadness about the panic and sadness that occurred during the outbreak.

When asked about the real-life associations with the film, most of the respondents first said "not much", but then named some objects that were related to the content of the film, such as another infectious disease (smallpox), the large number of deaths in the real epidemic and thus raised doubts about the content of the film, as well as some short-comings in the film's narrative ("...... There is no later data to support what happened with the vaccine...... it still (only) talks about the principle of the vaccine......").

The responses to this part of the question showed no significant differences between the respondents of the two groups. The responses shared by the groups show that the rational thinking of SIA's audience was always in the dominant position. They may have been touched by some associations with themselves and their life situations, but these associations were random and non-dominant.

Ethos

The majority of respondents said that authorship affects their trust in the content of the film. A film produced by an authoritative institution would increase their trust in the content. For the Hungarian Academy of Sciences, the producer of the sample film, some respondents said that although they did not know it, they would compare it to the Chinese Academy of Sciences, and thus would like to believe that they represent a high level of research capability at the national level; some respondents thought that although they did not know Hungary, it might represent a developed medical condition in Europe, and thus their trustworthiness was increased. Respondents mentioned that during the outbreak in the country, some of the information published by experts was proven to be false, leading to skepticism of subsequent statements made by the group of authors involved. Thus, while the identity and position of the author play an important role in the viewer's belief in the SIA, the author's own credibility has a decisive influence on the viewer's trust.

While the vast majority of respondents agreed that the identity of the author affects their trust in the content of the film, there were also dissenting voices. One interviewee over 60 said, "It doesn't matter who the author is, it's acceptable if what he says makes sense"; another interviewee over 60 said that he needs to be provided with more information about the author (Hungarian Academy of Sciences) to be able to build understanding and trust in the author; and one interviewee under 40 said "I cannot say that because he is an authority, he is right." From this, the spirit of using one's own knowledge base as an evaluation criterion and independent evidence-seeking is reflected. It is evident that the credibility of authors needs to be based on authentic credibility, professionalism, and facts.

As to whether they would search for the author's other works after seeing the sample film, some respondents expressed interest in whether the author has other health-related works. About half of the respondents said they were "not interested" in the author's other works because they were "too academic" and "less interesting to watch". About half of the respondents said they would not actively share the video. When asked what qualities they thought were needed in a person who makes "vaccination" recommendations, respondents cited professionalism (front-line scientific expert), a position similar to that of the interviewee (a doctor in their own family, not a vaccine manufacturer), and official certification (Academy of Sciences).

In terms of trust in authors, the respondents' opinions did not reflect significant differences due to the age factor.

Summarizing Reflections

In the overall reflection on the factors influencing acceptance, a clear explanation of the information was most often chosen as the most persuasive element, with the authority of authorship coming second and only a few respondents citing the work's fit with their personal characteristics as the main influencing factor in the film's persuasiveness.

Respondents' suggestions for improving the film to achieve effective acceptance included increasing the comprehensiveness, detail, and supporting evidence of the information presented, such as "adding explanations and descriptions of terms," "incorporating some real information about today's global epidemic," "explaining the positive and negative effects," "proof of clinical trials," and "indicating the source of the data," among others.

In addition, in terms of audio-visual presentation, the suggestion also includes "using easy-to-understand language"; one interviewee over 60 years old suggested that she would like the animation design "not to make those children (as characters), at least close to our age group (as characters)......", upon further questioning, this suggestion meant that it would be easier to understand if animation characters and elements were used that were similar to the age and lifestyle of older viewers. "The tone is too flat, suggest more rhythm", "There could be some metaphors or more humorous written expressions", "More people (characters) like in the cartoon", etc. These suggestions for the expression itself reflect the viewer's expectation that the presentation techniques in film and animation be applied to add interest to the film.

6 Discussion

Returning to the question posed at the beginning of this paper: Is there a barrier to the acceptance of SIA by older audiences, and what is the nature of the age factor and how does it affect the acceptance of SIA?

6.1 The Rhetorical Stance

In this study of older animation viewers over 60 years old, I found that despite the fact that the sample animated film was well produced and released by an authoritative organization, most viewers, including the older and younger groups, were skeptical of it. According to the Rhetorical Stance theory proposed by Wayne Booth [12], a work is well accepted when there is a state of balance between the author, the audience, and the point of view. It can be seen that the balance between the case animated short film and the older audience was not reached. According to the analysis above, the imbalance is reflected in:

(1) The audience's rustiness with the animation medium makes it difficult for them to interpret the animated images, which creates an imbalance between the audience's understanding and the animated representation.
(2) When the audience viewed the sample animated clips based on their own knowledge base and logical reasoning ability, they found that the content of the clips did not adequately provide persuasive arguments, thus creating an imbalance between the audience's reasoning and the arguments provided by the clips.
(3) A discrepancy between the creator's intention (e.g., application of color) and the audience's understanding of the image (e.g., interpretation of color), resulting in an imbalance between creation (encoding) and interpretation (decoding).
(4) Since serious information is closely related to audiences' personal interests, audiences have strict requirements for the reliability of the information providers, i.e. the sources, in short films. When the credibility of the information source is not enough to meet the audience's requirements, the rhetorical stance between the two is out of balance.

As seen by comparing the older group with the younger group, of the above unbalanced relationships between the sample films and the respondents, only the first one is characteristic of the older group and the remaining three are not related to the age factor.

6.2 The Essential of Age Factor

The older group did have some differences from the younger group in their responses after viewing the sample animation, such as whether they were accustomed to and skilled in the medium, but the way and conditions of understanding, judging, and accepting rational information were largely the same.

The common age-related characteristics reflected in the interviews stem from the influence of the external environment in which this group has lived for a long time. The external environment in which people live contains common education, technological conditions, values, social institutions, etc. These factors make the audience of a certain age have similar life experiences and show some discomfort in understanding and using new things. There are also differences and diversity within the 60+ group. This suggests that dividing audiences by age is only partially representative of their characteristics, and that dividing target groups purely by age will bury the diversity within this age group.

It can be seen that the essence of the age factor that influences the acceptance of SIA is the factor of life experience. The real factor that affects the acceptance of animation is actually the past experience of the audience. The audience group of SIA should be divided by the similarity of life experience, which can be more accurate than simply dividing by age.

Animation design deals with the minds of the audience, and the diverse characteristics of the mind are far richer than the physiological characteristics that the body exhibits at different ages. When we are used to using age as a yardstick to delineate a group of users (just like the age-appropriate design of transportation, digital devices, etc.), we must remember that in these designs, the way the design object interacts with the user's human body needs to address the decline of physiological functions brought about by increasing age, which is completely different from the way animation interacts with the viewer's mind.

The factor of the age of digital SIA audience obviously does not originate from the degeneration of physiological functions. The differences exhibited by older and younger viewers in viewing and evaluating serious information stem more from personal experience (e.g., work experience, lifestyle habits, knowledge base, etc.). The differences brought by age are essentially personal experiences created by the social environment of different historical periods (e.g., the experience of watching TV cartoons, or the experience of living in a time when mobile Internet devices were not developed, etc.).

Respondents over 60 years old "watched it again to understand it" and "watched it three times to understand it" tell us that we can be influenced by the accumulation of experience. In other words, we can improve the audience's familiarity with animation by increasing their experience in watching animation films, and thus improve their effectiveness and efficiency in receiving SIA.

This provided guidance for the creation of the SIA:

(1) The audience's life experience is used as a basis for understanding and classifying audience groups;
(2) The experience of the audience can be used as a basis for design decisions in SIA;
(3) Influence audience acceptance by cultivating the audience's experience, for example, by adding preparatory viewing processes before using SIA to disseminate content so that audiences become familiar with the viewing object and increase acceptance.

6.3 Integration of Animation, Drama Art and Design

When the truth and rigor of the information conflicts with the emotional experience and fun of viewing, ensuring truth and rigor should come first. sia is rational. The interviews showed that the overall viewing experience of the audience was calm, even bland and boring. Only a few respondents reported gaining a sense of joy in acquiring knowledge. This invariably limits the audience's interest in the animation of serious information and limits the dissemination of information.

The audience's comments for improvement reflect their desire for more interesting elements of animated films, animated characters, etc. to appear in the film. This reflects that animated films resulting from the combination of the animation medium and dramatic art have a strong appeal to the audience and therefore have good potential for application.

Authors producing engaging SIAs that can be effectively received by audiences still need to employ the narrative devices of the dramatic arts, but the expression is constrained by audience factors. SIA embodies the value of human-centeredness, which is the value of design. Thus, SIA is a product of theatrical art techniques being used in the field of design, requiring animation creators to break the original mindset of artistic expression and create with the mindset of design.

7 Limitations and Future Work

The SIA sample selected in this paper represents only one type of narrative form. In fact, animation has a variety of narrative forms. In my future research, I will further explore the impact of different narrative forms of animation on the audience's reception of serious information and gain a more comprehensive understanding of the association between SIA and audience reception.

The limited sample size of this study only tentatively established the association between individual audience factors and SIA, but the sample size could not cover the diversity of older audience groups, so I speculate that there may be more relationships between individual audience characteristics and acceptance that have not yet been revealed. In future studies, a wider range of audience groups can be studied to improve the system of individual audience characteristics related to SIA acceptance.

8 Conclusion

Using rhetoric as a theoretical framework, this paper first collects the post-viewing states of older and younger audiences of Covid-19 science animation shorts through one-on-one interviews. Their characteristics are obtained by comparison and induction, including the high rationality of audience, the high demand for authorial reliability and the coexistence of strengths and limitations in animation presentation. Subsequently, several sets of unbalanced relationships in the rhetorical stance between the author, the animation, and the audience are summarized, revealing the problems that affect older audiences accept the SIA. By comparing the older group with the younger group of audiences, it is found that the usual design idea of delineating users on the scale of age does not work for the design of SIA, because it is the audience's mind rather than their body that interacts with SIA. The audience's acceptance of SIA is influenced by factors originating from experience such as knowledge base and mindset, so it is more reasonable to divide the audience group of SIA by the similarity of experience than to divide the group based on age. The creation of SIA still relies on the medium of animation and theatrical expression techniques, but its core value has shifted from expression to human-centeredness; SIA is a usable design object that requires the creator of animation to break the original mindset of artistic expression and create with a design mindset.

References

1. Xiao, Y., Yue, S.: The model of internet + old-age service: the innovative development of old-age service in new era. Popul. J. **39**(01), 58–66 (2017)
2. Quan, H., Xiaodi, Z.: The influence factors of the digital divide in the elderly and the social integration strategy. J. Zhejiang Univ. Technol. (Soc. Sci.) **16**(04), 437–441 (2017)
3. Su, Y.: The persuasive impact of animation in health care sciences services: a rhetoric-based literature study. In: Stephanidis, C., Antona, M., Ntoa, S., Salvendy, G. (eds.) HCII 2022. CCIS, vol. 1654, pp. 458–465. Springer, Heidelberg (2022). https://doi.org/10.1007/978-3-031-19679-9_58
4. https://youtube.com/watch?v=UGPp7zdToKk
5. Housten, A.J., et al.: Does animation improve comprehension of risk information in patients with low health literacy? A randomized trial. Med. Decis. Making **40**(1), 17–28 (2020)
6. Scher, C., et al.: Usefulness and acceptability of an animation to raise awareness to grief experienced by carers of individuals with dementia. Dement.-Int. J. Soc. Res. Pract. **21**(2), 363–379 (2022)
7. Meppelink, C.S., van Weert, J.C., Haven, C.J., Smit, E.G.: The effectiveness of health animations in audiences with different health literacy levels: an experimental study. J. Med. Internet Res. **17**(1), e11 (2015)
8. Murray, J., et al.: A theory-informed approach to developing visually mediated interventions to change behaviour using an asthma and physical activity intervention exemplar. Pilot Feasibility Study **2**, 46 (2016)
9. Aristotle: On Rhetoric: A Theory of Civic Discourse. Oxford University, New York (2007)
10. Buchanan, R.: Strategies of design research: productive science and rhetorical inquiry. In: Design Research Now: Essays and Selected Projects, pp. 55–66 (2007)
11. Buchanan, R.: Design and the new rhetoric: productive arts in the philosophy of culture. Philos. Rhetor. **3**(2001), 183–206 (2017)
12. Booth, W.: The rhetoric stance. Now don't Try to Reason With me. University of Chicago Press, Chicago (1970)
13. Wiemker, V., et al.: Pilot study to evaluate usability and acceptability of the 'animated alcohol assessment tool' in Russian primary healthcare. Digit. Health **8** (2022)
14. Patell, R., et al.: Communication skills training for internal medicine residents using a brief animated video. J. Cancer Educ. **37**(2), 379–386 (2022)
15. Kang, E., et al.: Development of a web-based discharge education intervention to improve the postdischarge recovery of general surgical patients. J. Nurs. Scholarsh. **54**(2), 143–151 (2022)
16. Vandormael, A., et al.: Effect of a story-based, animated video to reduce added sugar consumption: a web-based randomized controlled trial. J. Glob. Health **11** (2021)
17. Stoll, J.A., et al.: Development of video animations to encourage patient-driven deprescribing: a team alice study. Patient Educ. Couns. **104**(11), 2716–2723 (2021)
18. Nishikawa, M., et al.: Japanese health and safety information for overseas visitors: protocol for a randomized controlled trial. BMC Public Health **21**(1) (2021)
19. Rose, J.S., et al.: A validated audio-visual educational module on examination skills in ophthalmology for undergraduate medical students in the COVID-19 season-an observational longitudinal study. Indian J. Ophthalmol. **69**(2), 400–405 (2021)

20. Duzkaya, D.S., et al.: The effect of a cartoon and an information video about intravenous insertion on pain and fear in children aged 6 to 12 years in the pediatric emergency unit: a randomized controlled trial. J. Emerg. Nurs. **47**(1), 76–87 (2021)
21. . do Nascimento, C.D., et al.: Cross-cultural validity of the animated activity questionnaire for patients with hip and knee osteoarthritis: a comparison between the Netherlands and Brazil. Braz. J. Phys. Therapy **25**(6), 767–774 (2021)
22. Kayler, L.K., et al.: Development and preliminary evaluation of an animation (simplifyKDPI) to improve kidney transplant candidate understanding of the Kidney Donor Profile Index. Clin. Transplantat. **34**(3) (2020)
23. Baris, A., Ozturkmen, Y.: The role of advanced technology product animations on informing patients with gonarthrosis preoperatively. Istanbul Med. J. **20**(6), 553–557 (2019)
24. Andraka-Christou, B., Alex, B., Madeira, J.L.: College student preferences for substance use disorder educational videos: a qualitative study. Subst. Use Misuse **54**(8), 1400–1407 (2019)
25. Krieger, J.L., et al.: A pilot study examining the efficacy of delivering colorectal cancer screening messages via virtual health assistants. Am. J. Prev. Med. **61**(2), 251–255 (2021)
26. Ghavami, A., et al.: Effects of observing real, animated and combined model on learning cognitive and motor levels of basketball jump shot in children. Biomed. Hum. Kinet. **14**(1), 54–60 (2022)
27. Shqaidef, A.J., et al.: A comparative assessment of information recall and comprehension between conventional leaflets and an animated video in adolescent patients undergoing fixed orthodontic treatment: a single-center, randomized controlled trial. Am. J. Orthod. Dentofacial Orthopedics **160**(1), 11-+ (2021)
28. Essop, H., Lubbe, I., Kekana, M.: Bringing literature to life: a digital animation to teach analogue concepts in radiographic imaging during a pandemic - lessons learnt. Afr. J. Health Prof. Educ. **13**(3), 186–188 (2021)
29. Templeton, M., Kelly, C., Lohan, M.: Developing a sexual health promotion intervention with young men in prisons: a rights-based participatory approach. JMIR Res. Protoc. **8**(4) (2019)

Using Persona Development to Design a Smartphone Application for Older and Younger Diabetes Patients – A Methodological Approach for Persona Development

Fatima Varzgani[✉], Soussan Djamasbi, and Bengisu Tulu

Worcester Polytechnic Institute, Worcester, MA 01609, USA
{fvarzgani,djamasbi,bengisu}@wpi.edu

Abstract. Personas are fictional but realistic representations of user groups of a product or service that focus on their goals, needs, behavior, and other characteristics that may impact the design of the product. Using personas in the early phases of the design process can help identify product features, and demonstrate how these features address user needs and challenges. Despite being used in research for over a decade, there is a lack of standardized methodology on the development of personas and how they are used in the design process. The objective of this paper is to develop a systematic approach to the persona development process and show its effectiveness through a case study where we followed the proposed methodology in the early design phase of a diabetes management smartphone application (app) targeted at older and younger users. The study was conducted in United States from January to June 2020. The findings of our study provided an empirical examination of the effectiveness and efficiency of the design process using personas.

Keywords: Persona Development · User-centered Design · User-experience Driven Innovations · Proto-Personas · User Personas · Older and Younger Users · Smartphone App

1 Introduction

One of the core aspects of user-centered design is understanding user needs and wants. Technologies that are developed keeping user needs and wants into consideration are often proven to be successful. Despite its importance, many organizations fail to start their design process with empathy building. This results in either inability of the product to reach its target users [1], or the product not being used the way it was intended. One way this challenge can be addressed is through developing personas. The persona development process captures users' mental model including their challenges, expectations, and anticipated behavior [2]. Users' goals, needs, behavior, and other characteristics that may impact the design of the product are then represented through personas, which

Q. Gao and J. Zhou (Eds.): HCII 2023, LNCS 14043, pp. 214–227, 2023.
https://doi.org/10.1007/978-3-031-34917-1_16

refer to fictional but realistic representations of user groups of a product or service [3]. Using personas can be very beneficial to organizations. Personas can help improve communication within an organization by building consensus about user needs among senior leadership and help them to work effectively together to address opportunities for innovation and other strategic goals [4].

Using personas in the early phases of the design process can help identify product features and demonstrate how these features address user needs and challenges [5], leading to the development of successful products. Robert et al. argued that 40% of the usability of applications depends on the visual aspects and user interaction (how the product looks and feels), whereas 60% depends on the product's ability to address user needs and challenges [6]. Personas add value by conveying crucial information about a user's expectations and usage scenarios to designers, thereby allowing them to make centric choices around user needs [7].

Different studies have used different methods for creating personas. Kneale et al. developed personas of homebound older adults, their caregivers, and their nursing staff by conducting a literature review of related case studies [8]. Bhattacharyya et al. developed personas of frail elderly and people with multiple chronic conditions and their caregivers from in-depth patient interviews [9]. Molen et al. developed personas of diabetic patients using patient interviews and a literature search [10]. LeRouge et al. developed personas of the aging population with multiple chronic diseases using data gathered from observation, survey data, and informal interviews [2]. Ekström & Loos developed personas from demographic data of older population to understand the process of becoming a third age eHealth consumer. They used the concept of cultural age, which refers to the way a person experiences her or his age, to develop personas of third age eHealth consumers [11].

Personas have been used in research on human-computer interaction for more than a decade [12]. Despite the progress in the use of personas in research, there is still no fixed methodology for creating them. Salminen et al. argued that there is a lack of standardized methods for creating personas, and provided persona guidelines on creatin data-driven personas from numerical data such as online user data [13]. However, to the best of our knowledge, there is a lack of standardized methodology for creating personas and how to use them in the early design phases of product development.

The objective of this paper is to develop a systematic approach to the persona development process. To assess the effectiveness of the process, we explored the following question: Is our proposed persona development methodology effective in guiding the early design phase of a diabetes management smartphone application (app) targeted at older and younger users?

2   Proposed Methodology for Developing Personas

Our proposed methodology consists of developing two types of personas; proto-personas and user personas. Proto personas are assumption-based personas that are created through indirect interaction with the users [4]. They are created by subject matter experts, such as members of an organization who possess immense knowledge about their customers. Developing proto-personas has multiple benefits. First, the proto-persona development process is relatively quick and cost-effective since it does not involve direct interaction with the users. Second, it creates consensus between different teams or members of an organization, such as senior leadership and product designers, which is extremely important for developing successful products [4]. User personas are the most accurate representation of the users as they provide a rich set of first-hand information from actual users. However, since they involve direct interaction with the users, their development typically requires more resources and takes longer. The organizational cost for developing user personas can be reduced by using the information gathered through proto personas development (reference Jain et. Paper). Hence, proto personas make a great starting point for understanding users and designing solutions as they make the entire design process more effective and efficient.

2.1 Proto Persona Development

For creating proto personas, the following major steps can be utilized: (1) identification of key user attributes that impact the product design, (2) user data collection from subject matter experts, and (3) analysis of the data collected from subject matter experts and creation of proto personas (Fig. 1). The outcome of this process will be proto personas that can then be used to gather requirements for designing a solution.

Fig. 1. Proto persona development process.

Key User Attribute Identification. Proto persona development should start with the identification of and shared understanding about key user attributes that may impact the design of the product. These attributes are non-binary user characteristics that provide meaningful differentiation between personas and have a direct or indirect impact on the design and usage of the product. For example, a user's level of comfort with smartphone usage can impact the design of a smartphone application, therefore, smartphone savviness can serve as a suitable and relevant attribute for designing smartphone applications.

There are multiple ways of identifying these attributes. The first way is utilizing subject matter experts' knowledge about the users. Asking organization members or project stakeholders about key user attributes and requirements of the product is generally a quick way of identifying these attributes. The second way is through a literature search. Searching literature and validated constructs about certain user attributes that lead to the successful adoption of similar products can serve as a good start as well. For example, for health management products or services, constructs such as Patient Activation Measure (PAM), a validated survey instrument that was developed to assess an individual's knowledge, skill, and confidence for self-management [14], can be used to identify relevant key user attributes for self-management health applications.

Once a set of key attributes are identified, the next step is to make sure that those who participate in proto-persona development process have the same understanding about what these attributes mean. Facilitating such shared understanding can be accomplished by asking the subject matter experts to come to an agreement about the list of the key user attributes and their definitions. For example, the subject matter experts can be asked to review them and make suggestions or modify the items or their definitions, and/or add any additional attribute that they may find important. All modifications are finalized via face-to-face or virtual discussions to make sure all participants agree on the list of identified attributes and their meaning. This step is crucial in creating a shared understanding between the subject matter experts and the designers as well as a shared language for communicating and sharing design ideas.

Data Collection from Subject Matter Experts. Once the key user attributes are identified, the second major step is to collect data about potential users from the subject matter experts. Since proto-personas are assumption-based, it is imperative to collect data from the people who have an accurate picture of the user base, otherwise getting the wrong information can lead to myopia [4].

Data can be collected through individual interviews or a workshop with the subject matter experts. Both methods follow a similar procedure. The interviews and the workshop can be started by giving an overview of what personas are to familiarize the experts with the concept. Next, the list of attributes and their definitions should be shared with the experts again to make sure they are all on the same page and agree with the definitions. This step is followed by the persona development activity, during which experts are asked to come up with as many personas as they can think of by completing a persona worksheet for each persona. Figure 2 provides an example of a persona worksheet.

Demographics	Facts and Interactions
Demographic information of persona such as gender, age, income, job, marital status, etc.	Persona's roles and responsibilities, routines and schedules, technology usage, habits; etc.
Challenges and Feelings	**Goals, Wants and Needs**
The challenges or feelings this persona faces.	Needs, wants, and goals of this persona; what this persona needs and what they try to achieve.

Fig. 2. Example of a persona worksheet.

If data collection is done through individual interviews, it is recommended that each expert is asked to complete a certain number of worksheets within a specified time duration. The number of worksheets to be completed depends on the total number of interviewees and the time allotted to the interviewees. Generally, for a one-hour interview, two worksheets per interviewee is a reasonable number to be expected to be completed.

If data is collected through a workshop, the attendees of the workshop should be divided into groups of three to five and asked to complete as many worksheets as they can in a specified amount of time.

Once the worksheets are completed, the experts should be asked to rate their developed personas on different spectrums for each of the attributes (Fig. 3). For example, smartphone savviness (defined as the degree to which a user feels comfortable with using new apps) can be rated on a scale of low to high. With the completion of this step, the interview or the workshop can be wrapped up.

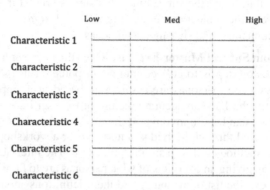

Fig. 3. Attribute ratings on different spectrums.

Data Synthesis. After data collection, the attribute ratings should be used to organize the completed worksheets into a smaller set of major persona groups with similar characteristics. Depending on available resources and expertise, this can be done in several ways. It can be done qualitatively or using both quantitative and qualitative methods. To make the process more efficient, we suggest using quantitative methods like Hierarchical Cluster Analysis (HCA) using the attribute ratings to form the initial set of clusters. The clusters formed through HCA or any clustering method should be then qualitatively analyzed to verify the similarities between the clusters and identify emerging themes.

After verification of the clusters, this iterative consolidation process will result in major clusters, each representing a distinct persona. These personas are then visualized using persona cards [4] which can be labeled either based on their characteristics or given a name to humanize them even further. While persona cards can be modified as needed to better match the project needs, the same format should be used for all persona cards within the same project.

Designing Solution Mockups. Developing personas help in identifying user needs and requirements that are unique to each persona or are shared by all the personas. The design efforts can be prioritized based on the organization's goals or the project objectives. If the solution is targeted at a particular persona, then the needs of that persona can be prioritized. If the solution is aimed at multiple personas, then the common needs among all personas can be identified and personalization options can be provided to cater to the needs of individual personas. The needs and requirements identified can be used to develop a set of design mockups that can be tested in the subsequent steps.

2.2   User Persona Development

The user persona development process starts by preparing interview questions for in-depth user interviews. The goal of user interviews is two-fold. First, these user interviews will help in understanding user needs and goals by refining the proto-personas and identifying any gaps for opportunities in the proto-personas and actual user base. Second, these user interviews can be used to gather feedback about the initial design mockups or prototypes developed using the information from proto personas.

For the first goal of the user interviews, interview questions should be related to persona verification, such as users' lifestyles and their needs, challenges, and goals (See persona development worksheet in Fig. 2). For the second goal, the design mockups or prototypes can be demonstrated to the interviewees to gather their feedback about their preferences, likes, and dislikes on the design choices, and how the designs can help address their needs. These user interviews should then be analyzed to identify any new emerging user patterns and group similar users together based on their needs and wants and expectations of the product. While the objective of mockups is to get user feedback on design, they often help to engage users in storytelling, which in turn can help gain a deeper understanding of user needs.

The final step in our proposed process is to compare the differences between the proto personas and the user personas to identify opportunities for extending and/or refining proto-personas.

The persona development process should be an ongoing process as persona needs keep on evolving. Before making any major design updates, the entire process should be repeated to stay up to date on the persona's needs and challenges. This process will allow organizations to assess and update their knowledge of their target market.

3   Case Study: Designing a Diabetes Management Application for Older and Younger Patients Using Persona Development

We implemented the process for developing a diabetes management smartphone app for older and younger patients with a diabetes management company. The study was conducted in United States from January to June 2020. For this study, we developed proto personas and user personas to understand patient needs and challenges and to develop low-fidelity design mockups of a diabetes management smartphone application.

3.1   Developing Proto Personas

Materials and Methodology. For developing proto personas, we conducted a workshop with eight members of an organization that specializes in diabetes management. These members included top management executives, clinical directors, and software and product designers.

We started the process by identifying and developing a set of 9 user attributes that could impact the design of the smartphone app (Table 1). These attributes were mostly derived from the Patient Activation Measure (PAM). We shared these attributes and their definitions with the workshop attendees prior to the workshop via email and asked them to add to the list if they can think of additional attributes. Along with the list of attributes, we also asked the workshop attendees some questions regarding their knowledge of their patients.

Table 1. Key user attributes and their definitions.

Key User Attribute	Definition
1. Physical health status	Level of physical wellness
2. Attitude toward a healthy lifestyle	Proactive vs. reactive attitude towards health
3. Smartphone savviness	Comfort level in using smartphones
4. Affordability	Patient's ability to afford the necessary treatment
5. Behavioral health status	Level of mental wellness
6. Access to Care	Degree of access to care
7. Involvement in decision-making	Level of patient activation (how much they know, how much they believe they can do), control, and involvement in decision making
8. Disease knowledge	Knowledge/awareness about one's health
9. Patient schedule	Patient's schedule: tight/busy, or flexible with plenty of free time

We started the workshop by reviewing the user attributes to clarify and verify their definitions. We also asked workshop attendees to make suggestions about removing and/or revising the items or their definitions. Based on this discission the set of attributes to be used was finalized (Table 1).

Next, we divided the workshop attendees into 3 groups and asked them to complete as many persona worksheets as they can in 40 min. The worksheet required respondents to provide information about demographics, daily routines, challenges, feelings, goals, wants, and needs of a persona (Fig. 4).

After completing the worksheets, we asked the workshop attendees to identify where their developed persona fell on the spectrums for each of the 9 attributes (Fig. 5).

Results. During the workshop, a total of 14 worksheets were completed. Using the attribute ratings, we first consolidated the worksheets into major clusters using Hierarchical Cluster Analysis. This resulted in 4 major persona groups. We then manually inspected the clusters to look for emerging themes and characteristics of the clusters (Fig. 6). The manual inspection revealed that two of the clusters had similar characteristics, therefore, we merged them. This left us with a set of 3 final proto personas (Fig. 7).

We used the information from the proto personas to gather user requirements and created a set of low-fidelity design mockups of the app based on the needs identified. To measure the effectiveness of the persona development process, we also used two other low-fidelity app mockups that were developed prior to the workshop without using the

Persona Worksheet

Facts Overview/ Demographics	Facts & Interactions
List the demographics info about your persona, e.g., gender, age, residence, background, income, job, marital status, children, faith, urban-suburban, rural, etc.	List any basic information about the Persona's roles and responsibilities, key information about their household and families, key information about Persona's health and their family's.

Persona's routines and interactions. What online platforms do they use for care services (technology usage?) |
| **Challenges and Goals** | **Wants and Needs** |
| List the relevant health challenges that this Persona faces.
List their relevant goals. | List what this persona wants from your service to meet their needs and goals and to overcome their challenges. |

Fig. 4. Persona worksheet used in the workshop.

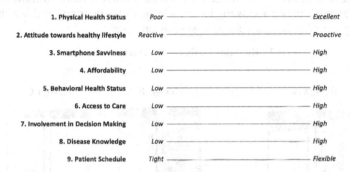

Fig. 5. User attributes used for persona clustering.

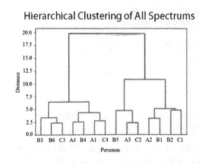
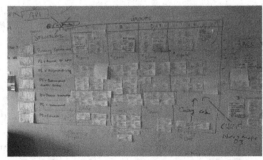

Fig. 6. Hierarchical Cluster Analysis (left) and manual inspection of worksheets (right).

information revealed in the proto personas (Fig. 8). These mockups were used in user persona interviews to compare the designs and get feedback about patient preferences.

- Active Abbey:
  - o Mostly belong to upper-middle-class socio-economic background. Either they are diagnosed with diabetes or have a kid with diabetes. They are very career-oriented, which leads to a very busy lifestyle. They are very smartphone savvy. They have a very proactive attitude towards life and take their health very seriously. They have very high disease knowledge.
- Hopeless Heather:
  - o Mostly belong to lower-middle-class socio-economic background. They experience multiple comorbidities and have limited access to healthcare. They have limited knowledge about their health issues and depend on others. They have low motivation in managing their health. They are not very smartphone savvy.
- Dallying Dani:
  - o Mostly belong to middle-class socio-economic background. They have irregular schedules most days. They have a reactive attitude towards health. They think they possess higher knowledge about their physical health than they actually do. They are avid smartphone users.

Fig. 7. Key user attributes and their definitions.

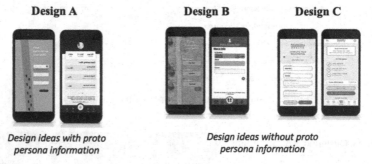

Design A   Design B   Design C

Design ideas with proto persona information   *Design ideas without proto persona information*

Fig. 8. Low-fidelity design mockups of the smartphone app.

3.2 Developing User Personas

Materials and Methodology. For user persona development, we conducted individual video conference interviews with participants. The goal of our user interviews was twofold. The first goal was to verify the results of our proto-persona development workshop. For this purpose, we prepared interview questions related to the personas' lifestyles, their current diabetes management routine, and their needs and challenges. The second goal of these interviews was to gather feedback about the app design mockups that we developed in the prior steps. For this purpose, we prepared a set of slides with screenshots of the designs created using the proto-persona information. We also showed the participants the designs that were created without the proto-persona information so that we could compare the feedback received on the design mockups.

    Participants were invited to participate in the study via mass email to the organization's mailing list and social media flyers. Our inclusion criteria included participants who were either patients or caregivers of patients diagnosed with either Type 1 or Type 2 diabetes, ages 18 and above, and could speak, read and write English. We excluded any participants who were diagnosed with moderate to severe intellectual disabilities.

We categorized participants between the ages of 18 and 46 as younger users and any participant above the age of 46 years as older users. We used relative terms such as "younger" and "older" for patient groups to highlight the comparative nature of age categorization in our study [15]. Our final set of participants included 21 diabetic patients (7 older patients with ages above 46 years, and 14 younger patients with ages between 18 and 46 years). Sixteen participants were female and five were male. Since the interviews were conducted via video conference calls, we recruited participants from all over the United States.

Results. We conducted user interviews to (1) verify the proto personas, and (2) get feedback about the app design mockups. The results of the interviews not only in the verification of the proto-personas but also revealed that patients belonging to the same persona group can have differences in their needs and challenges. For this reason, we created major persona groups and within these major groups, we identified persona subgroups (Fig. 9). We labeled the first major persona group identified as "Active Abbey" (n = 18). This persona is diagnosed with Type 1 diabetes, belongs to upper-middle class socio-economic status, has a very busy schedule due to their jobs, are outgoing, and has a proactive attitude towards health and life. Within this personas group, the first subgroup we identified is Younger Abbey (n = 9), who belongs to the 21–35 years age group, is either single or married without kids, faces challenges in managing their diabetes as they do not feel comfortable wearing or showing their glucose monitors in public settings. The second subgroup of the Active Abbey persona group is Abbey (n = 4), who belongs to the 36–46 years age group, is married with kids, and finds managing diabetes challenging with kids and jobs. The third subgroup is labeled as Older Abbey (n = 5), who belongs to the age group of 46 + years, have multiple chronic health issues, and find managing diabetes challenging along with other health conditions. We labeled the second persona group as "Heather" (n = 2). This persona group is diagnosed with diabetes Type 2, are 56 + years old, belong to middle-class socio-economic background, are either unemployed or work part-time. We identified two subgroups within this persona group, (1) Hopeless Heather (n = 1), who is physically inactive due to laziness, does not give priority to their health, has no health insurance, and follows an unhealthy lifestyle, and (2) Hopeful Heather (n = 1), who is physically active, have a proactive attitude towards health, have multiple chronic issues but still are motivated to self-manage their diabetes. The third persona group we identified is "Dani" (n = 1). This persona is diagnosed with Latent Autoimmune Diabetes in Adults, belongs to the 36–46 years age group, belong to lower socio-economic background, has multiple comorbidities, and has limited ability to make their own health decisions. We did not identify any subgroups within this persona group since one participant belonged to this persona.

The second goal of the user interviews was to get feedback about the app design ideas. For the second goal too, we had two subgoals. First was to assess the effectiveness of proto personas in the design process, and second to compare the feedback (preferences, approvals, and disapprovals) of younger and older users on the app designs.

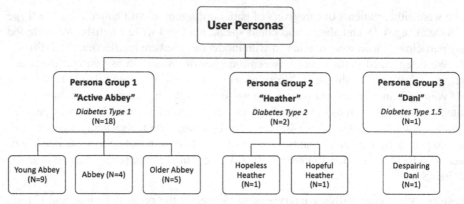

Fig. 9. Major personas and their subgroups.

Design A, the app design that was created using the information from the proto personas, was the most popular first choice among all participants (Fig. 10). Design A was the most preferred choice among younger user groups (Younger Abbey, Abbey, and Dani). Most of the younger participants liked the motivational quote on the Homepage of Design A. They said that the motivational quote made embarks a positive feeling in them. They also liked the colors, design, and layout of information in Design A. According to them, the layout of information made it easier to locate important information with minimal effort. One participant mentioned, "*I like Design A. It's simple yet very effective. Design B looks boring, and Design C looks very busy and overwhelming.*"

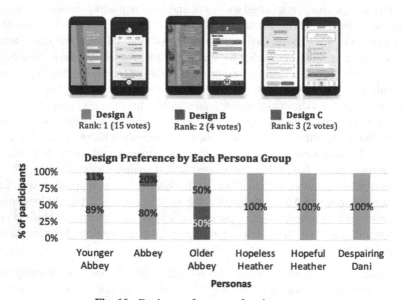

Fig. 10. Design preferences of each persona.

Within the older user groups, Design A was the most preferred choice in Hopeless Heather and Hopeful Heather personas, but in the Older Abbey persona group, Designs A and B had a tie. Older users who preferred Design A liked certain features such as the dashboard providing a summary of body vitals and the number of footsteps on the home screen. They found the information in the dashboard helpful and easily accessible According to one participant from Older Abbey persona, *"In Design A I like the easy thing at the top that says your heart rate, body temp. I really like that"*. They also found the minimalistic design of Design A to be more useful and easier to use. One participant said, *"I really like Design A. It's clean, simple, and straightforward."* Most common recommendation was using contrasting colors to present important information and have the option of adjusting the font size according to their preferences.

Older users from the Older Abbey persona who preferred Design B specifically liked the different colored text frames. According to them, the different colored text boxes made the information in them more prominent. One participant mentioned, *"One thing I like is the coloring, and how each box has a different color associated with it, distinguishing the information from one another."*

Both older and younger users showed similar preferences toward different app designs. Even though both groups preferred Design A, the reasons for choosing the design were vastly different. When asked about their preferences, older user groups preferred contrasting colors, bigger font sizes, and bigger and more prominent button sizes. This is because physical and cognitive abilities change with age, leading to declining in visual and motor capabilities in older adults [16]. On the other hand, younger users preferred Design A because its simplicity and visual appeal made the design look more user-friendly and efficient.

4 Discussion

Our results showed that our proposed process was successful in achieving its goals. Proto persona development process helped in identifying user needs and challenges and making the design process more effective and efficient. Based on the needs identified through proto personas, our team was able to create a low-fidelity design mockup that catered to the needs of all personas. This was reflected in the results of the user interviews. The user interviews revealed that despite being in different stages of life with varying needs and challenges, the design created using proto personas satisfied the needs of both the younger and older user groups. Design A seemed to satisfy the needs of different user groups, compared to the other designs, hence, proving the effectiveness of our proposed process.

Our user persona development process also proved to be more efficient as in the same interviews, we were able to refine our personas as well as gain valuable feedback from the users about the design choices.

5 Conclusion, Limitations and Implications for Future Research

The objective of this paper was to develop a systematic approach to the persona development process. To assess the effectiveness of the process, we explored the following question: Is our proposed persona development methodology effective in guiding the early design phase of a diabetes management smartphone application (app) targeted at older and younger users? Our study results provided evidence of effectiveness and efficiency of our proposed persona development methodology in early design process of the smartphone app. Developing proto-personas helped in eliciting user requirements for the diabetes management app, keeping user needs and wants into consideration. User personas helped in verifying the needs and wants of the patients as well as getting feedback on the app design mockups created using the information from proto-personas.

Our study, however, did have some limitations. We tested our proposed method on a small sample size of only 21 participants. A bigger sample size could result in better generalizability of the results. Moreover, we conducted our interviews via video conferencing, which is why we were able to attract participants who were already comfortable with technology use and had familiarity with different application types. Expanding our sample size to users who are not smartphone savvy can help identify different types of needs and challenges. Overall, our results are encouraging and can be replicated on different types of digital solutions catering to the needs of different populations. Our paper provides a systematic approach to the persona development process. For future research, we recommend using the persona development methodology proposed in this paper to increase the efficiency and effectiveness of the early design process.

References

1. Miaskiewicz, T., Kozar, K.A.: Personas and user-centered design: how can personas benefit product design processes? Des. Stud. **32**(5), 417–430 (2011)
2. LeRouge, C., et al.: User profiles and personas in the design and development of consumer health technologies. Int. J. Med. Inf. **82**(11), e251–e268 (2013)
3. Pruitt, J., Adlin, T.: The Persona Lifecycle: Keeping People in Mind Throughout Product Design. Elsevier, Amsterdam (2010)
4. Jain, P., Djamasbi, S., Wyatt, J.: Creating value with proto-research persona development. In: Nah, FH., Siau, K. (eds.) HCI in Business, Government and Organizations. Information Systems and Analytics. HCII 2019. LNCS, vol. 11589, pp. 72–82 (2019). Springer, Cham. https://doi.org/10.1007/978-3-030-22338-0_6
5. Salminen, J., et al.: Use cases for design personas: a systematic review and new frontiers. pp. 1–21 (2022)
6. Roberts, D., et al.: Designing for the user with OVID: Bridging the Gap between Software Engineering and user Interface Design. Macmillan Technical Publishing, Noida (1998)
7. Nielsen, L.: Personas-user focused design. vol. 1373, Springer, London (2013). https://doi.org/10.1007/978-1-4471-7427-1
8. Kneale, L., et al.: Using scenarios and personas to enhance the effectiveness of heuristic usability evaluations for older adults and their care team. J. Biomed. Inform. **73**, 43–50 (2017)
9. Bhattacharyya, O., et al.: Using human-centered design to build a digital health advisor for patients with complex needs: persona and prototype development. J Med. Internet Res. **21**(5), e10318 (2019)
10. van der Molen, P., et al.: Identifying user preferences for a digital educational solution for young seniors with diabetes. Diabetes Spectrum **30**(3), 182–187 (2017)
11. Ekström, M., Loos, E.: Constructing third age ehealth consumers by using personas from a cultural age perspective. In: Zhou, J., Salvendy, G. (eds.) Human Aspects of IT for the Aged Population. Design for Aging. ITAP 2015. LNCS, vol. 9193, pp. 35–43 (2015). Springer, Cham (2015). https://doi.org/10.1007/978-3-319-20892-3_4

12. Goh, C.H., Kulathuramaiyer, N., Zaman, T.: Riding waves of change: a review of personas research landscape based on the three waves of HCI. In: Choudrie, J., Islam, M., Wahid, F., Bass, J., Priyatma, J. (eds.) Information and Communication Technologies for Development. ICT4D 2017. IFIP Advances in Information and Communication Technology, vol. 504, pp. 605–616. Springer, Cham (2017). https://doi.org/10.1007/978-3-319-59111-7_49

13. Salminen, J., et al.: A survey of 15 years of data-driven persona development. Int. J. Hum.-Comput. Interact. **37**(18), 1685–1708 (2021)

14. Hibbard, J.H., et al.: The development and testing of a measure assessing clinician beliefs about patient self-management. Health Expect **13**(1), 65–72 (2010)

15. Varzgani, F., et al.: Effects of text simplification on reading behavior of older and younger users. In: Human Aspects of IT for the Aged Population. Technology Design and Acceptance: 7th International Conference, ITAP 2021, Held as Part of the 23rd HCI International Conference, HCII 2021, Virtual Event, 24–29 July 2021, Proceedings, Part I. (2021)

16. Nguyen, M.H., et al.: Optimising eHealth tools for older patients: collaborative redesign of a hospital website. Eur. J. Cancer Care **28**, e12882 (2019)

Effects of Health Science Popularization Platform on Older Adults' eHealth Literacy: From the Perspective of Digital Empowerment

Yixuan Wang[1](✉), Xiaoting Xu[2](✉), and Qinghua Zhu[1](✉)

[1] School of Information Management, Nanjing University, Nanjing 210023, China
mf21140119@sina.nju.edu.cn, qhzhu@nju.edu.cn
[2] School of Sociology and Population Studies, Nanjing University of Posts and
Telecommunications, Nanjing 210023, China
xtxu@njupt.edu.cn

Abstract. The world's population is currently aging significantly, and older adults have a significant need for health information while having a low level of eHealth literacy. With the implementation of the health China strategy, the construction of the health science popularization platform has been put on the agenda. However, it is unknown how digital technology will affect senior users. We looked into the particular impacts that the kinds of digital empowerment that the health science popularization platform has made available to older adults have on them. In this study, we also developed, from the perspective of digital empowerment, the mechanism model of the health science popularization platform on the eHealth literacy of older adults. This study employed a questionnaire survey approach to gathering data, primarily using an online platform to ask older persons with prior experience using a platform for the popularization of health science to fill out. 248 participants aged over 50 took part in the study and finished the survey up to standard. The SmartPLS4.0 program was used to analyze the data using the PLS-SEM approach. According to the findings, the health science popularization platform significantly affects older adults' capacity to look for and use health information, and as a result, older adults' self-efficacy and ease of use support their eHealth literacy. By enhancing information push, simplifying function operation, and other measures during the future development of the health science popularization platform, we may assist older adults in adjusting to digital technology and thereby advance eHealth literacy, finally help bridge the digital divide.

Keywords: EHealth literacy · Health science popularization platform ·
PLS-SEM · Older adults

1 Introduction

With the serious problem of global population aging, how to help older adults bridge the digital divide has become an important issue to enjoy their old age and adapt to the digital era. The Internet plays an important role in terms of the dissemination of health knowledge, with over 72% of Internet users in America seek health information online [1]. Even though there is broad agreement that online interactions should complement (but not substitute) traditional face-to-face encounters, for some people health science popularization platforms such as health forums represent the primary way of accessing medical information for convenience or financial reasons [2]. With the implementation of Health China 2030, a large number of health science popularization platforms have been under construction, and much barrier-free transformation has been carried out for older adults to help them improve digital literacy. Older adults are facing problems using digital technology, including privacy infringement, distortion of health information, unskilled operation, and fear of difficulty. During the COVID-19 pandemic, due to restrictions on offline activities, they begin to seek medical help and health science popularization online. Large amounts of older adults start learning to use health applications to obtain health information and conduct online communication in health communities. The changes in eHealth literacy in the process of older adults' exposure to digital technology, such as health science popularization platforms, are unknown and worth studying.

2 Literature Review

2.1 Health Science Popularization

The canonical understanding of popularization involves a one-way transmission or dissemination model of communication, whereby expert, esoteric knowledge is translated into language understandable by the public [3]. Popularization is a social process comprised of a wide variety of discursive-semiotic practices, such as mass media, books, the Internet, exhibitions and other communicative events, designed to spread scientific knowledge, opinions and ideologies of scholars among the public [4].

The popularization of medical information and medical technology can lead to improved health equity and digital health equity. The digital divide and disparities in healthcare access can create differences in the quality of care and treatment between different population groups [5]. Jisan Lee et al. reviewed the domestic and international use status, acceptance rates, and use cases for various types of medical information. This study concluded that healthcare providers should continually strive to popularize medical information and foster health equity and digital health equity [6]. P. ANESA & A. FAGE-BUTLER characterized the online health forum as a Web 2.0-style popularization tool, and investigated which explanatory tools (such as definitions, analogies, exemplifications, and generalizations) could help experts to explain complex or technical information [2].

At present, health popularization platforms in China are mainly of the following types: a)health columns on comprehensive websites, such as Baidu Doctor under Baidu and the health column under Sohu; b)specialized health websites, such as Tencent Medical Dictionary and 39 Health Network; c)platforms based on social software, such as the health official accounts on WeChat and Weibo. Recently, the short video social platform of Tiktok has attracted numerous health science popularization organizations. However, there is still relatively little research done into health science popularization platforms and the behaviors of senior users.

2.2 Digital Empowerment

In the field of management, the concept of "empowerment" was initially proposed by Follett in the 1920s to enhance organizational power through empowering individuals [7]. With the popularization and development of digital technology, the concept of digital empowerment has emerged, which is defined as a new phenomenon with enhanced digital capability [8]. From different perspectives, scholars have studied digital empowerment. Sociologists view digital empowerment as not only the result of individual use of technology, but also the ability to make society more inclusive through technology [9]. In addition, digital empowerment gives individuals new ways to solve problems and enables people to become capable subjects, who can take control of their lives and environment [10]. In the field of management, Lenka et al. put forth three core components of digital empowerment from the perspective of corporate value co-creation: intelligence ability, connectivity ability, and analysis ability. They explained the mechanism through which these three components and customers can jointly create value [11]. In general, digital empowerment can be divided into two categories based on the empowerment tools - resource empowerment [12] and structural empowerment [13] - as well as two categories based on actor relationships - platform empowerment [14] and ecological empowerment [15].

Although scholars have explored the connotation of digital empowerment from different perspectives, all definitions cover the following two aspects: a) The application of digital technology, which can help individuals gain more information and professional skills to innovate and adapt to digital society [16]. b) The improvement of the ability of the empowerment object, emphasizing knowledge literacy and increased innovation ability. To date, little attention has been paid to the health science popularization platform and its potential to help older adults bridge the digital divide. Digital empowerment can help them learn new skills, improve eHealth literacy, and ultimately use resources on health science popularization platforms to access, manage, process, and disseminate health information.

2.3 EHealth Literacy

EHealth literacy, which involves the ability to find, understand and evaluate online health information through electronic media, and make relevant decisions to solve their own health problems [17], has been investigated in the youth population [18] and the group of patients with chronic diseases [19]. However, research on the electronic health literacy of the older population is relatively scarce. Currently, studies on the eHealth literacy of older adults focus on the current situation, specific applications [20], and influencing factors [21]. Consequently, the use of health science popularization platforms can help to improve the eHealth literacy of older adults, which will play an important role in bridging the digital gap.

3   Theoratical Background and Research Hypothesis

3.1   Theoratical Background

Motivation-Opportunity-Ability (MOA) Theory. MOA theory believes that consumers' handling of marketing communication depends on three aspects: motivation, opportunity and ability. The effectiveness of marketing information can be achieved by developing a person's motivation, opportunity and ability level [22]. The MOA theory has a wide range of applications and is often used to explain the motivation of other information behaviors, including the use of social media [23], online gamer communication [24] and other fields. In this study, digital empowerment provided by the health science popularization platform has given older adults more opportunities to access and use health information and digital technology. The help and confidence of older adults themselves achieve have become their motivation for continuous use, and the ability improvement is reflected in the improvement of their eHealth literacy.

Technology Acceptance Model (TAM). The TAM model, proposed by American scholar David, aims to evaluate the perceived usefulness and ease of use of external variables, such as user characteristics, system design, organizational structure, and policy impact. These two variables will then affect the user's attitude towards the system and finally the behavior [25]. This model has been widely used in the field of information systems to research the user's use intention and service evaluation mechanism. In this study, to understand the impact of the health science popularization platform on the eHealth literacy of older users, we combine the TAM model and the MOA theory to create a conceptual model. This model will illustrate the digital empowerment mechanism of the health science popularization platform for senior users.

3.2 Perspectives of Health Science Popularization Platform

Health Information Seeking (HIS). Health Information Seeking is defined as the user's behavior of searching for information about the disease, health, and risk in specific situations [26]. The health science popularization platform has broken through the limitations of time and region and is increasingly favored by users. Through digital empowerment of the health science popularization platform, older adults can search for the health information they need, satisfy their health information requirements, and improve their sense of efficacy in the process. Because older adults are usually not proficient in digital technology, the information search function provided by platforms can also make them feel more receptive to digital empowerment. Based on the above analysis, this study proposes the following hypothesizes:

H1: The health information seeking ability empowered older adults by the health science popularization platform has a positive impact on their perceived usefulness.
H2: The health information seeking ability empowered older adults by the health science popularization platform has a positive impact on their perceived ease of use.
H3: The health information seeking ability empowered older adults by the health science popularization platform has a positive impact on their self-efficacy.

Personalization (PER). In the era of algorithm, personalization in the field of e-commerce focuses on how to mine valuable information and patterns from the mass data of consumers through big data, to better predict the requirements and preferences of consumers and provide them with more valuable products and services [27]. The personalized service of the health science popularization platform is based on the particularity of older adults and provides corresponding health information services according to their needs and preferences. Accurate personalized services and information push services help older adults have a better user experience and feel the usefulness and convenience of the platform's digital empowerment. Based on the above analysis, this study proposes the following hypothesizes:

H4: The personalized services provided by the health science popularization platform are positively affecting the perceived usefulness of older adults.
H5: The personalized services provided by the health science popularization platform are positively affecting the perceived ease of use of older adults.
H6: The personalized services provided by the health science popularization platform are positively affecting the self-efficacy of older adults.

Health Information Usage (HIU). In the study of users' incidental health information use behavior, researchers found that there was a positive correlation with users' mastery of health knowledge [28]. The health science popularization platform enables older adults to access health information and medical knowledge that are difficult to obtain before so that they can improve doctor-patient communication and guide daily health care. Digital technology reduces the threshold for older adults to apply health information and obtain health guidance, enabling them to feel the value of the health science popularization platform, reduce the resistance to digital technology, and improve their internal sense of efficacy in using health information. Based on the above analysis, this study proposes the following hypothesizes:

H7: The health information usage ability empowered older adults by the health science popularization platform has a positive impact on their perceived usefulness.
H8: The health information usage ability empowered older adults by the health science popularization platform has a positive impact on their perceived ease of use.
H9: The health information usage ability empowered older adults by the health science popularization platform has a positive impact on their self-efficacy.

3.3 Perspectives of Older Adults

Perceived Usefulness (PU). Perceived usefulness refers to the useful information of goods or services obtained by users in the environment, and is the effective information screening before generating behavioral intention [29]. When users can obtain more useful information from the platform, their perceived trust will be significantly enhanced, and their willingness to purchase and use will also be stronger [30]. If older adults feel that the information and services obtained from the health science popularization platform are useful, they will tend to continue to use the platform and apply their health advice, which will ultimately improve their electronic health literacy. Based on the above analysis, this study proposes the following hypothesis:

H10: The perceived usefulness of older adults using the health science popularization platform has a positive impact on their eHealth literacy.

Perceived Ease of Use (PEU). Perceived ease of use can positively affect users' acceptance of information systems and promote their continuous use [31]. For older adults, the ease of using the information system is of great significance for their sustainable use. If older adults feel relaxed and convenient in the process of using the health science popularization platform, and will be willing to use more digital technology and access more health information, to improve their electronic health literacy. Based on the above analysis, this study proposes the following hypothesis:

H11: The perceived ease of use of older adults using the health science popularization platform has a positive impact on their eHealth literacy.

Self-efficacy (SE). Self-efficacy refers to the self-evaluation of the individual's ability to organize and implement a series of actions to achieve the set goals [32]. Previous studies have shown that self-efficacy can promote users' willingness to invest in purchasing, learning, and using certain information systems [33]. The improvement of self-efficacy experienced by older adults while using the health science popularization platform will further promote their use of the platform, learn more health knowledge, and practice digital technology operation, thus promoting their eHealth literacy. Based on the above analysis, this study proposes the following hypothesis (Fig. 1 and Table 1):

H12: The self-efficacy of older adults using the health science popularization platform has a positive impact on their eHealth literacy.

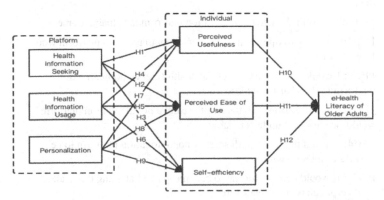

Fig. 1. Conceptual model of the impact mechanism of the health science popularization platform on older adults' eHealth literacy from the perspective of digital empowerment

Table 1. Measurement indicators and reliability of each variable

Variable	Item	Reference
HIS	HIS1: I have sought out health information on the health science popularization platform	[34]
	HIS2: I have looked to different online sources to obtain health information	
	HIS3: I have paid close attention to health information on the health science popularization platform	
	HIS4: I have actively searched on health science popularization platform for health information	
PER	PER1: The health science popularization platform offers personalized services based on my health situation	[35]
	PER2: The health science popularization platform offers personalized services based on my preferences	
	PER3: Based on my preferences and health situation, the health scicence popularization platform can provide me the kind of information or service that I might like	
HIU	HIU1: I will recommend others to seek health information through doctors in the health science popularization platform	[36]
	HIU2: I will make a health or medicine-related decision according to the information I sought in the health science popularization platform	
	HIU3: I will recommend others to use the health information from the health science popularization platform	
PU	PU1: The health science popularization platform can provide me with professional knowledge	[37]
	PU2: The health science popularization platform is helpful to answer my doubts	
	PU3: The health science popularization platform is valuable to me	
PEU	PEU1: Learning to operate health science popularization platform would be easy for me	[31]
	PEU2: I would find it easy to get the health science popularization platform to do what I want it to do	
	PEU3: My interaction with the health science popularization platform would be clear and understandable	
	PEU4: I would find the health science popularization platform to be flexible to interact with	
	PEU5: It would be easy for me to become skillful at using the health science popularization platform	
	PEU6: I would find the health science popularization platform easy to use	

(*continued*)

Table 1. (*continued*)

Variable	Item	Reference
SE	SE1: I can always manage to solve difficult problems if I try hard enough	[38]
	SE2: If someone opposes me, I can find means and ways to get what I want	
	SE3: It is easy for me to stick to my aims and accomplish my goals	
	SE4: I am confident that I could deal efficiently with unexpected events	
	SE5: Thanks to my resourcefulness, I know how to handle unforeseen situations	
	SE6: I can solve most problems if I invest the necessary effort	
	SE7: I can remain calm when facing difficulties because I can rely on my coping abilities	
	SE8: When I am cofronted with a problem, I can usually find several solutions	
	SE9: If I am in a bind, I can usually think of something to do	
	SE10: No matter what comes my way, I'm usually able to handle it	
EHL	EHL1: I know how to find helpful resources on the Internet	[39]
	EHL2: I know how to use the Internet to answer my health questions	
	EHL3: I know what health resources are available on the Internet	
	EHL4: I know where to find helpful health resources on the Internet	
	EHL5: I know how to use the health information I find on the Internet to help me	
	EHL6: I have the skills I need to evaluate the health resoures on the Internet	
	EHL7: I can tell high quality from low quality health resources on the Internet	
	EHL8: I feel confident in using information from the Internet to make health decisions	

4   Research Methodology

4.1   Research Design

In this study, the questionnaire survey method was used to collect data, and the PLS-SEM method was used for data analysis. Firstly, considering the particularity of older adults, the questionnaire distribution plan was conducted online and offline at the same time. Secondly, structural equation model method was used because PLS-SEM is the most simple but accurate to determine the dependency between multiple variables [40]. In the multiple linear regression analysis, the eHealth literacy of older adults was taken as the dependent variable, and the empowerment dimensions health science popularization platform provides to older adults were taken as the independent variables. The influencing factor model of the health science popularization platform on the eHealth literacy of older adults from the perspective of digital empowerment was established. Finally, the statistical analysis software program SmartPLS4.0 were used to collect, process, and analyze the data. Theoretical and practical discussions were conducted based on the data analysis results.

4.2 Data Collection

This study took older adults with experience in using the health science popularization platform as the research object, and set screening questions to ensure the accuracy of the object. We have distributed the questionnaire online for data collection through the Tencent questionnaire older adults' group, which is a special aging research service and has accumulated more than 500,000 older user resources.

This questionnaire mainly includes two parts. The first part is demographic variables, including gender, age, and education. The second part is about the investigation of the influencing factors of older adults' eHealth literacy, including 7 latent variables such as health information seeking and usage, et al. In terms of scale design, the measurement indicators in this paper were based on or adapted from previous studies, and were scenarioized based on the actual situation of older adults in China, using Likert 5-level scale. After several rounds of collection, a total of 289 complete questionnaires were finally obtained, and 248 valid questionnaires were obtained after eliminating invalid questionnaires such as age group inconformity (under 50).

5   Empirical Testing and Analysis

5.1   Participant Characteristics

The survey results show that there are slightly more males than females among the older adults interviewed; The age is concentrated in the age range of 55 to 65 years old, with 55 to 60 years old accounting for the largest proportion, and most of them have retired. The education level of the older adults interviewed is mainly high school education, followed by primary and middle school education, which indicates that the education level of older adults in China is still not ideal. Few older people have received graduate education (Table 2).

Table 2. Participant characteristics

Demographic variables		Frequency	percentage (%)
Gender	Male	138	55.6
	Female	110	44.4
Age	50–55	37	14.9
	55–60	141	56.9
	60–65	61	24.6
	65–70	5	2
	over 70	4	1.6

(*continued*)

Table 2. (*continued*)

Demographic variables		Frequency	percentage (%)
Working Status	Unretired	98	39.5
	Retired	130	52.4
	Reemployment after Retirement	20	8.1
Education	primary and middle school	56	22.6
	senior high school	80	32.3
	junior college	51	20.6
	undergraduate course	50	20.2
	Postgraduate course (master,PHD)	11	4.4

5.2 Reliability and Validity Analysis

The results show that Cronbach's α of all values are greater than 0.7, the standard load of each item factor corresponding to the latent variable of the model is greater than 0.7, and the combined reliability(CR) value is also greater than 0.7, indicating that there is high consistency and good reliability among the items. The average extraction variance of each variable is greater than 0.5, and the square root of the AVE value of each variable is greater than the correlation coefficient between this variable and other variables. The aggregate validity and differential validity of this paper are good. In addition, the VIF of each variable is less than 10, so there is no multicollinearity among the variables of this model (Table 3 and Table 4).

Table 3. Outer loadings, Cronbach' α, CR value and AVE value

Variable	Item	Outer loading	VIF	Cronbach's α	CR	AVE
Health Information Seeking(HIS)	HIS1	0.898	3.000	0.911	0.912	0.790
	HIS2	0.853	2.330			
	HIS3	0.897	3.281			
	HIS4	0.905	3.265			
Health Information Usage(HIU)	HIU1	0.895	2.832	0.860	0.861	0.782
	HIU2	0.848	1.718			
	HIU3	0.908	2.981			
Personalization(PER)	PER1	0.921	3.146	0.917	0.917	0.857
	PER2	0.930	3.379			
	PER3	0.927	3.239			
Perceived Usefulness(PU)	PU1	0.923	3.156	0.938	0.939	0.765
	PU2	0.919	3.025			
	PU3	0.908	2.665			

(*continued*)

Table 3. (*continued*)

Variable	Item	Outer loading	VIF	Cronbach's α	CR	AVE
Perceived Ease of Use(PEU)	PEU1	0.834	2.609	0.905	0.905	0.840
	PEU2	0.896	3.589			
	PEU3	0.911	4.268			
	PEU4	0.847	3.01			
	PEU5	0.864	3.202			
	PEU6	0.895	3.793			
Self-efficacy(SE)	SE1	0.768	2.421	0.950	0.950	0.690
	SE2	0.879	2.358			
	SE3	0.779	3.403			
	SE4	0.849	4.224			
	SE5	0.872	3.207			
	SE6	0.832	2.665			
	SE7	0.803	2.463			
	SE8	0.787	3.113			
	SE9	0.846	5.477			
	SE10	0.881	5.544			
eHealth literacy(EHL)	EHL1	0.835	3.009	0.937	0.938	0.693
	EHL2	0.824	2.902			
	EHL3	0.847	3.566			
	EHL4	0.869	3.619			
	EHL5	0.81	2.713			
	EHL6	0.825	3.01			
	EHL7	0.833	4.764			
	EHL8	0.817	4.814			

Table 4. Discriminate validity test results

Variables	EHL	HIS	HIU	PER	PEU	PU	SE
EHL	**0.833**						
HIS	0.696	**0.889**					
HIU	0.644	0.694	**0.884**				
PER	0.648	0.819	0.785	**0.926**			
PEU	0.803	0.783	0.745	0.776	**0.875**		
PU	0.675	0.756	0.767	0.801	0.789	**0.917**	
SE	0.811	0.629	0.659	0.627	0.804	0.656	**0.831**

5.3   Path Coefficients and Hypothesis Testing

In this paper, Smart PLS4.0 is used to estimate the path parameters of the research model, and the BootstrApplying repeated sampling method is used to test the significance of the path coefficients, with a sampling number of 5000 times. The results show that the positive effects of health information search and health information use on the perceived usefulness, perceived ease of use, and self-efficacy of older adults are established, and the personalized characteristics have a significant positive impact on perceived usefulness, while the hypothesizes of its impact on perceived ease of use and self-efficacy are not supported by data in this paper. The perceived ease of use and self-efficacy of older adults using the health science popularization platform have significant positive effects on their eHealth literacy, while the impact of perceived usefulness is unclear (Table 5 and Fig. 2).

Table 5. Results of Hypothesis Test

Hypothesis	Relationship	coefficient(β)	T-value	P-value	result
H1	HIS -> PU	0.253	2.905	0.004**	√
H2	HIS -> PEU	0.401	3.092	0.002**	√
H3	HIS -> SE	0.287	2.208	0.027*	√
H4	HIU -> PU	0.325	4.509	0.000***	√
H5	HIU -> PEU	0.301	3.309	0.001**	√
H6	HIU -> SE	0.396	3.161	0.002**	√
H7	PER -> PU	0.338	3.867	0.000***	√
H8	PER -> PEU	0.212	1.751	0.080	
H9	PER -> SE	0.081	0.537	0.591	
H10	PU -> EHL	0.084	1.116	0.265	
H11	PEU -> EHL	0.365	3.481	0.001**	√
H12	SE -> EHL	0.463	6.664	0.000***	√

*** P < 0.001, ** P < 0.05, * P < 0.01

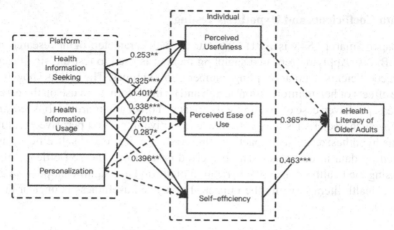

Fig. 2. Model path coefficient

6 Conclusions and Suggestions

6.1 Digital Empowerment of Health Science Popularization Platform

Significant Impacts of Health Information Seeking. Firstly, Health information seeking behavior significantly affects older adults' perceived usefulness. With such digital technology, they could search for health information arbitrarily and satisfy their multiple health information requirements on their own, which could make them agree with the value of the platform. Secondly, health information seeking behavior significantly positively affects older adults' perceived ease of use.

Significant Impacts of Health Information Usage. The ability of older adults to truly contact, use and disseminate health information is an important segment in the digital empowerment of the health science popularization platform, which is of great significance for them to integrate into the digital society and bridge the digital divide. Compared with passively accepting a massive volumn of health information, older adults can actively accept health information services and practice them in life, so that they can truly feel the importance of health science popularization platforms and realize the convenience of digital technology operations. Constant contact and practice help older adults build up confidence in their use of information technology so that they feel able to adapt to the digital era and improve their internal efficacy.

The Impact of Personalization is Inconspicuous. On the one hand, accurate recommendations of health information based on the individual needs and preferences of older adults can provide more help and improve the perceived usefulness of older users. On the other hand, large amounts of personalized health information may cause older adults to suffer from health information overload and affect their usage of the health science popularization platform. Previous studies have shown that information overload can cause anxiety and even confusion in users' behavior [41]. As older adults themselves are physically and psychologically weak, facing large numbers of health information pushes could easily generate negative emotions and generate doubts about their health status. Also, too complex health services will make older adults confused in terms of functions, and feel that the operation of the health science popularization platform is too complex to use, which will reduce their confidence in operating and result in insufficient self-efficacy.

6.2 Improvement of Older Adults' eHealth Literacy

PEU & Self-efficacy Have Significant Positive Impact on eHealth Literacy. Older adults' perceived ease of use could promote their eHealth literacy, as previous studies have shown that e-health literacy is related to the use of health care [42]. On the one hand, the operation of the health science popularization platform is simple, practical and easy to operate. The page design is easy to understand, in simple terms, and rich, and practical in content. The health suggestions put forward, such as diet, Chinese patent medicine, massage, and acupuncture, are operable, which is more conducive to the learning and practice of health knowledge for older adults. On the other hand, older adults feel that the health science popularization platform is easy to operate, which helps them overcome their fear of unfamiliar digital technology, and is willing to get in touch with other health information platforms, and finally achieve the improvement of electronic health literacy. Older adults' self-efficacy could also significantly promote their digital literacy. As older adults' self-confidence and sense of efficacy in the face of digital technology improve, they will reduce their previous fear of emerging technologies and massive information, and face the digital era with a more open attitude. Starting from the digital empowerment of the health science popularization platform, older adults will have the confidence to search for health information and obtain health services from more larger platforms, improve their electronic health literacy and even digital literacy, and successfully bridge the digital divide.

Perceived Usefulness Has No Significant Impact on eHealth Literacy. This issue can be explained from three aspects: in terms of health information, the information provided by the health science popularization platform is massive and of uneven quality for older adults. Health information overload reduces older adults' ability to judge the authenticity and practicality of information and does not play a substantive role in improving their eHealth literacy. In terms of platforms, for older adults in modern society, there are many other online and offline channels to obtain useful health services in addition to the health science popularization platform. While recognizing the value of the health science popularization platform, they may still choose traditional ways to obtain health information services, such as seeking help from family doctors, because of unadaptability, psychological resistance, and other reasons. From the perspective of older adults themselves, realizing the value of the health science popularization platform will also bring practical difficulties due to their own digital technology deficiencies. In particular, the family older adults group lacks the assistance of peer exchange of health information in social relations to promote eHealth literacy [43], which hinders the learning and practice of health knowledge.

6.3 Suggestions

For The Health Science Popularization Platform. On the one hand, strengthen the information and service quality of the health science popularization platform, and provide more practical and effective health advice for the elderly. Platforms should expand the communication and dissemination channels of health knowledge, help older adults to quickly find scientific and professional information content from the massive complex health information, promote their awareness and understanding of health information, and ultimately improve eHealth literacy. On the other hand, health science popularization platforms should simplify the operation and take more consideration of the requirements of older adults in design and function, to reduce their use burden. The personalized recommendation information for older adults should also be more simplified to avoid the pressure and anxiety caused by excessive health information push. The health science popularization platform can also use AIGC technology (robot, virtual reality, etc.) to assist the science popularization activities for older adults, enhance their sense of presence and perceived ease of use, finally make them more receptive to digital technology.

For Social Environment Construction. It is far from enough for the health science popularization platform to empower older adults with digital technology because older adults often lack the belief and ability to use the acquired authority, and it needs the joint efforts of all sectors of society to help older adults improve their digital literacy and use digital technology with the facility. For older adults with the social endowment, more actions could be taken to strengthen the publicity of the health science popularization platform, provide the tutorial and guidance of digital technology to promote older adults learning health knowledge, use online health communities, and finally improve electronic health literacy. In the case of older adults supported in the family, full use of close contact and full communication in the family environment should be made to promote intergenerational communication and teaching, so that older adults could fully immerse themselves in the environment of using digital technology to obtain health services, and improve their eHealth literacy.

For Older Adults Themselves. Older adults should also maintain an open mind to accept the fact that the digital era is coming and build confidence in the use of digital technology. In daily life, more online health service providers including the health science popularization platform should be used to obtain the required health information, practice the operation of digital technology, and apply the health knowledge learned to daily health care. The exchange of digital technology experience and health information through peer and intergenerational communications will also help older adults skillfully use information technology, judge distorted health information, improve their self-efficacy, and ultimately help them improve their eHealth literacy.

7 Contribution and Limitation

7.1 Contribution

Theoretically, this study can expand the research scope of digital empowerment and explore the aspects and effects of health science popularization on digital empowerment of older adults. It can also build an influential mechanism between health science platforms and older adults, which could help understand the relationship between these factors. Practically, this study can provide suggestions for the improvement of the health science popularization platform, help older adults to better access health information through the platform, and ultimately improve eHealth literacy. The aging of population is a distinctive global feature of the present era. More concrete measures should be taken to support older adults in the face of rising pension and medical costs. Improvement of health science popularization, and eHealth literacy of older adults, can help all generations equally benefit from improved health and education conditions.

7.2 Limitation

In terms of research objects, this study is mainly aimed at older adults in the Chinese Mainland, therefore the applicability to older adults in other regions is limited, and older people with experience in using the health science popularization platform may have a higher educational background, so the impact on other older adults' eHealth literacy is still unknown. In terms of the research scope, it is difficult to accurately measure the changes in eHealth literacy of older adults before and after using the health science popularization platform. Future research can be carried out longitudinally to track the behavior of older adults using the health science popularization platform and record the changes in their eHealth literacy. The control variable experiment method can also be used for scientific comparative analysis.

Future research can also explore the mechanism of digital empowerment in other situations, such as the impact on employees' innovation behavior and innovation performance. The relationship between different digital empowerment methods and the empowerment effects is worth exploring, and whether digital empowerment will cause negative effects such as excessive cognitive load on older adults is also an important issue.

Acknowledgments. This study was supported by the National Social Science Foundation of China (22&ZD327).

References

1. Fox, S., Duggan, M.: Health online 2013. Pew Research Center's Internet & American Life Project (2013). http://www.pewinternet.org/files/old-media/Files/Reports/PIP_Hea lthOnline.pdf. Accessed 17 Jan 2015
2. Anesa, P., Fage-Butler, A.: Popularizing biomedical information on an online health forum. Iberica **29**, 105–128 (2015)

3. Whitley, R.: Knowledge producers and knowledge acquirers: popularisation as a relation between scientific fields and their publics. In: Shinn, T., Whitley, R. (eds.) Expository Science: Forms and Functions of Popularisation, pp. 3–30 (1985)
4. Calsamiglia, H.: Popularization discourse and knowledge about the genome. Discourse Soc. **15**, 4 (2004). https://doi.org/10.1177/0957926504043705
5. Lee, J.: The impact of health information technology on disparity of process of care. Int. J. Equity Health **34**, 14 (2015)
6. Lee, J., Koh, J., Kim, J.Y.: Popularization of medical information. Healthc. Inf. Res. **27**, 110–115 (2021)
7. Overstreet, H.A., Follett, M.P.: The new state: group organization the solution of popular government. J. Philos. Psychol. Sci. Methods **16**, 21 (1919). https://doi.org/10.2307/2940024
8. Li, Z., Li, H., Wang, S.: How multidimensional digital empowerment affects technology innovation performance: the moderating effect of adaptability to technology embedding. Sustainability **23**, 15916 (2022)
9. Makinen, M.: Digital empowerment as a process for enhancing citizens' participation. E-Learn. Digit. Media **3**, 381–395 (2006)
10. Hermansson, E., Lena, M.: Empowerment in the midwifery context-a concept analysis. Midwifery **27**, 811–816 (2010)
11. Lenka, S., Parida, V., Wincent, J.: Digitalization capabilities as enablers of value co-creation in servitizing firms. Psychol. Mark. **34**, 92–100 (2017)
12. Günther, W.A., Mehrizi, M.H.R., Huysman, M.: Debating big data: a literature review on realizing value from big data. J. Strateg. Inf. Syst. **3**, 191–209 (2017)
13. Nambisan, S., Lyytinen, K., Majchrzak, A., Song, M.: Digital innovation management: reinventing innovation management research in a digital world. MIS Q. **41**, 223–238 (2017)
14. Yoo, Y., Boland, R.J., Lyytinen, K., Majchrzak, A.: Organizing for innovation in the digitized world. Organization Sci. **23**, 1398–1408 (2012)
15. Gupta, R., Mejia, C., Kajikawa, Y.: Business, innovation and digital ecosystems landscape survey and knowledge cross sharing. Technol. Forecast. Soc. Chang. **147**, 100–109 (2019)
16. Norcelly, C., Yan, C.U., Elkin, Q.: Digital empowerment: integration university, business and public policy for endogenous development. Revista Negotium **12**, 20–34 (2017)
17. Norman, C.D., Skinner, H.A.: Ehealth literacy: essential skills for consumer health in a networked world. J. Med. Internet Res. **8**, e9 (2016)
18. Briones, R.: Harnessing the web: how e-health and e-health literacy impact young adults' perceptions of online health information. Medicine **4**, e5 (2016)
19. Price-Haywood, E.G., Harden-Barrios, J., Ulep, R., Luo, Q.: Ehealth literacy: patient engagement in identifying strategies to encourage use of patient portals among older adults. Popul. Health Manag. **20**, 486–494 (2017)
20. Levy, H., Janke, A.T., Langa, K.M.: Health literacy and the digital divide among older Americans. J. Gen. Intern. Med. **30**, 284–289 (2015)
21. Choi, N.: Relationship between health service use and health information technology use among older adults: analysis of the us national health interview survey. J. Med. Internet Res. **13**, e33 (2011)
22. MacInnis, D.J., Jaworski, B.J.: Information processing from advertisements: toward an integrative framework. J. Mark. **53**, 1 (1989)
23. Pg, A., Ejn, B.: Studying the antecedents and outcome of social media use by salespeople using a moa framework. Ind. Mark. Manage. **90**, 346–359 (2020)
24. Xc, A., Vsl, B., Pbl, C., Yang, L.D.: The effects of bidder factors on online bidding strategies: a motivation-opportunity-ability (MOA) model. Decis. Support Syst. **138**, 113397 (2020)
25. Davis, F.D., Warshaw, B.P.R.: User acceptance of computer-technology - a comparison of 2 theoretical-models. Manag. Sci. **35**, 982–1003 (1989)

26. Rd, E.M.M., Sharon, W.R.: Exploring older adults' health information seeking behaviors. J. Nutr. Educ. Behav. **44**, 85–89 (2012)

27. Liu, C.T., Du, T.C., Tsai, H.H.: A study of the service quality of general portals. Inf. Manag. **46**, 52–56 (2009)

28. Tian, Y., Robinson, J.D.: Incidental health information use on the internet. Health Commun. **24**, 41–49 (2009)

29. Vijayasarathy, L.R.: Predicting consumer intention to use on-line shopping: the case for an augmented technology acceptance model. Inf. Manag. **41**, 747–762 (2004)

30. Pavlou, A.P.: Consumer acceptance of electronic commerce: integrating trust and risk with the technology acceptance model. Int. J. Electron. Commer. **7**, 101–134 (2003)

31. Davis, F.D.: Perceived usefulness, perceived ease of use, and user acceptance of information technology. MIS Q. **13**, 319–340 (1989)

32. Landon, S., Smith, C.E.: The use of quality and reputation indicators by consumers: the case of bordeaux wine. J. Consum. Policy **20**, 289–323 (1997)

33. Hartzel, K.: How self-efficacy and gender issues affect software adoption and use. Commun. ACM **46**, 167–171 (2003)

34. Lagoe, C., Atkin, D.: Health anxiety in the digital age: an exploration of psychological determinants of online health information seeking. Comput. Hum. Behav. **52**, 484–491 (2015)

35. Zhao, L., Lu, Y., Gupta, S.: Disclosure intention of location-related information in location-based social network services. Int. J. Electron. Commer. **16**, 53–90 (2012)

36. Wu, T., Deng, Z., Zhang, D., Buchanan, P.R., Zha, D., Wang, R.: Seeking and using intention of health information from doctors in social media: the effect of doctor-consumer interaction. Int. J. Med. Inform. **115**, 106–113 (2018)

37. Sussman, S.W., Siegal, W.S.: Informational influence in organizations: an integrated approach to knowledge adoption. Inf. Syst. Res. **1**, 14 (2003)

38. Zhang, J.X., Schwarzer, R.: Measuring optimistic self-beliefs: a Chinese adaptation of the general self-efficacy scale. Psychologia **38**, 174–181 (1995)

39. Norman, C.D., Skinner, H.A.: eHEALS: the eHealth literacy scale. J. Med. Internet Res. **8**, e27 (2006)

40. Ojha, P.K., Mitra, I., Das, R.N., Roy, K.: Chemometrics & Intelligent Laboratory Systems, vol. 107, pp. 194–205 (2011)

41. Jensen, J.D., Pokharel, M., Carcioppolo, N., Upshaw, S., Katz, R.A.: Cancer information overload: discriminant validity and relationship to sun safe behaviors. Patient Educ. Couns. **94**, 90–96 (2019)

42. Luo, Y.F., Yang, S.C., Chen, A.S., Chiang, C.H.: Associations of eHealth literacy with health services utilization among college student: scross-sectional study. J. Med. Internet Res. **20**, e283 (2018)

43. Paek, H.J., Hove, T.: Social cognitive factors and perceived social influences that improve adolescent ehealth literacy. Health Commun. **27**, 727–737 (2012)

Behavioral Intention Model for Online Consultation at Internet Hospitals Among Older People at Home

Mingwen Zhang, Liangchen Jing$^{(\boxtimes)}$, Qizhi Wei, and Cong Cao(iD)

Zhejiang University of Technology, Hangzhou, China
2112104203@zjut.edu.cn

Abstract. This paper discusses the specific factors that influence the decision-making shift of homebound older people towards online consultation from offline to internet hospitals. By combining the Theory of Planned Behaviour (TPB) and push-pull theory, this paper proposes a model of the behavioral intention of homebound older people to choose an Internet hospital for online consultation. The model is analyzed from two perspectives: the offline hospital (push factors) and the Internet hospital (pull factors). The model assumes that the shift in older people's decision-making at home results from the combined control of push and pull factors. The model applies not only to consultation services but also to other healthcare-related services and has good adaptability. The model provides full-cycle decision support for the development of the Internet hospital by looking at the problem from the perspective of the elderly at home. The ultimate goal of this paper is to promote the development of Internet hospitals and to build a new medical service model that integrates digital healthcare "online + offline".

Keywords: Behavioral intentions · Internet hospitals · Older People · Home · Behaviour

1 Introduction

With the advent of healthy China and the era of digital governance, a new medical service model that integrates digital medical services, "online + offline", is replacing the traditional offline hospital service model [1]. The development of Internet hospitals is one of the most important ways to address the lack of demand for medical resources [2]. The number of Internet hospitals in China increased dramatically during the 2019 coronavirus disease pandemic and played an essential role in preventing and controlling the outbreak [3]. Policy interventions by the Chinese government have also strongly contributed to the development of Internet hospitals [4]. Community-based home care is still the choice of most older people today, and the community-based home care model is one of the primary forms of elderly care [5]. However, as the population ages, the traditional home care model can no longer meet the growing needs of the elderly, and how to promote the elderly in a digital society has become a widely discussed issue [6].

© The Author(s), under exclusive license to Springer Nature Switzerland AG 2023
Q. Gao and J. Zhou (Eds.): HCII 2023, LNCS 14043, pp. 246–255, 2023.
https://doi.org/10.1007/978-3-031-34917-1_18

The use of online healthcare-related services in Internet hospitals by older people in the home care model has positive implications for all three parties: offline hospitals, older people, and online hospitals.

Although Internet hospitals have brought convenience to society, there are still many difficulties for older people to use online products and services such as Internet hospitals [7]. From the perspective of the elderly, their poor adaptability to digital technology and low acceptance of digital products is one of the primary reasons for the low usage rate of Internet hospitals [8]. From other perspectives, the product design of Internet hospitals also needs more age-appropriateness and complex pages [9]. Factors such as brilliant elderly assistance activities and the digital learning atmosphere of the elderly community also affect the use of Internet hospitals by the elderly.

Based on the Theory of Planned Behaviour (TPB) and push-pull theory, this paper constructs a model of online consultation behavioral intention that influences the decision-making shift of homebound older people from offline hospitals to internet hospitals. By building this model, an abstract representation of the decision-making shift of older people in the home care model is presented. Using this model, we can understand the reasons influencing the change in decision-making from offline to offline consultations and the use of internet healthcare-related services. The model will help to increase the use of Internet hospitals by older people, thus promoting the development of Internet hospitals and bringing convenience to the lives of older people.

2 Literature Review

The public's intention to seek medical treatment includes the public's choice of hospitals and doctors. The choice of public medical treatment behavior intention is affected by the resource conditions of medical institutions, the public's conditions, and the surrounding social environment. Many scholars have researched the public's choice of intention to see a doctor.

Summarize from the perspective of public selection of offline hospitals, Tengilimoğlu et al. [10] pointed out that the behavior and attitude of personnel, as a public relations activity supporting the hospital's reputation in public, is an essential factor in determining the choice of hospitals by consumers. He et al. [11] pointed out that the long waiting time in public hospitals is critical for patients to choose emergency rooms in private hospitals. In contrast, the high cost of emergency rooms in private hospitals is essential for patients to select emergency rooms in public hospitals. Gil et al. [12] developed a framework based on the Andersen Behavioural Model covering need, support, and personal factors to explain why outpatient service users choose state and public (rather than private) hospitals. Byamfo et al. [13] identified increased hospital reputation and type of illness as determinants of the public choice of hospital. Andaleb [14] pointed out that service quality perception and demographic characteristics can also predict patients' choice between public and private hospitals. Barnea et al. [15] identified patient trust, patient focus, and commitment of healthcare professionals as factors that serve as patients' choice of hospital.

Based on research at the Internet hospital level, Liu et al. [16] examined patients' choice of willingness to use different types of sponsored Internet hospitals and showed that gender, education, and consumer type were the main factors influencing patients' use of different supported types of Internet hospitals. Li et al. [17] pointed out that perceived behavioral control and perceived severity of illness were the most critical factors determining patients' use of online consultation services at Internet hospitals, the essential elements in determining patients' willingness to use online hospital consultation services.

The existing literature provides a detailed analysis of the factors influencing the public's behavioral choice to attend medical appointments, but they still need help with the following problems.

1. *The elderly as a particular group, the existing literature lacks research on the behavioral intention to visit the elderly at home.*
2. *As a new type of online hospital, the existing literature needs more research on the behavioral choice of online services in Internet hospitals.*
3. *Although the existing model applies to most of the population, it does not reflect the particular characteristics of the elderly group.*

3 Theory Development

This paper aims to develop a model of the behavioral intentions of homebound older people to visit a doctor online to reveal the shifts in decision-making regarding their choice of healthcare services. In the process of selecting a theoretical basis, the analysis and comparison of different theories on individual behavior generation led to the decision to choose the theory of planned behavior as the theoretical basis for the model and to combine the push and pull theory related to motivation and decision shifts with the theory of planned behavior model.

The Theory of Planned Behaviour (TPB) is one of the most influential theories about individual behavior. Other theories that we can use to explain individuals' behavioral intentions are the Technology Acceptance Model (TAM) [20], the Integrated Technology Acceptance Model (UTAUT) [20] developed based on the Technology Acceptance Model (TAM), the Theory of Rational Behaviour (TRA) [18], the Motivation Model (MM) [21], the Technology Acceptance Model and Planned Behaviour Theory Integration Model (C-TAM-TPB) [22], the Computer Utilization Theory (MPCU) [23], the Innovation Diffusion Theory (IDT) [24], the Social Cognitive Theory (SCT) [19], etc. We finally selected the Theory of Planned Behaviour (TPB) due to factors such as the complexity of research on older people's behavioral intentions and the mismatch between other models and this study. The Theory of Planned Behaviour was proposed by Icek Ajzen (1988, 1991). The theory was developed from the Theory of Rational Behaviour (TRA) to complement the Theory of Rational Behaviour. The Theory of Planned Behaviour considers behavioral attitudes, subjective norms, and perceived behavioral control as the three main variables that determine behavioral intentions. The Theory of Planned Behaviour (TPB) argues that an individual's will is influenced not only by behavioral purposes but also by the individual's abilities, opportunities, resources, environment, and other conditions of practical control [19].

The push-pull theory is essential for studying the causes of population mobility. The American scholar E.S. Lee proposed the push-pull theory. Push-pull theory suggests that the movement of people, i.e., the change from the place of migration to the place of migration, is influenced by both push and pull factors. Factors conducive to improving living conditions become pull factors, and factors not conducive to improving living conditions become push factors [25]. Population mobility is the result of a forward pull and a backward push. In this study, the shift in the decision-making of older people for some healthcare services from offline hospitals to internet hospitals can be considered as a migration from the place of migration to the place of migration. Therefore, the push and pull factors of the push-pull theory were selected to be combined with the theory of planned behavior in this model.

4 The Proposed Model

Based on the theory of planned behavior and push-pull theory, this paper constructs a model of the behavioral intention of the elderly at home to choose online consultation at an Internet hospital. Based on the push-pull theory, this paper treats the shift in the choice of healthcare services from offline hospitals to Internet hospitals as a change from a "moving-out place" to a "moving-in place". As shown in Fig. 1, the model discusses the influence and mechanism of older people's behavioral intention to choose online medical services in Internet hospitals in terms of both push and pull factors.

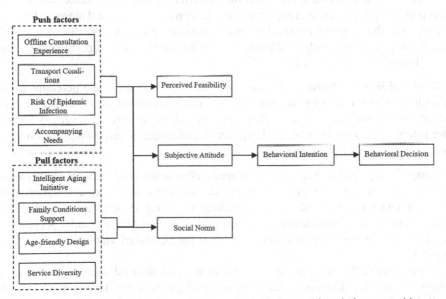

Fig. 1. Behavioral intention model for online consultation at Internet hospitals among older people at home.

4.1 Push Factors

In push-pull theory, push factors are often used as negative factors and are one of the main reasons people move out of the 'move-out' area [25]. Our model considers pushing factors as the main reason why homebound older people abandon offline hospitals. Among the push factors, we selected four main aspects for discussion and explanation: offline consultation experience, transport conditions, the risk of epidemic infection, and accompanying needs. Perceived feasibility refers to the degree to which an individual expects to feel in control or control of a particular behavior when in it. Subjective attitude refers to the positive or negative evaluation of an individual's performance of a specific behavior.

Offline Consultation Experience. The offline consultation experience refers to the psychological feelings that patients build up during their offline hospital visits. The consultation experience has become a crucial part of evaluating the quality of health-care services [26]. In the model, offline consultation experience is essential for offline hospitals. A poorer experience at an offline hospital can directly affect the patient's subjective attitude toward the hospital. Improving the overall patient experience can be done by intervening from the perspective of patient emotion and dignity [27]. How older people feel about their offline hospital experience is one factor driving a shift in decision-making.

Transport Conditions. In this model, transport conditions refer to considerations, including the distance between home and hospital, accessibility, and older people's ability to travel. Transport conditions affect the perceived feasibility of offline hospitals for older people. As a particular group, older people are more efficient and more challenging to travel with than younger people. Poorer access to transport can mean that older people have limited access to timely medical resources. The solution to this problem is to learn about the use of internet hospitals.

Risk of Epidemic Infection. The risk of epidemic infection is the potential for an individual to be infected by the virus in their social environment. Older people have reduced resistance due to aging. They are more likely to develop severe symptoms after infection than younger people [28]. The risk of epidemic infection is considered a secondary variable in this model.

Accompanying Needs. Accompanying needs refers to the need for a second person to help the individual psychologically or physically while performing a particular behavior or action. Older people need companionship more during medical appointments, and offline clinics have limited access to resources and services [29]. For older people with escort needs, the need for an escort can affect the perceived viability of the offline hospital.

As a negative factor in the model, the strength of the push factor will make the elderly at home feel less controllable about the offline hospital. That is, the perceived feasibility of the offline hospital will weaken, thus creating the psychology of avoiding going to the offline hospital as much as possible. This psychological change is the main reason for the old people at home to move out of the "emigration place". At the same time, the enhancement of the thrust factor will make the impression and attitude of the elderly at home to the offline hospital worse, thus making a negative evaluation, that is, the subjective attitude of the elderly at home to the offline hospital weakened. When the personal attitude and feasibility perception of the elderly to the offline hospital are diluted to a certain extent, the behavioral intention of the elderly at home to the offline hospital will be reduced, thus deciding to "move out" of the offline hospital.

Today's Internet hospitals cannot wholly replace offline hospitals, and offline hospitals still maintain their irreplaceable role in society [30]. We expand the scope of application of the model from consultation services to medically related services and divide the medically related services into two categories: medical-related services that Internet hospitals and medical-related services can replace that Internet hospitals cannot return. For the irreplaceable medical-related services of Internet hospitals, offline hospitals are still the only choice for the public. Therefore, enhancing the thrust factor is different from what we should do. On the contrary, weakening the thrust factor, improving the patient's medical experience, deepening the digital reform of offline hospitals, and promoting the integration of "online + offline" services are what today's offline hospitals should do.

4.2 Pull Factors

In the push-pull theory, the pull factor, as a positive factor, is one of the main reasons the "destination" attracts people to move in. In the model, we regard the pull factor as the main reason for the older adults at home to choose Internet hospitals actively. Among the pull factors, this model mainly explains and discusses the four aspects of the intelligent aging initiative, family conditions support, age-friendly design, and service diversity. Social norms refer to the cognition of social pressure individuals feel when they take a specific behavior.

Intelligent Aging Initiative. Intelligent aging initiatives are social activities that help the elderly use digital products and help them connect with digital life. The development of intelligent activities to help the elderly is not only to meet the objective needs of the aging society but also to love and help the elderly. It will become the shared responsibility of the whole society in the future. An exemplary implementation of intelligent elderly care activities in a region can form an excellent digital learning atmosphere, thus forming a social norm.

Family Conditions Support. He family conditions support in this model refers to the family's material conditions and spiritual support to help the elderly use digital products and services. It includes the intelligent equipment supplied for the elderly and the family's help in using digital products for the elderly.

Age-Friendly Design. Age-friendly design refers to the corresponding plan that entirely considers the physical function and action characteristics of the elderly. The aging design of Internet hospitals includes a friendly interface design style for the elderly, functional design to meet the actual needs of the elderly, etc. [31]. The method, in line with the characteristics and conditions of the elderly, can make the elderly feel friendly, thus improving their perception and evaluation of the feasibility of Internet hospitals.

Service Diversity. The service diversity in this model is for Internet hospitals. Although offline hospitals play an irreplaceable role, Internet hospitals also have unique advantages as a part of the Internet. Based on the online scene of Internet hospitals, we can conceive and create more innovative and practical services. For example, "cloud accompanying service" can meet the needs of elderly people who need to be accompanied.

As a positive factor in the model, the strength of the pull factor will lead to a migration behavior of the social environment from offline hospitals to Internet hospitals, thus strengthening the social norms of the elderly for Internet hospitals, leading to the active or forced choice of Internet hospitals by the elderly at home. At the same time, strengthening the pull factor will also show the elderly at home to positively evaluate Internet hospitals. When the social norms and subjective attitudes of Internet hospitals are strengthened to a certain extent, the behavioral intention of the elderly at home to "move into" Internet hospitals will increase, thus making the "move in" decision.

From the perspective of the relationship between supply and demand, the pull factor in the enhancement model is actually to expand the beneficiary group of Internet hospitals, which leads to an increase in the market for medical services of Internet hospitals. And with the deepening of aging, this demand will also expand further. On the other hand, the increase in demand will also stimulate the supply, thus promoting Internet hospitals to provide more creative and practical medical-related services. In the long run, increasing the pull factor in the model will help the elderly to bridge the "digital divide", bring convenience to their lives, and make Internet hospitals develop healthily and prosperously.

5 Fullcycle Support

Both the Internet hospitals established by well-known enterprises and those found by local hospitals serve the local need to connect with the local medical resources. Therefore, although Internet hospitals are offline services, they have regional differences. The elderly group is of great significance and value for the future development of Internet hospitals. Due to the guiding role of the elderly group in the development of Internet hospitals, we can regard the entire migration cycle of some medical-related services from offline hospitals to Internet hospitals for the elderly at home in a particular region as the development cycle of Internet hospitals in that region from initial establishment to prosperity. Based on this, this model can not only be used to study the behavior intention of the elderly at home for online consultation in Internet hospitals or their intention to use medical-related services but also be used to study the development of Internet hospitals at a particular time point, a certain period and even the entire cycle.

From the perspective of the development cycle of Internet hospitals, there are many problems in the early stage of the development of Internet hospitals, such as few types of services, weak social promotion, and impaired functions, which are not enough to attract the elderly and even the public. According to the model, we can promote the migration process by enhancing the pull factor. We should note that the impact of the thrust factor on the young group is far less than that of the elderly group, and the effect of the model on the young group is far less than that of the elderly group. Moreover, in the model, the thrust factor only plays an auxiliary role, which is not an issue that Internet hospitals need to pay attention to.

For some medical services that Internet hospitals cannot replace, offline hospitals are the only choice for the public. Therefore, from the perspective of offline hospitals, it is the best choice to reduce the thrust factor, strengthen its connection with local Internet hospitals, and build an online and offline integrated medical service model.

6 Conclusion

Based on the theory of planned behavior and push-pull theory, this paper proposes a model of the behavioral intentions of homebound older people toward choosing an internet hospital for online consultation. We can analyze the model from two perspectives: the perspective of the offline hospital (push factor) and the perspective of the Internet hospital (pull factor). The combined effect of the push and pull factors drives a shift in decision-making among homebound older people. This paper explains these variables' role in older people's home decision-making process by describing the specific components of push and pulls factors. At the same time, the model applies to online consultation services and other health-related services. We can categorize healthcare-related services into those that are substitutable by internet hospitals and those that are not substitutable by internet hospitals. For those healthcare-related services that are substitutable by internet hospitals, we analyze them from the perspective of internet hospitals. This is where the pull factor is the main propelling factor, and the push factor only plays a supporting role. For those medical-related services that are not substitutable by internet hospitals, we can analyze them from the perspective of offline hospitals. This is where the push factor plays a significant role, and the pull factor plays a secondary role.

In the context of society's vigorous promotion of Internet hospitals, the attitude of the elderly community towards Internet hospitals and their use is an issue that cannot be ignored in the development of Internet hospitals. It can be said that the elderly group determines the future of the development of Internet hospitals. Therefore, the model also applies to the study of Internet hospitals' current situation and development cycle and provides full-cycle support.

Existing models of behavioral intention to visit a hospital do not cover all influencing factors and lack a unique design for homebound older people. There needs to be more research on the behavioral choices of Internet hospital-related services. The home care model is most older people's primary mode of care. The model in this paper can help internet hospitals to analyze the behavioral intentions of the elderly population, which will help society to pay more attention to the elderly population. This model enriches the research on the behavioral intentions of home-based older people and the quantitative analysis on the use of Internet hospitals. The model also combines the theory of planned behavior and the push-pull theory, extending the scope of service to the scenarios of medical consultation behavioral intention and internet hospital application.

In summary, this model aims to build a new healthcare service model that integrates digital healthcare "online + offline". The model fills a research gap in this field and is a reference for developing Internet hospitals. This model's application also helps solve the real-life problems of social equity and the distribution of social and medical resources, which has vital practical and realistic significance. Using the model can also help older people cross the digital divide and access and use digital products, thus enriching and facilitating their lives.

Based on the existing literature and data and using an experimental research method, this paper proposes a behavioral intentional choice model based on the Theory of Planned

Behaviour for homebound older people to visit an internet hospital online. In the subsequent research, this paper will focus on data collection and analysis, validation, and modification of the model to provide better decision support for internet hospitals.

Acknowledgments. The work described in this paper was supported by grants from the General Scientific Research Projects of the Zhejiang Provincial Education Department, grant number Y202250161; the Zhejiang Provincial Federation of Social Sciences, grant number 2023N009; the Humanities and Social Sciences Research Project of Zhejiang Provincial Department of Education, grant number Y202248811; and the Zhejiang Province Undergraduate Innovation and Entrepreneurship Training Program, S202210337022.

References

1. Su, Y., Hou, F., Qi, M., Li, W., Ji, Y.: A data-enabled business model for a smart healthcare information service platform in the era of digital transformation. J. Healthcare Eng. **2021**, 1–9 (2021)
2. Ge, F., et al.: Experiences and challenges of emerging online health services combating COVID-19 in China: retrospective, cross-sectional study of internet hospitals. JMIR Med. Inform. **10**(6) (2022)
3. Xu, X., et al.: Assessment of internet hospitals in China during the COVID-19 pandemic: national cross-sectional data analysis study. J. Med. Internet Res. **23**(1), e21825 (2021). https://doi.org/10.2196/21825
4. Lai, Y., Chen, S., Li, M., Ung, C.O.L., Hu, H.: Policy interventions, development trends, and service innovations of internet hospitals in China: documentary analysis and qualitative interview study. J. Med. Internet Res. **23**(7) (2021)
5. Xu, M., Zhao, Y., You, J., Wang, B., Li, Z.: Preference and influencing factors of community home-based elderly care in community-living elderly people in Nanning. Chinese General Pract. **23**(18) (2020)
6. Yang, Z., Xia, S., Feng, S.: Network information security platform based on artificial intelligence for the elderly's health "Integration of Physical, Medical, and Nursing Care". Computational and Mathematical Methods in Medicine 2022 (2022)
7. Gao, W., Li, L., Xue, Y.: Analysis of the factors on learning digital cultural products for the elderly under active aging: the case of lifelong learning in China. In: 2022 IEEE 2nd International Conference on Educational Technology (ICET), pp. 175–179. IEEE (2022)
8. Li, S.: Synesthetic design of digital elderly products based on big data. Wirel. Commun. Mob. Comput. **2021**, 1–9 (2021)
9. Nassir, S.: Designing ICT to support positive ageing in Saudi Arabia. In: Proceedings of the 2016 ACM Conference Companion Publication on Designing Interactive Systems, pp. 41–42 (2016)
10. Tengilimoglu, D., Yesiltas, M., Kisa, A., Dziegielewski, S.F.: The role of public relations activities in hospital choice. Health Mark. Q. **24**(3–4), 19–31 (2008)
11. He, J., Hou, X.Y., Toloo, G., FitzGerald, G.: Patients' choice between public and private hospital emergency departments: a cross-sectional survey. Emerg. Med. Australas. **29**(6), 635–642 (2017)
12. Gil M.-R., Choi, C.G.: Factors affecting the choice of national and public hospitals among outpatient service users in South Korea. INQUIRY: J. Health Care Organ. Prov. Financ. **56**, 1–11 (2019)

13. Bamfo, B.A., Dogbe, C.S.K.: Factors influencing the choice of private and public hospitals: empirical evidence from Ghana. Int. J. Pharmaceut. Healthcare Mark. **11**(1), 80–96 (2017)

14. Andaleeb, S.S.: Public and private hospitals in Bangladesh: service quality and predictors of hospital choice. Health Policy Plan. **15**(1), 95–102 (2000)

15. Barnea, R., TurSinai, A., LevtzionKorach, O., Weiss, Y., Tal, O.: Patient preferences and choices as a reflection of trust—a cluster analysis comparing postsurgical perceptions in a private and a public hospital. Health Expect. **25**(5), 2340–2354 (2022)

16. Liu, L., Shi, L.: Chinese patients' intention to use different types of internet hospitals: cross-sectional study on virtual visits. J. Med. Internet Res. **23**(8), e25978 (2021). https://doi.org/10.2196/25978

17. Li, D., et al.: Determinants of patients' intention to use the online inquiry services provided by internet hospitals: Empirical evidence from China. J. Med. Internet Res. **22**(10), e22716 (2020). https://doi.org/10.2196/22716

18. Fishbein, M., Ajzen, I.: Belief, attitude, intention, and behavior: an introduction to theory and research (1977)

19. Bandura, A.: Social foundations of Thought and Action, pp. 23–28. Englewood Cliffs, NJ 1986 (1986)

20. Davis, F.D., Bagozzi, R.P., Warshaw, P.R.: User acceptance of computer technology: a comparison of two theoretical models. Manage. Sci. **35**(8), 982–1003 (1989)

21. Davis, F.D., Bagozzi, R.P., Warshaw, P.R.: Extrinsic and intrinsic motivation to use computers in the workplace 1. J. Appl. Soc. Psychol. **22**(14), 1111–1132 (1992)

22. Rogers, E.M., Singhal, A., Quinlan, M.M.: In An integrated approach to communication theory and research (2014)

23. Su, W., Bi, X.H., Wang, L.: Research on user acceptance model of internet of things based on UTAUT theory. Inf. Sci **5**(2013), 128–132 (2013)

24. Robinson, J.P., Shaver, P.R., Wrightsman, L.S.: Measures of Personality and Social Psychological Attitudes: Measures of Social Psychological Attitudes. Academic Press (2013)

25. Lee, E.S.: A theory of migration. Demography **3**, 47–57 (1966)

26. Mannonen, P., Kaipio, J., Nieminen, M.P.: Patient-centred design of healthcare services: meaningful events as basis for patient experiences of families. In: Building Capacity for Health Informatics in the Future. IOS Press. (2017)

27. Wong, E., Mavondo, F., Horvat, L., McKinlay, L., Fisher, J.: Victorian healthcare experience survey 2016–2018; evaluation of interventions to improve the patient experience. BMC Health Serv. Res. **21**(1), 1–13 (2021)

28. Alarnous, R., Albasalah, A., Alshawwa, S.: Empowering quality of life for elderly people during crisis and epidemics in Saudi Arabia. Period. Eng. Nat. Sci. **9**(4), 982–990 (2021)

29. Nijhof, D., Ingram, A., Ochieng, R., Roberts, E.J., Poulton, B., Ochieng, B.: Examining GP online consultation in a primary care setting in east midlands. UK. BMC Health Serv. Res. **21**(1), 1–10 (2021)

30. Li, J., et al.: Prevention and control of COVID-19 after resuming general hospital functions. Pathogens **11**(4), 452 (2022). https://doi.org/10.3390/pathogens11040452

31. Xiao, Y., Ye, Y., Liu, Y.: Research on the age-appropriate design of mobile phone APPs based on the experience of using smartphones for Chinese Young-Old. In: Gao, Q., Zhou, J. (eds) 8th International Conference on Human Aspects of IT for the Aged Population, ITAP 2022 Held as Part of the 24th HCI International Conference, HCII 2022, vol. 13330, pp. 248–262. Springer International Publishing, Cham (2022). https://doi.org/10.1007/978-3-031-05581-2_19

IT Support for Caregivers

17 Support for caregivers

A Study for Estimating Caregiving Contexts Based on Extracting Nonverbal Information from Elderly People at Home

Sinan Chen[1(✉)], Masahide Nakamura[1,2], and Kiyoshi Yasuda[3]

[1] Center of Mathematical and Data Sciences, Kobe University, 1-1 Rokkodai-cho, Nada, Kobe 657-8501, Japan
chensinan@gold.kobe-u.ac.jp, masa-n@cs.kobe-u.ac.jp
[2] RIKEN Center for Advanced Intelligence Project, 1-4-1 Nihonbashi, Chuo-ku, Tokyo 103-0027, Japan
[3] Osaka Institute of Technology, 5-16-1 Omiya, Asahi-ku, Osaka 535-8585, Japan
yasukiyo.12@outlook.jp

Abstract. In order to reduce the burden on family caregivers, machine-assisted estimation of situations (called "caregiving contexts") necessary for the care of elderly people at home is becoming increasingly important. Older adults at home usually express their feelings through nonverbal information such as facial expressions, movements, and postures, except in daily conversation. This study aims to examine a method for estimating the caregiving context based on extracting nonverbal information from older adults at home. Our key idea is to input real-time image data captured by a USB camera into a pre-trained model that can be run in an edge environment and subject the results to analysis that aggregates a set of features for each location in the home. We expect that the results of this research will allow us to build a classifier of caregiving contexts unique to each household and to analyze better and infer the caregiving needs of the elderly.

Keywords: Caregiving contexts · Images · Nonverbal information · Smart healthcare · Web application

1 Introduction

The most severe problem in caring for the elderly at home is the heavy burden on family members. Family members have to stay with the elderly for extended periods because it is difficult for them to grasp the real needs and timing of the elderly. So far, home monitoring systems using engineering technology have taken human movements from sensor devices [15] or acquired human physiological data from wearable devices [1]. However, it is difficult for machines to estimate the "mental" thoughts of the elderly. Many existing technologies are limited to simply notifying family members of abnormal values (e.g., leaving the bed or a slight change in heart rate).

Q. Gao and J. Zhou (Eds.): HCII 2023, LNCS 14043, pp. 259–268, 2023.
https://doi.org/10.1007/978-3-031-34917-1_19

Our research group has developed a computer-programmed robot with a character (called Mei-chan) that interacts with elderly people at home. It uses "voice" to automatically ask them about their daily living conditions (e.g., Have you eaten? How are you feeling today?) automatically. In addition, through conversation with Mei-chan, the elderly can conveniently use microservices such as video viewing and information retrieval through voice control [12]. Furthermore, the biometric information of an older adult conceived of a wearable device is linked to Mei-chan [13]. The system automatically asks Mei-chan about the causes of changes in the older adult's physical health that cannot be captured in words (i.e., there is no subjective sensation from the older adult) and performs an integrated analysis of different types of data [5]. In addition, Mei-chan can be reproduced by various devices as a virtual caregiver, and a video telephone function is also included [3].

However, except for voluntary conversation between the elderly and the robot, the elderly often expresses their emotional thoughts using nonverbal information such as facial expressions, movements, and hand postures. Examples include body movements when the older adult wants to go to the restroom, distressed facial expressions when the older adult forgets something, and hand postures when the older adult wants to pick up an item. It is impractical to output all of this nonverbal information in a conversation. Our interest is to introduce live images taken from a USB fixed-point camera into a web browser to extract nonverbal information. Further and estimate the necessary looking after situation (called the caregiving context) for caregiving. In recent years, analysis platforms such as TensorFlow have emerged, and many pre-trained models have been migrated from the cloud to local environments. In the edge environment of the home, techniques such as face recognition [4], skeleton estimation [11], and hand posture tracking [17] can be executed from a web browser. We consider that it is promising to use these technologies to extract nonverbal information about elderly people at home.

The purpose of this study is to investigate a method for estimating the caregiving context based on extracting nonverbal information from homebound elderly persons. Figure 1 shows the overall architecture of the proposed method. Our key idea is to create groups of nonverbal information for each human location in the image and build an estimation model using Python analysis. The approach is first to introduce live images taken from a USB fixed-point camera into the pre-trained TensorFlow.js. Next, for each human location in the output image, nonverbal information (e.g., 2D coordinates of feature points on the face, skeleton, and hands) is manually compiled. The set of nonverbal information for each location is then manually labeled. The labeled data is then used as training data. Together with the training data acquired commonly, it is applied to a multi-class neural network algorithm to construct and evaluate an estimation model. As a preliminary experiment, we set up a single subject to extract nonverbal information from live images of actual in-home care. We label the care context data and build and evaluate an individual-adaptive estimation model. Then, we evaluate the estimation performance for each care context label using

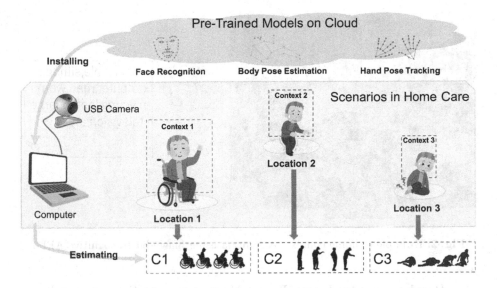

Fig. 1. Overall architecture of the proposed method.

a confusion matrix. In future work, we will use the results of these experiments as a reference to modify the model construction method when dealing with other elderly people. This study is expected to elucidate the effectiveness of caregiving context estimation for elderly people at home and to be helpful in sensing behavioral intentions associated with daily living activities.

2   Preliminaries

2.1   Aging Society and Assistive Technology

In recent years, societies around the world have been aging. Population, society, and disease structures are changing, and the number of people requiring nursing care is increasing yearly. In Japan, in particular, there is a chronic shortage of medical and welfare facilities and personnel, and the government calls for a shift from institutional care to home care. A serious problem is the significant mental and physical burden on family caregivers when older adults are cared for at home, where they are accustomed to being. In particular, when an older adult needs serious nursing care, the family caregiver must provide care 24 h a day. When so-called elderly couples mutually care for each other, the burden falls heavily on both the caregiver and the cared-for person.

In the field of support for home care using engineering technology, representative research is a system for monitoring older adult who requiring nursing care using Information and Communication Technology (ICT) and Internet of Things (IoT). Machines take over the manual observation of the caregiver's condition and ask the caregiver for assistance only when necessary. In this way, it dramatically reduces the burden on caregivers.

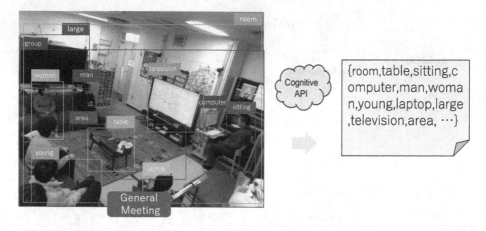

Fig. 2. Example of home context recognition using image-based cognitive API.

2.2   Previous Study: Image-Based Home Context Recognition [8]

Our previous study proposed an image-based fine-grained home context recognition technique [6]. Home context recognition mainly includes two types of context: residents' daily activities (e.g., eating, sleeping, cleaning, reading, etc.) and home environmental conditions (e.g., unoccupied, lights off, low temperature, high humidity, etc.). For each household, a user-defined home context is recognized through images [7]. In the proposed method, first, tags are extracted from images as features using the cognitive Application Programing Interface (API). Example of home context recognition using image-based cognition API is shown in Fig. 2. Next, we build a classifier combining cognitive API and analysis. Finally, an ensemble of features is trained using several different cognitive APIs [10]. By doing so, we achieved a recognition accuracy of 0.98 for user-defined in-home contexts.

2.3   Technical Challenges

We consider that the limitations of conventional elderly monitoring systems include the following two aspects. First, there is the issue of system installation and operation costs and the inability to respond to the different circumstances of each household. There are various challenges to the diffusion of the system to ordinary households, and it is not easy to spread widely in the home care field. It is difficult for the system to penetrate the home care field widely. On the other hand, the second issue is that the support is limited to simply detecting the subject with sensors and notifying the user. It is difficult to understand what the subject is seeking, and it is difficult to observe the "intentions" and "minds" of the caregiver and the subject.

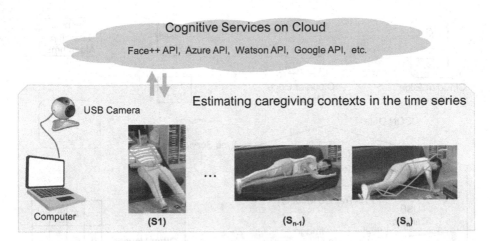

Fig. 3. Example of human pose estimation using cloud services.

2.4   Estimating Caregiving Contexts

Figure 3 shows an example of human pose estimation using cloud services. In recognizing the context of an older adult requiring care at home, it is essential to use nonverbal information to determine whether care is needed. For example, (S1) lying down, (S2) standing, (S3) sitting, (S4) walking, (S5) looking around, and so on. For this, more detailed human pose estimation is required. In addition, to estimate the intention of an older adult requiring care at home, we estimate the intention from the time series of the state. For example, if S3→S2→S5 is repeated, there is a possibility that the caregiver is looking for someone. Stream data analysis and processing in real-time is required. However, there is a performance limitation of the cognitive API. Although the accuracy of posture recognition is high, the communication overhead to the cloud is too significant for constant real-time use. Hence, a more Python image feature recognition technology is essential for recognizing the context of persons requiring care at home.

In recent years, PoseNet models have emerged that take advantage of edge computing technology [9]. It is a machine-trained posture estimation model that uses Google's TensorFlow.js library. It can recognize human posture in real-time on a web browser using a USB camera as input image data. On the other hand, the output results are from the web browser console, including the coordinates of 17 human body parts and the value of each score. The posture estimation model can also be executed in the local environment and adjusted from one or two-person mode. The Web browser can depict skeleton-only images without including the natural environment. In addition, pre-trained models in computer vision include face recognition, hand recognition [18], and object recognition [14]. In face recognition [4], 2D coordinates of human facial feature points can be extracted from images to estimate age, gender, and emotion. In this study, we aim to use these techniques to estimate the care context from nonverbal information of a person in need of care at home.

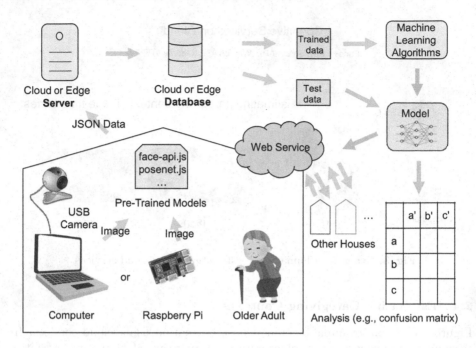

Fig. 4. Overall architecture of proposed method.

2.5 Proposed Method

The purpose of this study is to investigate a method for estimating the care situation of older adults at home based on the extraction of nonverbal information. Our key idea is to create a set of nonverbal information for each person's location in the image and build an estimation model using Python analysis. Figure 4 shows the overall architecture of the proposed method. For the nonverbal information set, we use a pre-trained model that can be run in an edge environment to aggregate the 2D coordinates of feature points on the human face, skeleton, and fingers and label the data set for each location. Furthermore, we separate the training data from the test data and use a Python analysis algorithm to build a classifier that can estimate the location and situation from a set of nonverbal information about a person. This allows us to determine where the older adult at home has always been and what kind of caregiving context he/she has often had. It is also expected to reduce the burden on family caregivers based on the pre-estimated caregiving context.

3   Experimental Evaluation

Table 1. Environment and application settings

Target space	Single-room (4 m × 5 m)
Experimental period	One day (2 July 2022)
Evaluated subject	An aged man (65s)
Shooting device	USB camera (Logitech OEM B500)
Shooting position	In a corner of the room
Shooting interval	1 s
Computer browser	Chrome (Version 84.0.4147.125)
Image resolution	320 × 240
Application device	Raspberry Pi 3 Model B [2]
Pre-trained model	PoseNet model
Estimation type	Single-person mode
Model architecture	ResNet50 [16]
Estimation threshold	0.5
Number of defined parameters	2

Environment and application settings are shown in Table 1. In this experiment, we use a human pose estimation model and focus mainly on the physical changes of older adults during the day. Figure 5 and Figure 6 shows the time series of changes in the body feature coordinates in this experiment. The visualized results of this experiment show that the subjects' head movements were mainly from 6:00 to 7:00 a.m., from 2:00 to 5:00 p.m., and around 6:00 p.m. The subjects' hand movements were also higher than the head movements. Conversely, from the results of shoulder and hand movements, etc., it can be inferred that there were few changes in coordinates between 8:00 a.m. and 1:00 p.m. and between 5:00 p.m. and 6:00 p.m., indicating a situation that would require nursing care. In addition, the values of 0 are mainly concentrated around 7:30 a.m. and between 2:30 p.m. and 5:00 p.m., and the subjects consider that they need special watchful waiting during these hours. However, even though we could guess whether the older adult was walking or not, it was still unclear what the older adult was doing. In the future, it will be essential to link the spoken dialogue agent with changes in the physical feature coordinates and to ask timely questions from the agent.

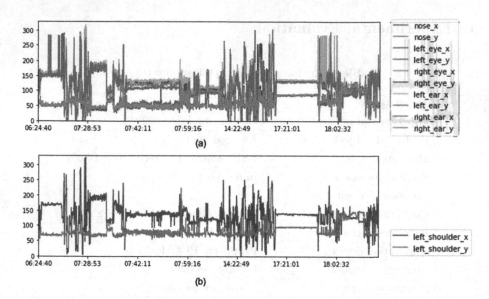

Fig. 5. Changes in physical features on the time series of this experiment: (a) Change in head features. (b) Change in shoulder features.

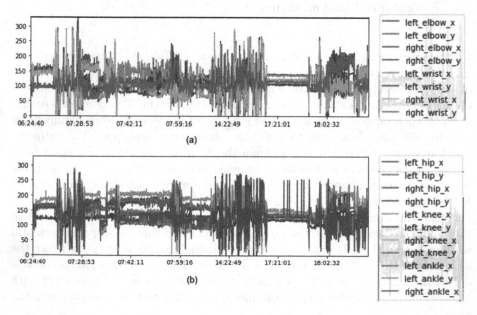

Fig. 6. Changes in physical features on the time series of this experiment: (a) Change in hand features. (b) Change in lower half of body features.

4   Conclusion

In this paper, we focus on older adults who need care at home and investigate a method for estimating the care context to reduce the burden on family caregivers. The proposed method uses a USB camera to input real-time image data to a pre-trained model that can be executed in an edge environment. The 2D coordinate data of human faces, fingers, and skeletons in the images are considered non-verbal information, and caregiving contexts are labeled for each location in the home. Finally, we separate the training data from the test data and build a classifier that can estimate the caregiving context for each location in the home. We conducted preliminary experiments using the proposed method. We analyzed nonverbal information from continuous image data of an older adult and applied Python analysis to construct a classifier of caregiving context. In the future, we plan to use multiple USB cameras to collect and reuse richer analysis results from multiple image data. We are also deeply interested in discovering individual adaptive factors of the elderly and assigning to the training data the factors of where and when they needed more care, such as always being prone to falls.

Acknowledgements. This research was partially supported by JSPS KAKENHI Grant Numbers JP19H01138, JP20H05706, JP20H04014, JP20K11059, JP22H03699, JP19K02973, Grant-in-Aid for JSPS Research Fellow (No. 22J13217), and Tateishi Science and Technology Foundation (C) (No. 2207004).

References

1. Al-khafajiy, M., et al.: Remote health monitoring of elderly through wearable sensors. Multimedia Tools Appl. **78**(17), 24681–24706 (2019). https://doi.org/10.1007/s11042-018-7134-7
2. Ansor, A., Ritzkal, R., Afrianto, Y.: Mask detection using framework tensorflow and pre trained CNN model based on raspberry pi. Jurnal Mantik **4**(3), 1539–1545 (2020)
3. Chen, S., Nakamura, M.: Designing an elderly virtual caregiver using dialogue agents and WebRTC. In: 2021 4th International Conference on Signal Processing and Information Security (ICSPIS), pp. 53–56. IEEE (2021)
4. Chen, S., Nakamura, M.: Developing a facial identification system using pre-trained model and spoken dialogue agent. In: 2022 International Balkan Conference on Communications and Networking (BalkanCom), pp. 62–67. IEEE (2022)
5. Chen, S., Ozono, H., Nakamura, M.: Integration analysis of heterogeneous data on mind externalization of elderly people at home. In: Gao, Q., Zhou, J. (eds.) HCII 2022. LNCS, vol. 13331, pp. 197–209. Springer, Cham (2022). https://doi.org/10.1007/978-3-031-05654-3_13
6. Chen, S., Saiki, S., Nakamura, M.: Evaluating feasibility of image-based cognitive APIs for home context sensing. In: 2018 International Conference on Signal Processing and Information Security (ICSPIS), pp. 1–4. IEEE (2018)
7. Chen, S., Saiki, S., Nakamura, M.: Proposal of home context recognition method using feature values of cognitive API. In: 2019 20th IEEE/ACIS International Conference on Software Engineering, Artificial Intelligence, Networking and Parallel/Distributed Computing (SNPD), pp. 533–538. IEEE (2019)

8. Chen, S., Saiki, S., Nakamura, M.: Integrating multiple models using image-as-documents approach for recognizing fine-grained home contexts. Sensors **20**(3), 666 (2020)
9. Chen, S., Saiki, S., Nakamura, M.: Nonintrusive fine-grained home care monitoring: characterizing quality of in-home postural changes using bone-based human sensing. Sensors **20**(20), 5894 (2020)
10. Chen, S., Saiki, S., Nakamura, M.: Toward flexible and efficient home context sensing: capability evaluation and verification of image-based cognitive APIs. Sensors **20**(5), 1442 (2020)
11. Gatt, T., Seychell, D., Dingli, A.: Detecting human abnormal behaviour through a video generated model. In: 2019 11th International Symposium on Image and Signal Processing and Analysis (ISPA), pp. 264–270. IEEE (2019)
12. Ozono, H., Chen, S., Nakamura, M.: Study of microservice execution framework using spoken dialogue agents. In: 2021 IEEE/ACIS 22nd International Conference on Software Engineering, Artificial Intelligence, Networking and Parallel/Distributed Computing (SNPD), pp. 273–278. IEEE (2021)
13. Ozono, H., Chen, S., Nakamura, M.: Encouraging elderly self-care by integrating speech dialogue agent and wearable device. In: Gao, Q., Zhou, J. (eds.) HCII 2022. LNCS, vol. 13331, pp. 52–70. Springer, Cham (2022). https://doi.org/10.1007/978-3-031-05654-3_4
14. Sanchez, S., Romero, H., Morales, A.: A review: comparison of performance metrics of pretrained models for object detection using the tensorflow framework. In: IOP Conference Series: Materials Science and Engineering, vol. 844, p. 012024. IOP Publishing (2020)
15. Tamamizu, K., Sakakibara, S., Saiki, S., Nakamura, M., Yasuda, K.: Capturing activities of daily living for elderly at home based on environment change and speech dialog. In: Duffy, V.G. (ed.) DHM 2017. LNCS, vol. 10287, pp. 183–194. Springer, Cham (2017). https://doi.org/10.1007/978-3-319-58466-9_18
16. Wang, W., Hasabnis, N.: Distributed MLPerf ResNet50 training on Intel Xeon architectures with tensorflow. In: The International Conference on High Performance Computing in Asia-Pacific Region Companion, pp. 29–35 (2021)
17. Yang, L., Chen, S., Yao, A.: Semihand: semi-supervised hand pose estimation with consistency. In: Proceedings of the IEEE/CVF International Conference on Computer Vision, pp. 11364–11373 (2021)
18. Zeng, H.: An off-line handwriting recognition employing tensorflow. In: 2020 International Conference on Big Data, Artificial Intelligence and Internet of Things Engineering (ICBAIE), pp. 158–161. IEEE (2020)

Caregiver Attitudes Toward Internet-Enabled Sources of Information

Adam Felts, Alexa Balmuth, Chaiwoo Lee[✉], Lisa D'Ambrosio,
and Joseph F. Coughlin

Massachusetts Institute of Technology, Cambridge, MA 02139, USA
cafelts@mit.edu

Abstract. Caregivers have an array of informational needs in order to accomplish tasks, solve problems, obtain peace-of-mind, and make sense of their caregiving situation, which spurs them toward the activity of information seeking. Technologically enabled information sources, especially the internet, play an important role in caregiver information seeking. An online survey was conducted to explore the information sources that family caregivers rely on and what qualities of information sources are most important to caregivers, with particular attention paid to online sources such as websites, social media, video apps, podcasts, and virtual assistants. The survey was completed by 324 people who belong to a research panel of caregivers. Results indicate that the internet is the most commonly used information source among caregivers, as well as among the top-three most preferred sources. However, despite receiving high marks for ease of use and helpfulness, internet-based sources tended to score poorly on metrics of trustworthiness and reliability. The biggest difficulty that caregivers experience when seeking information is having insufficient time in the day to search for information, which may contribute to their reliance on the internet as a source despite its shortcomings in certain key dimensions. The internet may also have value as an information source for caregivers beyond purely practical concerns – including as a way to satisfy curiosity. For these reasons, among others, the internet stands as an essential informational resource for many unpaid family caregivers, alongside medical professionals and family and friends.

Keywords: caregivers · family caregiving · information seeking · information sources · technology · internet

1 Introduction

Family caregivers manage a wide array of responsibilities, which can encompass the domains of finance, medicine, law, technology adoption and use, personal care, housekeeping, and many others. Accompanying this range of responsibilities is a variety of informational needs that caregivers may have to accomplish tasks, solve problems, obtain peace-of-mind, or make sense of their care-giving situation. Kernisan et al. (2010) identified a wide range of different topics on which caregivers may seek information, including health information, practical information on how to perform caregiving tasks,

© The Author(s), under exclusive license to Springer Nature Switzerland AG 2023
Q. Gao and J. Zhou (Eds.): HCII 2023, LNCS 14043, pp. 269–287, 2023.
https://doi.org/10.1007/978-3-031-34917-1_20

legal and financial matters, help with addressing behavioral and psychological issues, emotional support, information about housing, and information about older adults and driving.

Information seeking among caregivers may be performed for practical purposes, such as to acquire knowhow, solve problems, or to discern between possible options when making a decision. Kernisan et al. identified two primary themes that described the reasons for caregiver in-formation-seeking in a study of online information-seeking behavior: first, a desire for assistance with practical skills, and second, help for interpreting and planning for symptoms, behaviors, and interpersonal situations. Information-seeking may be proactive—that is, aimed toward preparing oneself for future situations—or reactive, to deal with existing problems or to address an ongoing crisis (Stajduhar, Funk, and Outcalt, 2013).

Information-seeking may also be done for psychological reasons, such as to satisfy a curiosity or to cope with emotions like anxiety and loneliness. Information-seeking may both be driven by emotions and may produce emotions, such as worry, relief, confusion, anger, helplessness, dis-appointment, or hopefulness (Savoleinen, 2014; Kuhlthau, 1990). In a study of online health in-formation seeking, Rupert et al. (2016) observed that caregivers sought information on their care recipient's illness or medical situation to relieve stress and to feel less lonely. Information-seeking may have psychological benefits as well by increasing feelings of control and self-efficacy (Wil-liams, Morrison, and Robinson, 2016).

Sources of information that caregivers may use include professionals such as health-care workers, financial professionals, lawyers, or social workers. Or they may take recourse to their peers, such as friends, family, or other caregivers. They may refer to companies and organizations such as health insurance providers, national advocacy organizations, or government entities. They may read books or magazines. Finally, they may turn to the vast compendium of formal and informal informational resources that can be found on the internet, using search engines, social media, or specific websites.

The use of the internet as an information source has grown drastically in the last twenty-five years, expanding the academic study of information seeking from the organization and user experience of libraries toward the investigation of information seeking performed online. As of 2016, for example, sixty percent of U.S. adults seek health information online (Rupert et al. 2016), and many obtained information from peer networks such as online forums and social media.

While the internet may be a predominant source of information for many people, it is often used as a supplement to more formal sources of information, such as medical professionals or other experts, rather than a replacement for those sources (Chio et al. 2008, Rupert et al. 2016). An information-seeker may value different aspects of a source of information, such as trustworthiness, convenience, usability, the capacity for empathy and understanding, and reliability, depending on the information-seeking task at hand and the resources available to the information-seeker.

This paper explores caregivers' use of various sources in the information seeking process, with particular attention paid to sources that are enabled by digital and computing technology, chiefly the internet. The qualities—both positive and negative—of these technologically enabled sources are highlighted by comparisons with caregivers' perceptions of other information sources. The reasons that caregivers turn to these technologically enabled sources, what benefits these sources offer, and their perceived limitations are also explored.

2 Study Design

2.1 Questionnaire Design

A questionnaire was developed to query unpaid family caregivers about the sources that they use to find information. The survey asked about what sources caregivers use most frequently, as well as the sources they most prefer to use. Respondents were also asked to evaluate the sources of information that they use across various dimensions. The survey also included items about the reasons that led respondents to seek information, feelings and emotions that respondents experienced when using different sources, and difficulties in searching for and finding information.

To develop the list of information sources that the questionnaire asked about, a pilot survey was administered to a group of adults who identified as former caregivers. The pilot survey included lists of topics and sources that were derived from a review of the literature, which were expanded by the inclusion of responses from the pilot survey respondents.

Relevant Survey Questions. Respondents were asked, "Thinking generally about when you look for information related to caregiving, how easy or difficult is each of the following for you?" The following items were provided for respondents to answer: "Finding a source of information that I can trust;" "finding the information I need when I need it;" "knowing where to go to find the information I need;" and "finding time in my day to search for the information I need." Response options comprised a five-item Likert-style scale as follows: Very easy, Easy, Neither easy nor difficult, Difficult, Very difficult.

Respondents were asked about the frequency with which they used information sources to find information related to providing care. Response options included Never, Rarely, Sometimes, and Often. The list of information sources that respondents were asked about can be found in Table 3. Of the information channels and sources that respondents reported using rarely, sometimes, or often, they were asked to selected up to three of their most preferred channels or sources.

Of the information sources that respondents reported using rarely, sometimes, or often, they were asked about how easy it was for them to use the selected sources, how helpful the selected sources were for them in finding information related to providing care, how reliable the selected channels or sources were in finding information related to providing care, how trustworthy they felt the caregiving-related information from the selected channels or sources was, how satisfied they were with the selected channels or sources in finding information related to providing care, and how much they felt the selected sources and channels understood their situation as a caregiver. Response options for each of these items comprised a five-item Likert-style scale (e.g., Not at all easy, A little easy, Somewhat easy, Quite easy, Extremely easy).

A battery of questions also asked respondents about the internet in particular as an information source.

For those respondents who reported using the internet as an information source, they were asked how often they started their information searches on the internet using a search engine versus going to a specific website. They were also asked which apps or websites that they used when they consulted the internet for caregiving-related information: Facebook, Twitter, YouTube, Instagram, Wikipedia, medical advice websites, a health insurer website, national organization or advocacy websites, government websites such as medicare.gov, caregiver support forums, or some other site or app.

A question asked respondents about qualities they observed and prioritized in internet-based sources: "When thinking about seeking information related to caregiving, how common is it that internet websites or apps have the following characteristics?" Six characteristics were listed: trustworthiness, reliability, ease of use, convenience, sympathy and understanding, and specificity and depth of information. The same question was asked about the importance of these six characteristics of internet websites or apps for respondents when seeking information related for caregiving.

Respondents were asked about the reasons that they used websites or apps to seek information related to caregiving, with the following response options: "I needed to solve a problem," "I wanted to learn how to do something," "I needed to understand something better," "I was just curious about something," "I was worried about something," "I wanted to feel less alone," "I was looking for something to make me feel hopeful," "I wanted to feel more confident about my caregiving," and an "other" option that allowed respondents to provide a reason not listed.

Respondents were also asked about the feelings or emotions they have experienced in relation to using the internet to seek information related to caregiving. A large set of response options was provided: frustration, compassion, love, determination, empowerment, gratitude, patience, helplessness, loneliness, stress, relief, fear, joy, anger, curiosity, confusion, anxiety, excitement, strength, hope, guilt or shame, disappointment, and sadness or depression, as well as the option to select "None of the above."

2.2 Survey Administration

An approximately 20-min online survey was conducted with family caregivers who were members of an ongoing caregiver research panel organized by the MIT AgeLab. A total of 324 participants residing in the US responded to the survey. The survey was fielded from June 29 to July 15, 2021.

Demographic information about the sample is included in Table 5 in the Appendix. Notably, 84 percent of respondents identified as women. 88 percent identified as white. 42.9 percent reported possessing a postgraduate degree. 55.7 percent of respondents reported that their care recipient was a parent.

3 Results

3.1 Difficulties in Seeking Information

The survey asked respondents about the level of difficulty of four features of the information-seeking process: finding time in the day to search for information, knowing where to go to find information, finding the information one needs when one needs it, and finding a trustworthy source of information.

Caregivers reported the greatest difficulty with finding time in their day to search for the information they need, as reported in Table 1. Reported difficulty in one feature was often associated with reported difficulty in the other features.

Table 1. Difficulty of the information-seeking process.

Difficulty of…	Mean (N = 324)
Finding time in my day to search for the information I need	3.15
Knowing where to go to find the information I need	2.89
Finding the information I need when I need it	2.88
Finding a resource of source of information that I can trust	2.85

Notes: 1 = Very easy, 2 = Somewhat easy, 3 = Neither easy nor difficult, 4 = Somewhat difficult, 5 = Very difficult

3.2 Use of Information Sources

Respondents were shown a list of 27 information sources and were asked to indicate the *frequency* with which they used each source. Of those sources that respondents did not report "never" using, respondents were also asked to select their three *most preferred* information sources. While presumably not exhaustive, the list of sources was intended to capture a wide range of plausible sources of caregiving-related information. Respondents' most frequently used and most preferred information sources are listed in Tables 6 and 7, respectively, in the Appendix.

In general, respondents consulted a relatively wide range of sources for caregiving information. On average, caregivers reported having used 15 of the 27 provided information sources.

The *most frequently used* source from the list was internet/web search, followed by the care recipient's doctor or other healthcare provider, and family or friend(s) who are/were caregivers. While these were also the top three *most preferred* channels/sources that emerged, the order shifted, with human sources—family or friend(s) who are/were caregivers, and the care recipient's doctor—rising significantly above internet/web search in preference. Notably, those two most preferred sources were among the top three for over half of respondents.

Other technologically enabled information sources asked about in the survey were virtual assistants such as Siri and Alexa, online communities and social media, and video apps such as YouTube and TikTok. Among these sources, online communities and social media was the fifth-most frequently used information source among respondents; video apps were the 11th-most used; and virtual assistants were the second-least-used source.

3.3 Evaluating Positive Attributes of Information Sources

To better understand caregivers' attitudes toward the sources of information that they used, those who used each given source were asked to evaluate it along six different dimensions: *ease of use* of the source in finding information about caregiving; *helpfulness* of the source in finding information; *reliability* of the source; *trustworthiness* of information from the source; *satisfaction* with the source; and the extent to which the source was *understanding* of the respondent's situation as a caregiver. Each was rated on a five-point scale (1 = not at all; 2 = a little; 3 = somewhat; 4 = quite; and 5 = extremely). Respondent' mean attribute scores for each information source are reported in Table 8 in the Appendix.

Within each individual source, dimensions were highly correlated, with Cronbach's alpha scores for each of the 27 sources ranging between .862 (internet/web search) and .941 (hospice care provider or staff). Exploratory factor analyses within each source also consistently revealed all six of the dimensions for each source loading on a single factor, suggesting that caregivers tended to evaluate a given source relatively consistently across dimensions.

Across dimensions, caregivers on average rated the helpfulness of these information sources as relatively lower and the trustworthiness of these sources as relatively higher. There was greater variation in caregivers' ratings of how well different sources understood them as caregivers and less variation in assessment of the helpfulness and reliability of and satisfaction with these information sources.

Ease of Use. The internet/web search was rated highest in terms of ease of use of sources to find information related to caregiving, joined in the top 10 easiest-to-use sources by other widely and publicly available media: books, newspapers, or magazine/journal articles; video websites or apps; and podcasts. Online communities and social media were also rated among the easiest sources to use, as were national organizations or advocacy groups for particular disease conditions and national organizations or advocacy groups for caregiving more generally, which may also be accessed online. Family and friends who were caregivers rated seventh overall in terms of ease of use, and the top 10 were closed out by pharmacists, the care recipient's doctor, and digital assistants/AI devices. Among the top ten sources for ease of use, only two professional sources emerged: pharmacists and the care recipient's doctor or other healthcare provider.

Despite the high correlations of the different source attributes with each other, ease of use of the information source appeared a little more distinctive than the other dimensions. Except for digital assistants, all the media channels included in the list of sources (internet/web search, books, newspapers, magazine/journal articles, video websites or apps, and podcasts) appeared among the top ten highest-rated sources for ease of use. In fact, two of the channels—podcasts and digital assistants, both of which are newer among these technology-enabled sources—ranked among the lowest ten sources for all of the dimensions except for ease of use.

Helpfulness of the Source in Finding Information Related to Caregiving. The sources rated highest in terms of helpfulness generally tended to be other people with caregiving experience and healthcare professionals. Family and friends who were caregivers, online communities and social media, and national organizations and advocacy groups for a particular disease condition and those for aging/caregiving more generally all ranked among the ten highest-rated sources on helpfulness. Professional sources in the top ten included ones that are more likely to have regular contact with the care recipient and address his or her medical needs, notably the care recipient's doctor or other healthcare provider, hospice care providers or staff, and home health aides. Media channels—internet/web search, books, newspapers, magazines and journals, and video websites and apps—rounded out the ten highest-rated sources on helpfulness.

In contrast, a number of different professionals ranked comparatively lower on helpfulness, notably lawyers and eldercare attorneys, financial professionals, hospital staff, and hospital social workers. Podcasts were not particularly helpful to caregivers as a source of information for caregiving, nor were digital assistants/AI virtual assistants. Family and friends who were not caregivers were also lower on helpfulness, as were religious leaders. Health insurance providers for the care recipient and the caregiver ranked second-to-last and last on helpfulness, respectively.

Reliability of the Source in Finding Information Related to Caregiving. Professionals—notably healthcare professionals—tended to be among the highest-rated sources of information in terms of reliability. Among the top ten sources in terms of reliability were the care recipient's doctor or other healthcare provider, hospice care providers or staff, the caregiver's doctor or healthcare provider, visiting nurses, and pharmacists. Other professionals in the top ten were lawyers and eldercare attorneys. Rounding out the top ten were national organizations or advocacy groups for particular disease conditions and for general aging or caregiving, family and friends who were caregivers, and books, newspapers, and magazine/journal articles.

Sources rated among the least reliable reflected a mix of different types, including financial professionals and religious leaders. Among media channels, video websites or apps, podcasts and digital assistants/AI were rated relatively low on reliability; online communities and social media were also among the lower-rated.

Trustworthiness of the Source for Information Related to Caregiving. Healthcare professionals dominated most of the top ten most trustworthy information sources. Caregivers rated their care recipient's doctor, their own doctor, family therapists or counselors, pharmacists, hospice care providers, visiting nurses and hospital staff more highly. Family and friends who were caregivers also appeared among the highest-rated sources in terms of trustworthiness, as did lawyers and eldercare attorneys. National organizations for particular conditions and for aging or caregiving more generally were also more highly rated.

In contrast to the ease-of-use dimension, media channels rated lower on trustworthiness. Books, newspapers, magazines and journals, internet and web searches, podcasts, video websites or apps, and digital assistants/AI were all among the ten lowest rated sources on trustworthiness. Family and friends who were not caregivers and online communities or social media were also ranked lower.

Understand you as a Caregiver. Caregivers rated other family and friends who were also caregivers highest in terms of serving as a source of information who understood their situation as a caregiver. Healthcare professionals, notably family therapists, hospice care providers, the care recipient's doctor, home health aides, visiting nurses, and the caregiver's doctor, were also relatively highly rated on this attribute compared with other sources. National organizations and advocacy groups for particular conditions and for aging or caregiver generally were relatively highly rated as understanding the caregiver's situation, as were geriatric care managers.

Faring less well in terms of overall rank in understanding the caregiver's situation were media channels: books, newspapers, magazine and journal articles; podcasts; internet and web searches; video websites and apps; and digital assistants. Several professionals also ranked lower on this dimension, notably religious leaders and financial professionals. Family and friends who were not caregivers and health insurers for both the care recipient and the caregiver were also among the lowest ranked sources.

Satisfaction with the Source for Information for Caregiving. As with trustworthiness, healthcare professionals dominated most of the top ten highest-rated sources in terms of satisfaction for information related to caregiving. Caregivers rated their care recipient's doctor highest on average, but also among the top ten were pharmacists, family therapists or counselors, the caregiver's own doctor, hospice care providers and visiting nurses. Family and friends who were caregivers also ranked among the highest in terms of satisfaction—second only to the care recipient's doctor—as did national organizations or advocacy groups for particular disease conditions and then for aging or caregiving more generally. Internet and web searches were also rated among the top ten for information source satisfaction.

Caregivers rated video websites or apps, podcasts, and digital assistant/AI channels relatively lower on satisfaction. Hospital social workers, religious leaders, online community and social media, and family and friends who were not caregivers also were among the lowest ranked on satisfaction, as were area agencies on aging and health insurers for both the care recipient and the caregiver.

3.4 The Internet as Caregiving Information Source

The survey included a more in-depth battery of questions about caregivers' use of and attitudes toward the internet as an information source.

The survey asked those respondents who used the internet as an information source how they used the internet to find information—whether they turned to a specific website or started with a search engine—and what websites they most consulted for caregiving information. When using the internet for information seeking, starting with a search engine was typically utilized by most caregivers. Most caregivers said they "almost always" (60.2%) or "most of the time" (25.8%) start with a search engine as opposed to going a particular website.

The most-used websites or apps were medical advice websites, followed by national organization or advocacy websites and government websites—all three of which were utilized by over half of the sample. Generally speaking, social media websites/apps were the least commonly used, as shown in Table 2.

Table 2. Using websites to find information: frequency of use

Websites used	Frequency (N = 256)
Medical advice website	74.6% (n = 191)
National organization or advocacy website	59.0% (n = 151)
Government website	54.7% (n = 140)
Caregiver support forum	33.2% (n = 85)
Health insurer website	23.4% (n = 60)
YouTube	18.8% (n = 48)
Wikipedia	18.4% (n = 47)
Facebook	18.0% (n = 46)
Instagram	3.9% (n = 10)
Twitter	3.5% (n = 9)
Other	13.3% (n = 34)

Frequency of use and higher ratings of positive qualities of the internet were significantly and positively correlated with one another, though some variation in these measures did occur. The same top three most important characteristics that emerged for internet websites/apps were trustworthiness, reliability, and specificity and depth of information. Notably, these did not align with the most common characteristics of the internet, which included convenience, ease of use, and reliability, as shown in Table 3.

Further, importance and prevalence were significantly and positively correlated—though only weakly—for reliability ($r = .150$, $p < .05$), ease of use ($r = .220$, $p < .01$), convenience ($r = .276$, $p < .01$), and sympathy and understanding ($r = .267$, $p < .01$), but were not significantly correlated for trustworthiness or specificity and depth of information. These findings suggest a discrepancy between the most important attributes of internet sources for caregivers and the attributes that are most prevalent in such sources.

Caregivers most often reported using the internet for information-seeking because they "needed to understand something better" (87.0%), though some caregivers did select each of the given reasons, as shown in Table 4.

Caregivers also selected a variety of feelings and emotions that they have experienced in relation to using the internet to seek information related to caregiving; the top three were curiosity, frustration, and stress. The emotions that caregivers reported experiencing when using the internet as an information source are reported in Table 9 in the Appendix.

Table 3. Using websites to find information: importance and prevalence of positive attributes

Attributes	Mean importance (N = 253)	Mean prevalence (N = 251)
Trustworthiness	4.65	3.27
Reliability	4.59	3.37
Specificity and depth of information	4.43	3.23
Ease of use	4.09	3.43
Convenience	3.93	3.47
Sympathy and understanding	3.34	2.83

Notes: For both importance and prevalence, 1 = Not at all, 2 = A little, 3 = Somewhat, 4 = Quite, 5 = Extremely

Table 4. Using websites to find information: reasons for using

Reasons for using Internet Websites/apps	Percent (N = 253)
I needed to understand something better	87.0%
I needed to solve a problem	64.0%
I wanted to learn how to do something	57.3%
I was worried about something	57.3%
I was just curious about something	47.4%
I wanted to feel more confident about my caregiving	37.5%
I was looking for something to make me feel hopeful	19.8%
I wanted to feel less alone	17.4%
Other	7.9%

4   Discussion

Caregivers may seek information from a wide variety of sources, with respondents selecting 15 of 27 of the sources listed in the survey on average. However, a few sources received a relatively outsized amount of use by the respondents, suggesting a core set of information sources that many caregivers rely on. The top two most-preferred sources—the care recipient's doctor and friends and family who were caregivers—were chosen by over half the sample. The internet is the source of information that caregivers most frequently turn to, followed by the care recipient's doctor and family and friends who were also caregivers.

While the internet is the most frequently used source of information among caregivers, it may not be the most preferred source under every circumstance—the internet appeared among the top three most preferred sources for just over a third of the sample. While the internet ranked among the top 10 information sources when the six surveyed attributes (trustworthiness, reliability, satisfaction, helpfulness, convenience, and ease of use) were scaled together, medical professionals such as doctors, pharmacists, and counselors and sources of specialist knowledge such as disease advocacy groups scored higher—and family and friends who were caregivers were the top source. Additionally, the internet ranked poorly in terms of trustworthiness, an attribute that the respondents valued highly both in general and specifically for internet-based sources.

The discrepancy between the frequency of use of the internet by caregivers and its shortcomings in certain key attributes might be explained by its extremely high ratings for convenience and ease of use. When ease of use was removed from the scale of positive attributes, the internet fell significantly in the ranking of sources, suggesting that this is the key attribute for its appeal among caregivers. The appeal and occasional necessity of ease and convenience in the information seeking process may result in caregivers frequently consulting convenient information sources even if they are lacking in other valued attributes.

This privileging of ease and convenience in their actual use of information sources—if not in their evaluation of the most important aspects of those sources—is likely associated with challenges that caregivers experience related to time management. Having time in the day to search for information was the most difficult aspect of information-seeking among the respondents. For caregivers who are often short of time, convenience and ease of use may be essential attributes of a useful source of information, even if they are not the most valued.

Given the high prevalence of use of the internet as an information source, providing technology support to caregivers and designing easier-to-use technological platforms may significantly reduce barriers to finding information. For organizations seeking to act as sources of information for caregivers, recognizing caregivers' needs for convenience as well as their preference for trustworthy sources—and attending to both needs—may be the best way to meet their information seeking needs. Online sources that are able to connect caregivers with validated expertise—or caregiving peers—may be optimal if not comprehensive.

The internet may also satisfy other information-seeking needs for caregivers that other sources cannot as easily fulfill. One of the top three reasons for using the internet as a source of information among caregivers was to satisfy a curiosity. Additionally, curiosity was one of the top three emotions that respondents reported feeling when using the internet to search for information. No other source was strongly associated with curiosity as a reason for use or as an associated emotion. The enormous variety of information across different domains on the internet and its easy accessibility may make it uniquely suited for satisfying curiosity. The internet's capacity to satisfy curiosity may further contribute to its high levels of usage as an information source among caregivers.

Acknowledgments. We would like to acknowledge the sponsors of the MIT AgeLab CareHive consortium for their support of this research, and the CareHive Caregiver Panel members for their invaluable insights.

Appendix

Table 5. Sample characteristics (N = 324)

Caregiver characteristics		Count	%
Age	Silent Generation and older (born 1945 or earlier)	20	6.3%
	Older Boomers (born 1946~1954)	85	26.6%
	Younger Boomers (born 1955~1964)	113	35.3%
	Generation X (born 1965~1980)	86	26.9%
	Millennials and younger (born 1981 or after)	16	5.0%
Gender	Male	51	15.7%
	Female	272	84.0%
	Prefer not to say	1	0.3%
Household income	Less than $25,000	22	6.8%
	$25,000~$49,999	35	10.8%
	$50,000~$74,999	47	14.5%
	$75,000~$99,999	47	14.5%
	$100,000~$149,999	55	17.0%
	$150,000~$199,999	22	6.8%
	$200,000 or more	31	9.6%
	Prefer not to answer	65	20.1%
Ethnicity	White	285	88.0%
	Black or African American	10	3.1%
	Hispanic or Latino	6	1.9%
	Asian or Asian American	20	6.2%
	Native American	1	0.3%
	Hawaiian or Pacific Islander	2	0.6%
	Other	7	2.2%
Highest level of education completed	High school diploma	4	1.2%
	Some college	41	12.7%
	Trade/technical/vocational school or associate's degree	21	6.5%
	College degree	82	25.3%
	Some post-graduate work	37	11.4%
	Post-graduate degree	139	42.9%

(*continued*)

Table 5. (*continued*)

Caregiver characteristics		Count	%
Employment status	Employed full-time	111	34.3%
	Employed part-time	43	133%
	Self-employed	31	9.6%
	Not employed	32	9.9%
	Homemaker	20	6.2%
	Student	6	1.9%
	Retired	99	30.6%
	Other	27	8.3%
Care recipient's relationship to caregiver	Spouse or partner	78	24.1%
	Parent	180	55.7%
	Parent-in-law	14	4.3%
	Grandparent	4	1.2%
	Aunt or uncle	8	2.5%
	Sibling	9	2.8%
	Child	16	5.0%
	Other	14	4.3%
Length of time caregiving	Less than 6 months	10	3.1%
	6 months or more but less than 1 year	20	6.2%
	1 year or more but less than 5 years	136	42.1%
	5 years or more but less than 10 years	89	27.6%
	10 years or more	68	21.1%
Total number of care recipients	One	248	76.8%
	Two	69	21.4%
	Three or more	6	1.9%
Care recipient's condition(s)	Long-term physical condition	28	73.5%
	Short-term physical condition	22	6.8%
	Memory problem	193	59.6%
	Emotional/mental health problem	85	26.2%
	Behavioral issue	32	9.9%
	Developmental/intellectual disorder	21	6.5%
	Other	45	13.9%

(*continued*)

Table 5. (*continued*)

Caregiver characteristics		Count	%
Living arrangement between caregiver and care recipient	Living together	161	49.7%
	Within walking distance of each other	24	7.4%
	Short driving distance from each other (less than 1 hr drive)	88	27.2%
	Longer distance (drive of 1 hr or more but less than 2 hrs)	22	6.8%
	Far distance from each other (drive of 2 hrs or more but less than 8 hrs)	10	3.1%
	Very long distance from each other (drive of 8 hrs or more)	19	5.9%
Caregiver responsibilities sharing	I am the only caregiver for my care recipient	113	35.0%
	I share some of the responsibilities with another family member	92	28.5%
	I share some of the responsibilities with a paid caregiver	37	11.5%
	I share some of the responsibilities with a family member and a paid caregiver	51	15.8%
	Other	30	9.3%

Table 6. Frequency of using different information channels/sources

Channels/sources	Mean frequency (N = 319)
Internet/web search	3.37
My care recipient's doctor or other healthcare provider for him/her	3.04
Family or friend(s) who are/were caregivers	2.82
Books, newspapers, or magazine/journal articles	2.78
Family or friend(s) who are/were not caregivers	2.50
Online community or social media	2.30
My doctor or other healthcare provider for me	2.21

(*continued*)

Table 6. (*continued*)

Channels/sources	Mean frequency (N = 319)
National organization or advocacy group for caregiving or aging	2.15
National organization or advocacy group for a particular disease or condition (e.g., Alzheimer's Association, American Cancer Society, etc.)	2.13
Hospital staff (e.g., nurses, doctors in hospital)	2.09
Video website or app (e.g., YouTube, Tiktok)	2.06
Pharmacist	1.98
Area agency on aging	1.97
A financial professional	1.96
Local aging agency	1.95
Care recipient's health insurance provider	1.90
Home health aide	1.89
Lawyer or eldercare attorney	1.86
Visiting nurse	1.77
Family therapist or counselor	1.69
Social worker from hospital	1.64
Podcast	1.61
My health insurance provider	1.53
A religious leader	1.45
Digital assistant/AI virtual assistant	1.44
Geriatric care manager (paid for out of pocket)	1.40
Hospice care provider or staff	1.36

Notes: 1 = Never, 2 = Rarely, 3 = Sometimes, 4 = Often

Table 7. Most preferred information channels/sources

Channels/sources	Percent placing in top 3
Family or friend(s) who are/were caregivers	59.1%
My care recipient's doctor or other healthcare provider for him/her	55.6%
Internet/web search	34.2%
Geriatric care manager (paid for out of pocket)	27.4%
Hospice care provider or staff	26.9%

(*continued*)

Table 7. (*continued*)

Channels/sources	Percent placing in top 3
National organization or advocacy group for a particular disease or condition (e.g., Alzheimer's Association, American Cancer Society, etc.)	22.2%
Visiting nurse	19.8%
Family therapist or counselor	19.1%
Home health aide	15.6%
Lawyer or eldercare attorney	15.4%
My doctor or other healthcare provider for me	14.6%
Area agency on aging	14.3%
Books, newspapers, or magazine/journal articles	13.9%
Family or friend(s) who are/were not caregivers	13.5%
Social worker from hospital	13.5%
Online community or social media	13.2%
National organization or advocacy group for caregiving or aging	13.1%
Local aging agency	11.7%
A financial professional	11.5%
Hospital staff (e.g., nurses, doctors in hospital)	9.2%
Pharmacist	8.8%
A religious leader	7.1%
Care recipient's health insurance provider	5.5%
Video website or app (e.g., YouTube, Tiktok)	4.2%
My health insurance provider	3.4%
Podcast	2.9%
Digital assistant/AI virtual assistant (e.g., Siri, Amazon Echo)	2.8%

Table 8. Mean attribute scores for each information source

Source	Ease	Helpfulness	Reliability	Trustworthiness	Satisfaction	Understand you	N of cases
1 Family or friend(s) who are/were caregivers	3.44	3.46	3.48	3.79	3.52	3.8	227–271
2 Family or friend(s) who are/were not caregivers	3.04	2.62	2.69	3.09	2.77	2.71	220–262

(*continued*)

Table 8. (*continued*)

Source	Ease	Helpfulness	Reliability	Trustworthiness	Satisfaction	Understand you	N of cases
3 A financial professional	3.06	2.78	3.11	3.38	3.16	2.9	144–178
4 Lawyer or eldercare attorney	2.7	2.89	3.4	3.68	3.21	3.17	152–180
5 Geriatric care manager (paid for out of pocket)	2.86	3	3.16	3.43	3.09	3.27	62–78
6 A religious leader	2.93	2.57	2.99	3.41	2.87	2.99	84–98
7 My doctor or other healthcare provider for me	3.19	3.08	3.46	3.84	3.4	3.36	169–202
8 My care recipient's doctor or other healthcare provider for him/her	3.27	3.35	3.68	3.91	3.54	3.48	246–292
9 Hospital staff (e.g., nurses, doctors in hospital)	2.57	2.76	3.18	3.54	3.09	3.11	168–205
10 Home health aide	3.06	3.18	3.11	3.3	3.16	3.44	126–158
11 Visiting nurse	2.96	3.01	3.43	3.54	3.25	3.41	119–148
12 Hospice care provider or staff	3.15	3.26	3.5	3.64	3.25	3.51	49–65
13 Social worker from hospital	2.58	2.73	2.99	3.38	3.04	3.08	108–133
14 Pharmacist	3.29	3.1	3.42	3.72	3.48	3.24	154–190
15 My health insurance provider	2.63	2.44	2.74	3.01	2.9	2.53	88–109
16 Care recipient's health insurance provider	2.62	2.52	2.83	3.01	2.7	2.41	143–173

Table 9. Using websites to find information: related emotions

Emotions – Internet	Percent (N = 252)
Curiosity	52.0%
Frustration	51.6%
Stress	46.0%
Anxiety	37.7%
Relief	36.5%
Empowerment	34.5%
Determination	33.7%
Confusion	29.8%
Disappointment	29.8%
Hope	27.0%
Sadness or depression	20.2%
Compassion	19.4%
Gratitude	19.4%
Helplessness	18.7%
Patience	17.9%
Strength	17.5%
Fear	14.7%
Anger	11.9%
Loneliness	6.7%
Excitement	6.7%
Love	6.3%
Guilt or shame	6.3%
Joy	2.0%
None of the above	6.7%

References

Chiò, A., et al.: ALS patients' and caregivers' communication preferences and information seeking behaviour. Eur. J. Neurol. (2007). https://doi.org/10.1111/j.1468-1331.2007.02000.x

Chua, G.P., Ng, Q.S., Tan, H.K., Ong, W.S.: Caregivers of cancer patients: what are their information-seeking behaviours and resource preferences? Ecancermedicalscience **14**, 1068 (2020). https://doi.org/10.3332/ecancer.2020.1068

Diviani, N., Zanini, C., Jaks, R., Brach, M., Gemperli, A., Rubinelli, S.: Information seeking behavior and perceived health literacy of family caregivers of persons living with a chronic condition the case of spinal cord injury in Switzerland. Patient Educ. Counsel. **103**(8), 1531–1537 (2020). https://doi.org/10.1016/j.pec.2020.02.024

Kernisan, L.P., Sudore, R.L., Knight, S.J.: Information-seeking at a caregiving website: a qualitative analysis. J. Med. Internet Res. **12**(3), e31 (2010). https://doi.org/10.2196/jmir.1548

Kuhlthau, C.: Inside the search process: Information seeking from a user's perspective. J. Am. Soc. Inf. Sci. **42**(5), 361–371 (1991)

Mason, N.F., Francis, D.B., Pecchioni, L.L.: Health information seeking as a coping strategy to reduce Alzheimer's caregivers' stress. Health Commun. **37**(2), 131–140 (2022). https://doi.org/10.1080/10410236.2020.1824665

Rupert, D.J., et al.: Peer-generated health information: the role of online communities in patient and caregiver health decisions. J. Health Commun. **21**(11), 1187–1197 (2016). https://doi.org/10.1080/10810730.2016.1237592

Savolainen, R.: Emotions as motivators for information seeking: a conceptual analysis. Libr. Inf. Sci. Res. **36**(1), 59–65 (2014). https://doi.org/10.1016/j.lisr.2013.10.004

Schook, R.M., et al.: Why do patients and caregivers seek answers from the internet and online lung specialists? A qualitative study. J. Med. Internet Res. **16**(2) (2014). https://doi.org/10.2196/jmir.2842

Soong, A., Au, S., Kyaw, B. Theng, L.N., Car, L.T.: Information needs and information seeking behaviour of people with dementia and their non-professional caregivers: a scoping review. BMC Geriatr. **20**(61) (2020). https://doi.org/10.1186/s12877-020-1454-y

Stajduhar, K.I., Funk, L., Outcalt, L.: Family caregiver learning—how family caregivers learn to provide care at the end of life: a qualitative secondary analysis of four datasets. Palliat. Med. **27**(7), 657–664 (2013). https://doi.org/10.1177/0269216313487765

Williams, K.L., Morrison, V., Robinson, C.A.: Exploring caregiving experiences: caregiver coping and making sense of illness. Aging Ment. Health **18**(5), 600–609 (2014). https://doi.org/10.1080/13607863.2013.860425

What to Do Next? An Activity Scheduling Schema for Social Assistance Robots for Older Adults

David Gollasch(✉) ⓘ and Gerhard Weber ⓘ

Technische Universität Dresden, Nöthnitzer Straße 46, 01062 Dresden, Germany
{david.gollasch,gerhard.weber}@tu-dresden.de

Abstract. Due to an aging population, stressed caregivers within a stressed care sector as well as the wish of aging at home, there is an urgent need to provide solutions to cope with these challenges today and in the future. Finding technological, i.e., robotic, solutions is an interesting approach and is a highly frequented research topic. However, engineering social assistance robots (SARs) to a satisfying degree of usability and technology acceptance is challenging, because fulfilling user's expectations – especially with older adults as key user group – means to implement naturally-feeling robotic behaviour which leads to emulate a semi-human-like task execution behaviour. Within our work, we addressed the scheduling of robotic activities based on aspects such as parallelisability for multi-task execution, user- and system-triggered commands, as well as task priorities to allow interruption or stopping of running activities or dismissing incoming commands. We assessed user's expectations within a survey-based requirements analysis and derived a decision-making concept for scheduling incoming activities. We implemented the concept within a small app to evaluate the schema according to the acceptance of the resulting robotic behaviour. With this concept, we set a starting point to engineering well-accepted SARs from a behavioural perspective next to the finally implemented use cases and specific situations to use a SAR in the environment of older adults. This is crucial to move towards accepted technological solutions to the social challenges mentioned above that arise with an aging population.

Keywords: Human-Robot Interaction · Social Assistance Robots · Older Adults · Robot Behaviour · Activity Scheduling

1 Introduction

Assistance robots for use cases in the environment of older adults and care situations is a lively research field for a good reason: This research field addresses an increasingly urgent challenge of today's society and upcoming trends following future predictions regarding demographic changes and the development of the healthcare and caregiving sector. The United Nations predict that, globally, the number of older adults relative to the whole demography will double within the next three decades [1]. This increase

Q. Gao and J. Zhou (Eds.): HCII 2023, LNCS 14043, pp. 288–306, 2023.
https://doi.org/10.1007/978-3-031-34917-1_21

will lead to a rising demand for care services which is supposed to be overwhelming due to a shortage in caregivers [2]. For instance, the WHO already quantified the global lack of caregivers in 2013 to 7 million and predicted this number to increase to 13 million in 2035 [3]. For sure, this lack cannot only addressed by making more people want to become caregivers but by finding solutions to reduce the demand of caregivers, for instance, by developing concepts to allow people to age at home (for as long as possible) instead of care facilities. Therefore, providing technological solutions in the form of assistive technology can be promising [4]. Those assistive technologies can be of different shape, for instance, ambient assisted living (AAL) is an umbrella term to describe home-embedded electronic devices and services to provide support in everyday-life situations (so called activities of daily living, ADLs). While research within the AAL field primarily focusses on health-related issues such as monitoring the physiological condition of older adults or detecting emergency situations like falls, the development of embodied assistive agents (i.e., assistance robots) that provide support and cognitive stimulus is still in its infancy but a very motivating vision to cope with challenges such as social isolation, loneliness, depression, or even symptoms of mild cognitive impairments and early-stage dementia, that arise alongside the major trend of aging population [5, 6].

To move towards engineering feasible assistance robots for older adults, the design of a usable and accepted user interface to accommodate a fruitful human-robot interaction (HRI) is crucial besides the more specific and use-case-related functional robotic assets. While industrial robots in production environments in most cases only must fulfil a well-defined sequence of tasks or activities, the robotic activities of assistance robots or social assistance robots (SARs = agent-based user interface within assistance robots to, e.g., emulate a social entity) are invoked by triggers coming from users or the environment. Those triggers lead to a non-predictable sequence of robot activities and, thus, derives conflicting situations between multiple triggers as well as between triggered events and currently running activities. Furthermore, Feil-Seifer et al. [7] describe the requirement to design an HRI user interface in a way that it offers a responsive design based on the specific needs and preferences of older adults. More specifically, the robot should be easy to use, self-explanatory and controllable, and there should not be the need for an expert operator or a lengthy training. Especially the aspects of controllability and self-explanatory design highlights the need for a fitted mechanism to solve the described scheduling conflicts within the activity execution order. For instance, listening to a users' command is an activity that needs to be executed at almost any moment in time, even when the robot is busy with another task. Or, for instance, fetching an object, keys or similar, from another room and give information on something the robot is asked for, the weather for example. Moving to a room, looking for the object to fetch and talk simultaneously should be feasible, because it is not a problem for a human being, but a task scheduling challenge for robots.

To develop such a smart and fitted mechanism to solve occurring scheduling conflicts of robot activities, we address the following research question within this paper:

RQ. How can a first concept of a strategy for a task queue processing sequence with potentially parallelisable tasks for an assistance robot for older adults to ensure good usability and technology acceptance look like?

To move towards an answer to that question, we started to examine the actual need for parallelisation in HRI, focussing on older adults as key target user group, following a user-centred design approach [8, 9]. We did that by means of a short survey among older adults and people involved in different care situations based on their experiences related to support requirements during typical ADLs. We analysed the identified scenarios regarding their potential to cause scheduling conflicts anyway to elaborate the aspects regarding parallelisation and prioritisation of assistance activities that need to be considered when designing a feasible scheduling mechanism. With the important requirements being known, we proposed a concept in form of a scheduling model to provide a decision mechanism to select a feasible execution order for incoming new activities/tasks for the robot. To evaluate the model regarding technology acceptance [10] and to match users' expectations, we implemented the model within a tiny Android app prototype to run a quick evaluation to validate the matching to the initially considered requirements.

2 Background and Related Work

The user-centred design (UCD) process is crucial for designing interactive systems that meet the needs and preferences of their target user group. This is especially true for service robots, as the characteristics and requirements of the users can vary greatly between different groups. For example, the interaction between service robots and children is different from that between robots and older adults, with various factors such as the user's perception and evaluation of the interaction, their emotional connection, and the robot's adaptive behaviour playing a role as highlighted by Maitreyee et al. [11]. In addition, the applications and purposes of service robots are different between children and older adults with special needs. While the primary focus for service robots with children is to support inclusive education for those with disabilities, the focus for older adults is to assist with their limitations and provide support to both the older adults and their caregivers within a caregiving context.

The use of robots in caring for the elderly is a promising and growing field [12] that offers new opportunities within an ambient assisted living (AAL) environment. Fortunately, the acceptance of companion robots has increased in recent years [13], which drives the desire for interaction with these robots.

AAL focuses on providing technical assistance to older adults in their homes through smart home devices integrated into their homes and furniture. The goal of AAL products and services is to allow older adults to remain at home rather than moving to a care facility. However, the majority of AAL solutions focus on medical needs [14], such as emergency and fall detection and tracking daily habits and activities (ADLs), which can provide insight into behaviour changes for individuals with dementia.

Robots have the potential to enhance the AAL setup and the recognition of daily habits and activities by adding features such as activation and cognitive stimulation. An embodied user agent in the form of a robot may be an effective tool for this purpose [15]. Sauzéon et al. [16] have demonstrated a human-centred AAL platform that can incorporate assistive technology tailored to the individual user's needs and preferences, including those with dementia, cognitive impairments, and visual impairments using virtual reality technology.

In addition to activation and cognitive stimulation, other potential applications for robots include: a) using robots as agents in cognitive behavioural therapy to address issues such as anxiety, social stress, depression, and loneliness, which are becoming increasingly prevalent among older adults [17]; b) supporting people with early-stage dementia in performing daily activities [18–20]; and c) providing social assistance during the COVID-19 pandemic [21].

Humanoid robots or those with a human-like appearance typically use voice interaction as the main mode of communication. This is due to the ease of using natural language-based interaction, which has greatly improved in recent years with the widespread use of voice assistants like Siri and Alexa on smartphones and smart speakers. Studies have found that older adults are highly motivated to use voice-controlled robots in their daily lives [22, 23] (addressing technology acceptance). There is a growing focus on designing user-friendly voice user interfaces (VUIs) for these robots in the elderly care sector [24, 25] (addressing usability and user experience). In addition to voice interaction, there is interest in incorporating other forms of interaction, such as sentiment recognition, facial expressions, and gestures [26, 27], or using virtual, augmented, or mixed reality environments [28, 29]. However, to effectively address the specific needs and limitations of older adults, there is a need for user-centred design and collaboration with this target group [30, 31]. This will help to create effective and accessible robotic solutions for our aging society and relieve the stress on the elderly care sector.

The above-mentioned scenarios and use cases emphasise the importance of offering helpful features for older adults through social assistance robots (SARs). It's important to note that the needs and preferences of different groups of users vary, which highlights the significance of adopting a user-centred design (UCD) process when designing user interfaces for SARs [8, 9]. Despite a lot of research being done on robots for older adults, particularly in Asia, it is still unclear how to design a multi-purpose social assistance robot that acts as a general assistant and companion (similar to a personal butler) and what behaviour users want [32]. One challenge that needs to be addressed is how the robot should handle multiple commands. This paper aims to provide a starting point for designing solutions for this specific issue.

3   Requirements for Scheduling Triggered Activities

In advance to developing a feasible scheduling scheme for robot activities for SARs with older adults as key target user group, we need to identify the requirements which need to be considered and can be used to derive the actual decisions the concept should be able to make.

To retrieve information on user's expectations, we designed a survey among older adults and people with caring experiences. The survey comprises a questionnaire with the following structure:

1. User demographics (age, gender, role in elderly care and duration of being in that role)
2. Questions to assess expectations for an assistance robot based on statements related to specific and direct robot behaviour and activities. Participants evaluate on a 5-point Likert scale.
3. For the statements the participants agreed on: How should robotic support look like? A selection of activities is given, and participants are asked to evaluate the desirability of receiving support by means of an assistance robot. The desirability is evaluated on a 5-point Likert scale and an open question is added to describe that support in detail.
4. Open question to describe concerns related to SARs in care situations for older adults.
5. Open question to describe wished related to SARs in care situations for older adults.

The questionnaire has been presented among 19 participants. Slightly more than half of the participants are part of the target user group of older adults of age 65 and above (10 participants). The remaining 9 participants are younger but do have experience in the care sector. Form a gender perspective, the study involved 12 female and 5 male participants. Running this survey, we identified resulting statements as that we used to derive requirements for a decision-making schema for SAR activities (requirements analysis as part of the UCD process), cf. Table 1.

Table 1. Results or the requirements analysis for scheduling triggered robot activities

Statement	Resulting Requirement
The participants stated that following user expectations and keep controllability is an important factor of trustworthiness. In detail, they demand a predictable behaviour of the robot and before executing a task, the robot should ask for permission first	Ask users whenever necessary. Avoid potentially surprising behaviour
The availability of multitasking capabilities has not been deemed as very important	Parallelisability of tasks is not critical
(a) There was no obvious trend for or against the availability of self-initiated activities. (b) In terms of self-initiated activities, most of the participants preferred to keep communicating with the user and ask for permission (i.e., allow to stop activities or influence the robot's decisions and behaviour) instead of making decisions for itself	Provide proactive behaviour only when necessary. Ask for permission when possible

(continued)

Table 1. (*continued*)

Statement	Resulting Requirement
Since SARs offer an agent-based user interface to interact with the robot, we asked the participants for their perspective onto the robot itself. Thus, would they perceive the robot rather as a tool and utility or rather as a colleague. The answer was clear: All participants would perceive the robot as a tool and not as a colleague	Avoid chatting. The robot shall not mimic a friend
To sum up the concerns related to assistance through robots given by the participants, there is hesitation regarding data privacy-related issues (privacy concerns), regarding the level of human likeness in interaction (interaction concerns), and regarding the occurrence of dangerous situations caused by the robot in case of system failure (safety concerns)	Avoid threatening situations concerning privacy and safety
Apart from the mentioned concerns, the participants stated wishes towards the application of robots in care situations. Especially, they formulated the wish for meaningful support and interaction. Hence, the provided functionality should go beyond reminders or providing weather information and telling the news. Providing real cognitive stimulation or offering useful support during difficult ADLs or emergency situations is desired. Furthermore, the participants stated the demand for technical refinement related to HRI usability as well as the specific robot behaviour	Usefulness is the most important criterion

4 Parallel Execution of Tasks

The presented survey revealed that actual concurrency in executing tasks or activities is not a crucial capability of an SAR. Nevertheless, as stated above, it should be possible to combine multiple activities in situations that seem obviously reasonable and feasible such as the mentioned example of fetching an object from another room (movement and object recognition task) and answering a question (voice assistance task) at the same time. This drills down the technical challenge of task concurrency to the level of identifying and reacting on resource conflicts with resources being hardware components that cannot be accessed and controlled simultaneously. In case there is a conflict recognised, the competing activities cannot be executed concurrently, and, thus, need to be scheduled by means of the later presented schema. But in case there is no resource conflict, the two activities can be executed simultaneously.

Identifying resource conflicts prior to activity execution is the implementation challenge that we will only cover on a superficial level as implementation mechanisms may vary among different robots and depend on the software architecture to run activities and the implementation of hardware access (e.g., based on service bindings or using hidden access structures within abstraction frameworks). The crucial component that needs to be implemented and is part of the realisation strategy of the scheduling schema presented in this paper, is the resource conflict identification unit that compares the set of required resources for each activity and permits the concurrent task execution in case there is an empty intersection set for a pair-wise comparison of the given sets. If the intersection is not empty, the scheduling schema leads to a decision-making process as described below. To identify the required resources and build the named sets, the resources can either be stated directly within the programming code as (static) arrays for abstract classes for each activity. Or the resources can be derived from the implementation by, for instance, identifying service binding calls which reveals the used resources that cannot be accessed simultaneously as service bindings need to be unbound before another activity is allowed to set a new service binding for the same resource.

In case the parallel execution of activities is of no further relevance for the specific use cases and scenarios, especially since this criterion is of lower priority for the users, this step of identifying resource conflicts to allow multi-tasking can be skipped in the process and the task execution can proceed within the scheduling schema to – always – identify a (serialised) sequence of activity execution.

5 Handling Incoming Activities or Tasks

SARs are, in opposition to industrial and production robots, faced with incoming new commands in an unpredictable and unsorted timing. Furthermore, incoming commands cannot be handled as first-in-first-out FIFO queue, because commands may have different sources (coming from a user in front of the robot, coming from external triggers, or caused by pre-scheduled events) and varying priority (receiving weather information is less important than getting help in an event of emergency). And lastly, not all commands trigger activities that can be processed in parallel as seen above. Hence, we need to define a scheduling schema, that considers all mentioned aspects and lead to a robot behaviour that is a) feasible, b) makes sense related to the activity that needs to be scheduled (e.g., a postponed ringtone for an incoming call is obsolete), and c) is perceived as usable and accepted by the SAR's user(s).

A key distinguishment of incoming commands or triggers we make is whether an activity is triggered by an explicit user command or by an event that leads to proactive behaviour of the robot. Without looking at specific exceptions, explicitly formulated user commands always have a high priority compared to incoming triggers from external events. Furthermore, some participants of our requirements analysis study were sceptical towards proactive self-initiated robot activities, such that turning off those latter actions should be possible while user-initiated activities should not be affected here.

Optionally, in case specific proactively triggered activities should not be executed automatically, only for those non-user-triggered commands there could be a mechanism to ask the user for permission to execute the task in advance.

While, until now, we distinguished user-initiated and externally triggered events, assuming that those external triggers are based on sensory data or timers, we shall not forget that in a caring environment, next to the older adults, caregivers might be stakeholders or even users as well. Although when we use the term users, we primarily consider older adults, caregivers could as well perform configuration tasks with the robot that might lead to, for instance, reminding activities which, in the event of reminding, are perceived as self-initiated or proactive activities. Or in other words: proactive tasks can be originally caused by other people as well and are not *actually* proactive.

That is one side of non-user-triggered behaviour. On the other side, there are events triggered by the SAR's sensors observing the environment (e.g., fall detection) or external triggers, such as incoming calls (although a call is usually triggered by another human, we do not consider him or her to be a user or stakeholder of the robot).

As a result, we categorise the triggers as follows: There are (1) user commands that will (mostly) be executed directly, and (2) proactive tasks that need to be scheduled separately, whereas we have (2.1) indirect user commands, such as timer functions (user command: set timer; leads to trigger at a given time; leads to proactive behaviour at that given time), (2.2) sensory triggers, such as recognised falls or a room temperature decrease and (2.3) external triggers such as incoming calls.

5.1 User-Triggered Activities

Now, we focus on scheduling incoming commands in case another task or activity is already running, and the new incoming task cannot be executed in parallel. At first, we look at incoming commands that are triggered by the user, for instance, by asking directly to provide a weather forecast or ask for help finding an umbrella before going outdoors. One key requirement that needs to be considered throughout the whole process is that the user must always be able to stop all activities to ensure controllability.

Figure 1 illustrates the decision-making process (as flowchart from top to bottom) we propose for handling incoming user commands. The process handles incoming user commands as follows:

We assume to have two competing tasks A and B with A being the already executing activity (no matter if A has been triggered by a user or by an event) and B being the new incoming activity that has been triggered explicitly by the user.

The first conditional construct embeds the mechanism to check for parallelisability of the given tasks as described above. We already described that in case A and B are parallelisable, they can be executed concurrently, and if not, we follow the scheduling mechanism further down below.

We propose to distinguish between short and not necessarily short tasks regarding their duration to finish the activity. A threshold of when to categorise a task as short could be defined by the user or as a result of a requirements analysis for the specific SAR and application context, but we propose to consider short tasks to be activities that only briefly give some information, such as telling the time or providing calendar-based information for a daily schedule. In case the incoming task B is such as short task, there is a chance to briefly interrupt the running task A for executing B and resume A afterwards. We propose this behaviour if A is not an as "short" categorised task. In case A and B are both short tasks, the robot should wait for A to finish and execute B directly afterwards.

Commands that trigger tasks that are not categorised as "short" shall ask for permission to interrupt a currently running activity. Thus, the user should be notified that the upcoming activity could take a moment and leads to the interruption of a current activity. Given the user declines the request to execute B, A can continue running while B will be dismissed. We propose to not move B onto a queue, because the moment A is finished, and B takes over the robot's focus could be perceived as surprising behaviour. We recommend that the user then triggers B manually.

Given the user agrees to interrupt A in favour to execute B, we introduce one waiting slot for memorising a paused activity and that waiting slot needs to be empty at first. We do not recommend introducing a queue with multiple slots here as it is unlikely that users remember a sequence of paused activities rather than one which would otherwise cause unexpected behaviour as well. But there is one special case: If the duration of B is undefined and could be infinitely long (e.g., playing radio music), it would be pointless to let A wait for B to finish and resume with A then. Hence, in case of an open task B, we propose A to be stopped and dismissed. If B is not an open task, A will be paused and moved to the waiting slot while B can be executed. As soon as B is finished, resuming A should be notified to the user. So, we propose to ask the user for permission to continue running A.

The described mechanism distinguishes multiple types of tasks depending on their execution duration and decides, based on this information and a thoughtful selection of user involvement points to avoid unpredictable behaviour, which execution order is feasible, reasonable, and foreseeable.

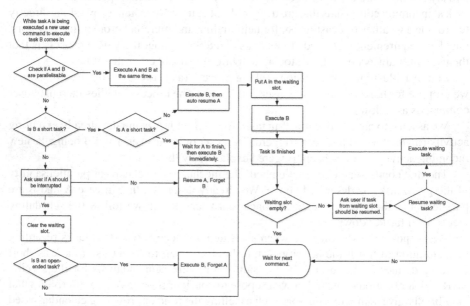

Fig. 1. Proposed decision-making process to handle conflicting incoming user tasks

5.2   System-Triggered (Proactively Executed) Activities

There are various reasons why an assistance robot might start to do something without being triggered by a user command. For instance, if it is possible to do video calls using the SAR, an incoming call needs to cause a notification for the user; or recognising emergency situations such as a fall should lead to calling help. Depending on what event triggered an action, the scheduling schema needs to decide when to interrupt running activities, when to append the incoming task to a queue (and onto which position) or when to dismiss incoming tasks. The resulting robot's behaviour should still be predictable and avoid surprising situations and – most importantly – any interruption must happen safely without any information loss or physical harm.

To generate a feasible behaviour, system-triggered tasks need to be categorised. We propose the following five categories with different priorities as described further down below in this section: We distinguish (a) emergency tasks such as calling help when a call is detected, (b) activities with high priority such as incoming calls, (c) tasks with medium priority such as alarms or timers, (d) tasks with low priority such as reminders or notifications, and (e) circumstantial activities that are not time critical at all.

Further, we introduce a queue that we call *proactive queue*. This queue should be sorted by category/priority first (emergency is the highest priority and circumstantial the lowest) and by time of adding an item (FIFO). Hence, whenever there we put a new task onto that proactive queue, we ensure to rearrange the items following this sorting.

The following Fig. 2 visualises the first of two parts of the scheduling process for system-triggered tasks. This first part focusses on the filling process for the mentioned proactive queue. The following procedure is shown: Firstly, we assume an event occurred and there now is a trigger to execute a new task. The incoming task enters the diagram from the top. If there is no other task already running, the robot may execute the incoming task right away. In case there is already a task running, we check for possible concurrency to execute both tasks simultaneously if supported. If that is not the case, we need to get into the scheduling mechanism based on priorities.

At first, we want to catch tasks with a low, non-time-critical priority. Thus, if the task is labelled as circumstantial, we propose to ask the user how to proceed. The user can choose between three options: he or she can skip the task to dismiss it, choose to reschedule the task to postpone execution or choose to execute the task which means to put the task onto the proactive queue. For any other task category, we directly forward the task onto the proactive queue, because we assume a certain time-critical activity which should not be dismissed or postponed. Whenever a new task is appended to the proactive queue, we ensure that all items in that queue are sorted based on priority (first) and time of appending (second) as described above.

Figure 3 continues the scheduling schema. We now have a sorted queue with tasks to execute one after another, beginning with the most important tasks and if there are multiple tasks of the same priority given, we select the longest-awaiting task first (FIFO).

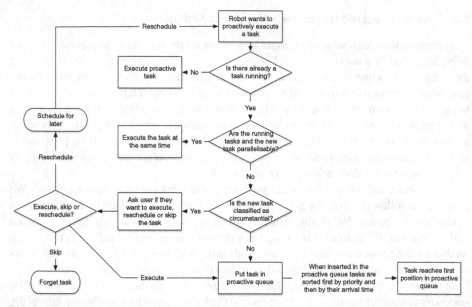

Fig. 2. Proposed decision-making process for system-triggered tasks. This figure comprises the first part of this process describing the filling and sorting process of the proactive queue.

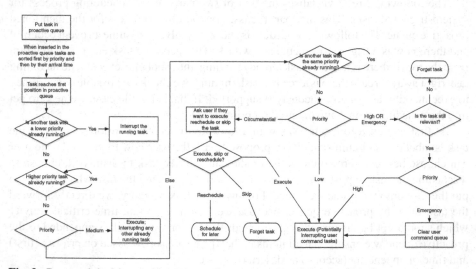

Fig. 3. Proposed decision-making process for system-triggered tasks. This figure comprises the second part of this process describing the FIFO and scheduling mechanism to empty the proactive queue.

If the currently running task is of lower priority than the task we select from the queue, we interrupt the running task in favour of the new, more important task. That step is required to ensure forwarding of incoming high-priority tasks such as emergency activities. In any other case, as the queue is already sorted, we always pick the most important tasks first, such that usually there is no less important task already being executed.

The next step forces the task execution to await finishing of the current, higher-prioritised task first. As soon as there is no higher-prioritised task still running, we check for medium-categorised tasks. If our task is of category medium, the activity shall be executed and is allowed to interrupt any other already running task (we already know that any task that could still be running is not of higher priority and we allow medium tasks to interrupt other medium tasks).

If we did not catch a medium task, we only see circumstantial, low, high, or emergency tasks here. If another task with the same priority is already running, we await that activity to be finished.

If the task to be executed is an emergency-rated activity, we propose to briefly check if the activity is still relevant (dismiss the task if the answer is no), clear the whole task queue and execute the activity right away (and interrupt any potentially running task, even user-triggered activities).

If the task to be executed a high-priority-rated activity, we proceed identical to the emergency case but without deleting the queue. Clearing the queue is only there to ensure no other activity could block very time-critical actions or the necessary steps to cope with the challenging situation of an emergency. High-categorised tasks are time-critical as well but do not handle dangerous situations.

As medium-rated tasks are already being handled, the next category is class of low-rated activities. They still are time-related although their slightly delayed execution is considered acceptable. Thus, now they can be executed after all more important tasks are done.

Finally, there are the non-time-critical circumstantial tasks. We assume that there has been a filled queue to process, and a reasonable amount of time passed by until we, finally, see the circumstantial task to be executed again. That is why we propose to ask the user again to process that activity now. The user has the same three options as before (execution now, postpone the task or dismiss the command).

With the described scheduling schema, we dealt with all upcoming situations of incoming tasks: based on user commands or external triggers (sensory data or scheduled events) and generated an execution order that is predictable from a user's perspective, involves the user in selected situations and ensures time-critical and important events to fast-forward within this flowchart.

6 Evaluation

Testing the feasibility of the presented scheduling schema means to identify logical issues which lead to unexpected behaviour. With that in mind, we implemented this schema within an activity simulation prototype within an Android app that can easily be tested by evaluation participants even during the pandemic-related limitations. This app can run on any Android-based smartphone and offers an abstract and simplified user interface that allows to directly trigger events with the press of a button and as a result, the app shows currently running activities to evaluate the simulated robotic behaviour.

Our small prototype that incorporated the scheduling schema should be sufficient to answer the rather abstract question of how users feel about the implemented workflow and behaviour as proposed in this paper. Therefore, we asked the participants to trigger certain events and answer some questions related to their experience using the prototype. We addressed the following two questions:

1. Does the concept make sense to the users, are there any system actions that are surprising or confusing, will they understand the robot's actions?
2. Do users accept the concept as is or do they wish some things would have been done differently?

We conducted an evaluation based on a qualitative study design based on the Thinking Aloud methodology. The participants were invited to articulate thoughts right during using the prototype. The tasks the users should fulfil are given verbally. For this brief evaluation, we invited 5 participants (of different age and gender) to take part. For the sake of testing the schema, we assume a pilot study to be sufficient. A study design with more participants and with special attention to the target user group is reasonable for final implementations of that scheduling schema within a specific SAR with a defined context.

The first set of tasks are related to the user commands. Our study design incorporated the following scenarios and specific tasks:

Scenarios:

- Short task interrupts already running task → interrupted task is automatically continued
- A finite task interrupts an already running task → when finished, ask if interrupted task should be continued
- A task that can be executed concurrently to an already running task → optional resource
- Two parallel running tasks are interrupted by a task that interrupts them both.
- Two parallel running tasks are interrupted by a task that interrupts one of them.

Tasks:

- Play music, then ask for the time and temperature
- Ask for the weather forecast, during the execution of that task request to see the map.
- Show the map while playing music. Then start the recipe activity.
- Show the map while playing music.

The second set of tasks are related to the proactive activities of the robot. Our study design incorporated the following scenarios and specific tasks:

Scenarios:

- Emergency blocks everything, even other emergency

- A circumstantial task appears → A dialog pops up, asking if the user wants the robot to execute, reschedule or skip the task
- Tasks accumulate in the sorted queue while a high priority task is being executed
- Low or circumstantial priority task waits for another task of the same priority
- A medium priority task interrupts another same priority task

Tasks:

- Alarm clock → Fire → Patient fell
- Call → News → New email → alarm clock
- Email → Reminder: take medication
- Alarm clock → Timer

After the Thinking-aloud phase, we asked a subset of the SUS questionnaire (with 5-point Likert scale) to get a rough evaluation of the overall usability impression. We reduced this set of questions, because the presented prototype is only an abstract representation of an SAR. The following questions were asked:

1. Did you feel like the robot actions were predictable or surprising? Did you like that?
2. Were there any system actions that were confusing or was the system easy to understand?
3. Did you observe a pattern in the robot's behaviour, or did you feel the robot behaved inconsistently?
4. Did you always feel like you were in control?
5. Would you accept a robot behaving in that way?
6. What things do you wish should be handled differently?

Both Table 2 and 3 summarise the results of our pilot study. The first table addresses the first set of tasks (user commands) while the second table addresses the second set of tasks (proactive behaviour). Each table contains the answers of our five test users (#1 to 5).

The test users mostly agreed with the presented concept and stated general acceptance towards an actual SAR with the described behaviour. The most notable complaint was related to the questions the robot is asking questions, i.e., to confirm a choice before interrupting another task. This contradicts the results of our requirements analysis study. The requirements analysis revealed a demand for control and being asked for permission in some situations. As the interaction modality with the prototypical app surely differs from the interaction with an actual SAR (for instance, a SAR could be controlled via voice instead of GUI buttons), the perception of confirmation questions and checks of the robot might be different as well. Overall, we did not identify logical or feasibility-related issues with the presented scheduling schema.

Table 2. Comparing the answers for the final questions for the user command prototype

Question	#1	#2	#3	#4	#5
Predictable or surprising	predictable	Mostly predictable	predictable	Somewhat surprising	Predictable
Confusing or easy to understand	Easy to understand	Easy to understand	Easy to understand	Easy to understand	Easy to understand
Pattern observed or inconsistent behaviour	pattern	inconsistent	Somewhat inconsistent	Partly a pattern observed	Pattern
Feeling of control	yes	yes	yes	yes	Yes
Accept the behaviour	yes	yes	yes	No, because the robot asks too many questions	yes
Wishes	none	More consistency regarding when the robot checks back	Change rules for when to ask for confirmation for task interruption	Fewer questions	none

Table 3. Comparing the answers for the final questions for the proactive tasks prototype

Question	#1	#2	#3	#4	#5
Predictable or surprising	predictable	both	Mostly predictable	Mostly predictable	predictable
Confusing or easy to understand	Easy to understand	Rather easy to understand	Easy to understand	Easy to understand	Easy to understand
Pattern observed or inconsistent behaviour	pattern	Slightly inconsistent	pattern	pattern	pattern
Feeling of control	yes	yes	yes	No, because the robot made all decisions	yes
Accept the behaviour	yes	Probably yes	yes	yes	Yes
Wishes	none	Change priorities	Change some priorities, more personalisation	More personalisation	none

7 Discussion

As subject to be discussed, we want to address three aspects: the opposing results of the requirements analysis and the prototype evaluation, the aspect of individualisation and customisability next to the fixed scheduling mechanism, and the open question of adding further types of tasks which might lead to additional task categories to distinguish.

Firstly, the opposing results of the requirements analysis and the prototype evaluation are surprising. Before designing the scheduling schema, we considered the need for re-prompts and checking questions to be plausible as it correlates with the demand for keeping full control of the robot's behaviour, especially to avoid surprising and unexpected situations. We clearly accept that too many questions of how to proceed might be disturbing at some point but identifying the sweet spot of right dose of questions is subject to further evaluation of specific SARs that implement our scheduling mechanism. Probably, the number of re-prompts can be reduced by changing system settings to, for instance, always allow (or reject) the execution of circumstantial activities.

This leads to the second discussion point of customisability within the scheduling schema. Next to the number of checks and re-prompts, the perception of the robot's behaviour might vary individually as well. We did not pay attention on keeping the schema extendable but there are ideas of how to customise the flowchart to incorporate an individualised behaviour of the robot. For instance, the robot could store prior made decisions related to the execution of circumstantial tasks, such that asking again for the same type of task might be avoidable. Another variation-point for extending the model is by adding a queue (probably with a fixed number of slots) instead of the one waiting slot for the user-commands-related model. Based on the cognitive abilities of the user, it might be desired to give a list of commands at once that the SAR should execute one after another.

Finally, it is an open question how to extend the model in case further priority levels or duration classifications shall be introduced. Our assumption is that less categories are favourable to reduce unnecessary complexity within the scheduling mechanism. Thus, we identified typical scenarios and ADLs that could be relevant to engineering SARs and derived different kinds of robotic activities from these ADLs, which we then categorised as presented (distinguishment between short, not-necessarily short, and potentially infinitely long-lasting tasks; plus, the five priorities from circumstantial to emergency events). There is no obvious solution of where to add further branching within the flowcharts to incorporate further categories. Thus, manual re-engineering of the schema and a new evaluation of feasibility is required then.

8 Conclusion and Outlook

The initial research question referred to the feasibility of a scheduling mechanism for activities of an SAR that leads to an acceptable behaviour. This acceptable behaviour is given for those strategies that avoid unpredictable and surprising situations and by ensuring that controllability is always given. Based on our requirements analysis, the designed scheduling strategy, and the positive feedback from our prototype evaluation, we provided a feasible structure to implement the complex task execution methodology that is required for robots that interact with real users. How this schema performs under real-world conditions within a specific SAR is still an open question and needs further implementation and evaluation. Especially the need for concurrency heavily depends on the specific use cases of an SAR.

Regarding the usability evaluation, the provided user feedback was mostly positive, and most participants said that they would accept a robot behaving as described in the concept. However, some users expressed disagreement with some of the task prioritisations or the robot's ongoing questions to confirm their choice to execute a task. Nevertheless, the goal of our research was to develop a first concept with an acceptable user evaluation and met user expectations which is fulfilled as the feasibility is shown by means of the prototype and the agreement with the behaviour is given by the participants.

Future research should focus on the implementation of the given schema in real-word application scenarios to put the scheduling under test. That helps to spot the aspects for improvement within the model or reveal missing cases that we did not identify by means of our requirements analysis. That implementation within a SAR can as well be evaluated with the actual target user group to investigate the implications on usability and technology acceptance related to the scheduling mechanism and task fulfilment strategy of the robot.

Those implementations in actual SARs lead to specific models for those SARs. It would be advantageous to merge improvements to the scheduling scheme into the abstract flowcharts presented within this paper, hence, to offer a generalised approach to implement robotic behaviour with a high degree of user acceptance.

References

1. United Nations Department of Economic and Social Affairs, Population Division: World population ageing 2020 Highlights: living arrangements of older persons. United Nations, New York (2020)
2. Martinez-Martin, E., Escalona, F., Cazorla, M.: Socially assistive robots for older adults and people with autism: an overview. Electronics 9, 367 (2020). https://doi.org/10.3390/electronics9020367
3. Thomas, G., Reddy, S., Oliel, S.: WHO | Global health workforce shortage to reach 12.9 million in coming decades. https://apps.who.int/mediacentre/news/releases/2013/health-workforce-shortage/en/index.html. Accessed 08 Feb 2023
4. Macis, D., Perilli, S., Gena, C.: Employing socially assistive robots in elderly care. In: Adjunct Proceedings of the 30th ACM Conference on User Modeling, Adaptation and Personalization, pp. 130–138 (2022)
5. Yamazaki, K., et al.: Home-assistant robot for an aging society. Proc. IEEE 100, 2429–2441 (2012). https://doi.org/10.1109/JPROC.2012.2200563
6. Samaddar, S., Desideri, L., Encarnação, P., Gollasch, D., Petrie, H., Weber, G.: Robotic and virtual reality technologies for children with disabilities and older adults. In: Miesenberger, K., Kouroupetroglou, G., Mavrou, K., Manduchi, R., Covarrubias Rodriguez, M., Penáz, P. (eds.) Computers Helping People with Special Needs. LNCS, vol. 13342, pp. 203–210. Springer, Cham (2022). https://doi.org/10.1007/978-3-031-08645-8_24
7. Feil-Seifer, D., Mataric, M.J.: Defining socially assistive robotics. In: 9th International Conference on Rehabilitation Robotics, ICORR 2005, pp. 465–468 (2005)

8. Bradwell, H.L., Edwards, K.J., Winnington, R., Thill, S., Jones, R.B.: Companion robots for older people: importance of user-centred design demonstrated through observations and focus groups comparing preferences of older people and roboticists in South West England. BMJ Open **9**, e032468 (2019)

9. Bulgaro, A., Liberman-Pincu, E., Oron-Gilad, T.: Participatory design in socially assistive robots for older adults: bridging the gap between elicitation methods and the generation of design requirements. arXiv Prepr. arXiv:2206.10990 (2022)

10. Martín-García, A.V., Redolat, R., Pinazo-Hernandis, S.: Factors Influencing Intention to Technological Use in Older Adults. The TAM Model Aplication. Res Aging. 1640275211063797 (2021). https://doi.org/10.1177/01640275211063797

11. Lindgren, H.: Younger and older adults' perceptions on role, behavior, goal and recovery strategies for managing breakdown situations in human-robot dialogues. In: Proceedings of 9th International Conference on Human-Agent Interaction (2021). https://doi.org/10.1145/3472307.3484679

12. Abdi, S., de Witte, L., Hawley, M.: Emerging technologies with potential care and support applications for older people: review of gray literature. JMIR Aging **3** (2020). https://doi.org/10.2196/17286

13. Huang, T., Huang, C.: Elderly's acceptance of companion robots from the perspective of user factors. Univ. Access Inf. Soc. **19**(4), 935–948 (2019). https://doi.org/10.1007/s10209-019-00692-9

14. Queirós, A., da Rocha, N.P.: Usability, Accessibility and Ambient Assisted Living. Springer, Cham (2018). https://doi.org/10.1007/978-3-319-91226-4

15. Gasteiger, N., et al.: Robot-delivered cognitive stimulation games for older adults. ACM Trans. Hum.-Robot Interact. **10**, 1–18 (2021). https://doi.org/10.1145/3451882

16. Sauzéon, H., Edjolo, A., Amieva, H., Consel, C., Pérès, K.: An ambient assisted living platform for supporting aging in place of prefrail and frail older adults: rationale, HomeAssist plaform, quasiexperimental design, and baseline characteristics (2021)

17. Hedman, E., Ljótsson, B., Lindefors, N.: Cognitive behavior therapy via the internet: a systematic review of applications, clinical efficacy and cost-effectiveness. Expert Rev. Pharmacoccon Outcomes Res. **12**, 745–764 (2012). https://doi.org/10.1586/erp.12.67

18. Vasudavan, H., Balakrishnan, S., Murugesan, R.K.: A study on activity recognition technology for elderly care. Int. J. Curr. Res. Rev. **13**, 107–111 (2021). https://doi.org/10.31782/ijcrr.2021.131225

19. Smith, R., Dragone, M.: A dialogue-based interface for active learning of activities of daily living. In: 27th International Conference on Intelligent User Interfaces (2022). https://doi.org/10.1145/3490099.3511130

20. Striegl, J., Gollasch, D., Loitsch, C., Weber, G.: Designing VUIs for social assistance robots for people with Dementia. Presented at the Mensch und Computer 2021 (2021). https://doi.org/10.1145/3473856.3473887

21. Getson, C., Nejat, G.: Socially assistive robots helping older adults through the pandemic and life after COVID-19. Robotics **10**, 106 (2021). https://doi.org/10.3390/robotics10030106

22. Song, Y., Yang, Y., Cheng, P.: The investigation of adoption of voice-user interface (VUI) in smart home systems among Chinese older adults. Sensors **22**, 1614 (2022). https://doi.org/10.3390/s22041614

23. Koebel, K., Lacayo, M., Murali, M., Tarnanas, I., Çöltekin, A.: Expert insights for designing conversational user interfaces as virtual assistants and companions for older adults with cognitive impairments. In: International Workshop on Chatbot Research and Design, pp. 23–38 (2021)

24. Murad, C., Munteanu, C., Cowan, B.R., Clark, L.: Revolution or evolution? Speech interaction and HCI design guidelines. IEEE Pervasive Comput. **18**, 33–45 (2019)

25. Gollasch, D., Weber, G.: Age-related differences in preferences for using voice assistants. Presented at the Mensch und Computer 2021 (2021). https://doi.org/10.1145/3473856.347 3889
26. Pollmann, K.: The modality card deck: co-creating multi-modal behavioral expressions for social robots with older adults. Multimodal Technol. Interact. **5**, 33 (2021). https://doi.org/10.3390/mti5070033
27. Swoboda, D., Boasen, J., Léger, P.-M., Pourchon, R., Sénécal, S.: Comparing the effectiveness of speech and physiological features in explaining emotional responses during voice user interface interactions. Appl. Sci. **12**, 1269 (2022). https://doi.org/10.3390/app12031269
28. Zeng, D., et al.: SHECS: A Local Smart Hands-free Elderly Care Support System on Smart AR Glasses with AI Technology. arXiv:2110.13538v1 (2021)
29. Giri, G.S., Maddahi, Y., Zareinia, K.: An application-based review of haptics technology. Robotics **10**, 29 (2021). https://doi.org/10.3390/robotics10010029
30. Bardaro, G., Antonini, A., Motta, E.: Robots for elderly care in the home: a landscape analysis and co-design toolkit. Int. J. Soc. Robot. (2021). https://doi.org/10.1007/s12369-021-00816-3
31. Bradwell, H., Winnington, R., Thill, S., Jones, R.B.: Prioritising design features for companion robots aimed at older adults: stakeholder survey ranking results. In: Li, H., et al. (eds.) ICSR 2021. LNCS (LNAI), vol. 13086, pp. 774–779. Springer, Cham (2021). https://doi.org/10.1007/978-3-030-90525-5_70
32. Müller, S.: Realisierung nutzeradaptiven Interaktionsverhaltens für mobile Assistenzroboter (2016)

Technologies and Services to Support Care: Family Caregivers' Experiences and Perspectives

Chaiwoo Lee, Alexa Balmuth[✉], Lisa D'Ambrosio, Adam Felts, and Joseph F. Coughlin

AgeLab, Massachusetts Institute of Technology, Cambridge, MA, USA
abalmuth@mit.edu

Abstract. Many technology-enabled products and services have the potential to support family caregivers. There is limited understanding, however, of how and why caregivers adopt and use technologies. An online survey explored family caregivers' attitudes toward and use of technology both for themselves and in their role as a caregiver, as well as how the use of technology has impacted caregivers' lives. This paper reports on responses from 339 caregivers who belong to an ongoing research panel and are currently involved in providing care to an adult family member. Results indicated that caregivers were generally active users of technology for themselves for general purposes not specific to caregiving, but that their use of technologies to support care lagged behind. Caregivers who used technology for caregiving reported generally positive experiences and were satisfied overall with what they used, rating technologies as useful, and found them easy to use and to incorporate into care arrangements. A causal analysis found that ease of use and ease of integrating technologies into the care context were significant predictors of overall satisfaction with technologies for caregiving. Study results point to a need to ensure greater access to general platform technologies – notably smartphones and laptops – and to explore further issues around costs associated with using technologies.

Keywords: Caregiving · Family Caregivers · Informal Care · Technology Adoption

1 Introduction

An aging population, coupled with declining birth rates, is challenging the current supply of professional and informal care. Today, more than one in five Americans provide care to a loved one [1], and current demographic trends predict that an increasing number of adults will face caregiving demands [2]. Family caregivers are responsible for a wide range of tasks, encompassing domains including health care, transportation, meal preparation, home maintenance, housework, service coordination, personal hygiene, financial management, and keeping company. The demands of caregiving, often coupled with responsibilities like work and childcare, require caregivers' expenditure of financial resources, physical energy, emotional bandwidth, and time.

Q. Gao and J. Zhou (Eds.): HCII 2023, LNCS 14043, pp. 307–330, 2023.
https://doi.org/10.1007/978-3-031-34917-1_22

Technologically advanced consumer products and services – including smart home products, internet-enabled services, communication technologies, and personal computers – have altered how many people carry out their day-to-day tasks. Many technologies and services developed to make life easier for the general population also have the potential to assist older adults and those who provide care to them.

Recent studies have explored the potential role that technology-enabled products and services may play in supporting family caregivers. A report based on an expert roundtable organized by the National Alliance for Caregiving emphasized that technology-based solutions may help caregivers to coordinate tasks and address complexities, leading to reduced burdens with caregiving [3]. Similarly, existing and emerging technology solutions can help ease caregiving burdens and make life better for caregivers [4]. A review study on intervention strategies to support caregivers observed that technology-based interventions were generally positively perceived and accepted by caregivers, and that technology could improve convenience, cost-effectiveness, and flexibility in accessing caregiving resources as well as provide social support for caregivers [5]. Other reviews pointed out possible ways that specific technology products and services may support caregivers. It was suggested that internet-based home technologies could assist informal caregiving and to help older adults live independently [6]; another study focused on the potential usefulness of social media, online communities and forums, health-related smartphone apps, and telemedicine for family caregivers [7]. In an empirical approach, a survey of 30 family caregivers found that those who used technology to support their care responsibilities found it useful, and that technology was often used to help save time and to ease emotional burdens [8].

However, there remains an incomplete understanding of which, if any, technologies caregivers prefer to use, how and why they use them, and which characteristics of a technology are most conducive to its adoption by caregivers. Many existing technologies and services – including those expressly designed to assist caregivers, such as medication monitoring tools – are not widely used by caregivers despite their potential usefulness [9]. A survey study reported that technology usage was limited among caregivers and that many technology products and services were not widely adopted for caregiving, and found that this adoption gap was due to limited awareness and availability rather than due to a lack of interest in technologies [8]. The importance of awareness and availability was also emphasized by [4], which argued that the integration of new technology solutions into people's lives cannot happen if caregivers do not know what is available to them. Prior research has also discussed other barriers that contribute to low adoption and utilization of technology among caregivers, including unfamiliarity, time restriction, complexity and distrust [10]; and issues around cost-effectiveness, accessibility, and integration with existing practices need to be addressed to facilitate effective use of technology [5].

Existing models and frameworks that describe various factors, determinants, and barriers related to technology use can be applied to describe how technology acceptance and utilization may take place in a caregiving context. The Technology Acceptance Model (TAM) suggested perceived ease of use and perceived usefulness as the main determinants of acceptance [11]. The unified theory of acceptance and use of technology

(UTAUT), originally created as an adaptation of TAM, confirmed the effects of perceived ease of use and usefulness with newly defined factors of performance and effort expectancy, and emphasized that individual characteristics (e.g., age, gender, related experience) play key roles in determining technology adoption [12]. In a study that evaluated how technology may be used to support remote caregiving, usability measures including efficiency and effectiveness, which closely relate to ease of use and usefulness, were utilized along with satisfaction [13]. Furthermore, a review study suggested that the compatibility between a technology and a user's lifestyle could impact adoption and user experience [14].

In this study, an online survey was conducted with a large group of family caregivers to examine their attitudes toward and use of consumer technologies. The survey included questions about their general feelings regarding technology use for themselves and specifically for caregiving. This paper presents findings on the technological attitudes and behaviors of caregivers, with attention to differences by gender, age, care arrangements, and caregiving role and responsibilities. It will explore which technologies caregivers use to help with caregiving, how and why they use them, and what they perceive as the impacts of use, in addition to highlighting potentially useful products and services that have heretofore met with scarce adoption among family caregivers.

2 Study Design

2.1 Questionnaire Design

An approximately 20-min questionnaire was developed with items about caregivers' use of technology in general and the ways in which they may use technology in their role as a caregiver. The questionnaire included 25 technology-enabled products and services commonly used by the general population and may be used to support caregiving (Table 1).

Table 1. Technologies included in the study

Category	Items
General-purpose technologies	Computer or laptop; cellular phone (not a smartphone); smartphone; tablet; ereader; video chat platform; instant messaging platform; task management/scheduling/calendar tools or apps; social media
Home and health technologies	Home security system; smart energy utilities and monitoring systems; smart home appliances; medication management platform or smart dispenser; fitness and physical activity management tool; health or body metric tracker; personal assistant, smart speaker; smart entertainment system
Internet-based services	Grocery delivery service; meal-kit delivery service; online food ordering & delivery service; ridesharing service; on-demand entertainment streaming service; housework service; pet care service; caregiving assistant service[a]

[a] Caregiving assistant service was not listed when asked about general use

Caregivers who indicated that they currently used a given technology for caregiving were asked additional questions about each selected item related to the nature of its use, experiences of use, and the outcomes and impacts of use. The survey also asked about the reasons that led respondents to use a given technology product or service, the tasks and activities a given technology was used for, and the outcomes that they had experienced from using it. The reasons and outcomes were adapted from a previous study conducted to explore caregivers' use of technology with a small sample [8]. The list of tasks and activities was adapted from existing definitions and descriptions of basic and instrumental activities of daily living (ADLs and IADLs, respectively) [15], and based on responses to a brief intake questionnaire that participating caregivers filled out upon joining the study panel.

A review of existing models and frameworks that describe usability, user experience, and user acceptance and adoption of technology [11, 12, 14] was conducted to develop additional measures around caregivers' attitudes toward technologies for caregiving. Variables were included in the questionnaire to capture: perceived ease of use, perceived ease of integrating the technology into their caregiving role, perceived usefulness, and satisfaction. The questions used in analysis for this paper are summarized in Table 2.

Table 2. Questionnaire items

Category	Question
General attitudes and experience	How would you rate your overall level of experience with technology/with using technology to help with your caregiving responsibilities?
	How would you rate your overall level of trust in technology/technology to help with your caregiving responsibilities?
	How interested are you in learning about new technologies/technologies that can be used to help with your caregiving responsibilities?
Technology use process and objectives[a]	How would you rate the ease of use of each of the following technologies or services for caregiving?
	How well do you or did you feel the following technologies or services fit into your role as a caregiver?
	What are some of the reasons you use(d) the following technologies or services for caregiving? Please select all that apply
	What are some of the activities for which you use(d) the following technologies or services for caregiving? Select all that apply

(*continued*)

Table 2. (*continued*)

Category	Question
Technology use outcomes and impacts[a]	How would you rate the usefulness of each of the following technologies or services for caregiving?
	How have each of the following technologies or services impacted your caregiving experience? Please select all that apply
	Overall, how satisfied are you or were you with each of the following technologies or services for caregiving?

[a] These questions were asked for all products and services selected as "use or have used" out of technologies listed in Table 1

2.2   Survey Administration and Sample Characteristics

An online survey was conducted with family caregivers who were members of an ongoing caregiver research panel organized by the MIT AgeLab. Data collection took place between July 6–20, 2020. The online questionnaire was initially sent to 1,107 caregivers, and 477 complete responses were collected with an overall response rate of 43.1%. The analysis here focused on 339 respondents who were involved in providing care to an adult family member including a parent, a grandparent, a spouse, or another older relative, excluding caregivers who were providing care to an adult child or a sibling.

The sample used for analysis represented a wide range of demographic characteristics and caregiving arrangements. The characteristics of the sample are summarized in Table 3.

Table 3. Sample characteristics (N = 339)

Caregiver characteristics		%
Caregiver age	Silent Generation and older (born 1945 or earlier)	8.0%
	Older Boomers (born 1946–1954)	22.7%
	Younger Boomers (born 1955–1964)	40.1%
	Generation X (born 1965–1980)	24.2%
	Millennials and younger (born 1981 or after)	5.0%
Caregiver gender	Male	19.8%
	Female	80.2%
	Prefer not to say	0.0%
Caregiver household income	Less than $25,000	5.3%

(*continued*)

Table 3. (*continued*)

Caregiver characteristics		%
	$25,000–$49,999	10.0%
	$50,000–$74,999	13.6%
	$75,000–$99,999	17.7%
	$100,000–$149,999	18.9%
	$150,000–$199,999	8.3%
	$200,000 or more	10.9%
	Prefer not to answer	15.3%
Caregiver highest level of education completed	High school diploma	0.6%
	Some college	10.3%
	Trade/technical/vocational school or associate's degree	8.0%
	College degree	24.5%
	Some post-graduate work	11.5%
	Post-graduate degree	45.1%
Caregiver employment status	Employed in any condition (full, part, self)	44.8%
	Employed full-time	29.2%
	Not employed, looking for work	1.8%
	Not employed, not looking for work	4.4%
	Furloughed	1.2%
	Laid off	1.2%
	Employed part-time	3.2%
	Homemaker	4.1%
	Self-employed full-time	8.3%
	Self-employed part-time	5.0%
	Student	2.1%
	Retired	32.4%
Care recipient's relationship to caregiver	Spouse or partner	30.4%
	Parent or parent-in-law	65.8%
	Grandparent, aunt or uncle	3.8%
Length of time in caregiving	Less than 2 years	14.5%

(*continued*)

Table 3. (*continued*)

Caregiver characteristics		%
	2 years or more but less than 5 years	33.0%
	5 years or more but less than 10 years	31.0%
	10 years or more	21.5%
Time spent per week providing care	1–9 h	32.4%
	10–19 h	20.9%
	20–39 h	23.9%
	40+ h	22.7%
Total number of ADLs[a] caregiver is helping with	0 ADL	48.7%
	1–2 ADLs	26.0%
	3+ ADLs	25.4%
Total number of IADLs[b] caregiver is helping with	0–3 IADLs	14.7%
	4–5 IADLs	26.3%
	6–7 IADLs	30.4%
	8 IADLs	28.6%
Care recipient's condition(s)	Long-term physical condition	69.6%
	Short-term physical condition	11.2%
	Memory problem	55.8%
	Emotional/mental health problem	24.2%
	Behavioral issue	10.3%
	Developmental/intellectual disorder	4.7%
	Alzheimer's or other dementia	33.0%
	Other	18.9%
Living arrangement between caregiver and care recipient	Living together	53.1%
	Within walking distance of each other	6.2%
	Short driving distance (less than 1 h drive)	28.0%
	Longer distance (drive of 1 h or more but less than 2 h)	4.4%
	Far distance (drive of 2 h or more but less than 8 h)	4.1%
	Very long distance (drive of 8 h or more)	4.1%
Caregiver responsibilities sharing	I am the only caregiver for my care recipient	31.3%

(*continued*)

Table 3. (*continued*)

Caregiver characteristics		%
	I share responsibilities with another family member	28.9%
	I share responsibilities with a paid caregiver	14.2%
	I share responsibilities with family and a paid caregiver	15.9%

[a] Activities of daily living (ADLs) include moving from one place to another (e.g., walking, getting up and sitting down); bathing and showering; getting dressed and undressed; eating and feeding; getting to and from toilet; and helping with incontinence or diapers

[b] Instrumental ADLs included transportation; grocery and other shopping; housework; preparing meals; taking and managing medications; social activities and interactions; arranging services and appointments; and managing finances

3 Results

3.1 General Attitudes Toward and Experience with Technology

Caregivers who participated in the survey were found to be generally experienced with, trusting of, and interested in learning about technology. When asked about using technology to help with caregiving responsibilities, however, respondents indicated that they were less experienced and less trusting than in their general use. In contrast, interest in learning about new technologies was consistent across the two contexts of use – general and caregiving. These results, illustrated in Fig. 1, suggest that while caregivers are generally open to using technologies to help with caregiving, they may not be using them extensively in the caregiving context, potentially due to limited awareness or familiarity.

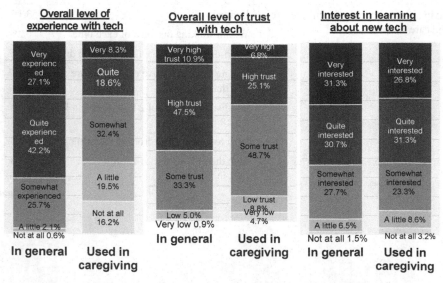

Fig. 1. Caregivers' overall experience with and attitudes toward technology

Caregivers were asked to report their use of technology products and internet-based services in association with their caregiving experience. In general, caregivers were active users of technology and had incorporated related products and services into their caregiving experience, with most respondents (83.5%) using at least one technology product or service in association with caregiving. When asked about a total of 25 technology products and services currently available on the consumer market, caregivers reported using on average 4 to 5 different technologies to help with their caregiving responsibilities. 'General' technologies were the most widely used, while internet-enabled services were comparatively less popular, and home/health technologies were rarely used in the context of caregiving (see Table 4).

Table 4. Prevalence of technology use among caregivers (See Table 1 for technology items)

Technology category	Caregiving-related use		General use	
	Average count	% using one or more	Average count	% using one or more
General (9 total)	2.640	81.7%	5.988	97.3%
Home/health (8 total)	0.723	38.9%	2.071	74.6%
Internet-based service (8 total[a])	1.106	53.4%	2.024	87.6%
Total	4.691	83.5%	10.024	97.3%

[a] Caregiving assistant service was not listed when asked about general use

Use of technology products and services for caregiving, however, was found to be relatively limited when compared with caregivers' use of technologies for themselves or for general purposes not specific to caregiving. Caregivers reported using on average about 10 of the 24 (excluding caregiving assistant service) given technologies generally, significantly larger than the average number of technologies (about 4.7 out of 25) used to help with their caregiving responsibilities. The biggest gap was observed for home/health technologies, with only 38.9% of caregivers using these technologies for caregiving compared to 74.6% using them for general purposes; on average less than one home/health technology was reported being used for caregiving, compared with about two technologies on average for general purposes.

Among technologies included in the questionnaire, the smartphone was the most popular tool, with about two-thirds of caregivers using it to help with their caregiving responsibilities. Other widely adopted technologies for caregiving included computers or laptops, video chat platforms, grocery delivery services, on-demand entertainment services, tablets, and task management or scheduling tools, as shown in Table 5. While most of the home/health technologies included in the survey were used by 20% or more of the sample (except for smart home appliances and medication management platforms), only a small subset used any of these technologies for caregiving. This adoption gap between general use and caregiving-related use was also evident for general technologies and internet-enabled services, however. Specifically, while most caregivers indicated that they used a computer or laptop, a smartphone, a video chat platform, an on-demand entertainment service, social media, and instant messaging for themselves, adoption rates for these technology products and services in the context of caregiving was much lower.

Table 5. Caregivers' adoption of technology products and services

Technology category	Technology item	Caregiving use (%)	General use (%)
General	Smartphone	65.5%	91.2%
	Computer or laptop	60.5%	95.3%
	Video chat platform	45.4%	87.0%
	Tablet	26.3%	63.4%
	Task management/scheduling/calendar tools or apps	25.7%	64.0%
	Instant messaging platform	14.2%	71.1%
	Social media	13.3%	77.9%
	Cellular phone (NOT a smartphone)	10.3%	12.1%
	eReader	2.9%	36.9%
Home/health	Health or body metric tracker	16.8%	25.4%
	Personal assistant, smart speaker	15.0%	37.8%
	Smart entertainment system	11.5%	45.1%
	Home security system	10.9%	24.5%
	Smart energy utilities and monitoring systems	6.5%	26.0%
	Fitness and physical activity management tool	4.7%	33.9%
	Medication management platform or smart dispenser	4.4%	2.4%
	Smart home appliances	2.4%	12.1%
Internet-based service	Grocery delivery service	28.9%	38.9%
	On-demand entertainment streaming service	27.4%	79.9%
	Ridesharing service	14.5%	34.8%
	Online food ordering & delivery service	13.6%	30.1%

(*continued*)

Table 5. (*continued*)

Technology category	Technology item	Caregiving use (%)	General use (%)
	Caregiving assistant service	7.1%	n/a
	Meal-kit delivery service	5.6%	6.5%
	Housework service	2.9%	2.4%
	Pet care service	1.5%	3.8%

Few differences in adoption of technologies for caregiving-related applications were observed across caregivers of different demographic characteristics, but some did emerge by age, gender, income, and education. For example, Generation X (born 1965–1980) caregivers reported a higher rate of adoption and a higher number/variety of technologies for their own use than for caregiving. Male caregivers reported being more likely to use technologies than female caregivers. Caregivers with higher household incomes and those with higher levels of education used a larger number of technologies on average.

Different care arrangements were also related to varied prevalence of technology use. While those who provided care for less than 5 years were more likely to use at least one technology for caregiving, caregivers with 5 or more years of experience used a greater number of technologies on average. Caregivers assisting with at least one ADL (activity of daily living) used more technologies on average than those who did not help with any ADLs. Caregivers' involvement in helping with IADLs (instrumental ADLs) appeared to be positively associated with the number of different technologies that caregivers were using. Caregivers living at a short distance or a very far distance from their care recipients were more likely to use technologies for caregiving, while caregivers at a medium distance were slightly less likely to do so. Other characteristics associated with higher adoption of technology for caregiving included sharing responsibilities with other family, providing care to a parent or parent-in-law, and spending 40+ h per week providing care.

3.2 Drivers of Technology and Service Use Among Caregivers

As shown in Table 6, caregivers typically used technologies to address several different caregiving tasks or challenges rather than to solve or support just a single issue. General technologies, notably smartphones and computers/laptops, were on average used to support a higher number of different caregiving tasks than home/health technologies or internet-based services.

A majority of caregivers (62.2%) who used a smartphone to support their caregiving reported using it for communications with their care recipient, but substantial segments also used smartphones to assist with attending medical appointments, managing transportation, shopping and meal preparation, managing finances, and entertainment. Computers/laptops were most often used to support managing care recipient's finances (64.4%), but they were also used by sizeable numbers of caregivers to aid with entertainment, shopping, meal preparation, and attending medical appointments. Overall, for

Table 6. Caregiver perceptions of and experiences with technology products and services

Technology item		Mean numbers/ratings			
		Associated tasks[a]	Reasons for use[b]	Ease of use[c]	Ease of integration[d]
General	Computer or laptop	2.955	4.367	4.427	4.307
	Cellular phone (not a smartphone)	1.960	3.500	3.909	3.848
	Smartphone	3.368	4.530	4.401	4.481
	Tablet	2.229	3.296	4.364	4.046
	eReader	1.000	2.333	3.800	3.100
	Video chat platform	1.560	3.380	3.974	3.914
	Instant messaging platform	1.524	3.030	3.864	3.636
	Task management tool	2.292	3.708	4.235	4.238
	Social media	1.423	3.310	4.395	3.857
Home/health	Home security system	0.333	1.963	4.286	4.265
	Smart energy utilities monitoring	1.125	2.267	3.905	3.950
	Smart home appliances	1.000	2.800	3.333	4.500
	Medication management platform	1.111	3.600	4.200	4.467
	Fitness and activity management	0.333	3.000	3.938	3.688
	Health or body metric tracker	0.600	2.469	4.268	4.321
	Personal assistant, smart speaker	1.545	3.233	3.860	3.680

(continued)

Table 6. (*continued*)

Technology item		Mean numbers/ratings			
		Associated tasks[a]	Reasons for use[b]	Ease of use[c]	Ease of integration[d]
	Smart entertainment system	1.040	2.036	3.703	4.029
Internet-based service	Grocery delivery service	1.097	3.060	4.051	4.124
	Meal-kit delivery service	1.538	2.933	3.938	4.000
	Online food ordering & delivery	1.286	2.529	3.913	3.864
	Ridesharing service	1.564	3.135	3.857	3.833
	On-demand entertainment streaming	1.027	2.075	4.108	4.087
	Housework service	1.400	3.250	3.500	3.800
	Pet care service	0.000	2.250	3.800	3.800
	Caregiving assistant service	1.765	4.095	3.609	3.591

[a] Range for number of associate tasks: 0–8 (Managing finances; managing transportation; shopping and meal preparation; housecleaning and home maintenance; communications with my care recipient; managing medications; attending medical appointments; entertainment)
[b] Range for number of reasons for use: 0–10 (To support my care recipient's health; to ensure my care recipient's safety; to ease my physical strain; to ease my financial strain; to ease my emotional strain; to save me time; to help with tasks I don't have the skills for; to improve communication; to keep things organized; to provide pleasure or joy)
[c] Average of scores ranging from 1 (not easy to use at all) to 5 (very easy to use)
[d] Average of scores ranging from 1 (not at all well) to 5 (very well)

general technologies, the tasks most typically supported were communication with the care recipient, attending medical appointments, and entertainment.

Technologies in the home/health category were more frequently used to support individual care tasks tied to the technology's particular function. For example, 56.4% of caregivers using smart entertainment systems reported using them for entertainment, and 60% of those using medication management platforms reported using them to help manage medications. Smart speakers were used to entertain and communicate with the care recipient. Similarly, many of the internet-based services primarily supported single care tasks. On-demand streaming services were used to support entertainment of the care recipient; ridesharing was employed to support transportation; and grocery delivery, online food ordering and delivery, and meal-kit services aided with shopping and meal preparation.

Caregivers also typically reported multiple reasons for using a technology, as shown in Table 6. General technologies had on average more reasons selected for their use (category average of 3.495 reasons) compared with home/health technologies and internet-based services (category averages of 2.671 and 2.916 reasons, respectively). Caregivers reported the greatest number of reasons to use smartphones and computers/laptops, with number of reasons selected over four on average.

Across all three categories, however, three reasons broadly emerged for caregivers' use of a given technology or service: supporting the care recipient's health, saving the caregiver's time, and easing the caregiver's emotional strain. Easing financial strain was less likely to be selected as a reason to use a technology/service across the three categories.

Other reported reasons were more likely to be associated with a particular category or with a particular technology/service. Improving communication, to provide pleasure or joy, and to keep things organized more strongly emerged as reasons people used general technologies to support caregiving. Phones (both smartphones and cellular phones) were more often used to ensure the care recipient's safety, and task management tools were more often used to keep things organized, to support the care recipient's health, and to save the caregiver time. Among home/health technologies, the reasons caregivers reported using a particular device or service were often tied to the device's key functions: health/body metric trackers were primarily used to support the care recipient's health; and home security systems were mostly used to ensure the care recipient's safety. While smart entertainment systems were used first to provide pleasure or joy, they secondarily were used to reduce caregivers' emotional strain. Personal assistants/smart speakers were used for a wider variety of different reasons that more closely followed patterns of reasons among general technologies; reasons included supporting care recipient health and safety, to ease caregiver emotional strain, to save time, to improve communication, and to provide pleasure or joy.

For internet-based services, easing the caregiver's physical strain emerged more strongly as a reason for use compared to other technologies or services. Except for entertainment streaming services, which primarily were used to provide pleasure or joy, internet-based services were also used by caregivers to save time. Reasons to use streaming services reflected those selected to use smart entertainment systems – the primary reason to use was to provide pleasure or joy, but the secondary reason for each was to reduce caregivers' emotional strain. Caregivers often reported using grocery delivery services and caregiving assistant services to support their care recipient's health. Ensuring the care recipient's safety was also more likely to be selected as a reason for use among caregivers using ridesharing services or caregiving assistant services. Assisting with tasks the caregiver lacked the skills for, improving communication, and keeping things organized were more often selected as reasons for use of caregiving assistant services.

3.3 Integrating Technology Use into the Caregiving Experience

As shown in Table 6, caregivers typically reported favorably on the ease of use of each of the technologies or services they used; average ratings reflected that they were "quite" or "very" easy to use. General technologies – notably computers/laptop, tablets, smartphones and social media – were more likely to be "quite" or very "easy to use." Task management tools were also likely to rate more highly on ease of use. About one-third of users of instant messaging platforms and of cellular phones reported them as being less easy to use (saying they were "somewhat," "a little" or "not at all" easy to use).

Among home/health technologies, home security system users were most likely to report that the technology was easy to use, followed by health or body metric trackers, smart entertainment systems, and smart energy utilities/monitors. Users of smart home appliances indicated relatively greater difficulty, but the average rating still reflected that they were "somewhat" to "quite" easy to use. Internet-based services also generally rated favorably in assessment of their ease of use. People using entertainment streaming services were most likely to find these easier to use, and grocery delivery services also rated highly. Caregivers who used caregiving assistant services were more likely to indicate issues with ease of use, but still found that they were "somewhat" to "quite" easy to use.

In addition to ease of use, how well a technology integrates into the caregiver's life and routine is a key factor for adoption and retention. Caregivers generally indicated that most of the technologies integrated well into their role, as shown in Table 6. Reported ease of integration of the technology into the caregiving role was highest among the top two technologies caregivers reported using for themselves outside of their caregiving roles: smartphones and computers/laptops. Most caregivers using these tools to support their caregiving (84.7% of smartphone users; 79.5% of computer or laptop users) said that they integrated "quite" or "very" well into their caregiver roles. Home security system users were also likely to rate the ability of incorporating these into their caregiving quite highly (73% reporting "quite" or "very" high integration). Among those technologies or services that respondents reported greater difficulties with integrating into their caregiving were caregiving assistant services (41.7% saying these were "not at all," "a little" or "somewhat" easy to integrate into their caregiving roles).

3.4 Impacts and Outcome of Technology Use on the Caregiving Experience

Most technologies and services included in the survey rated favorably on their usefulness for caregiving, with many of the general-purpose and home/health technologies generally rated higher than internet-based services. Smartphones topped the list again when it came to usefulness, with 59.9% of users rating them as "very useful." Home security systems, computers or laptops, task management tools or apps, and grocery delivery services were close behind. Although offered specifically for caregiving support, caregiving assistant services appeared among the least useful technologies and services for caregivers on average, along with e-readers, social media, instant messaging platforms, fitness and physical activity management tools, and personal assistants or smart speakers (see Table 7).

Caregivers' reports of the impacts of their use of a technology were analyzed to delve deeper into the specific ways that technologies and services have affected their lives. When asked to select all that applied from five positive and five negative impacts, respondents reported that medication management tools, smartphones, grocery delivery services, housework services, and computers or laptops had larger numbers of positive impacts, with caregivers reporting nearly three positive impacts of each on average (see Table 7). Most often, these positive impacts were saving time, making life easier, relieving stress and worries, and solving problems; making life easier followed by relieving stress were the most commonly cited positive impacts across different technologies. Time saving also emerged as a positive impact of using general technologies and internet-based services. Across technologies, however, cost and financial impacts appeared in a less positive light. Very few caregivers noted a positive impact of technologies on financial savings. Cost arose as the primary negative impact, specifically for internet-based services such as online food ordering and delivery, ridesharing services, and grocery delivery services.

Caregiver satisfaction with the use of a technology was measured to capture the success of various technologies and services from the perspective of users broadly. In general, caregivers' average ratings reflected a high level of satisfaction with the technologies or services they used for caregiving, as shown in Table 7. There was, however, some variation across specific technologies and services. On average, caregivers reported the highest levels of satisfaction with the two most widely used general technologies – smartphones and computers or laptops. Entertainment streaming services also scored high in satisfaction, in addition to health or body metric trackers. In contrast, caregivers reported lower levels of satisfaction with caregiving assistant services, meal-kit delivery services, housework services, smart home appliances, and personal assistants or smart speakers, but average ratings still indicated that they are "somewhat" to "quite" satisfied with these.

Table 7. Perceived impacts of using technology for caregiving

Technology item		Mean numbers/ratings			
		Positive impacts[a]	Negative impacts[b]	Usefulness[c]	Satisfaction[d]
General	Computer or laptop	2.781	0.202	4.226	4.348
	Cellular phone (not a smartphone)	2.038	0.423	3.576	3.594
	Smartphone	2.963	0.254	4.449	4.395
	Tablet	2.324	0.176	3.841	4.140
	eReader	1.778	0.000	3.600	3.400
	Video chat platform	2.070	0.194	4.020	3.833
	Instant messaging platform	1.500	0.368	3.556	3.773
	Task management tool	2.737	0.105	4.271	4.202
	Social media	1.472	0.306	3.698	3.905
Home/health	Home security system	1.742	0.226	4.171	4.000
	Smart energy utilities monitoring	2.444	0.222	3.950	3.950
	Smart home appliances	2.750	0.000	4.333	3.500
	Medication management platform	3.273	0.000	4.500	4.133
	Fitness and activity management	1.533	0.467	3.563	3.625
	Health or body metric tracker	1.808	0.058	4.070	4.309
	Personal assistant, smart speaker	1.955	0.182	3.592	3.580

(*continued*)

Table 7. (*continued*)

Technology item		Mean numbers/ratings			
		Positive impacts[a]	Negative impacts[b]	Usefulness[c]	Satisfaction[d]
	Smart entertainment system	1.594	0.344	3.946	3.941
Internet-based service	Grocery delivery service	2.866	0.598	4.155	3.938
	Meal-kit delivery service	2.118	0.706	3.444	3.333
	Online food ordering & delivery	2.105	0.500	3.778	3.705
	Ridesharing service	2.436	0.564	3.837	3.750
	On-demand entertainment streaming	1.488	0.202	3.946	4.217
	Housework service	2.857	0.714	3.778	3.333
	Pet care service	2.200	0.600	3.600	3.600
	Caregiving assistant service	2.053	0.579	3.583	3.409

[a] Range for number of positive impacts: 0–5 (saved me or my care recipient time; made life easier; relieved stress and worries; solved problems; reduced expenses)
[b] Range for number of negative impacts: 0–5 (wasted my or my care recipient's time; made life more complicated; created stress and worries; caused problems; increased expenses)
[c] Average of scores ranging from 1 (not useful at all) to 5 (very useful)
[d] Average of scores ranging from 1 (not satisfied at all) to 5 (very satisfied)

3.5   Determinants of Caregivers' Satisfaction with Technology

A linear regression analysis was carried out to collectively examine the impacts of possible drivers of caregivers' satisfaction with the technologies they use for caregiving. In this analysis, caregivers' ratings of satisfaction with technology was used as the dependent variable. Predictors included the total number of reasons for using the given technology, the total number of different tasks that the given technology was used in association with, perceived ease of using the technology, perceived ease of integrating the technology into the caregiving experience, perceived usefulness of the technology, whether or not the technology had positive impacts (i.e., saved time, made life easier, relieved stress, solved problems, and/or reduced expenses), and whether or not the technology had the negative impact of increasing expenses. Other possible negative impacts asked about in the survey (i.e., wasted time, made life more complicated, created stress, caused problems) were not included as they were only selected by a small subset of the sample across all technologies. Regression models were fitted for the individual technology products and services covered in the survey, and they were also developed for different technology groups using averages calculated for the included variables, as summarized in Table 8.

Across all groups/types of technologies included in the survey, perceived ease of use and integration were significant and the most impactful drivers of satisfaction with a technology in the caregiving context. In other words, caregivers were more satisfied with technology products or services when they could easily use them and integrate them with their caregiving experience. Perceived usefulness was also found to have a significant impact on satisfaction for general technologies, carrier/platform systems and add-on services. This suggests that for many technologies used for caregiving, satisfaction with the technologies may hinge on how useful or helpful they are in assisting with caregiving responsibilities. The importance of ease of use and usefulness observed from this analysis aligns closely with past studies were these factors were identified as key drivers to adoption [11, 12, 14].

Experiencing positive impacts significantly affected caregivers' satisfaction with most of the technologies covered in the survey. Time saving was a significant driver to increased satisfaction for general and carrier/platform technologies, while making life easier significantly impacted satisfaction with home/health technologies and internet-based or add-on services. Satisfaction with general technologies was also significantly driven by whether they solved problems for caregivers, and satisfaction with internet-based services also depended significantly on whether they relieved caregivers' stress. The negative impact of increase in expenses was not found to significantly impact satisfaction. However, it should be noted that this may be a result of very few caregivers reporting the negative impact of increased expenses in the survey, and we do not consider this to be sufficient evidence to conclude that the financial costs of a technology – or more broadly, negative experiences with technology generally – have limited impacts on satisfaction.

For home/health technologies, the total number of associated tasks had a negatively significant impact on satisfaction – that is, fewer associated tasks correlated with greater satisfaction with the technology. This may be a result of technologies in this category being generally used for a smaller number of tasks that are closely tied with their intended functions (see Table 6), but it could also be an indication that caregivers may be more satisfied with home or health technologies that are focused around a smaller set of functions rather than technologies that seek to address a larger number of responsibilities.

Table 8. Regression analysis predicting caregivers' satisfaction with technologies

Predictor variables	General	Home/health[a]	Internet-based services[a]	Carriers/platforms[a,b]	Add-on systems[c]	Add-on services[a,d]
Total # of associated tasks	0.006	−0.167*	0.008	0.055	−0.033	0.010
Total # of reasons for use	−0.078	0.024	−0.003	−0.061	0.062	−0.016
Ease of use	0.417**	0.450**	0.480**	0.415**	0.505**	0.468**
Ease of integration	0.316**	0.427**	0.278**	0.325**	0.468**	0.210**
Impact – saved time	0.088	0.016	−0.113	0.096*	0.072	−0.070
Impact – made life easier	0.101*	0.197*	0.154*	0.080	0.053	0.130*
Impact – relieved stress	0.029	−0.149	0.278**	0.017	−0.073	0.041
Impact – solved problem	0.101*	0.080	−0.091	0.018	0.052	0.092
Impact – reduced expense	−0.050	0.044	−0.016	−0.013	0.048	0.078
Impact – increased expense	0.012	0.025	−0.055	−0.020	n/a	−0.006
Usefulness	0.124*	0.103	0.017	0.163**	−0.052	0.152*
R square	0.728	0.776	0.709	0.691	0.703	0.633
F	55.870	16.670	21.446	42.855	8.057	27.587
Subset size (n)	277	114	152	268	104	245

Tables entries are standardized beta coefficients. *$p < 0.05$, **$p < 0.01$.

[a] Entertainment technologies (smart entertainment system and on-demand entertainment streaming within service) were excluded as they were different from other technology products and services included in the survey regarding reasons for using and associated tasks.

[b] Carriers/platforms: Technology that can operate on its own and can be used to run additional features/apps (computer or laptop, smartphone, tablet, and personal assistant or smart speaker).

[c] Add-on systems: Systems that are typically device-based but require or are complemented with applications that run on a carrier technology (home security system, smart energy utilities and monitoring system, smart home appliances, medication management platform or smart dispenser, fitness and physical activity management tool, and health or body metric tracker).

[d] Add-on services: Services or applications that requires a carrier technology for operation and use (video chat, instant messaging, task management/scheduling/calendar, social media, grocery delivery, meal-kit delivery, online food ordering & delivery, ridesharing service, housework service, pet care service, caregiving assistance service).

4 Discussions and Conclusion

4.1 Summary and Conclusion

In this study, a large and diverse group of caregivers was surveyed on their attitudes toward and experiences with using various types of technology-enabled products and services to support their caregiving. Findings from the online survey showed that their usage in the caregiving context lags far behind their use in general, non-care-related contexts. Caregivers were also found on average to be less experienced with and less trusting of technologies to help with caregiving compared to technologies for general, non-care-related purposes. Interest in learning about new technologies, on the other hand, did not differ much between general and caregiving-related use, suggesting that limitations in caregivers' current experiences using technology to support their role may be due to a lack of awareness rather than a lack of interest or perceived utility.

Although caregivers' current usage of technology for caregiving was relatively limited, those who did use technology generally reported positive experiences. Across most of the technology products and services covered in the survey – spanning general-purpose technologies, home and health technologies, and internet-based services – caregivers reported using them to support multiple caregiving tasks and indicated positive impacts of their use in multiple domains. Caregivers were generally satisfied with the technologies they used and found them easy to use, easy to integrate into their caregiving role, and useful.

Results from a regression analysis to understand how various aspects of experience with a technology affect overall satisfaction with it showed that perceived ease of use and integration were the most impactful and significant drivers to satisfaction. Perceived usefulness and experiences with a subset of positive impacts (i.e., saving time, making life easier, relieving stress and solving problems) were also found to be significant drivers for some but not all of the technology groups/types covered in the survey. These results suggest that while the outcomes and impacts of technology use may be important, for the caregiving context, the process of learning about a technology and fitting it into existing caregiving arrangements and routines may be weighed more heavily.

4.2 Implications

Results from this study also point to several practical implications around using technologies to support family caregivers and to improve the caregiving experience:

Smartphones and Computers/Laptops are Foundational Technologies In general, smartphones and computers/laptops emerged as foundational technologies for caregiving. These two technologies were the most frequently used, were used for more tasks and for more purposes, and yielded some of the highest satisfaction ratings overall and in terms of ease of use, integration and usefulness among caregivers. In addition, these two technologies are essential for accessing other technological supports for caregiving, including running other hardware or software to support care. Ensuring that caregivers have access to and are leveraging at least one of these foundational technologies may be a key consideration in promoting the adoption of technologies and services to support the care that caregivers provide.

There is a Need to Understand Non-users of Technology Better to Address the Awareness-Usage Gap. The current study included descriptions of technologies that caregivers were currently using to support care, and descriptions of factors that may influence successful utilization of technologies that have already been adopted. However, the study did not positively examine the non-use of different technologies and services among caregivers, which may reveal other barriers to use or reasons caregivers do not use them. A deeper understanding of the factors that drive lack of use should further illuminate barriers to and facilitators of technology adoption for caregivers.

The persistent usage gap between general use of technology and particular use of technology for caregiving indicates a potential selection effect at work. In particular, these data do not reveal if reported non-users have never used a technology or if they are no longer users of a technology for caregiving. It could be that those who are not satisfied with a technology or service simply stop using it; as such, it would be useful to know not only the drivers of satisfaction with technology or service use, but what the drivers of lack of satisfaction are. We might raise questions about how caregivers who struggle more with using new technologies – for example, those who found a technology different to learn to use – go about the process of adopting and integrating technology into their lives. How long do caregivers persist with attempting to learn to use a new technology or service? Does it vary based on their expectations about the benefits it might yield? To what extent do caregivers who expect to struggle to learn to use a new technology simply abandon any attempt to adopt it – that is, they never bother to try it because they expect it will be too difficult to learn to use?

Furthermore, along these lines, if the non-user pool is primarily comprised of people who have never used a technology or service for caregiving, the questions key to promoting and supporting technology for caregiving then become centered around why caregivers have not done so. Do the barriers to use lie around factors we know and understand better, such as access to a technology or service or to the financial resources to use them, or do they lie in other factors, such as caregivers' concerns about whether they will be able to use the technology or service, or an inability to envision how adopting a new technology might have a significant positive impact on the care they provide or their care experiences?

Cost Should be Further Explored as a Factor for Adoption and Use. While cost did not affect satisfaction with using a technology in this study's analysis, we should continue to study cost as a significant factor for the initial and continued use of different technologies and services. Many of the technologies and services people reported using have significant associated costs, and their use may not help to reduce or offset other costs of providing care. While it may be worthwhile for some caregivers to reap the benefits (e.g., saving time, make life easier, stress relief, etc.) of paying for and using technologies for caregiving, the financial practicality of their purchase or use should be considered, as well as the corresponding potential for uneven adoption patterns to exacerbate existing economic inequalities for those who provide care.

4.3 Directions for Future Research

This research found that caregivers who were using different technologies and services identified different kinds of benefits and positive impacts of using them, but these results raise additional questions. In particular, among caregivers who use these technologies, how do they actually experience the benefits? Are there additional benefits that we are not capturing with current measures? Further, which reasons for using the technology or services and which positive impacts are most important and valuable for caregivers – and how might these differ, if at all, from general use? Finally, which benefits are most likely to support caregiver persistence in overcoming any challenges of learning to use and to integrate new technologies or services into their lives?

Additionally, it should be noted that the survey was conducted during the COVID-19 pandemic, when a general trend toward an increased use of technology-enabled solutions was observed in various application areas and across people of different characteristics. How caregivers' perceptions of and experiences with using technology to support caregiving may have been aligned with the general public shift toward increased technology utilization amid the pandemic remains an issue to be understood.

Future research can also aim to investigate questions around how technologies and services can be easily utilized and integrated into the lives of their users, which were among the most significant and impactful drivers to satisfaction. For example, while ease of use and ease of integration were highly correlated for most technologies, there were a few technologies for which the association was weaker (e.g., e-readers, smart entertainment systems), which may indicate that caregivers may struggle to fit even technologies that are very easy to use into their caregiving experiences. A more in-depth look into ease of use and integration may uncover ways to develop and design technological products and services that are more successful in meeting the needs of caregivers and reducing the demands of care.

Acknowledgment. We would acknowledge the sponsors of the MIT AgeLab CareHive consortium for their support of this research, and the CareHive Caregiver Panel members for their invaluable insights.

References

1. AARP & National Alliance for Caregiving: Caregiving in the U.S. (2020). https://www.aarp. org/content/dam/aarp/ppi/2020/05/full-report-caregiving-in-the-united-states.doi.10.26419-2Fppi.00103.001.pdf
2. Redfoot, D., Feinberg, L., Houser, A.: The aging of baby boom and the growing care gap: a look at future declines in the availability of family caregivers. AARP Public Policy Institute (2013). https://www.aarp.org/content/dam/aarp/research/public_policy_institute/ltc/2013/baby-boom-and-the-growing-care-gap-insight-AARP-ppi-ltc.pdf
3. Adler, R., Mehta, R.: Catalyzing Technology to Support Family Caregiving. National Alliance for Caregiving (2014). https://www.caregiving.org/wp-content/uploads/2020/05/Catalyzing-Technology-to-Support-Family-Caregiving_FINAL.pdf
4. Andruszkiewicz, G., Fike, K.: Emerging technology trends and products: how tech innovations are easing the burden of family caregiving. Generations **39**(4), 64–68 (2015)

5. Schulz, R., Beach, S.R., Czaja, S.J., Martire, L.M., Monin, J.K.: Family caregiving for older adults. Annu. Rev. Psychol. **71**, 635–659 (2020)
6. Park, G., Robinson, E.: A systematic review of in-home smart technology adoption to improve older adult health and family caregiving. Innov. Aging **4**(Supplement 1), 409 (2020)
7. Eifert, E.K., Adams, R., Morrison, S., Strack, R.: Emerging trends in family caregiving using the life course perspective: preparing health educators for an aging society. Am. J. Health Educ. **47**(3), 176–197 (2016)
8. Lee, C., Ward, C., Ellis, D., Brady, S., D'Ambrosio, L., Coughlin, J.F.: Technology and service usage among family caregivers. In: Zhou, J., Salvendy, G. (eds.) Human Aspects of IT for the Aged Population 2017. LNCS, vol. 10298, pp. 420–432. Springer, Cham (2017)
9. Fox, S., Duggan, M., Purcell, K.: Family Caregivers are Wired for Health. Pew Research Center (2013). https://www.pewresearch.org/internet/2013/06/20/family-caregivers-are-wired-for-health/
10. Zulman, D.M., Piette, J.D., Jenchura, E.C., Asch, S.M., Rosland, A.M.: Facilitating out-of-home caregiving through health information technology: survey of informal caregivers' current practices, interests, and perceived barriers. J. Med. Internet Res. **15**(7), e123 (2013)
11. Davis, F.D.: Perceived usefulness, perceived ease of use, and user acceptance of information technology. MIS Q. **13**(3), 319–340 (1989)
12. Venkatesh, V., Morris, M.G., Davis, G.B., Davis, F.D.: User acceptance of information technology: toward a unified view. MIS Q. **27**(3), 425–478 (2003)
13. Lee, C., Orszulak, J., Asai, D., Myrick, R., Coughlin, J.F., de Weck, O.L.: Integration of medication monitoring and communication technologies in designing a usability-enhanced home solution for older adults. In: IEEE International Conference on ICT Convergence (ICTC 2011), New York, NY, USA, pp. 390–395. IEEE (2011)
14. Lee, C., Coughlin, J.F.: Older adults' adoption of technology: an integrated approach to identifying determinants and barriers. J. Prod. Innov. Manag. **32**(5), 747–759 (2015)
15. Katz, S.: Assessing self-maintenance: activities of daily living, mobility and instrumental activities of daily living. J. Am. Geriatr. Soc. **31**(12), 721–726 (1983)

Observations of Caregivers of Persons with Dementia: A Qualitative Study to Assess the Feasibility of Behavior Recognition Using AI for Supporting At-Home Care

Wilson Lozano[✉] , Sayde King , and Tempestt Neal

Department of Computer Science and Engineering, University of South Florida,
Tampa, FL, USA
{wilsonlozano,saydeking,tjneal}@usf.edu

Abstract. Dementia, characterized by a decline in cognitive abilities, is known to disrupt one's life, leading to aggressive behavioral and psychological symptoms of dementia (aBPS), like agitation, anxiety, and depression, that lower one's quality of life. While population-based studies around the world suggest a trend of declining risk of dementia in high-income countries over the past two decades, it is estimated that 135.5 million people will be diagnosed with dementia by 2050. As such, non-pharmaceutical tools have emerged to further understanding of dementia using human-computer interaction and artificial intelligence (AI) approaches. In this work, we explore the acceptability of AI for monitoring behavioral patterns during at-home care, with specific focus on aBPS, by engaging 10 caregivers of persons with dementia in semi-structured interviews. Our interview questions are designed to identify relationships between aBPS and behavioral cues, such as body movement and gestures, language and speech, one's physical location, and social context, that are commonly used in other AI applications. This study represents an initial investigation of an at-home automated aBPS monitoring system specifically designed for persons with dementia and their caregivers, particularly for predicting the onset of distress to ultimately contribute to improving quality of life.

Keywords: Dementia · Behavioral Recognition · Sensing

1 Introduction

Generally resulting from Alzheimer's disease, dementia is characterized by a decline in cognitive abilities [7]. As such, dementia is known to disrupt one's life, potentially leading to aggressive behavioral and psychological symptoms

Research reported in this publication was supported by the Alfred P. Sloan University Center of Exemplary Mentoring under award number G-2017-9717.

Q. Gao and J. Zhou (Eds.): HCII 2023, LNCS 14043, pp. 331–344, 2023.
https://doi.org/10.1007/978-3-031-34917-1_23

(aBPS), such as agitation, anxiety, and depression, that lower one's quality of life [5,6,17,18,27]. The current approach for addressing the needs of people diagnosed with dementia focuses on pharmaceutical cures [23]. However, before an effective medication will emerge, millions of people will develop dementia. While population-based studies around the world suggest a trend of declining risk of dementia in high-income countries over the past two decades [15], it is estimated that 135.5 million people will be diagnosed with dementia by 2050.

Prior studies have emerged to further understanding of dementia using human-computer interaction and artificial intelligence (AI) approaches. For example, some studies focus on detecting or assessing Alzheimer's disease or Alzheimer's dementia from speech language cues and speech-to-text transcripts using machine and deep learning models [1,14,19,21]. Similarly, Yeung et al. [28] used changes in language and speech to detect mild cognitive impairment (MCI), while Chen et al. [22] used gait information to predict different types of MCI. Multimodal approaches have been proposed as well using wearable sensors [11,12,26], while others have explored smart home technologies, like voice assistants and smart home sensors, to detect patterns associated with dementia, such as those from sleep and mobility [8,16]. Smith et al. [25] also suggested that the area of affective computing could be useful for addressing inadequacies in current screening and diagnostic approaches for persons with dementia (PwD).

Another group of prior work focuses on the detection of anxiety, distress, or agitation in aging individuals diagnosed with dementia or Alzheimer's disease. For instance, Fletcher-Lloyd et al. [20] proposed a classification model using ambient temperature, body temperature, movement, and entropy as features to predict agitation risk in PwD. Khan et al. [10] applied a computer vision model to video recordings of PwD in long-term care homes to detect agitation by treating agitation as an anomaly in behavior. Other approaches include data-driven forecasting using environmental features or medical records of the PwD [3,9], classification of Alzheimer's disease and MCI patients into depressive and non-depressive [2], and use of gesture recognition in PwD as a promising tool for Alzheimer's disease-related applications [13].

In this work, we also aim to increase understanding of dementia from the perspective of using AI to monitor behavioral patterns, with specific focus on assessing the feasibility of detecting aBPS in at-home care. To do so, we engaged with caregivers of PwD to qualify observed relationships between aBPS and behavioral cues, such as body movement and gestures, language and speech, one's physical location, and social context, in 10 semi-structured interviews. Our interview questions focused on gathering caregivers' observations of

1. behavioral patterns of the PwD that often correlate with their emotional state, especially those characterized by aBPS;
2. aBPS triggers, like unrealistic expectations, forgetfulness, or weakened communication skills;
3. conversational patterns that often correlate with aBPS;
4. environmental elements, such as noise, location, and social context, that often trigger aBPS;

5. and caregivers' comfort with the use of smart devices, like wearable devices, smartphones, and smart home assistants, to monitor the PwD to provide real-time prediction or detection of aBPS.

Analysis of the interview data show interesting insights concerning 10 themes, characterized by the caregivers' behavioral observations of their loved ones and their perceptions of a proposed AI-based technology for monitoring their loved one's behaviors that are likely predictive of aBPS. The former includes patterns in behavior and aBPS-related behaviors associated with one's state of mind, conversational topics, environment, and facial expressions. The latter captures interviewees' preferred modalities, methods for receiving notifications, features of the technology, and barriers of use in at-home care of the AI.

The paper is outlined as follows. Section 2 details our methodology, Sect. 3 presents the study's findings, and Sect. 4 discusses the results and concludes the article.

2 Methodology

Semi-structured qualitative interviews were conducted to potentially identify behavioral markers and triggers of distress, including anger, anxiety, frustration, and depression, that have been observed by actual caregivers of persons with dementia. This study received Human Subjects approval by the University of South Florida's Institutional Review Board (Study #004257).

We recruited 10 consenting adults (18+ years old) that self-identified as the primary caregiver of a PwD via e-mail and phone calls. The demographics of the participants are reported in Table 1. Most participants identified as White females over the age of 40.

Table 1. Participant Demographics

Participant	Age Range (in years)	Biological Sex	Spanish, Hispanic, or Latino Origin	Race
P1	50–59	F	No	White
P2	40–49	F	Yes	White
P3	50–59	M	Yes	White
P4	50–59	F	No	Black
P5	30–39	M	No	White
P6	30–39	F	No	Asian
P7	70–79	F	No	White
P8	60–69	F	No	White
P9	70–79	M	No	White
P10	50–59	F	No	Black

The interview guide consisted of the following questions:

1. Have you observed any relationships between symptoms of dementia, like memory loss, poor judgment, difficulty expressing thoughts, wandering, or repeating questions, and behavioral or psychiatric problems indicative of distress in your loved one? If so, can you describe your observations?
2. Can you describe any facial gestures or cues that you've noticed that indicated to you that your loved one was experiencing distress?
   (a) Have you noticed any patterns in this behavior?
   (b) Were you able to use facial expressions to predict the onset of distress?
3. When your loved one has experienced distress, did you notice that these moments were often tied to conversations on a particular topic or set of topics?
   (a) Can you describe these experiences? For example, are there noticeable patterns of behavior associated with the conversation itself that often trigger distress?
4. Can you talk a bit about any specific words that might be related to certain people or objects that generally result in forgetfulness or frustration?
5. Can you talk about any specific places or locations that you notice generally results in forgetfulness or frustration?
   (a) Are there any commonalities between these places, for instance, they all usually have a crowd of people that you can think of, especially anything that you notice are not present in places where your loved one seems to be calmer and more relaxed?
6. Do you find that the severity of your loved one's symptoms tends to correlate with their mood?
7. What do you think are some features a smart agent that can detect behavioral cues of distress should have?
8. Can you share any ideas on how this tool should be deployed?
9. How comfortable do you think your loved one might be with a smart agent in the home for the purpose of monitoring for emotional distress?
   (a) What about you? Would you find this useful?
   (b) How would you want the tool's information to be relayed to you and/or your loved one?
   (c) How do you think you would use this information?
   (d) Do you think it would be a useful resource to have, and if so, how?
   (e) Can you think of any barriers of use? Why wouldn't you want something like this in your home?
   (f) Are there certain platforms you are more comfortable with for collecting data, for example, a camera set-up, smartwatch, or voice assistant?

Interviews were conducted via the Microsoft Teams video conferencing service. The average interview time was approximately 35 min, with a minimum of 17 min and maximum time of 54 min. Interviews in English ($n = 8$) were audio recorded and transcribed using the AI-enabled transcription service, Temi[1]. Interviews in Spanish ($n = 2$) were audio recorded and transcribed in

---

[1] https://www.temi.com.

English using the AI-enabled transcription service, Sonix[2]. All transcriptions were reviewed by a researcher for accuracy. Participants were compensated with $15 electronic gift cards for their participation.

3 Findings

The qualitative interview data were analyzed by two independent coders using structured coding methods following a narrative analysis approach [24] to provide insight on which data signals (e.g., audio, video, inertial/movement measurements, physiological signals, speech, Bluetooth sightings as a measure of social context) show the most promise for in-home use as indicated by caregivers, along with insights concerning usability, design, and acceptance of an AI-based technology for monitoring and reporting the onset of aBPS in the PwD to the caregiver in real-time.

In total, 274 utterances were coded and included in our qualitative analysis. The coding process was four-fold. First, each coder independently read and reviewed seven interview transcripts. At this time, the coders generated their own generic codes based on the research goals and interview questions of the study. Next, both coders met to discuss and develop topics of interest, themes, and codes. All utterances coded by either coder were then assigned a topic and theme pair. Any disagreements between coders were discussed until the coders agreed on a single topic-theme pair for each utterance. After this assignment, coders independently re-coded the seven interviews and coded the remaining three in accordance to the new coding scheme and assigned topic-theme pairs. Through this process, we defined two overarching topics, *Behavioral Observations of PwD from Caregivers* and *Perceptions of the AI from Caregivers*, which included ten themes. Last, the coders independently assigned codes to each utterance and its assigned topic-theme pair.

We calculated inter-rater reliability (IRR) on the independent data. Cohen's κ [4] averaged 0.57 (min: 0.17, max: 0.86, SD: 0.173) across the 10 themes, corresponding to moderate agreement. Each coder was allowed to select multiple codes for a single utterance. Agreement was met with matching codes, including for utterances with one or multiple codes from coders. That is, disagreement resulted from any deviation of a single code between pairs of codes. For example, for the utterance below with the topic-theme pair *Behavioral Observations of PwD from Caregivers* and *aBSPD and State of Mind*, coder C_A may have assigned the codes **present** and **forgetfulness**, while coder C_B assigns the code **present**. In this case, we note agreement for assignment of **present** and disagreement for the lone mismatch of the code **forgetfulness**.

She can be very animated because she is cheerful and then suddenly change and become sad because [she] doesn't remember things.

---

[2] https://www.sonix.ai.

The theme with the lowest reported agreement was *aBSPD and Environment*. We attribute this low agreement in this theme to the coders not having a complete shared understanding of the meaning of the presence of the aBPS relationship with an environment.

Table 2 displays the themes organized into the two overarching topics and their assigned definitions. The coders also specified a total of 43 codes for the

Table 2. Themes and their definitions grouped by overarching topics.

Topic	Theme	Definition
Behavioral Observations of PwD from Caregivers	Behavioral Patterns	Observation of behavioral patterns that might correlate with an emotional state characterized. by aBPS
	aBPS and State of Mind	Observation of aBPS triggers, like unrealistic expectations, forgetfulness, or weakened communication skills.
	aBPS and Conversational Topics	Observation of whether conversational patterns correlate with aBPS.
	Environment and aBPS	Observation of whether environmental elements, such as noise, location, and social context, triggers aBPS.
	aBPS and facial expression or gestures	Observation of whether facial expressions or gestures correlate with an emotional state characterized by aBPS.
Perceptions of the AI from Caregivers	Preferred Modalities	Preferences of the caregiver, if any, about sensing modalities that might be used.
	Preferred Notifications	Preferences of the caregiver, if any, about the type of notifications that might be used for communicating the outcomes of the AI with the caregiver.
	Suggested Features	Suggested features that the caregiver feels should be added to an at-home AI-supported monitoring system.
	Barriers of Use	Barriers of use, from the caregiver's perspective, for an at-home AI-supported monitoring system.
	Caregiver's Comfort	How comfortable, from the caregiver's perspective, the PwD and the caregiver might be having an at-home AI-supported monitoring system

predefined themes. These codes, their definitions, and their assigned themes are listed in Table 3.

Table 3. Coding scheme of PwD behaviors and caregiver's perspectives

Code Themes	Definition
Behavioral Patterns	
wandering	The PwD was observed wandering prior to or while experiencing aBPS.
fidgeting	The PwD was observed making repeated small movements, especially of the hands to an object or to their own body, prior to or while experiencing aBPS.
refusing to follow instructions	The PwD refused to follow instructions or breaks a routine prior to or while experiencing aBPS.
aggression	The PwD is aggressive prior to or while experiencing aBPS.
other	Any other behavioral pattern was observed prior to or while experiencing aBPS.
aBPS and State of Mind	
present, not present	Situations, including unrealistic expectations, forgetfulness, or weakened communication skills, were observed in the PwD prior to or while experiencing aBPS.
forgetfulness	Forgetfulness was observed in the PwD prior to or while experiencing aBPS.
other	Another state of mind was observed prior to or while experiencing aBPS.
aBPS and Conversational Topics	
present, not present	A conversation's topic, a word or a set of words were identified (or not) as a trigger of an aBPS in the PwD.
Environment and aBPS	
present, not present	The PwD consistently experiences aBPS when entering or visiting specific places.
aBPS and Facial Expressions or Gestures	
facial exp present, not present	Facial expressions were observed in the PwD prior to or while experiencing aBPS.
gesture present, not present	Gestures were observed in the PwD prior to or while experiencing aBPS.
Preferred Modalities	
camera, audio, movement, measurements, physiological signals	The caregiver mentioned or suggested the use of a specific modality in the list (or set of modalities) to monitor the PwD.
other	The caregiver mentioned or suggested a modality not included in the list.
Preferred Notifications	
text, visual, sound, wearable	The caregiver mentioned or suggested a communication method included in the list.
Suggested Features	
location, physiological signal, vitals, wearables, sound analysis, provide advice	The caregiver mentioned or suggested a feature included in the list
Barriers of Use	
privacy, other	The caregiver mentioned privacy or other barrier of use of an at-home AI-supported monitoring system.
Caregiver's Comfort	
comfortable, uncomfortable	The caregiver mentioned their level of comfort for having an at-home AI-supported monitoring system for a PwD
useful, not useful	The caregiver mentioned how useful it might be to have an at-home AI supported monitoring system for a PwD.

3.1 Behavioral Observations of PwD from Caregivers

Theme 1: Behavioral Patterns. Theme 1 captures caregivers' observations of any behavioral patterns of PwD which they found to correlate with an emotional state associated with aBPS. Such identification of behavioral patterns prior to or during an aBPS-related episode, especially those observed in real-world instances, is critical for identifying potential behaviors that might be supported in an AI-based monitoring system.

We asked caregivers about any behaviors that they have observed to be indicative of distress in the PwD they care for. We found that most participants (7 out of 10 (70%)) indicated observing some behavioral pattern related to distress.

"... what happened is she would sit in a chair and she would ... be scratching her head and pulling her hair out... " [Participant 7]

Of the behavioral patterns mentioned by caregivers, aggression was the most common with seven occurrences in comparison to fidgeting or wandering which each occurred twice. Commonly, caregivers made a distinction between physical aggression, which may have involved harming others or themselves, and verbal aggression as characterized in the quote below.

"He would have some angry outbursts that included... [being] verbally aggressive, but never physically aggressive." [Participant 1]

Theme 2: aBPS and State of Mind. Theme 2 captures the relationship between caregivers' observations of aBPS triggers in the PwD they care for with the PwD's emotional and mental state. Overwhelmingly, nearly all (90%) caregivers provided observations that characterized such a relationship.

"Whenever someone talks about her mother, around like almost midnight, you would hear her crying..." [Participant 6]

Fifty percent of caregivers (five out of ten) characterized the manifestation of the relationship between aBPS triggers and mental state as forgetfulness.

"[If she's] sitting down and saying 'I'm going to get a pencil and stands up... The moment she stops and forgets she's going for the pencil. Then, she starts fighting with herself." [Participant 2]

Such observations might prove valuable for identifying which behaviors are relevant in an AI-based monitoring system, particularly concerning monitoring of one's affective state given the relationship between affect and aBPS.

Theme 3: aBPS and Conversational Topics. Theme 3 captures the responses of caregivers when asked if there were certain topics of conversation that often led to distress seen in the PwD that they care for. In this case, if the caregiver indicated or recalled a specific topic that generally acts as an aBPS trigger, we determined the presence of a relationship between conversation and aBPS. Although the specific topic of conversation may vary from one PwD to another, the confirmation of this relationship could help assess the feasibility of possibly integrating natural language and speech processing into the AI tool.

When asked about specific conversations or words that cause distress in the PwD, seven out of ten (70%) caregivers recounted their experiences with a specific word or topic of conversation that triggered aBPS.

" So when I would try and talk to my mother about not driving, that would start a fight." [Participant 7]

Interestingly, of the seven caregivers who reported the presence of this relationship, three later reported there were no particular topics or words that triggered aBPS.

"She was separated from her husband, so if I mentioned his name...she'd kind of get angry about that." [Participant 10 at 4:51]

"No, I really can't remember any one thing that just triggered [depression, distress, or frustration]." [Participant 10 at 5:34]

Theme 4: aBPS and Environment. Theme 4 represents instances where caregivers observed a relationship between the environmental elements of a particular location as triggers of an aBPS (or reported the absence of this relationship). Similar to Theme 3, while locations or environments that commonly lead to distress in one PwD may differ from another, verifying the presence or absence of this relationship could help to identify the relevance of including environmental sensors in an at-home AI-supported monitoring system.

Few (four out of ten caregivers) when asked if they have noticed any specific locations or places that lead to aBPS triggers explicitly shared that they have not noticed this relationship.

"Nothing like frustration. No, no, no. There are no places that produce it." [Participant 2]

Interestingly, both caregivers with experience working with larger populations of PwD (20% of participants) (i.e., caregiver in facilities with PwD and nurse/home health aid) reported the presence of this relationship.

"Frustration, yes... Like getting in the bathroom... you know, trying to ... convince 'em that they have dentures. Cause they don't remember having dentures." [Participant 5]

Theme 5: aBPS and Facial Expressions/Gestures. Theme 5 captures the relationship between facial expressions that may or may not precede or occur during an aBPS as observed and reported by PwD caregivers. The confirmation (or refusal) of the presence of facial expressions, prior to or during an aBPS, could help to assess the use case for computer vision and/or affect recognition as a part of the monitoring system.

When asked to describe facial expressions or gestures made by the PwD they care for indicating distress, several (seven out of ten) caregivers reported making such observations.

"Yes, yes. On several occasions. Especially the wrinkling of the face. That, with the words, 'this head of mine'. That is, is almost as important." [Participant 3]

Surprisingly, only one caregiver (10% of participants) reported the presence of gestures in relation to the onset or occurrence of an aBPS.

"Here is a gesture that he does a lot and that is to hold his head in his hands when he does not remember." [Participant 2]

3.2 Perceptions of the AI from Caregivers

Theme 6: Preferred Modalities. Theme 6 details any preferred data collection modalities specified by caregivers for the potential AI monitoring system. The identification of preferred modalities, from the caregiver's perspective, might guide the selection of an appropriate sensor or set of sensors to be used in a home setting.

Surprisingly, just four (40%) caregivers reported interest in the use of cameras. Caregivers who reported the preference of a camera noted being able to check in on the PwD without having to go to their physical location, noting the benefits of observing and recording their movements.

"I think obviously having a, a camera and recording someone's movements and behavior is probably the best thing you could do." [Participant 8]

Physiological signals, including temperature, heart rate, and blood pressure, were also mentioned by a few (three out of ten) caregivers.

"I don't know if the pulsations or something about the accelerating heartbeat when they are in those moments of stress that could help detect it to provide faster support." [Participant 3]

Theme 7: Preferred Notifications. Theme 7 reports on the preferred type of communication between the AI and the caregiver. Such insight is critical for ensuring transparency and developing trust for the technology.

Overwhelmingly, 80% of caregivers reported a preference for receiving notifications in a text-based format. For example, these notifications could potentially include an e-mail summary of behaviors detected or a SMS alert indicating a temperature rise.

"I personally would probably appreciate either a written, you know, summary of what was noticed, what was recorded, and/or a phone call." [Participant 8]

An equal number of caregivers (four out of ten) indicated interest in audio-based notifications as well as notifications via some wearable device.

"I would say definitely a wearable device that's placed on the carer and one for the patient and that way they can monitor any obvious physical changes." [Participant 4]

Theme 8: Suggested Features. Theme 8 focuses on features noted by interviewees that should be included in the AI. Suggestions from caregivers were given at various points in the semi-structured interviews. Our codes for this theme included location, physiological signals, vitals, sound analysis, provide advice, wearable, and other. Nearly all (80% of) caregivers shared suggestions associated with the code other due to the diversity in the suggestions. We also found that a common desire among 30% of caregivers included some indicator of a PwD's need to use the restroom.

"You could make like a mobile bladder scanner." [Participant 5]

Another popular suggestion from 50% of caregivers mentioned a desire for prediction or detection of distress associated with some action (e.g., falling or leaving the stove on).

"If you could program ... or get information that they went and turned the stove on, or turned the water on and then walked away."[Participant 7]

Theme 9: Barriers of Use. Theme 9 captures any mentioned potential barriers of use of the proposed system. This insight could be useful for navigating various usability issues, such as varying technology literacy levels, privacy and ethical concerns, and lack of adoption.

Fifty percent (five out of 10) of caregivers reported privacy as a potential barrier to acceptance of the proposed monitoring system. Caregivers also elaborated on the potential of data access and security of the monitoring system to hackers.

"I'd have to make sure as to where all the data is going and who would have access to the particular data. That would be the only time that I would be reluctant." [Participant 4]

Theme 10: Caregiver Comfort Level. Theme 10 reflects the level of comfort of the caregiver with interacting with an AI to monitor aBPS in their loved one. Such insight could help characterize the perceived usefulness of the technology.

Eighty percent (eight out of ten) of caregivers indicated that they would find such a monitoring system useful. Additionally, caregivers shared examples of how they would use the notifications and information provided by the system.

"You can always assess...assess and adjust. You know, you can adjust certain things like caregiver times or how the person is dealt with..."[Participant 8]

Most (60%) reported being comfortable with the idea of such an AI-enabled monitoring tool in the home.

"I think it is quite useful to have such a tool." [Participant 3]

4   Discussion and Conclusion

We conducted 10 semi-structured interviews to primarily (1) identify or establish if key factors exist in the behavior and environment of a PwD that might be used to infer or predict emotional states of interest and (2) to identify the suitable options to deploy a system/agent that is acceptable by PwDs and their caregivers in their homes. Such an AI could leverage a variety of approaches, such as affective computing, natural language processing, automated speech analysis, computer vision, and biometrics.

Findings suggest that behavioral patterns may be a strong indicator of aBPS. Seventy percent of interviewees reported the occurrence of a pattern prior to or during the PwD experiencing aBPS. Similarly, 70% of the interviewees reported the presence of facial expressions indicative of distress. Specifically, wandering, fidgeting, and facial expressions emerged as potential indicators of aBPS. Findings also suggest the use of natural language processing and affective computing to help combat aBPS associated with forgetfulness, the onset of aBPS due to certain conversational topics, or the use of specific words during conversation. However, we did not find a significant relationship of one's environment with distress (only 20% of the interviews identified the locations as related to an aBPS). Further research is required to investigate specific factors like noise, location, and social context.

Many modes for data collection were noted as well, like cameras, audio, and movement tracking. However, we note that no specific modality was mentioned over all others. Interestingly, 30% of the caregivers (including those with experience working with large populations) suggested the use of physiological signals. When asked about the features they would like to see in such an AI, many were noted, including location, physiological sensing, recording of vitals, sound analysis, providing advice, and being suitable for a wearable device. While no one particular feature emerged as prominent, this is an indication that caregivers prefer a broad set of data sources.

Concerning interacting with the AI, 80% of the interviewees selected text as the preferred notification method, indicating a need for fast communication to the caregiver. Visual and sound notifications were also suggested, but not required. Further, in general, the major concern associated with the use of the AI system was privacy concerning data breaches, invading the family's privacy, and data use. However, most (80%) felt the AI would be useful, while 60% felt they would be comfortable with such a tool. Thus, to further this work, future work should consider a broader range of participants, with special attention placed on the diversity of the participants, to determine if our findings generalize. Further, it is important to also consider other aspects of the tool, such as computational and hardware requirements, how caregivers might respond to erroneous output, and how other members of the household might adopt such a technology.

References

1. König, A., et al.: Automatic speech analysis for the assessment of patients with predementia and Alzheimer's disease. Alzheimer's Dementia 1(1), 112–24 (2015). https://pubmed.ncbi.nlm.nih.gov/27239498/
2. Abdallah, B.B., Abdallah, A.A., Ratte, S.S.: Detecting depression in Alzheimer and mci using artificial neural networks (ANN). In: ACM International Conference Proceeding Series, pp. 250–253 (2021). https://doi.org/10.1145/3460620.3460765
3. Byeon, H.: Predicting the anxiety of patients with Alzhcimer's dementia using boosting algorithm and data-level approach. Int. J. Adv. Comput. Sci. Appl. 12(3), 107–113 (2021). https://doi.org/10.14569/IJACSA.2021.0120313
4. Cohen, J.: A coefficient of agreement for nominal scales. Educ. Psychol. Measur. 20(1), 37–46 (1960). https://doi.org/10.1177/001316446002000104
5. Duxbury, J., Pulsford, D., Hadi, M., Sykes, S.: Staff and relatives' perspectives on the aggressive behaviour of older people with dementia in residential care: a qualitative study. J. Psychiatric Ment. Health Nurs. 20(9), 792–800 (2013). https://doi.org/10.1111/jpm.12018. https://onlinelibrary.wiley.com/doi/abs/10.1111/jpm.12018
6. Fujii, M., Ishizuka, S., Azumi, M., Sasaki, H.: Hypothesis of behavioral and psychological symptoms of dementia (2010)
7. Gottesman, R.T., Stern, Y.: Behavioral and psychiatric symptoms of dementia and rate of decline in Alzheimer's disease. Front. Pharmacol. 10 (2019). https://doi.org/10.3389/fphar.2019.01062. https://www.frontiersin.org/articles/10.3389/fphar.2019.01062
8. Harish, S., Gayathri, K.: Smart home based prediction of symptoms of Alzheimer's disease using machine learning and contextual approach. In: 2019 International Conference on Computational Intelligence in Data Science (ICCIDS), pp. 1–6 (2019). https://doi.org/10.1109/ICCIDS.2019.8862163
9. HekmatiAthar, S.P., Goins, H., Samuel, R., Byfield, G., Anwar, M.: Data-driven forecasting of agitation for persons with dementia: a deep learning-based approach. SN Comput. Sci. 2(4), 1–10 (2021). https://doi.org/10.1007/s42979-021-00708-3
10. Khan, S.S., et al.: Unsupervised deep learning to detect agitation from videos in people with dementia. IEEE Access 10, 10349–10358 (2022). https://doi.org/10.1109/ACCESS.2022.3143990
11. Khan, S.S., et al.: Agitation detection in people living with dementia using multimodal sensors. In: 2019 41st Annual International Conference of the IEEE Engineering in Medicine and Biology Society (EMBC), pp. 3588–3591. IEEE (2019)
12. Khan, S.S., et al.: DAAD: a framework for detecting agitation and aggression in people living with dementia using a novel multi-modal sensor network. In: 2017 IEEE International Conference on Data Mining Workshops (ICDMW), pp. 703–710 (2017). https://doi.org/10.1109/ICDMW.2017.98

13. Kibbanahalli Shivalingappa, M.S., Ben Abdessalem, H., Frasson, C.: Real-time gesture recognition using deep learning towards Alzheimer's disease applications. In: Frasson, C., Bamidis, P., Vlamos, P. (eds.) BFAL 2020. LNCS (LNAI), vol. 12462, pp. 75–86. Springer, Cham (2020). https://doi.org/10.1007/978-3-030-60735-7_8

14. Ilias, L., Askounis, D.: Multimodal deep learning models for detecting dementia from speech and transcripts. Front. Aging Neurosci. **14**, 830943 (2022). https://pubmed.ncbi.nlm.nih.gov/35370608/

15. Langa, K.M.: Is the risk of Alzheimer's disease and dementia declining? Alzheimer's Res. Therapy **7**(1), 1–4 (2015)

16. Liang, X., et al.: Evaluating voice-assistant commands for dementia detection. Comput. Speech Lang. **72** (2022). https://doi.org/10.1016/j.csl.2021.101297

17. Logsdon, R.G., Gibbons, L.E., McCurry, S.M., Teri, L.: Quality of life in Alzheimer's disease: patient and caregiver reports. J. Mental Health Aging **5**, 21–32 (1999)

18. Logsdon, R.G., Gibbons, L.E., McCurry, S.M., Teri, L.: Assessing quality of life in older adults with cognitive impairment. Psychosom. Med. **64**(3), 510–519 (2002)

19. Luz, S.: Longitudinal monitoring and detection of Alzheimer's type dementia from spontaneous speech data. In: 2017 IEEE 30th International Symposium on Computer-Based Medical Systems (CBMS), pp. 45–46 (2017). https://doi.org/10.1109/CBMS.2017.41

20. Fletcher-Lloyd, N., Soreq, E., Wilson, D., Nilforooshan, R., Sharp, D.J., Barnaghi, P.: Home monitoring of daily living activities and prediction of agitation risk in a cohort of people living with dementia. Alzheimer's Dementia J. Alzheimer's Assoc. **17**, e058614 (2021). https://pubmed.ncbi.nlm.nih.gov/34971120/

21. Petti, U., Baker, S., Korhonen, A.: A systematic literature review of automatic Alzheimer's disease detection from speech and language. J. Am. Med. Inform. Assoc. **27**(11), 1784–1797 (2020)

22. Chen, P.H., Lien, C.W., Wu, W.C., Lee, L.S., Shaw, J.S.: Gait-based machine learning for classifying patients with different types of mild cognitive impairment. J. Med. Syst. **44**(6), 107 (2020). https://pubmed.ncbi.nlm.nih.gov/32328889/

23. Powell, T.: Health policy and dementia. Curr. Psychiatry Rep. **20**, 1–5 (2018)

24. Saldaña, J.: The coding manual for qualitative researchers. In: The Coding Manual for Qualitative Researchers, pp. 1–440 (2021)

25. Smith, E., et al.: Affective computing for late-life mood and cognitive disorders. Front. Psych. **12**, 2380 (2021)

26. Spasojevic, S., Nogas, J., Iaboni, A., Ye, B., Mihailidis, A., Wang, A., Li, S.J., Martin, L.S., Newman, K., Khan, S.S.: A pilot study to detect agitation in people living with dementia using multi-modal sensors. J. Healthc. Inform. Res. **5**(3), 342–358 (2021). https://doi.org/10.1007/s41666-021-00095-7

27. Torisson, G., Stavenow, L., Minthon, L., Londos, E.: Reliability, validity and clinical correlates of the quality of life in Alzheimer's disease (QoL-AD) scale in medical inpatients. Health Qual. Life Outcomes **14**(1), 1–8 (2016)

28. Yeung, A., et al.: Correlating natural language processing and automated speech analysis with clinician assessment to quantify speech-language changes in mild cognitive impairment and Alzheimer's dementia. Alzheimer's Res. Therapy **13**(1), 109 (2021)

Engagement as a Goal and Process for Improving Support for Informal Caregivers: The Cremona Beside Caregiver Project

Michele Paleologo[1,5]([✉]) [iD], Eleonora Gheduzzi[3,5] [iD], Rita Bichi[1,5] [iD],
Maria Grazia Cappelli[5,6], Matteo Donelli[5,6], Niccolò Morelli[4,5] [iD],
Cristina Masella[3,5] [iD], and Guendalina Graffigna[2,5] [iD]

[1] Università Cattolica del Sacro Cuore, 20123 Milan, MI, Italy
michele.paleologo@unicatt.it
[2] Università Cattolica del Sacro Cuore, 26100 Milan, CR, Italy
[3] Politecnico di Milano, 26100 Milan, CR, Italy
[4] Università degli Studi di Genova, 16126 Genoa, GE, Italy
[5] Comune di Cremona, 26100 Cremona, CR, Italy
[6] Camera di Commercio di Cremona, 26100 Cremona, CR, Italy

Abstract. The role of the caregiver is essential in the management of older people's care processes, provide unpaid care and assistance to aged family members and act as case managers. Despite this they are in a potentially dangerous situation for his or her own health. The article discusses the importance of involving stakeholders in social and health service delivery and how this involvement is critical to creating value for patients and caregivers, paying attention to involve the most vulnerable citizens. The Cremona Beside Caregiver research project was conducted in the Cremona area with the aim of improving the quality of support for informal caregivers of older people in partnership with the City of Cremona and the Cremona Chamber of Commerce and with financial support from the Fondazione Comunitaria della Provincia di Cremona. The project was organized and developed in four main phases: socio-demographic analysis of the area was first carried out, then mapping of services and resources for the caregiver, then a phase of stakeholder engagement and an exploration of their outlooks and finally, exploration of caregivers' needs and expectations was conducted to understand the caregivers' point of view. The research project yielded several lessons which can be applied to future research projects in the area of informal caregiving. The results show that the increase of the ageing population in the area is putting a strain on the network of public services, and also showed an area rich in services and resources but lacking in integration and communication between actors. This lack of coordination and sharing among stakeholders leads to a misinformation of existing services among the population, with negative implications on the accessibility of services, paving the way for two intervention solutions.

Keywords: informal caregiver · active ageing · multistakeholders research · participatory research · ageing · older people · caregiver burden · caregiver engagement; patient engagement

© The Author(s), under exclusive license to Springer Nature Switzerland AG 2023
Q. Gao and J. Zhou (Eds.): HCII 2023, LNCS 14043, pp. 345–356, 2023.
https://doi.org/10.1007/978-3-031-34917-1_24

1 Introduction

1.1 The Importance of Informal Caregivers

As age and any comorbidities progress, it may become necessary for an older person to have someone to care for him or her in various capacities and to varying degrees. One can then speak of formal caregivers, if they are paid and trained people who assist the aged person, or of informal caregivers, if on the other hand the care and assistance is provided free of charge by someone who has a link-for example, kinship-with the caregiver [1].

This need for care, despite the health and social welfare system, is widespread to the point that in Italy we can count almost 3 million citizens who care for their dependent family members [2]. These, can be said to represent "the invisible and silent backbone of the health care system" [3], indeed, despite the fact that they are often forgotten by welfare systems and policy makers [4, 5], their role is essential in managing the care processes of the senior citizens and coordinating the services they use, representing a true case manager of the older [6].

The role of the caregiver, not without effort, becomes especially crucial when the old person is allowed to age in his or her own living and community context [7]. This practice is called aging in place and is recognized as a factor in improving the quality of life of the senior and the sustainability of social welfare [8, 9]. Moreover, even when there are multiple sources of care for the senior, the care provided by the family caregiver presents some advantages. Indeed, they turn out to be more attuned to their loved one and, for example, are more accurate in assessing the presence of physical symptoms and pain than other caregivers such as nurses [10, 11].

1.2 The Caregiver's Needs and Burden

Despite the importance of his or her work, the caregiver is in a potentially dangerous situation for his or her own health, not only reporting more fatigue, insomnia, anxiety, depression, weight loss or gain, but also manifesting a tendency to neglect his or her own health and needs [12].

This condition of psychophysical distress that goes by the name of caregiver burden [13] can be amplified by various contextual aspects, for example, as the older person's functional abilities diminish and thus his or her dependence on the caregiver increases [14] or as their dementia condition progresses [15]. Aspects and characteristics of the caregiver may also influence the level of caregiver burden. The literature shows that the female gender is in a higher burden situation [15–17]. The age of the caregiver also plays a key role, and sources of distress may exist at both poles of the caregiver's age evolution; in fact, older people face their caregiving task differently and their burden may be greater due to the feeling of being cut off from their lives, neglecting themselves in the last phase of their existence [18], at the same time younger caregivers may suffer more from the difficulty of reconciling the role of caregiver with their other life roles (parent, worker, husband, etc.) [19]. The informal caregiver who is therefore faced with the challenge of caring for their loved one brings with them a multitude of needs that are rarely met [20]. Prominent among these is the need to be informed of the resources and services available to them in order to care for their loved one in the best possible way [20, 21]. In addition, family caregivers manifest many other needs: related to economic aspects [20, 21], the possibility of receiving qualified home care assistance to care for their loved one, peer welfare policies a better work-family balance [20], training for both one's own role and for possible pathologies of the older [3, 21] and psychological support [21, 22] to name a few particularly emphasized in the relevant scientific literature.

To address these needs, it is necessary to think about services, policies and welfare systems that can solve them concretely [22] by recognizing caregivers their fundamental role in caring for the frail older people. A possible approach increasingly appreciated and adopted in the literature imply the direct involvement (engagement) of citizens in the definition of new health and social policies and services [23].

The next section explores the most suitable approaches and methodologies for moving in this participatory direction.

1.3 Caregiver Engagement as a Goal and as a Method

In order to promote caregiver engagement, there are many approaches and methodologies with related tools and techniques, derived from different fields of application and different theoretical roots. Our intention here is precisely to provide clarity and build an initial compass that can help guide one in choosing the approach best suited to one's context.

Speaking of participation in health care, a large body of scientific and health policy literature addresses the importance of fostering caregiver engagement and protecting the most fragile segments of the population to ensure equitable opportunities for all citizens to participate; however, today, concrete and systematic caregiver engagement initiatives are still rare [24].

A standard definition for caregiver engagement refers to the ability of caregivers to actively seek information related to the health and care of their loved one and to participate (and support their loved one's participation) in sharing treatment choices. We therefore refer to an underlying psychological dimension that can not only be supported but, first and foremost measured. Indeed, it is possible to identify four main stances toward taking a proactive role in the health care journey in which caregivers may find themselves: denial and avoidance, hyperactivation, self-denial and drowning, and balancing and equilibrium (for further discussion see Barello et al., 2019).

The active role of the caregiver should also be considered in the process of shared decision making related to the planning of the patient's daily and life activities [25]. The engagement of this character is also shown to be a crucial factor in the relationship with caregivers, for a better therapeutic alliance and more effective communication with the care team (Morelli et al., 2019). In this case, collaboration occurs at the 'micro' level between the professional, the caregiver and the older people. The goal of the exchange between these actors is the structuring and delivery of the care pathway for the aged.

1.4   Caregiver Engagement in Shaping Health and Social Services and Policies

Building participatory research pathways can be a successful way to create solutions that fully meet the needs of the most fragile citizens that are often overlooked and under-explored [26]. Let us therefore see how such participation can take place.

The caregiver can also be involved in the definition, implementation, and evaluation of health and social services and policies. Unlike the micro level where the exchange occurs more between individuals, in this case collaboration occurs between two (or more) homogeneous groups of actors. At the meso level, collaboration occurs between a group of professionals and a group of caregivers; at the macro level, between a group of policy-makers and a group of caregivers (and/or patients). The object of discussion also changes. While at the micro level the caregiver collaborates with the professional in defining and delivering their loved one's care pathway, at the meso level the object of discussion is health and social services, and at the macro level it is standards and guidelines [27].

In addition to the object of discussion and the actors involved, it is important to define the level of caregiver influence on the decision-making process. In some cases, caregivers' involvement might be for informational purposes only. In other cases, however, caregivers might be involved as partners in the design of a new service or legislation with the goal of creating a more democratic and inclusive service delivery [28]. The literature suggests several scales that attempt to conceptualize and organize forms of involvement by level of citizen influence on decision-making, among them the continuum suggested by [29]) is among the best known. It provides for four levels of involvement: information, consultation, participation, and co-involvement. The first level, information, rather than collaboration, is a one-way relationship in which service providers provide information to users but do not listen to their input or preferences. The consultation level involves a two-way exchange between providers and users, but allows users to make only minimal contributions to the process. At this level, users can express their preferences regarding a specific set of options and scenarios presented by practitioners. Following the moment of consultation, practitioners can decide for themselves how to use the collected feedback. At the participation level, users and providers are involved in a public dialogue and exchange that provides a higher level of input than the consultation level. Users are involved in decision-making processes and discuss their opinions by actively interacting with the rest of the participants. This gives much more space for users to express their preferences and engage with professionals. The co-production level sits at the top of this continuum. It differs from the participation level in that users provide substantial input on decision making {Citation} [30]. Users are considered "experts by experience"; they are not only recipients of a care pathway, service, or policy, but are also its creators [31].

Anyway, this differentiation of levels of collaboration and involvement is only intended to organize and guide professionals in the involvement of caregivers. In fact, it is not correct to state which level of collaboration and/or involvement is superior to another. The level must be chosen according to the objective of the exchange [32].

1.5   How to Engage Caregivers in an Inclusive Way?

The more or less active involvement of caregivers, especially when aimed at change and intervention, requires the involvement of other stakeholders for at least two reasons.

First, the involvement of a broad group of stakeholders ensures that their expectations and needs are considered and, where possible, used to develop initiatives in response to them. Second, the effect of a service (or regulation) results from direct and indirect exchange and integration among actors and related resources in the relevant service ecosystem [33]. In other words, the effect of a service for family caregivers will depend not only on how the service is delivered by professionals, but also on how the service is communicated and told to the citizen by local authorities, the sources of funding that local authorities make available, the skills and professionalism that the provider will be able to attract to deliver the service, and so on. In this sense, the involvement of stakeholders involved directly and indirectly in social and health service delivery is intended to be useful in creating greater coordination and integration among entities, maximizing the effect of service delivery in the area.

At the same time, it should be emphasized that the only actor that generates value is the service user (in this case the patient and caregiver dyad) [34]. A care pathway, service or regulation that is not enjoyed and experienced by one or more patients and/or caregivers does not generate any effect. For this reason, it is, yes, critical to involve the different stakeholders in the service ecosystem, but it is equally critical to include patients and/or their caregivers. The value created will depend on the ability of the ecosystem actors to organize and coordinate with each other to best meet the needs and expectations of users.

Despite the fact that the purpose of participatory approaches to research is precisely to help and involve those who are in situations of fragility, vulnerability and who therefore need help and support one of the risks to which attention needs to be paid lies precisely in the danger of failing to involve the 'less fortunate,' those who finding themselves in particularly stressful and overburdened situations exclude themselves from participation due to lack of time and resources [35–38]. Empirical evidence has shown that citizens involved in participatory processes are often the 'ordinary citizens,' that is, citizens with excellent dialogic skills, a high level of education, good health status, and sufficient free time to participate in participatory moments [39].

To facilitate the involvement of the most vulnerable citizens, which includes family caregivers, some interesting suggestions and recommendations can be found in the most recent literature. First, time should be spent on getting to know each other and therefore building relationships between professionals (or policy-makers) and these vulnerable citizens. This initial phase, called phase zero, helps identify inequalities and power dynamics and incentivizes motivation and exchanges among participants [26]. The creation of initial trusting relationships between caregivers and professionals is a key factor in the success of participatory processes [40]. At the same time, it should be emphasized/as mentioned above, creating these types of relationships require time, dedication, and resources [41]. To overcome this problem, it is good practice to leverage any pre-existing relationships with target groups to facilitate the engagement process [42]. Second, it is important to clarify from the outset the objectives and consequently also the roles of the participants in the collaboration process. Full transparency about the activities and modes of collaboration prevents misalignments between the expectations of the participants and those of the sponsoring entity [43]. An additional suggestion is to plan activities carefully, choosing the collaborative methods and tools best suited to the target participants [44]. Some vulnerable citizens may need time to share their experiences and formulate their opinions. Therefore, in order to be able to gather their input as well, the collaboration must extend for as long as necessary by organizing more participatory moments [45].

Finally, it is important to organize collaborative moments in which all participants are able to provide input. Indeed, not only is it difficult to fully understand the perspectives and needs of participants, but collaboration between professionals and vulnerable actors with very different backgrounds can become complex because the language and considerations of the former may be difficult for the latter to understand. To overcome this problem, it may be important to provide training moments on the topic of discussion prior to the collaborative moments and to encourage professionals (or policy-makers) to use simple terminology [46].

2 Methods

We now want to clarify how we moved from theory to practice and what pragmatic implications and lessons can be learned for the future with a case history of a research project conducted between 2021 and 2022 in the Cremona area (North Italy) entitled *"Cremona Beside Caregiver: un progetto per assistere chi assiste"*.

2.1 Study Design

This research project was established with the aim of improving the quality of support for informal caregivers of older people in the Cremona area through an in-depth understanding of the context and needs of the entire service ecosystem. To this end, an interdisciplinary project was set up with the participation of the EngageMinds Hub Research Center, the Department of Sociology of the Università Cattolica del Sacro Cuore, the Department of Management Engineering of the Politecnico di Milano, the City of Cremona and the Cremona Chamber of Commerce with financial support from Fondazione Comunitaria della Provincia di Cremona. The research project was organized and developed in four main phases with different approaches and methodologies.

Socio-Demographic Analysis of the Area. Statistical analysis was conducted on the demographic composition of the territory, the economic and health aspects of the over-65 resident population, the supply and use of social and health services aimed at the older people, and the presence and activism of the associative fabric in the Cremona area. The data analyzed emerge from Inps and Istat processing and to the Open Data of the Lombardy Region. This phase could be considered the −1 phase which allowed us to get an initial quantitative picture.

Mapping Services and Resources for the Caregiver. Secondly, and in concurrent, a desk analysis was conducted of health, social and social services in favor of the frail older and their caregiver provided by the formal caregiver network using the websites of the main organizations and institutions in the Cremona area and Regional Resolutions;

A desk analysis of the services provided by the informal caregiver network in favor of the caregiver was conducted in parallel and subsequently using the websites and social media of the associations.

Stakeholder Engagement and the Exploration of Their Outlooks. Approximately, phase zero begin between this and the previous phase. About twenty-one one-hour semi-structured interviews were conducted with social, health, and social and health care stakeholders. Thus, seeking not only to meet the knowledge objectives set up, but also to expand the number of stakeholders to be involved according to the community itself. During those interviews participants were asked to reflect with the researcher about the condition of older people and their caregivers, any available data and databases, any entities involved or to be involved, changes from the past, practices and projects in place, future plans or desire and aspects related to training of both caregivers and operators.

Then, two workshops were held with social, health and social-health stakeholders. In addition, four Workshops were also organized with two Cremona neighborhoods, involving an average of five neighborhood association representatives per workshop with a duration of about one and a half hours.

Finally, a press conference was organized inviting partners, involved stakeholders, and the public.

Exploration of Caregivers' Needs and Expectations. Eventually, to deeper understand the caregivers point of view, twenty semi-structured interviews of approximately one hour duration were conducted with caregivers of frail older people residing in their own homes and in residences for the aged. During those interviews researchers reflected with the participants on their caregivers experience, their needs, their lifestyle and how they have changed, their relationship with formal assistance network and any availability of an informal assistance network (i.e. parents, friends and so on).

3 Results

This initial ground-breaking research in the area allowed us to build a picture of the lives of both seniors and their caregivers from a multidimensional and multistakeholder perspective and, especially, to engage a network of stakeholders with whom we can develop new solutions by always continuing through a participatory research approach.

The demographic and socio-economic investigation showed an increasing weight of the older population in the total population, a negative trend in the birth rate, a negative demographic balance, and high administrative and geographic fragmentation that threatens to create further discrimination for the older and their caregivers in the more remote and rural areas. A good earning capacity of the area's retirees certainly emerges, a positive finding that, however, risks delaying the perception of malfunctions in the public service network by encouraging a shift to privatization with the risk of bequeathing to new, less affluent generations a system insufficient to meet their needs.

Service mapping enriched the statistical investigation by identifying services and resources in the Cremona area. The results revealed an area rich in services and resources especially from the third sector and small associations although mainly for the frail older people and less for the caregiver, both professional and informal. Upon investigating the stakeholders' point of view in the field, it is evident that there is a vast network of supply for seniors in the territory, which, however, is lacking in integration and communication among the actors, affecting the efficiency and quality of the services offered.

It also appears that the Italian funding system based on calls and projects, especially in the Third Sector, creates conditions of competition rather than collaboration, risking, according to some stakeholders involved, the dispersion of already meager resources. Indeed, a recurring theme among all sectors, especially the health sector, is the lack of financial and human resources. In addition, all stakeholders complained of a difficulty in sharing patient information and data among different entities and organizations, mainly due to lack of interoperable systems and privacy laws. A major consequence of the lack of coordination and sharing among stakeholders is a misinformation of existing services among the population, with inevitable negative implications on the accessibility of services. One of the main consequences of the lack of coordination and sharing among actors is a misinformation of existing services among the population, with inevitable negative implications on the accessibility of services. At the same time, a data access and management problem also emerges, partly due to bureaucracy and partly to a conflict between different technological systems, an aspect that is exacerbated by a digital literacy that is not always high, especially among the operators of voluntary associations.

Instead, from the perspective of the caregiver, several practical problems and a situation of psychological burden emerge that would need to be further investigated and quantified in the population. What is most evident, however, is the caregiver's difficulty in navigating the fragmented multitude of services to support him or her. In this regard, not only do some caregivers show a lack of familiarity with digital media also due to their age, but in several cases general confusion is also reported regarding online information and access to services via digital means. For this reason, the present scenario highlights two potential levels of intervention to be carried on in conjunction.

A first, more organizational and informational level that sets out to respond to the fragmentation of service offerings exacerbated by the lack of resources and problems in communication and collaboration among stakeholders and to the practical and informational needs of caregivers for which it is necessary to identify solutions that represent points of contact between the actors involved, allowing both to optimize the resources present and to highlight any inefficiencies and opportunities for improvement.

Once these needs have been at least partially resolved, it will be easier to think about a second level of intervention oriented focused on quality and to improve the effectiveness and efficiency of the network of service provision, the quality of life of caregivers, with particular attention to psychological and engagement needs and, finally, the well-being and motivation of professionals and volunteers involved in the delivery of health, social and social services.

4   Discussion

We think there are four main reasons of interest for this case-study. First, the project set out to involve the entire ecosystem of services for the caregiver and the frail older people, thus seeking not to exclude relevant figures and to maximize the confluence of diverse knowledge. In addition, Involving the entire ecosystem of services provided a comprehensive view of how service provision works and the relationships and exchanges between different stakeholders.

Second, the project deepened the analysis of the service ecosystem by performing an additional focus on two neighborhoods in Cremona. This approach allowed the research team to fully understand the dynamics and relationships between the local population and the territorial entities belonging to both the formal and informal service network. In addition, it allowed the establishment of trusting relationships and opportunities for confrontation with the social fabric of reference by grasping the peculiarities and specificities of the context analyzed.

Third, the project directly involved caregivers by collecting their experiential knowledge, expectations and needs through semi-structured interviews. Direct involvement of caregivers early in the project facilitated understanding of caregivers' difficulties and building trusting relationships between caregivers and the research team. Finally, this project allows us to explore both the micro level, delving into the relationship that caregivers have with professionals in the daily management of elder care, and the meso level, analyzing the relationships between different stakeholders in the service ecosystem and the latter's ability to respond to caregivers' needs.

In conclusion, we think it is important to reflect on how participatory research can be linked to caregiver engagement and why this should be conceived as both a goal and a method. In fact, during this research project it further became clear how this construct is to be considered simultaneously as the product of an effective system and as the driver of the participatory process that can lead to such an effective system. In fact, during the consultation and involvement of caregivers, it became clear that those who for particular reasons, probably to be found in their own micro-context of reference and predispositions, are already more integrated and engaged with the service network, were not only in a less distressed condition, but are also those who can (and will) most easily contribute to the shared production of knowledge and, therefore, in turn improve the quality of life and engagement of other caregivers.

Therefore, considering the importance of the caregiver to society and also given the situation of neglect and forgetfulness in which they often find themselves, this virtuous circle can be a key lever to give rise to project realities that improve their conditions, increasing engagement in small steps, starting with those who are already engaged.

Implementing solutions that allow for monitoring, mapping and consequently supporting and increasing the level of engagement of caregivers in a given area can be a master way to lighten its load with all the attendant benefits we discussed at the beginning of the chapter. To this end, in the light of the outcomes of this project, we intend to move forward with the design of a communication system between all the organisations involved in caring for the older person and his or her caregiver by building a digital interconnection platform to be managed by trained operators and disseminated throughout the territory in special spaces and counters open to citizens.

Indeed, introducing welfare measures in this direction would make it possible to move from a situation in which caregivers represent "the invisible backbone of the social and health care system" [3] to one in which they represent, where possible, an extension of it that enriches its effect, thanks to the affective dimension and knowledge of the assisted one, as well as his or her desire to participate in the health care journey of his or her loved one.

Funding. This study was conducted thanks to funding from Fondazione Comunitaria della Provincia di Cremona. The authors declare that the funders had no role in the study design, in interpretation of the results or in the decision to publish the results.

References

1. LoboPrabhu, S.M., Molinari, V.A., Lomax, J.W.: Supporting the Caregiver in Dementia: A Guide for Health Care Professionals. JHU Press (2006)
2. Istat: Conciliazione tra lavoro e famiglia (2019)
3. Morelli, N., Barello, S., Mayan, M., Graffigna, G.: Supporting family caregiver engagement in the care of old persons living in hard to reach communities: a scoping review. Health Soc. Care Community **27**, 1363–1374 (2019). https://doi.org/10.1111/hsc.12826
4. Applebaum, A.: Isolated, invisible, and in-need: there should be no "I" in caregiver. Palliat. Support. Care **13**, 415–416 (2015). https://doi.org/10.1017/S1478951515000413
5. Levine, C.: Putting the spotlight on invisible family caregivers. JAMA Intern. Med. **176**, 380–381 (2016). https://doi.org/10.1001/jamainternmed.2015.8002
6. Bookman, A., Harrington, M.: Family caregivers: a shadow workforce in the geriatric health care system? J. Health Polit. Policy Law **32**, 1005–1041 (2007). https://doi.org/10.1215/036 16878-2007-040
7. Horner, B., Boldy, D.P.: The benefit and burden of "ageing-in-place" in an aged care community. Aust. Health Rev. **32**, 356–365 (2008). https://doi.org/10.1071/ah080356
8. Rodriguez-Rodriguez, V., et al.: The impact of COVID-19 on nursing homes: study design and population description. Int. J. Environ. Res. Public Health **19**, 16629 (2022). https://doi.org/10.3390/ijerph192416629
9. Sánchez-González, D., Rojo-Pérez, F., Rodríguez-Rodríguez, V., Fernández-Mayoralas, G.: Environmental and psychosocial interventions in age-friendly communities and active ageing: a systematic review. Int. J. Environ. Res. Public Health **17**, 8305 (2020). https://doi.org/10.3390/ijerph17228305
10. Dawber, R., Armour, K., Ferry, P., Mukherjee, B., Carter, C., Meystre, C.: Comparison of informal caregiver and named nurse assessment of symptoms in elderly patients dying in hospital using the palliative outcome scale. BMJ Support. Palliat. Care **9**, 175–182 (2019). https://doi.org/10.1136/bmjspcare-2015-000850
11. Ruben, M.A., Blanch-Hartigan, D., Shipherd, J.C.: To know another's pain: a meta-analysis of caregivers' and healthcare providers' pain assessment accuracy. Ann. Behav. Med. **52**, 662–685 (2018). https://doi.org/10.1093/abm/kax036
12. Wolff, J.L., Spillman, B.C., Freedman, V.A., Kasper, J.D.: A national profile of family and unpaid caregivers who assist older adults with health care activities. JAMA Intern. Med. **176**, 372–379 (2016). https://doi.org/10.1001/jamainternmed.2015.7664
13. Adelman, R.D., Tmanova, L.L., Delgado, D., Dion, S., Lachs, M.S.: Caregiver burden: a clinical review. JAMA **311**, 1052–1060 (2014). https://doi.org/10.1001/jama.2014.304
14. Fuhrmann, A.C., Bierhals, C.C.B.K., dos Santos, N.O., Paskulin, L.M.G.: Association between the functional capacity of dependant elderly people and the burden of family caregivers. Rev. Gaúcha Enferm. **36**, 14–20 (2015). https://doi.org/10.1590/1983-1447.2015.01.49163
15. Park, M., Sung, M., Kim, S.K., Kim, S., Lee, D.Y.: Multidimensional determinants of family caregiver burden in Alzheimer's disease. Int. Psychogeriatr. **27**, 1355–1364 (2015). https://doi.org/10.1017/S1041610215000460

16. Connors, M.H., Seeher, K., Teixeira-Pinto, A., Woodward, M., Ames, D., Brodaty, H.: Dementia and caregiver burden: a three-year longitudinal study. Int. J. Geriatr. Psychiatry **35**, 250–258 (2020). https://doi.org/10.1002/gps.5244

17. Srivastava, G., Tripathi, R.K., Tiwari, S.C., Singh, B., Tripathi, S.M.: Caregiver burden and quality of life of key caregivers of patients with dementia. Indian J. Psychol. Med. **38**, 133–136 (2016). https://doi.org/10.4103/0253-7176.178779

18. Spatuzzi, R., et al.: Does family caregiver burden differ between elderly and younger caregivers in supporting dying patients with cancer? An Italian study. Am. J. Hosp. Palliat. Care **37**, 576–581 (2020). https://doi.org/10.1177/1049909119890840

19. Edwards, A.B., Zarit, S.H., Stephens, M.A.P., Townsend, A.: Employed family caregivers of cognitively impaired elderly: an examination of role strain and depressive symptoms. Aging Ment. Health **6**, 55–61 (2002). https://doi.org/10.1080/13607860120101149

20. Plöthner, M., Schmidt, K., de Jong, L., Zeidler, J., Damm, K.: Needs and preferences of informal caregivers regarding outpatient care for the elderly: a systematic literature review. BMC Geriatr. **19**, 82 (2019). https://doi.org/10.1186/s12877-019-1068-4

21. Rossi Ferrario, S., Zotti, A.M., Ippoliti, M., Zotti, P.: Caregiving-related needs analysis: a proposed model reflecting current research and socio-political developments. Health Soc. Care Community **11**, 103–110 (2003). https://doi.org/10.1046/j.1365-2524.2003.00410.x

22. Sousa, L., Gemito, L., Ferreira, R., Pinho, L., Fonseca, C., Lopes, M.: Programs addressed to family caregivers/informal caregivers needs: systematic review protocol. J. Personalized Med. **12**, 145 (2022). https://doi.org/10.3390/jpm12020145

23. Fusco, F., Marsilio, M., Guglielmetti, C.: Co-production in health policy and management: a comprehensive bibliometric review. BMC Health Serv. Res. **20**, 504 (2020). https://doi.org/10.1186/s12913-020-05241-2

24. Barello, S., Castiglioni, C., Bonanomi, A., Graffigna, G.: The Caregiving Health Engagement Scale (CHE-s): development and initial validation of a new questionnaire for measuring family caregiver engagement in healthcare. BMC Public Health **19**, 1562 (2019). https://doi.org/10.1186/s12889-019-7743-8

25. Guida, E., et al.: An Italian pilot study of a psycho-social intervention to support family caregivers' engagement in taking care of patients with complex care needs: the Engage-in-Caring project. BMC Health Serv. Res. **19**, 541 (2019). https://doi.org/10.1186/s12913-019-4365-x

26. Mulvale, G., Robert, G.: Special issue- engaging vulnerable populations in the co-production of public services. Int. J. Public Adm. **44**, 711–714 (2021). https://doi.org/10.1080/01900692.2021.1921941

27. Palumbo, R.: Contextualizing co-production of health care: a systematic literature review. Int. J. Public Sect. Manag. **29**, 72–90 (2016). https://doi.org/10.1108/IJPSM-07-2015-0125

28. Loeffler, E., Bovaird, T.: User and community co-production of public services: what does the evidence tell us? Int. J. Public Adm. **39**, 1006–1019 (2016). https://doi.org/10.1080/01900692.2016.1250559

29. Loeffler, M.: Citizen Engagement. Routledge (2015). https://doi.org/10.4324/9781315693279-25

30. Bovaird, T., Loeffler, E.: Public Management and Governance. Routledge (2015)

31. Le Cam, Y., Bolz-Johnson, M.: Expert by experience: valuing patient engagement in healthcare. In: Pomey, M.-P., Denis, J.-L., Dumez, V. (eds.) Patient Engagement. OBH, pp. 233–267. Springer, Cham (2019). https://doi.org/10.1007/978-3-030-14101-1_9

32. Loeffler, E., Bovaird, T.: From participation to co-production: widening and deepening the contributions of citizens to public services and outcomes. In: Ongaro, E., van Thiel, S. (eds.) The Palgrave Handbook of Public Administration and Management in Europe, pp. 403–423. Palgrave Macmillan, London (2018). https://doi.org/10.1057/978-1-137-55269-3_21

33. Frow, P., McColl-Kennedy, J.R., Hilton, T., Davidson, A., Payne, A., Brozovic, D.: Value propositions: a service ecosystems perspective. Mark. Theory **14**, 327–351 (2014). https://doi.org/10.1177/1470593114534346

34. Osborne, S.P.: From public service-dominant logic to public service logic: are public service organizations capable of co-production and value co-creation? Public Manag. Rev. **20**, 225–231 (2018). https://doi.org/10.1080/14719037.2017.1350461

35. Clark, J.K.: Designing public participation: managing problem settings and social equity. Public Adm. Rev. **78**, 362–374 (2018). https://doi.org/10.1111/puar.12872

36. Fung, A.: Varieties of participation in complex governance. Public Adm. Rev. **66**, 66–75 (2006). https://doi.org/10.1111/j.1540-6210.2006.00667.x

37. Lalani, M., Bussu, S., Marshall, M.: Understanding integrated care at the frontline using organisational learning theory: a participatory evaluation of multi-professional teams in East London. Soc. Sci. Med. **262**, 113254 (2020). https://doi.org/10.1016/j.socscimed.2020.113254

38. Weaver, B.: Co-production, governance and practice: the dynamics and effects of User Voice Prison Councils. Soc. Policy Adm. **53**, 249–264 (2019). https://doi.org/10.1111/spol.12442

39. Alonso, J.M., Andrews, R., Clifton, J., Diaz-Fuentes, D.: Factors influencing citizens' co-production of environmental outcomes: a multi-level analysis. Public Manag. Rev. **21**, 1620–1645 (2019). https://doi.org/10.1080/14719037.2019.1619806

40. Gheduzzi, E., Masella, C., Morelli, N., Graffigna, G.: How to prevent and avoid barriers in co-production with family carers living in rural and remote area: an Italian case study. Res. Involvement Engagement **7**, 16 (2021). https://doi.org/10.1186/s40900-021-00259-0

41. Burgess, R.A., Choudary, N.: Time is on our side: operationalising 'phase zero' in coproduction of mental health services for marginalised and underserved populations in London. Int. J. Public Adm. **44**, 753–766 (2021). https://doi.org/10.1080/01900692.2021.1913748

42. Eriksson, E.M.: Representative co-production: broadening the scope of the public service logic. Public Manag. Rev. **21**, 291–314 (2019). https://doi.org/10.1080/14719037.2018.1487575

43. Liabo, K., et al.: Public involvement in health research: what does 'good' look like in practice? Res. Involvement Engagement **6**, 11 (2020). https://doi.org/10.1186/s40900-020-0183-x

44. Dovey-Pearce, G., Walker, S., Fairgrieve, S., Parker, M., Rapley, T.: The burden of proof: the process of involving young people in research. Health Expect. **22**, 465–474 (2019). https://doi.org/10.1111/hex.12870

45. Nygren, J.M., Lindberg, S., Wärnestål, P., Svedberg, P.: Involving children with cancer in health promotive research: a case study describing why, what, and how. JMIR Res. Protoc. **6**, e19 (2017). https://doi.org/10.2196/resprot.7094

46. Rayment, J., Lanlehin, R., McCourt, C., Husain, S.M.: Involving seldom-heard groups in a PPI process to inform the design of a proposed trial on the use of probiotics to prevent preterm birth: a case study. Res. Involvement Engagement **3**, 11 (2017). https://doi.org/10.1186/s40900-017-0061-3

Live Classification of Similar Arm Motion Sequences Using Smartwatches

Sergio Staab$^{(\boxtimes)}$, Lukas Bröning, Johannes Luderschmidt, and Ludger Martin

RheinMain University of Applied Sciences, 65195 Wiesbaden, Hesse, Germany
{Sergio.Staab,Lukas.Broening,Johannes.Luderschmidt,
Ludger.Martin}@hs-rm.de

Abstract. This work provides an approach to monitoring the activities of people with dementia. Classification of daily activities helps automate caregivers' documentation of activities and can provide information about disease progression and disease-related changes. The prototype developed combines smartwatch technology with a neural network to classify activities in real time. A smartwatch offers the opportunity to integrate sensor technology into a patient's daily life without disruption.

To identify promising combinations of sensor data, accelerometer, gyroscope, gravity, and attitude data are sampled 20 Hz (Hz) and sent to a recurrent neural network called Long Short-Term Memory (LSTM) for real-time classification. In this work, we systematically compare how well an LSTM works in combination with different sensor combinations in detecting different activities. Using triaxial user acceleration, gravity, position, and gyroscope data, the trained model achieves over 90% accuracy.

The implemented real-time classification provides a direct statement at which time and with which probability one of the four activities was carried out.

This approach performs significantly better than previous tests using classification algorithms and also stands out from similar approaches in the literature. We achieve flexible, location-independent classification of very similar activities based on smartwatch sensor data. In doing so, the classification of the novel prototype is performed in real-time. This also provides room for interpretation of how the knowledge gained can be used to detect motor skills in the care of patients with neurological diseases.

Keywords: Human Motion Analysis · Machine Learning

1 Introduction

The goal behind this work is to facilitate the daily routine of caregivers. In cooperation with two dementia care homes, it has been found that the documentation of motor skills is an indicator for the detection of disease-related changes. The documentation of the patients' activities depending on the degree of mobility

Q. Gao and J. Zhou (Eds.): HCII 2023, LNCS 14043, pp. 357–376, 2023.
https://doi.org/10.1007/978-3-031-34917-1_25

is very time-consuming. We have developed an approach to digitize it. In the form of a nursing documentation platform in which activities can be recorded by ticking next to a list of activities, according to Staab et al. [29]. However, although such a platform makes caregivers' jobs easier, the work still needs to be done manually, which still results in a heavy workload, Staab et al. [28] said. In addition, there is a risk that staff may not notice certain activities due to the high workload. The focus of this work is on live classification arm movement sequences, from four activities. Based on feedback from the care teams, the following four activities were identified: drinking, eating, using the phone, and blowing the Nose. To be clear, the arm movement sequences are nearly identical for all four activities, making classification considerably more difficult. We talk about arm movement sequences in the classification analysis, as these are what our network recognizes, since each arm movement sequence then targets exactly one activity, the two terms can be interpreted as synonyms in this work. In this paper, we present an approach to automatically detect specific activities by having smartwatches send live sensor data to a recurrent neural network that directly analyzes it. After consultation with different care teams, a smartwatch offers the possibility of integrating sensor technology into a patient's daily routine without disturbing them, as many patients wear watches without. Nadal et al. [24] substantiated this statement, interacting with smartwatches reduces the perceived sense of shame during treatment because monitoring occurs unconsciously. Liu [21] and Guo [14] also argue that wearable health monitoring provides an opportunity to achieve effective collaboration among hospitals, communities, families, and individuals. Smartwatch-generated health data are seen by the majority of clinical staff as a way to reduce workload, according to Alpert et al. [1].

This paper makes the following contributions:

- an approach to live recognition of very similar arm motion sequences with smartwatches
- an insight into which sensor types are most promising in monitoring near-identical arm motion sequences
- a way to visualize the detection of activities live

This work is organized as follows. Section 2 presents related work in the field of health information technologies, human activity recognition, and recurrent neural networks. Section 3 describes the project structure, watchOS application, sensor technology, and then elaborates on sensor data aggregation and machine learning tool. Section 4 describes and discusses the activation detection process and results. Section 5 summarizes the work and takes a look into the future.

2   Related Work

The following is a listing of related work on health informatics, recurrent neural networks, and long short-term memory network. All of these topics are in the context of human motion analysis using wearables. We then discuss the state of research and the added value of this work.

2.1 Health Informatics

The technological progress of the twenty-first century has given rise to new smart devices such as smartwatches, whose use in everyday life is increasing, according to Lopes de Faria and Vieira [13]. In this regard, according to a statistic [30], 44% say they use their smartwatch for health reasons.

Alpert et al. [1] summarize in their paper that smartwatch-generated health data is seen by the majority of clinical staff as a way to reduce workload, motivate of patients, and improve the relationship with the patient.

In the work of Vijayan et al. [32], it is highlighted that the accuracy of step count and heartbeat measurement is dependent on the device and its price range. Thereby, all tested devices have a precision of 92% up to 99%, depending on the device and application.

Wearable health monitoring systems have become one of the emerging research areas attracting much attention today, according to Liu [21]. Brezmes et al. [8] have successfully measured various human activities using an accelerometer. Shoaib et al. [27] have used both smartphones and smartwatches together to identify various daily human activities.

In addition to activity classification, the rapid progress of the use of smartwatches in the health sector should also be highlighted. Various works exist in this regard, such as that of Bienhaus [7], in which he suggests the basics and the application of smartwatches to the reader. The author discusses the rapid development of smartwatches in the health sector. It also becomes evident that smartwatches make a positive contribution to improving the quality of life due to their health features and are therefore becoming increasingly attractive.

To understand the growing interest in smartwatches for healthcare, England and Azzopardi-Muscat's paper published in The European Journal of Public Health 2017 [12] is ideally suited. The authors reflect the demographic changes in Europe. Statistics are used to provide clear evidence of a society that continues to age. Across topics in 2019, the authors Bräunel and Häber [9] write about the possible future of smartwatches in application among people of high age. The potential of smartwatches in terms of positively enhancing quality of life specifically for long-term care patients is evident in this book. In 2018, Askari, Huldtgren and IJsselsteijn [5] researched the acceptance of smartwatches among seniors. It is clear that this is not true due to lack of education and proximity of the technologies by the smartwatch providers, although as previously mentioned, a healthier lifestyle can be achieved with the help of smartwatches. This becomes clear by means of field tests on suitable test persons.

2.2 Recurrent Neural Networks

Lipton et al. [20] in their work describe that RNNs allow sequential data processing because unlike feedforward neural networks, RNNs are able to store information that was calculated from previous inputs, thus allowing them to model sequences of data that correlate to each other.

Bhattacharjee et al. [6] compare the performance of a wide variety of supervised learning methods in the context of human activity recognition. The authors show that RNNs provide the highest accuracy of 97.55%. Support Vector Machine, perceptron neural network and back-propagation neural network on the other hand, achieved a maximum accuracy of 59.11%, 94.10%, and 97.40%, respectively. The authors use a dataset collected with a Samsung Galaxy S II smartphone 50 Hz, consisting of the acceleration, as well as angular velocity data from the smartphone.

The work of Mauldin et al. [22] also shows that RNNs are excellent for the task of classifying human motion activity. The authors of this work developed a system to detect falls using a smartwatch. In doing so, they show that compared to Support Vector Machines and Naive Bayes, an RNN is able to provide a better detection rate, as well as better adaptability to new users. The authors use a dataset of 7 volunteers, with ages ranging from 21 to 55 years, which was recorded at 31.25 Hz as training and test data. The classification of the activity is run on the user's smartphone, thus a simple network architecture with gated recurrent units (GRU) was chosen. Using this neural network, the authors are able to achieve up to 85% accuracy in detecting falls, while Naive Bayes can only achieve 65% and Support Vector Machines up to 73% accuracy. Both of these works show that RNNs are well suited for human activity detection and classification, each providing the highest accuracy in classification tasks, compared to other methods.

However, a particular challenge in the use of RNNs is the vanishing gradient problem described by Hochreiter [17]. Here the influence of the gradients of the network drops very quickly. Thus, the network is not able to learn longer temporal correlations, rendering it unsuited for many classification tasks. Hochreiter proposes several ways to solve the vanishing gradient problem in his work, including the use of a LSTM instead of a standard RNN. In Hochreiter's experiments, it is notable that LSTMs can produce particularly accurate results, while at the same time, they also learn faster than other proposed methods.

2.3 Long Short-Term Memory (LSTM)

Ashry et al. [4] developed a bidirectional long short-term memory (Bi-LSTM) that continuously detects human activity and incorporates future context unlike standard LSTM. The deep learning model processes sensor data streams from Series 4 Apple Watches that include triaxial accelerometer, gyroscope, and gravity readings and rotational displacement data at a sampling rate 50 Hz. The database was created by 25 subjects performing ten daily activities with a smartwatch on their right hand, the authors say. The ten activities include, among others, brushing teeth, eating, drinking, and combing hair. To prepare the data for the Bi-LSTM, Ashry et al. use a sliding window of 10 s that segments the data as time series data for input. Finally, the online system developed by Ashry et al. allows real-time classification of the ten activities with 91% accuracy.

Mekruksavanich et al. [23] investigated activity recognition based on smartwatch sensor data. For this purpose, the authors used a hybrid LSTM network that combines an LSTM with a Convolutional Neural Network (CNN). The authors used the publicly available WISDM dataset as the data basis. This comprises triaxial accelerometer and gyroscope data from smartwatches recorded by 51 volunteers performing 18 predefined activities at a sampling rate 20 Hz. Activities include various physical efforts such as walking, jogging, and climbing stairs, as well as eating various meals such as soup, sandwiches, and chips, and other activities such as writing or typing, among others. Mekruksavanich et al. find that CNN-LSTM provide better activity recognition and outperform alternative models in comparison. In their study, the authors achieve 96.2% accuracy in activity recognition.

Oluwalade et al. [25] also used the WISDM dataset in their study, in which they compared the performance of LSTM, Bi-LSTM as well as CNN-LSTM and CNN. To prepare the data for the LSTM, Oluwalade et al. performed scaling of the data set. Looking at the recognition accuracy of the LSTM, an average accuracy of 84.1% was achieved for the six non-hand-oriented activities. Hand-oriented activities, nine in total, were recognized with an average accuracy of 80.7%.

This work highlights the potential that smartwatches offer for the health sector. RNNs are ideally suited for the task of classifying human locomotor activities, to which LSTMs are successfully used for classifying general activities.

However, the state of research is fraught with four critical issues:

- The tracking of movements by means of cameras cannot be realized in everyday life.
- The tracking of movements by means of different sensors on the whole body cannot be realized in everyday life.
- Classifying motion sequences like walking, sleeping, or sitting is far too simple and not sufficient to cover everyday activities.
- Achieving flexible, location-independent data analysis by classifying activities based on sensor data in real-time. Sending smartwatch data to a server, processing the data, classifying it using an LSTM, allowing the real-time recognition and visualization of a subject's activities.

Accordingly, our work is an extension of the previously mentioned work that solves the three problems. In the following we will explain our prototype in more detail.

3   Project Structure

In this work, a watchOS application is implemented based on this sensor technology, which enables the aggregation and provision of movement and health data via an interface. The Apple Watch Series 6 is used, which is equipped with the latest sensor technology.

According to Apple Support [2], the Apple Watch Series 6 is equipped with a certain number of sensors that form the basis for tracking interaction and health data.

From the previous chapter, it is clear that general activity detection is possible using accelerometers and gyroscopes. The work of Weiss et al. [33] confirms that the aforementioned sensors can be used individually and in combination to detect a user's movements.

Since reliable arm motion detection is the goal of this work, it is desirable to collect motion data as fine-grained as possible. For this purpose, in addition to the basic data of the accelerometer and the gyroscope, further sensors and attributes are added and it is also examined whether more accurate measurements and a more reliable arm motion detection can be achieved by combining these.

This paper presents a standalone, state-of-the-art watchOS application for the Apple Watch Series 6 that offers various functionalities. The application includes methods for retrieving motion and health data, a temporary backup to the smartwatch memory, methods for tagging data, and an interface for exchanging sensor data with a web server via WebSocket. In case of complications, the backup methods can initiate a resend of the sensor data generated in a session.

Figure 1 provides an overview of the work. Data generation, data handling, and data saving are part of the tracking, the visualization of the labeled data and the classification of the data.

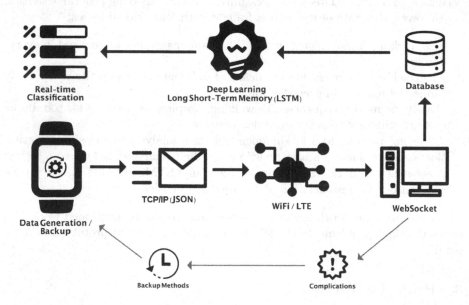

Fig. 1. Overview from data generation to live classification

The sensor technology in focus of this work consists of the accelerometer, gyroscope, magnetometer, position sensor and heart rate sensor. The different sensor systems are described below.

3.1 Smartwatch Sensor Technology

The application implemented in this project generates data based on various built-in sensors. The focus here is particularly on the accelerometer, gyroscope, magnetometer, altimeter, pedometer, GPS, heart rate and blood oxygen sensor as well as microphone, all of which can be controlled by the application.

Accelerometers are electromechanical devices that detect accelerations due to physical effects and convert them into electrical signals for further processing, according to Hering and Schönfelder [16]. They are used to measure instantaneous acceleration in multidimensional space [3], which describes the rate of change of velocity over time [26].

In the case of the Apple Watch Series 6, a triaxial sensor is installed, which, according to Apple Developer Documentation, provides acceleration values in three dimensions and thus in each direction of the orthogonal axes X, Y and Z (see Fig. 2). The unit of the values is g, where 1 g represents the gravitational acceleration caused by the Earth's gravitational field, which is standardized to be 9.81 m/s^2 in one direction on the Earth's surface.

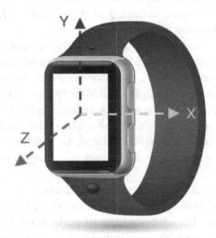

Fig. 2. Visualization of the three axes of the acceleration sensor of a smartwatch. Source: Cole et al., 2017 [10]

For the accelerometer, as with some other sensors on the smartwatch, both raw and processed data are provided to the developer. Raw data is data that is provided without prior correction. Accordingly, confounding factors and external influences such as acceleration due to gravity are included in the acceleration values of the three axes. According to the Apple Developer Documentation, the processed data is acceleration data that has been freed from distortions. The values are therefore already adjusted for distortions such as acceleration caused by gravity. With respect to the accelerometer, the processed data map the user-induced acceleration, but at the same time provide the extracted gravity values in three dimensions. In this work, it is generally decided to query processed data instead of collecting raw data from the sensor system. This is because, unlike querying individual raw data from each sensor, querying processed data returns an entire CMDeviceMotion object that contains all the motion data and thus data from the accelerometer, the gyroscope, as well as combined data such as the device orientation, also called attitude, and the magnetic field vectors.

An additional query of the raw data of the individual sensors can thus be avoided. The undistorted data also makes it easier to handle the motion data, since only the user-initiated motion can be worked with, and interfering factors have already been subtracted.

According to Hering and Schönfelder [16], gyroscopes are angular rate sensors that measure the rotational speeds of a body. The rotational speed is measured as an angle in radians per second, rad/s, about a respective axis by the gyroscope, which, like the accelerometer of the Apple Watch, measures the rotational values in three dimensions.

According to Henriksen et al. [15], smartwatches in general mainly use acceleration data for activity recording and health analysis. Accordingly, accelerometer data specifically enables the detection and analysis of physical activities, sleep, and movement patterns, counting of steps, and analysis of a user's energy consumption and fitness status.

Although acceleration data consequently already appear promising, the data basis is to be significantly expanded in the present project. In addition to accelerometer and gyroscope data, the processed data object also provides combined data for device orientation, also called 'attitude'. These are the aggregated values of pitch, roll and yaw as specific attitude angles to describe the orientation of a device in three-dimensional space. Thus, the above three values reflect the position of a smartwatch in space relative to a defined reference frame. The rotation values are specified in radians rad and range from $-\pi$ to π around a specific axis.

While gyroscope data describe an instantaneous angular velocity, attitude values consequently represent the steady orientation of the device relative to a certain reference frame. For this reason, attitude is evaluated as promising for the present work, as it provides meaningful values independent of active arm movements of a user and thus enables a steady position determination in space. Consequently, this can serve a more fine-grained detection of arm movements.

To the best of its knowledge, Apple does not disclose details about the so-called attitude. However, a commonly used method to calculate it is sensor fusion. Wu et al. [34] describe a corresponding method for determining the attitude by combining multiple sensors and applying mathematical methods like Kalman or complementary filters. Here, accelerometer, gyroscope, and magnetometer contribute to the mathematical calculation of the device attitude. Gravity acceleration can be used to determine where 'down' is, and magnetic field vectors can be used to determine where north is from the device's point of view. The gyroscope rotation values are integrated to estimate the deviation from the previous position. The combination of multiple sensors is thus used to calculate the attitude, using the strengths of each sensor to compensate for or minimize the weaknesses of each sensor, according to Wu et al. [34].

Since an accelerometer picks up all forces, such as vibrations, this can lead to undesirable interference. Gyroscopes can also provide erroneous values due to the so-called gyroscope drift. However, the accelerometer and magnetometer data can compensate for this drift. Disturbances of the magnetic fields, on the other hand, can strongly affect the measurements of the magnetometer. Magnetic perturbations only affect the Yaw value, since pitch and roll are derived from the accelerometer and rotation values only, while for yaw the magnetometer is used to correct the heading. Wu et al. [34] show that despite strong magnetic distortions, robust yaw values can be calculated using special algorithms.

A magnetometer is a measuring instrument for measuring magnetic flux density in T (Tesla) and is measured from 10^{-15} T to 10, so Loreit et al. [31]. It is assumed that in the Apple Watch, the magnetometer, accelerometer, and gyroscope all contribute to the mathematical calculation of the device's attitude.

Data queries are also implemented for a number of other sensors that can provide additional information about the smartwatch user. These include querying data from the altimeter to determine the device's air pressure and altitude changes, querying data from the GPS sensor to determine the current coordinates, altitude meters and movement speed, and device orientation. In addition, data from the pedometer provides information on the number of steps, distance traveled and walking speed, while the magnetometer is used to record magnetic field vectors. On the health data side, the optical or electrical heart sensor can be used to measure heart rate or activity, while the blood oxygen sensor can be used to measure blood oxygen saturation. Additionally, measurements through the smartwatch's microphone could provide information about what activities are being operated when there is no movement and no clearly classifiable posture of the smartwatch. The developed application is configurable and extensible so that additional sensors and attributes can be integrated in the future as needed.

In this paper, we will limit ourselves to a selection of sensor data, including user-initiated acceleration, acceleration due to gravity, gyroscope, and attitude values.

According to Apple Developer Documentation, the services provided by the Apple-provided framework called Core Motion allow the user to control the sensor technology used to collect motion-related data, configure data queries, and access the hardware-generated data. There are two ways to access the processed data. On the one hand, the motion data can be retrieved exactly when it is needed. On the other hand, the core motion framework provides a service that allows continuous retrieval of motion data at defined time intervals.

Since the goal of this work is a continuous data stream, continuous retrieval is consequently implemented. This means that all motion data received at a given frequency during a query is continuously acquired.

Continuous polling of motion data takes place at an individually adjustable time interval, the frequency. The maximum frequency 100 Hz when using an Apple Watch Series 6. Thus, a maximum of 100 motion data objects can be generated per second. At this point, it must be questioned which frequency of the query meets the requirements of this work. If more objects are generated than required, this leads to a noticeable increase in the load on the CPU and battery due to the increased number of queries, in addition to the redundancies. In this work, therefore, a standard frequency 20 Hz is initially specified, especially since, according to Dadafshar [11], the natural movements of a human do not exceed 12 20 Hz.

3.2   Long Short-Term Memory Neural Network

Long short-term memory (LSTM) originally dates back to the work of Hochreiter and Schmidhuber [18] and represents a special architecture of an artificial recurrent neural network (RNN). A typical LSTM memory cell has several gates and parameters. The behavior of each memory cell can be controlled by these. Through the activation function of the gates, the state of each memory cell can be controlled. The central elements of an LSTM memory cell are, in short, an input gate, a forget gate, and an output gate, as well as an activation function. With the LSTM, Hochreiter and Schmidhuber attempted to solve the vanishing gradient problem, which prevents temporal dependencies from being captured over longer context windows.

An LSTM is particularly suited to process sequential streams of sensor data due to a flexible gating mechanism, according to Ashry et al. [4]. In particular, according to Ashry et al., the key advantage over comparable machine learning models is that an LSTM considers the temporal context of the sensor data. According to Oluwalade et al. [25], the neural network architecture is designed to learn time-related dependencies and remember significant sequences.

The present work also aims to find out how accurately the activities of dementia patients can be detected with a standard LSTM. For this purpose, a dataset was created specifically for this use case. The data set for the present project was generated by ten users who each labeled the four similar activities of drinking, eating, talking on the phone, and blowing their noses 40 times each over a 10-second period.

First, the data was preprocessed, and the relevant data was extracted from the dataset, which includes other activities and sensor data as well. A check was made to ensure that the data set was balanced and that the activities were each equally distributed. The classes were recorded about the same number of times, making them balanced. In a train-test split, it was decided to contrast users. With an appropriate split of users between test and training data, a 75:25 split was realized. Furthermore, a normalization of the data was performed. The normalization converts the data relatively into a range from 0 to 1 using an MinMaxScaler. According to Laurent et al. [19], this allows lower training times to be achieved, for instance. Since the LSTM network can only accept numeric values, the labels were encoded accordingly. To provide the LSTM with data, a time series is generated from the data set. Batches for training and validation with a predefined window size are generated from the individual samples. An appropriate window size of 120 was evaluated by experimentation and will be considered in more detail in the results.

Architecturally, the input layer appropriately consists of 120 units, followed by a flatten layer, a dense layer with 64 units, and another dense output layer with four units for the number of classes. The first dense layer contains the activation function Relu, the last one the Softmax. In addition, the Adam optimizer was used in the compilation. The LSTM was implemented with Tensorflow 2.4.0. With all twelve features, the respective triaxial user acceleration, gravity, attitude, and gyroscope data, the trained model achieves more than 90% accuracy when trained over 35 epochs.

The best model was exported in a hdf5 file, so that the model can be further used for the targeted classification of sensor data in real-time on a server. Accordingly, the model is loaded on the server and can accept data in real-time by pre-processing it for prediction in a manner analogous to the approach used for training, ultimately serving as input. Finally, an output stream is obtained that indicates at which point in time and with which probability one of the four activities was performed. For the described process, Flask in particular plays a central role. Flask is a popular web framework written in Python. It allowed us to develop a web service to quickly control and monitor the LSTM while providing a wide range of features.

3.3 Visualization

In order to create a classification for data in real time, the user visits a web page, that renders a basic interface for the user to select his username and delay between classifications. The user is then able to start the classification process. After the page is served to the client, communication between client and server happens exclusively via asynchronous web sockets. Once the user starts the classification of his live data, the individual classes and their respective probabilities are sent to the client as a JSON object repeatedly, after being classified on the server using the exported model. The client then displays the results in a bar chart on the web page.

Such a graph is exemplified in Fig. 3. The Y-axis represents the classification probability, the X-axis the timestamp of the classifications. Each classified activity is assigned a unique color in this diagram, which is used to color the associated bars. Since each classification contains the probability for each of the four classes, the probabilities of all four charts in a classification amounts to 100%. Using the bar chart, the user is thus able to track the classification of his activity data in near real time.

4   Activity Recognition

To train the previously described LSTM model, ten subjects were included, each generating 40 label sequences, i.e., 400 labels.

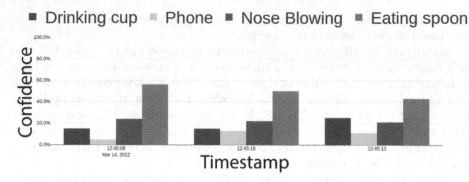

Fig. 3. Example of a graph generated by our LSTM-System

4.1   Movements

Figure 4 shows different arm position sequences of the nearly identical motion sequences (drinking, eating, telephoning and nose blowing).

The red arrows indicate the range of motion of the arm and wrist. Especially here it is noticeable that the movements of eating, drinking, phoning, and nose blowing are almost identical.

The arm moves toward the face and simply the position of the hand provides information about the different activity. This makes the recognition of the respective activity so complicated. In the following, we will elaborate a bit more on the movement sequences (see Fig. 4).

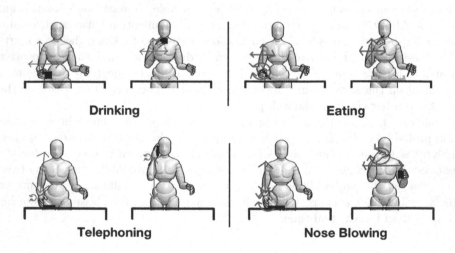

Fig. 4. Arm position sequences

In the following, Fig. 5 shows the previously described motion sequences based on all sensor systems for the four motion sequences overlapping color-coded: drinking (blue), eating (turquoise), nose blowing (orange), and telephoning (red).

It becomes evident here how important each individual sensor can be depending on the movement. Especially the sensors of the arm rotation detection (gravity, gyroscope, and attitude) play an important role.

Each sequence consists of arm positions and each activity was performed for 10 s. The measurement rate 20 Hz results in 10 (seconds)*10 (subjects)*20 (Hz)*4 (motion sequences) = 160,000 data sets per test series. The subjects always wore the watch on their dominant right hand. The test and training data were created separately, i.e., the data of one subject were compared with the data of the other nine subjects. The data range from 0 to 200 records, resulting from the previously described calculation 20 Hz*10 s label time.

Drinking from a cup starts with picking up the cup, a steady movement of the arm towards the mouth and a short dwell in front of the face. During the drinking movement, the hand tilts more and more slightly towards the face, from almost 90° at the beginning to 150° when the cup is empty. The movement ends as it began with a possibly now faster movement towards the table. Figure 5 shows the characteristics of this motion sequence. A clear shift in gravity can be seen as soon as the cup has to be tilted.

When eating with a spoon, starting with the dipping of the spoon, the hand is slowly guided towards the mouth. This is followed by a short dwell time with a slight inclination towards the mouth of 90° to 120°. Finally, there is a rapid lowering of the spoon. Figure 5 shows the characteristics of this motion sequence. The shift in attitude can be seen several times in this motion sequence, although it is significantly smaller.

When using a cell phone, the first movement, assuming that the phone is lying on the table, is to reach for the phone itself. In the following, the phone is picked up by a movement of the arm and hand, turned towards the subject and then moved towards the head. After that, the phone remains on the ear and, in our scenario, is not picked up again until the end of the label. Figure 5 shows the characteristics of this motion sequence. Picking up and examining the screen, which requires a movement of the hand, can be clearly seen here at the beginning. The subsequent resting phase is also a good indicator.

Nose blowing again follows a similar pattern. The paper tissue is taken from the table and then shaken up with the dominant hand. The paper tissue is taken from the table and then shaken up with the dominant hand, where the sensory system is attached. This is followed by the movement towards the head. The blowing is done only by holding the paper in front of the nose and one or two short movements towards the nose. In our scenario, the tissue is not put down again. Figure 5 shows the characteristics of this motion sequence. Here, after a quiet phase, the movement of shaking up the tissue stands out, followed by a quiet movement of the wrist in all directions. Especially with the similar movement of nose blowing, it becomes clear that the more unique a movement is, the easier it becomes to classify it. If one thinks of previous work that distinguished between walking and sitting, the degree of difficulty of the present work becomes clear.

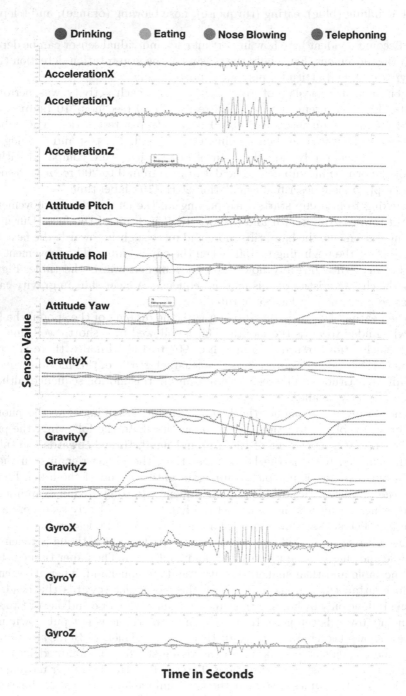

Fig. 5. Arm position sequences - four motion sequences (Color figure online)

It can be seen well in the example of a sensor that not all movements stand out well. Obviously, the sensor that contains only 1/4 of the used sensor technology and not each of the four movements is not the optimal sensor. Depending on the movement, the combination of different sensor technology is crucial.

The following compares the validation capability of different sensors with different window sizes based on the four movements.

4.2 Results

In order to analyze with which data, the LSTM achieves the best prediction accuracy, different sensor data combinations were tested (see Table 1).

Table 1. Comparison of the model accuracy of different sensor combinations for the classification of the activities eating, drinking, telephoning, and nose blowing

Sensor combination	Validation accuracy
Acceleration	25.27%
Attitude	88.93%
Gyro	25.42%
Gravity	84.66%
Acceleration, Attitude	63.62%
Acceleration, Gyro	25.72%
Acceleration, Gravity	84.66%
Attitude, Gyro	87.46%
Attitude, Gravity	88.82%
Gyro, Gravity	84.03%
Attitude, Gravity, Acceleration	80.97%
Attitude, Gyro, Acceleration	84.1%
Attitude, Gyro, Gravity	89.14%
Acceleration, Gyro, Gravity	82.94%
All four sensors	90.59%

Firstly, the sensors were tested individually, i.e., their three characteristics were used for training and testing. It is noticeable that both the acceleration and gyroscope data alone do not provide sufficient results. The accuracy in each case is just over 25%, which is similar to the probability of simply guessing the correct activity. Attitude and Gravity, on the other hand, are each significantly more informative, at 88% and 84%, respectively, when the sensors are used alone. All other combinations are in the range of about 82% to 90% with the exception of the combination of Acceleration and Position, which only reaches a bit more than 63%. However, the best accuracy was achieved with the combination of all

four sensors, respectively all twelve features, showing a validation accuracy of
90.59%.

Before investigating the different sensor combinations, different window sizes
used to feed the LSTM were tested with all four sensors, thus all twelve features.
The tests were performed with six different window sizes, the results of which
are recorded in Table 2. This revealed that a window size of 6 s, or 120 samples,
produces the best results for the data used, at 90.59%. Both a higher and lower
window size could not achieve better results.

Table 2. Comparison of the evaluation metric validation accuracy at different window
sizes for all four sensors.

Window size	Accuracy	Epochs (50 total)
30 (1.5s)	74.94%	22
60 (3s)	81.87%	46
100 (5s)	83.74%	45
120 (6s)	90.59%	35
200 (10s)	87.56%	12
360 (18s)	86.68%	23

4.3   Discussion

Based on the research presented here, the interaction of accelerometer, attitude,
gyroscope, and gravity proves to be the strongest sensor combination for classifying the activities investigated.

It should be noted that as a sole sensor, the triaxial data of the Attitude (X,
Y, and Z) perform best.

The test series with the heart rate hardly affected the results, so we decided
to leave it out of the results. The heart rate plays a minor role in arm position
sequences so far. Later, however, heart rate could play an interesting role.

Looking more closely at Table 1, it can be seen that both the accelerometer
and gyroscope data alone do not provide sufficient results. With hardly more
than 25% accuracy each, the prediction probability is barely above the probability of guessing the correct activity. This may be due in particular to the fact
that these are instantaneous sensor data values, which, in contrast to Attitude
and Gravity, cannot permanently describe a position of the smartwatch in the
room. Attitude and Gravity alone achieve values of almost 89% and 85%, respectively, and are thus much more meaningful. It is noticeable that especially the
combinations which include both Attitude and Gravity show a higher accuracy,
which again supports the statement from before regarding the informative value
of the individual sensors.

It is shown that the prototype can classify even very similar movements with
a high probability. Thus, the contribution of this work is to gain knowledge

about detection and classification algorithms that allow a solid prediction of very similar motion sequences.

A crucial point is the informative value of the sensor technology that continuously measures the posture of the hand. It has simply become clear that the movement patterns of the hand have significantly more significance for similar movements than the movement patterns of the arm itself.

This also supports the results of Xia and Sugiura [35], who showed that simply increasing the number of sensors for static activities does not lead to a significant increase in the recognition rate. The movement and rotation of the hand must be tracked in detail.

This knowledge can now be transported into further work with the goal of identifying motion sequences over a desired period of time.

Especially during the development of the LSTM, the web service created served as a central tool for visualizing the results and performance of the model. It allows the model to be tested with live data from the real world, rather than having to rely on previously generated data sets in a database. In addition, the Flask-framework makes it possible to easily extend the visualization capabilities in the future.

5   Conclusion

In this work, a systematic comparison was performed to determine the best combinations of sensors and window size (size of the data stream for classification input) of a Long Short-Term Memory network for identifying the arm motion sequences of eating, drinking, phoning, and blowing the nose.

These motion sequences are nearly identical. It was found that the combination of the accelerometer, position sensor, gyroscope, and G-sensor sensor values with a window size of 6 s gave the best performance for 10-second-long labels. The prediction accuracy was 90.59%.

Another finding is that hand motion and rotation play an important role in discriminating similar arm motion sequences. We initially assumed that heart rate and arm movements would provide unique data on the respective activities; however, this assumption was incorrect. Over 90% of the performance was due to hand motion and rotation recognition. This is a critical finding because it implies that more importance must be placed on the sensor values used. The sensor values, especially Attitude and Gravity, are a crucial factor that enables the recognition of nearly identical motion sequences.

Based on this work, it is now possible to develop a system that makes statements about the probability of each activity over a period of several hours, which basically automates or at least significantly supports caregiver documentation. After consultation with two dementia care teams, this would greatly facilitate the review and understanding of the progression of the chronic disease. Such a system would also allow for new approaches to evaluation and long-term documentation.

Future efforts will be to further improve the performance of the LSTM network, in particular to develop and compare different variants. In addition, more daily activities of dementia patients shall be included, as well as a default class (i.e. movements that do not belong to any of the activities relevant for classification).

References

1. Alpert, J.M., et al.: Secondary care provider attitudes towards patient generated health data from smartwatches. NPJ Digit. Med. **3**(3) (2020). https://doi.org/10.1038/s41746-020-0236-4
2. Apple Inc.: Apple watch series 6 - technical specifications (2021). https://support.apple.com/kb/SP826
3. Apple Inc.: Cmmotionmanager — apple developer documentation (2021). https://developer.apple.com/documentation/coremotion/cmmotionmanager. cMMotion-Manager
4. Ashry, S., Ogawa, T., Gomaa, W.: CHARM-deep: continuous human activity recognition model based on deep neural network using IMU sensors of smartwatch. IEEE Sens. J. **20**(15), 8757–8770 (2020)
5. Askari, S.I., Huldtgren, A., IJsselsteijn, W.: Wear it or fear it - exploration of drivers & barriers in smartwatch acceptance by senior citizens. In: Bamidis, P., Ziefle, M., Maciaszek, L. (eds.) Proceedings of the 4th International Conference on Information and Communication Technologies for Ageing Well and e-Health, pp. 26–36. No. 11 in 1, SCITEPRESS - Science and Technology Publications, Funchal, Portugal (2018). https://doi.org/10.5220/0006673000260036
6. Bhattacharjee, S., Kishore, S., Swetapadma, A.: A comparative study of supervised learning techniques for human activity monitoring using smart sensors. In: 2018 Second International Conference on Advances in Electronics, Computers and Communications (ICAECC), pp. 1–4 (2018). https://doi.org/10.1109/ICAECC.2018.8479436
7. Bienhaus, D.: Smartwatch und Wearables im Gesundheitsbereich: Grundlagen und Anwendungen. Gesellschaft für Informatik e.V, Bonn (2016)
8. Brezmes, T., Gorricho, J.-L., Cotrina, J.: Activity recognition from accelerometer data on a mobile phone. In: Omatu, S., et al. (eds.) IWANN 2009. LNCS, vol. 5518, pp. 796–799. Springer, Heidelberg (2009). https://doi.org/10.1007/978-3-642-02481-8_120
9. Bräunel, B., Häber, A.: Wearables – Zukunftstechnologie für die geriatrische Pflege? In: Pfannstiel, M.A., Da-Cruz, P., Mehlich, H. (eds.) Digitale Transformation von Dienstleistungen im Gesundheitswesen VI, pp. 311–332. Springer, Wiesbaden (2019). https://doi.org/10.1007/978-3-658-25461-2_16
10. Cole, C.A., Anshari, D., Lambert, V., Thrasher, J.F., Valafar, H.: Detecting smoking events using accelerometer data collected via smartwatch technology: Validation study. JMIR mHealth and uHealth **5**(12), e189 (2017)
11. Dadafsha, M.: Accelerometer and gyroscopes sensors: operation, sensing, and applications (2014). https://pdfserv.maximintegrated.com/en/an/AN5830.pdf
12. England, K., Azzopardi-Muscat, N.: Demographic trends and public health in Europe. Eur. J. Public Health **27**(suppl._4), 9–13 (2017). https://doi.org/10.1093/eurpub/ckx159

13. Igor Lopes de Faria, V.V.: A comparative study on fitness activity recognition. In: Proceedings of the 24th Brazilian Symposium on Multimedia and the Web, WebMedia 2018, pp. 327–330. Association for Computing Machinery, New York (2018). https://doi.org/10.1145/3243082.3267452

14. Guo, M., Wang, Z.: Segmentation and recognition of human motion sequences using wearable inertial sensors. Multimedia Tools Appl. **77**(16), 21201–21220 (2018). https://doi.org/10.1007/s11042-017-5573-1

15. Henriksen, A., et al.: Using fitness trackers and smartwatches to measure physical activity in research: analysis of consumer wrist-worn wearables. J. Med. Internet Res. **20**(3), e110 (2018)

16. Hering, E., Schönfelder, G. (eds.): Sensoren in Wissenschaft und Technik: Funktionsweise und Einsatzgebiete, IArC monographs on the evaluation of carcinogenic risks to humans, 1st edn, vol. 102. Vieweg+Teubner Verlag, Wiesbaden (2012). https://doi.org/10.1007/978-3-8348-8635-4. https://monographs.iarc.fr/wp-content/uploads/2018/06/mono102.pdf

17. Hochreiter, S.: The vanishing gradient problem during learning recurrent neural nets and problem solutions. Int. J. Uncertain. Fuzziness Knowl.-Based Syst. **6**, 107–116 (1998). https://doi.org/10.1142/S0218488598000094

18. Hochreiter, S., Schmidhuber, J.: Long short-term memory. Neural Comput. **9**(8), 1735–1780 (1997)

19. Laurent, C., Pereyra, G., Brakel, P., Zhang, Y., Bengio, Y.: Batch normalized recurrent neural networks. In: 2016 IEEE International Conference on Acoustics, Speech and Signal Processing (ICASSP), Lujiazui, China, pp. 2657–2661. IEEE (2016). https://doi.org/10.1109/icassp.2016.7472159

20. Lipton, Z.C., Berkowitz, J., Elkan, C.: A critical review of recurrent neural networks for sequence learning. arXiv abs/1506.00019 (2015)

21. Liu, Y., Pharr, M., Salvatore, G.A.: Lab-on-skin: a review of flexible and stretchable electronics for wearable health monitoring. ACS Nano **11**(10), 9614–9635 (2017)

22. Mauldin, T.R., Canby, M.E., Metsis, V., Ngu, A.H.H., Rivera, C.C.: Smartfall: a smartwatch-based fall detection system using deep learning. Sensors **18**(10) (2018). https://doi.org/10.3390/s18103363. https://www.mdpi.com/1424-8220/18/10/3363

23. Mekruksavanich, S., Jitpattanakul, A., Youplao, P., Yupapin, P.: Enhanced hand-oriented activity recognition based on smartwatch sensor data using LSTMs. Symmetry **12**(9), 1570 (2020)

24. Nadal, C., et al.: Integration of a smartwatch within an internet-delivered intervention for depression: protocol for a feasibility randomized controlled trial on acceptance. Contemp. Clin. Trials **103**, 106323 (2021). https://doi.org/10.1016/j.cct.2021.106323. https://www.sciencedirect.com/science/article/pii/S1551714421000598

25. Oluwalade, B., Neela, S., Wawira, J., Adejumo, T., Purkayastha, S.: Human activity recognition using deep learning models on smartphones and smartwatches sensor data. In: Proceedings of the 14th International Joint Conference on Biomedical Engineering Systems and Technologies - HEALTHINF, Vienna, Austria, pp. 645–650. INSTICC, SciTePress (2021). https://doi.org/10.5220/0010325906450650

26. Prechtl, A.: Zeit. raum. bewegung. In: Prechtl, A. (ed.) Vorlesungen über die Grundlagen der Elektrotechnik, pp. 1–14. Springer, Vienna (1994). https://doi.org/10.1007/978-3-7091-3833-5_1

27. Shoaib, M., Bosch, S., Scholten, H., Havinga, P., Incel, O.: Towards detection of bad habits by fusing smartphone and smartwatch sensors. In: 2015 IEEE Interna-

tional Conference on Pervasive Computing and Communication Workshops (Per-Com Workshops), PerCom Workshops, pp. 591–596. IEEE (2015). https://doi.org/10.1109/PERCOMW.2015.7134104

28. Staab, S., Luderschmidt, J., Martin, L.: Recognition of usual similar activities of dementia patients via smartwatches using supervised learning. In: International Conference on Progress in Informatics and Computing, Sessions in Shanghai and Tampere. IEEE (2021). https://doi.org/10.1109/PIC53636.2021.9687025. pIC

29. Staab, S., Martin, L.: Informationsplattform INFODOQ. In: 56. Jahrestagung der Deutschen Gesellschaft für Sozialmedizin und Prävention, Leipzig Germany, vol. 1 (2021). dGSMP

30. Statista GmbH: Ganz allgemein, warum nutzen sie ihre smartwatch? (2016). https://de.statista.com/statistik/daten/studie/588913/umfrage/umfrage-zu-nutzungsgruenden-einer-smartwatch-in-deutschland/

31. Fritz, D., et al.: Der elektronische kompaß. Design & Elektronik Sensortechnik, pp. 28–30 (1995)

32. Vijayan, V., Connolly, J.P., Condell, J., McKelvey, N., Gardiner, P.: Review of wearable devices and data collection considerations for connected health. Sensors **21**(16) (2021). https://doi.org/10.3390/s21165589. https://www.mdpi.com/1424-8220/21/16/5589

33. Weiss, G.M., Timko, J.L., Gallagher, C.M., Yoneda, K., Schreiber, A.J.: Smartwatch-based activity recognition: a machine learning approach. In: 2016 IEEE-EMBS International Conference on Biomedical and Health Informatics (BHI), Las Vegas, NV, USA, pp. 426–429. IEEE (2016). https://doi.org/10.1109/BHI.2016.7455925

34. Wu, J., Zhou, Z., Chen, J., Fourati, H., Li, R.: Fast complementary filter for attitude estimation using low-cost MARG sensors. IEEE Sens. J. **16**(18), 6997–7007 (2016)

35. Xia, C., Sugiura, Y.: Wearable accelerometer optimal positions for human motion recognition. In: 2020 IEEE 2nd Global Conference on Life Sciences and Technologies (LifeTech), Kyoto, Japan, pp. 19–20. IEEE (2020). https://doi.org/10.1109/LifeTech48969.2020.1570618961

Technology Service Design for the Older Adults with Dementia

Wang-Chin Tsai[1]([✉]), Chia-Fen Chi[2], and Yu-Hsing Huang[3]

[1] Department of Creative Design, National Yunlin University of Science and Technology, Yunlin, Taiwan
wangwang@yuntech.edu.tw
[2] Department of Industrial Management, National Taiwan University of Science and Technology, Taipei, Taiwan
chris@mail.ntust.edu.tw
[3] Department of Industrial Management, National Pingtung University of Science and Technology, Pingtung, Taiwan
yhh@mail.npust.edu.tw

Abstract. The purpose of this study is to explore the interpersonal interactions and lifestyles of elderly people with dementia, and to provide a care-oriented service design that can reduce the physical and mental burden of caregivers by combining the interactive care network system constructed by Smart Life. Caregivers will be interviewed in this study to observe and document the care problems of elderly people with dementia due to wandering; workshops and affinity diagrams will be conducted to explore the pain points of caring for elderly people with dementia. This study aims to further develop a system for searching for wandering elderly people or a care service interface and to produce the prototype of an anti-wandering wearable device. The results of this study can be used as a reference for the design of wandering prevention products for elderly people with dementia.

Keywords: Service Design · Older Adults · Dementia

1 Introduction

1.1 Older Adults and Technological Caregiving

The problems caused by aging populations in many advanced countries have become apparent, as there are social security systems of social welfare, support, and medical care in addition to economic problems such as reduced productivity. It has become an issue worthy of attention to design more user-friendly products so that elderly people with declining physiological functions can enjoy their lives in a healthy, comfortable, and safe manner. In advanced countries, such as Europe, the United States, and Japan, issues related to the aging society have already been considered from the perspective of normalization and social well-being. The government is currently promoting policies related to local caregiving, such as the Long-Term Care 2.0 policy so that caregivers can have their physical and mental burden reduced if they have access to relevant information

Q. Gao and J. Zhou (Eds.): HCII 2023, LNCS 14043, pp. 377–391, 2023.
https://doi.org/10.1007/978-3-031-34917-1_26

and use the services and technologies. Thus, the use of technological devices in caregiving can reduce the stress of caregivers and gradually change the way they interact with each other and care for each other. However, the issue of personal privacy arises when using technological devices as a platform for capturing relevant physical or behavioral information (e.g., cloud-based platforms) [1]. Relevant carriers can be roughly divided into invasive (e.g., implanted chips and tattooed QR-core) and wearable (e.g., bracelets, necklaces, and clothing) in terms of the loading approach. This study proposes to use wearable devices as assistive tools to avoid the controversies associated with invasive devices and to reduce the caregiver's stress due to the patient's cognitive impairment. It will make an in-depth exploration on elderly people with dementia, the caregivers, and the service design platform of technological aids and care for wearable devices. From the characteristics of the physical and mental functions of elderly people with dementia, the interaction and lifestyle of elderly people with dementia and their caregivers will be explored, and the service design with care as the core and smart life as the goal will be constructed through the technology care network platform, which is the motive of this study.

Caregiving is not an easy task, and there are many differences in caregiving patterns between Eastern and Western cultures due to the local conditions. For example, in Western societies, people make the decision of living in institutions easily when they are old, while in Eastern societies, caregivers may have to bear the moral risk of un-filiality when they send the elderly away from their homes to live in institutions [2]. Home care is a better way of caring for patients with dementia in a familiar environment to alleviate their symptoms. However, caring for a person with dementia at an advanced age is not an easy task from the perspective of the physician, the family, or the caregiver. The peripheral symptoms of wandering (getting lost or even missing) in the caregiving process are often the most stressful for the caregiver in the process of caring for or looking for the patient [3]. If there is a comprehensive approach or service platform that allows unprofessional people, such as family members or on-site caregivers, to improve their knowledge of dementia prevention and care [4], understand how to conduct assessments, piece together the fragmented information puzzle, and adjust their care or coping patterns, it can not only improve the quality of care for people with dementia but also effectively reduce the psychological stress faced by caregivers.

As mentioned above, one of the most important design issues at present is how to design technology products that meet the needs of elderly people with dementia and their caregivers to reduce their ability to operate the products due to their physical and mental deterioration, or to compensate for their physical and mental deterioration through technology [5]. This study aims to investigate the interpersonal interaction and lifestyle of elderly people with dementia, and to provide care-oriented service design by combining the interactive care network system constructed by Smart Life. Reducing the physical burden and psychological needs of institutional caregivers is also one of the research purposes.

1.2 Dementia and Assistive Devices

The cognitive impairment of dementia can be assisted by technological products and technologies to maintain the best functional status of the patient and to prevent or inform the occurrence of accidents, reduce the burden of care and improve the quality of life of both the patient and the caregiver [6]. In recent years, there has been a lot of investment in the development of technology for dementia care in foreign countries, but it is still in its infancy in Taiwan, with a lack of information, products, and welfare benefits. It is the wish of this study to have a development as soon as possible to benefit the patients of dementia and caregivers. In general, the most common cognitive symptoms of patients with mild to moderate dementia are memory deficits (e.g., forgetting to take the medication or the location of frequently used items), the loss of higher-order cognitive functions (e.g., computational skills, planning skills, and problem-solving skills), psycho-behavioral problems (e.g., hallucinations, anxiety, and agitation), and imbalance in daily routines (e.g., waking at night and loss of energy). The higher the severity of dementia, the higher the frequency of life problems caused by cognitive impairments, such as the interference behaviors of repetitive questioning and mood disorders, and the cognitive problems of forgetfulness and communication difficulties. Various specific phenomena reflect the caregiver's difficulties in life care [7]. In order to reduce the burden of caregivers, the first step is to make use of the care services provided by the government or to utilize the day care and short-term care services of related organizations, which can reduce the symptoms of patients and the stress of caregivers [8]). A shift system among family members can be established to ensure the caregiver's personal time; or other family members may be asked to help share caregiving responsibilities, as it can be a great help even if they can only help in the evening.

In fact, when older adults with dementia wander, they are bound to wear relevant clothing. If not dressed or wearing shoes, they will attract the attention of others around them. Clothing reflects one's values, ethics, and aesthetics, and is an important part in the history of human development and civilization. With the advent of the Internet of Things, the world is moving towards multi-functional clothing - smart clothing that is more difficult to integrate in order to meet different needs. When going out, people must have experienced the situation of forgetting their smartphones or wallets, especially for elderly people with dementia. Elderly people with dementia may have discomfort or aversion toward wearing bracelets or necklaces with an anti-wandering function, not to mention the sensors and locators which can record and report the location and situation of the wearer at any time. Clothing is like the second skin of human beings, people may forget to wear accessories to their body, such as smartphones, watches, and bracelets, but not clothes. Therefore, the use of sensor fusion, with various clothing-based wearable devices sewn onto the body of elderly people with dementia, can reduce the time spent searching for them and the occurrence of their getting lost, and reduce the burden on caregivers at the same time [4]. Therefore, this study proposes to use clothing/apparel and technology, supported by other care platforms or systems, to monitor or sense elderly people with dementia. With a simple user interface, the location of the target can be obtained in real-time or the wearer can be warned if they are in a dangerous site. This way, the psychological stress of the caregiver can be reduced and depression may be prevented.

1.3 Service Design and Elderly People with Dementia

"Service design" refers to the design of holistic experience; it is possible to identify the touch points between users and each service through the service design model. The 4D's design process is mainly based on the stages to "discover, define, develop, and deliver". In different stages, problems are identified, summarized and developed, and user-friendly research results may be presented [2]. Design ethnography is a structured process to build a deeper understanding of the target group in service design, to design new design concepts conforming to the viewpoints of users from daily life and regular behaviors, and to communicate the findings to cross-disciplinary members to ensure that all stakeholders understand and accept the findings, creating synergy and playing a central role in the design process. Because of the differences in the living environments and personalities of elderly people with dementia, the needs of elderly people with dementia are diverse. The psychological gaps of elderly people with dementia can be closely identified through service designs. That is, the 4D's design process can provide a deeper understanding of and complete care for elderly people with dementia, reducing the caregivers' psychological stress, and improving their quality of life. Although elderly people with dementia are very different from each other, the proximity of the living area (home or community), the way of care (active or passive), and the design of life services (physical or psychological) can be used as the starting point to implement this study. The design is centered on elderly people with dementia and is divided into three major directions (caregiver and care; care and technology; and technology and elderly people with dementia) and is implemented with related community, neighborhood network, and service design concepts. It is expected that through the proposed " Caring Service Design Study for Elderly People with Dementia", this study can make recommendations for the development of the "Content of Caring Service Design Study for Elderly People with Dementia" for age-friendly cities which has been advocated by the World Health Organization and key partners for many years, to "Create Happiness through Care".

1.4 Physical and Mental Needs of Elderly People with Dementia in Care Service Technology

As caregivers age, their physical and mental functions gradually decline, and elderly people with dementia experience the same problems and inconveniences when using various products. Therefore, understanding the physical and mental characteristics of the elderly is helpful for the elderly in using technology products. The physical and mental functions related to the design of products for the elderly can be divided into motor functions, perceptual functions, cognitive functions, and information device usage factors, which are individually described below:

(1) Motor Functions

Motor functions include muscle strength, dexterity, and speed. The muscle strength of elderly people decreases with age due to the reduction of myogenic fibers (Fujiwara, Sotoyuki, & Tateno, 1996). At the same time, the central nervous system control of muscle movement is reduced, which will affect the sensitivity and speed of the elderly (Vercruyssen, 1997), so the operation time for a task needs to be increased. Furthermore, the operation time of different elderly people varies greatly for tasks with more complex and difficult contents, and the required operation time is approximately 1.4 to 2.0 times that of young people [2].

(2) Perceptual Functions

Regarding visual aspects, in order to make the product interface easy to operate for the elderly, the text size should be at least 12–14 points in a left-aligned sans-serif font and designed to be adjustable in size in the design of a touch interface. In addition, dynamic text can reduce the reading ability (including speed, correctness, and willingness) of the elderly, and a static, high-brightness contrast between text and background is preferred. In terms of hearing, because older adults are less likely to understand computer speech, the use of synthetic voices should be avoided, and slower speech speed is preferred. In terms of volume, elderly people tend to prefer a volume of 74–85 dB.

(3) Cognitive Functions

The mental state of the elderly affects their cognitive abilities, and the provision of appropriate communication and interaction through technology can improve this problem. However, attention should be paid to the mental load of the elderly to avoid over-learned functions. Technology anxiety is a problem for older adults in technology operations, and incorrect operating experiences may increase their aversion to technology. The complexity of the functions and interfaces of information technology (IT) products and the physical and mental deterioration of the elderly, as well as the lack of previous experience in using IT products have caused many problems for the elderly in using IT products [3]. As learned from the in-depth understanding of the operation of technology-related products by the elderly, the most important problem is the decline in memory and attention due to cognitive deterioration, which makes it difficult to operate and creates a sense of rejection [2]. In addition, cognitive functions-visual attention, working memory, and planning functions also affect the use of information technology as older adults age. For example, poor visual attention can lead to an increase in search time and even the turning of a blind eye to the searched object. If working memory is weakened, the reading time will increase when an older adult is reading and understanding [3].

(4) Problems with the Usage of Information devices

Elderly people with dementia may reject or forget to wear anti-lost products due to cognitive impairment. Therefore, if elderly people wander around and are lost without the device, the prevention and monitoring functions of the device are meaningless. Either way of wearing the device cannot ensure the safety of the wearer. Even if one is able to pinpoint the location of the elder, it is still a chore to find them in the middle of the night. Furthermore, the positioning of the elderly does not guarantee their being brought home immediately. Hence, it still requires a social care system platform to avoid putting caregivers in a state of fear 24 h a day.

Currently in Taiwan, although the caregivers or home helpers of elderly people with dementia may be young, the reality is that most of the caregivers are older adults. There is a trend of elderly people taking care of elderly people in Taiwan. Both the caregiver and the care recipient, whether they are elderly or elderly people with dementia, may encounter difficulties when assisting in the operation and donning of devices due to physical or mental (cognitive) impairment. For example, it requires flexion and extension of the limbs, bending, turning, and manipulation of both hands for putting on and taking off the clothing, pants, shoes, and socks. Therefore, when joint mobility or muscle strength is insufficient, it will affect the activities of dressing and undressing. The way clothing is put on or secured creates the need for the manipulation techniques for buttons, zippers, velcro straps (Velcro), buckles, elastic bands, and straps. Elderly people with dementia are often overwhelmed or forgetful during the operation steps and are unable to put on and take off the devices. This study is designed from the service design perspective to meet the needs of caregivers and to reduce their physical and mental stress.

1.5 Summary

Long-term care is still the goal of caring for elderly people with dementia in their daily life and home treatments, whether in the middle or late stages of the disease. Therefore, this study aims to explore the psychological needs of elderly people with dementia from the perspective of service design and hopes to develop care products and service design platforms for elderly people with dementia from shared values and designs based on their homes and communities. Because of the significant differences in the physical and mental functions of elderly people with dementia, this study will explore the elderly people with dementia of different living styles and symptoms, and design care products and services that meet the physical and mental functions and living styles of elderly people with dementia through the integration of cross-border technology, so that elderly people with dementia can achieve the purpose of interaction and care with the family, friends, and community.

2 Research Method

This study will first explore the care and stress issues faced by elderly caregivers due to the wandering of elderly people with dementia. Through the review of related Taiwanese and international literature, we may discover suitable home care fields for elderly people with dementia, and define the problems and care service interface design of wearable devices that could potentially arise from the wandering and disappearing of elderly people. Consequently, this study aims to make two preliminary design proposals for anti-wandering wearable devices as shown in Fig. 1.

2.1   Phase 1: Literature Review and Analysis

Although this study has already collected data on elderly people with dementia, elderly caregivers, wearable devices, positioning technology, and care services, it is still necessary to conduct an in-depth literature review to further understand the status of domestic and international research. By doing so, this study can collect research and analyses on the physical and mental functions, as well as the lifestyles of elderly people with dementia, the technological adaptability of elderly people with dementia and their caregivers, the needs of elderly people with dementia for care service platforms, positioning technologies, and the design of cognitive aids for daily life. It aims to further explore the needs of service design in care and practical applications in order to effectively reduce the physical and mental stress of elderly caregivers. The stereotyping, durability, and battery life of anti-wandering wearable devices, the collaborative searching system, and current technology development and applications will also be discussed in depth. Furthermore, the relationship between caregivers, wearable devices, and care platforms will also be explored as the basis for the next stage of implementation.

Fig. 1. Basic Concept for the interface Framework

2.2   Phase 2: Care Field Survey, and Problem Identification and Definition

Based on the research results of the first phase, this study will conduct caregiver interviews, and observations and documentations on the daily living environment of elderly people with dementia, with a specific focus on the problem of wandering. Through expert consultation meetings, recommendations will be made for family responses, collaborative searching approaches, care settings, service design needs, and care models. Then, three caregivers of elderly people with dementia will be invited to participate in a focus group for face-to-face discussions with digital cameras and audio recorders. The patients' wandering symptoms due to cognitive impairment, the caregivers' search in the case of wandering, the collaborative searching process, and the problems faced by caregivers in caring for the patients in order to develop various devices, care model concepts, and design plans as shown in Fig. 2.

Fig. 2. Interface planning and development

2.3 Phase 3: Proposal for Prototype of Wearable Care Products

This study will draw affinity diagrams and behavioral models for the corresponding care model for elderly people with dementia and the care service design approach. In addition, it will plan the feasibility of wearable products with indoor departure detection sensors and outdoor location monitoring to reduce the search time and the probability of wandering and reduce the pressure of caregivers' vigilance throughout the day. This study plans to design three or more anti-wandering wearable devices for care service design proposals so that the products are not only in conformity with the design but also meet the requirements for durability and safety as shown in Fig. 3.

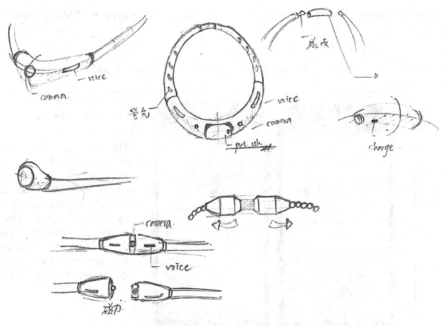

Fig. 3. Idea planning and development

3 Results and Discussion

3.1 Research Results

Upon the completion of the design study of care services for elderly people with dementia, the participations in universal design and related design competitions are expected using the findings of this study. In addition, the research results and recommendations will be compiled and published to contribute to the field of usability design for elderly people with dementia.

The above care platform is named "Elderly Care" which divides the care of elderly people with dementia into four major areas: biological condition and status, medical care, lifestyle, social activities, and relatives' companionship. The caregivers will fill in relevant data and information according to the different characteristics of the older adults. With the aid of technology, caregivers can effectively take care of elderly people with dementia even in remote locations.

Together with the wearable device of "Elderly Ware", the software and hardware can help caregivers to provide more comprehensive care for elderly people with dementia. The Elderly Ware is equipped with audio, camera, and positioning functions to match the platform's functionality and has an earthy tone and a simple shape to suit the preferences of older adults.

The following Table 1 explains how to use the care platform of "Elderly Care" in detail.

Table 1. Result of the care platform of "Elderly Care"

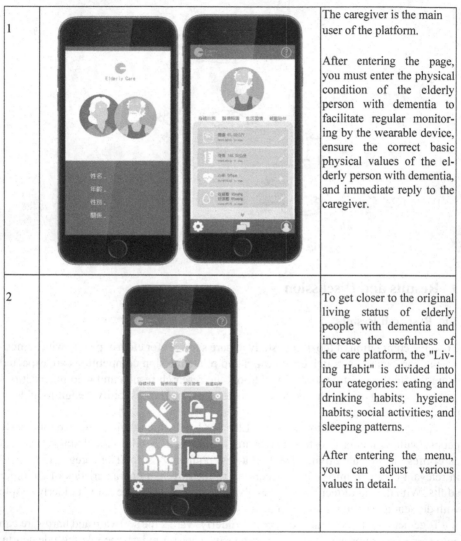

| 1 | | The caregiver is the main user of the platform. After entering the page, you must enter the physical condition of the elderly person with dementia to facilitate regular monitoring by the wearable device, ensure the correct basic physical values of the elderly person with dementia, and immediate reply to the caregiver. |
| 2 | | To get closer to the original living status of elderly people with dementia and increase the usefulness of the care platform, the "Living Habit" is divided into four categories: eating and drinking habits; hygiene habits; social activities; and sleeping patterns. After entering the menu, you can adjust various values in detail. |

(continued)

Table 1. (*continued*)

| 3 | 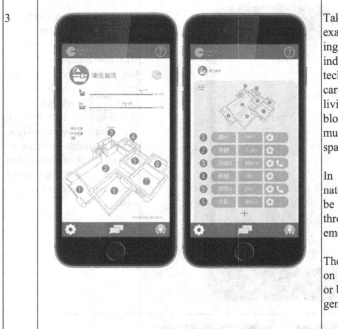 | Taking hygiene habits as an example, to prevent fainting or unconsciousness, indoor space scanning technology is used to allow caregivers to divide the living space into multiple blocks and set the maximum length of stay in each space.

In the case of an unfortunate event, caregivers can be notified in real-time through care platforms for emergency treatments.

The camera can be turned on by the wearable device or by calling a preset emergency contact. |
| 4 | 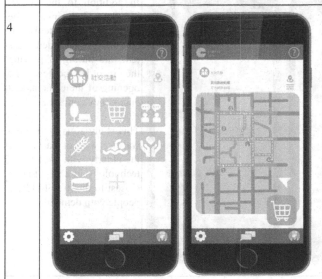 | Using social activities as an example, GPS technology is used to track the exact outdoor location of elderly people with dementia.

Caregivers can set the route of going out according to the different living conditions of the elders, and set the distance beyond the predetermined route to send an alert. |

(*continued*)

Table 1. (*continued*)

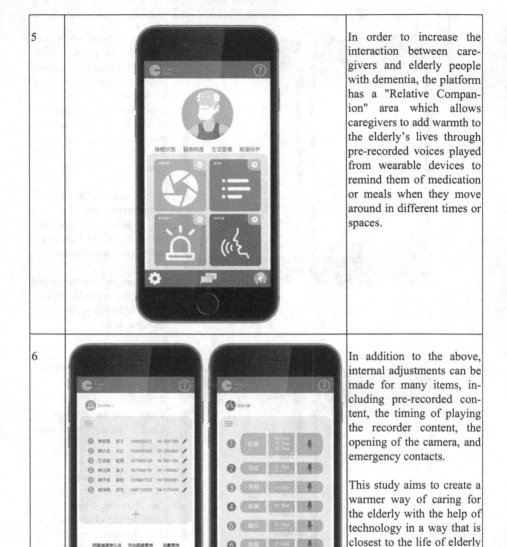

5		In order to increase the interaction between caregivers and elderly people with dementia, the platform has a "Relative Companion" area which allows caregivers to add warmth to the elderly's lives through pre-recorded voices played from wearable devices to remind them of medication or meals when they move around in different times or spaces.
6		In addition to the above, internal adjustments can be made for many items, including pre-recorded content, the timing of playing the recorder content, the opening of the camera, and emergency contacts. This study aims to create a warmer way of caring for the elderly with the help of technology in a way that is closest to the life of elderly people with dementia.

The following Table 2 explains the use and structure details of the "Elderly Ware" wearable device.

Table 2. Result of the usage and structure details of the "Elderly Ware" wearable device

1		After selection and discussion, this study decides to set the wearable device as a waterproof necklace. The shape is simple and clean to increase the willingness of the elderly in wearing it.
2		A skin-friendly, breathable material has been chosen for the neck ring, and a conservative brown color is chosen to increase the elderly's willingness to wear it.
3		The neck ring is used magnetically to minimize the difficulty of putting it on and taking it off.
4		In the center of the device is a small lens, which can be turned on in case of emergency to understand the situation in real-time. The long and narrow recesses on the left and right are for the pre-recording voice function in the "Elderly Care" of the platform.

(*continued*)

Table 2. (*continued*)

5	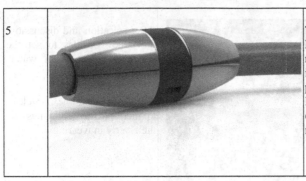	There is a USB port on the Elderly Ware for charging and reading some of the device's information. In the case of a person with dementia getting lost, one may quickly access emergency contact information.

4 Conclusion and Suggestions

This study discusses the lifestyles of caregivers and elderly people with dementia and explores the service needs of care products for elderly people with dementia. In addition, it will present empirical findings on the physical and mental functions of caregivers for the applications of designed care products, system platforms, and service design-related products. Through the integration of the project, the design results will be validated in various fields to evaluate the acceptance, satisfaction, and user experience of the care products by caregivers and elderly people with dementia, and the subsequent application reports will be written. Finally, this study will propose the promotion strategies of the care products and system platform services for elderly people with dementia. It will also complete the integration of field systems to achieve the goal of elderly people with dementia living independently while aging successfully and locally.

Acknowledgements. The authors hereby extend sincere thanks to National Science and Technology Council (NSTC)of the Republic of China (Taiwan, ROC) and Innovation-Oriented Trilateral Proposal for Taiwan Tech, Yun Tech and Ping Tech for their financial support of this research, whose project code is MOST 111-2410-H-224-027 -. It is thanks to the generous patronage of NSTC and Taiwan Tech, Yun Tech and Ping Tech that this study has been smoothly performed.

References

1. Bosco, A., Schneider, J., Coleston-Shields, D.M., Orrell, M.: Dementia care model: promoting personhood through co-production. Arch. Gerontol. Geriatr. **81**, 59–73 (2019). https://doi.org/10.1016/j.archger.2018.11.003
2. Chen, L., Liu, Y.: Affordance and intuitive interface design for elder users with dementia. Procedia CIRP **60**, 470–475 (2017). https://doi.org/10.1016/j.procir.2017.02.015
3. Chiu, C., Tasi, W., Yang, W., Guo, J.: How to help older adults learn new technology? Results from a multiple case research interviewing the internet technology instructors at the senior learning center. Comput. Educ. **129**, 61–70 (2019)

4. Czaja, S.J., Boot, W.R., Charness, N., Rogers, W.A.: Designing for Older Adults-Principles and Creative Human Factors Approaches, 3rd edn. CRC Press, Boca Raton (2019)
5. Hendriks, N., Huybrechts, L., Slegers, K., Wilkinson, A.: Valuing implicit decision-making in participatory design: a relational approach in design with people with dementia. Des. Stud. **59**, 58–76 (2018). https://doi.org/10.1016/j.destud.2018.06.001
6. Nygard, L., Starkhammar, S.: The use of everyday technology by people with dementia living alone: mapping out the difficulties. Aging Ment. Health **11**(2), 144–155 (2007)
7. Petrovčič, A., Slavec, A., Dolničar, V.: The ten shades of silver: segmentation of older adults in the mobile phone market. Int. J. Hum.-Comput. Interact. **34**(9), 845–860 (2018)
8. Tan, B., Fox, S., Kruger, C., Lynch, M., Shanagher, D., Timmons, S.: Investigating the healthcare utilisation and other support needs of people with young-onset dementia. Maturitas **122**, 31–34 (2019). https://doi.org/10.1016/j.maturitas.2019.01.003

Effectiveness of Support Programmes for (in)Formal Caregivers of Older Dependent People to Design Technologies

Vanessa Zorrilla-Muñoz[1,2]([✉]), Alberto Veira-Ramos[2,3],
María Silveria Agulló-Tomás[2,3], Nicolas Garcia-Aracil[1], and Eduardo Fernandez[1,4]

[1] Bioengineering Institute, Miguel Hernández University of Elche, Elche, Spain
{vzorrilla,nicolas.garcia,e.fernandez}@umh.es
[2] University Institute on Gender Studies, University Carlos III of Madrid, Getafe, Spain
{aveira,msat}@polsoc.uc3m.es
[3] Department of Social Analysis, University Carlos III of Madrid, Getafe, Spain
[4] CIBER BBN, Elche, Spain

Abstract. The growing number of older dependent population in Spain has incremented the demand for programmes and services aimed to provide support to (in)formal caregivers. Current legislation does not provide clear standardized practices for the results evaluation of such programmes which can constitute a guideline for public or private organizations, including NGOs. One strategy to successfully cope with this situation is the implementation of self-administered questionnaires as an essential part of a cycle of continuous improvement of programmes and services. This paper is based on results from survey data collected from a sample of managers of programmes, suggests that entities using self-administered questionnaires can, indeed, improve the effectiveness of their programmes significantly. The result of this study could contribute to the design and develop devices and software to improve care of older people and provide caregivers complementary assistance, especially, for older women.

Keywords: Ageing · Caregivers · Support programmes · Effectiveness assessment/evaluation · care technologies · care devices · Gender

1 Introduction

World's population projections point towards an accelerating ageing during the oncoming decades. Although significant improvements in the health care systems of most developed countries are helping people to live longer and healthier lives, the absolute numbers of older dependent people will grow considerably over the next decades. This trend is unlikely to be reversed unless cures for neurodegenerative diseases such Alzheimer are developed and made available to the public. Such context will constitute a serious challenge for governmental and non-governmental organizations involved in the provision of formal and informal care to the dependent older population (Leadley et al. 2014; Sixsmith et al. 2014; Jin et al. 2015; Stein and Sadana 2015; Steptoe et al.

2015). In this vein, projects implemented to monitor the increase of dependent older people and their needs[1] point to a growing demand for professional and semi-professional care which will require effectiveness of support services. Campbell et al. (2000) defines effectiveness as '[…] the extent to which care delivers its intended outcome or results in a desired process, in response to need. […]'. Lam Díaz et al. (2008) considers effectiveness in terms of a health system as the expression of the impact measure that a procedure has on the population health. Therefore, effectiveness considers the level with which tests, procedures, treatments and services are provided and the degree to which patient care is coordinated between health persons, institutions and time. Effectiveness is an attribute that can only be evaluated in real practice. For Van Mierlo et al. (2012), the effective support can contribute to reduce caregivers' negative outcomes (i.e. overburden and psychosocial illnesses).

Caregivers constitute a segment of the population that is expected to increase along with the number of dependent older adults. In fact, the evaluation of programmes for caregivers of older people has already a long history (see authors such as NHS Executive 1994; Giacinto 1996; Hodgson, et al. 1998; Collins et al., 2002; Woolham and Challis 2008). Particularly, three international projects (EUROFAMCARE[2], CARMEN and CAREKEYS) analyse programmes for caregivers of older people (IMSERSO 2005). More specifically, EUROFAMCARE applies several assessment tools to service providers and program managers for caregivers of older people with the purpose of analysing the caregiving services with respect to effectiveness and efficiency. The results of EUROFAMCARE demonstrate that older women assume the traditional role of informal caregiving within the family. Furthermore, the EUROFAMCARE reports inform about the negative consequences associated to caregiving activities (i.e. the lack of time for caregivers to take care of themselves and the loneliness that can frequently lead to the caregiver into social exclusion) and the need to strengthen support for caregivers. Yet, EUROFAMCARE reports indicate that an overwhelming majority of carers (over 75%) never used support services. This is mainly due to their high cost (Poland), the complexity in the bureaucratic process (Italy), or non-availability or difficult accessibility (Greece). At the same time, data from these studies also reveals that caregivers who have access to these programmes are highly satisfied with them.

Triantafillou et al. (2010, 2011) (INTERLINK team) in its report "Informal Care in Long Term Care System. European Overview Paper" provides a comparative overview of policies by identifying deficiencies and best practices in supporting informal caregivers of older people. INTERLINK team notices that there is no definition of the principles from which to establish policies to support comprehensive character for informal caregivers in many of the examined countries.

The extensive review of projects and bibliography highlights the necessities in the field of support for caregivers in different countries. Research papers in European countries like Bień et al. (2013); Chiatti et al. (2013); Lüdecke et al. (2012); Di Rosa et al. (2011); Krevers and Öberg (2011); Alwin et al. (2010); Lamura et al. (2008); Lamura et al. (2006); Stoltz et al. (2004) point out how in Europe the level of older people needs'

---

[1] See for example PROCARE, PRO ELDERLY HEALTH, DAPHNE or CAREKEYS.

[2] See more information and detailed description about the project here:https://www.uke.de/ext ern/eurofamcare/beschreibung.php.

coverage does not reach the expected levels. In a non-European countries' context, it is also worth mentioning research papers like Espín Andrade (2003); and Huenchuan et al. (2009). Keefe et al. (2008) has developed a tool to enable practitioners to understand caregivers' needs and situations in Canada. Moreover, some papers emphasize the need for best practices analysis in the care of older people –i.e. Hickman et al. (2007), Moyle et al. (2008)–.

Situation of older people caregivers' programmes and their evaluation in Spain.

In Spain, the first studies based on older people caregivers' samples were developed in the 90s. During this decade, the main focus was on evaluation of services provided to older people like residences and day-care and night-care centres or telecare (Medina et al. 1998). However, few programmes were adequately evaluated at that time (Agulló-Tomás 2002).

Implementation and development of support programmes to caregivers' fostered during the first decade of the century. EUROFAMCARE, for instance, reported about five of such programmes implemented in five different regions of Spain in 2006: 'Training program for caregivers' (Canary Islands), 'Sendian' caregiver support program (Basque Country), 'Welfare Check' (Galicia), 'Carer Subsidy' (Madrid) and 'Vida als Anys' (Catalonia).

Some authors analysed the development and implementation of psychosocial support programmes: Crespo and López (2007) assessed the development of programmes for caregivers trying to foresee "how to maintain well-being in ageing". This study was conducted through an experimental, psychological and individual methodology based on preventing and minimising caregivers' stress. Additionally, intergenerational programmes were aimed to alleviate the loneliness of older persons (Ayala et al. 2021) wich included the program "Close to you" from 2010 (IMSERSO with FEMP, Red Cross, Caritas and ADESSTA). Other authors evaluate the intervention programmes, i.e. the paper of Torres et al. (2008) analyses publications –appeared in the previous ten years– of various programmes and interventions to support informal caregivers in Spain. This analysis demonstrates that there is very little research based on evidences draw from programmes' results.

Some programmes have already been implemented and evaluated for a long period, i.e. 'The Ageing Report' (EC 2012) explores caregivers' programmes in Spain and describes different future scenarios by considering variables such as dependency rates - demographic scenario or constant disability scenario, between others - by the projection of receiving formal care. Agulló-Tomás et al. (2018, 2019) have described the necessities and demands related to older women caregivers. They have discussed about the necessities of implementation and, evaluation of programmes aimed to support caregivers of older people, because these types of program remain almost negligible in Spain. In this line, other authors, for example, Val-Calvo et al. (2019), Catalan et al. (2021) and Zorrilla-Muñoz et al. (2022) emphasize research need about new technologies and methodologies applied and developed for a better care of older people with disabilities, specially women.

Our work is based on results from a research project funded by the Spanish government to assess the potential impact of legislation reform ('Ley de Dependencia', -Dependency Act- approved in 2010) on the older dependents support improves. This project aimed to broad the scope of social research on ageing in Spain by targeting also caregivers.

This chapter aims to contribute to existing literature on the challenges of ageing by filling an existing gap in the reaserch on caregiving services, which is still underdeveloped. Most particularly, this article provides insight on how implementing self-evaluation questionnaires can improve effectiveness of the programmes aimed to provide support to caregivers of old dependents. The focus of this paper is the intermediaries (managers and coordinators of the companies providing services to older adults) because the outcomes focus are the process oriented.

This article responds to the following research questions:

1. Is effectiveness dependent on the program's *design*, when controlling for relevant factors such as *programme impact* on beneficiaries and participation?
2. Could self-administrated surveys be regarded as a valid methodology for the self-evaluation of performance and the identification of potential measures for improvement support services to caregivers?
3. Could this questionnaire be implemented in current devices designed for (in)formal care help?

2 Methods

The applied method is divided in two phases:

First phase: A questionnaire was designed to be completed by managers of programmes providing (in)formal support to old dependents and their caregivers. The Questionnaire for Responsible on Programmes Caregiver Support (QRPC) collected information about the characteristics of entities providing support to caregivers of old dependents and the type of programmes they implement, the number and profile of beneficiaries and the estimated budget and geographical scope of their activities. Additionally, the questionnaire includes several items which could be used by each entity to self-evaluate its performance.

The list of initial targets was elaborated in cooperation with various organizations, Public Administration, Non-Profit Organizations and independent vendors, all of which provided a directory of contacts of potential providers of services of some sort to older adults: 1) One directory was provided by the Spanish Confederation of Families with Alzheimer's and other Dementias CEAFA with over 1,229 addresses. This organization was founded in 1990s and is formed by 270 associations grouped in 19 regional federations representing more than 200,000 families (see http://ceafa.es). 2) Another directory was acquired from "Fundamental Negocios, SL" which provided additional 2,915 addresses of private companies providing services to older adults like Day-care centres and residences. 3) A third directory was acquired from the Company Web Municipal Councils with additional 8,112 addresses of public regional and local institutions. 4) Finally, In addition to these directories, the research team conducted its own mailing based on the exploration of web sites of various organizations. Then, a non-probabilistic sampling dynamic type "snowball" for sending multiple partners was initiated.

Despite de initial large number of addresses not all were updated, many emails were returned and most of them did not have programmes aimed to caregivers of old dependents. Therefore, a phase of filtering was conducted after which a sample size of n = 969 programmes coordinated by 435 managers of different institutions was defined.

Before the distribution of the questionnaire by E-mail, a pre-randomized trial of the questionnaire was administrated to 101 entities meeting certain criteria: 1) To have professional staff with experience on Social Work, Education Social Psychology, Nursing, Physiotherapy or Sociology; 2) To have staff with experience working as manager/director in the entity and; 3) To offer support programmes for caregivers of old dependents.

Finally, a total of 338 managers and coordinators completed our questionnaire providing information about 439 programmes. The software to analyses questionnaire was STATA.

The Questionnaire for Responsible on Programmes Caregiver Support (QRPCS) was constructed to assess which services are provided, how were they designed and implemented and the profile of beneficiaries. Additionally, items to measure effectiveness, impact on beneficiaries and participation were included. Its design (see Table 1) was based on some of the proposed items of EUROFAMCARE "Questionnaire service providers" (SPQ) and other resources such as: 1) Web pages of analysed entities: 530 programmes that appear in different Web pages; 2) Expert seminar based on the consideration of evaluation from a classical perspective (Epting et al. 1971; Rossi et al. 1988; among others); 3) Participatory approaches, such as Patton (2003) or CIPP model (Stufflebeam 2003); 4) The Spanish context through Bañón et al. (2003), Bustelo (2003); 5) The recommendations of the Evaluation and Quality Agency (hereinafter AEVAL) and the Spanish Evaluation Society (hereinafter SEE).

Each item of the questionnaire used in the quantitative analyses presented in this article was formulated through a Likert scale of 3 points by considering the following scores: Disagree (1), not disagree and not agree (2) and agree (3). All relevant items used in the models presented in this article are listed in Table 1.

Table 1. Cronbach α and average inter-item correlation factor for the CSPQ factors: Design, Participation design, Program effectiveness, Impact on beneficiaries.

CSPQ factors by group	Cronbach α	AIIC (Average Inter-Item Correlation)
	0.9961	0.3413
Design	0.9116	0.4424
Participation design	0.9322	0.6627
Program effectiveness	0.9119	0.3928
Impact on beneficiaries	0.9683	0.6163

A second phase complements the results of this study with a qualitative exploratory method through the discourses of ENCAGE-CM[3], ENVACES and ENCAGEn-CM, where were extracted 118 documents and testimonies of LEDYEVA project were also

---

[3] see https://encage-cm.csic.es/.

exploited[4] with 124 codes (generated from the previous scripts) and the following sub-codes: "Programmes" (284 discourses)"Technologies" (103 discourses) and "Image" (182 discourses) and "Care" (296 discouses). Based on these codes/variables, the relationship or co-occurrences were assessed, and the citations/verbatims where codes/topics appeared more frequently were compared. The interviews were completely transcribed and anonymized, before carrying out a content analysis using the ATLAS.ti program (v8).

3 Results

First, basic descriptive statistics based on sample data are provided and results of factor analysis and regression models are presented. Second, discourses of the qualitative analysis were commented.

At least 43.96% of sampled entities are Non-profit organizations (NGOs) and 36.90% belong to the Public Administration. Private entities and Foundations do not reach 20% altogether (9.34% and 9.79% respectively). Most of the entities operate locally (44.65%) and only 18.68% at national level. The rest acts in mancomunal (14.92%), provincial (8.88%) and regional level (13.67%). NGOs have the smallest available estimated budget to implement this type of programmes (mean budget of 13,001.77 EUR) which constitutes about a quarter of the mean budget reported by Public Administration entities (53848.67 EUR). Private entities have a budget of 25417.25 EUR and private Foundation 35868.67 EUR.

Regarding the type of services offered, the most frequently mentioned by respondents are training programmes, (36.4%), followed by groups of psychosocial support (29.9%) and, individual psychosocial support programmes (15.1%). Leisure programmes represent only 3.3% of the total although tend to be highly valued by beneficiaries, according to respondents. Information and management programmes and indirect/mixed programmes account for 8.6% and 6.8% respectively. Completion rate of programmes offered by all sampled entities is on average 72.99%.

About 60% of programmes are bidirectional, because they intend to help caregivers to take care of themselves and help them to take better care of the dependent older person they oversee. The most frequent profile of beneficiary is that of an unpaid woman (78% of participants). Most programmes are in fact specifically addressed to housewives or retired women. This analysis coincides with other mentioned researches such INTERLINK or EUROFAMCARE project. Finally, it should be mentioned that 206 programmes correspond to entities without a quality management certificated system, of which 121 are NGOs.

A total of 57 items from the questionnaire were examined. The AIC and BIC defined a minimum number of 46 statistical factors with four cases of Heywood over the 57 selected. Nine factors were validated through an initial plotter of data. The outcome was refined through the plot of four accumulated selective factors which were labelled as "design", "participation", "effectiveness" and "impact" of programmes. Cronbach analysis was calculated for each group of variables – grouped into 4 factors - as represented in Table 2 -.

---

[4] see http://cuidadoresdemayores.blogspot.com/.

Table 2. Statistical results of Design, Participation, Effectiveness and Impact factors.

Item		Mean	±	SD	KMO	FD	UV	Cronbach α	AIIC
Design	Internal_meetings	1.5148	±	0.0457	0.9413*	0.7891	0.3129	0.8181	0.8989
	Implemented_program	0.9379	±	0.0518	0.8563*	0.6267	0.3491	0.6603	0.9067
	Rules/opinions	1.0976	±	0.0550	0.8693*	0.6137	0.4040	0.6643	0.9065
	Pre_assessment_study	1.1923	±	0.0511	0.9418*	0.7006	0.4112	0.7432	0.9027
	Goals_expressions	1.4615	±	0.0460	0.9598*	0.8413	0.2586	0.8473	0.8974
	Program_schedule	1.5267	±	0.0469	0.9072*	0.8781	0.1654	0.8717	0.8962
	Goals_results_program	1.5917	±	0.0445	0.9099*	0.8884	0.1425	0.8776	0.8959
	Indicators_results_program	1.3669	±	0.0482	0.9381*	0.8232	0.2479	0.8321	0.8982
	Activities_services_program	1.5237	±	0.0467	0.9124*	0.8342	0.2647	0.8398	0.8978
	Methodology_program	1.5651	±	0.0452	0.9560*	0.8976	0.1343	0.8879	0.8953
	Resources_program	1.4911	±	0.0448	0.6712*	0.8603	0.2289	0.8642	0.8966
	Known_program	1.6006	±	0.0458	0.6873*	− 0.0168	0.4405	0.0527	0.9314
	Updated_program	1.7988	±	0.0423	0.6901*	0.0531	0.4900	0.0970	0.9298
Participation	Participation_definition	1.9319	±	0.0367	0.9466*	0.7777	0.3836	0.8216	0.9245
	Program_design_participation	1.2337	±	0.0584	0.9240*	0.7960	0.3217	0.8288	0.9236
	Program_design_development	1.4852	±	0.0519	0.9106*	0.8502	0.2394	0.8687	0.9185
	Program_design_evaluation	1.5030	±	0.0527	0.9100*	0.8582	0.2382	0.8748	0.9177
	Interaction	1.8047	±	0.0430	0.9207*	0.7975	0.3275	0.8320	0.9232
	Objectives_achievement	1.8669	±	0.0407	0.8918*	0.8183	0.2668	0.8452	0.9215
	Institutional_collaboration	1.6183	±	0.0492	0.9451*	0.7906	0.3592	0.8306	0.9234
Effectiveness	Quality_certification	1.5384	±	0.0537	0.9409*	0.7431	0.3431	0.7699	0.9025
	Program_coverage	1.9083	±	0.0395	0.9252*	0.7963	0.2591	0.7951	0.9015
	Achieved_objectives	1.8047	±	0.0428	0.9616*	0.8258	0.2790	0.8323	0.9001
	Program_influence_employment	2.8669	±	0.0231	0.2905*	− 0.0712	0.5427	0.1750	0.9221
	Program_influence_phys_health	1.6834	±	0.0407	0.7825*	0.3453	0.6762	0.3660	0.9163
	Program_influence_emotions	2.1864	±	0.0453	0.3953*	− 0.0267	0.4421	0.1815	0.9219
	Program_influence_social	2.3817	±	0.0437	0.4115*	0.1497	0.5000	0.2582	0.9196
	Program_impl_res_service	1.6213	±	0.0481	0.9297*	0.8068	0.2516	0.8109	0.9009
	Program_impl_res_develop	2	±	0.0353	0.9514*	0.8254	0.2641	0.8308	0.9002
	Optimal_results_persons	1.9349	±	0.0396	0.9101*	0.8455	0.1461	0.8211	0.9005
	Optimal_results_time	1.9586	±	0.0388	0.8726*	0.8389	0.1192	0.7998	0.9013
	Optimal_results_money	1.8787	±	0.0431	0.9427*	0.8255	0.2386	0.8131	0.9008
	Efficiency_compared	1.94083	±	0.0413	0.9555*	0.7435	0.3762	0.7633	0.9027
	Assess_less_expensive	1.0710	±	0.0638	0.9352*	0.7306	0.3797	0.7447	0.9034
	Benefits_overtime	1.8521	±	0.0402	0.9655*	0.7709	0.3642	0.7799	0.9021
	Program_viability	1.8846	±	0.0415	0.9465*	0.7603	0.3369	0.7600	0.9028

(*continued*)

Table 2. (*continued*)

Item		Mean	±	SD	KMO	FD	UV	Cronbach α	AIIC
Impact	Program_supported_external	1.3402	±	0.0573	0.9683*	0.7603	0.3330	0.7762	0.9669
	Program_known_society	1.3461	±	0.0514	0.9609*	0.8146	0.2384	0.8239	0.9662
	Program_acc_bar_administrative	0.9142	±	0.0640	0.9453*	0.8880	0.0690	0.8784	0.9655
	Program_acc_bar_economic	0.9024	±	.0646292	0.9546*	0.8782	0.0861	0.8695	0.9656
	Program_acc_bar_culture	0.9556	±	.0627376	0.9598*	0.8731	0.0937	0.8647	0.9657
	Program_acc_bar_geographycal	1.1568	±	.0596057	0.9728*	0.8342	0.2028	0.8363	0.9660
	Program_acc_bar_temporary	1.4319	±	.0561351	0.9645*	0.7376	0.3402	0.7503	0.9672
	Program_acc_bar_information	1.2278	±	.0566429	0.9728*	0.8143	0.2473	0.8212	0.9663
	Program_framework_promotion	1.396	±	.054865	0.9602*	0.7392	0.3419	0.7566	0.9671
	Program_relevancy_institutional	1.7958	±	.044436	0.9381*	0.7586	0.2296	0.7708	0.9669
	Program_relevancy_economic	1.7899	±	.0443541	0.9529*	0.7694	0.2513	0.7822	0.9668
	Program_relevancy_social	1.9615	±	.0361069	0.9512*	0.7634	0.2650	0.7777	0.9668
	Program_changes	1.3047	±	.0572713	0.9667*	0.7699	0.3195	0.7836	0.9668
	Careers_return_participation	1.7722	±	.0438938	0.9707*	0.7768	0.3038	0.7928	0.9666
	Careers_recommendation	1.9349	±	.0384693	0.9446*	0.7369	0.2805	0.7522	0.9672
	Program_continuation	2.0710	±	.0319528	0.9579*	0.7712	0.2489	0.7855	0.9667
	Program_resources_continuation	1.5710	±	.0524031	0.9601*	0.7208	0.3339	0.7393	0.9674
	Detection_problems	1.6035	±	.0491241	0.9594*	0.7736	0.2585	0.7874	0.9667
	Program_improve	1.6301	±	.0455924	0.9726*	0.7960	0.3037	0.8099	0.9664

* Bartlett test p < 0.01 and multivariate analysis p < 0.01.

SD (Standard Deviation), KMO (Kaiser-Meyer-Olkin), FD (Load factor), UV (Uniqueness Variance), AIIC (Average Inter-Item Correlation).

KMO statistical sampling frequencies provided adequacy (from 0.79 to 0.88). Bartlett's test (p < 0.01) and Multivariate statistics (p < 0.01) were also applied. Load factor (FD) and uniqueness variance (UV) calculated comply with the FD < 0.4 and UV > 0.6. Thus, it was found that selected factors were suitable for statistical analysis. After items' correction over the initial 57 items, the factor-solution was determined by the plot analysis and screen printing. Statistical results are illustrated in Table 3 for a final 55 items selected (2 items were eliminated of the model for not reaching the minimum statistical levels tested). The mean and standard deviation are also indicated in Tables.

Table 3 shows the final version of the 55 selected items which are included in the 4 factors: "Design", "participation", "effectiveness" and "impact" of programmes. The table illustrates the load factor, mean, standard deviation and correlation item-subscale corrected for each element. The variables of all items revealed the internal consistency analysis with α Cronbach of. 0.9961 and the average inter-item correlation (AIIC) test was 0.3413.

The prediction of effectiveness was calculated through multiple regressions. The results demonstrated that the model using the total scores of the effectiveness (ANOVA analysis with P < 0.01) as a criterion variable and the total scores for design, participation and impact of programmes (ANOVA analysis with p < 0.01) as predictor variables,

Table 3. Multiple regression analysis model depending on entities.

Entities	Number of entities	R2	F
Total	338	0.9245	3, 334 (1362.59)*
Without quality certification	206	0.9325	3, 231 (929.77)*
Public Administration entity	90	0.9672	3, 286 (845.65)*
Private entity	31	0.9589	3, 27 (209.99)*
Foundation	34	0.8840	3, 30 (76.19)*
Non-profit organization	183	0.9197	3, 179 (683.37)*

* $p < 0.01$

is statistically significant (adjusted $R2 = 0.8096$, $F(3, 334) = 473.40$, $p < 0.01$). Standardized beta coefficients are $\beta = 0.1181$, and $t = 4.20$ $p < 0.01$ for the design; $\beta = 0.0298$, $t = 0.084$ for the participation; and $\beta = 0.4070$, $t = 0.0296$ and $p < 0.01$ for the impact of programmes.

A second model was calculated by considering only entities without quality certification ($n = 206$). For this case, the results obtained improved $R2 = 0.9325$, and $F(3, 231) = 929.77$, $p < 0.01$.

Alternative models were calculated splitting the sample by type of entity. Results for Public Administration organizations are interesting because they often show the best available estimated budget. The model provides high significance levels for Public Administration entities, $R2 = 0.9672$, $F(3, 179) = 845.65$, $p < 0.01$; Private entities, $R2 = 0.9589$, $F(3, 27) = 209.99$, $p < 0.01$; and Non-Profit Organizations, $R2 = 0.9197$, $F(3, 286) = 683.37$, $p < 0.01$. In comparison, fitness and explanatory power of the Model decreases slightly when applied to private Foundations: $R2 = 0.8840$, $F(3, 30) = 76.19$, $p < 0.01$.

Some of the discourses reveal programmes (where technologies and device are used) are positive for both: Older people and caregiver. In this sense, programmes offer the use of technology and devices could help to improve autonomy and independence of older people if the devices are designed for the person, that is, person-centred with usability technologies.

> *If I understand the use of this technology, then, I could become somewhat more independent or autonomous (EPS_OSC_170615, older man, voluntary in a Non-profit organization).*

In relationship of the technology programs offered to (in)formal caregivers, some of the discourses comment the need to design new digital accessible technologies available in different lands and spaces. For example, rural spaces are usually non-accessible due to the lack of Internet connectivity.

> *We continue to have a problem in rural areas [...] and in the villages if the network and Internet does not reach you, then you already have a tremendous gap there (EPS_OSC_170512, woman, expert, Non-profit organization).*

Moreover, efficient programmes could reinforce technologies to help caregiver for a better care and improving the quality of life of older persons with disease. Some discourses indicate the importance of offer preventive control of diseases. This also applies to the design of preventive-based technologies that can be included in rehabilitation and therapy programs.

[…] so from a healthy life to suffering from illnesses, to starting in the critical moment that we begin to decompensate, and that they begin to give us a poor quality of life that makes us dependent that finally we die. […] we are not going to achieve it if it is not also distancing the disease backwards (because we do not forget that a person loses their autonomy and becomes dependent because he has a series of diseases). A person is not dependent because today you decide to be dependent. It is because the diabetes that he has made him already dependent, or the hypertension that he had was not well controlled, he did not take care of himself, or that percentage that escapes good care, and has a stroke, and has become a hemiplegic (EPS_INS_170425, woman, expert, Institution).

At the same time, some programs increasingly offer technological support, to help the person feel cared for and close. In this sense, it should be remembered that technology can facilitate the person cared for (and the person who cares for them) to the resources and the professional person.

Some personas have lived a terrifying isolation what you have to do is give it oxygen, right? Oxygen to accompany them, to make them feel… One from Ireland has come to us […] he saw us on the internet and he has come here and he is with us in this. But he is still a person who has always been very active. He continues to have and is very independent (EP_OSC_170407, older men, expert, Non-profit organization)

4 Discussion

The research suggests that self-administered questionnaires can, indeed, enhance effectiveness in a context of 1) unclear regulation and 2) scarcity of (human and financial) resources, particularly among NGOs, (a fast-developing sector, given the lack of sufficient services provided by the Public administration and the Private sector).

The implementation of self-administered questionnaires is a comprehensive instrument to be used for 1) measuring effectiveness of programmes and 2) providing feedback on what measures to undertake to improve the quality of the services provided to caregivers of old dependents and, 3) used for design new technologies connected to older people and their (in)formal caregivers.

Effectiveness of programmes was measured through the regression model by using three items' groups: Design, participation and impact on beneficiaries. This model suggests that using scales to measure effectiveness such as those included in the QRPCS could help to improve knowledge on the level of older people needs' coverage per program and the feedback of participants. This knowledge and feedback could be very valuable to implement improvements on the programmes' design during the self-evaluation process.

In the broader context of the socio-health sector, the design of a programme is often included in certification schemes which apply standards such as UNE 158101 residential centres, UNE 158201 day / night centres, UNE 158301 home help, and UNE 158401 telecare. The implementation of these standards has innumerable internal advantages, among which it stands out that they facilitate the compliance of the legislation, provide an efficient, safe and professional management, consolidating through indicators, and also, are addressed to the evaluation and monitoring of the quality of the service offered. However, the certification schemes for older people caregivers' programmes are still insufficient due to: 1) the lack of precise laws, regulations and standards and; 2) the lack of sufficient provision of such services by the public administration or the private sector; 3) the lack of technologies evaluating the convenience of used programs as resources to improve better care and facilities for the (in)formal caregiver. Under this perspective, new platforms to connect professional and the care environment are in development and introduce rehabilitation and therapy services integrated through video calls or games, which in turn is favoring the reduction of the "digital divide" for older people and the person who care them. Also, care professionals are conscious that new programmes could include technologies address to prevention and health promotion in integrated care programs related to home care (Lette et al., 2020). Examples of technology is the robot iDRhA[5] designed for patients with brain damage to do rehabilitation program at home and preventive accidents devices, such as EGARA (http://bastonegara.es/)[6] who detects and prevents collisions and obstacles outside the home, allowing the person to be more autonomous and independent.

Increasing need to compensate the lack of resources available to caregivers in Spain has led NGOs originally specialized on the provision of services to old dependents to adapt diversifying their activities in order to include also programmes for their (in)formal caregivers. Thus, lack of clear procedures and standards on how to provide such services has arisen as a major challenge for directors and managers of these newly implemented programmes of training, support and relief aimed to caregivers.

One strategy to successfully cope with this situation is the implementation of self-administrated questionnaires as an essential part of a cycle of continuous improvement of programmes and services provided, most particularly in this type of organizations.

In the older people care sector, the application of best practices standards may improve caregivers' programmes –such as ISO certificates and other certificates in process based on the person-centred and integrated model of care, provide service meets specific requirements which include needs for the continuous improvement of programmes, or Balanced Scorecards (BS) that help organizations to transform strategy into measurable operational objectives and interrelated by enabling the behaviour of the key people in the organization and resources are strategically aligned (Baraybar, 2011: 10–11)– which may enable to development strategies to improve quality of programmes.

From the analysis of data on how design, participation and impact items influence effectiveness, especially for the case of entities without quality certification system, it can be concluded that organizations providing support to caregivers could rely on strategies such as BS, helping to success in relation to bureaucratization (Chow et al., 1998; Inamdar et al., 2001) to generate insight into the effectiveness of the programmes they are offering.

---

[5] https://idrha.es/

[6] For more information, see https://catedraretinosis.org/

In addition, BS may promote an improvement on financial strategies which can be used to obtain greater investments and investors who can facilitate the consolidation and transfer of adjusted programmes to beneficiaries based on the older people caregivers' programmes' effectiveness measurement.

Under these considerations, the QRPCS questionnaire could be used into a context of socioeconomic and quality implementation strategies by organizations which provide older people caregivers' programmes.

Sample design took into account the total number of existing organizations providing services for caregivers, but clusters based on the nature (type) of the entity (private, NGO, Public, Foundation) were not used. All questionnaires received by respondents were processed. For this reason, the results consider qualitative analysis of ENCAGEn-CM database.

Effectiveness of programmes aimed to provide support services to caregivers comprises more components than those measured in our study (design, impact and participation).

After controlling for other factors, the model displays similar results on effectiveness for entities with and without quality certificates.

The results clearly point out that adopting relatively low-cost measures, such as self-administrated questionnaires, organizations providing services to caregivers could evaluate their effectiveness. This goes in line with Gandoy *et al.* (1999) who demonstrated that low cost supporting programmes can prevent institutionalization of patients if quality care in their own home is provided. Nonetheless, full confirmation regarding this relationship between best practices covered in our questionnaire and likelihood of institutionalization and de-institutionalization can't be assessed.

The approach of the model confirms that the program design, participation and impact on beneficiaries influence the programmes' effectiveness and depends on the entity type. Also, QRPCS could facilitate the review of good practices in organizations and supporting policy for older people caregivers. The research findings suggest how Non-profit Organizations of older persons' carers' programmes, which have less economic resources in comparison to Public and Private entities, can improve quality of results in terms of programmes' effectiveness, which can also implemented in new designed technologies and devices to care to assess the effectiveness of both: Program and technology.

Acknowledgements. The authors gratefully acknowledge the contributions of María Victoria Gómez and Alba Gil. We would like to thank our two anonymous referees and the editor of this publication for their comments and suggestions that substantially improved this contribution.

Fundings and Grants. This research has also been supported by CM:LEDYEVA Project "Carers of the older people: the situation regarding the Dependency Act and evaluation of programs for caregivers" (funded by MINECO, "Ministry of Economy and Competitiveness", Ref: CSO2009–10290, National R&D Plan, 2009–2013, Spain): http://cuidadoresdemayores.blogspot.com.es. The project was granted by Fundacion Pilares (2020) as "especial mention research". The project was considered (2013) "Good Practice" by the Network at European level "WeDO Partnership" (For Wellbeing and Dignity of Older People) which regroups various organizations and countries linked to these issues. https://www.fundacionpilares.org/red-de-buenas-practicas/premios-fundacion-pilares/ediciones-anteriores/iv-premios-fundacion-pilares-edicion-2020/. Also obtained (2012) the recognition of "good practice" by Fundacion Pilares.

This work is part of: ENCAGen-CM R&D Activities Program (Active Ageing, Quality of Life and Gender. Promoting a positive image of old age and aging against ageism) (Ref. H2019/HUM-5698) (Community of Madrid-FSE. PR: G. Fernandez-Mayoralas, C Rodriguez-Blázquez, MS Agulló-Tomás, MD Zamarrón, and MA Molina).

This contribution takes parts of the grant "Multimodal telerehabilitation assisted by robotic devices to maximize motor recovery" co-financed by FEDER funds, within the FEDER operational program of the Valencian Community (2014–2020) and the grant PROMETEO/2019/119 from the Generalitat Valenciana and the Bidons Egara Research Chair of the University Miguel Hernandez to Eduardo Fernandez. Moreover, this contribution has been supported by the Spanish Ministry of Science and Innovation, through the projects PID2019-108310RB-I00, TED2021-130431BI00 and PLEC2022-009424; and the AVI (https://innoavi.es/es/) throught the project INNTA1/2022/2023 "Innovation Agent for the Bioengineering Institute for the Miguel Hernandez University of Elche". The fieldwork for the qualitative analysis was financed by the ENVACES R&D + i project (MINECO-FEDER, ref. CSO2015–64115-R. PR: F. Rojo-Perez) and the ENCAGE-CM R&D Activities Program (Community of Madrid-FSE, ref. S2015/HUM-3367. LR: G. Fernandez-Mayoralas).

Appendix

Appendix I. Comparison Item Categorized EUROFAMCARE SPQ, QRPCS and Defined Variables.

Groups of items proposed in EUROFAMCARE SPQ	Groups of items identified in QRPCS	Defined variables
Service providers to families, goals, monitoring needs / as caregivers / as family, program information	**Program design**: Objectives, establishment of program services, execution of the program Conditions regarding time, targets, indicators for analysis, methodology and State-guaranteed defined resources	**Design variables:** How has been designed the program to establish the needs of caregivers? "Internal_meetings": Through internal meetings; "Implemented_program": Implemented program has been applied by other entities; "Rules/opinions": Rules/opinions of official bodies have been used; "Pre_assessment_study": Pre-assessment study has been applied (survey, data, or other representers caregivers of groups); Goals_expressions: How have the goals been expressed in concrete and clear criteria and indicators?; "Program_schedule" Has the program a timing, schedule, planning?; "Goals_results_program:? Are still goals maintained to achieve some results ?; "Indicators_results_program": Have been established indicators to achieve results?; "Activities_services_program": Does the program develop activities or provide services?; "Methodology_program": Does the program follow a clear methodology (in sequencing tasks, phases, etc.) ?; "Resources_program": Has the program enough resources to achieve the objectives?; "Known_program": Is the program sufficiently known?; "Updated_program": Has been updated the program?

(continued)

(continued)

Groups of items proposed in EUROFAMCARE SPQ	Groups of items identified in QRPCS	Defined variables
Items on background: the need to use the service organization by / as family caregivers	**Participation design in the programs:** Selected participants / -participation as caregivers / as in the design, development and evaluation of programs-, program coordination, coordination and management	**Participation variables:** "Participation_definition": Is it clearly defined who will participate in the program and how?; Are caregivers involved in the program design? "Program_design_participation": Are caregivers involved in the program design?; ""Program_design_development: Are caregivers involved in the program application and development?; "Program_design_evaluation": Are caregivers involved in the program monitorization and evaluation?; "Interaction": Have been coordination and participation stimulated between different actors?; "Objectives_achievement": Do you think that the coordination and management have contributed to the achievement of objectives?; "Institutional_colaboration": Do you think that institutional collaboration have contributed to the achievement of results?; "Benefits_overtime": When the program has been finished: Do you consider that benefits achieved will last over time (in the medium and long term)?; "Program_viability": Is the program viable at different levels?

(continued)

(continued)

Groups of items proposed in EUROFAMCARE SPQ	Groups of items identified in QRPCS	Defined variables
Main benefits, satisfaction, development Programs in the future and improvement	**Impact of programs on beneficiaries:** Futures over time, continuity, benefits, recommendation and dissemination, future viability, resources, barriers, correcting problems, review, improvement and satisfaction with the programs	**Impact variables:** "Program_supported_external": Is the program supported (funding, dissemination, for example) by other external entities?; "Program_known_society": Do you think that the program is sufficiently known by society as a whole?; Do you think that caregivers have found barriers to access to programs? "Program_acc_bar_administrative": Administrative barriers; "Program_acc_bar_economic": Economic barriers ?; "Program_acc_bar_culture": Culture barriers; "Program_acc_bar_geographycal": Geographical barriers; "Program_acc_bar_temporary" Temporary barriers (i.e. They cannot leave the older person to anyone to attend the activity) ?; "Program_acc_bar_information": Barriers due to the lack of information or knowledge of the program; "Program_framework_promotion": Do you think that the current legal framework promotes the program to achieve its objectives?; Is the program appropriate-relevant (or appropriate to the context) from the point of view…? "Program_relevancy_institutional": Political and institutional; "Program_relevancy_economic": Economical; "Program_relevancy_social": Social and cultural; "Program_changes": Have been changes in the program context which may affect the program initially established?; "Careers_return_participation": Do caregivers return to the entity requesting to participate in other programs?; "Careers_recommendation": Are programs recommended by caregivers?; "Program_continuation": Should the program continue in the future?; "Program_resources_continuation": Are resources available to continue with the program activities?; "Detection_problems": Are mechanisms foreseen for the detection and correction of program problems?; "Program_improve": Do you think that the program could be improved?

(continued)

(continued)

Groups of items proposed in EUROFAMCARE SPQ	Groups of items identified in QRPCS	Defined variables
Opportunities and demand for assistance / caregivers as / as, vision caregivers / as, resources and strategies for future development	**Effectiveness of programs:** Quality expectations and demands, achieved goals, influence of the program on / as caregivers / as, resource efficiency, utilization and resource efficiency, future achievement of objectives	**Effectiveness variables:** "Quality_certification": Has the entity established a system to ensure quality in the provision of services?; "Program_coverage": Is the program suitable to meet the expectations, demands and needs of caregivers?; "Achieved_objectives": Have expected objectives been achieved?; Is the program influencing…? "Program_influence_employment":… The employment situation (labour standards and/or, insertion, between others)?; "Program_influence_phys_health":… Physical well-being and health?; "Program_influence_emotions":… Emotional and psychological well-being?; "Program_influence_social":… Social welfare and social relations?; "Program_impl_res_service": Are the assigned resources enough for program implementation and service delivery?; "Program_impl_res_develop": Are (economic, material and human) resources appropriate for program development which are used ?; Is there an optimal relationship with…? "Optimal_results_persons":… Effort, human resources (personnel involved) ?; " Optimal_results_time":… Time spent ?; "Optimal_results_money":… Invested money ?; "Efficiency_compared": Are efficient use of resources allocated to the program compared with other possible alternative uses made? (i.e. service-program offering or giving money for it); "Assess_less_expensive": Does the likelihood assess of achieving the same results in a less expensive more economically?

References

1. Agulló-Tomás, M.S.: Mujeres, cuidados y bienestar social: el apoyo informal a la infancia ya la vejez: Instituto de la Mujer (2002). https://www.inmujeres.gob.es/publicacioneselectron icas/documentacion/Documentos/DE1470.pdf
2. Agulló-Tomás, M.S., Zorrilla-Muñoz, V., Gómez-García, M.V.: Género y evaluación de programas de apoyo para cuidadoras/es de mayores. Prisma Social: revista de investigación social (21), 391–415 (2018).http://revistaprismasocial.es/article/view/2469
3. Agulló-Tomás, M.S., Zorrilla-Muñoz, V., Gómez-García, M.V.: Aproximación socio-espacial al envejecimiento y a los programas para cuidadoras/es mayores. Int. J. Dev. Educ. Psychol. **1**(1), 221–228 (2019)

4. Alwin, J., Öberg, B., Krevers, B.: Support/services among family caregivers of persons with dementia—perceived importance and services received. Int. J. Geriatr. Psychiatry **25**(3), 240–248 (2010). https://doi.org/10.1002/gps.2328

5. Bañón, R., Caballero, V., Sánchez Medero, G.L: Evaluación de la acción y de las políticas públicas. Una visión desde la bibliografía. La Evaluación de la Acción y de las Políticas Públicas, compilado por Rafael Bañón i Martínez, Ediciones Díaz de Santos SA, Madrid, pp. 215–250 (2003)

6. Baraybar, F.A.: El Cuadro de Mando Integral «Balanced Scorecard»: ESIC Editorial (2011)

7. Bień, B., et al.: Disabled older people's use of health and social care services and their unmet care needs in six European countries. Eur. J. Pub. Health **23**(6), 1032–1038 (2013). https://doi.org/10.1093/eurpub/cks190

8. Bustelo, M.: La evaluación y los planes de igualdad en el estado español. Cómo evaluar las políticas públicas desde la perspectiva de género, 127–152 (2003)

9. Campbell, S.M., Roland, M.O., Buetow, S.A.: Defining quality of care. Soc. Sci. Med. **51**(11), 1611–1625 (2000). https://doi.org/10.1016/S0277-9536(00)00057-5

10. Catalan, J.M., Blanco, A., Bertomeu-Motos, A., Garcia-Perez, J.V., Almonacid, M., Puerto, R., Garcia-Aracil, N.: A modular mobile robotic platform to assist people with different degrees of disability. Appl. Sci. **11**(15), 7130 (2021). https://doi.org/10.3390/app11157130

11. Chiatti, C., Di Rosa, M., Melchiorre, M.G., Manzoli, L., Rimland, J., Lamura, G.: Migrant care workers as protective factor against caregiver burden: results from a longitudinal analysis of the EUROFAMCARE study in Italy. Ageing Ment. Health **17**(5), 609–614 (2013). https://doi.org/10.1080/13607863.2013.765830

12. Chow, C.W., Ganulin, D., Haddad, K., Williamson, J.: The balanced scorecard: a potent tool for energizing and focusing healthcare organization management. J. Healthc. Manag. **43**(3), 263–280 (1998). https://doi.org/10.1097/00115514-199805000-00010

13. Collins, K.S., Hughes, D.L., Doty, M.M., Ives, B.L., Edwards, J.N., Tenney, K.: Diverse Communities, Common Concerns: Assessing Health Care Quality for Minority Americans. Commonwealth Fund, New York (2002)

14. Crespo López, M., López Martínez, J.: El apoyo a los cuidadores de familiares mayores dependientes en el hogar: desarrollo del programa "Cómo mantener su bienestar": Imserso (2007)

15. Di Rosa, M., et al.: A typology of caregiving situations and service use in family carers of older people in six European countries: the EUROFAMCARE study. GeroPsych: J. Gerontopsychol. Geriatr. Psychiatry **24**(1), 5 (2011). https://doi.org/10.1024/1662-9647/a000031

16. Epting, F.R., Suchman, D.I., Nickeson, C.J.: An evaluation of elicitation procedures for personal constructs. Br. J. Psychol. **62**(4), 513–517 (1971). https://doi.org/10.1111/j.2044-8295.1971.tb02066.x

17. Espín Andrade, A.M.: Estrategia para la intervención psicoeducativa en cuidadores informales de adultos mayores con demencia. Cuidad de la Habana 2009 (2003)

18. EC. The Ageing Report. Economic and budgetary projection for the 27 EU Member States (2010–2060). Brussels (2012)

19. Gandoy Crego, M., et al.: Evaluación y resultados de la instauración de un programa de terapia de grupo dirigido a un colectivo de cuidadores familiares de enfermos de Alzheimer (1999)

20. Giacinto, G.: Caring for older europeans: comparative studies in 29 countries. Aldershot: Arena (1996)

21. Hodgson, C, Higginson, I., Jefferys, P.: Carers' Checklist. An outcome measure for people with dementia and their carers. The Mental Health Foundation, London (1998)

22. Huenchuan, S., Roqué, M., Arias, C.: Envejecimiento y sistemas de cuidado:¿ oportunidad o crisis. Santiago de Chile: Naciones Unidas (2009)

23. Inamdar, N., Kaplan, R., Bower, M.: Applying the balanced scorecard in healthcare provider organizations. J. Healthc. Manage./Am. Coll. Healthc. Executives **47**(3), 179–195 (2001). Discussion 195–176. https://doi.org/10.1097/00115514-200205000-00008

24. IMSERSO: Redes y Programas Europeos de Investigación V PROGRAMA MARCO DE LA UE (1998–2002). Boletín sobre el envejecimiento, 19 & 19 (2005)

25. Jin, K., Simpkins, J.W., Ji, X., Leis, M., Stambler, I.: The critical need to promote research of ageing and ageing-related diseases to improve health and longevity of the elderly population. Ageing Dis. **6**(1), 1 (2015). https://doi.org/10.14336/AD.2014.1210

26. Keefe, J., Guberman, N., Fancey, P., Barylak, L., Nahmiash, D.: Caregivers' aspirations, realities, and expectations: The care tool. J. Appl. Gerontol. **27**(3), 286–308 (2008). https://doi.org/10.1177/0733464807312236

27. Krevers, B., Öberg, B.: Support/services and family carers of persons with stroke impairment: perceived importance and services received. J. Rehabil. Med. **43**(3), 204–209 (2011). https://doi.org/10.2340/16501977-0649

28. Lam Díaz, R. M., Hernández Ramírez, P.: Los términos: eficiencia, eficacia y efectividad¿ son sinónimos en el área de la salud?. Revista Cubana de Hematología, Inmunología y Hemoterapia **24**(2) (2008). http://scielo.sld.cu/scielo.php?script=sci_arttext&pid=S0864-02892008000200009

29. Lamura, G., et al.: Group, EUROFAMCARE 2008 Family carers' experiences using support services in Europe: empirical evidence from the EUROFAMCARE study. Gerontologist **48**(6), 752–771 (2008). https://doi.org/10.1093/geront/48.6.752

30. Lamura, G., et al.: Erfahrungen von pflegenden Angehörigen älterer Menschen in Europa bei der Inanspruchnahme von Unterstützungsleistungen. Z. Gerontol. Geriatr. **39**(6), 429–442 (2006). https://doi.org/10.1007/s00391-006-0416-0

31. Leadley, R.M., Armstrong, N., Reid, K.J., Allen, A., Misso, K.V., Kleijnen, J.: Healthy ageing in relation to chronic pain and quality of life in Europe. Pain Pract. **14**(6), 547–558 (2014). https://doi.org/10.1111/papr.12125

32. Lette, M., Ambugo, E.A., Hagen, T.P., Nijpels, G., Baan, C.A., y De Bruin, S. R.: Addressing safety risks in integrated care programs for older people living at home: a scoping review. BMC Geriatr. **20**(1), 1–13 (2020)

33. Lüdecke, D., Mnich, E., Kofahl, C.: The impact of sociodemographic factors on the utilisation of support services for family caregivers of elderly dependents—results from the German sample of the EUROFAMCARE study. GMS Psycho-Soc.-Med. **9** (2012)

34. Medina, M.E., et al.: Evaluación del impacto en cuidadores de usuarios del Servicio de Ayuda a Domicilio. Anales de Psicología **14**, 105–126 (1998)

35. Executive, N.H.S.: Developing NHS Purchasing and GP Fundholding: Towards a Primary Care-led NHS. Department of Health, Heywood (1994)

36. Patton, M.Q.: Utilization-focused evaluation. In: Kellaghan, T., Stufflebeam, D.L. (eds.) International Handbook of Educational Evaluation, Kluwer International Handbooks of Education, vol. 9, pp. 223–242. Springer, Dordrecht (2003). https://doi.org/10.1007/978-94-010-0309-4_15

37. Ayala, A., et al.: Influence of active and healthy ageing on quality of life changes: insights from the comparison of three european countries. Int. J. Environ. Res. Public Health **18**(8), 4152 (2021). https://doi.org/10.3390/ijerph18084152

38. Rossi, P.H., Freeman, H.E., Hofmann, G.: Programm-Evaluation: Einführung in die Methoden angewandter Sozialforschung: Enke (1988).

39. Sixsmith, J., et al.: Healthy ageing and home: The perspectives of very old people in five European countries. Soc. Sci. Med. **106**, 1–9 (2014). https://doi.org/10.1016/j.socscimed.2014.01.006

40. Stoltz, P., Uden, G., Willman, A.: Support for family carers who care for an elderly person at home–a systematic literature review. Scand. J. Caring Sci. **18**(2), 111–119 (2004). https://doi.org/10.1111/j.1471-6712.2004.00269.x

41. Stein, C., Sadana, R.: The world health organization – the case for measuring wellbeing in Europe. In: Glatzer, W., Camfield, L., Møller, V., Rojas, M. (eds.) Global Handbook of Quality of Life, International Handbooks of Quality-of-Life, pp. 763–769. Springer, Dordrecht (2015). https://doi.org/10.1007/978-94-017-9178-6_34

42. Steptoe, A., Deaton, A., Stone, A.A.: Subjective wellbeing, health, and ageing. Lancet **385**(9968), 640–648 (2015)

43. Stufflebeam, D.L.: The CIPP model for evaluation. In: Kellaghan, T., Stufflebeam, D.L. (eds.) International Handbook of Educational Evaluation, Kluwer International Handbooks of Education, vol. 9, pp. 31–62. Springer, Dordrecht (2003). https://doi.org/10.1007/978-94-010-0309-4_4

44. Torres Egea, M., Ballesteros Pérez, E., Sánchez Castillo, P.D.: Programas e intervenciones de apoyo a los cuidadores informales en España. Gerokomos **19**(1), 9–15 (2008). https://doi.org/10.4321/S1134-928X2008000100002

45. Triantafillou, J., et al.: Informal care in the long-term care system. Executive Summary (2011). http://interlinks.euro.centre.org/sites/default/files/WP5%20Informal%20care_ExecutiveSummary_FINAL.pdf

46. Triantafillou, J., et al.: Informal care in the long-term care system European Overview Paper (2010)

47. Val-Calvo, M., Álvarez-Sánchez, J.R., Ferrández-Vicente, J.M. Fernández, E.: Optimization of real-time EEG artifact removal and emotion estimation for human-robot interaction applications. Front. Comput. Neurosci. **13**, 80 (2019). https://doi.org/10.3389/fncom.2019.00080

48. Van Mierlo, L.D., Meiland, F.J., Van der Roest, H.G., Dröes, R.M.: Personalised caregiver support: effectiveness of psychosocial interventions in subgroups of caregivers of people with dementia. Int. J. Geriatr. Psychiatry **27**(1), 1–14 (2012). https://doi.org/10.1002/gps.2694

49. Woolham, J., Challis, R.: Performance indicators in social care for older people. Ageing Soc. **28**(3), 437 (2008). https://doi.org/10.1017/S0144686X08007101

50. Zorrilla-Muñoz, V. et al.: Older women images and technologies to increase gender peace in crisis and COVID-19 times. In: Gao, Q., Zhou, J. (eds.) Human Aspects of IT for the Aged Population. Technology in Everyday Living. HCII 2022. LNCS, vol 13331. Springer, Cham (2022). https://doi.org/10.1007/978-3-031-05654-3_30

Aging, ICT Use and Digital Literacy

Intergenerational Solidarity: Perceptions of Young Adults

Inês Amaral[1,2]([✉]), Ana Marta Flores[1,3], and Eduardo Antunes[1]

[1] Faculty of Arts and Humanities, University of Coimbra, Coimbra, Portugal
ines.amaral@uc.pt, {amflores,eduardo.antunes}@fl.uc.pt
[2] Centre for Social Sciences, University of Coimbra, Coimbra, Portugal
[3] NOVA Institute of Communication, Lisboa, Portugal

Abstract. This paper focuses on the intergenerational solidarity perceptions of young adults (aged between 18 and 30) in Portugal regarding how solidarity is intertwined with digital media uses, appropriations, and embodiments during the pandemic context. Therefore, this research departs from the following questions: (RQ1) Do Portuguese young adults perceive to use of the Internet to communicate with family members? If so, with whom do they communicate? (RQ2) How is solidarity intertwined with digital media uses, appropriations and embodiments? Data collection was performed between 8 and 17 October 2021, and according to the representative sample of 1500 young adults in Portugal, using the Internet to communicate with any family member is an almost unanimous activity (96.2%). Furthermore, results show that digitally mediated relationships with relatives over 65 mobilised structural, associational and affectual intergenerational solidarity.

Keywords: intergenerational digital relationships · digital practices · intergenerational solidarity

1 Introduction

Especially in the last decade, social and cultural changes in practices have been described by mediatic intensification, in particular, of digital-based media, which fall under the idea of living in "media-saturated societies" [1]. In the case of the widespread digital media [2], such transformations have been modifying the practices of publics/audiences in terms of their everyday lives [3]. Digital media have exponentially opened possibilities of interactiveness [4, 5]. Audience usage combination of several different media platforms has been described as cross-media [6–8], which differs from generation to generation [9].

Such a generational media gap can be addressed, for example, as the "digital divide" [10], which is reinforced by widespread rhetoric that generations do not interact with and through digital media and that they tend to increase such separation. Intergenerational relationships, contacts and interactions may be understood as 'cross-generations' connections performed by people with other people. This second one is from a different generation than the first one. In fact, traditional mass media representations reinforce

Q. Gao and J. Zhou (Eds.): HCII 2023, LNCS 14043, pp. 413–425, 2023.
https://doi.org/10.1007/978-3-031-34917-1_28

that idea of dividedness. Especially in times of crisis, those media representations exacerbate the dividedness between different groups of people, against one another, including generations as a social divide factor [11].

Western societies emphasise an idea that may be considered as opposed to solidarity: independence. If solidarity contemplates close bonds of intimacy and affection, it can be seen as opposed to the development of independence while children grow and become adults [12]. Derpmann [13] shows that "solidarity" is frequently used when facing adversities, crises and emergencies. The idea of solidarity became central to everyone's lives in the last couple of years due to the COVID-19 pandemic. Appeals to the solidarity of different natures emerged, either international solidarity, national solidarity, or intergenerational solidarity; for example, all were part of media discourses through the most difficult pandemic times [14].

Since the older generation was the one more challenged, health-wise, with the COVID-19 pandemic, the mediatised general idea of solidarity usually included the notion of intergenerational solidarity, which gained a connotation of social responsibility [13–16]. Without detriment to health issues, the COVID-19 pandemic presented a range of other difficulties to older generations, including the capacity to use media and digital media tools to mitigate the pandemic's consequences [17]. In fact, such a generation is provided with opportunities but also with challenges in terms of their capacity to use digital media tools [18]. Differences in digital media access are associated with a range of socio-demographic variables, including age, education, financial/economic capacity or gender [19–22].

This paper is focused on age as an important factor in the digital divide, aiming to emphasise solidarity as a key aspect of intergenerational relationships. Considering mere communication as the basis for intergenerational interactions and, consequently, intergenerational solidarity, if existing. Communication processes and dialogues across generations are essential aspects to address and prospect societies grounded in solidarity, functioning in a collaborative manner [10], even when it comes to media and technology.

This study addresses intergenerational solidarity according to the perceptions of 1500 surveyed young adults (aged between 18 and 30) in Portugal (a representative sample with socio-demographic quotas). The idea is that "intergenerational solidarity comprises, on the one hand, specific behaviour and, on the other hand, a feeling of belonging and close connection between family generations" [23]. For that matter, this paper intends to further developments in this area and is conducted with the research questions: RQ1: Do Portuguese young adults perceive to use of the internet to communicate with family members? If so, with whom do they communicate? RQ2: How is solidarity intertwined with digital media uses, appropriations and embodiments?

1.1 Intergenerational Solidarity and ICT

Studies show that older generations use ICT-mediated communication to strengthen relations with family and friends [24–28]. Studies in the field of games also pay attention to how intergenerational experiences can stimulate the participation of older people. Co-design that involves people of different generations to interact both with each other and with the game designers is one of the proposals made to develop this social interaction [46]. In addition, intergenerational digitally mediated relationships may lead to overcoming social and digital inequalities, enabling personal ties and adopting and using Internet technologies [29]. Furthermore, intergenerational solidarity may induce social cohesion and can be a form of empowerment [30].

From interpersonal relationship theories, Bengtson and Roberts [30] developed an intergenerational solidarity model based on six types of solidarity: i). Associational solidarity (interaction patterns facilitating integration and combating isolation); ii). Affectual solidarity (understanding, respect and trust); iii). Normative solidarity (stressing family commitments); iv). Consensual solidarity (consensus concerning sharing life values and beliefs); and v). Structural solidarity (a network that provides physical proximity and support) [3]. Following this perspective, Harper and Hamblin [31] contend that "the traditional contract between the generations is based on a system of intergenerational reciprocity". Therefore, intergenerational learning within families allows for breaking down barriers and promoting digital literacy by focusing on social capital [32] through "identifiable social relationships" [33].

According to Taipale [34], ICTs are connected with associational and functional patterns of solidarity across generations, encouraging social bonding via platforms and improving autonomy through intergenerational learning [35], combating social isolation [36] and allowing to overcome the digital divide [37].

Scientific literature is often focused on internet use as personal use [37] rather than participatory use [38]. Moreover, intergenerational uses are participatory and go beyond the instrumental logic of technology, enhancing intergenerational learning in multiple dimensions of daily life. It follows that creating social support networks across generations can be centred on technology exponentiating social capital and overcoming a set of socio-demographic factors and economic resources that characterise the digital divide [39, 40]. These social support networks that focus on technology use and intergenerational relationships promote processes of informal and occasional learning [41]. Likewise, these networks materialise through ICTs and may avoid ageism [42] and promote active ageing [35].

Age-related circumstances impact social relations and functional capacities [43, 47]. Therefore, intergenerational digitally mediated relationships with family and friends may provide social connectivity and help complete everyday tasks [43].

In the last decades, intergenerational digitally mediated relationships have risen due to social media widespread use. Furthermore, mobile media use improved family solidarity [44], increasing the feeling of closeness during the pandemic [45]. Moreover, the use of these technologies has slowly driven the focus on functional dependence on the intergenerational solidarity framework [30] to "emphasising how emotional and social support between generations extends to the use of communication technology" [44].

The study presented in this article is twofold and took place during the pandemic after two states of emergency declared by the Portuguese government, between 8 and 17 October 2021, which resulted in the isolation of the population. The results suggest linking social support to combat digital inequality and foster self-sufficiency from an intergenerational solidarity perspective.

2 Method

The approach followed in this paper is a quantitative-extensive methodological strategy. By focusing on how young adults in Portugal (N = 1500 aged between 18 to 30 years old) perceive their intergenerational solidarity, especially with a generation of family members over 65 years old, this article presents findings of an applied online questionnaire survey. Such a questionnaire was applied to a representative sample of 1500 young adults, aged between 18 to 30 years, with quotas by gender and region (including mainland Portugal and islands) distributions.

Adopting a critical perspective of contemporary forms of digital media, this article intends to focus on the intergenerational solidarity perceptions of young adults in Portugal (RQ1: Do Portuguese young adults perceive to use of the internet to communicate with family members? If so, with whom do they communicate?) in terms of how much solidarity is intertwined with digital media uses, appropriations, and embodiments (RQ2: How is solidarity intertwined with digital media uses, appropriations and embodiments?).

The online questionnaire survey was conducted by an external contracted company, with a margin of error of ± 2.53% at the 95% confidence level. Using IBM SPSS statistical analysis software and other digital programs for statistical procedures, the data were analysed according to both descriptive and inferential (bivariate) statistical procedures.

Table 1 reveals a sample distribution which is particularly balanced in terms of age group and gender, which also considers other socio-demographic variables, such as socioeconomic and education. However, not all options constitute samples with significant statistical difference distribution. Therefore, the intersections presented in this article are the ones which have produced more statistically significant results, according to the inferential (bivariate) statistical analytical procedures. In the case of a specific statistically significant difference, such frequency is accompanied by a letter corresponding to the column to which such frequency is statistically significantly different. Such inferential (bivariate) procedures allow establishing appropriate comparisons between proportions, in that way indicating statistically significant differences through applied z-tests in the cases of sample sizes being bigger than 30, with a significance level of 0.05 (5%), which corresponds to a z-level of 1.96. Hence, admitting that such differences observed are statistically significant at a 95% confidence level.

Table 1. Sample distribution

Heading level	Count N	Count %
Age		
18 - 24	747	49.80%
25 - 30	753	50.20%
Gender Identity		
Man	696	46.40%
Woman	796	53.07%
Non-binary	6	0.40%
Agender, genderqueer or genderfluid	5	0.33%
In question	3	0.20%
Rather not answer	1	0,07%
Marital Status		
Single	1145	76.33%
Married or in Non-marital partnership	349	23.27%
Divorced or Separated	6	0.40%
Widower	0	0.00%
Other	0	0.00%
Education		
Basic education	48	3.20%
High school	655	43.67%
Bachelor's degree	516	34.40%
Master's degree	260	17.33%
PhD	21	1.40%
Occupation		
Student	425	28.33%
Self-employed	130	8.67%
Employee	459	50.60%
Liberal worker (Freelancer)	36	2.40%
Unemployed	150	10.00%

Source: Authors

3   Results and Discussion

According to the representative sample of 1500 young adults in Portugal, using the internet to communicate with any family member is an almost unanimous activity, with only 56 young adults (3,73%) responding negatively to such a question, which answers positively to the first part of RQ1 (Do Portuguese young adults perceive to use of the internet to communicate with family members?). However, online communication with family members is not equally distributed. In fact, there are statistically significant differences in terms of which family members the young adults affirm to communicate with. According to Table 2, young adults in Portugal reveal they mostly communicate through the internet with their mothers (75.21%), followed by their brothers/sisters (67.59%) and cousins (66.97%). 935 respondents affirm they communicate online with their fathers, which represents 64.75%, which is more than 10% less than the young adults who say that they communicate with their mothers.

Regarding older family members, more than 23% of young adults in Portugal affirm they communicate online with their grandmothers, which got higher percentages than grandfathers (17.73%) and other family members over 65 years old (15.17%). In fact, Table 2 indicates a gendered tendency in the family members with whom the respondents communicate. For example, either in a comparison between mother and father or in a comparison between grandmother and grandfather, there are higher percentages of young adults affirming they communicate by internet-based media with their female family members instead of their male ones.

Table 2. Family members with whom respondents communicate online

Family Members	Count N	Count %
Mother	1086	75.21%
Brothers/Sisters	976	67.59%
Cousins	967	66.97%
Father	935	64.75%
Uncle/Aunt	851	58.93%
Grandmother	333	23.06%
Grandfather	256	17.73%
Family members over 65	219	15.17%

Source: Authors

Between young adults in Portugal who affirm they communicate with their family members through internet-based media, there are statistically significant differences in terms of the gender of the young adults' respondents and as well as in terms of the marital status of such respondents. By using inferential (bivariate) statistical analytical procedures, Table 3 reveals such differences. Despite the representative sample of 1500 young adults being composed of 14 people who actively identify beyond the binary of man and woman, such a small-sized sample does not produce significant statistical data. The same applies to the small sample of young adults in Portugal who are divorced or separated (6 people), which does not constitute statistically relevant data. Therefore, Table 3 presents the percentages of family members with whom the respondents affirm they do online communication, intersected with the respondent's gender ("man" or "woman" as response options) and with the respondents' marital status ("single" or "married or in non-marital partnership" as options).

Regarding gender, Table 3 reveals three distinct statistically significant differences for a significance level of 0.05 (5%). First, young women adults reveal statistically significantly higher tendencies in online communication with their cousins and their uncle/aunt (71.71% and 64.34%, respectively) compared with the percentages of men's respondents (61.14% and 52.56%, respectively). On the other hand, young men adults in Portugal reveal a statistically significant tendency for online communication with their father (68.22%) in comparison with women respondents (61–76%).

When considering marital status differences in terms of respondents' online communication with family members, there are two specific statistically significant differences, as revealed in Table 3. Young adults in Portugal who are married or in a non-marital partnership show statistically significant higher tendencies in terms of internet-based communication with their mother and with their brothers/sisters (79.64% and 72.75%, respectively) in contrast with the respondents who are single (73.82% and 65.94%, respectively).

Since this article focuses on an intergenerational aspect, brothers/sisters and cousins only partially fit the scope, as those family members tend to be of the same generation as the respondents. Nonetheless, Table 3 has still revealed statistically significant different frequencies, regarding gender and marital status, for online intergenerational communication with the respondent's family members.

Table 3. Percentages of respondents by gender and marital status who use the internet to communicate with family members

	GENDER		MARITAL STATUS	
	Man (A)	Woman (B)	Single (C)	Married Or In Non-Marital Partnership (D)
Mother	76.05%	74.55%	73.82%	79.64% C
Brothers/Sisters	66.72%	68.48%	65.94%	72.75% C
Cousins	61.14%	71.71% A	65.76%	70.96%
Father	68.22% B	61.76%	64.76%	64.97%
Uncle/Aunt	52.56%	64.34% A	58.42%	60.48%
Grandmother	23.19%	22.87%	21.92%	26.95%
Grandfather	18.67%	16.67%	17.30%	18.86%
Family members over 65	14.61%	15.63%	15.04%	15.27%

Source: Authors

When solidarity is emphasised in terms of intergenerational activities and relationships, there is a tendency to look for connections between the younger and oldest generations. In this article's case, the online questionnaire applied to a representative sample of young adults in Portugal, aged between 18 and 30 years old, which implies a more specific focus on such respondents' interactions with their grandmothers, grandfathers and any other family members over 65. Therefore, solidarity is linked with young adults helping the older generations of family members deal with media, especially digital media tasks and activities. Thus, respondents were asked to indicate the frequency of categories of tasks/activities performed with their older family members. Such intergenerational solidarity results are revealed in Table 4.

Table 4 reveals the results of six different categories of tasks carried out through digital media by young adults, which are embedded in the idea of intergenerational solidarity since the young adults perform them with an auxiliary purpose to their family members' generation of grandparents and other relatives over 65 years old. The six categories of digital media-based tasks are: "digital communication/relationship", "assistance with economic/financial tasks", "civic and political participation", "digital leisure activities", "consulting legitimate news", and "seeking information on health and state services". In addition, respondents' perceptions of frequencies were inquired, according to a Likert Scale with five options, such being: "everyday", "several times a week", "once a week", "rarely", and "never". Z-tests had processed results revealed by Table 4 with a 95% confidence level to determine if any digital media intergenerational solidarity category of tasks is statistically significantly more or less frequent than any other category of tasks.

Several statistically significant results indicate that young adults in Portugal tend to frequently be in solidarity with their grandparents and other relatives over 65 years old in categories like "digital communication/relationship", "consulting legitimate news", and also "seeking information on health and state services". In fact, respondents who affirm they everyday intergenerationally perform such three categories of solidary tasks (14.80%, 16.00% and 15.67%) are statistically significantly more than the ones who affirm they perform the remaining three digital-media-based categories of tasks. In terms of digital communication/relationship tasks, respondents answered statistically significantly more "everyday", "several times a week," and "once a week" than either three or four different categories of tasks. Therefore, the 22.44% who perceive performing the "digital communication/relationship" category of tasks once a week is the highest answered percentage for this frequency option, which constitutes the most mid-level option amongst the five available frequencies. In point of fact, 22.44% are statistically significantly higher than the remaining categories of tasks, with the only exception being "seeking information on health and state services" (with 21.56% of respondents perceiving to once a week perform digital-media-based tasks that fit into such category of intergenerational solidarity).

Reinforcing the previously mentioned results, respondents who affirm they perform digital communication/relationship tasks "rarely" or "never" are statistically significantly inferior at those same frequency options regarding almost all the other five categories of tasks. For example, in the case of categories of tasks like "assistance with economic/financial tasks" and "civic and political participation", young adults in Portugal who perceive never to do the two categories as mentioned above (32.44% and 31.89%, respectively) are statistically significantly more than the respondents to affirm never to do the remaining categories of intergenerational solidarity digital-media based tasks: "digital communication/relationship" (13.87%); "digital leisure activities" (20.56%); "consulting legitimate news" (17.78%); "seeking information on health and state services" (18.11%). The percentages of young adults in Portugal who perceive never to do the "assistance with economic/financial tasks" and "civic and political participation" categories of tasks are the only two results with more than 30% of perceived frequency answers.

The "digital leisure activities" and "seeking information on health and state services" categories of tasks reveal peculiar statistically significant results. According to Table 4, young adults' perceptions of the frequency of such intergenerational solidarity tasks are very balanced. For instance, in the case of "digital leisure activities", 24.00% of respondents who perceive to realise several times a week such category of tasks are statistically significantly more than the "several times a week" percentages for the following three categories: "assistance with economic/financial tasks" (15.67%); "civic and political participation" (15.44%) and "seeking information on health and state services" (19.56%). At the same time, respondents who affirm they "rarely" or "never" do digital leisure activities (25.00% and 20.56%, respectively) are statistically significantly higher than the ones who perceive to rarely or never realise digital communication/relationship intergenerational solidarity digital media based tasks.

Likewise, the "seeking information on health and state services" category of tasks is the only category of intergenerational solidarity digital-media-based tasks with statistically significant differences for all five frequency options.

Table 4. Frequency perceptions of categories of tasks by the respondents with their grandparents or other relatives over 65 years old in a scale ranging from "Everyday" to "Never"

	CATEGORIES OF TASKS		
	Digital Communication/ Relationship (A)	Assistance with Economic/ Financial Tasks (B)	Civic and Political Participation (C)
Everyday	14.80% BCD	9.44%	9.67%
Several times a week	27.16% BCF	15.67%	15.44%
Once a week	22.44% BCDE	17.33%	16.67%
Rarely	21.73%	25.11% A	26.33% A
Never	13.87%	32.44% ADEF	31.89% ADEF
	Digital Leisure Activities (D)	Consulting Legitimate News (E)	Seeking Information on Health and State Services (F)
Everyday	11.89%	16.00% BCD	15.67% BCD
Several times a week	24.00% BCF	24.67% BCF	19.56% BC
Once a week	18.56%	18.00%	21.56% BC
Rarely	25.00% A	23.56%	25.11% A
Never	20.56% A	17.78% A	18.11% A

Source: Authors

4   Conclusions, Limitations and Implications for Future Research

In this paper, we focused on the perceptions of young adults about the intergenerational relationships they establish with their relatives. Regarding the first research question (RQ1), as we intended to understand if and with whom Portuguese young adults perceive to use of the Internet to communicate with family members, the results show that close relatives such as mothers, brothers and sisters, cousins and parents are with whom young adults communicate the most. However, 31.16% reveal that they interact with relatives over 65, with grandmothers and grandfathers standing out. There are no significant statistical differences in intergenerational digital relationships with family members over 65 in terms of gender. However, young people who are married or in a non-marital partnership are the ones who most use the Internet to communicate with grandmothers, grandfathers and other relatives over 65.

In addition, we tried to understand with whom they communicate through the Internet and if there is intergenerational solidarity in digital media uses, appropriations and embodiments (RQ2). In terms of intergenerational solidarity, the study concludes that functional solidarity is the most common, with young adults helping the older generations of family members deal with media, especially digital media tasks and activities. Furthermore, we identified six activities where intergenerational solidarity occurs: i). Digital communication/relationship; ii). Assistance with economic/financial tasks; iii). Civic and political participation; iv). Digital leisure activities; v). Consulting legitimate news; and vi). Seeking information on health and state services.

The data shows that most young adults help their relatives over 65 to carry out daily activities that focus on three key categories: digital communication/relationship, consulting legitimate news, and seeking information on health and state services. Therefore, the most mobilised modes of solidarity are structural, associational and affectual.

Future research should focus on older citizens' perceptions on intergenerational solidarity concerning digitally mediated relationships with younger generations.

Acknowledgements. Financial support from Portuguese national funds through FCT (Fundação para a Ciência e a Tecnologia) in the framework of the project "Mediated young adults' practices: advancing gender justice in and across mobile apps" (PTDC/COM-CSS/5947/2020).

References

1. Encheva, K., Driessens, O., Verstraeten, H.: The mediatization of deviant subcultures: an analysis of the media-related practices of graffiti writers and skaters. Mediekultur: J. Med. Commun. Res. **29**(54), 8–25 (2013)
2. van Krieken, K.: Multimedia storytelling in journalism: exploring narrative techniques in snow fall. Information **9**(5), 1–14 (2018)
3. Amaral, I., Flores, A.M., Antunes, E., Brites, M.J. (2022). Intergenerational digitally mediated relationships: how portuguese young adults interact with family members over 65+. In: Gao, Q., Zhou, J. (eds) Human Aspects of IT for the Aged Population. Technology in Everyday Living, HCII 2022. Lecture Notes in Computer Science, vol. 13331, pp. 335–348. Springer, Cham (2022). https://doi.org/10.1007/978-3-031-05654-3_23

4. Erjavec, K.: Readers of online news comments: why do they read hate speech comment. In: ANNALES Histoire, Sciences Sociales, pp. 451–462 (2014)
5. Reis, C.: Estudos narrativos mediáticos. In: Reis, C. (Ed,) Dicionário de Estudos Narrativos, pp. 132–145. Almedina, Coimbra (2018)
6. Schrøder, K.C.: Audiences are inherently cross-media: Audience studies and the cross-media challenge. CM Komunikacija i mediji 6(18), 5–27 (2011)
7. Lee, H., Yang, J.: Political knowledge gaps among news consumers with different news media repertoires across multiple platforms. Int. J. Commun. 8(1), 597–617 (2014)
8. Kõuts-Klemm, R., Brites, M.J.: How digital converges cross-media news typologies across countries: a comparative study of news consumption in Estonia and Portugal. Participations 14(2), 464–483 (2017)
9. Jenkins, H., Ito, M., Boyd, D.: Participatory Culture in A Networked Era: A Conversation on Youth, Learning, Commerce, and Politics. Polity Press, Cambridge (2016)
10. Hayes, T., Walker, C., Parsons, K., Arya, D., Bowman, B., Germaine, C., Lock, R., Langford, S., Peacock, S., Thew, H.: In it together! Cultivating space for intergenerational dialogue, empathy and hope in a climate of uncertainty. Child. Geograph, 1–16 (2022)
11. Blau, Z.S.: OttI Age in a Changing Society. Franklin Watts, New York (1997)
12. Derpmann, S.: Gründe der Solidarität. Mentis, Münster (2013)
13. Ellerich-Groppe, N., Pfaller, L., Schweda, M.: Young for old—old for young? ethical perspectives on intergenerational solidarity and responsibility in public discourses on COVID-19. Eur. J. Ageing 18(2), 159–171 (2021). https://doi.org/10.1007/s10433-021-00623-9
14. Barry, C., Lazar, S.: Justifying lockdown (2020). https://www.ethicsandinternationalaffairs.org/2020/justifying-lockdown/
15. Brglez, M., Duda J., Ijabs, I., et al.: Solidarity between generations must guide the EU response to and recovery from COVID-19. https://towardsanagefriendlyep.files.wordpress.com/2020/05/letter-to-ec-and-council_solidarity-between-generations.pdf
16. Ellerich-Groppe, N., Schweda, M., Pfaller, L.: #StayHomeForGrandma–Towards an analysis of intergenerational solidarity and responsibility in the coronavirus pandemic. Soc. Sci. Hum. Open 2(1), 100085 (2020)
17. Van Jaarsveld, G.M.: The effects of COVID-19 among the elderly population: a case for closing the digital divide. Front. Psychiatry 11 (2020)
18. Malwade, S., et al.: Mobile and wearable technologies in healthcare for the ageing population. Comput. Meth. Programs Biomed. 161, 233–237 (2018)
19. Friemel, T.N.: The digital divide has grown old: determinants of a digital divide among seniors. New Media Soc. 18(2), 313–331 (2016)
20. Nimrod, G.: Older audiences in the digital media environment. Inf. Commun. Soc. 20(2), 233–249 (2017)
21. Chipeva, P., Cruz-Jesus, F., Oliveira, T., Irani, Z.: Digital divide at individual level: evidence for Eastern and Western European countries. Gov. Inf. Q. 35(3), 460–479 (2018)
22. Zhou, Y., He, T., Lin, F.: The digital divide is aging: an intergenerational investigation of social media engagement in China. Int. J. Environ. Res. Public Health 19(19), 12965 (2022)
23. Szydlik, M.: Intergenerational solidarity and conflict. J. Comp. Fam. Stud. 39(1), 97–114 (2008)
24. Sinclair, T.J., Grieve, R.: Facebook as a source of social connectedness in older adults. Comput. Hum. Behav. 66, 363–369 (2017)
25. Quinn, K.: Cognitive effects of social media use: a case of older adults. Soc. Med.+ Soc. 4(3), 1–9 (2018)
26. Silverstein, M., Bengtson, V.L.: Do close parent-child relations reduce the mortality risk of older parents? J. Health Soc. Behav. 32(4), 382–395 (2009)

27. Taipale, S., Petrovcic, A., Dolnicar, V.: Intergenerational solidarity and ICT usage : empirical insights from finnish and Slovenian families. In S. Taipale, T.-A. Wilska, C. Gilleard (Eds.), Digital Technologies and Generational Identity : ICT Usage Across the Life Course, pp. 69–86. Routledge (2018)
28. Rainie, L., Wellman, B.: Networked The New Social Operating System. MIT Press, Cambridge (2012)
29. Dolničar, V., Grošelj, D., Hrast, M.F., Vehovar, V., Petrovčič, A.: The role of social support networks in proxy Internet use from the intergenerational solidarity perspective. Telematics Inform. **35**(2), 305–317 (2018)
30. Bengtson, V.L., Roberts, R.E.: Intergenerational solidarity in aging families: An example of formal theory construction. J. Marriage Fam. 856–870 (1991)
31. Harper, S., Hamblin, K.: International Handbook on Ageing and Public Policy. Edward Elgar Publishing, Cheltenham (2014)
32. Newman, S., Hatton-Yeo, A.: Intergenerational learning and the contributions of older people. Ageing Horiz. **8**(10), 31–39 (2008)
33. Field, J., Schuller, T.: Norms Networks and Trust. Adults Learn. **9**(3), 17–18 (1997)
34. Cruz-Saco, M.A.: Intergenerational solidarity. In: Cruz-Saco, M.A., Zelenev, S. (eds.) Intergenerational Solidarity, pp. 9–34. Palgrave Macmillan US, New York (2010). https://doi.org/10.1057/9780230115484_2
35. Patrício, M.R., Osório, A.: Intergenerational learning with ICT: A case study. Studia paedagogica **21**(2), 83–99 (2016)
36. Lee, O.E.K., Kim, D.H.: Bridging the digital divide for older adults via intergenerational mentor-up. Res. Soc. Work. Pract. **29**(7), 786–795 (2019)
37. Dolničar, V., Hrast, M.F., Vehovar, V., Petrovčič, A.: Digital inequality and intergenerational solidarity: The role of social support in proxy internet use. AoIR Selected Papers of Internet Research (2013)
38. Selwyn, N., Gorard, S., Furlong, J.: Whose Internet is it anyway? Exploring adults'(non) use of the Internet in everyday life. Eur. J. Commun. **20**(1), 5–26 (2005)
39. Hargittai, E.: Second-level digital divide: Mapping differences in people's online skills. arXiv preprint cs/0109068 (2001)
40. Loos, E.: Generational use of new media and the (ir)relevance of age. In: Colombo, F., Fortunati, L. (eds.) Broadband Society and Generational Changes, pp. 259–273. Peter Lang, Berlin (2011)
41. Reisdorf, B.C., Axelsson, A.-S., Söderholm, H.M.: Living Offline A Qualitative Study of Internet Non-Use in Great Britain and Sweden. Selected Papers of Internet Research: IR 13.0 Technologies (2012)
42. Ayalon, L., et al.: Aging in times of the COVID-19 pandemic: avoiding ageism and fostering intergenerational solidarity. J. Gerontol.: Ser. B **76**(2), e49–e52 (2021)
43. Leek, J., Rojek, M.: ICT tools in breaking down social polarization and supporting intergenerational learning: cases of youth and senior citizens. Interact. Learn. Environ. 1–16 (2021)
44. Nouwen, M., Duflos, M.: Displaying intergenerational solidarity on TikTok during the COVID-19 pandemic: understanding the implications in the grandparent-grandchild relationship. J. Fam. Stud. 1–20 (2022)
45. McDarby, M., Ju, C.H., Carpenter, B.D.: Frequency of contact and explanations for increased contact between grandchildren and their grandparents during the COVID-19 pandemic. J. Intergenerational Relat. **19**(2), 163–178 (2021)

46. Loos, E.F., de la Hera Conde-Pumpido, T., Simons, M., Gevers: Setting up and conducting the co-design of an intergenerational digital game: A state-of-the-art literature review. In: Zhou, J., Salvendy, G. (Eds.), Human Aspects of IT for the Aged Population. Design for the Elderly and Technology. 5th International Conference, ITAP 2019, Held as Part of the 21st HCI International Conference, HCII 2019, Orlando, FL, USA, 26–31 juli 2019, Proceedings, Part I, pp.56–69. Springer, Cham (2019)
47. de la Hera Conde-Pumpido, T., Loos, E.F., Simons, M., Blom, J.: Benefits and factors influencing the design of intergenerational games: a systematic literature review. Societies **7**, 18 (2017)

Understanding ICTs in Older Life: A Scope Review of 'The Gerontologist' and 'Research on Aging'

Simone Carlo(✉) ⓘ and Sara Nanetti ⓘ

Università Cattolica del Sacro Cuore, Milan, Italy
simone.carlo@unicatt.it

Abstract. Aging is an inevitable process for all human beings. Aging not only affects the personal life of individuals, but also has an impact on society as a whole: a country with many elderly people is a more fragile, less innovative country, with higher costs in terms of health and pension expenditure. In this context, information and communication technologies (ICT) can offer an important support in addressing some of the challenges related to ageing, improving communication between generations, access to information and the possibility of remaining active and involved in society, mitigating the negative effects of aging and transforming the elderly into a resource for the community.

The complexity and importance of the topic has led different disciplines to study (from different points of view) the relationship between aging and the use of ICT. The present study aims to investigate the theme of aging and how it is studied in relation to digital technologies from an interdisciplinary perspective. Due to the heterogeneity of perspectives and analyses in this field of study, a careful examination of interdisciplinary scientific journals focused on aging processes was required. Therefore, the analysis of scientific production was focused on two international scientific journals: The Gerontologist and Research on Aging.

Keywords: Ageing · Scoping review · ICTs

1 Introduction

1.1 Ageing and ICTs

Aging is an inevitable process for all human beings. As we age, the body and mind undergo changes that can affect the quality of life: less mobility, risk of isolation and loneliness, health problems. But aging not only affects the personal life of individuals, but also has an impact on society as a whole: a country with many elderly people is a more fragile, less innovative country, with higher costs in terms of health and pension expenditure. In this context, information and communication technologies (ICT) can offer an important support in addressing some of the challenges related to ageing, improving communication between generations, access to information and the possibility of remaining active and involved in society, mitigating the negative effects of aging

Q. Gao and J. Zhou (Eds.): HCII 2023, LNCS 14043, pp. 426–442, 2023.
https://doi.org/10.1007/978-3-031-34917-1_29

and transforming the elderly into a resource for the community. However, there are also the more problematic aspects of the relationship between the elderly and technologies, such as the scarce diffusion of ICT among the over 65s, a certain frustration in using some IT services and also the risk of an unconscious use by of the elderly of some digital resources.

The complexity and importance of the topic has led different disciplines to study (from different points of view) the relationship between aging and the use of ICT.

The adoption of information and communication technologies by older adults is an established research area in countries such as the USA [1], Europe, the UK [2] and the Scandinavian countries [3]. in which the domestic penetration of the Internet occurred early and rapidly, also significantly involving the older sections of the population.

Even in historically less digitized (but sometimes older) countries a reflection on the role of ICTs in the daily life of the elderly is developing. In the last few years has Italy begun to reflect with a certain constancy on the processes of diffusion and adoption of technologies by the over 65s [4]: particular attention is been placed both on the reasons and ways in which the elderly use technologies, and on the motivations that make many elderly people resistant to the use of ICT, making the Grey Digital Divide in Italy (i.e. the difference in the penetration of technologies between the elderly and the rest of the population) very accentuated compared to other European countries [5].

A large part of this reflection is part of a more extensive attempt to encourage the use of ICT by the Older people, emphasizing the positive effects (personal and social) deriving from the process of digitization of daily life also of the over 65s. The Covid-19 pandemic and the forced adoption of digital communication tools to counter closures and isolation has further spread the idea in society that digitization is a process that is not only positive in itself, but inevitable, and the resistance to change - or even just a certain caution against its effects - a traditionalist attitude. In particular, much reflection has revolved and revolves around the ability "per se" of ICTs to bridge gaps, problems, emerging tensions in society, such as the generational divide, for example, or the effects of excessive aging of society [6].

But beyond the enthusiasm around the processes of diffusion of technologies even among the elderly, academic research, sociology and psychology must continue to study what are, in reality, the contexts of use and non-use of digital technologies by part of the elderly, such as the reasons that lead the elderly and families to adopt or not a communication technology and such as the effects of the Internet and smartphones on identity and intergenerational relationships [7].

1.2 The State of the Art on Research on the Elderly and ICT

To reconstruct, with the necessary conciseness, the current scenario of studies on the relationship between aging and ICTs, we will resume here the results of two recent systematic reviews. The first systematic review concerns the "quantitative" studies conducted by Hunsaker and Hargittai [8]. The researchers note that the growth in the diffusion of ICTs among the elderly has led to growing attention to the skills and uses of digital technologies by the elderly: studies show that age is negatively correlated with digital skills, while digital skills they are high when the level of education and income is higher.

This growing attention from scientific research towards digital skills occurs simultaneously with the growth of public attention towards initiatives related to the organization of courses for digital literacy for the elderly.

Hunsaker and Hargittai also underline how progressively quantitative studies on the elderly are having increasing attention not only on "who are the digital elderly" but also on "what the digital elderly do": there is a growing interest in the digital practices of the elderly, who are varied, articulated, heterogeneous. In particular, the authors underline how the quantitative studies studied are often longitudinal studies and thus set themselves the goal of tracing the evolution over time of the use of digital media by the elderly.

If quantitative research on the use of ICTs by the elderly is now numerous and consolidated, only in recent years has there been a growth in qualitative studies on the relationship between ICTs and ageing: these studies have been little systematized. This is why Bonifacio [6] concentrated his efforts on a systematic review of qualitative studies on the relationship between the elderly and technologies.

A first interesting element that emerges from Bonifacio's revision is how the definition of "what an elderly person is", that is, from what age it is right to consider "elderly" people, is extremely variable: some papers consider people even well under 60 to be elderly and this risks overestimating the use of technologies by the "elderly", who perhaps are not "completely elderly". A second element of interest is the lack of studies on the use of ICTs among the elderly that are comparative between different countries and different cultural contexts. A third element concerns the dissemination of intervention research with the aim of evaluating some potential technological solutions to problems related to aging or to reduce the digital divide: most of the studies investigated deal with digital training and to confirm or (deny) the relationship between active aging and ICT use. Bonifacio's research collected papers up to 2018 and did not have the opportunity to investigate how the 2020 Covid-19 health crisis led to a possible change in the topics addressed by the most recent papers. Also for this reason, we consider it useful to continue mapping, studying, reviewing papers and scientific research on the relationship between the use of ICTs and ageing.

2   Methods and Sample

2.1   Research Questions

In recent years, there has been a significant increase in the adoption of digital technologies among older adults. The use of technology has the potential to enhance the quality of life and well-being of this population, particularly in terms of maintaining social connections and accessing health information. However, this group also faces several barriers in adopting digital technologies, including limited access, low digital literacy, and negative attitudes towards technologies. To better understand the current state of the field and identify future research directions, scoping reviews on the use of digital technologies among older adults have been conducted. There are numerous scoping reviews that have focused on specific aspect of the elderly's interaction with new digital technologies in various areas of interest, from digital applications in the medical field [9], referring to the impact of digital technology on the processes of care and assistance for the elderly population [10] and the impact digital technology on loneliness and social isolation in older people [11] to older adults' involvement in digital technology use [12].

The present study aims to investigate the theme of aging and how it is studied in relation to digital technologies from an interdisciplinary perspective. Due to the heterogeneity of perspectives and analyses in this field of study, a careful examination of interdisciplinary scientific journals focused on aging processes was required. Therefore, the analysis of scientific production was focused on two international scientific journals: The Gerontologist and Research on Aging.

2.2 Identifying Relevant Studies

Scoping reviews can be used by researchers to identify knowledge gaps, clarify concepts, and investigate research conduct, and can be useful precursors to systematic reviews. While scoping reviews are conducted for different purposes than systematic reviews, they still require rigorous and transparent methods to ensure trustworthy results. In summary, scoping reviews are a valuable tool in evidence synthesis, and proper conduct and guidance can lead to more efficient and effective research [13]. Scoping reviews have become increasingly popular across multiple disciplines as a means of synthesizing knowledge. While some scoping reviews have been conducted on intergenerational programs, none have yet synthesized evidence of intergenerational practices associated with program outcomes. Therefore, the present study aimed to undertake a scoping review to locate evidence-based practices used during intergenerational programming to further understand which evidence-based practices demonstrate appropriateness, effectiveness, meaningfulness, and feasibility within intergenerational programming.

2.3 Charting and Extraction of the Data

The scoping review is a crucial step in any research endeavor and must guarantee that the most pertinent information in the area of study is gathered from a vast array of documents. This process, referred to as the literature review or state of the art, involves a comprehensive examination of a particular subject. For this investigation, we plan to conduct a survey of the latest scholarly literature concerning aging, the use of technology by the elderly population, the limitations, and resources that technology can offer to the elderly, and the impact of technology on social relationships.

1. Each of the topics of interest addresses more specific issues:
2. The impact of COVID-19 on the digitalization processes.
3. The use of digital technologies in the daily life of the elderly.
4. The connection between the use of digital technologies and bio-psycho-social well-being.
5. The relationship between digital technologies and social relationships.
6. The main limitations encountered by the elderly in the use of digital technologies.
7. The advantages of using digital technologies for the elderly population.

The scoping review will particularly focus on the most recent (from 2019 to 2022) scholarly production of two international journals: The Gerontologist and Research on Aging. The choice of focusing the literature analysis on these two journals stems from the need to understand how interdisciplinary scientific reflection has approached the topic of aging and its relationship with digital technologies. Both peer-reviewed journals, in fact, concentrate on interdisciplinary research on aging and related issues, publishing articles, reviews, and comments that cover a wide range of topics related to aging from a geriatric, psychological, sociological, technological, and health perspective. Furthermore, they are considered among the leading journals in the field and have a high impact factor and are indexed in many important databases, including PubMed, Scopus, and the Web of Science.

From the extraction of all articles published from the journals, a total of 564 articles were analyzed for The Gerontologist and 171 for Research on Aging (Table 1).

Table 1. Sample (N°)

Years	The Gerontologist	Research on ageing
2019	138	41
2020	78	29
2021	131	38
2022	217	63
TOT	564	171

From the total sample of extracted articles, those that included the terms "Technology" and "Digital" were selected based on a text analysis of the abstracts and keywords. It was not necessary to add the textual criteria of "ageing" and/or "elderly," as these are specialty journals. Based on these criteria, a total of 41 articles were extracted, 39 articles for The Gerontologist and 2 articles for Research on Aging.

From the database searches, the data has been exported to an Excel spreadsheet for review and selection of the articles.

The following data was extracted from each article: title, author, country of author, country of study, methodology, subject matter, analyzed technology type, challenges and benefits of ICT use, the social dimension in the use of digital technologies, key themes, and key findings,

After extracting the key information from the articles included, a narrative summary of the main conclusions and concepts for each topic of interest was made.

3 Results

Table 2. Sample

Ref	Authors	Keywords	Main Topics	Methodology
[14]	(Chai and Kalyal 2019)	Cell phone use, happiness, China, rural–urban differences	(2) Use of ICT and well-being	Quantitative (survey)
[15]	(Schlomann et al. 2020)	Community-dwelling, digitalization; fourth age; technology	(1) ICT Care model	Longitudinal Quantitative Research
[16]	(Schroyer 2021)	Long-term care; Mental health (services, therapy); Social isolation; Covid	(4) Covid pandemic	*Review/commentary*
[17]	(Sipocz, Freeman, and Elton 2021)	Generational identity; Intergenerational conflict, Social media, Covid	(6) Ageism	Qualitative content analysis
[18]	(Chu et al. 2021)	Aging; Health behavior; Information-seeking; Protective measures; Worry, Covid	(4) Covid pandemic	Qualitative (media diary)
[19]	(Kim et al. 2021)	Evaluation, Geriatric care model, Implementation science, Long-term care	(1) ICT Care model	Trial – Intervention research (qualitative)
[20]	(Akhter-Khan 2021)	Caregiving; Ageism; Feminist economics; Healthy aging;	(3) Relational dimension	*Review/commentary*
[21]	(Ang, Lim, and Malhotra 2021)	Health-related difficulty; Internet use; Quality of life; Social support	(2) Use of ICT and well-being	Quantitative (survey)
[22]	(Zhang et al. 2021)	Emotional health; Internet use; Social networking sites (SNS)	(3) Relational dimension	Longitudinal Quantitative Research
[23]	(Kozlov et al. 2021)	Advance care planning; Communication; Decision making; Families	(1) WEB Care model	Trial – Intervention research (qualitative)

(continued)

Table 2. (*continued*)

Ref	Authors	Keywords	Main Topics	Methodology
(24)	(Williams et al. 2021)	Continuing education; Dementia; Elderspeak; Person-centered care; Staff-resident interactions, Online education	(1) WEB Care model	Intervention research (qualitative)
[25]	(Wei et al. 2022)	Aging in place; Measurement; Social isolation; Social networks; Technology	(3) Relational dimension	*Scoping review*
[26]	(Szabo et al. 2019)	Use of Internet, quality of life	(3) Relational dimension	Longitudinal Quantitative Research
[27]	(Fang et al. 2019)	Digital divide, intersectionality	(5) Digital divide	*Scoping review*
[28]	(Nam et al., 2019)	Health behaviors, Internet use	(2) Use of ICT and well-being	Longitudinal Quantitative Research
[29]	(Grates et al. 2019)	Design of technology for older adults, participatory design	(1) WEB Care model	Quantitative (survey) + qualitative interviews
[30]	(Mitchell et al. 2019)	Health disparities, Minority issues, Cohort differences	(5) Digital divide	Quantitative (survey)
[31]	(Pruchno 2019)	Digital Divide, Well-being, Robotics, Community, Nursing Home	(1) ICT Care model	*Review/commentary*
[32]	(Sood et al. 2019)	Gaming, Dementia	(1) WEB Care model	*Systematic review*
[33]	(Lee et al. 2019)	Computer self-efficacy, Technology adoption	(2) Use of ICT and well-being	Longitudinal Quantitative Research
[34]	(Westerhof et al. 2019)	Mental health (digital services, therapy)	(1) WEB Care model	Pilot randomized controlled trial
[35]	(Peine and Neven 2019)	Science and technology studies, Gerontechnology	(2) Use of ICT and well-being	*Review/commentary*
[36]	(Schmidt and Wahl 2019)	Technology, Autonomy and self-efficacy, Task performance	(2) Use of ICT and well-being	Quantitative (survey)

(*continued*)

Table 2. (*continued*)

Ref	Authors	Keywords	Main Topics	Methodology
[37]	(Croff et al. 2019)	African American, Gentrification, Social engagement, App	(1) App Care model	Qualitative interviews
[38]	(Mitzner et al. 2019)	Computer system specifically designed for older users. Trail	(2) Use of ICT and well-being	Qualitative (trial)
[39]	(Choi et al. 2020)	Attitudes and perception toward aging/aged, Gender issues	(5) Digital divide	Quantitative (survey)
[40]	(Liu et al. 2020)	Disparities in access to online health-related technology and health care utilization	(1) WEB Care model	Quantitative (survcy)
[41]	(Burholt 2020)	Technology-mediated communication, familiar relationships, isolation and loneliness	(3) Relational dimension	Longitudinal Quantitative Research
[42]	(Grigorovich and Kontos 2020)	Ethical, social, and policy implications of using technology in institutional care	(1) ICT Care model	*Critical review*
[43]	(Köttl, Tatzer, and Ayalon 2022)	Media coveraga, older ICT user, Covid pandemic	(4) Covid pandemic	Qualitative (media discourse critical analisys)
[44]	(Boot 2022)	Cognitive change, use of ICT	(1) WEB Care model	Book review
[45]	(Rush et al. 2022)	Health promotion; Technology acceptance model	(1) WEB Care model	*Systematic review*
[46]	(Kim and Han 2022)	Cognitive decline, ICT uses	(2) Use of ICT and well-being	Longitudinal Quantitative Research
[47]	(Chu et al. 2022)	Digital Ageism, AI for Older People	(6) Ageism	Review
[48]	(Haghzare et al. 2022)	Assistive technologies; Care partners; Driving;	(1) Automated vehicles (AVs)	Qualitative interviews
[49]	(Yeung et al. 2022)	Using of PC, cognitive function	(2) Computer uso benessere	Pilot randomized controlled trial

(*continued*)

Table 2. (*continued*)

Ref	Authors	Keywords	Main Topics	Methodology
[50]	(Ng and Indran 2022a)	Generational stereotypes; Intergenerational tension; TikTok; Videos. Ageism	(2) Use of ICT and well-being	Qualitative content analysis
[51]	(Ng and Indran 2022b)	Aging narratives; Social construction of old age; Social media. Ageism	(6) Ageism	Qualitative content analysis
[52]	(Døssing and Crăciun 2022)	Age stereotypes; Stereotype content model; Twitter. Agesim, Covid	(4) Covid pandemic	Qualitative content analysis
[53]	(Averbach and Monin 2022)	Accessibility; Arts and health; Technology; Visual arts; Wellness	(1) ICT Care model	Trial, experimental, qualitative

3.1 An Overview About Relevant Topics

As can be seen from Table 2 the selected articles focus on six main topics: 1) the analysis or experimentation of new digital technologies (Web, App, ICT, Internet) aimed at caring for the elderly, promoting their well-being, achieving new levels of autonomy, or assisting caregivers in their care tasks; 2) the ways in which the elderly population approaches digital technologies (Computers, smartphones, Internet) and the relationship that usage has with perceived well-being; 3) the relational dimension of new technologies that allow the elderly to combat loneliness and reinforce their social and care networks through their use; 4) the effects that the Covid pandemic has had on numerous digitalization processes and how the elderly have reacted to these changes; 5) the relevance of the digital divide phenomenon with respect to a multiplicity of factors that, from an intersectional perspective, include not only age but also gender, ethnicity, and numerous social factors; 6) the phenomenon of widespread ageism through social media.

3.2 Criticalities and Advantages of the Use of ICTs

In his review of the literature, Bonifacio [6] underlines how a reflection on the advantages that the elderly would have from the use of ICTs is well present in the corpus of articles analysed, while instead the reflection on the possible risks in the use of ICT by the elderly is more marginal (almost non-existent).

Also in our review the advantages for the elderly of using ICT are well present: thanks to the use of digital media, the elderly would have better mental health [46], more effective communication with one's own social network (even intergenerational) [23] and in isolated contexts [14]. The elderly find in ICTs a new source of entertainment

[53], more effective tools to heal themselves and be healed [46], to feel supported [20, 22], for greater autonomy, more effective information channels [18].

The literature on the relationship between the elderly and ICT has over the years been more attentive to underlining the positive aspects of the relationship between technologies and ageing, both in macrosocial terms (e.g. savings in public health costs [45]) both in microsocial terms (the positive impact in the daily life of the elderly): "ICTs are often promoted as a solution to a set of emergent problems related to Western aging societies. Besides the policy discourse, even several scientific studies currently share this research perspective" (6, p.34). The real risk, for the elderly, is therefore that of remaining disconnected [54].

However, a growing focus on emerging critical issues is gaining ground in the most recent academic literature.

For example, Schroyer [16] underlines how excessive time spent in front of the TV and in the use of digital media can have negative effects on the elderly, especially in contexts of isolation, sedentary lifestyle, illness, communication crises and anxiety-provoking situations (Covid-19).

Among the elements of difficulty and criticality in the use of ICT is the issue of privacy. Privacy is understood both as an element that slows down the use of technologies by the elderly (concerned about the risk of seeing their autonomy/independence undermined) and as a concern on the part of researchers regarding the non-aware use by the elderly of own data and information. A further element of criticism concerns the difficulties that the elderly would have in understanding the reliability of news on the Internet, especially those related to health: using the Internet for health information is risky because it favors the confirmation bias [16].

A concern linked to the Internet as a place in which processes of discrimination against the elderly take shape clearly emerges [50].

In particular, social networks (Twitter and Tik Tok) are represented as places of manifestation of ageism by the younger generations [17, 51]. Such conflicts are statutes exacerbated by the Covid-19 pandemic in which the elderly have simultaneously been the subjects to be protected more than others but also, for some, the cause of the personal limitations that the younger generations have had. [52]. "The pandemic seemed to have acted as an amplifier, further exacerbating and perpetuating stereotypical, dichotomous, but also empowering aging images. [...] "Aging-and-innovation" discourses have contributed to the construction of an overly negative imagery of older persons as frail and needy, due to the fact that the majority of designed products for older people focuses on health care/assistive technologies" [20, p. 421].

Furthermore, critical positions are beginning to emerge with respect to the role of technologies in the healthcare system, in its accessibility, universality but also sustainability when fully operational: for example: "monitoring technologies may introduce new types of risks, such as disruption of care, increased workload related to data management, and technology maintenance, may undermine otherwise good intentions with the use of these technologies" [20, p.1198].

3.3 Social Dimension

The study conducted by Szabo et al. highlights, through a longitudinal analysis of a panel of subjects between 60 and 70 years old, the indirect impact of Internet use for social, informational, and instrumental purposes on the well-being of older adults, through reducing loneliness and supporting social engagement [26]. The article shows that not all modes of online content consumption have the same impact on subjects in terms of well-being and social engagement. Three different ways of using the internet were considered: for social purposes (e.g., connecting with friends/family), with instrumental purposes (e.g., banking), and for informational purposes (e.g., reading health-related information). Social use indirectly influenced well-being through the reduction of loneliness and the increase of social engagement, while informational and instrumental use indirectly influenced well-being through engagement in a wider range of activities; however, they were not correlated with loneliness. In summary, Internet use can support the well-being of older adults, but not every form of engagement has the same impact on well-being and social engagement.

Another investigation presented by Zhang et al. addresses the association between internet use and social relationships, but with a focus on social media use [22]. Once again, the proposed analysis highlights a strong correlation between social media use and a decrease in perceived loneliness levels. In this case, social media communication was associated with higher levels of perceived social support and social contact, which were related to lower levels of loneliness among older adults.

The broad reflection proposed by Akhter-Khan, highlighting the important role played by the elderly in providing care and support and how this is positively correlated with their well-being, addresses the relationship with digital technologies as follows: on the one hand, as a potential tool through which the elderly can extend their care and emotional support to children and grandchildren; on the other hand, as tools through which they can remain integrated in their communities through volunteering activities on social media platforms [20].

The study proposed by Burholt et al. focuses on the daily practices of older adults in their familial context and the use of technology-mediated communication, demonstrating how synchronous and asynchronous forms of communication have some functional equivalence to face-to-face contact. Telephone calls, text messages, and emails are used as a substitute or supplement to in-person contact and have reduced the influence of face-to-face contact on social isolation for older adults. However, none of the forms of communication have emotional equivalence to the "gold standard" of physical presence. The authors note that the contact provided through technology-mediated communication does not match older adults' expectations regarding familial relationships [41].

Wei et al.'s scoping review aimed to identify studies that aimed to improve health or social care for older adults and used technology to measure social networks. The review highlighted how technology facilitates objective and longitudinal data collection on the social interactions and activities of older adults. However, the use of technology to measure older adults' social networks is primarily in an exploratory phase. Multidisciplinary collaborations are needed to overcome operational, analytical, and implementation challenges [25].

In conclusion, the reviewed articles demonstrate how the psychological well-being of older adults is strongly linked to social connections, while information and communication technologies (ICT) have been identified as a tool to increase social engagement. The use of social media and other internet-based communication technologies, such as the social platform aimed at increasing seniors' participation in public life [29], have been identified as factors that can improve well-being and reduce loneliness. However, important issues remain open regarding accessibility and the digital divide, which appears strongly correlated with the availability of immaterial-cultural and material-economic resources. The use of technology for health management is lower among minority groups and those with lower socioeconomic status. Living arrangements also simultaneously influence the use and benefits of technology for older adults. Furthermore, the relationship between cognitive functions and technology use is influenced by living arrangements and the social environment. Age and negative perceptions of aging are also linked to less frequent internet use, especially among women. Overall, the interplay between technology, social environment, and cognitive functions in later life should be considered for a better understanding of the use and effects of technology for older adults.

3.4 Methodologies, Sample, Technologies

The papers analyzed show an extreme variety of methodologies applied. Quantitative research is the most numerous and often uses and analyzes secondary data sources already available such as the Health and Retirement Study - USA [28, 39, 40], and samples already collected from institutions and public bodies. In particular, there are few studies that construct ad hoc questionnaires and samples, designed to specifically and in-depthly investigate the relationship between ICT and ageing: many of these ad hoc surveys are conducted in Asia, where many of the paper with a cross-sectional approach [14, 21].

Among the quantitative research (above all from the United States, Canada, New Zealand but also from Europe) a growing attention emerges for longitudinal research, with the attempt to understand the changing relationship between the elderly and ICT over the years. In particular, these are studies that seek to study the processes of reducing the access digital divide and the emergence of gaps of various nature (for example on skills) [15, 22, 26].

As regards research with qualitative methodologies, they are less numerous and often linked to intervention research and clinical contexts [24].

As far as age and the personal definition of the elderly are concerned, several researches that use secondary data from national surveys already consider people over 50 to be elderly [22, 39, 49]. Apart from some specific research conducted within nursing homes where the age considered is often over 75, generally the elderly considered are people over 60 years of age.

A separate reflection concerns desk research (both quantitative and qualitative) which focuses on the analysis of texts (posts on social media, articles on the Internet) and is research in particular related to the theme of the representation of the elderly (often stereotyped) on the Internet [17, 51].

The number of reviews present in our sample is also significant, demonstrating the growing production of papers and research on the relationship between the elderly and aging but also the result of the need to systematize an often fragmented, heterogeneous, unconsolidated scientific production.

Finally, as regards the technologies studied, on the one hand there are studies that focus on the use of communication technologies and digital services currently available on the market (Internet, social media, smartphones).

On the other hand, especially intervention research in clinical and healthcare contexts, the effects and effectiveness of specially developed technologies and services are analysed. These technologies and services are mainly attributable to "environment-based technology", i.e. "hardware designed for and installed in living spaces such as in private homes or nursing homes" [33, p 428] and, more marginally, to "person-based technology", i.e. hardware that is wearable. "This technology includes cameras and Global Positioning System (GPS) sensors in smartphones, accelerometers, and heart rate detectors installed in smartwatches and wearable sensors" (ibidem).

Furthermore, reflections are emerging about the impact of new technologies and services (such as Artificial Intelligence [47] and Automated vehicles [48]) on aging.

4   Conclusion

At the end of our article, we can make some reflections, which emerge from the reading and review of the numerous articles present in our sample.

A first consideration concerns the type of elderly person that emerges from the papers analysed. Life expectancy is growing in all countries of the world and the onset of old age is moving further and further ahead of the life course. Despite this, academic research often begins to consider "elderly" subjects who in society they are now considered adults or mature and have not yet entered the third stage of life. We are talking about those researches that consider elderly subjects under 60 years old, sometimes even under 55 years old.

Classifying such young subjects as "elderly" is certainly an advantage and a simplification for the recruiting phase of the research (the very elderly are more difficult to find respect the young elderly) but there is a risk of having distortions in the results, especially if the use of ICTs is analysed.

A second reflection concerns the social and relational dimension of the elderly. If the most recent literature on the digital divide and the processes of learning and using technologies underline the need to study the use of ICTs in the social contexts in which it is articulated, not all research still gives space to the relational dimension to understand the relationship between aging and use of ICTs. In particular, quantitative research continues to reflect on the personal characteristics and dimensions of the elderly, to apply a "methodological individualism" [55] that reduces the complexity of the real contexts of learning and use of ICTs. On the other hand, it has been highlighted that articles focusing on the relationship between ICTs and the social participation of the elderly have shown interesting connections between the use of ICTs and an increase in social relationships or a decrease in loneliness [26]. These findings warrant further investigation and exploration.

A third element of reflection concerns the contexts of analysis and the nature of the samples. The analysis of secondary data of large samples (already structured) is a fairly common practice. Less widespread is the construction of ad hoc questionnaires and samples. As far as qualitative research is concerned, nursing homes continue to represent an interesting place for research and for understanding the relationship between aging and technologies (especially health). But is the analysis of these contexts really useful for understanding the aging processes in society? Aren't these contexts too characterized, where the aging processes are peculiar and cannot be extended to the whole of society?

COVID-19 has played a catalytic role in the phenomenon of ageism in the analyzed literature. On the one hand, disparities, and inequalities of access, particularly to information, have been highlighted, and on the other hand, distorted and stereotypical representations of aging in relation to new technologies have emerged in social media narratives. According to the findings, the pandemic amplified stereotypes regarding the relationship between older adults and emerging information and communication technologies (EICT), but also led to discussions on positive aging trends and innovation, highlighting the crucial role of media in raising awareness about power imbalances and reducing ageism related to EICT use [43]. Even social media has played a significant role in polarizing the discourse on aging between hostile and benevolent ageism [52]. Access to information during the Covid-19 pandemic has revealed numerous weaknesses, particularly with respect to the most vulnerable populations [16]. Indeed, it has been shown that having more sources of information in the context of a public health crisis provides greater incentives to adopt higher health protective behaviors [47].

References

1. Saunders, E.J.: maximizing computer use among the elderly in rural senior centers. Educ. Gerontol. **30**(7), 573–585 (2004)
2. Haddon, L.: Social exclusion and information and communication technologies: lessons from studies of single parents and the young elderly. New Media Soc. **2**(4), 387–406 (2000)
3. Naumanen, M., Tukiainen, M.: Guided participation in ICT-education for seniors: Motivation and social support. In: 2009 39th IEEE Frontiers in Education Conference, pp. 1–7 (2009)
4. Colombo, F., Aroldi, P., Carlo, S.: 'Stay tuned': The role of ICTs in elderly life. Active Ageing Healthy Living: Hum. Cent. Approach Res. Innov. Source Qual. Life **1**(203), 145–156 (2014)
5. Sala E, Gaia A.: Older People's Use of «Information and Communication Technology» in Europe. The Italian Case. AL. 2019 (2019)
6. Bonifacio F. The Relationship Between Older Adults and ICTs: A Systematic Review of Qualitative Studies. Relat. Between Older Adults ICTs: Syst. Rev. Qual. Stud. 21–37 (2021)
7. Colombo, F., Aroldi, P., Carlo, S.: 'I use it correctly!' : the use of ICTs among Italian grandmothers in a generational perspective. Hum. Technol. [Internet]. 2018 **14**(3) (2021). https://jyx.jyu.fi/handle/123456789/60473
8. Hunsaker, A., Hargittai, E.: A review of Internet use among older adults. New Media Soc. **20**, 3937–3954 (2018)
9. Wilson, J., Heinsch, M., Betts, D., Booth, D., Kay-Lambkin, F.: Barriers and facilitators to the use of e-health by older adults: a scoping review. BMC Public Health **21**(1), 1556 (2021)
10. Chelongar, K., Ajami, S.: Using active information and communication technology for elderly homecare services: A scoping review. Home Health Care Serv. Q. **40**(1), 93–104 (2021)

11. Döring, N., Conde, M., Brandenburg, K., Broll, W., Gross, H.M., Werner, S., et al.: Can communication technologies reduce loneliness and social isolation in older people? A scoping review of reviews. Int. J. Environ. Res. Public Health **19**(18), 11310 (2022)

12. Kebede, A.S., Ozolins, L.L., Holst, H., Galvin, K.: The digital engagement of older people: systematic scoping review protocol. JMIR Res. Protoc. **10**(7), e25616 (2021)

13. Munn, Z., Peters, M.D.J., Stern, C., Tufanaru, C., McArthur, A., Aromataris, E.: Systematic review or scoping review? Guidance for authors when choosing between a systematic or scoping review approach. BMC Med. Res. Methodol. **18**(1), 143 (2018)

14. Chai, X., Kalyal, H.: Cell phone use and happiness among Chinese older adults: does rural/urban residence status matter? Res. Aging **41**(1), 85–109 (2019)

15. Schlomann, A., Seifert, A., Zank, S., Rietz, C.: Assistive technology and mobile ICT usage among oldest-old cohorts: comparison of the oldest-old in private homes and in long-term care facilities. Res. Aging **42**(5–6), 163–173 (2020)

16. Schroyer, D.: Media effects on individual worldview and wellness for long-term care residents amid the COVID-19 virus. Gerontologist **61**(1), 8–12 (2021)

17. Sipocz, D., Freeman, J.D., Elton, J.: "A toxic trend?": generational conflict and connectivity in twitter discourse under the #BoomerRemover hashtag. Gerontologist **61**(2), 166–175 (2021)

18. Chu, L., Fung, H.H., Tse, D.C.K., Tsang, V.H.L., Zhang, H., Mai, C.: Obtaining information from different sources matters during the COVID-19 pandemic. Gerontologist **61**(2), 187–195 (2021)

19. Kim, H., Jung, Y.I., Kim, G.S., Choi, H., Park, Y.H.: Effectiveness of a technology-enhanced integrated care model for frail older people: a stepped-wedge cluster randomized trial in nursing homes. Gerontologist **61**(3), 460–469 (2021)

20. Akhter-Khan, S.C.: Providing care is self-care: towards valuing older people's care provision in global economies. Gerontologist. **61**(5), 631–639 (2021)

21. Ang, S., Lim, E., Malhotra, R.: Health-related difficulty in internet use among older adults: correlates and mediation of its association with quality of life through social support networks. Gerontologist. **61**(5), 693–702 (2021)

22. Zhang, K., Kim, K., Silverstein, N.M., Song, Q., Burr, J.A.: Social media communication and loneliness among older adults: the mediating roles of social support and social contact. Gerontologist **61**(6), 888–896 (2021)

23. Kozlov, E., McDarby, M., Duberstein, P., Carpenter, B.D.: The feasibility and acceptability of an intergenerational, web-based intervention to enhance later-life family care planning. Gerontologist. **61**(7), 1153–1163 (2021)

24. Williams, K.N., Coleman, C.K., Perkhounkova, Y., Beachy, T., Hein, M., Shaw, C.A., et al.: Moving online: a pilot clinical trial of the changing talk online communication education for nursing home staff. Gerontologist **61**(8), 1338–1345 (2021)

25. Wei, S., Kang, B., Bailey, D.E., Caves, K., Lin, Y., McConnell, E.S., et al.: Using technology to measure older adults' social networks for health and well-being: a scoping review. Gerontologist **62**(7), e418–e430 (2022)

26. Szabo, A., Allen, J., Stephens, C., Alpass, F.: Longitudinal analysis of the relationship between purposes of internet use and well-being among older adults. Gerontologist **59**(1), 58–68 (2019)

27. Fang, M.L., Canham, S.L., Battersby, L., Sixsmith, J., Wada, M., Sixsmith, A.: Exploring privilege in the digital divide: implications for theory, policy, and practice. Gerontologist **59**(1), e1-15 (2019)

28. Nam, S., Han, S.H., Gilligan, M.: Internet use and preventive health behaviors among couples in later life: evidence from the health and retirement study. Gerontologist **59**(1), 69–77 (2019)

29. Grates, M.G., Heming, A.C., Vukoman, M., Schabsky, P., Sorgalla, J.: New perspectives on user participation in technology design processes: an interdisciplinary approach. Gerontologist **59**(1), 45–57 (2019)

30. Mitchell, U.A., Chebli, P.G., Ruggiero, L., Muramatsu, N.: The digital divide in health-related technology use: the significance of race/ethnicity. Gerontologist **59**(1), 6–14 (2019Jan 9)

31. Pruchno, R.: Technology and aging: an evolving partnership. Gerontologist **59**(1), 1–5 (2019)

32. Sood, P., Kletzel, S.L., Krishnan, S., Devos, H., Negm, A., Hoffecker, L., et al.: Nonimmersive brain gaming for older adults with cognitive impairment: a scoping review. Gerontologist **59**(6), e764–e781 (2019)

33. Lee, C.C., Czaja, S.J., Moxley, J.H., Sharit, J., Boot, W.R., Charness, N., et al.: Attitudes toward computers across adulthood from 1994 to 2013. Gerontologist **59**(1), 22–33 (2019)

34. Westerhof, G.J., Lamers, S.M.A., Postel, M.G., Bohlmeijer, E.T.: Online therapy for depressive symptoms: an evaluation of counselor-led and peer-supported life review therapy. Gerontologist **59**(1), 135–146 (2019)

35. Peine, A., Neven, L.: From intervention to co-constitution: new directions in theorizing about aging and technology. Gerontologist **59**(1), 15–21 (2019)

36. Schmidt, L.I., Wahl, H.W.: Predictors of performance in everyday technology tasks in older adults with and without mild cognitive impairment. Gerontologist **59**(1), 90–100 (2019)

37. Croff, R.L., Witter Iv, P., Walker, M.L., Francois, E., Quinn, C., Riley, T.C., et al.: Things are changing so fast: integrative technology for preserving cognitive health and community history. Gerontologist **59**(1), 147–157 (2019)

38. Mitzner, T.L., Savla, J., Boot, W.R., Sharit, J., Charness, N., Czaja, S.J., et al.: Technology adoption by older adults: findings from the PRISM trial. Gerontologist **59**(1), 34–44 (2019)

39. Choi, E.Y., Kim, Y., Chipalo, E., Lee, H.Y.: Does perceived ageism widen the digital divide? and does it vary by gender? Gerontologist **60**(7), 1213–1223 (2020)

40. Liu, D., Yamashita, T., Burston, B., Keene, J.R.: The use of online health-management tools and health care utilization among older Americans. Gerontologist **60**(7), 1224–1232 (2020)

41. Burholt, V.: Technology-mediated communication in familial relationships: moderated-mediation models of isolation and loneliness. Gerontologist **60**(7), 1202–1212 (2020)

42. Grigorovich, A., Kontos, P.: Towards responsible implementation of monitoring technologies in institutional care. Gerontologist **60**(7), 1194–1201 (2020)

43. Köttl, H., Tatzer, V.C., Ayalon, L.: COVID-19 and everyday ICT use: the discursive construction of old age in German media. Gerontologist **62**(3), 413–424 (2022)

44. Boot, W.R.: Designing, evaluating, and disseminating novel technology solutions to support older adults with cognitive impairments. Gerontologist **62**(7), 1095–1096 (2022)

45. Rush, K.L., Singh, S., Seaton, C.L., Burton, L., Li, E., Jones, C., et al.: Telehealth use for enhancing the health of rural older adults: a systematic mixed studies review. Gerontologist **62**(10), e564–e577 (2022)

46. Kim, Y.K., Han, S.H.: Internet use and cognitive functioning in later life: focus on asymmetric effects and contextual factors. Gerontologist **62**(3), 425–435 (2022)

47. Chu, C.H., Nyrup, R., Leslie, K., Shi, J., Bianchi, A., Lyn, A., et al.: Digital ageism: challenges and opportunities in artificial intelligence for older adults. Gerontologist **62**(7), 947–955 (2022)

48. Haghzare, S., Delfi, G., Stasiulis, E., Mohamud, H., Dove, E., Rapoport, M.J., et al.: Can automated vehicles be useful to persons living with dementia? the perspectives of care partners of people living with dementia. Gerontologist **62**(7), 1050–1062 (2022)

49. Yeung, D.Y., Chow, L.C., Ho, A.K.K., Chung, E.K.H.: The effect of information and communications technology use on the well-being of older Hong Kong Chinese adults. Educ. Gerontol. 1–16 (2022)

50. Ng, R., Indran, N.: Hostility toward baby boomers on TikTok. Gerontologist **62**(8), 1196–1206 (2022)

51. Ng, R., Indran, N.: Not too old for TikTok: how older adults are reframing aging. Gerontologist. **62**(8), 1207–1216 (2022)

52. Døssing, M.V., Crăciun, I.C.: From hostile to benevolent ageism: polarizing attitudes toward older adults in German COVID-19-related tweets. Gerontologist **62**(8), 1185–1195 (2022)
53. Averbach, J., Monin, J.: The impact of a virtual art tour intervention on the emotional well-being of older adults. Gerontologist **62**(10), 1496–1506 (2022)
54. Lee, B., Chen, Y., Hewitt, L.: Age differences in constraints encountered by seniors in their use of computers and the internet. Comput. Hum. Behav. **27**(3), 1231–1237 (2011)
55. van Dijk, J.A.G.M.: The evolution of the digital divide - the digital divide turns to inequality of skills and usage. Digit. Enlightenment Yearbook **2012**, 57–78 (2012)

Applying PBL Model to Technological Learning Strategies for Older Adults

Kuei-Yuan Chang(✉) ⒾⒹ and Chang-Franw Lee

Graduate School of Design, National Yunlin University of Science and Technology, Yunlin, Taiwan

ken.chang.1011@gmail.com, leecf@yuntech.edu.tw

Abstract. With the aim of integrating the concepts of PBL learning philosophies and learning communities, this study discussed and worked out a technological teaching strategy suitable for older adults. It was expected that this study could explore and deepen the learning experience of older adults through personally experiencing the situation and through problem exchange to assist them in improving their technological literacy and the ability to learn independently. This study held a participatory workshop and invited 18 older adults to participate in a technological learning course to further probe into the learning effectiveness and the opinions of older adults.

This study showed that when learning in technological courses, the participants had great individual differences, were interest- and practical-oriented, had a lack of self-confidence, had a community effect, and had requirements for immediate discussion and assistance. Assisted by two kinds of PBL models, the participants received significant positive effects on the desire for technical learning, the perceived usefulness, and their psychological well-being. Moreover, the participants also had the thought and motivation to continue pursuing independent learning.

Keywords: PBL Model · Older Adults · Learning Community

1 Introduction

1.1 Older Adults and Technological Learning

The public often misunderstands older adults' attitudes toward learning technology. Many people believe that older adults do not understand and do not need to use technology. In fact, older adults also have the potential to use technological products. Although older adults may find it difficult to learn independently and often make mistakes due to a lack of relevant technological experience, they can also use technology skillfully after receiving appropriate guidance [1]. In addition, many older adults believe that technology can improve their life quality and life satisfaction [2–4], and they expect to use it to strengthen their connections with relatives and friends [5].

© The Author(s), under exclusive license to Springer Nature Switzerland AG 2023
Q. Gao and J. Zhou (Eds.): HCII 2023, LNCS 14043, pp. 443–456, 2023.
https://doi.org/10.1007/978-3-031-34917-1_30

Learning information technology and network applications are useful for older adults to receive new information and to promote study while achieving the purpose of social connectedness [6], thus improving all aspects of their life quality [4, 7]. This study divided the above-mentioned normal factors affecting older adults' use of information technology and the benefits into three categories:

1. Self-efficacy: For older adults, learning technology and staying up to date with technology are signs of self-challenge and of maintaining vitality in addition to understanding young people's life. These actions are helpful for them to establish confidence.
2. Social connection: Older adults' use of information technology helps to promote social connections, command social development, maintain relationships with families and friends, promote interpersonal relations, and manage self-image.
3. Psychological well-being: Older adults' use of information technology includes aspects of leisure, entertainment, and living needs and eliminates the sense of loneliness for older adults. It also provides extra channels for shopping, amusement games, inquiry about health information, and knowledge learning.

In brief, for older adults, learning how to use technological products can promote a positive perception of life, satisfy social connectedness requirements, and improve self-efficacy.

1.2 Learning Philosophies of Problem-Based Learning

In recent years, learner-centered learning has attracted much attention and become a trend in education policy. Problem-based learning (PBL) is a reflection of a kind of behavioral education in which the learning is situational and life-like. It pursues the concepts of student-centered learning and uses problem-based teaching materials, group-based platforms, and discussion-based modes. With the interpretation and application differences in different teaching scenes, two explanations of problem-based learning and project-based learning have derived from PBL. Although the core of both explanations is to organize the learning process based on problems and to regard problems as the starting point of the learning process [8], there are differences in the learning connotation, problem structure, and achievement category.

- **Problem-Based Learning**

Problem-based learning (PBL) starts with an ill-defined abstract problem. The purpose of learning is learning, and the key of learning is the process of solving a problem, not the ultimate answer. Problem-based learning can also be regarded as a kind of divergent learning mode. Based on an indefinite problem or description, it guides learners to form different sub-topics in the process of solving the initial problem [9, 10]. Learners should try different strategies or methods to experience the connotation of knowledge during the practical application in order to avoid inflexible knowledge.

The thinking situation of problem-based learning is similar to that of the learning of knowledge through self-exploration. When trying to learn the initial goal, more sub-topics available for exploration can be identified. With the understanding of different perspectives, a personalized comprehension model for the initial goal is constructed at last. This kind of learning model can be applied to an abstract learning objective such as learning of science and technology products which has multiple uses and is different from person to person. It can provide the opportunity to make up for the cognitive gaps of individual learners on practicality caused by standardized course content. In addition, under the structure of the same goal, through the learning process of practical application, learners can establish knowledge understanding in accordance with their requirements.

- **Project-Based Learning**

A driving question is the core of project-based learning which can also be regarded as a convergent learning mode. Sub-topics are formed based on the observation of different life phenomena or try of different factors. Learners understand the initial driving question which they intend to solve based on the study of sub-topics [11].

The characteristics of project-based learning are similar to the thinking situation when an individual conducts the learning behavior to complete something. In the process of trying to complete a task, after learning multiple aspects, learners can finally learn the skill of how to complete the initial task. This kind of learning process can be applied to the learning of compound skills composed of multiple single functions. It can also be applied to converge fragmented knowledge into a unified concept. Science and technology products have many functions and their application situations are different. Older adult learners may not be able to integrate many concepts learned in the classroom and apply them to their life situations. Therefore, this study suggested that the characteristics of project-based learning are appropriate for after–class exercise. Based on the designated core task, project learning assists the learners to integrate the knowledge learned into a practical skill that can be used in daily life. At the same time, learners can experience the practicability of the skill during the exercise.

1.3 Learning Communities for Older Adults

Cooperative learning is a systematic strategy in which the participants have a common learning goal that can improve their cognitive and social development and promote learning from each other. Cooperative learning has key factors such as positive interdependence, individual and group accountability, promotive interaction, appropriate use of social skills, and group processing [12, 13]. During the process of cooperative learning, learners will receive recognition from themselves and others because of mutual encouragement and support. When this learning mode is connected with the social requirements of older adults for learning, extra learning benefits can be generated to promote learning motivation. In addition, through the application of community networks, older adults can have more opportunities to present themselves, participate in society, and integrate into the people around them [6, 7]. Moreover, they can create a positive impact through mutual assistance with other older peers. Therefore, this study suggested that community networks are suitable as an auxiliary tool for cooperative learning and a sharing platform for connecting learners.

1.4 Summary

Through a literature analysis in the previous section, this study explored this issue from three dimensions: (1) older adults and technological learning; (2) PBL learning philosophies; and (3) learning communities for older adults. These three dimensions are regarded as references for designing technological learning courses for older adults. This study intended to integrate the concepts of two kinds of PBL learning philosophies and learning communities into a technological learning course for older adults that could meet the special requirements of older adults for technological learning.

The comparison of the two types of PBL learning philosophies with the characteristics of older adults' technological learning revealed that the application of these two philosophies on older adults' technological learning has application potential. Specifically, PBL satisfies the goal orientation need of older adults regarding technological products and attaches importance to the requirements of practicability, which can help learners to integrate the knowledge learned into skills that can be used practically. In the process of problem-based learning, older adults were allowed to construct a model of a personalized understanding through self-exploration to make up for the cognitive gap of individual learners on practicality caused by standardized course content.

The concept of a learning community satisfies the special requirements for social participation and interpersonal interaction of older adults when participating in technological learning courses. In addition, regarding PBL learning philosophies, the concept of a learning community provides a discussion channel that is free of time and space limitations. Therefore, the benefits of a learning community and PBL learning philosophies play a complementary role.

This study aimed to integrate in-person courses with the online learning community to provide a new course design strategy for the trend of older adults' learning on technology. The integration was tested practically to receive experience feedback. It was expected to bring benefits to older adults, researchers, teachers, and designers in the relevant field of technological learning.

2 Research Method

2.1 Cross-Sectional Investigation

This study entered the field of older adults' learning in communities to implement a cross-sectional investigation of the shortage and research gap in the design of current technological courses for older adults. Through semi-structured interviews, six experts with experience teaching technological courses for older adults were invited for interviews to provide practical experiences at the teaching scene, the current activity arrangements community leisure courses, and the content appetite of older adults taking these courses.

After sorting out the interview results, it was found that when taking technological courses, older adults have characteristics such as great individual differences, being interest- and practical-oriented, a lack of self-confidence, community effect, and requirements for immediate discussion and assistance. According to the documents and interview results, this study put forward a design architecture (Fig. 1) for technological courses aimed at older adults that combined PBL learning philosophies with the application of a learning community. The older adults' requirements of goal orientation and attaching importance to practicability for technological products are satisfied by the PBL learning philosophies. While the older adult learners practice after class, they can also apply all skills learned in the classroom in their lives. In addition, the online learning community established by the older adults from the same class not only promotes personal interaction and learning from one another but also provides immediate discussion channels after class. Assisted by the teaching materials, the course may help the learners to learn constantly and prolong their learning enthusiasm and memory to avoid losing opportunities to practice and confidence due to momentary setbacks.

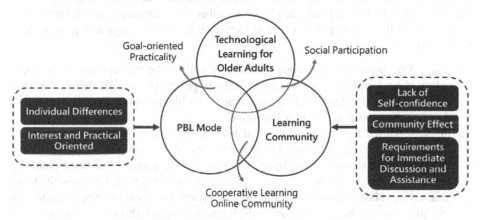

Fig. 1. Design architecture of the proposed course

2.2 Design Technological Learning Courses for Older Adults

The design of the technological learning course for older adults created in this study was implemented in a number of thematic units. Each thematic unit consisted of three parts (Fig. 2) that stretched over two offline classes, with a time interval of one week between them. The after-class exercise between two in-person classes was presented in the online community group, extending the learning field and time to the life scenes of learners.

In-person Class	Online Community	In-person Class
Learning Basic Functions	Assignment (Project)	Ask Questions (Problem)
The teacher assisted the learners face-to-face in solving operational problems during the class and helped them practice basic application situations.	The teacher assigned a compound exercise after class. The learners applied the knowledge in daily life scenes and in the environment they were interested in using their own devices at home.	The teacher assisted the learners to converge the extra-diverged learning problems, solve relevant questions about the topic and summarize the topic before starting the next thematic unit.

Fig. 2. Phased tasks in the class

The course design and learning process in this study are shown in Fig. 3. The topic of the course started in the second half of the first class and ended in the first half of the second class, which could link the classes together. The learning tasks and process of the learners in the learning cycle could be explained in detail through four phases (A, B, C, and D):

1. Phase A occurred at the beginning of the course unit. The learners learned the application of basic functions of this topic in the in-person course. The teacher assisted the learners face-to-face in solving operational problems during the class and helped them practice basic application situations.

2. Phase B started at the end of the first half of the course. The teacher assigned a compound exercise after class. The learners applied the knowledge learned in class in daily life scenes and in the environment they were interested in using their own devices at home. Based on the concept of project-based learning, this phase included an exercise to be completed after class as the core driving question. According to their requirements and the actual situation, the learners decided on how to complete the task and formed their own sub-topics based on their attempts through different methods or under different circumstances. Through the learners' exploration on the sub-topics, they gradually learned the functions acquired in class and finally understood the skills to be conveyed to the learners in the course unit.

3. In phase C, each learner performed the exercise in different scenes (which were sub-topics) and had the opportunity to discover additional functions or usages during the experience, thereby generating new questions. At this time, in addition to the original core driving question (the after-class exercise), the learners generated different sub-questions. The sub-question generation by every learner was a process of forming problem-based learning centering on a fuzzy structure problem which was exploring and familiarizing the relevant functions of the topic. By trying diverged strategies and methods, learners eventually formed a functional application mode in their own style.

4. In phase D, after the learning process of the convergence of phase B and the divergence of phase C, the learners brought the skill or questions newly identified to the offline class for discussions with the teacher. In addition, the teacher assisted the

learners to converge the extra-diverged learning problems, solve relevant questions about the topic and summarize the topic before starting the next thematic unit.

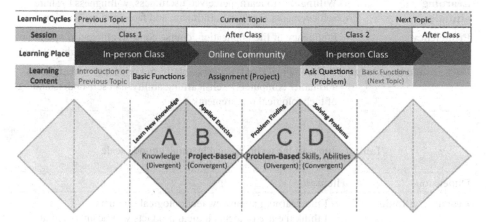

Fig. 3. The architecture of course design and learning process

2.3 Research Process and Method

In reference to the analysis result of the review data, this study designed a course model for older adults in the form of a community leisure course. In total, three course units addressing one technological topic were arranged. The action research method was used at the same time. The researcher observed and reflected in the teaching process and dynamically adjusted the next course unit immediately. As shown in Table 1 and Table 2, after the end of the course, a Technological Learning Attitude scale was used to analyze the changes in participants' learning attitude, proficiency, and background knowledge before and after the technology course. Then, through a semi-structured interview, this study further investigated the learning effectiveness and opinions of the older adult learners and put forward the PBL teaching results conforming to older adults' requirements in technological learning. It also proposed advice for the design of technological learning courses for older adults to provide convenience for the usage and reference of the following relevant research.

2.4 Research Scope and Subjects

The experimental objectives of this study were to (1) record the learning process and effectiveness of older adults; (2) analyze the influence of the course on older adults' attitude toward technological learning, operation proficiency, and technological knowledge; and (3) understand the relevant opinions and satisfaction of older adults with the teaching design presented in this study.

Table 1. Abstract of the topic of Technological Learning Attitude scale

Dimension	Abstract of the topic discussed in this study
Learning attitude	Willingness to learn, perceived usefulness, willingness to share achievements, sense of fulfillment, and feeling of satisfaction
Proficiency	Frequency of life application, course content, efficiency, operation autonomy, cognitive difficulty, and confidence (in teaching others)
Background knowledge	Technological tool type, cross-platform knowledge (smartphones and tablet computers), self-learning ability, and self-understanding of technological requirements

Table 2. Items of the technological learning attitude scale

Dimension	Item
Learning attitude	1. I like learning about new technological products 2. I think the use of technological products will be an essential ability in future life 3. Learning to use technology makes me feel satisfied and successful 4. I am looking forward to sharing my learning experience with my relatives and friends 5. I will be curious about how others use technological products 6. I have the idea and motivation to learn technological products independently
Proficiency	7. I think it is easy to handle things with smartphones 8. I often use my smartphone to accomplish tasks in my life 9. I am confident that I can teach my skills to my friends and relatives 10. I think a smartphone can improve my life efficiency or quality 11. I can skillfully operate the technological products I own
Background knowledge	12. I can understand the characteristics and differences between smartphones, tablet computers, and computers 13. I can use others' smartphones or tablet computers smoothly even though they are not the kind I am familiar with 14. I know that smartphones have more functions besides those that I have learned about 15. I already know roughly what kind of smartphone features I need (photo function, battery capacity, screen size, and audio function)

The experimental site was a community care center. A smartphone learning course was conducted once a week for about 2.5 h each time, with a total of four classes. The main experimental tools were the subject's smartphones and a six-inch smartphone using the Android operating system provided by the researcher. During the study process, the experimental results were recorded through cameras, paper questionnaires, and smartphone screenshots.

The recruited subjects were older adults aged 55 to 70 who had the ability to learn. A total of 18 subjects, including four males and 14 females, participated in the whole experimental process, and their average age was 64.7 years (ranging from 70 years old to 55 years old, with a standard deviation of 5.81 years).

2.5   Experimental Procedures

This research conducted a study on technological learning through courses in the community activity field for older adults. The course content centered on the topic of learning how to use a smartphone. The content preferences were situational topics and topics that could be shared. Therefore, the core of the teaching content was the situational tasks. The course architecture continued the thematic unit form designed in this study and made the learners experience and complete the arranged PBL learning task by connecting three course cycles through an online learning community group.

Three course units were designed in this study: how to use LINE's picture editor, how to use the Foodie camera app, and how to use Google Maps. Upon completion of the course, this study invited the subjects to complete after-class questionnaires and participate in semi-structured interviews. While implementing the experiment, the researcher observed from the side and recorded the problems or phenomena identified during the experiment, of which the findings were provided as a reference for teaching design adjustments on the following week and the reference of the study result.

The topic of the first unit of the course was how to use the built-in picture editor of the LINE messaging app and how to interact in the course group after being added to the group. In accordance with the PBL model adopted in this study, a learning task based on project-based learning was arranged to be completed after class. In this task, older adults were asked to take their favorite photos and then use the functions learned during class to edit the photos, add patterns or texts, and finally share them in the course group. In this way, older adult learners attempted to complete the whole operating procedure and experience the pleasure of creation and sharing. In addition, through the learning community group, the teacher assisted the older adults to carry out discussions and exchanges to promote the learning confidence of older adults and interactions within the community group.

The second course content and exercise tasks focused on the various tools in the software for editing pictures and their effects. Then, the older adults were able to see and understand the meaning of the values and the changes before and after adjustments. The purpose of the second course was to enable the learners to learn to shoot and edit pictures in daily life and post them to social media. The exercise themes were developed by the learners themselves at home. This was an advanced task that could only be completed by connecting the learning content of this course with that of the previous course. Based on the practical operation and combination of multiple tools, the older adult learners experienced the practicality of the functions and finally integrated them into a skill that could be practically used.

The third course was the relevant application of Google Maps to provide convenience for older adults when making appointments with relatives and friends and when planning travel itineraries. In reference to the PBL model, the after-class exercise this time was to find a scenic spot, plan an itinerary to visit it, and share it through the LINE community group. This was a compound operating task that required the use of two applications. It was more difficult for the older adults, but if they could acquire this skill smoothly, they would have more opportunities to use it as the skill is very practical in real-life situations.

3 Results and Discussion

3.1 Research Results

According to the result of the Technological Learning Attitude scale (as shown in Table 2 and Table 3), after completing the three course units, the subjects indicated positive effects on aspects such as the desire for technological learning, the perceived usefulness, and the psychological well-being of the subjects. They also had the thought and motivation to engage in independent learning. There was no change in the result of item 4 about the willingness to share achievements. However, its average score was already the highest in the pretest stage, echoing the pilot study of expert interviews which found that sharing and community communication was one of the main motivations for the older adults to participate in technological learning. Regarding the subjects' proficiency, after learning, the subjects' command of the course content was significantly improved, and they were more inclined to believe that learning new technology could improve their life quality and efficiency. Items 9 and 11 showed a slight decrease in values between the questionnaires taken before and after the course. Although the values of items 9 and 11 were still in the range of positive perspectives, the result indicated that the older adults had become more conservative regarding their familiarity with their own devices and their confidence in teaching others after learning and exploring more unknown functions.

According to the summary of the interview result and the record of the action research, the purposes of older adults' learning and use of smartphones were mainly related to tourism, life records, graphic creation, information sharing, and efficiency improvement. During the process of learning and exploring, they experienced the usefulness of smartphones through actual practice. At the same time, they felt disturbed by the need for cross-platform and cross-device usage and failed to develop confidence in teaching their peers, resulting in the development of a more conservative attitude than before the learning and creating an obstacle to their exchange and discussion.

This study also identified that in addition to normal usage, during the exercise process, older adults also often discovered special application modes themselves. For example, they greeted relatives and friends with self-made cards and used the street view function of Google Maps to travel around the world. It could be seen that after class, the older adults' usage of their devices, together with their life situations, effectively stimulated learning achievements that were more in line with themselves and that deepened the impression of the newly learned content.

On the other hand, the older adults said that the arrangement of the exercises after class in this study helped deepen their learning impression and ability to share knowledge with their relatives and friends, which aroused their appreciation. This indicates that in addition to learning, the action of learning also generated social function. In the minds of the subjects, apart from the function of viewing class information, the course group was also a place to practice as the learners did not have to worry about the impact of

Table 3. Result of the technological learning attitude scale (rounded to the second decimal place)

Dimension	Item (Table 2)	Before	After	t-value	p-value (2-tailed)
Learning attitude	1	4.06	4.69	3.48	0.003*
	2	4.13	4.69	3.09	0.007*
	3	4.00	4.56	3.09	0.007*
	4	4.50	4.50	0.00	1.000
	5	3.94	4.44	2.45	0.027*
	6	3.69	4.50	4.33	0.001*
Proficiency	7	3.75	4.38	2.83	0.013*
	8	3.63	4.06	1.82	0.089
	9	4.13	4.00	−0.62	0.544
	10	3.69	4.25	3.58	0.003*
	11	3.81	3.75	−0.21	0.835
Background knowledge	12	3.63	3.56	−0.21	0.835
	13	3.19	2.94	−1.00	0.333
	14	3.75	4.44	3.91	0.001*
	15	3.19	4.19	4.90	0.000*

* $p < 0.05$

operational errors on other unknowing relatives and friends. All the above phenomena showed that the demand of older adults for technological learning was closely related to social sharing and life records. The PBL exercises and the assistance of the online learning group helped the older adults experience the convenience of technological functions and further strengthened their learning willingness.

3.2 Discussion

In order to meet the requirements and characteristics of older adults in learning technological products, this study incorporated two PBL learning philosophies with the use of learning community strategies as the main architecture of the course. The two philosophies and learning community respectively meet the goal orientation, practical learning preferences, and requirements for social and interpersonal interactions of older adults, all of which had corresponding usages in each phase of the learning process.

It could also be seen from the changes after the course experience that after experiencing the learning content of the course, the older adults were more confident that learning technology could improve their life quality and efficiency while improving their willingness to apply it in their daily lives.

In this teaching strategy, the theory of two PBL models was applied successively. According to the literature review and the findings of this study, when older adults understand the usefulness and importance of technology to themselves, they will have good learning motivation and positive experiences. Therefore, for the exercise after class, the project-based learning mode was adopted to assist the learners with integrating the knowledge they had learned into a practical skill they could use and in perceiving its practicality based on the designated core task. After completing the after-class exercise, the learners began to enter the phase of self-exploration. During this process, they gained opportunities to identify new solutions or usages according to their requirements. In this case, the experience of problem-based learning of the second PBL model made up for the cognitive gaps of individual learners on practicality caused by standardized course content. Based on the subjects' self-exploration, the problem orientation assisted them in constructing a personalized knowledge understanding that was more in line with their requirements.

4   Conclusion and Suggestions

4.1   The Current Situation and Opportunities of Older Adults' Technological Learning

Before learning about technological products, older adults usually need an appropriate scene or full imagination to smoothly accept a new technological application. When technological learning can effectively meet the requirements of older adults for social interaction and self-efficacy, it can have a significant positive impact on their willingness to learn, perceived usefulness, social participation, and psychological well-being, thereby making up for some of their physiological and psychological difficulties. The learning content which is practical and sharable is more appropriate for older adults in entry-level topic planning for technological learning.

4.2   PBL Learning Strategies in Line with the Technological Learning Requirements of Older Adults

Based on two PBL learning philosophies, this study integrated the characteristics of in-person courses and online group interaction. The participants applied what they had learned to the environments in line with their situations and interest, thereby improving the positive effects on their independent technological learning and social interaction. Course design that is in line with the PBL learning philosophy can enable learners to use their own life situations to practice the learnt skill and to personally feel the practicality and usefulness of this skill, all of which could increase learners' motivation and willingness to learn. Learning communities can enable learners to get instant help and maintain their sense of participation at home. The sharing of learning achievements causes discussion, provides social fun for older adults, builds confidence and self-satisfaction, and at last effectively improves the negative factors of purely digital courses, such as the lack of interpersonal interaction, lack of peer support, and isolation.

4.3 The Learning Experience Process and After-Class Effectiveness of Older Adults on the Course

According to the result of the teaching experiment, during the learning process, older adults could combine multiple single functions into practical compound skills through PBL exercises arranged by the teacher and experience the practicality of the skills during the exercise. The self-exploration process could help older adults to live and personalize their technological knowledge, understand their technological requirements, and develop the habit and motivation of continuous learning. The incorporation of an online learning community could guide older adults to understand the expected results of a course during the early stages of learning, generate topics, and induce learning motivation. The community could also provide immediate assistance and discussion while learning, thereby maintaining the learning enthusiasm and participation of older adults. After learning, older adults could feel encouraged to share their learning effectiveness to establish confidence and receive self-satisfaction.

This study analyzed the current technological learning situation and opportunities of older adults. It proposed a PBL teaching strategy that was in line with the technological learning requirements of older adults and provided a new course design strategy to meet older adults' preferences for learning technology, which was tested, and experiences and feedback were obtained. The findings of this study could bring benefits to older adults as well as researchers, teachers, and designers in the field of technological learning.

References

1. Wakefield, R., Wakefield, K.: Social media network behavior: a study of user passion and affect. J. Strateg. Inf. Syst. **25**(2), 140–156 (2016). https://doi.org/10.1016/j.jsis.2016.04.001
2. Dorin, M.: Online education of older adults and its relation to life satisfaction. Educ. Gerontol. **33**(2), 127–143 (2007). https://doi.org/10.1080/03601270600850776
3. Erickson, J., Johnson, G.M.: Internet use and psychological wellness during late adulthood. Can. J. Aging/La Revue canadienne du vieillissement **30**(02), 197–209 (2011). https://doi.org/10.1017/S0714980811000109
4. Xie, B., Watkins, I., Golbeck, J., Huang, M.: Understanding and changing older adults' perceptions and learning of social media. Educ. Gerontol. **38**(4), 282–296 (2012). https://doi.org/10.1080/03601277.2010.544580
5. Zhou, J., Rau, P.-L.P., Salvendy, G.: Older adults' use of smart phones: an investigation of the factors influencing the acceptance of new functions. Behav. Inf. Technol. **33**(6), 552–560 (2014). https://doi.org/10.1080/0144929X.2013.780637
6. Sinclair, T.J., Grieve, R.: Facebook as a source of social connectedness in older adults. Comput. Hum. Behav. **66**, 363–369 (2017). https://doi.org/10.1016/j.chb.2016.10.003
7. Quinn K.: The cognitive benefits of social media use in later life: results of a randomized, controlled pilot study. In: 8th International Conference on Social Media & Society. Social Media for Good or Evil, Toronto, Canada (2017). https://doi.org/10.1145/3097286.3097340
8. Kolmos, A.: Problem-based and project-based learning. In: Skovsmose, O., Valero, P., Christensen, O.R. (eds.) University Science and Mathematics Education in Transition. Springer, Boston (2009). https://doi.org/10.1007/978-0-387-09829-6_13
9. Delisle, R.: How to Use Problem- Based Learning in the Classroom. Association Supervision and Curriculum Development, Alexandria (1997)

10. Helle, L., Tynjälä, P., Olkinuora, E.: Project-based learning in post-secondary education theory, practice and rubber sling shots. High. Educ. **51**(2), 287–314 (2006). https://doi.org/10.1007/s10734-004-6386-5
11. Krajcik, J.S., Blumenfeld, P.C., Marx, R.W., Soloway, E.: A collaborative model for helping middle grade science teachers learn project-based instruction. Elementary School J. **94**, 483–497 (1994)
12. Johnson, D.W., Johnson, R.: Cooperation and Competition: Theory and Research. Interaction Book Company, Edina (1989)
13. Johnson D.W., Johnson, R.: Cooperation and Competition. 2nd edn. Elsevier, Amsterdam (2015). https://doi.org/10.1016/B978-0-08-097086-8.24051-8

ICTs in Later Life and Post-pandemic Challenges

Fausto Colombo[✉] [iD], Piermarco Aroldi[iD], and Simone Carlo[iD]

Università Cattolica del Sacro Cuore, Milan, Italy
fausto.colombo@unicatt.it

Abstract. The article aims to assess the long post-Covid-19 phase from the point of view of the relationship between seniors and ICTs, with an Italian focus. During the first phase of the pandemic (in some ways the most acute and dramatic, because of its newness and the uncertainties to be able to face it) an increase in the overall production and consumption of digital contents and tools was at large empirically observed. At that stage, interesting hypotheses were formulated based on the assumption that the pandemic should spread the ICTs even among the most resistant categories, including the seniors. Three years after the pandemic outbreak, it is time to empirically test how reasonable this hypothesis was, how well it is borne out by the facts, and what general interpretations regarding the effect of major events and crises on the diffusion of technologies among seniors can be made. Our thesis is that, in Italy, the effect on current seniors in terms of diffusion is limited if not null. Instead, the data show that the pandemic has strengthened the divide between seniors and younger generations, and consequently supports the interpretation of technologies as markers for second-level digital divide.

Keywords: older people · digital media · Covid-19 · digital divide

1 Introduction

The article aims to assess the long post-covid phase from the point of view of the relationship between seniors and ICTs, with an Italian focus.

We can consider the first phase of the Covid-19 pandemic in Italy that which begins at the end of February 2020 and ends in May 2020: this phase goes from the first outbreaks identified in northern Italy, passes through the first local lockdowns and the induction of the national lockdown (March 8, 2020) and ends with the end of the national lockdown (May 4, 2020). The second phase of the pandemic in Italy begins on 13 October 2020, with a series of severe restrictions that are eased from until May 2021. The third phase, linked in particular to the dissemination of vaccines but also to the endemization of the virus, ends on March 31, 2022 with the end of the state of emergency introduced by the government.

During the first phase of the pandemic (in some ways the most acute and dramatic, because of its newness and the uncertainties to be able to face it) an increase in the overall production and consumption of digital contents and tools was at large empirically

© The Author(s), under exclusive license to Springer Nature Switzerland AG 2023
Q. Gao and J. Zhou (Eds.): HCII 2023, LNCS 14043, pp. 457–471, 2023.
https://doi.org/10.1007/978-3-031-34917-1_31

observed. At that stage, interesting hypotheses were formulated based on the assumption that the pandemic should spread the ICTs even among the most resistant categories (according to, for instance, Rogers' classic categorization, [1]), including the seniors. Regarding the latter, it was assumed that the need to stay in touch with family members and acquaintances, would have generated a digital literacy effect that would not be dampened with the slowdown and (hopefully) the definitive control of the virus. Three years after the pandemic outbreak, it is time to empirically test how reasonable this hypothesis was, how well it is borne out by the facts, and what general interpretations regarding the effect of major events and crises on the diffusion of technologies among seniors can be made. As we shall see, our thesis is that the effect on current seniors in terms of diffusion is limited if not null. Instead, the data show that the pandemic has strengthened the divide between seniors and younger generations, and consequently supports the interpretation of technologies as markers for second-level digital divide. This understanding, in turn, prompts us to adopt an alternative perspective drawing on the assumption that technological diffusion is more as a stratification of diffusion and practices rather than a linear development. On this basis, several hypotheses can be made on the effects of the pandemic in the coming years both for current and future seniors, starting with the fundamental role played by the socialization to technology occurring at work. Further enquiries concerning the intergenerational role of major global events and crises, of which the pandemic is a significant example, should be made.

The article is divided into three parts. At first it is focused on the analysis perspective oriented towards the recognition of digital divide not only as a starting point for the spread of digital technologies and related practices, but rather as a permanent context even reinforced by the pandemic crisis. The second aims to demonstrate the co-relationships between trend of technology diffusion among seniors and theories of stratification. The third draws some conclusions, formulating some hypotheses for future development.

2 ICT, Ageing, Digital Divide

2.1 The Origin of Digital Divide

In recent years processes of technology diffusion and adoption by the over 65s [2, 3] has been at the core of the academic debate also in Italy: particular attention has been paid both to reasons and ways in which the older people use technologies and to those reasons making many older people resistant to the use of ICTs, making the Grey Digital Divide (i.e. the difference in technology penetration between the older people and the rest of the population) very pronounced in Italy compared to other European countries [4].

The first studies on the adoption and use (and non-use) of ICTs by the older people were made within the theoretical framework of the digital divide. The digital divide literature argues that exclusion from the digital, IT and connected society impacts all aspects of life, such as education, sociability, culture and entertainment, personal interactions, and political participation [5].

The concept of the digital divide was basically originated in reference to the disadvantage in access to communication platforms and the resulting disadvantage in terms of access to information [6]. In the context of the so-called 'first-level digital divide', research initially studied the socio-demographic characteristics and differences between those having technologies and connections to the Internet (or telephone line) and those who have not [7]. This so-called dichotomous or binary interpretation, based exclusively on the categories of 'have' and 'have-nots', certainly facilitated the initial framing of the digital divide phenomenon, but risked giving rise to simplistic interpretations of reality, such as, for example, thinking that in order to overcome inequalities, it would be enough to foster technological endowments (i.e. to solve what is defined by Dijk as the 'first-level digital divide' [8]), instead disregarding the skills to use such communication technologies (defined as the 'second-level digital divide'). Starting from this initial theoretical framework, which stemmed from political concerns and the harmonious development of society [9], progressively, there was an awareness that in addition to the divide in terms of access to the Net, there were profound differences in terms of the use of technologies [10].

2.2 The 'Second-Level Digital Divide'

In recent years, the universe of meanings to which the term digital divide has come to refer has widened over time, moving decisively away from the technocentric approach of its origins, i.e.. Based exclusively on gaps in ownership and use of technologies [11]. There has been a shift in assuming that in addition to the divide in terms of access to ICTs and the Internet, inequalities between people were mostly in the use of technologies: this is a 'second-level digital divide' [8].

The digital divide has started to be conceived as an evolving social phenomenon: it is no longer to be meant as a single gap, but as a variety of social, economic, and technological differences defining together the complexity of the phenomenon. In recent years, the literature on the digital divide has therefore been enriched by theorists who have placed the relationship between ICT, technology diffusion, skill acquisition and social issues at the center of their reflection [12]. Research in recent years has focused on the study of different types of skills (technical, verbal, mathematical), qualitative differences in the use of technologies, and the relationships between use and broader economic and social trends. According to this understanding of the digital divide, what matters is not the possession of technologies, but rather the skills and competences of people in and to be able manage their risks and opportunities [13]. With respect to the topic of e-skills, digital skills do not only mean to be able technically to know how to use a media, but also a to manage and evaluate the information resources on the Internet and to make use of the opportunities offered by the Net [14].

2.3 Grey Digital Divide, Normalization, Stratification

From the very beginning, the debate around the digital divide (both first and second level) has regarded age as one of the most important socio-demographic variables influencing the diffusion and use of ICTs, and the level of digital skills. For some authors, the 'grey digital divide' [15] is a purely generational phenomenon, destined to disappear on its own over time: the next digital generations will displace the old analogue generations.

Such an interpretation is consistent with what is termed the 'normalization' hypothesis aimed to solve digital divides: this hypothesis is based on the prediction that over time a level of saturation in the diffusion of technologies will be reached hence allowing even those groups and individuals who were initially in late to close the gap with early adopters.

Over time, because of those policies lowering prices, or thanks to the evolution of technologies in terms of greater ease of use, the distance between users and non-users will be bridged.

This is a hypothesis often supported by public decision-makers (who believe, for instance, that lowering prices of technologies is enough to ensure their diffusion, see 16) but also by early academics dealing with digital divides [6] (Fig. 1).

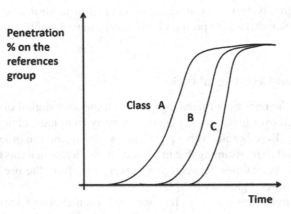

Fig. 1. Model of normalization

The reflection around digital divides has in recent years broadened to a new hypothesis on the diffusion of technologies, that of 'stratification'. The stratification model is more focused to the concept of inequality and argues that, due to greater capital of knowledge and availability of access, those who are in a position of relative advantage with respect to technology, will increase their privileges; conversely, groups characterized by a slow and difficult adoption of the new technology will never fill the gap [5] (Fig. 2).

Therefore, if the hypothesis of normalization foresees a closure of the gaps (over time), that of stratification considers it impossible to close - without adequate public policies - digital gaps, since they are rooted in social inequalities. Van Dijk underlines how this second model well represents the long-term trend of digital inequalities, because it takes into account uneven access, connected in turn with the personal, relationship and social characteristics and skills of individuals (age included, see [17]).

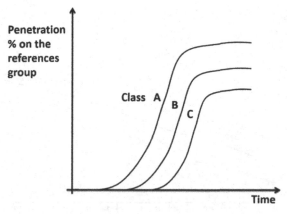

Fig. 2. Model of stratification

3   The Use of ICT in Different Age Cohorts in Italy

3.1   Research Question, Data and Methods

Taking the into account this literature, these theories can be tested with regards to the pandemic crisis. The research question that arises is: has the Covid-19 crisis and the rapid digitization of large sectors of European society reduced, increased, or left unchanged the digital divide of the Italian older people compared to younger generations/cohorts?

In the following paragraphs we will show some secondary data taken from the "Digital Agenda Key Indicators" database, a service of the European Commission [18], which selects various indicators, divided into thematic groups, illustrating some key dimensions of the European digital market. These include data on telecommunications, broadband, mobile, Internet usage, Internet services, eGovernment, eCommerce, eBusiness, digital skills, and research and development. It is a very diverse data source: data regarding digital consumption and demand come from Eurostat. The indicators constructed allow us to compare the development of European countries over time, and much of the data on technology consumption/ownership is offered broken down by age cohorts.

Due to the nature of data, our aim is not to give an in-depth analysis, but an overview able to show a longitudinal trend of digital divide between the Italian older people and the rest of the coexisting generations.

Let us point out, preliminarily, that the data we are using concern subjects aged 75 at the most, which, especially in Italy, constitutes a strong limitation, given that subjects over 75 represent an increasingly significant slice (over 10%) of the Italian population. We shall see in the conclusions how this bias can be assimilated to some extent in our interpretative inferences.

3.2 Internet Use

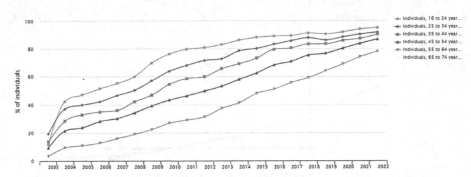

Fig. 3. Individual who are frequent Internet users (every day or almost every day), by Age (6 groups) 2003–2022. Source: European Commission, Digital Scoreboard

The graph shows the trend over time of Internet access by Italian citizens, divided by age groups, between 2003 and 2022. As we can see, the digitalization processes of the older age groups (65–74 years) have been steadily growing since 2003, but only in some stages faster than the general digitalization of the population. On the contrary, between 2006 and 2015 the digitalization of the older people, although starting from lower percentages, increased more slowly than that of the younger age groups. The same happened between 2019 and 2020 (the start of the pandemic): despite the compulsory digitalization of services and of many aspects of daily life, the over-65s with frequent Internet use increased less quickly than the younger cohorts, from 38.1% to 41.8% (a delta of + 3.7%), while frequent use among the mature 55–64-year-olds increased by 4.9%, starting from already large percentages of Internet users. Between 2020 and 2021, the 6.7% increase in frequent Internet users among the older people was slightly higher than the increase recorded for the other age groups (+5.2% for those aged 55–64). But this seems to be only a sort of delayed 'technical rebound' compared to the general post-pandemic digitalization process, with growth between 2021 and 2022 levelling off again. In essence, between 2019 and 2022 (the years of Covid-19), the growth in the frequency of use by the older people did not go faster than in the previous three years (2016–2019) and only partially narrowed the gap with the younger cohorts, which grew at the same rate or, in the case of the younger and already heavily digitized population, at a still sustained rate. On the other hand, it seems to be the middle-aged cohorts (55–64, but also 45–54) narrowing the top-level digital divide in recent years (well before Covid). From these data it can therefore be argued that Covid-19 can be conceived neither as increasing the frequency of Internet use among the population nor as reducing age-related gaps nor as allowing the older people to increase the frequency of use of digital technologies in general and of the Internet in particular (Fig. 3).

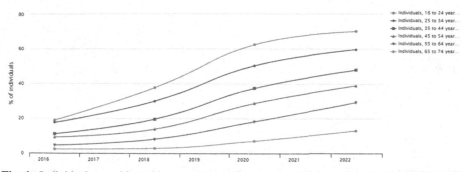

Fig. 4. Individuals watching video on demand from commercial services. Italy. (2016–2022). Source: European Commission, Digital Scoreboard

3.3 Consumption of Digital Content, Information Resources and Communication Tools

Regarding some specific digital contents, it is interesting to note how the dynamics widening the gap between the older people and the young population began in the middle of the last decade: it was at that time, in fact, that after years of niche use of such contents, the acceleration of the digital offer of movies, music and games resulted in a rapid increase of consumption by the younger generations. However, the phenomenon was not replicated among older generations, who remained on the margins of consumption of such products. In recent years, consumption has risen markedly in all cohorts, but among older people it has grown much slower, even during 2022. The distance to the younger cohorts has thus increased. As Fig. 4 shows, while more than 70% of people between 16 and 24 habitually have watched video on demand, among the older people this percentage drops to 12%.

Same trend can also be seen in the data concerning playing or downloading games, images, movies, or music. As regards to online practices, between 2013 and 2016, there was a significant growth among young people and younger adults, while this growth among the older people was much slower, thus increasing the delta and the difference between the older people and the young. In 2020, users aged 65 to 74 years playing or downloading games, images, movies, or music were 27.6 per cent compared to 85 per cent of 16- to 24-year-old. The difference in growth between 2019 and 2020 among 65- to 74-year-olds was minimal, while it was more significant among the mature (55–64 years old), who, during the pandemic, seemed to be the cohort increasing the most their digital consumption (Fig. 5).

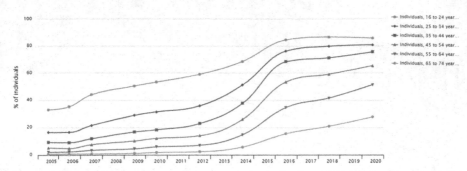

Fig. 5. Individuals have used Internet, in the last 3 months, for playing or downloading games, images movies or music. Italy. (2005–2020). Source: European Commission, Digital Scoreboard

The gap between younger and older age groups has not been narrowed even in standard and less technically complex uses of the Internet, such as reading news and online newspapers. Between 2019 and 2022, the consumption of online news in younger courts increased at the same rate or even faster than in the over 65s, despite the fact that the percentage of online newspaper readers among young people and adults was already higher. Among people aged 65–74, online news reading increased by about 10% in 3 years (from 24.1% to 34.7%), in line with other cohorts or even less than other cohorts: people between the ages of 35 and 44, for example, recorded an increase from 50% to 62% (Fig. 6).

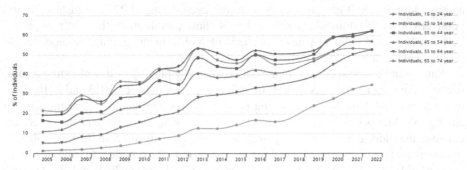

Fig. 6. Individuals used the Internet, in the last 3 months, for reading / downloading online newspapers / news magazines (2005–2022). Source: European Commission, Digital Scoreboard

Finally, data regarding phone and video calling usage are also interesting because they again show how the growth in the use of these tools has not been homogeneous. The need to communicate in a context where seeing each other was more difficult and complicated led many people to start using some digital communication services. While this certainly occured for the younger and already largely digitized age groups, for the older people this digitalization process was significantly slower. Between 2019 and 2022 the use of online phone calls and videocalls increased among 65–74 y/o 'only' by 16.4%, compared to + 20.6% among 55–64 y/o, 21.5% among 45–54 y/o, and 20% among 35–55 y/o. This slower pace was combined with an already low diffusion of such services among the older people and made the gap between young and old even wider in 2022, with 36.5% of the older people using such services against 86.5% of the 16–24 y/o. Again, the acceleration of digitalization due to Covid-19 has widened rather than narrowed the generational gaps (Fig. 7).

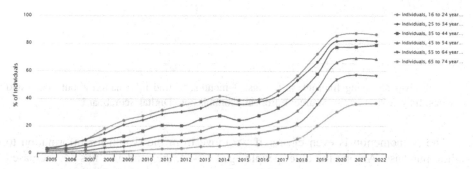

Fig. 7. Telephoning or video calls (via webcam) over the Internet (2005–2022). Source: European Commission, Digital Scoreboard

3.4 Information and Consumption of Commercial Goods and Services

Among the changes introduced by the pandemic in people's daily lives is the area of purchases and information on the goods to be purchased. The ongoing closure of stores, a certain supply difficulty, the fear of contagion had increased the popularity of online purchasing services and the choice of products. The number of people using these services had increased. Again, this growth was not equally distributed throughout the population, but was accelerated in some cohorts and less significantly in others.

The years between 2020 and 2021 represented a season of great changes, even here however recording a more moderate growth among the older people over 65. Between 2019 and 2022 the search for information on goods and services increased less by 10% among people between 65 and 74, against +16% of people between 54 and 65, 15.2% of people between 45 and 54 and 12% of people between 25 and 34 years. Starting from data showing that the older people use less of these services, the gap between the younger generations and the older people had further increased (Fig. 8).

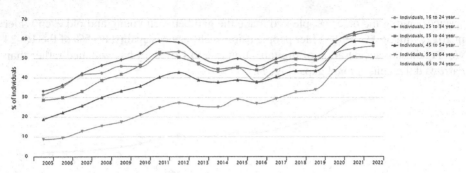

Fig. 8. Individuals using Internet, in the last 3 months, to find information about goods and services. Italy. (2005–2022). Source: European Commission, Digital Scoreboard

The phenomenon is even clearer if we move from the search for information to online purchase. Among the older people aged 65–74, the pandemic has not increased the (already existing) slow growth in the online purchase of goods, while for the other cohorts it has significantly increased the percentages of subjects online purchasing. This has led to growing gaps between the younger cohorts (with almost 70% of 25–34 y/o shopping online) and the older ones, among whom only 20% of people have bought something in last 12 months (Fig. 9).

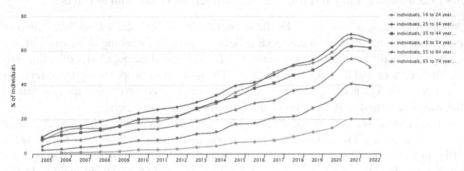

Fig. 9. Individuals ordering goods or service online in the last 12 months, for private use. Italy. (2005–2022). Source: European Commission, Digital Scoreboard

The graph allows us to further reflect. After the peak of 2020, some online behaviors, and habits due to the effects of the pandemic have kept on changing. In all age groups, for example, the percentage of individuals shopping online has fallen down. The return to normality has led some individuals to re-engage in established habits, such as shopping in physical stores. This reminds us of how the digitalization process can in some cases be 'reversible' and not necessarily that certain behaviors which have been 'digitized' in an emergency period will remain as such in the future. For instance, not all users prefer to buy online when they can go back offline and when the situation (re-opening of shops, increased mobility) allows it.

Conversely, other online services seem to continue the growth that started during the Covid-19 period (but often much earlier) and that does not seem to stop. This is the case of online banking, which has been steadily increasing in terms of usage for years (with a significant bust in 2013 almost as significant as 2020–2021) and which does not seem to be stopping (and which, again, risks widening the gap between older and younger people, who have already been digital users for several years) (Fig. 10).

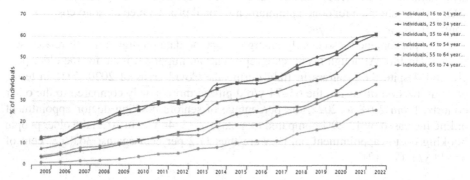

Fig. 10. Individuals using the Internet, in the last 3 months, for online banking. Italy. (2005–2022). Source: European Commission, Digital Scoreboard

3.5 eGovernment and eHealth

Among the services that have rapidly digitized with the pandemic are those related to public administration and in particular health services. Also in this case, a certain journalistic narrative and discourse on the part of the institutions has told how the digitalization of public administrations has been followed by a widespread use of these new digital services.

Indeed, even in this case it is useful to look at the data. The pandemic has indeed given a strong boost to the use of digital eGovernment services, but in an unequal way, with some age cohorts (e.g. 34–44 y/o) accelerating much more than others (the older people, above all), increasing the gap between age groups (Fig. 11).

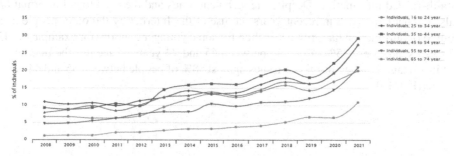

Fig. 11. Individuals submitting completed forms to public authorities, over the internet, last 12 months. Italy. (2008–2021). Source: European Commission, Digital Scoreboard

Tale fenomeno emerge chiaramente anche dai dati sui servizi digitali legati alla salute (eHealth). Nonostante la cura della salute rappresenti per gli anziani un tema importante e nonostante i progressi in Italia durante la crisi Covid del 2020–2021 in termini di digitalizzazione della salute, i 65–74 y/o si sono digitalizzati con più lentezza rispetto alle altre coorti.

Dal 2018[1] al 2022 la percentuale di anziani che prendono un appuntamento con il proprio medico via Internet è aumentata del 13,29% contro un + 23% dei 35–44 y/o. Nel 2022 gli anziani che prendono appuntamento con il proprio medico sono così il 17,2% contro il 36,4% dei 35–44 y/o.

This phenomenon also clearly emerges from the data on digital health-related services (eHealth). Although health care represents an important issue for the older people and despite the progress in Italy during the Covid crisis of 2020–2021 in terms of digitalization of health, the 65–74 y/o digitized more slowly compared to the other cohorts. From 2018 to 2022, the percentage of seniors booking doctor appointment online increased by 13.29% compared to + 23% of 35–44 y/o. In 2022, the older people booking doctor appointment online were thus 17.2 per cent against 36.4 per cent of 35–44 y/o (Fig. 12).

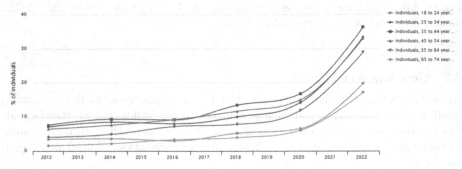

Fig. 12. Making an appointment with a practitioner via a website (2012–2022). Source: European Commission, Digital Scoreboard

This trend is also confirmed when focusing on the use of the Internet to obtain health-related information. Despite the turbulent times and the need to get information (also) about Covid-19, in recent years the use of the Internet by the older people as a source of information has grown less than for some younger cohorts (for example the 45 -54 years old): only 35% of people between 65 and 74 years of age use the Internet to get information on health-related issues against 58% of people between 35 and 44 years of age (Fig. 13).

---

[1] This case refers to two-years data. There are no data split off for 2019.

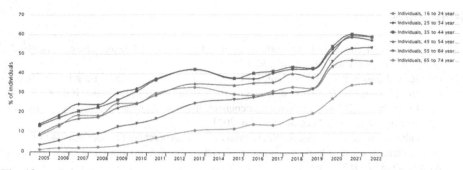

Fig. 13. Individuals using the Internet in the last 3 months, seeking information about health: injury, disease, nutrition, improving health, etc. Italy. (2005–2022). Source: European Commission, Digital Scoreboard

4 Conclusion: Implication for Future Research

The data we have considered seem to unequivocally show that the hypothesized reduction of the digital divide between seniors and the other age cohorts - at least in Italy - has not occurred [18]. Indeed, we can go further. On the basis of other empirical evidence in past researches, which show how the group following that of 65/75 year old, i.e. that of old seniors (75+) is even less digitally literate and more resistant to literacy, it must be assumed that the divide has increased even more than what is shown here.

Of course, further research will also have to deal with some contextual issues. For example, old seniors hospitalized in nursing homes had access for a short time to video-conferencing systems that allowed them to be connected with family members. However, this access was mediated by some facilitators (the staff of the nursing homes themselves or the family members themselves) and certainly decreased once the doors of the nursing homes were reopened for visits. However, everything seems to contribute to demonstrating both the relevance of the second-level divide and the stratification hypothesis, whereby the inertias in the use of previous media - rooted in everyday practices - heavily affected the technological consumption diets of subjects, and in these cases in particular of older people subjects.

In the light of the data we have shown, and pending further insights, we can however add a working hypothesis regarding the determining factors of the second level digital divide [12]. This hypothesis consists in attributing a particular significance to the social-ization of technologies that takes place in the workplace [19]. In fact, as other researches, including ourselves, have shown, the role of professional networks, production environments and the impact of technological innovation on working practices seems to be very high, and constitutes a very strong discriminating element between those who work (and is more easily exposed to the encounter with innovation), and who instead, outside the world of work, can only count on the informal network of peers and family members to find motivations [20]. We plan to work on this hypothesis in the future.

References

1. Rogers, E.M.: Diffusion of innovations, p. 367. Free Press of Glencoe, New York (1962). https://bac-lac.on.worldcat.org/oclc/301676794
2. Pirone, F., Pratschke, J., Rebeggiani, E.: Un'indagine sull'uso delle Ict tra gli over 50: considerazioni su nuovi fattori di disuguaglianza sociale e territoriale. SOCIOLOGIA DEL LAVORO, Jul 15 2008. http://www.francoangeli.it/Riviste/SchedaRivista.aspx?IDarticolo=33789&lingua=IT. Accessed 28 May 2021
3. Colombo, F., Aroldi, P., Carlo, S.: Nuevosmayores, viejas brechas: TIC, desigualdad y bienestar en la tercera edad en Italia. Comunicar: Revista Científica de Comunicación y Educación **23**(45), 47–55 (2015)
4. Sala, E., Gaia, A.: Older people's use of «information and communication technology» In: The Italian Case, Europe (2019)
5. Warschauer, M.: Reconceptualizing the Digital Divide. First Monday Jul 1 2002. https://journals.uic.edu/ojs/index.php/fm/article/view/967. Accessed 12 Feb 2021
6. Compaine, B.M.: The Digital Divide: Facing a Crisis or Creating a Myth?, p. 374. MIT Press, Cambridge, Mass (2001)
7. Loges, W.E., Jung, J.Y.: Exploring the digital divide: internet connectedness and age. Commun. Res. **28**(4), 536–562 (2001)
8. Van Dijk, J. A.: The Evolution of the digital divide - the digital divide turns to inequality of skills and usage. In: Digital Enlightenment Yearbook 2012, pp. 57–78 (2012)
9. Gunkel, D.J.: Second thoughts: toward a critique of the digital divide. New Media Soc. **5**(4), 499–522 (2003)
10. Ragnedda, M., Muschert, G.W.: The digital divide: the internet and social inequality in international perspective. UNITED KINGDOM. Taylor & Francis Group, London (2013). http://ebookcentral.proquest.com/lib/unicatt-ebooks/detail.action?docID=1221501. Accessed 16 Jan 2023
11. Fang, M.L., Canham, S.L., Battersby, L., Sixsmith, J., Wada, M., Sixsmith, A.: Exploring privilege in the digital divide: implications for theory, policy, and practice. Gerontologist **59**(1), e1-15 (2019)
12. Hargittai, E., Hinnant, A.: Digital inequality: differences in young adults' use of the internet. Commun. Res. **35**(5), 602–621 (2008)
13. Livingstone, S., Haddon, L., Görzig, A.: Children, risk and safety on the internet: research and policy challenges in comparative perspective. In: Livingstone, S., Haddon, L., Görzig, A. (eds.) Policy Press, Bristol, p. 408 (2012). http://www.policypress.co.uk. Accessed 28 May 2021
14. Hargittai, E.: The digital divide and what to do about it. In: Jones, D.C. (ed.) New Economy Handbook, pp. 822–841. Academic Press, San Diego, CA (2003)
15. Millward, P.: The 'grey digital divide': Perception, exclusion and barriers of access to the Internet for older people. First Monday, Jul 7 2003. https://www.firstmonday.org/ojs/index.php/fm/article/view/1066. Accessed 25 May 2021
16. Carlo, S., Sourbati, M.: Age and technology in digital inclusion policy: a study of Italy and the UK. ESSACHESS – J. Commun. Stud. **13**(2(26)), 107–27 (2020)
17. The Deepening Divide. SAGE Publications Inc. (2021). https://us.sagepub.com/en-us/nam/the-deepening-divide/book226556. Accessed 2 Jan 2022
18. European Commission. Digital Scoreboard (2023). https://digital-agenda-data.eu/

19. Carlo, S., Buscicchio, G.: Condizionelavorativa, uso delle ICT e invecchiamento: una indagine descrittiva-correlazionale del contesto italiano. SALUTE E SOCIETÀ (2022). https://www.francoangeli.it/riviste/SchedaRivista.aspx?IDArticolo=71258&lingua=It. Accessed 22 Feb 2023
20. Zaccaria, D., Sala, E., Respi, C.: Le competenze digitali dei lavoratori anziani in Italia. SALUTE E SOCIETÀ (2022). https://www.francoangeli.it/riviste/SchedaRivista.aspx?IDArticolo=71255&lingua=It. Accessed 5 Dec 2022

Digital Media Use and the Role of Internet Self-efficacy Among Older Technology Volunteers – A Baseline Study from the Project "DiBiWohn"

Michael Doh[✉] [iD], Joshua L. Schlichting[iD], David Leopold[iD], Linda Göbl[iD], and Mario R. Jokisch[iD]

Catholic University of Applied Sciences, Karlstr. 63, 79104 Freiburg, Germany
michael.doh@kh-freiburg.de

Abstract. How can older residents in assisted living and inpatient care facilities participate in digital education and social activities? This is the aim of the German interdisciplinary research project "Digital Educational Processes for Older Residents in Assisted Living Arrangements and Care Facilities" (DiBiWohn). Central to the project is a peer mentoring concept, in which older volunteers are trained as technology volunteers who assist in the learning process of digital technology novices from the aforementioned institutions. The paper first describes the project and the peer-to-peer concept. Then, findings from a nationwide online survey conducted in the spring of 2021 with $n = 171$ active technology volunteers ($M = 70.4$ years, 60–89 years) are presented, including everyday use of digital media, digital competencies, and attitude towards technology. The findings are related to a comparison group with $n = 160$ persons ($M = 70.4$ years, 60–90 years) who are equally educated, but do not volunteer in the field of technology. Inferential statistical analyses are applied to identify relevant determinants of Internet self-efficacy in both groups. The findings emphasize that information and communication technologies, such as the Internet and smartphones, are already used on a daily basis in both groups. However, the level of digital competencies and self-efficacy is significantly higher among the active technology volunteers. They thus represent "digital best agers" who have the prerequisites to be learning companions and role models for older people who are inexperienced in digital technologies.

Keywords: Media Gerontology · Internet self-efficacy · Information and Communication Technology · Age · Technology Volunteers

1 The Project "DiBiWohn"

The joint interdisciplinary project "Digital Educational Processes for Older Residents in Assisted Living Arrangements and Care Facilities" (DiBiWohn) [1] is set to run from September 2020 to August 2025 with funding from the German Federal Ministry of Education and Research. The project is aimed at older residents in assisted living and inpatient care facilities – a group which has not been adequately targeted by educational

© The Author(s), under exclusive license to Springer Nature Switzerland AG 2023
Q. Gao and J. Zhou (Eds.): HCII 2023, LNCS 14043, pp. 472–488, 2023.
https://doi.org/10.1007/978-3-031-34917-1_32

and digitalization offers so far. The research group brings together disciplines such as gerontology, media education, educational science, sociology and nursing science. Collaborating on the project are the Catholic University of Applied Sciences Freiburg, the Center for General Scientific Continuing Education (ZAWiW) at Ulm University, the Media Competence Forum Southwest Foundation (MKFS) Ludwigshafen and the Evangelische Heimstiftung GmbH Stuttgart, and the Institute for Gerontology at Heidelberg University (co-opted).

The project links research with practice, and basic and applied research with participatory research methods. One focus is on educational-theoretical and media-gerontological research, investigating fundamental questions about (digital) educational processes in older and old age and their effects on education and technology biographies, identity work and living environment. Another research focus concerns educational and media practice, including the development and design of informal and non-formal digital educational formats. Using participatory methods and a peer-to-peer concept for digital education in old age, the target group will acquire digital access (such as tablets and the Internet). Moreover, opportunities for promoting and maintaining social and societal participation in the social space will be explored. In addition, digital educational technologies for the technology volunteers with the purpose of networking and (further) education activities will be explored and developed. The education program is initiated in selected institutions in Baden-Württemberg and Rhineland-Palatinate. The findings will then be used to develop concepts of education and action, resulting in a transfer concept capable of being scaled nationwide to other educational and residential facilities for older people.

2   Peer-to-Peer Concept with Older Technology Volunteers

In peer-to-peer concepts, persons of the same age act as role models in the sense of Bandura's social-cognitive learning theory [2] to support and promote self-efficacy, competencies and empowerment. This approach has been used in the field of adult education and education for older people since the 1980s [3], with a focus on health behavior and addiction prevention [4]. In Germany, it was only in the 2000s that the approach was applied to older adults learning the use of information and communication technologies (ICT). Initially, this was mostly in the context of fixed-term promotion programs and research projects, e.g. the nationwide initiative of "Senior Technology Ambassadors" (2012–2014) [5, 6], or regional projects such as the Quartiers-NETZ in Gelsenkirchen (2014–2018) [7] or "Kommunikation mit intelligenter Technik" (KommmiT) in Stuttgart (2015–2020) [8, 9]. Nowadays, there are various peer mentoring programs all over Germany on municipal, regional and supra-regional level [10, 11] as well as singular networks on federal state level like the "Netzwerk Senioren-Internet-Initiativen Baden-Württemberg" (sii) with more than 600 older technology volunteers [12] or the network "Digital Botschafterinnen & Botschafter Rheinland-Pfalz" with more than 400 members [13].

It is characteristic for such mentoring concepts to train older volunteers as learning companions for older people who are inexperienced in or uncertain about technology, in order to familiarize them with ICT. The mentoring takes place primarily in tandem or in small groups and represents a low-threshold, informal learning setting. In this, geragogical guiding principles such as an "orientation towards living environment, competencies, biography, and autonomy" [14, p. 208f.] of the novices are taken into account. The goals are to reduce fears and insecurities regarding the technology, and to increase self-efficacy through self-directed learning. According to Bandura [2], self-efficacy expectancy can arise from observing the mentor (vicarious experience) and, particularly, from trying things out for oneself (mastery experience). Self-efficacy is related to technology biographical experiences and is important for mentors as well as for novices in overcoming challenges on the internet [15]. Mentors and novices relate to each other in that they belong to a similar technology generation; i.e. both groups were socialized in a "pre-digital" era of technology [16]. Due to their shared experience, people from the same technology generation can be expected to demonstrate similar media use [17, 18]. For the learners, this connection provides a ground for identification, allowing them to perceive companions as role models and as "door openers to the digital world" [6, 9, 19]. Peer-to-peer concepts aim to introduce learners to a "warm expert" in the sense of Bakardjieva: Someone who is familiar with the technology that the learner wants to learn about, but also familiar with and therefore empathic towards the specific needs and background of the learner [20].

3 Research Question

Previous research projects by the authors involving peer-to-peer mentoring in the context of ICT have shown that older TV generally have a high affinity, experience and expertise with regard to ICT. Moreover, they tend to have a positive attitude towards technology due to their technology biography [6, 9, 19]. They often are so-called "early adopters" [21], who are quick to familiarize themselves with technical and digital innovations [6]. As such, they can play a crucial role in the further diffusion of innovations among the broader population [22]. In the following, we will verify these findings with descriptive analyses on the basis of the new survey. Specifically, we will examine the group differences between TV and CG with regard to their use of ICT. In a second step, we will contrast the factors associated with Internet self-efficacy in the two groups using hierarchical linear regressions.

4 Method: Baseline Study of Older Technology Volunteers

The project setting first required to review the current state of research and the level of digital transformation in assisted living and care facilities and in the two target groups (residents and technology volunteers). This was achieved through a literature research carried out in the last quarter of 2020. Based on the findings, several baseline studies using quantitative methods were designed and carried out in the first and second quarter of 2021.

Recruitment. The survey of older technology volunteers was carried out nationwide in May and June 2021 – in the midst of social restrictions due to the COVID-19 pandemic – in the form of an online survey. The questionnaire focused on media gerontological constructs (including media equipment, media use, online activities, subjective ICT knowledge, Internet self-efficacy, attitude towards technology, and obsolescence) as well as on aspects of participation in the social space, voluntary and educational activities. Participants were acquired via mailing lists and networks of the project partners as well as via associations for education and for older people operating on federal state level (Baden-Württemberg and Rhineland-Palatinate) and on national level (e.g., the German National Association of Senior Citizens' Organisations BAGSO).

Study Variables and Measures. *Media equipment* was measured with a list of 15 common devices and media (e.g. smartphone, Internet connection). Participants were asked to tick each that is present in their household. To measure the *frequency of media use* 13 devices were rated on a six-point scale from 0 ("never") to 5 ("multiple times a day"). Furthermore, the intensity of use of three key media (television, radio set, Internet) was collected by asking for a subjective estimate of the average daily usage time in minutes per day.

Usage of Internet applications was measured for 14 activities (e.g. "sending and receiving e-mails", "using search engines such as Google"). Participants indicated their frequency of use on a six-point scale ranging from 0 ("never") to 5 ("multiple times a day").

Motives for Internet use included 14 motives based on the ARD/ZDF Massenkommunikations Langzeitstudie [23] which were rated on a five-point Likert-type agree-disagree scale. The motives cover aspects of cognition (e.g., "because I want to inform myself"), entertainment (e.g., "because I have fun"), and uniqueness of the Internet (e.g., "because there is content there that I can only find there").

For *subjective ICT knowledge,* participants were asked to grade their overall knowledge of PC/Laptops, Smartphones, Tablets and the Internet on a scale from 1 ("very good") to 6 ("very bad"). An overall score for ICT knowledge was computed as mean of the four grades.

Attitude towards technology captures the endorsement of digitization and technologization includes two statements derived from Mollenkopf and Kaspar [24], e.g. "Technological progress is needed, therefore some unavoidable disadvantages must be accepted", rated on a five-point Likert-type agree-disagree scale. An overall score was computed as mean of the two items.

Technology biography is a measure of previous engagement with technology. It includes four statements, also from Mollenkopf and Kaspar [24], e.g. "I have always had a lot to do with technology in my life", rated on the same scale, of which an overall mean score was computed.

Obsolescence is the perception of current times. It was measured with five statements about the perception of current times derived from Brandstädter and Wentura [25] (e.g. "Life is getting more complicated and harder for me to understand"), which were rated on a five-point Likert-type agree-disagree scale. An overall score was computed as mean of the five items.

Internet self-efficacy is the believe in the own ability to cope with challenges that may occur when using the Internet. Participants indicated their agreement to a total of six items on a five-point Likert-type agree-disagree scale. Three items concern general aspects of Internet usage taken from Eastin and LaRose [26] (e.g. "I feel confident understanding terms/words relating to the Internet") In addition, three items were self-developed, which target health and communication areas of Internet usage (e.g. "I feel confident to research relevant health-related information on the Internet"). An overall score was computed as mean of the six items.

Subjective age is a measure of the subjective evaluation of one's "felt age". Following Rubin and Berntsen [27], participants gave an answer in years to the question: "Some people feel either older or younger than their actual age, other people feel just as old as they are. Regardless of your actual age, how old do you feel at the moment?".

Awareness of Age-Related Gains and Losses: These two dimensions are based on the concept of "Awareness of Age-Related Change" (AARC, [28]), each measured with five statements (e.g. "As I get older, I notice that..." gains: "...I recognize my own needs better"; losses: "...my mental capacity declines"), which were rated on a five-point Likert-type agree-disagree scale. An overall mean score was computed for each dimension.

Volunteer status was obtained by asking participants "Are you volunteering in the field of ICT (e.g. tablet, smartphone, AAL, Wearables, Internet) as a conveyor of knowledge (companion, ambassador, mentor, lecturer)?".

Sample. The sample included $n = 171$ active technology volunteers (TV) aged 60 to 89 years ($M = 70.4$ years). In addition, a comparison group (CG) with $n = 160$ persons of the same age was generated ($M = 70.4$ years, 60 to 90 years) who did not define themselves as TV. The CG is even higher educated (87% with university entrance qualification and higher compared with 78% among TV; Table 1) and is comprised of more women (CG: 45%, TV: 33%). Overall, members of both groups have various socioeconomic, health-related and psychological resources: They do not feel alienated or excluded from society (obsolescence), they also feel remarkably younger than their chronological age (by more than nine years), and they have high levels of general life satisfaction. Hence, they are typical representatives of an active, healthy and mobile "young age" or "third age".

Table 1. Sample Description.

Variable	Total	TV	CG	Group comparison	
	$N = 331$	$n = 171$	$n = 160$	Test statistic	p value
Age (M, SD)	70.44 (5.76)	70.43 (5.75)	70.44 (5.78)	$t(329) = -0.017$	.986
Gender (female)	39.0%	33.3%	45.0%	$\chi^2(1) = 4.730$	.030
Education level[a]				$\chi^2(2) = 8.200$	.017
Low	7.3%	11.1%	3.1%		
Medium	10.6%	11.1%	10.0%		
High	82.2%	77.8%	86.9%		
Income				$\chi^2(2) = 2.580$	.275
<1,000€	1.5%	2.2%	0.8%		
1,000-2,000€	13.0%	15.6%	10.3%		
>2,000€	85.4%	82.2%	88.9%		
Family status (married)	75.2%	76.6%	73.8%	$\chi^2(1) = 0.362$	.547
Household size (> 1)	74.9%	77.2%	72.5%	$\chi^2(1) = 0.969$	.325
Retired/receiving pension	92.1%	91.2%	93.1%	$\chi^2(1) = 0.411$	.521
Disabled person's pass holders	14.8%	13.5%	16.3%	$\chi^2(1) = 0.514$	.474
Care degree	1.8%	0.6%	3.1%	$\chi^2(1) = 2.997$	.083
Subjective health (M, SD)[b]	2.47 (0.96)	2.47 (1.00)	2.46 (0.92)	$t(329) = 0.050$	.960
Life satisfaction (M, SD)[b]	1.95 (0.89)	1.93 (0.96)	1.98 (0.80)	$t(329) = -0.526$	.599
Obsolescence[c]	1.95 (0.65)	1.90 (0.65)	2.01 (0.64)	$t(329) = -1.668$	.096
Subjective age (difference to chronological age)	-9.65 (8.76)	-9.65 (9.31)	-9.65 (8.16)	$t(328) = -0.001$	.999
Awareness of age-related changes[d]					
Gains	3.48 (0.58)	3.52 (0.61)	3.44 (0.54)	$t(329) = 1.224$	.222
Losses	2.00 (0.60)	2.00 (0.58)	1.99 (0.63)	$t(329) = 0.005$	.996
Attitude towards technology[e]	4.21 (0.77)	4.27 (0.81)	4.15 (0.72)	$t(327.713) = 1.418$	.157
Technology biography[f]	3.97 (0.85)	4.22 (0.72)	3.71 (0.90)	$t(305.338) = 5.661$	< .001
Need for support[g]	3.27 (1.58)	2.73 (1.44)	3.85 (2.06)	$t(282.352) = -5.724$	< .001
Volunteering	80.4%	100.0%	59.4%	$\chi^2(1) = 86.444$	< .001
Hours per month (M, SD)[h]	17.55 (27.86)	26.15 (31.51)	8.73 (20.10)	$t(277.723) = 5.944$	< .001
(Further) education activities (hours per month; M, SD)	33.67 (28.03)	32.79 (29.34)	34.60 (26.63)	$t(328) = -0.584$	.560
Internet self-efficacy (M, SD)[i]	4.32 (0.64)	4.50 (0.53)	4.14 (0.70)	$t(294.772) = 5.290$	< .001

[a]Low = no school diploma or lower secondary school diploma with or without apprenticeship, Medium = secondary school diploma, High = at least advanced technical college certificate.
[b]Rated in school grades, ranging from 1 (highest grade) to 6 (lowest grade).
[c]Mean of 5 items, ranging from 1 ("do not agree at all") to 5 ("fully agree").
[d]Mean of 5 items each for gains and losses, ranging from 1 ("do not agree at all") to 5 ("fully agree").
[e]Mean of 2 items, ranging from 1 (very negative) to 5 (very positive).
[f]Mean of 4 items, ranging from 1 (little experience) to 5 (much experience).
[g]Ranging from 1 (none at all) to 10 (very much).
[h]Volunteering in the field of ICT and in other fields; non-volunteers received the value 0.
[i]Mean of 6 items, ranging from 1 ("do not agree at all") to 5 ("fully agree").

5   Results

5.1   Empirical Findings on the Use of ICT

Both groups are well equipped with media and digital devices. Almost all households have a computer or laptop, smartphones, and Internet connection, as well as televisions and radio sets. Nevertheless, the TV group is even more affine towards digital devices, as indicated by significant group differences in the proportion of people equipped with tablets (TV: 87%, CG: 64%), smartphones (TV: 99%, CG: 92%), activity trackers (TV: 36%, CG: 22%) and digital voice assistants (TV: 28%, CG: 18%; Fig. 1). Looking at the experience with ICT use, the only group difference is found in the first phase of digitization: The TV have been using a computer or laptop for an average of almost 29 years, compared with 26 years of experience in the CG. With regard to the second phase of digitization, Internet use, the average experience is 21 years in both groups. Similarly, the groups are even regarding the third phase of digitization, mobile Internet use: Smartphones have been in use for just over ten years and tablets for seven years in both groups.

In both groups, numerous analog and digital media and devices are an integral part of everyday media life. The Internet, computer, smartphone, television, and newspaper are used daily by almost all respondents; tablet and radio set by over 80% and digital voice assistants and e-book readers by around 40% daily. The groups differ in their daily use of the telephone, which is more frequent among TV (TV: 89%, CG: 75%), and in reading books, which is more frequent in the CG (TV: 61%, CG: 84%, Fig. 2).

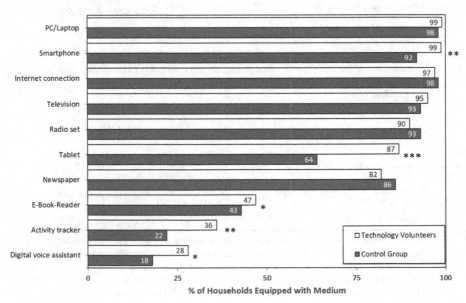

Fig. 1. Media equipment of surveyed households among TV and CG. Significance levels of χ^2-tests for group differences are indicated by stars: *** $p \leq .001$, ** $p \leq .01$, * $p \leq .05$.

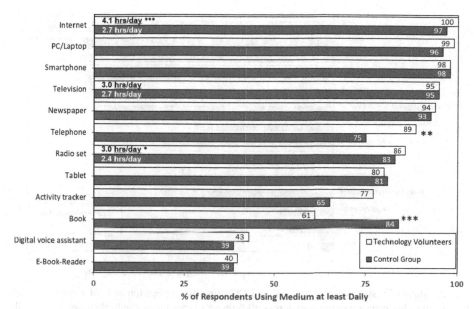

Fig. 2. Share of respondents among TV and CG using the medium at least daily in the subsample of respondents equipped with the medium. χ^2-tests for group differences are conducted across all 6 response categories (multiple times a day, daily, weekly, monthly, rarely, never). Mean daily use among both groups is indicated for Internet, television and radio and tested for group differences with t-tests. Significance levels are indicated by stars: *** $p \leq .001$, ** $p \leq .01$, * $p \leq .05$.

In addition, the TV use mass media much more intensively than the CG. According to their self-assessments, the TV use the Internet for more than four hours a day and listen to the radio for more than three hours a day; in the CG, the daily Internet use is below three hours and the radio use is around 2.5 h. The groups do not differ significantly in their television use, which is around three hours daily. While television and the Internet share the status of the most widely used media in the CG, the Internet dominates among the TV.

Next, looking at Internet usage, it can again be noted that both groups have a very broad usage of the Internet. Almost all respondents use online applications and activities such as e-mailing, search engines and news at least once a week. However, the TV are significantly more active on the Internet – the share of weekly use is higher among TV than in the CG for almost all the applications included in the survey. For example, 81% of the TV use online banking on a weekly basis, compared with 69% in the CG; equally large differences appear in the frequency of use of video platforms, video calls, social networks and digital neighborhood platforms (Fig. 3).

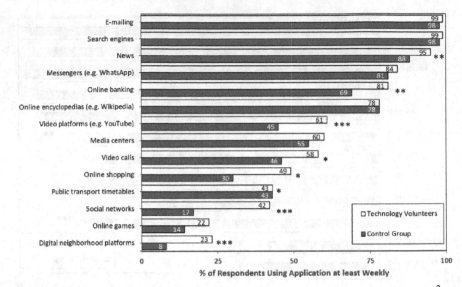

Fig. 3. Share of respondents among TV and CG using the application at least weekly. χ^2-tests for group differences are conducted across all 6 response categories (multiple times a day, daily, weekly, monthly, rarely, never). Significance levels are indicated by stars: *** p ≤ .001, ** p ≤ .01, * p ≤ .05.

The extraordinary relevance of the Internet for the TV can be supported by further findings. The diverse use of the Internet is accompanied by a broad spectrum of motives for Internet use: While almost all respondents in both groups use the Internet "to obtain information", more than 60% of the TV indicated that they use the Internet "for opportunities to exchange", "to get food for thought", "because of content that can only be found there", "to maintain social contacts", "because the personal environment uses it as well", and "because it is fun". Herein, the agreement of the TV with almost all of the items is remarkably higher than in the CG (Fig. 4).

Furthermore, the Internet is the most important source of information in both groups when it comes to "information about a problem of personal importance" (TV: 89%, CG: 75%; percentages excluding respondents who aren't interested in this topic), "new products" (TV: 83%, CG: 61%), "information about Covid-19" (TV: 59%, CG: 44%), and "health and care" (TV: 53%, CG: 43%). Only when it comes to "current happenings in your region", daily newspapers still dominate (TV: 59%, CG: 62%), and when it comes to "current happenings in the world", television is most important (TV: 50%, CG: 46%; Fig. 5). These findings demonstrate the advancement of the digital transformation of everyday media life particularly among TV.

In both groups, this is accompanied by fundamental knowledge and skills in using the Internet and digital devices, although the TV attribute themselves significantly higher competencies with regard to the Internet (school grade 1.9 to 2.5, where 1 is the highest and 6 is the lowest possible grade), computers (1.8 to 2.5), smartphones (2.1 to 2.8) and tablets (2.3 to 3.2; Fig. 6).

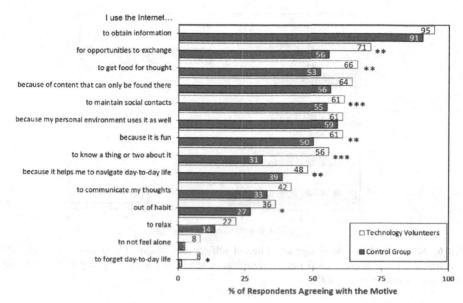

Fig. 4. Share of respondents among TV and CG agreeing with the motive for Internet use. χ^2-tests for group differences are conducted across all 5 response categories (strongly agree, agree, neither/nor, disagree, strongly disagree). Significance levels are indicated by stars: *** $p \leq .001$, ** $p \leq .01$, * $p \leq .05$.

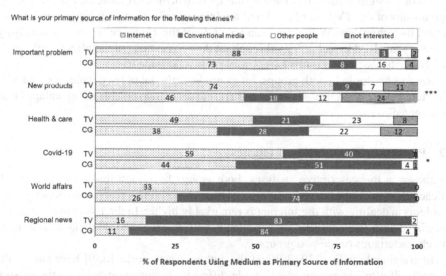

Fig. 5. Most important source of information among TV and CG for various themes. "Conventional media" include television, radio, newspaper and magazines. "Other people" include family, partner, friends, neighbors. χ^2-tests for group differences are conducted dichotomously for "Internet" vs. "Other sources". Significance levels are indicated by stars: *** $p \leq .001$, * $p \leq$ .05.

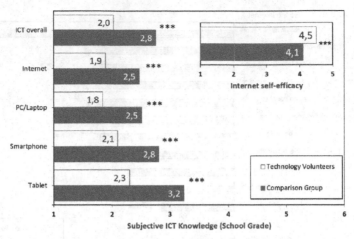

Fig. 6. Subjective ICT knowledge and Internet self-efficacy among TV and CG. Internet self-efficacy is a mean score over 6 items. Significance levels of *t*-tests for group differences are indicated by stars: *** $p \leq .001$.

Finally, the TV have much higher levels of Internet self-efficacy (Fig. 6). For instance, 75% of the TV are confident in "trouble shooting Internet problems", while only 43% of the CG feel confident about this. Accordingly, the need for support when using modern technology is significantly lower among the TV than in the CG (Table 1). This particularly high affinity of the TV towards ICT and the Internet reflects in their biography which is shaped by technology: While, for example, 74% of the TV agree that they have always been very involved in technology throughout their lives, this only applies to 45% of the CG. Nevertheless, both groups have a very positive attitude toward technology: In both groups, for example, eight out of ten people share the view that "technological progress is needed, therefore some unavoidable disadvantages must be accepted".

5.2 Predictors of Internet Self-efficacy

As shown in the descriptive analyses, both groups have high levels of Internet self-efficacy. However, the TVs' confidence in their own abilities regarding challenges and problems in dealing with the Internet is remarkably higher. In the following, the factors associated with this self-efficacy expectancy will be examined, looking at differences and characteristics of the two groups.

International studies [29, 30] and the authors' own works [6, 9] have shown that Internet self-efficacy among older people differs by sociodemographic characteristics: It is generally higher among men, among people with high education levels, and people of younger age. In this study, (small) corresponding correlations are found in both groups. One exception is that education level does not correlate significantly with Internet self-efficacy among TV. This means that Internet self-efficacy is lower for female TV and for older TV, but not for TV with lower formal education. As expected, self-efficacy is associated with self-assessed skills and knowledge in using ICT (Internet, PC/laptop, tablet, smartphone), and with the portfolio of online applications (number of applications used at least weekly). Here, the correlations are large among the CG and medium-sized among the TV. Only in the CG, self-efficacy correlates with the extent of volunteer work (hours per month) and there is a non-significant tendency for higher self-efficacy when spending more time on (further) education activities (in person or online, including self-learning; Table 2).

Table 2. Correlation coefficients of the predictors with Internet self-efficacy for the total sample and the two groups. Spearman-correlations were calculated for ordinal variables, and Pearson-correlations for metric variables. Conventions after Cohen [31]: .3 = medium, .5 = large.

| | Technology Volunteers | | Control Group | | | |
| | Total Sample | | Technology Volunteers | | Control Group | |
	r	p	r	p	r	p
Age	-.24	< .001	-.23	.003	-.27	< .001
Gender (m=0, f=1)	-.19	< .001	-.22	.003	-.12	.117
Education level (low/medium=0, high=1)	.10	.074	-.01	.852	.30	< .001
ICT knowledge[a]	.64	< .001	.53	< .001	.63	< .001
Internet applications[b]	.48	< .001	.36	< .001	.49	< .001
(Further) education activites (online or in-person; hrs/month)	12.	.032	.03	.726	.23	.002
Volunteering (ICT or other fields; hrs/month)	.14	.009	.02	.793	.13	.093

[a]Mean of 5 items, ranging from 1 (little knowledge) to 5 (much knowledge).
[b]Sum of applications used at least monthly, max. 14.

Next, hierarchical linear regression analyses were applied to examine the predictive power of the factors correlated with Internet self-efficacy and to determine their specific contributions to the explained variance in self-efficacy in the two groups. Model 1 includes sociodemographic predictors and shows that a higher age predicts lower self-efficacy in both groups. Beyond that, female gender predicts lower self-efficacy among the TV, and a high level of education predicts higher self-efficacy in the CG. For both.

groups, the largest share of variance is explained in model 2 by adding the media-related variables ICT skills and broadness of Internet usage. This is not surprising, since conceptual aspects such as "confidence", "perceived competence" and "scope of use" are closely related. It is noteworthy that in the CG, other variables can explain additional variance in model 3: The extent of volunteer involvement in particular, but also the extent of (further) education activities predict Internet self-efficacy in this group. In other words, persons from the CG who are more involved in general voluntary work, or who invest more time in educational opportunities such as lectures, courses or self-study, generally have a higher Internet self-efficacy. However, in the TV group no relation of these factors with Internet self-efficacy could be found, which may be due to the fact that this group already has very high levels of self-efficacy. This could also explain why the explained variance of the overall model is only moderate in this group. In contrast, the overall model has a good fit in the CG, achieving over 50% of explained variance (Table 3).

Table 3. Hierarchical linear regression analysis of Internet self-efficacy for the two groups

	Model 1	Model 2	Model 3	Model 1	Model 2	Model 3
Age (z-standardized)	-23 **	-.10	-.09	-.27 ***	-.09	-.11
Gender (m=0, f=1)	-.23 **	-.12	-.11	-.10	-.06	-.04
Education level (low/medium=0, high=1)	-.01	-.03	-.03	.28 ***	.18 **	.14 *
ICT knowledge[a]		.42 ***	.43 ***		.48 ***	.51 ***
Internet applications[b]		.18 *	.19 **		.18 *	.16 *
(Further) education activities (online or in-person; hrs/month)			-.05			.13 *
Volunteering (ICT or other fields; hrs/month)			.01			.24 ***
adjusted R^2	8,6%	31,6%	31,0%	15,2%	45,3%	51,6%
F-test of model prediction	6.921 ***	16.622 ***	11.843 ***	10.512 ***	27.360 ***	25.247 ***

[a]Mean of 5 items, ranging from 1 (little knowledge) to 5 (much knowledge).
[b]Sum of applications used at least monthly, max. 14. *** $p \leq .001$, ** $p \leq .01$, * $p \leq .05$.

6   Summary and Outlook

The results demonstrate that both groups of highly educated older people have high levels of openness to technology in general and to ICT and the Internet in particular. They are equipped with a broad portfolio of digital media, use their digital devices intensively and for a diverse range of online applications. Nevertheless, the group of technology volunteers stands out against the comparison group in that their everyday media life is much more digital. In this group, the Internet has now become the leading medium in specific areas. In addition, members of this group have even higher levels of digital knowledge and skills. Due to their manifold person-related and digital-technology-related resources, they have very good prerequisites for "digital volunteering in old age". In this, they can act as role models and "door openers", also called "warm experts", for digitally inexperienced or insecure older people, since both volunteers and novices belong to the same pre-digital technology generation. These concepts can also be transferred to other areas: Especially when new digital health services are introduced, "digital best agers" can contribute to the dissemination of health knowledge and digital health competencies among older adults [32].

For the DiBiWohn research project, this study afforded a fundamental understanding of this special group of "digital best agers". This baseline study represents a benchmark for all technology volunteers participating in the project. It will allow to map person- and technology-related processes of change, development, and mediatization over the course of the active technology mentoring and the continuous online and in-person training programs. Beyond that, the data opens up possibilities for comparative analyses with the parallel survey of residents in assisted living facilities and with the representative study "Senior citizen, Information, Media" (SIM), also from the spring of 2021, including over 3,005 private residents aged 60 and over [33].

7 Limitations

The study is accompanied by a number of limitations. First, the sample is a highly selective group of older adults of "younger old age" who are highly educated and have a lot of experience and competencies with regards to technology and digital media. Therefore, the results cannot be generalized to all older persons. This applies in particular to the correlations shown between Internet self-efficacy and the personal and media-related influencing factors. Further research is needed to examine whether these relationships also apply to older adults with fewer resources, competencies, and technical experience.

Second, due to the cross-sectional study design, no causal statements can be made and all directions of effect are only theoretical. For this purpose, older adults should be monitored and surveyed over a longer period of time to better understand the effects of volunteering on constructs such as subjective age, self-efficacy or attitudes towards technology.

References

1. Project "Digitale Bildungsprozesse für ältere Menschen in seniorenspezifischen Wohnformen der institutionalisierten Altenhilfe" [Digital Educational Processes for Older Residents in Assisted Living Arrangements and Care Facilities] (DiBiWohn) Homepage. https://dibiwohn.org/en/. Accessed 27 Dec 2022
2. Bandura A.: Self-Efficacy: The Exercise of Control. W.H. Freeman, New York (1997). https://doi.org/10.5860/choice.35-1826
3. Parkin, S., McKeganey, N.: The rise and rise of peer education approaches, drugs: education. Prevent. Policy 7(3), 293–310 (2000). https://doi.org/10.1080/09687630050109961
4. Hoffman, S.B.: Peer counselor training with the elderly. Gerontologist 23(4), 358–360 (1983). https://doi.org/10.1093/geront/23.4.358
5. Zhou, J., Salvendy, G. (eds.): ITAP 2015. LNCS, vol. 9193. Springer, Cham (2015). https://doi.org/10.1007/978-3-319-20892-3
6. Doh, M., Jokisch, M. R., Rupprecht, F. S.: Förderliche und hinderliche Faktoren im Umgang mit neuen Informations- und Kommunikations-Technologien im Alter – Befunde aus der Initiative der „Senioren-Technik-Botschafter" [Factors facilitating or hindering

the use of new information and communication technologies in old age - Findings from the "Older Technology Ambassadors" initiative]. In: Kuttner, C., Schwender, C. (eds.) Mediale Lernkulturen im höheren Erwachsenenalter, vol. 12, pp. 223–242. Schriftenreihe Gesellschaft – Altern – Medien, kopaed, Munich (2018)

7. Stiel, J., Brandt, M., Bubolz-Lutz, E.: Technikbotschafter*in für Ältere werden – Lernformate im freiwilligen Engagement „Technikbegleitung" [Becoming a technology ambassador for older people - Learning formats in "technology accompaniment" volunteering]. In: Kuttner, C., Schwender, C. (eds.) Mediale Lernkulturen im höheren Erwachsenenalter, vol. 12, pp. 201–222. Schriften-reihe Gesellschaft – Altern – Medien, kopaed, Munich (2018)

8. Doh, M., Jokisch, M.R., Jäkh, S.D., Scheling, L., Wahl, H.-W.: Das Projekt KommmiT – Kommunikation mit intelligenter Technik. Ergebnisbericht der wissenschaftlichen Begleitung [The KommmiT Project – Communication with intelligent technology. Report of the accompanying research]. LfK (2021). https://www.lfk.de/medienkompetenz/seniorinnen-und-senioren/kommmit

9. Jokisch, M.R., Doh, M., Brehm, M., Tatsch, I.: Schulung älterer Menschen zum Technikbegleiter – Ein Praxisbericht aus dem Digitalen Projekt KommmiT [Training older people to become technology volunteers - A practice report from the digital project KommmiT]. In Schramek, R., Steinfort-Diedenhofen, J., Kricheldorff, C. (eds.) Diversität der Altersbildung. Geragogische Handlungsfelder, Konzepte und Settings, pp. 201–212. Kohlhammer, Stuttgart (2022)

10. Doh, M.: Auswertung von empirischen Studien zur Nutzung von Internet, digitalen Medien und Informations- und Kommunikations-Technologien bei älteren Menschen [Evaluation of empirical studies on the use of the Internet, digital media, and information and communication technologies among older people]. In Hagen, C., Endter, C., Berner, F. (eds.) Expertisen zum Achten Altersbericht der Bundesregierung. Deutsches Zentrum für Altersfragen, Berlin (2020).https://www.achter-altersbericht.de/fileadmin/altersbericht/pdf/Expertisen/Expertise-Doh.pdf

11. Schramek, R., Stiel, J.: Förderung von Technik- und Medienkompetenz älterer Menschen aus der Perspektive der Geragogik [Promoting technology and media knowledge in older people from the perspective of geragogy]. In Hagen, C., Endter, C., Berner, F. (eds.) Expertisen zum Achten Altersbericht der Bundesregierung. Deutsches Zentrum für Altersfragen, Berlin (2020). https://www.achter-altersbericht.de/fileadmin/altersbericht/pdf/Expertisen/Expertise-Schramek-und-Stiel.pdf

12. Netzwerk für Senior-Internet-Initiativen Baden-Württemberg [Network for initiatives regarding older people and the Internet in Baden-Württemberg]. https://netzwerk-sii-bw.de/. Accessed 20 Dec 2022

13. Project "Digital-Botschafterinnen und -Botschafter für Rheinland-Pfalz" [Digital ambassadors for Rhineland-Palatinate]. https://digital-botschafter.silver-tipps.de/. Accessed 20 Dec 2022

14. Bubolz-Lutz, E., Gösken, E., Kricheldorff, C., Schramek, R.: Geragogik: Bildung und Lernen im Prozess des Alterns. Das Lehrbuch [Geragogy: Education and learning in the process of aging. The textbook]. Kohlhammer, Stuttgart (2010)

15. Jokisch, M.R., Schmidt, L.I., Doh, M., Marquard, M., Wahl, H.-W.: The role of internet self-efficacy, innovativeness and technology avoidance in breadth of internet use: Comparing older technology experts and non-experts. Comput. Human Behav. 111, 106408 (2020). https://doi.org/10.1016/j.chb.2020.106408

16. Sackmann, R., Winkler, O.: Technology generations revisited: the internet generation. Gerontechnology 11(4), 493–503 (2013). https://doi.org/10.4017/gt.2013.11.4.002.00

17. Ivan, L., Loos, E.F., Bird, I.: The impact of technology generations on older adults' media use: Review of previous empirical research and a seven country comparison. Gerontechnology 19(4) (2020)

18. Loos, E., Ivan, L.: Not only people are getting old, new media are too: technology generations and the changes in new media use. New Media Soc. (2022)
19. Jokisch, M. R.: Altern in einer digitalisierten Gesellschaft: Studien zur Selbstwirksamkeit, Technikakzeptanz und dem Obsoleszenzerleben bei älteren Erwachsenen [Aging in a digitized society: Studies on self-efficacy, technology acceptance and perceived obsolescence among older adults] (dissertation, Ruprecht-Karls-Universität Heidelberg), Heidelberg (2021). https://doi.org/10.11588/heidok.00032076
20. Bakardjieva, M.: Internet Society The Internet in Everyday Life. Sage Publications, London (2005)
21. Rogers, E.M.: Diffusion of Innovations. Free Press, New York, New York (2003)
22. Loos, E., Peine, A., Fernández-Ardèvol, M.: Older people as early adopters and their unexpected & innovative use of new technologies: deviating from technology companies' scripts. In: Gao, Q., Zhou, J. (eds.), HUMAN ASPECTS OF IT FOR THE AGED POPULATION, HCII 2021, LNCS vol. 12786, pp. 156–167. Springer, Cham (2021). https://doi.org/10.1007/978-3-030-78108-8_12
23. Breunig, C., Engel, B.: Massenkommunikation 2015: Funktionen und images der medien im vergleich [mass communication 2015: comparing functions and images of the media]. Media Perspektiven 7(8), 323–341 (2015)
24. Mollenkopf, H., Kaspar, R.: Technisierte Umwelten als Handlungs- und Erlebensräume älterer Menschen [Technisized environments as spaces for action and experience of older people]. In: Backes, G.M., Clemens, W., Künemund, H. (eds.) Lebensformen und Lebensführung im Alter. Alter(n) und Gesellschaft, vol 10. VS Verlag für Sozialwissenschaften, Wiesbaden (2004). https://doi.org/10.1007/978-3-663-10615-9_10
25. Brandtstädter, J., Wentura, D.: Veränderungen der Zeit- und Zukunftsperspektive im Übergang zum höheren Erwachsenenalter: Entwicklungspsychologische und differentielle Aspekte [Changes in time and future perspective at the transition to old age: Developmental psychological and differential aspects]. Zeitschrift für Entwicklungspsychologie und Pädagogische Psychologie 26(1), 2–21 (1994)
26. Eastin, M.S., LaRose, R.: Internet self-efficacy and the psychology of the digital divide. J. Comput.-Med. Commun. 6(1), JCMC611 (2000). https://doi.org/10.1111/j.1083-6101.2000.tb00110.x
27. Rubin, D.C., Berntsen, D.: People over forty feel 20% younger than their age: subjective age across the lifespan. Psychon. Bull. Rev. 13(5), 776–780 (2006). https://doi.org/10.3758/BF03193996
28. Kaspar, R., Gabrian, M., Brothers, A., Wahl, H.W., Diehl, M.: Measuring awareness of age-related change: development of a 10-item short form for use in large-scale surveys. Gerontologist 59(3), e130–e140 (2019). https://doi.org/10.1093/geront/gnx213
29. Czaja, S.J., et al.: Factors predicting the use of technology: findings from the center for research and education on aging and technology enhancement (CREATE). Psychol. Aging 21(2), 333–352 (2006). https://doi.org/10.1037/0882-7974.21.2.333
30. Jokisch, M.R., Scheling, L., Doh, M., Wahl, H.W.: Contrasting internet adoption in early and advanced old age: does internet self-efficacy matter? J. Gerontol.: Ser. B 77(2), 312–320 (2022). https://doi.org/10.1093/geronb/gbab096
31. Cohen, J.: Statistical Power Analysis for the Behavioral Sciences, 2nd edn. L. Erlbaum Associates, Hillsdale (1988)

32. Jokisch, M., Schmidt, L., Doh, M.: Acceptance of digital health services among older adults: findings on perceived usefulness, self-efficacy, privacy concerns, ICT knowledge, and support seeking. Front. Public Health **10**, 1073756 (2022). https://doi.org/10.3389/fpubh.2022.107 3756
33. Medienpädagogischer Forschungsverbund Südwest (mpfs): SIM-Studie 2021 – Senior:innen, Information, Medien. Basisuntersuchung zum Medienumgang von Personen ab 60 Jahren in Deutschland [SIM Study 2021 – Older people, information, media. Baseline study on media use of people aged 60 and over in Germany] (2022). https://www.lfk.de/fileadmin/PDFs/Pub likationen/Studien/SIM-Studie/sim-studie-2021.pdf

First and Second-Level Digital Divides and Cultural Capital: Framing Digital Lives of Seniors in Portugal and Europe

Tiago Lapa[1]([envelope]) [iD], Teresa Martinho[2] [iD], and Célia Reis[3] [iD]

[1] Iscte– Instituto Universitário de Lisboa, Av das Forças Armadas, 1649-026 Lisboa, Portugal
tjfls1@iscte.pt
[2] ICS, Av. Professor Aníbal de Bettencourt, 9, 1600-189 Lisboa, Portugal
[3] Instituto Politécnico de Leiria, Campus 2, Morro do Lena – Alto do Vieiro, Apartado 4163, 2411-901 Leiria, Portugal

Abstract. Although research has been mainly focused on mapping individual determinants of digital exclusion, stressing the role of schooling, less attention has been paid to explore the role of pre-existing cultural practices and capital, beyond formal education, as determining factors of first-level and second-level divides among seniors and across western societies. The diffusion of digital devices with access to the internet is reaching a level close to 90% in European societies. However, the digital divide is still a noticeable issue when comparing generations and among seniors of age 65+ years (Friemel, 2016). As access to the internet, digital literacy, and use of digital services are increasingly prerequisites for public life and accessing public and commercial services in Europe and elsewhere (Alexopoulou, Åström, Karlsson, 2022), it is pertinent to look at the digital lives (or lack of) of seniors. Therefore, our study explores the influence of variations in cultural capital on the digital divide among seniors (aged 65+) in Portugal and Europe. The analyses are based on data from Eurobarometer and a representative survey concerning cultural practices on and offline in Portugal. The first part of the study introduces a comparative perspective of different regions of the European Union (EU) concerning the distribution of digital access and of online practices with cultural purposes, tracing digital first and second-level digital divides across Europe according to indicators of social and cultural inequality. The second section focuses on the results of the national survey regarding Internet use for cultural consumption. In the third part, also based on the same national data, we explore the association of various offline and online practices related to culture with types of digital divide. With this analysis we hope to find alternate ways of considering the links between technology usage and seniors and go beyond traditional analysis of this relationship.

Keywords: Internet · seniors · digital inclusion · social inclusion · ICT

Q. Gao and J. Zhou (Eds.): HCII 2023, LNCS 14043, pp. 489–504, 2023.
https://doi.org/10.1007/978-3-031-34917-1_33

1 Introduction

Past research has been mainly focused on tracing individual factors of digital exclusion, emphasizing the role of schooling. Less consideration has been paid to investigate the role of pre-existing cultural practices and capital, beyond formal education, as influential factors of first-level and second-level divides among seniors across western societies, albeit the digital transformations of, at least, part of the senior population in Europe and elsewhere.

Among seniors, the digital divide is still an evident issue, especially when comparing seniors of age 65+ years with younger generations (Friemel, 2016). Besides access to digital technologies, digital literacy, and use of digital services are increasingly prerequisites for public life and accessing public and commercial services in Europe and elsewhere (Alexopoulou, Åström, Karlsson, 2022). Therefore, it is appropriate to glance at the digital lives (or lack of) of seniors. In this line of research, our study explores the influence of variations in cultural capital on the digital divide among seniors (aged 65+) in Portugal, placing the country in an European comparative perspective. Our analysis is based on data from Eurobarometer and a national representative survey regarding cultural practices on and offline in Portugal.

2 Seniors and Digital and Social Inequalities

As recognized by the European Declaration on Digital Rights and Principles, technological advances bring about transformations in our lives, offering opportunities for learning, socialization, entertainment and promoting opportunities for access to health and culture (EC, 2022). Furthermore, it recognizes that the recent COVID-19 pandemic has accelerated the pace of digitization by further perennating the role it plays in society and the economy.

Similarly, digital inclusion policies are now a priority of the Portugal Digital Programme (Government of Portugal, 2020) that fosters the digital transformation of companies, public bodies, and people's training in media and digital literacy. However, this brings us to the critical point of the intersection between digital and social inequalities that lead to social exclusion. Social inequalities are both the negative cause and consequence of e-exclusion, especially in countries like Portugal where there are notable percentages of people without access or limited access to the Internet, and/or with the lack of capacity or skills to use Information and Communication Technologies (ICT). An example of this is older people who are deprived of access to services that have been digitized, namely public services. The access and use of technologies such as the computer and mobile phone as means of digital inclusion is relevant (Dias, 2012). In addition, as Helen Helsper (2008, 2009 and 2012) argues, access, use, skills, and attitudes are the mediating factors of digital inclusion that, consequently, lead to social inclusion. In Portugal 87.3% of households have internet connection at home, where 84.1% of this connection is by broadband (INE, PORDATA, 2021). Table 1 shows an increase in internet use from 68.6% in 2015 to 82.3% in 2021. While younger cohorts already reached a plateau, this increase happened because of the growing digital inclusion of older cohorts. As shown in Table 1, in 2015 only 27.2% of individuals between

65 and 74 years had access to the Internet, today the figures are almost double with 47.7% (2021), but still below 50%. Furthermore, the data analyzed by age group reveals a consistent gap between cohorts, with internet usage declining as age advances. In this sense, first-level digital inequalities (related to access) increase from younger to older age groups, to the extent that people without access or limited access to the internet are deprived of access to digitized services (Neves, 2021) and away from online public participation. Specially if we consider social network sites and other online services as new forms of culture that bring new arrangements of socialization (Amaral & Sousa, 2012).

Table 1. Internet use in Portugal from 2015 to 2020 by age group (%).

	16–24 years	25–34 years	35–44 years	45–54 years	55–64 years	65–74 years	Total
2015	99,3	94,9	87,5	64,6	42,0	27,2	68,6
2016	99,1	97,2	88,8	71,6	47,0	28,3	70,4
2017	99,0	97,6	93,2	75,2	55,1	31,1	73,8
2018	99,4	98,2	92,9	78,7	53,4	32,7	74,7
2019	99,5	98,0	95,1	78,4	57,3	33,1	75,3
2020	99,5	98,2	95,7	82,7	65,3	39,0	78,3
2021	99,7	98,4	96,4	88,2	71,0	47,7	82,3

Source: Pordata (2021)

It is noticeable that although there is a greater democratization in access to ICT, that is a decrease in first-level digital inequalities, albeit late in European standards, there is still a digital gap in usage and types of use (related to second-level inequalities) (Lapa & Vieira, 2019). The European Community (EC, 2022) also recognizes that the COVID-19 pandemic has increased the digital divide throughout the European Union, not only between urban and rural areas, but also that weak access to connectivity and internet access has been notorious, in addition to limitations in digital skills and understanding of ICT, causing major risks of social cohesion.

At the same time, other countries, such as Switzerland in particular, Digital Senior 2020 (Swissinfo et al., 2020) reported that, at the time of the study, 74% of individuals over 65 used the internet, a situation that in 2009 the figures were 38%. The study also points out that the use of internet on mobile phones and tablets amounts to 68% and that this evolution of digital inclusion was due to the offer of courses that allowed older people to explore the new ICT. As Cunha (2017) states for greater social integration, technological inclusion is needed, and positive experiences and interactions are needed for technologies to be accepted and adopted by them.

Gil and Easter (2018) identified that learning ICT by seniors is related to their participation and inclusion in the digital society, so it will be important to reflect whether the non-use of ICT by older people is associated with the non-relevance they consider for their lives (Helsper, 2009; Neves, 2013) or for the lack of interest in the use of the Internet because they consider it not for you, do not have usability capacity or do not have access (Helsper, 2009). However, it is still worth considering that there are differences between the younger and the older seniors, because older adults are the most infoexcluded, "(…) these represent citizens with the lowest rates of access to and use of digital technologies". (Gil, 2019). This author constifies that the digital fracture entails with him not only a potential social exclusion, but also everything that this involves, and the consequences inherent to it.

When talking about social exclusion based on internet studies, we should consider the first-level digital divisions dependent on the lit, where people do not have information, do not know, or do not want to be linked to the forms of use, motivations, interests, and competencies that can be barriers in this use (Gómez, 2018). At a second level, the use in whose abilities may be a barrier (DiMaggio & Hergittai, 2001). And finally, to a third level linked to the benefits they can enjoy online, namely the social benefits of using the internet at the social, economic, political, health and culture level (Van Dursen, 2010).

In fact, even with a greater democratization in access to ICT in our country, the reality is that there is still a digital gap in terms of use and types of use (Lapa & Vieira, 2019). As identified by the Eurobarometer (Standard Eurobarometer 84 Autumn 2015 - Media use in the European Union), in a study in the member countries, there are three types of Internet users among the oldest (between 65 and 99 years old): digitally immersed communicators, where internet use is more frequent and diverse; Asynchronous communicators, individuals accustomed to the Internet, but with a less regular use than the previous group; and Phone enjoyers, who have less communication activity and frequency of internet use, as well as with fewer paid Internet services compared to previous users (Vulpe and Crăciun, 2020).

Still, Gil (2019) states that we may be facing a new digital fracture associated with inter or intragenerationality, because there is a clear notion that digital literacy and the digital skills associated with them are only present before, according to the author, "(…) a critical and reflective attitude in the use and mobilization of digital technologies to the detriment of more functional or instrumental aspects."

If, on the one hand, Loos (2012) argues that when it comes to the search for information in an internet context the concepts of "digital natives" and "digital immigrants" have no reason to exist, on the other hand, Lapa & Di Fátima (2019) explain so that we are faced with a more complex model where the life cycle and the form of socialization with the media or physical limitations can make us better understand the online behavior of seniors.

However, older users acquire digital skills through greater internet experience and their time of use with online tools, as technologies become more user-friendly, enabling a continuous improvement in their digital literacies (DiMaggio el al., 2004).

Seniors are a heterogeneous social group associated with life experiences and digital literacy is associated with their routines and interests (Gil, 2019; Barroso, 2021), where for some technology is perceived and part of their daily routines (Berker et al., 2006), where mobile phones, the internet and computers are central in the lives of some people (Haddon, 2011).

3   Digital Divides Among Seniors in Portugal and Europe

By the turn of the 20th century to the 21st century, the European Union had already identified the problem of 'digital divide' (van Dijk 2009) and digital inequality, a term that some authors consider more rigorous to mention the cleavages that go beyond having access or not to use the Internet, and which refer to very different degrees of competence, variety of objectives, social support and conjugation with offline life (DiMaggio and Hargittai 2001). Digital inequality is among a group of European Union countries, representative of the Nordic, Mediterranean, central and eastern regions, where Portugal was among those whose proportion of Internet users aged 16 to 74 were below the EU average rate (Table 2) in 2021. The contrast between the situation of the Mediterranean countries (except for Spain), and the eastern one and the panorama of the states of central and northern Europe is noteworthy. In Nordic countries, in 2010, Internet users varied between 88% (Denmark) and 91% (Sweden). The discrepancy observed is characteristic of countries whose political and economic path denotes the later promotion of the so-called information society, as a programmatic orientation of public policies and the economy. Demographic and educational reasons have also contributed to explain the softer pace of appropriation of new information and communication technologies in the Portuguese context.

Regarding the Portuguese society, the lower use of the Internet ends up reflecting its demographic structure, since the population is one of the oldest in the EU-27. The results of a recent survey on cultural practices in Portugal (Martinho and Lapa, 2022) reaffirm a very sharp generational divide (Lapa and Vieira, 2019): while internet use was around 100% among Portuguese aged 15 to 34, only 26% among those aged 65 or older said they used the Internet. Eurostat data for 2021 also show the low levels of digital inclusion of older people in Portugal: less than half of The Portuguese aged 65 to 74 were internet users (Table 2), and there was still a significant recovery in the last decade, compared to the proportions that the group assumed in 2010 (10%) and 2005 (2%). The e-exclusion of Portuguese seniors correlates closely with academic qualifications, since the generation aged 65 and over represents the social group that can least benefit from the expansion of the educational system in the country, and with economic resources.

The appropriation of digital culture and connectivity anywhere and anytime is currently seen in about 77% of European citizens aged 65 to 74, with the mobile phone or smartphone as the predominant web access technology (Table 3). This indicator reveals the progressive familiarization of Portuguese s and niores with mobile phones, adhering to a much lesser extent the 'other mobile devices' to access the internet, such as smart TV, smart speakers, console game, e-book reader, smart watch, predominantly suitable by Finland, Netherlands, and Spain.

An in-depth analysis of the data collected in the Eurobarometer (Standard Eurobarometer 84 Autumn 2015 – Media use in the European Union) identified, in all member countries, three types of older Internet users, from 65 to 99 years: digitally immersed communicators, denoting a more frequent and diversified internet use; the A synchronous communicators, familiar with the Internet, but more distant from its use than the previous group; and Phone enjoyers, with lower levels of communication activity, paid Internet services and Internet use frequency (Vulpe and Crăciun, 2020). The study concludes

Table 2. Share of individuals aged 65–74 years and 16 to 74 years who used the internet in the last 3 months (2005, 2010 and 2021).

	65–74 years			16 to 74 years		
	2005	2010	2021	2005	2010	2021
European Union	na	25	65	na	67	89
Portugal	2	10	48	32	51	82
Spain	4	14	73	44	64	94
Greece	1	4	35	22	44	78
Italy	4	11	52	34	51	82
Denmark	30	56	95	77	88	99
Finland	18	43	85	73	86	97
Sweden	27	58	90	81	91	97
Netherlands	34	56	90	79	90	95
Germany	20	41	74	65	80	91
Belgium	12	35	77	58	78	93
Ireland	8	20	97	37	67	99
Slovenia	na	12	62	47	68	89
Hungary	5	13	62	37	61	89
Czechia	2	19	56	32	66	89

na: not available
Source: Statistics I Eurostat (europa.eu)

that in the Northern regions, the type of users that prevails is Asynchronous communicators. The situation is similar in Western European countries, but the category of Digitally immersed communicators is higher in this area, unlike Northern countries. In the Southern and in Eastern Europe, the dominant profile is "mobile phone enjoyers".

In the approach to the online dimension, Eurostat's cultural statistics consider two axes: the use of the internet for selected cultural activities and the use of the internet for purchasing selected cultural goods and services. Considering the first axis, the most accomplished activity, without cutting of ages, corresponds to 'watching internet streamed TV or videos' (72%), followed by 'reading on line news sites/newspapers/news magazines' (71%), 'listening to music (e.g. web radio, music streaming) or downloading music' (60%) and 'playing or downloading games' (32%) (Eurostat 2022). But there are particularities related to the different adhering of different age groups (Table 4). Thus, while the audiovisual domain is markedly juvenilized, the practice of 'reading on line news sites/newspapers/news magazines' is the only one in which there is an overall growth in the passage of the age range '16–24 years' to the group '25–54 years'; moreover, even if it tends to decline among those between 65 and 74 years old, it represents the online cultural activity preferred by European seniors, including the Portuguese. In the survey conducted in Portugal in 2020, it was found that online activity reinforced

Table 3. Devices to access the Internet among people aged 65 to 74 years old. Percentage of individuals who used the internet in the last 3 months (2021).

	Desktop computer	Mobile phone or smartphone	Other mobile devices (smart TV, smart speakers, console game, e-book reader, smart watch)
European Union	37	77	12
Portugal	31	83	8
Spain	26	100	30
Greece	33	75	9
Italy	42	88	8
Denmark	35	79	4
Finland	27	80	53
Sweden	38	83	14
Netherlands	46	87	30
Germany	41	65	7
Belgium	34	69	13
Ireland	24	87	27
Slovenia	47	79	10
Hungary	43	59	4
Czechia	44	55	25

Source: Statistics | Eurostat (europa.eu)

by the group of 65 and over, in the stages of social confinement, was 'reading books, newspapers and magazines', while 'watching films and TV series' assumed a low expression. Another aspect that stands out in Eurostat data is the most pronounced decrease in 'listening to music (e.g., web radio, music streaming) or downloading music' in the transition of the group '25–54' to those between 65 and 74 years old.

The study of the uses that seniors have with the use of the Internet and the bonuses they remove from it is still in a very exploratory phase in Portugal. Concluding from the research so far conducted, senior internet users are generally young elderly (average equivalent to 68 years), considering that although Internet use is not among the most important activities of their routines it is hardly expendable. The data show that they mostly access the Internet from home and the motivations that mobilize them more, and from which they derive greater gratification, are access to information, communication with family and friends, entertainment, and memory sharing (Oliveira, 2019; Rebelo, 2013). The use of this medium also contributes to the strengthening of self-esteem, citizenship, and the sense of utility of some seniors (Oliveira, 2019).

Table 4. Using the internet for cultural purposes, by age group. Percentage of individuals who used the internet in the last 3 months (2022).

	Watching internet streamed TV or videos			Reading online news sites/newspapers/news magazines			Listening to music (e.g., web radio, music streaming) or downloading music			Playing or downloading games		
	16–24	25–54	65–74	16–24	25–54	65–74	16–24	25–54	65–74	16–24	25–54	65–74
European Union	88	77	49	67	74	65	86	66	28	60	32	17
Portugal	91	75	39	87	85	68	95	78	35	73	34	22
Spain	95	90	63	77	85	71	94	83	41	64	36	19
Greece	90	70	33	85	90	86	97	77	38	77	31	8
Italy	91	83	57	55	66	61	84	66	29	62	33	17
Denmark	99	96	70	87	91	82	97	88	43	74	52	32
Finland	100	98	86	92	96	90	99	89	49	78	50	21
Sweden	94	95	68	73	88	79	92	89	47	73	47	24
Netherlands	100	98	81	75	89	79	96	84	46	73	57	40
Belgium	90	78	38	59	73	61	86	67	26	66	38	23
Ireland	95	85	61	71	81	76	89	75	36	45	22	11
Slovenia	95	85	61	71	81	76	89	75	36	45	22	11
Hungary	95	89	67	93	94	87	93	80	48	57	30	14
Czechia	98	86	50	84	93	93	97	70	23	62	27	8

Source: Statistics I Eurostat (europa.eu)

4 Methodology

For the present research, we also used data from the Survey of Cultural Practices of the Portuguese 2020, representative of the Portuguese reality, applied between September 12th and December 28th, 2020, with the aim of carrying out a pioneering survey carried out on a national scale of cultural practices. Culture of the Portuguese, whether offline or online. It also encompasses the survey of how, given the change in offline activities due to the constraints imposed by the pandemic, individuals have adapted to new forms of online participation and changed their consumption habits of media and cultural activities.

This article focuses on the quantitative analysis in SPSS of data referring to respondents aged over 65, which covers n = 513 (which corresponds to 33% of the total number of respondents and reflects the national demographic pyramid), with 40.5% male and 59.5% female. Still, with the aim of perceiving the differences between younger and older seniors, a segmentation by age was chosen: 65–74 years (55.4%); and over 75 years old (44.6%).

Relevant data from the sample, which were weighting factors in the analysis of the results, are the fact that 89.6% of the sample is made up of retired or disabled individuals; 77.5% have an education up to the 3rd cycle; 50.3% are married and 36.9% are widowed. Still on the sample, the composition of the household is essentially composed of one (39.4%) or two people (50.2%) reflecting the predominance found in terms of marital status. And regarding the use of the internet, only 25.6% of respondents are users, which is why the rate of e-excluded is still high in this age group in Portugal, although 74.4% of individuals are non-users. If we look at the age group of 65–74 years old, 36.6% use it and 63.4% do not use it; while among seniors over 75 years old, 11.8% use the internet and 88.2% do not, meaning that the older the age, the lower the rate of internet use.

5 Portuguese Seniors in Digital Transformation

The European Union (EU) (2007) focuses on the importance of e-inclusion in order to ensure social justice and to ensure equity in the knowledge society. And in this sense, it made public the i2010 Initiative measures to combat inequalities and e-exclusion among older people.

E-exclusion is a relevant factor and quite evident in seniors in Portugal. The representative data used by this study shows the main reasons that lead to the non-adhering to the use of the Internet by seniors. There are two main factors associated with non-use of the Internet: not seeing utility and lack of interest (45.4%) and illiteracy regarding the way of using the Internet or because it feels confused by technology (42.7%). Then with less relevance are the issues related to the lack of access to a computer or the internet (8.8%) and the lack of economic conditions (2.3%) to bear the cost of the internet.

From the point of view of the type of technology most used in internet access, we can say that technological seniors today use their smartphone (17.3%) more frequently than the laptop (8.8%), the desktop computer (6.1%) and tablets (3.8%). Access through SmartTV (0.8%) and Game Console (0.2%) have little expression in this age segment.

The growing expansion of smartphone use in Portugal in recent years (Marktest, 2018) has allowed better access conditions. In addition, ease of use and more affordable prices has given older age groups the opportunity to have access and open their horizons in the technological field.

And while smartphones allow easy access to the internet that may contribute to greater digital inclusion of seniors, some studies in this area show that the use by these older individuals is linked to the perception of benefits (Mohadis & Ali, 2014) and they need to feel motivated (Rosales & Fernández-Ardèvol, 2016).

The Model of Acceptance and Adoption of Technology by Seniors (Renaud & Biljon, 2008) states that for seniors to accept and adopt technology it is essential to understand that it is useful and effective to them, as it is easy to use and learn. On the other hand, in the appropriation of mobile devices by seniors it is necessary that they are encouraged to use the technologies and informed of their potential (Rodrigues & Morgado, 2019). With this, these authors determined the three levels of mobile phone appropriation: the first encompasses the evaluation of the utility and is called "Motivation"; the second linked to those who are willing to explore and experiment, is called "Try/Adopt"; and the third when they are part of the routines and in different areas, it is called "Integrate".

Helsper et al. (2020) developed, through a study with young people, the Youth Digital Skills Indicator (yDSI), a tool that allows the evaluating of digital skills and digital knowledge issues, which can be used for large-scale population research. According to the authors (Helsper et al., 2020): "A review of the literature led to a framework identifying four dimensions that constitute digital skills: (1) technical and operational skills; (2)

information navigation and processing skills; (3) communication and interaction skills; and (4) content creation and production skills. Across all four dimensions a distinction should be made between being able to use the functionalities of information and communication technologies (ICTs) (ICTs) and understanding why ICTs are designed and content is produced in certain ways and being able to use that knowledge in managing interactions in and with digital spaces (critical aspects)."

It is therefore important to reflect that digital skills should be weighed in older ages; digital skills should be weighed in the approaches to data analysis. If technical and operational skills are considered, in the context of seniors in Portugal; navigation and information processing skills; communication and interaction skills; and content creation and production skills, one can explain the percentages corresponding to the activities developed and expressed in this study, as well as the impact that digital skills are important for motivation, experimentation/adoption and integration, as Rodrigues & Morgado (2019) argues.

There are two main functions of internet access. The first focused on access to information that, although not regular activities, but accessing one or several times a year, but not every month, seniors use the internet to search for information. However, it can be observed that the online activities developed by older individuals in their routines about the search for cultural information are still very low.

The frequency of use from monthly to daily increases, there are fewer seniors who carry out this type of activities, being the most sought after activity or several times a year, but not every month, "Search for information about museums, galleries, art, archaeological sites" (4.6%), followed by "Search for information on books, music, cinema and shows" (3.7%). This data is reversed when it comes to analyzing a more frequent search, from one to several times a month, but not every week, where "Search for information about books, music, cinema and shows" (2.2%) is the most used activity, followed by "Listening to music from the internet (Through any streaming service like Spotify) " (1.8%), similarly the same happens with the activities performed most frequently (one or several times a week, but not every day), which reveal the same behavior: "Search for information about books, music, cinema and shows" (1.6%) and "Listen to music from the internet (Through any streaming service like Spotify)" (1.5%).

Every day, the internet can be used as entertainment, with 1.3% of respondents describing listening to music from the internet (Through any streaming service like Spotify). The other activities developed, considering, however, their little expression, are associated with entertainment, and demonstrate a greater ability to use technology: buy or download music (0.3%); share cultural content (Videos, music, images, others) generated by themselves (0.2%); and interact online on culture-related topics (Placing messages and likes on social networking sites and other virtual groups) (0.1%).

This study also shows that respondents still have an interest in other activities, but without much expression. It can be noted that about 5.8% of respondents expressed interest in daily news sites (not including newspapers and magazines) and that 6.1%, use the internet to, one or several times a month, but not every week, to search for accurate information (meaning of words, historical facts, etc.), although 3.3% do so one or several times a year, but not every month, and 1.9% perform these tasks one or several times a week, but not every day.

6 Seniors, Practices, and Online Cultural Consumption

Lifelong learning has been a concern of the United Nations Educational, Scientific and Cultural Organization (UNESCO) which considers that in this way people prepare to act, reflect and respond to the various social, political, economic, cultural and technological challenges (UNESCO, 2009). And, if, on the one hand, aging can allow positive activities such as educational activities (Martin, 2007), consequently, cultural organizations need to implement changes in their practices to attract, educate and listen to a wider audience (Holden, 2010).

We believe that ICT can be a contribution to encouraging cultural practices among seniors, particularly in terms of online consumption, but as Lapa & Vieira (2019) refer, although there is already a greater democratization in the use of ICT, the digital gap between use and types of use is still significant. The Digital News Report Portugal 2021 (OberCom, 2021) states that: "Television and the Internet (including social networks) continue to be the most used sources by the Portuguese for access to news – about three quarters of respondents say they used these sources in the previous week. Television is the main source of news for 57.7%, the Internet (excluding social networks) for 17.4% and social networks alone to 13.4%. The press is the main source of news for 7.3% and the radio for 4.2%."

Following this trend that television is the most used media by the Portuguese in access to information, the data from the study of the Survey on Cultural Practices 2020 reveal that the news, reports, and information are in the list of television programs that individuals usually see the most (87.8%), and 97,8% of individuals watch TELEVISION daily, and of these 98.7% do so through the television set. Furthermore, at the informative level the debates (pros and cons, Circulation of the square, Axis of evil) and the interview programs (e.g., High definition, Great interview) are still of interest with 20.5% and 20.6%, respectively.

Also, and based on the data of the study, in addition to informing television is still the main entertainment medium for seniors, to the extent that 52.9% have in their list of programs that usually see soap operas, then 37.5% other contests (e.g.: Right Price, Got Talent Portugal, etc.), 33.4% General culture competitions (e.g. Who wants to be a millionaire, Mental samurai); 32.8% films; 31.1% documentaries and entertainment programs (reality shows, talk shows, humor, etc.); 31% sports shows (games, news, debates, etc.); 27.9% Mass or other religious programs.

Other cultural consumptions seen on television reveal less interest among older individuals when: 17.7% watch series; 9.9% look for other cultural programs; 4.9% are interested in theater; 3.2% watch programs related to books and reading; and 3% other performing arts programs (circus, opera, etc.). In terms of musical interests, respondents seek to see on television: concerts of popular music (8.1%); other music programs (7.6%); and classical music concerts (4.3%).

7 Pandemic and the Change in Cultural Habits and Digital Consumption by Seniors

Television has always been the most consumed medium by the Portuguese, according to the ERC study (2016) 99% of respondents say they regularly watch television programs. Although there have been significant changes in media consumption practices in recent years, television content continues to generate the most interest among the Portuguese population, and according to the Survey on the Cultural Practices of the Portuguese in 2020 (Pais, J. M.; Magalhães, P. & Antunes, M. L., 2020) 90% of people said they see content in this medium daily. This study also revealed that the age group of 65 years or more is the most exposed to television, of which 98% use daily, and in global indicators women (92%) watch more television than men (87%).

Following the analysis of the data, 81.2% of men maintained their television watching habits during the pandemic, as well as 79.9% of women. However, males (17.3%) started to use more than females (15.2%) and the reverse happens when women (2.6%) started using less television during this pandemic period than men (0.5%).

TV viewing had an increase in use by seniors during the pandemic period, considering that there would be a longer time available on the part of these individuals, the search for information and entertainment may be the answer to these data obtained.

With the deprivation of offline cultural consumption during the pandemic period, the internet could be a means of access to culture contributing even to greater entertainment and occupation of more free time. As Barroso (2021) demonstrated in his study, in a pandemic time "greater isolation of seniors from the social world contributed to the increase in their digital literacy". However, the results of the Survey on The Cultural Practices of the Portuguese 2020 express that 74.3% of individuals over 65 years of age were omitted in their answers about the use of the Internet to access cultural activities during the pandemic. It is evidenced in this study that, despite being in low percentages, seniors only started to use the internet more for access to information, such as reading books, newspapers and magazines online (2.1%), and to entertain themselves when they see music shows (1.4%), eventually accessing platforms such as YouTube, followed by seeing movies (1%), dance shows (0.8%), theater shows (0.6%), visit library and archive sites (0.5%) and visit museum sites, historical monuments, archaeological sites and art galleries (0.5%).

It should be addressed that the rates of use of the internet and digital services for access to culture by seniors are not of significant relevance, only 13.3% maintained the use to watch movies and 13.2% to read books, newspapers and magazines online, with the remaining activities positioned in the range of 11.1% and 11.8%. It is relevant to understand that these data reflect, similarly, that as observed in the Study of RCS (2016), 100% of people over 65 years of age use television to watch entertainment content, and only 0.9% do so through the computer.

8 Conclusion

Many digital policies implemented in the past and implemented in the present patent a focus on the younger sectors and education, the modernization of the economic fabric and the administrative machine of the State. However, it is in the seniors, in the low-skilled or uninserted sectors of the labor market, and away from urban centers, that we find the most evident cases of e-exclusion and that constitute the groups that most distance Portugal from other European partners. It should be remembered that current seniors were of mature age when 15 years ago the "technological shock" occurred and were young adults in the 1990s, when policies for the information society began to be implemented. The data suggest, therefore, the lack of a better evaluation, a reduced impact of technological policies on the lives of many Portuguese and, most likely, below the intended and expectations created. Many public policy initiatives have focused on infrastructure and the "device model", with the first-order aspects of the digital divide, i.e. access, and within the adult population, left out particularly vulnerable sectors of society.

The approach developed in this article makes evident the importance of lifelong learning of Portuguese seniors, not only for the personal development of individuals as participatory citizens in the political, economic, social and cultural life of a country, but also for its digital inclusion that is reflected in its cultural inclusion.

It is concluded, demonstrating through the consumption of cultural activities, that today's seniors are transported to new consumption habits and activities through what technology provides them. But there is still a digital divide between the various individuals belonging to this group, which are associated with limited technical skills and availability of these means in a digitally excluded cohort.

Likewise, the study showed that the Pandemic eventually brought new habits and digital consumption to part of this group of individuals, supported by the social distancing and isolation to which they were obliged. Creating more skills in online forms of socialization (Barroso, 2021) and bridging excess free time.

As limitations of this study, we can consider the lack of focus of the study on the relevance of online social networks in the development and promotion of cultural practices, and currently they are part of the global world and are used by many organizations and even the media to disseminate, inform and interact. So, we consider it to be an approach to integrate into future studies. Are these new ICT also a way to inform and motivate the increase in cultural practices among seniors in Portugal? We believe that by increasing the digital skills of seniors we are developing society in a fairer and more competitive way at economic, social, and cultural level.

References

Amaral, I., Sousa, H.: Redes sociais no Twitter. Ciberjornalismo, modelos de negócio e redes sociais, Bastos, Helder; Zamith, Fernando (org.). Edições Afrontamento/CETAC.MEDIA, pp. 149–162 (2012)

Barroso, C.: Os seniores na sociedade em rede em Portugal: O contributo das Redes Sociais Online no seu Capital social. [Tese de Doutoramento, ISCTE – Instituto Universitário de Lisboa]. Repositório do ISCTE (2021)

Berker, T., Hartmann, M., Punie, Y., Ward, K.J.: Domestication of Media and Technology. Open University Press, London (2006). https://www.researchgate.net/publication/259257339_Dom estication_of_Media_and_Technology

CE: Comunicação da Comissão ao Parlamento Europeu, ao Conselho, ao Comité Económico e Social Europeu e ao Comité das Regiões que estabelece uma Declaração Europeia sobre os Direitos e Princípios Digitais para a Década Digital (2022)

Cunha, C.S.L.: Promoção do uso de Tecnologias computadorizadas na população idosa [Dissertação de Mestrado, Escola de Ciências Sociais e Humanas, Departamento de Psicologia Social e das Organizações, ISCTE-IUL]. Repositório ISCTE-IUL (2017). http://hdl.handle.net/10071/15304

Dias, I.: O uso das tecnologias digitais entre seniores: motivações e interesses. Sociologia, Problemas e Práticas, 68, pp. 51–77. Bruxelas (2012)

DiMaggio, P.J., Hargittai, E.: From the 'Digital Divide' to 'Digital Inequality': Studying Internet Use as Penetration Increases. Working Paper 15. Princeton University Center for Arts and Culture Policy Studies, Princeton (2001). https://doi.org/10.1002/bem.20484

DiMaggio, P., Hargittai, E., Celeste, C., Shafer, S.: Digital inequality: from unequal access to differentiated use. In: Neckerman, K. (org.) Social Inequality. Nova Iorque, Russell Sage, pp. 355–400 (2004)

ERC: As novas dinâmicas do consumo audiovisual em Portugal (2016)

Gil, H.: A Literacia Digital e as Competências Digitais para a Infoinclusão: por uma inclusão digital e social dos mais idosos. Re@D – Revista Educação a Distância e Elearning, vol. 2, no. 1, V2(1). Competências Digitais (2019). https://doi.org/10.34627/vol2iss1pp79-96n

Gil, H., Páscoa, G.: O bem-estar através das tecnologias digitais: um estudo em populações 50+. INFAD Revista de Psicología 1(2), 33–42 (2018). ISSN 0214-9877. https://www.researchgate.net/deref/http%3A%2F%2Fdx.doi.org%2F10.17060%2Fijodaep.2018.n2.v1.1144

Gómez, D.C.: The Three Levels of the Digital Divide: Barriers in Access, Use and Utility of Internet among Young People in Spain. Interações Sociedade e as novas modernidades (2018). https://doi.org/10.31211/interacoes.n34.2018.a4

Azevedo, A.A.: Apresentação do Portugal Digital [Discurso do Secretário de Estado para a Transição Digital] e Plano de Ação para a Transição Digital de Portugal. Portugal Digital. Fundação Champalimaud: Lisboa (2020)

Haddon, L.: Domestication analysis, objects of study, and the centrality of technologies in everyday life. Can. J. Commun. 36(2), 311–323 (2011). https://doi.org/10.22230/cjc.2011v36n2a2322

Helsper, E.: Digital inclusion: an analysis of social disadvantage and the information society. Department for Communities and Local Government, London, UK (2008). ISBN 9781409806141. http://eprints.lse.ac.uk/26938/

Helsper, E.: The ageing Internet: digital choice and exclusion among the elderly. Working with Older People, vol. 13, no. 4, pp. 28–33. Media and Communications, London School of Economics and Political Science (2009). http://eprints.lse.ac.uk/id/eprint/26686

Helsper, E.: A corresponding fields model for the links between social and digital exclusion. Commun. Theory 22(4), 403–426 (2012). http://eprints.lse.ac.uk/id/eprint/45013

Helsper, E.J., Schneider, L.S., van Deursen, A.J.A.M., van Laar, E.: The youth Digital Skills Indicator: Report on the conceptualisation and development of the ySKILLS digital skills measure. KU Leuven, Leuven: ySKILLS (2020)

Holden, J.: Culture and Class. Counterpoint, London (2010)

INE, 2017, 2021

Lapa, T.: A infância em rede: Media e quadros de existência infantis na Sociedade em rede [Tese de Doutoramento, ISCTE-IUL]. Repositório do ISCTE (2014). http://hdl.handle.net/10071/12331

Lapa, T., Fátima, B.: Novos media e gerações. Pensar as veredas da literacia. In book: Literacia dos novos media. Mundos Sociais. Lisboa (2019)

Lapa, T., Vieira, J.: Divisões digitais em Portugal e na Europa. Portugal ainda à Procura do comboio Europeu? Sociologia online **21**, 62–82 (2019)

Loos, E.: Senior citizens: digital immigrants in their own country? Observatorio **6**, 1–23 (2012). http://dare.uva.nl/record/461270

Krause, A.: The role and impact of radio listening practices in older adults' everyday lives. J. Front Psychol. (2020). https://doi.org/10.3389/fpsyg.2020.603446

Marktest: Bareme Rádio (2010)

Marktest: Os Portugueses e as Redes Sociais 2018 (2018)

Martin, A.: Gerontologia educativa: Enquadramento disciplinar para o estudo e intervenção socioeducativo com idosos. In: Osório, A., Pinto, F. (eds.) As pessoas idosas: Contexto social e intervenção educativa. Instituto Paiget. Lisboa (2007)

Martinho, T.D., Lapa, T.: Internet, práticas culturais online e distinção. In: Pais, J.M., Magalhães, P., Antunes, M.L. (coords.) Práticas Culturais dos Portugueses. Inquérito 2020, pp. 55–98. Imprensa de Ciências Sociais, Lisboa (2022)

Mauritti, R.: A construção da intimidade nos protagonismos do viver só. Barometro Social (2011)

Mohadis, H., Ali, N.: A study of smartphone usage and barriers among the elderly. Em 3rd International Conference on User Science and Engineering (i-USEr), pp. 109–114 (2014). https://doi.org/10.13140/2.1.1732.8321

Neves, B.B.: Social capital and internet use: the irrelevant, the bad, and the good. Sociology Compass 7/8 (2013). http://onlinelibrary.wiley.com/doi/10.1111/soc4.12059/abstract

Obercom: Digital News Report Portugal 2021. OberCom – Reuters Institute for the Study of Journalism (2021). https://obercom.pt/wp-content/uploads/2021/06/DNR_PT_2021_final.pdf

Pinheiro, J., Martins, J.: A relação afetiva do idoso com o rádio: Histórias e lembranças 2012 (2012)

Pais, J.M., Magalhães, P., Antunes, M.L.: Inquérito às Práticas Culturais dos Portugueses em 2020. Síntese de resultados. Instituto de Ciências Sociais da Universidade de Lisboa (ICS-UL) (2020)

Pordata (2021). https://www.pordata.pt/Portugal/Indiv%C3%ADduos+com+16+e+mais+anos+que+utilizam+computador+e+Internet+em+percentagem+do+total+de+indiv%C3%ADduos+por+grupo+etário-1139

Renaud, K., Biljon, J.V.: Predicting technology acceptance and adoption by the elderly: a qualitative study [Conferência]. In: Annual Research Conference of the South African Institute of Computer Scientists and Information Technologists, Wilderness, South Africa (2008). https://doi.org/10.1145/1456659.1456684

Rodrigues, C., Morgado, L.: Apropriação de Dispositivos Móveis no Quotidiano dos Seniores: Investigação sobre um Protótipo de Modelo de Formação. Em Marques, C.G., Pereira, I., Pérez, D. (eds.) Book of Proceedings of the 21st International Symposium on Computers in Education, pp. 137–142. Instituto Politécnico de Tomar, Tomar (2019). http://hdl.handle.net/10400.2/9719

Rosales, A., Fernández-Ardèvol, M.: Smartphones, apps and older people's interests: from a generational perspective. In: MobileHCI 2016: Proceedings of the 18th International Conference on Human-Computer Interaction with Mobile Devices and Services, pp. 491–503. ACM Press, New York (2016). 10.1145/ 2935334.2935363

Swissinfo, M.A.R., Yang, X., Fenazzi, S., Uda, K.: Idosos cada vez mais presentes na Internet. Pro Senectute (2020). https://www.swissinfo.ch/por/idosos-cada-vez-mais-presentes-na-Internet/46178210

UE: European i2010 initiative on e-inclusion – "Be parto f the information society". European Commission, Brussels (2007)

UNESCO: Relatório global sobre aprendizagem e educação de adultos (2009). http://unesdoc.unesco.org/images/0018/001886/188644por.pdf

Van Deursen, A.J.A.M.: Internet Skills. Vital assets in an information society [Tese Doutoramento, University of Twente] (2010). https://doi.org/10.3990/1.9789036530866

Vulpe, S., Crăciun, A.: Silver surfers from a European perspective: technology communication usage among European seniors. Eur. J. Ageing **17**(1), 125–134 (2020). https://doi.org/10.1007/s10433-019-00520-2

Influence of Cognitive Function and the Mental Model on ICT Use – Examined by TAM Model

Taiga Nohara[1], Kaoru Takagi[1], Ikuko Sugawara[2,3], Yasuyuki Gondo[4], and Misato Nihei[1,2(✉)]

[1] The University of Tokyo, Chiba, Japan
nohara-taiga852@g.ecc.u-tokyo.ac.jp, kaorutkg@gmail.com,
mnihei@edu.k.u-tokyo.ac.jp
[2] Institute of Gerontology, The University of Tokyo, Tokyo, Japan
sugawara@iog.u-tokyo.ac.jp
[3] Seibu Bunri University of Hospital, Saitama, Japan
[4] Osaka University, Osaka, Japan
y.gondo.hus@osaka-u.ac.jp

Abstract. The Covid-19 pandemic has led to the development of the Communication Tool (CT), which facilitates non-face-to-face communication and is used by a wide range of generations. But seniors are often reluctant to use such tools, so it is important to consider a UI with high acceptability. In this study, we attempted to understand the factors that influence the aging characteristics of seniors on their intention to use CT, with the TAM model, which is used to explain individual acceptance or intention to use new technologies. Specifically, we investigated subjective evaluation and aging characteristics using the TAM questionnaire for existing CTs and new CTs for which mental models can be formed easily and aim to clarify the influence on the ease-of-use (PEOU) and behavioral intention to use (BI) of CTs. The results suggest that age-related attentional decline affects interest in new products and thereby behavioral intention to use (BI), and the ability to form mental models affects perceived ease of use (PEOU).

Keywords: Socially assistive robot · Risk assessment · Dementia

1 Introduction

The Covid-19 pandemic has led to the widespread use of online communication, and Communication Tool (CT), which facilitates non-face-to-face communication, and is used by a wide range of generations. In addition, ICTs and CTs with various UIs are available due to the efficiency of development through platforms for application development. However, seniors, who have been using dial telephones, are often reluctant to use them. In order to solve the digital divide between generations, it is important to consider UI with high acceptability.

The Technology Acceptance Model (TAM) is one of the widely used models when considering the acceptability of new devices [1]. As shown in Fig. 1, in TAM, behavioral

© The Author(s), under exclusive license to Springer Nature Switzerland AG 2023
Q. Gao and J. Zhou (Eds.): HCII 2023, LNCS 14043, pp. 505–518, 2023.
https://doi.org/10.1007/978-3-031-34917-1_34

intention to use (BI), which means "the degree to which one plans whether or not to perform a certain action in the future," is said to be affected by the perceived usefulness (PU), perceived ease of use (PEOU), and attitude toward use (A) variables. In the TAM model, there are also external variables such as gender, age, and education as variables that affect perceived usefulness (PU) and perceived ease of use (PEOU).

For UI design, Cho et al. [2] proposed a model that incorporates perceived UI design (PUID) as a new variable in the technology acceptance model and reported that PUID has a PEOU impact. Hong et al. [3] also showed that screen design affects perceived ease-of-use PEOU. Among ICTs, CTs are considered to have a significant impact on the behavioral intention to use (BI) not only by the UI design for displaying information but also by the UI for inputting information (input UI), due to the nature of exchanging information. However, no previous study has clarified the relationship between input UI and usage intention, especially in CT.

Therefore, this study attempts to figure out the factors that influence the aging characteristics of seniors on the intention to use CTs using the TAM model, which has been used to explain individual acceptance or intention to use new technologies. Specifically, we will investigate subjective evaluation and aging characteristics using the TAM questionnaire for existing CTs and new CTs for which mental models can be easily formed, and aim to clarify the influence on the perceived ease-of-use (PEOU) and behavioral intention to use (BI) of CTs. In this study, as aging characteristics, we focused on attentional and executive functions, which are cognitive functions that thought to be related to the input of information, and mental models of operation, which are models and images that humans have of interacting with artifacts [4].

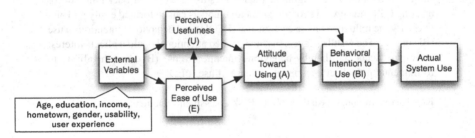

Fig. 1. TAM model diagram [1]

2 Method

2.1 CTs Used in the Experiment

There are three types of communication tools targeted in this study: e-mail, LINE [5] and CT with handwritten UI (handwritten CT) shown in Fig. 2(d). E-mail and LINE are the smartphone applications that are usually used by seniors as identified by the preliminary survey. Handwritten CT was developed based on the assumption that mental models are easily formed.

2.2 Evaluation Method of Three Abilities to Form Mental Models of Operations

To evaluate the ability of forming mental models, based on Doi et al.'s study [6, 7], we created tasks which pictures of the equipment's control panel and CT's screen were printed on paper, and show it to the participants, then they were asked to answer what operations they should perform to achieve a specific requirement. Higher performance in the operating procedures task means higher prediction of equipment and app behavior, in other words, higher performance in the operating procedures task means higher ability to form mental models of equipment and apps.

The target UIs were, a microwave that three difficulty levels are set, and the three mentioned CTs. Three types of microwave models with different operating methods were targeted, as shown in Table 1. Table 2 and Fig. 2 show the content and presented images for operating procedure tasks for each device and application. Answers are rated on a 5-point scale. The scoring criteria are shown in Table 3.

Table 1. Information and operation of each microwave

Code	Model	Brand	Operation procedures
A	ER-AA17A	Toshiba Lifestyle	Set power and time with separate dials
B	YRB-177	Yamazen	Set power and time with buttons
C	ARE-S19	Amadana	Set power and time with a single dial

Table 2. Contents of operating procedure tasks for each device and application

Device and application	Task
Microwave	(Presenting the microwave body and control panel) What operation should you perform to put frozen meat in the microwave and defrost it at 200W for 5 min?
E-mail	(Presenting the draft screen of the e-mail) How do you send an e-mail with an image attached?
LINE	(Presenting a fictitious LINE chat screen) How do you send the image to the other party?
Handwritten CT	(Presenting the screen of Handwritten CT) How do you send a handwritten message to the other person about today's business?

Table 3. Scoring criteria of operating procedure tasks

Device and application	Scoring criteria
Microwave A	Turn the output dial [1 point] Set output to 200W [1 point] Turn the time dial [1 point] Set the time to 5 min [1 point] No description of unnecessary operations [1 point]
Microwave B	Press the button for 200W [1 point] Press the button for 1 min [1 point] Press 5 times [1 point] Press the start button [1 point] No description of unnecessary operations [1 point]
Microwave C	Use the dial to set the output [1 point] Turn the dial to the left to set the output [1 point] Use the dial to set the time [1 point] Turn the dial to the right to set the time [1 point] No description of unnecessary operations[1 point]
E-mail	Press the button [1 point] Press the correct button [2 point] Select a photo (no details required) [2 point]
LINE	Press the button [1 point] Press the correct button [2 point] Select a photo (no details required) [2 point]
Handwritten CT	Operate the Date Picker [1 point] Set the date to today [1 point] Handwritten Entry [1 point] Entering an errand [1 point] No unnecessary operation description [1 point]

2.3 Participants and Experimental Protocol

Thirteen healthy male and seven healthy females (72.8 ± 4.0 years old) were recruited for the experiment through the Silver Human Resources Center. The experimental procedures are as follows.

1. The participants were asked to answer questionnaires regarding basic information such as their age and gender.
2. The TAM questionnaire and operating procedures task will be administered for the three types of microwaves.
3. The TAM questionnaire and operating procedures task will be administered for the email application. Then perform the actual operation task and administer the TAM questionnaire again.
4. The TAM questionnaire and operating procedures task will be administered for LINE.

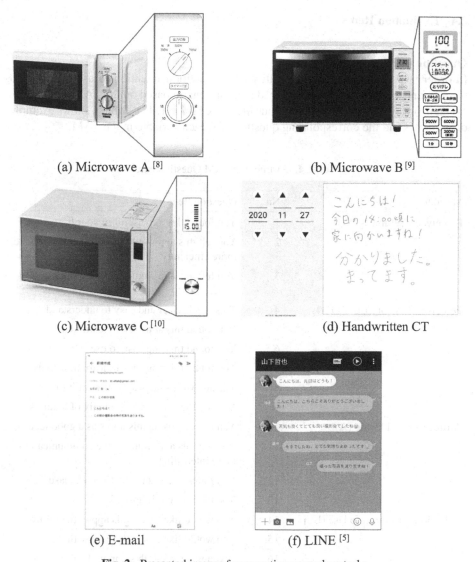

(a) Microwave A [8]

(b) Microwave B [9]

(c) Microwave C [10]

(d) Handwritten CT

(e) E-mail

(f) LINE [5]

Fig. 2. Presented images for operating procedure tasks

5. The TAM questionnaire and operating procedures task will be administered for the handwritten CT. Then perform the actual operation task and administer the TAM questionnaire again.
6. Cognitive function tests (TMT, KWCST) are performed.

2.4 Evaluation Items

Questionnaire and Survey

In order to evaluate subjective usability and Behavioral Intention to use (BI) towards devices and applications, we developed a questionnaire based on the TAM (TAM questionnaire) with reference to the previous literature [1, 2, 11, 12]. Table 4 shows examples of variables and the corresponding questions for each variable in the TAM.

Table 4. Example of TAM Questionnaire

Variable	No.	Question Item
Perceived Usefulness (PU)	1	You found this app useful in your life
	2	You felt this app would help you communicate more efficiently
	3	You felt this app would make communication easier
Perceived Ease of Use (PEOU)	4	This app is clear and easy to understand
	5	You found this app easy to learn to use
	6	You found this app easy to use
	7	You found this app easy to learn how to use
	8	The app works the way you want it to
	9	You felt the app had a good mix of features
Attitude toward Using (A)	10	You felt that using this app was a good idea
	11	You felt this app would make communication more interesting
	12	You found using this app to be a pleasure
	13	You like using this app
Behavioral Intention to Use (BI)	14	You would like to use this app in the future
	15	You would like to use this app with others
	16	If you were to use this app in the future, you would use it more often
	17	You think using this app is important for your future
	18	You think it is worthwhile to use this app

The evaluation was conducted using a 7-point Likert scale, and each variable is converted to a score out of 100.

Questionnaires were also administered regarding the experience and frequency of use of each device and application, the final education level, and interest in new products. For interest in new products, the following questions were asked based on the five strata (innovator, early adopter, early majority, late majority, and laggard) of the innovator theory [13].

1. Interested in new products and want to be the first to buy them when they are released
2. Interested in new products and will buy them if they are expected to be effective and efficacious
3. If others start using it and it is expected to be effective, you will buy it.
4. If it becomes popular in the world, you will buy it.
5. Not interested in new products

Actual Operation Tasks

In addition to the operation procedure tasks for the e-mail and handwritten CT, the users were asked to operate the actual applications using tablet devices. The contents of the tasks are shown in Table 5. Answers are evaluated on a 5-point scale.

Table 5. Contents of the actual operation tasks for each application

Device and application	Task
E-mail	Similar to the operating procedure task, attach the image to the email from the email draft screen that is displayed
Handwritten CT	After teaching the participants verbally how to draw and erase lines, let them interact with the person in charge of the experiment. After that, they circle the letters and turn them red. Then they are asked to operate the date dial to see the next day's information

Cognitive Function Test

In this experiment, the Trail Making Test (TMT) and the Keio version of the Wisconsin Card Sorting Test (KWCST) [14] were used to measure cognitive functions related to attention and executive functions. The TMT consists of two tests, A and B. Performance is evaluated by the time required for both tasks and the difference between them, and a large difference in the time required for each task or the time required for both tasks indicate a reduced attentional turnover [15]. The KWCST is a test that sorts cards based on specific sorting rules (color, number, or shape). Using the number of correctly classified categories and the number of misclassified categories as evaluation indices, the KWCST measures concept formation, concept or set conversion, and inhibition of inappropriate responses. In this experiment, the test was conducted on a laptop computer using testing software [16] running on a Windows OS.

3 Results

3.1 TAM Scores for Each CT

Figure 3 shows the box-and-whisker plots of the TAM questionnaire scores for e-mail, LINE, and handwritten CT. The scores for e-mail and handwritten CT were obtained after the actual operation tasks. The mean scores for all items were higher in the order of Handwritten CT, e-mail, LINE. And for PEOU, Handwritten CT had significantly higher scores than e-mail and LINE (p < 0.01).

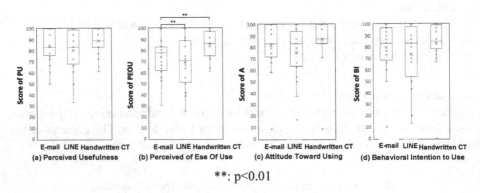

**: p<0.01

Fig. 3. Result of the TAM questionnaire for each CT

3.2 Cognitive Decline and Intended Use of CT

For the three types of CTs, grouping was conducted based on the CT with the highest score of BI from the TAM questionnaire in the actual operation tasks within an individual. As a result, there were eight participants in the handwritten CT group, three in the e-mail group, and nine in the group with the same BI of handwritten CT and e-mail. Due to the small number of participants in the e-mail group, we decided to compare two groups in this study: the handwritten CT group and the other group.

Figure 4 shows the scores of the cognitive function test between the handwriting input CT group and the other group. t_B and Δt were showed to have significant differences, indicating that the higher BI of handwriting CT, the higher the results of the cognitive function test related to attention function.

3.3 Cognitive Decline and Interest in New Products

Figure 5 shows the relationship between interest in the new product and performance on the cognitive function test. It indicates that there is a correlation between score of Δt and interest in the new product ($r = 0.63$), with lower performance indicating weaker interest in the new product.

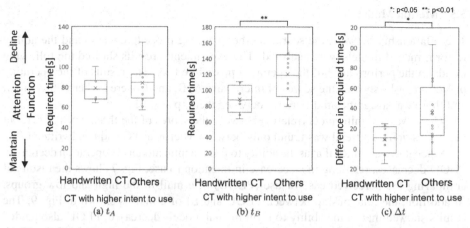

Fig. 4. Cognitive function test results for the handwritten CT group and the other group

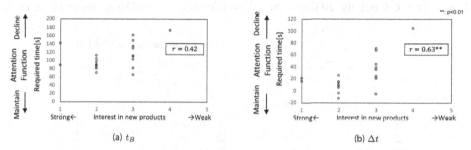

Fig. 5. Interest in new products and TMT performance

3.4 Impression Changes by Operating the Actual UI

Figure 6 shows the amount of increase in TAM questionnaire scores after the actual operation task in handwritten CT for each participant. A trend toward an increase in TAM scores with actual use was shown.

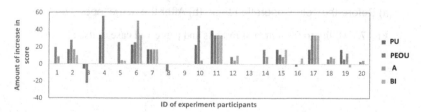

Fig. 6. Amount of increase in TAM questionnaire scores after the actual operation task in handwritten CT

3.5 Mental Model

The relationship between the scores on the operating procedures tasks and the ability to form mental models were analyzed. The experimental results showed the following trends in the performance of the operating procedure task. The results of the operating procedure tasks showed the scores of microwave A, B, and C were higher in that order, and there was a significant difference between them (p < 0.01).

There was a significant correlation between the scores of the three types of CT, but the only significant trend was found only between Microwave C and handwritten CT.

Since it was assumed that as the ability to form mental models in operation decreases, PEOU decreases, resulting in a decrease in intention to use, Fig. 7 shows the results of comparing the perceived ease of use (PEOU) of e-mail in the high and low groups. In addition, the relationship between PEOU and BI of e-mail is shown in Fig. 9. The results showed that as the ability to form mental models decreased, PEOU also tended to decrease. The result also showed that there is a correlation between PEOU and BI. On the other hand, Fig. 8 shows the relationship between mental model and TAM in handwritten CT and Fig. 10 shows the relationship between PEOU scores and BI scores.

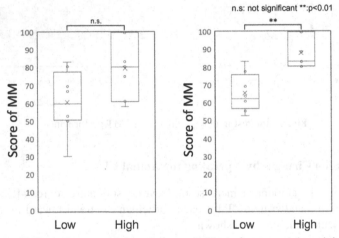

(a) Before the actual operation task (b) After the actual operation task

Fig. 7. Ability to form mental models and perceived ease of use of e-mail

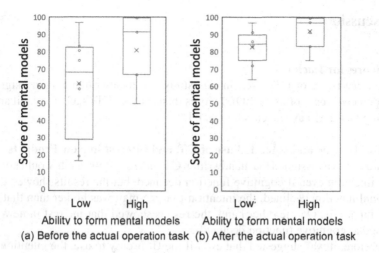

(a) Before the actual operation task (b) After the actual operation task

Fig. 8. Ability to form mental models and perceived ease of use of handwritten CT

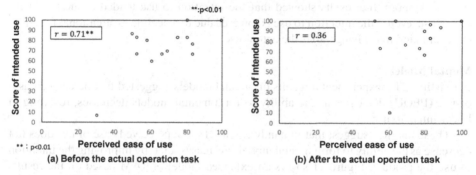

Fig. 9. Perceived ease of use scores and intent to use scores for e-mail

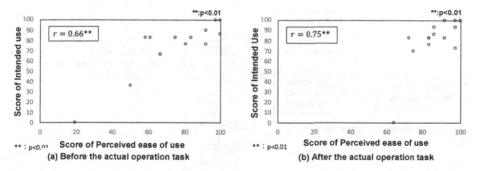

Fig. 10. Perceived ease of use scores and intent to use scores for handwritten CT

4   Discussion

TAM Scores for Each CT
For the three types of CTs used in this study, the handwritten CT had significantly higher perceived ease of use (PEOU) scores than existing CTs such as e-mail and LINE, indicating that they have an easy-to-use UI.

Cognitive Decline and Intended use of CT, and Interest in New Products
In this study, it was assumed that handwritten CT with easy-to-use UIs would not decrease the use intention even if cognitive function declined, but the results showed that when attentional function declined, the intention to use e-mail was higher than that of handwritten input UIs. On the other hand, the results showed that interest in new products weakened as cognitive function declined.

Therefore, it was suggested that even if the UI is easy to use, the intention to use it may decrease as it perceived as a new product (possibility of status quo orientation due to cognitive decline).

Furthermore, the results showed that the intention to use tended to increase with actual use, even if the intention to use is lowered due to a decline in attentional function, the evaluation may change after the actual use.

Mental Model
In existing CTs, experimental results on mental models suggested that perceived ease-of-use (PEOU) decreases as the ability to form mental models decreases, resulting in lower intent to use.

These findings suggest that in handwritten CTs, the perceived ease of use does not decrease as the ability to form mental models decreases, thereby improving the intention to use the product. Figure 11 shows an extended model of TAM based on the results obtained from this study.

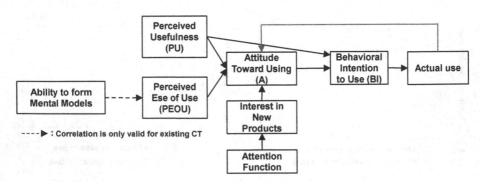

Fig. 11. Extended model of TAM based on findings from this study

5   Conclusion

In the study, we focused on cognitive functions and the ability to form mental models of operation, which are thought to be related to the BI of new CT in senior's population, and investigated their effects. As a method to measure the ability to form mental models, we developed a series of microwave operation tasks with different levels of difficulty. In addition, we compared and evaluated CTs by investigating the relationship between subjective evaluation using the TAM questionnaire and cognitive function tests for hand-written CT, which is comparatively new to existing CTs such as e mail and LINE but do not require new formation of mental models. It was suggested that the decline in cognitive function (attentional function) with aging was not related to the perceived ease of use (PEOU) of the UI, but was affected by the interest in the new product and thereby behavioral intention to use (BI). The ability to form mental models also influenced perceived ease of use (PEOU), which could lead to behavioral intention to use (BI). Furthermore, the results suggested that BI improves with actual, rather than assumed, trial. Finally, the relationship between cognitive functions (attentional functions) and the ability to form mental models was explained using the TAM model.

Acknowledgments. We would like to thank the participants of the interviews and the experiment for their cooperation and Chan Chi Tao for English language editing.

References

1. Davis, F.D.: Perceived usefulness, perceived ease of use, and user acceptance of information technology. MIS Q. Manag. Inf. Syst. **13**(3), 319–339 (1989)
2. Cho, V., Cheng, T.C.E., Lai, W.M.J.: The role of perceived user-interface design in continued usage intention of self-paced e-learning tools. Comput. Educ. **53**(2), 216–227 (2009)
3. Hong, W., Thong, J.Y.L., Wong, W.M., Tam, K.Y.: Determinants of user acceptance of digital libraries: An empirical examination of individual differences and system characteristics. J. Manag. Inf. Syst. **18**(3), 97–124 (2001)
4. Harada, E.: What do cognitive aging studies tell us? Implications of memory and cognitive engineering research. Psychol. Rev. **52**(3), 383–395 (2009). (in Japanese)
5. LINE Corporation: Communication Application (in Japanese). https://line.me/ja/. Accessed 23 Feb 2023
6. Doi, T., Ishihara, K., Yamaoka, T.: The proposal of the level of mental model building measurement scale in user interface. Des. Stud. **60**(4), 69–76 (2013). (in Japanese)
7. Doi, T., Tominaga, S., Yamaoka, T., Nishizaki, Y.: The element for structring the mental model in operation of user interfaces. Des. Stud. **58**(5), 53–62 (2012). (in Japanese)
8. Toshiba Lifestyle: ER-SS17A_ER-SS17B. https://www.toshiba-lifestyle.com/jp/microw aves/er-ss17a_er-ss17b/. Accessed 23 Feb 2023
9. Yamazen: YRB-177. https://book.yamazen.co.jp/product/cook/oven/entry-10554.html. Accessed 23 Feb 2023
10. Amadana. https://www.amadana.com/. Accessed 23 Feb 2023
11. Ministry of Health, Labor and Welfare: Community-based comprehensive care system (in Japanese).https://www.mhlw.go.jp/stf/seisakunitsuite/bunya/hukushi_kaigo/kaigo_ koureisha/chiiki-houkatsu/. Accessed 23 Feb 2023

12. Bao, S., Hoshino, S., Hashimoto, S., Shimizu, N.: Factors influencing internet adoption in rural areas of Hubei Province, China: on the basis of UTAUT. J. Rural Plann. **33**(1), 54–62 (2014). (in Japanese)
13. Rogers, E.M.: Diffusion of Innovations. Free Press, New York (1995)
14. Kashima, H.: Wisconsin card sorting test (Keio Version) (KWCST). Brain Spirit Med. **6**, 209–216 (1995). (in Japanese)
15. Kashima, H.: Attention disorders and frontal lobe damage. Rehabil. Med. **32**(5), 294–297 (1995)
16. Japan Stroke Data Bank: Wisconsin Card Sorting Test Ver.2.0. http://strokedatabank.ncvc. go.jp/archive/. Accessed 23 Feb 2023

A Social Justice-Oriented Perspective on Older Adults Technology Use in HCI

Three Opportunities for Societal Inclusion

Linnea Öhlund[✉] [iD]

Department of Informatics, Umeå University, Umeå, Sweden
`Linnea.ohlund@umu.se`

Abstract. There is a growing strand of research on social justice in HCI. While many contemporary HCI studies are being conducted and analyzed in a social justice context, still few studies examine how this plays out among older adults and their use of technology. In this paper, three streams of HCI and HCI-connected research are mapped out describing personal characteristics, economic benefits, and age-related vulnerability at the forefront of older adults' technology use. Through an empirical study and a social justice-oriented perspective, I establish how HCI research on older adults' technology use fails to include important societal factors and misses out on valuable insights such as how societal structures can affect senior's life and technology use. Contributions posit three opportunities into how a social justice-oriented perspective can benefit research regarding older adults' technology use in HCI.

Keywords: HCI · Social Justice · Older adults · Ageism

1 Introduction

Research on older adults technology use rarely discuss social injustice such as, pressure of technology use in society, isolation from society interlinked with technology and exclusion from social and private digital services (see: [9, 21, 29, 33]). Such partial perspectives could potentially lead to negative effects for older adults because they center personal shortcomings and misses out on valuable insights on how societal structures affect important parts of older adults lives [9, 29]. In some regards, older adults are perceived as a vulnerable group because of aspects related to aging, such as cognitive and/or physical decline [9, 21, 29]. This presumed vulnerability is usually explored in the context of personal characteristics, economic benefits, and age-related vulnerability [7, 21, 30]. Technology has massive potential to positively influence and affect the lives of older adult users by, for example, reducing isolation, supporting at-home independence, and inspiring creativity [17, 23, 32]. Research has moreover explored personal robotics, eldercare robotics, and acceptance models for technology use, aiming to create positive changes in the lives of older adults [1, 4, 6, 16, 31]. Although the topic of older adults technology use is much explored within HCI, little research has taken into consideration

© The Author(s), under exclusive license to Springer Nature Switzerland AG 2023
Q. Gao and J. Zhou (Eds.): HCII 2023, LNCS 14043, pp. 519–532, 2023.
https://doi.org/10.1007/978-3-031-34917-1_35

societal structures such as pressure of technology use in society, isolation from society interlinked with technology, exclusion from social and private digital services, and how these structures can cause negative effects [29].

In this paper, We look beyond factors of personal characteristics, economic benefits, and age-related vulnerability within HCI and HCI-connected research to understand how societal structures can affect senior's life and technology use. We set out to explore the following research question: *What are the opportunities to incorporate societal factors of technology use affecting the lives of older adults?* Accordingly the, aim of this paper is to highlight the need Of incorporating societal factors in research about older adults and technology use in HCI. Moreover, societal factors is understood as large structural governmental laws or initiatives that affect the lives of our participants.

1.1 Social Justice in HCI

Social justice is a concept currently growing within HCI (See: [5, 10, 26, 27]). The concept aims to explore systemic societal structures interlinked with vulnerable groups of people. Notions such as power, privilege, access, and vulnerability are often discussed within the field [8, 11, 13, 26]. Social justice has come to emerge in HCI predominately in the last ten years, [18, 20, 21]. One of the most cited papers on social justice in HCI discusses design strategies for a social justice orientation in interaction design [8]. Dombrowski et. al [8] argues for an understanding of social justice as an orientation consisting of modes and sensitivities towards, e.g., marginalized voices and inequality. The paper takes a stance in political theorist H.P.P Lötters arguments about justice. Lötter discuss social justice as multidimensional and defines the philosophical stance as," justice is to give everyone their due." They furthermore use the work of Lötter to analyze the potential role of social justice in design and interaction design. Another definition of social justice in HCI is provided by Strohmayer et al. [26]. The article centers around a sex-worker organization in Canada and analyzes the usage of a tool to help sex-workers report abusive customers. Strohmayer [26] discuss a gap within justice-oriented literature in HCI, proclaiming that a more nuanced discussion of the implications and meanings of justice is needed. By interlinking the idea of Fraser's multidimensional justice with previous HCI literature, authors develop three implications for developing digital technologies for stigmatized, criminalized, and often misrepresented communities. Moreover Irani et al., [13] discuss postcolonial computing in an HCI context. Notions of social justice are described as power, authority, legitimacy, and participation in the context of globalization. Moving to other works, social justice has been attributed to many various studies in HCI with a major focus on groups who are vulnerable or in some sense, stigmatized, marginalized, or discriminated such as sex workers, women living under heavy patriarchal structures, gentrified communities, and other groups discriminated against [8, 11, 22]. From existing literature on social justice in HCI, a group rarely mentioned emerges as older adults. Older adults may not directly be seen as marginalized or discriminated in a larger sense, instead, other aspects of injustice can unite senior communities, such as class, ethnicity, or gender. However, in this paper and the study conducted, the general unifying aspect of vulnerability is age. Analyzing older adults technology use using a social justice perspective is done by highlighting societal structures such as such as pressure of technology use in society, isolation from society interlinked with technology, and exclusion from digital services.

2 Age and Older Adults in HCI

To frame the research question, below we present research on older adults and technology use from HCI, Cognitive Science, Psychology and Behavior and Information technology.

2.1 Capabilities, Adoption and Acceptance in Technology Use

The barriers between age and technology use are often described as capabilities, adoption and acceptance [2, 4, 7, 15, 21, 33]. Capabilities, adoption, and acceptance imply that a person may not use technology because of physical or psychological obstacles or because of personal choice and attitudes. There has been attempts at extending concerns of acceptance by not only looking directly at personality and acceptance but also social support and prior experience [2, 15]. For example, [16] extends the TAM (technology acceptance model), a commonly used acceptance model within HCI, with additional phases building out theories to create a bigger understanding of what makes mobile technologies accepted by Older adults [16]. Extension of the TAM includes aspects that, on the one hand, includes prior experience and peer-support, but on the other hand does not include aspects of how life could be of good quality even without mobile technologies. Similarly, [28] extends the discourse on Older adults and technology use in HCI and wants to"go beyond seeing Older adults as merely old or limited" when it comes to system design. They see a huge impact on what groups of Older adults are included in their study and states that many of their findings should not be"over-generalized" due to missing factors. Moreover, they also discuss how the results point to a more complex perspective on social connection from technology use and how this could, for example, be accommodation differences of infrastructures.

2.2 Age as an Economic Opportunity for Technology Development

In business, economics, and HCI, aging is often discussed concerning an economic perspective. As the population of the world is getting older with fewer individuals being able to care for Older adults, how can technology aid with rising costs of eldercare [11, 18, 26]. Mosthagel [27] discuss how studies on older adults' attitudes towards technology often lack a business and economic perspective. Accordingly, one example of how to lower the cost of care for older adults is to design digital technologies that help older adults live at home longer if possible. Such technologies would not only help many older adults, who wish to live more independently at home but may also lower senior care costs The potential of using technology to aid with the dilemma of cost vs. care is, according to [6] very high, and benefits can include social interaction, medical providing, and assistance. On the other hand, even though launching technology to help not only with eldercare costs, easier management for care providers and older adults to maintain at home independence, other ethical risks can arise.

Sharkey et al. [24], discuss practical risks of having in-home technologies in the form of robots to help older adults in their everyday life. The arising risks include privacy risks, information obtaining risks, and possible shortcomings from the in-home technology potentially leading to physical harm. Likewise, [12] discuss how assuming that older adults will use assistive technologies just to maintain their independence or to gain social interaction is highly overstated and that technologies should see to each individual's diversity addressing the functional, emotional, and social needs. Moving from such statements of ethical considerations and overstated potential of at-home technologies for older adults, other challenges arise when technology is only discusses as positive when trying to solving large societal challenges such as care vs. costs without going deeper into how this change might take place and affect the lives of older adults in a particular society.

2.3 Ageism and Stigma in Technology Development

Technology development for older adults is often built on ageist discrimination creating a vicious circle according to Ivan et al., [14]. They describe how technology design and development is often conducted by youth for the youth market therefore alienating older adults rendering them to not want to use such technologies. Similarly, [19] discusses how the digital divide is often researched in relation to older adults and their internal characteristics such as technophobia, physical and cognitive decline, and computer literacy. They discuss how the factor of ageism defined as age discrimination is not sufficiently explored in research about older adults and technology. Designing and building technology for older adults and older adults may not only center around a youth market as in [14] but may also be built on negative stereotypes around aging [18] causing a product development to not meet the correct needs of the target group. Stigmatization amongst older adults is discussed by [29] as stemming from a discourse that has relied on the biomedical aspects of aging in contrast to the psychological and behavioral. They argue that much HCI research further elongates stigma since less focus is put on other aspects than physical and medical. These arguments stem from earlier work of [9] which bases conclusions on funding decisions made in the US. This funding was primarily put into biomedical research on aging instead of humanities, behavioral sciences, and psychology. [29] continues to build on these conclusions and discusses how this focus on the biomedical aspects of aging has tipped over into public spheres and, in the end, mass media, meaning that a social view on aging as pathological or abnormal has grown. This view has according to [9] led to a collective discourse of aging where much HCI research is conducted with a notion that ageing can be solved by better and more expensive technology and medical services. This view that technology can aid with certain age relating problems and issues is much explored within HCI [4, 6, 21, 25, 33]. A large proportion of this research scratch the surface of discussing technology use interlinked with or structures of a society but none of them further develop arguments for why such aspects may be regarded as having major impacts on older adults' technology use and lives. In summary [14, 18, 19] points to bias technology development for older adults, excluding insights on ageism and negative stereotypes on aging as damaging for Older adults and technology development. [9, 29] further points to how much research in HCI is researched with the concern that age can be bettered or solved with technology.

3   Data Collection and Method

In this paper, research on a social justice perspective to highlight societal structures surrounding older adults' technology use is centered. The aim is to is to highlight the need for incorporating of societal factors in research about older adults and technology use in HCI. To do this, i conducted an interview study with 15 older adults living in Sweden. The call for participation was done through senior citizen organization websites in the north of Sweden. I contacted individuals who worked in the organization and had their emails officially posted on each website. By focusing directly on these organizations participants was certain to be an older adult and "senior" according to themselves. I choose to contact half of the individuals from four different websites and sent out an email containing information about the study and the focus of the interview questions.

Participants were asked if they were available through phone and their preferred time of the interview. Initially, 11 men and 18 women were contacted whereas 3 men and 8 women responded. Through the first interviews, participants recommended additional individuals (4 extra women) who also considered to take part in the study. In the end, 15 older adults were interviewed, 11 from initial contact and 4 from snowball selection. At the time of the interviews the Covid-19 pandemic was still affecting the lives and routines of our participants and we therefore choose to conduct the interview through telephone. I recorded each call with the consent of our participant by putting them on speaker phone and recording with quick time player on a computer standing next to the phone. Each interview lasted from 20–50 min.

I created an interview guide which was divided into two parts. The first part included questions about participants' life situations and the influence of the COVID-19 period. I asked about their daily routines and how they were different from before the pandemic. I also asked them about their home and social life. The second part included questions about the participant's technology use, such as what they have at home, what they use every day and if/how they had used technology more or different since the start of the Covid-19 pandemic.

3.1   Analysis

After conducting the interviews, the audio files were transcribed non-verbatim to word documents. The data-transcripts were analyzed in a team of three researchers using a thematic analysis [3] and we started by initially coding the data, highlighting experts that aligned with the research aim. After coding the transcripts, we sorted the codes into categories formed by similar codes. Lastly, we sought to group once again our categories into three overarching themes. From our thematic analysis we posit three themes, i) the importance of technology to live a connected life, ii) Force and frustration from the technological push in society and iii) Societal exclusion from technological divides.

Table 1. Participants overview

Participant no.	Gender	Age	Living status	Earlier occupation
1	Male	70	Married	Economy manager
2	Female	71	Married	Teacher
3	Female	76	Lives alone	Manager
4	Female	70	Married	Nurse
5	Female	69	Lives alone	Nurse
6	Female	70	Married	Occupational therapist
7	Female	77	Lives alone	Teacher
8	Female	74	Married	Tax-worker
9	Female	73	Lives alone	Teacher
10	Male	70	Lives alone	It-specialist
11	Female	76	Lives alone	Cultural worker
12	Female	80	Married	Technician
13	Male	70	Lives alone	Administrator
14	Female	71	Lives alone	Manager
15	Female	79	Married	Teacher

4 Findings

In this paper we center the research question: *What are the opportunities to incorporate societal factors of technology use affecting the lives of older adults?* Foregrounding a social justice perspective, we proceed to analyze how our participants uptake technology living within the Swedish digital society, how the Covid-pandemic of 2020 and forward changed their usage and how this period made visible those who do not use technology and the negative effects arising from this.

4.1 The Importance of Technology to Live a Connected Life

As the Covid-19 pandemic proceeded, older adults saw many of their daily activities become more restricted. For example, many physical meetings held by various senior citizen organizations started to shut down to protect their members from infection. Similarly, gyms, restaurants, and museums, started to restrict their hours and space. This process of social distance had an effect on many of the older adults in our study. However, at the same time many also started using technological tools to connect with their former physical activities. Participant 2, describes a scenario where she and her husband attempted to use a video call app to attend their niece's graduation ceremony:" *Well, we were supposed to connect to my niece's graduation, and it was fun because we had made a little sign and sang for her, so that was amazing*".

As many participants had started to use their technology more and in a different way than before, others had already gotten used to technological tools as a way of socializing. Participant 3 shares how she used to see her grandchild through zoom before the pandemic: *"Before my younger daughter moved here from Stockholm, and her son was about three, I would read stories to him through my phone and we would sometimes play hide and seek. Now we don't do that anymore when they live here instead we see each other in real-life"*.

Similarly, to participant 3, participant 14 would also use technology to connect with family members who were because of distance or the pandemic out of reach. Participant 14 mentions her mother who lives in an eldercare home: *"I have to say that I have appreciated facetime very much. My almost 100-year-old mom is still around, she turns 100 in February and where she lives they have been wonderfully good in reaching out through face time. Its just great!"*.

Technological tools in participants everyday life were discussed effortlessly as a vital part taken for granted, many had for years used both apps such as messenger and WhatsApp to text with friends and family, and facetime was for example, also used by participant 8 to talk with her grandchildren: *"We use our smartphones daily many times and we have for example messenger and facetime where we mostly talk with our grandchildren who live in. Its fun to see them and we have a good connection even though they live so far away"*.

Likewise, participant 9, describes her use of her smartphone money transfers and social media updates as *" easy to use for everything most of the time, its easiest like that"*. As participants turn to at home technology, extending their social connections online, a parallel discussion on pressure and force arises. Participants reflect on how society plays a role in a strong technological implementation and force below.

4.2 Force and Frustration from Technological Advances

When discussing technology use amongst older adults and relations to technology, feelings of force and frustration emerged amongst several participants. These feelings were by participants linked to the large implementation of technology all throughout Swedish society and how society itself plays a part in this technological force. P11 explains how older adults may not want to use technology simply because they do not want to and critiques society: *"Society forces people in their last stages of life into something they don't want (technology) and makes them feel totally lost"*.

P14 makes similar statements and discusses acquaintances suffering from negative consequences due to not using technology: *"Basically, there is nothing you can do without using technology at this point, you are completely dependent on it... One can barely go shopping without technology, that's how it is today. I. have an acquaintance who is single and alone, and she can barely pay bills via computers. Stuff like that is completely alien to her, it's like a nightmare"*. P7 extends their feelings of anger to age discrimination and technology: *"Sometimes I think about age discrimination that I experience sometimes. I get so angry thinking on how society establishes how it is necessary to have a computer and a cellphone"*.

Further feelings of frustration were connected to public services such as access to money and banking options. P12 described an event in their life where they wanted help from the bank with a bank app for money transfer: *"I tried to get help at the bank with an app for transferring money, but I couldn't get any because there were some darn codes that I was supposed to hand in. It was something with six digits that I could not remember. so that wasn't nice"*. Participant 8 similarly thought that the money question was an issue:*"I think paying with my card is easier but at the same time I think it is terrifying that you can't use cash. I think about not having a computer and how it makes you completely powerless, you can't pay bills or send emails, it is a vulnerable system I tell you"*.

Participant 3 likewise reflects on digital money transfer services:*" I cannot understand how people manage without computers in these days. It's just something that you need to have today"*.

When encountering new technologies or having to adjust to new features, participant 12 would talk herself into not backing down reflecting over the positive outcomes that learning could bring:*" The technology we have at home is really good, I would definitely not manage without them. I am not shy learning new technologies or learning new stuff... I have a saying: technology cannot win over me"*.

Similarly participant 9 briefly reflected on not having technologies:*" it's hard to imagine being without technologies, I take it for granted, if it was not there life would very different., it's just there and I expect it do work, it would probably be a disaster if it wasn't there"*.

As participants discussed their own reflections of technological force and opportunities, many reflect on their family and friends who for various reasons did not have the same opportunities or will to use technology causing negative consequences.

4.3   Societal Exclusion Through Technological Assertation

Family or friends who did not use digital technology would often feel left out from certain societal areas For example, participant 2 discuss how her older mother felt dejected because of not having the same opportunities to information or housing as others who had access to the internet:*"Just look at my mother she is a lost generation, she feels very disregarded and angry, sometimes a commercial says just enter www. but she can't... .10–15 years ago when she became a widow, we showed her a computer we were going to plug in, but she didn't want it. Now she says, what if I had listened to you?"*.

When turning a certain age, some people would feel that technology was simply not a part of their life that they wanted to explore. But this preference could according to Participant 7 lead to negative consequences as they discussed an acquaintance who felt too old to use technology but still felt left out despite having the choice:*"sometimes I think of my 98-year-old neighbor that doesn't have a computer. She doesn't feel there is any need for her to have a computer at her age, which is perhaps understandable. But I mean you need a computer to put yourself in a queue for a retirement home.... It is the same with the bank and there is no one to talk to. You have to go through the internet and that makes me so upset because I feel like everyone should have the right to a functioning everyday life. No one should be forced to do something that you don't have the possibility to do and there is no help to get"*.

Many participants generally felt frustrated about the fact that in the Swedish society, digital change is happening at such a fast pace causing some people to get completely left behind. P8, says:*"Some people don't have a computer and they are actually quite many; they are left behind and that's sad for them"*. Discussing how the development of the digital society has negative implications for many senior individuals, participant 14 extends:*"There needs to be an understanding for Older adults who can't learn technology because of their age or income. There have to be opportunities for all of us despite knowledge levels.... It speaks for itself that a person who has never in their working-life used a computer or a mobile phone and is 85 cannot naturally understand how to pay bills digitally. There has to be opportunities for all of us to make every-day life work"*.

Reflecting on how her own journey with technology is progressing, p11 discusses how it has simultaneously made her think on older adults that does not keep up with the same speed therefore becoming excluded:*"As of right now I have a better relationship with technology, I have started to understand how important it is. But I have also started to understand how difficult and dangerous the digitalization has become. I'm fine, but what about those who are older? They don't even know how to do some stuff; they don't have a computer but all the time they are being told to find services on their computer? I can't help to think about older people that constantly feels like crap. They are really being excluded!"*. As these findings point out there is a concern amongst those who are efficient in technology about the strong force and pressure to use technology in order to be connected to vital societal services and opportunities. We move to discuss our findings and present three opportunities for HCI research to bridge a social justice perspective with research on older adults and technology use.

5 Discussion

By illustrating how society and technology is interlinked through the empirical study opportunities are framed around how a social justice perspective can benefit research about older adults' technology use in HCI. The opportunities framed, gives HCI researchers ways to go beyond research about older adults' technology use that does not incorporate societal factors which can create partial biased perspectives. We cater to the research question: What are the opportunities to incorporate societal factors of technology use affecting the lives of older adults? In answering this question, we advance a series of three opportunities: *1. Dismantling negative societal negative effects from technological implications* 2. *Understanding how technology excludes older adults from services*, and 3. *Acknowledging ageism in society*. These opportunities aim to support HCI researchers in designing technologies for and with older adults that account for how societal structures can affect older adults' life and technology use.

5.1 Misdirected Focus: Capability, Adoption, and Acceptance

The first gathered stream of research was called"capabilities, adoption and acceptance of technology connected to age". The section showed how research often rely on older adults' personal characteristics, such as how capable they are and if they will adopt or accept technology in their life [2, 4, 7, 15, 21, 33]. Much of this research do not take into consideration factors of society such as pressure of technology use in society, isolation from society interlinked with technology or exclusion from social and private digital services causing negative effects living in society. [16, 28] make attempts to extend models and frameworks about acceptance and capabilities in older adults technology use technology use. Both argue for extending scholarly work centered around technology use for older adults, moving beyond, for example,"seeing older adults as merely old or limited" or to include aspects of prior computational experience in research. Despite efforts, neither provide deeper material about societal factors and how that may play a large part in conducting such research. As illustrated in our study, societal factors have a large impact into how some participants discussed struggling to access certain opportunities through technology. Despite many of them using technology on a daily basis, socially connecting with friends and family, participants 7, 14, 2, 8 and 11 all mentioned family, friends, and acquaintances directly suffering in their daily life from not wanting nor being able to use digital technologies and as an extension created negative feelings. P2's mother had earlier felt that she was too old to use a computer but now regretted her earlier choices to not become a computer user due to the negative effects of not using one. P11 expressed frustration about how there is a lack of empathy and opportunities for older adults who does not use technology and how such individuals are constantly being told that they need computers. P8 discussed how older adults who does not have a computer is completely powerless and how the system (society) is very vulnerable for those who have chosen not to use technology. These examples from P2, P8 and P11 all highlight individuals that do not use technology because they have at some point chosen not to. This choice has resulted in negative consequences for them and their lives. Wanting and not wanting to use technology is a choice likewise is for example acceptance. But older adults may not have been fully aware of the potential consequence's their choice would render. Therefore, capability, adoption and acceptance factors can be misdirected in that it does not recognize how some older adults does not want to use technology and how these choices should be respected. This poses a challenging dilemma but likewise a social justice perspective opportunity for the HCI discourse:

- *Opportunity 1: Dismantling negative societal effects from technology implications* HCI have the opportunity to focus beyond capabilities, adoption and acceptance to acknowledge how older adults that does not want to use technology are affected negatively in society. A social justice-opportunity would not seek to aid or solve senior's situation with more technology for them, but rather to form technology to dismantle such negative societal effects they experience. For example, how could HCI be engaged in local or national policies that forces older adults to use certain technologies or platform to obtain information or services? Would it be possible to have personal physically engaging with older adults who wants help them as a part of a service provided by the government or municipality?

5.2 Technological Exclusion from Non-use

In many recent studies, of the rising population of elders vs. lowering the costs of eldercare with technology is discussed [6, 21, 25]. Such statements of the immense potential of technology for eldercare rarely include societal factors and as a result miss out on valuable insights [12, 24]. [21] creates arguments for how research on Senior's technology use lacks a business and economics perspectives. In this stated shortcoming by they do not look into how a societal perspective might frame thoughts of economy. I frame these arguments about technology as tools for lowering costs of eldercare insufficient because it rarely discusses the importance of societal factors and we urge researchers to frame such dilemmas with a perspective on societal, cultural, emotional, and political instead of only economical. In our study connections was made to certain services that would make older adults lives better. These services were for example, paying bills digitally, being able to transfer money digitally, finding information and housing opportunities. P7's neighbor couldn't enter them self into a queue for a retirement home and was ultimately excluded from a housing opportunity because of this. P2 discussed her mother that could not get information on products or services because all information she wanted to access existed exclusively online. P12 discussed an unpleasant situation in the bank resulting in not being able to use a common money transferring app. Moreover, the discussions from P7, P14, P2, P8, P11 illustrates how not using technology can result in exclusion from many important social and private services meant to make life better. This causes a dilemma but likewise an opportunity for HCI:

– *Opportunity 2: Service provision for technological non-use*

The HCI community have a social justice opportunity to shift our attention from the economic benefits of technology to understand how older adults not using technology may be excluded from social and private services rendering their lives less manageable and with less economic opportunities. Such services can include but are not limited to, housing opportunities, paying bills, and transferring money. Can we offer for example, analogue banking options for those who prefer them, and more person-to-person services for those who would like help? Could it be possible to hold onto analogue services for as long as people need them and when the interest for them lessens only then discontinue those services? Could we imagine a local housing bureau for older adults who do not use the internet that they can go visit in real life?

5.3 Fostering a Deeper Understanding of Ageism

Research about older adults technology use often criticizes related research for not acknowledging ageism or age-discrimination [14, 19]. Both on terms of having bias youth producing technologies for a youth market and making products not wanted or adapted for senior users. Similarly [18] urges researchers to include older adults in every stage of technology design and argues for how ageism might play a role in their adaptation of technology. [14, 18]. All make important arguments for how ageism and discrimination should be an included factor in research about older adults' technology use. Without such acknowledgments much valuable insights about how older adults experience their place in society may never be reached and instead research with partial perspectives will be reproduced, in the end causing negative effects [14, 18]. Such insights on age discrimination and ageism are discussed in our study where many participants expressed frustration against strong technological force in society. Participants 11,14,7,12 all expressed negative feelings and experience when discussing certain situations about technology. P11 meant that the societal force of technology made some older adults feel totally lost, similarly P14 meant that without out technological skills it is barley possible to perform basic tasks, making life feel like a nightmare. P7 linked this force to age discrimination saying that individuals need to have a computer in order to get by in society. Furthermore, stigmatization can be found both in the public and in

HCI discourse according to [9, 29] and they argue how ageing is often framed as problem manageable with technology. Stigma and a partial perspective portrayal of age in technology can prohibit HCI from developing beyond such arguments and continuously reproduce such perspectives that does not recognize how societal structures can affect senior's life and technology use. But opportunities also arise.

– *Opportunity 3: Acknowledging ageism in society*

The thirds social justice opportunity HCI can acknowledge draws on feelings and opinions on ageism of participants or target groups. To include such acknowledgments, this could be done by consulting participants about their life situations and by going deeper into aspects of stigma and marginalization. This acknowledgement would frame HCI research about older adults beyond general age-related vulnerability and include societal factors into how ageism is experienced. By for example, discussing the background of participants, do they have extensive experience of technology from their work, if not do they want more knowledge? How can society, the government, municipality, or community takes these steps to actually incorporate older adults in such education. However, research should always acknowledge that those who do not wish to use technology should still have the same societal opportunities as those who do.

6 Conclusion

This paper aimed to highlight the opportunities to include societal factors of older adults' technology use and to look beyond for example capabilities, acceptance and economic benefits. From a literature background including HCI, cognitive science, psychology and behavioral and information technology research, qualitative interviews with 15 older adults were conducted. Through a social justice perspective where the data was analyzed focusing on how societal structures in technology development and implications affect older adults three opportunities arise: *1. Dismantling negative societal negative effects from technological implications, 2. Understanding how technology excludes older adults from services,* and *3. Acknowledging ageism in society.* These three opportunities contribute to an ongoing discourse of social justice in HCI.

References

1. Beacker, R., et al.: Technology to reduce social isolation and loneliness. In: Proceedings of the 16th International ACM SIGACCESS Conference on Computers & Accessibility - ASSETS 2014, Rochester, New York, USA, pp. 27–34 ACM Press (2014). https://doi.org/10.1145/266 1334.2661375
2. Beer, J.M., Takayama, L.: Mobile remote presence systems for older adults: acceptance, benefits, and concerns. 8
3. Braun, V., Clarke, V.: Using thematic analysis in psychology. Qual. Res. Psychol. 3(2), 77–101 (2006). https://doi.org/10.1191/1478088706qp063oa
4. Charness, N., Boot, W.R.: Aging and information technology use: potential and barriers. Curr. Dir. Psychol. Sci. 18(5), 253–258 (2009). https://doi.org/10.1111/j.1467-8721.2009.01647.x

5. Corbett, E., Loukissas, Y.: Engaging gentrification as a social justice issue in HCI. In: Proceedings of the 2019 CHI Conference on Human Factors in Computing Systems, pp. 1–16. Association for Computing Machinery, New York (2019). https://doi.org/10.1145/3290605.3300510

6. Deegan, P., et al.: Mobile manipulators for assisted living in residential settings. Auton Robot. 24(2), 179–192 (2008). https://doi.org/10.1007/s10514-007-9061-8

7. Dogruel, L., et al.: The use and acceptance of new media entertainment technology by elderly users: development of an expanded technology acceptance model. Behav. Inf. Technol. 34(11), 1052–1063 (2015). https://doi.org/10.1080/0144929X.2015.1077890

8. Dombrowski, L., et al.: Social justice-oriented interaction design: outlining key design strategies and commitments. In: Proceedings of the 2016 ACM Conference on Designing Interactive Systems, pp. 656–671. Association for Computing Machinery, New York (2016). https://doi.org/10.1145/2901790.2901861

9. Estes, C.L., Binney, E.A.: The biomedicalization of aging: dangers and dilemmas. Gerontologist. 29(5), 587–596 (1989). https://doi.org/10.1093/geront/29.5.587

10. Fox, S., et al.: Exploring social justice, design, and HCI. In: Proceedings of the 2016 CHI Conference Extended Abstracts on Human Factors in Computing Systems, pp. 3293–3300. Association for Computing Machinery, New York (2016). https://doi.org/10.1145/2851581.2856465

11. Fox, S., et al.: Social justice and design: power and oppression in collaborative systems. In: Companion of the 2017 ACM Conference on Computer Supported Cooperative Work and Social Computing, pp. 117–122. Association for Computing Machinery, New York (2017). https://doi.org/10.1145/3022198.3022201

12. Hirsch, T., et al.: The ELDer project: social, emotional, and environmental factors in the design of eldercare technologies. In: Proceedings on the 2000 conference on Universal Usability - CUU 2000, Arlington, Virginia, United States, pp. 72–79 ACM Press (2000). https://doi.org/10.1145/355460.355476

13. Irani, L., et al.: Postcolonial computing: a lens on design and development. In: Proceedings of the 28th International Conference on Human Factors in Computing Systems - CHI 2010, Atlanta, Georgia, USA, p. 1311 ACM Press (2010). https://doi.org/10.1145/1753326.1753522

14. Ivan, L., Cutler, S.J.: Ageism and technology: the role of internalized stereotypes. Univ. Tor. Q. 90(2), 127–139 (2021). https://doi.org/10.3138/utq.90.2.05

15. Jia, P., et al.: Designing for technology acceptance in an ageing society through multi-stakeholder collaboration. Procedia Manufact. 3, 3535–3542 (2015). https://doi.org/10.1016/j.promfg.2015.07.701

16. Kim, S., et al.: Acceptance of mobile technology by older adults: a preliminary study. In: Proceedings of the 18th International Conference on Human-Computer Interaction with Mobile Devices and Services, Florence, Italy, pp. 147–157. ACM (2016). https://doi.org/10.1145/2935334.2935380

17. Kitazaki, M., et al.: Connected resources - empowering older people to age resourcefully. In: Extended Abstracts of the 2019 CHI Conference on Human Factors in Computing Systems, p. 1. Association for Computing Machinery, New York (2019). https://doi.org/10.1145/3290607.3311774

18. Mannheim, I., et al.: Inclusion of older adults in the research and design of digital technology. Int. J. Environ. Res. Public Health 16(19), 3718 (2019). https://doi.org/10.3390/ijerph16193718

19. McDonough, C.C.: The effect of ageism on the digital divide among older adults. J. Gerontol. Geriatr. Med. 2(8), 1–7 (2016)

20. McMurtrey, M.E., et al.: Seniors and technology: results from a field study. J. Comput. Inf. Syst. 10 (2011)

21. Mostaghel, R.: Innovation and technology for the elderly: systematic literature review. J. Bus. Res. **69**(11), 4896–4900 (2016). https://doi.org/10.1016/j.jbusres.2016.04.049

22. Rose, E.J.: Design as advocacy: using a human-centered approach to investigate the needs of vulnerable populations. J. Tech. Writ. Commun. **46**(4), 427–445 (2016). https://doi.org/10.1177/0047281616653494

23. Seo, J.H., et al.: Re-powering senior citizens with interactive art making: case study with independent older adults. In: Extended Abstracts of the 2018 CHI Conference on Human Factors in Computing Systems, pp. 1–6. Association for Computing Machinery, New York (2018). https://doi.org/10.1145/3170427.3188476

24. Sharkey, N., Sharkey, A.: The eldercare factory. Gerontology **58**(3), 282–288 (2012). https://doi.org/10.1159/000329483

25. Sokoler, T., Svensson, M.S.: Embracing ambiguity in the design of non-stigmatizing digital technology for social interaction among senior citizens. Behav. Inf. Technol. **26**(4), 297–307 (2007). https://doi.org/10.1080/01449290601173549

26. Strohmayer, A., et al.: Technologies for social justice: lessons from sex workers on the front lines. In: Proceedings of the 2019 CHI Conference on Human Factors in Computing Systems, pp. 1–14. Association for Computing Machinery, New York (2019). https://doi.org/10.1145/3290605.3300882

27. Sultana, S., et al.: Design within a patriarchal society: opportunities and challenges in designing for rural women in Bangladesh. In: Proceedings of the 2018 CHI Conference on Human Factors in Computing Systems, pp. 1–13. Association for Computing Machinery, New York (2018)

28. Sun, Y., et al.: Being senior and ICT: a study of seniors using ICT in China. In: Proceedings of the SIGCHI Conference on Human Factors in Computing Systems, pp. 3933–3942. Association for Computing Machinery, New York (2014). https://doi.org/10.1145/2556288.2557248

29. Vines, J., et al.: An age-old problem: examining the discourses of ageing in HCI and strategies for future research. ACM Trans. Comput.-Hum. Interact. **22**(1), 2:1–2:27 (2015). https://doi.org/10.1145/2696867

30. Wandke, H., et al.: Myths about older people's use of information and communication technology. GER **58**(6), 564–570 (2012). https://doi.org/10.1159/000339104

31. Wang, S., et al.: Technology to support aging in place: older adults' perspectives. Healthcare **7**(2), 60 (2019). https://doi.org/10.3390/healthcare7020060

32. Yang, S.-Y., John, S.: Team bingo: a game that increases physical activity and social interaction for seniors in a community setting. In: Extended Abstracts of the 2020 CHI Conference on Human Factors in Computing Systems, pp. 1–6. Association for Computing Machinery, New York (2020). https://doi.org/10.1145/3334480.3381653

33. Zhang, C., Shahriar, H.: The adoption, issues, and challenges of wearable healthcare technology for the elderly. In: Proceedings of the 21st Annual Conference on Information Technology Education, pp. 50–53. Association for Computing Machinery, New York (2020). https://doi.org/10.1145/3368308.3415454

Value Co-creation Perspectives on Digital Literacy Training for Older Adults: A Call to Action Research

Yuxiang (Chris) Zhao[✉]

Nanjing University of Science and Technology, Nanjing 210094, China
yxzhao@vip.163.com

Abstract. Despite evidence of an increasing trend in the adoption and use of digital technology, recent studies suggest that older adults continue to face significant challenges in surviving in the digital age. There is an urgent need to enhance the digital literacy of older people, so that more of them can enjoy the benefits of digital technology in their later years, with the joint attention of academia and industry. In this opinion paper, I argue for exploring ways and responses to foster digital literacy among older adults from the value co-creation perspective. In particular, promoting digital literacy among older adults requires special attention from families, tech companies, communities, policymakers, and other professions. I call for more action research to investigate theoretical insights and practical implications in digital literacy training for older adults. Research agenda and actionable items are proposed for future discussion.

Keywords: Digital Literacy · Older Adults · Value Co-creation · Action Research · Social Information Practices

1 Introduction

The development and advancement of Information Communication Technologies (ICTs) have greatly facilitated the use of computers, the Internet, and social media for older adults. The technology-afforded digital sphere has brought convenience to seniors in their daily lives, recreation, social activities, and personal health management, promoting their social participation and inclusion and further enhancing their sense of well-being [1, 2]. At the same time, however, the rapid growth of the digital society has not benefited a segment of the older population [3, 4]. Due to uneven regional development, differences in socio-economic levels, inadequate digital infrastructure, and varying levels of education, the digital divide is prevalent among older adults [5, 6]. A significant disconnect exists between the perceived affordance of ICTs for the elderly and the constraints of adoption, access, and use [7]. Meanwhile, digital ageism is a problem that cannot be ignored and needs to be taken seriously for older people [8, 9]. Given the globally aging population and proliferation of ICTs, there is a pressing need to critically examine the age-related bias in the adoption and use of digital technology [10]. Although there is a "generational lag" in technology use among older adults [11], this does not mean that older adults are rejecting digital products and refusing to learn digital skills [12].

© The Author(s), under exclusive license to Springer Nature Switzerland AG 2023
Q. Gao and J. Zhou (Eds.): HCII 2023, LNCS 14043, pp. 533–542, 2023.
https://doi.org/10.1007/978-3-031-34917-1_36

Digital literacy is defined as "the set of skills, knowledge and attitudes required to access, create, use, and evaluate digital information effectively, efficiently, and ethically" ([13], p. 2243). Theoretical and practical exploration of digital literacy for older adults is an essential step in helping them take full advantage of the dividends of the digital age [14]. Prior work suggests that a "second digital divide" may exist among older adults, which deals with issues of digital literacy and efficacy [15, 16]. In this paper, digital literacy for older adults is defined as the ability to locate, access, organize, share, and evaluate digital information. It also involves using digital technologies and tools to solve problems, critically understand digital content, and make decisions. An expanding body of literature discusses the measurement of digital literacy among older adults [14], with increasing attention to the benefits of their use of ICTs and how using these digital technologies can fulfill their diverse needs [15]. Another part of the research focuses on digital literacy training for older adults, including the main factors that influence digital literacy among elders and ways to improve the effectiveness and success of the training [7, 8, 16–18].

In this opinion paper, digital literacy training for older adults is regarded as a type of social practice that draws on the socio-technical systems' perspective to understand the cultivation of digital literacy. It is worth emphasizing that simply involving older adults in technology is not effective in enhancing their digital literacy. In other words, digital literacy cultivation cannot be achieved by providing materiality alone. As Park [19] suggested, digital literacy is learned through social practice and community-level interaction, rather than simply facilitating technology engagement. The concept of digital literacy indicates how learning is a social process. Thus, digital literacy is best acquired in real-life settings where family members, peers, mentors, and professionals come together to provide a sociocultural environment for exploration [15]. Although existing studies have mentioned the participation of multiple actors in digital literacy training for older adults [7], they have not yet risen to the theoretical level to explore the shaping of actor networks and the role played by sociomateriality in value creation in the process of digital literacy practice. It is worth noting that a practice-oriented approach to digital literacy training does not mean it is possible to ignore theoretical underpinnings and interpretations. Given this, I call for introducing value co-creation theory to explore the underlying mechanism and value-sensitive design of digital literacy training for older adults. At the same time, as a social information practice, digital literacy training for elders is situated in rapidly evolving social, cultural, and technological contexts. Digital literacy training for older adults should not be limited to micro-level controlled experimental studies, but it should consider drawing on an action research approach to explore multi-stage, multi-actor, multi-scene, and media-rich information practices. The use of action research, which "brings together researchers and practitioners in a joint attempt to ameliorate a problematic situation while simultaneously contributing to scholarly knowledge" ([20], p. 851), is one way to bridge the long-standing gap in digital literacy research. Therefore, I call for more rigorous action research in digital literacy training for older adults, i.e., designing action research programs based on theory and executing action research to contextualize and/or expand the original theory.

2 A Brief Review on Digital Literacy Training for Older Adults

Since digital literacy is a multifaceted concept with varying definitions, this paper does not aim to discuss its conceptualization and measurement or the differences between it and related concepts, as previous research has addressed these topics [21–23]. Instead, this paper focuses on discussing effective interventions for promoting digital literacy among older adults to enhance their digital competence, skills, and transformation. While numerous initiatives for digital literacy training exist, most of them target younger generations. Digital literacy training for older adults has focused on the use of digital devices such as computers, iPads, and the Internet [5, 24, 25], and much of the relevant research has been done on computer literacy, information literacy, and media literacy in earlier years [21, 26, 27]. However, as technology has advanced, the umbrella concept of digital literacy has evolved [28]. For instance, social media's emergence has generated a plethora of conflicting information, and older individuals' ability to screen and evaluate this information's credibility has become an essential aspect of digital literacy training today [29, 30]. Additionally, algorithms, which were once hidden behind internet applications, are now being brought to the forefront. While older individuals do not need to understand the algorithms' specific operations, understanding how they work is crucial for algorithmic literacy training, an essential aspect of digital literacy training.

The lack of digital literacy among older adults has reduced them to digital refugees and made it difficult for them to integrate into digital society [31]. Especially after the COVID-19 outbreak, more and more older adults are becoming aware of the importance of digital literacy in their daily lives. Many projects are being carried out to cultivate digital literacy among older adults. For example, the Office of Economic Development and Community Partnerships at Johns Hopkins University offers a free digital literacy program for older adults. The European Commission and the Board of Education and Culture under the Lifelong Learning Project have joined forces with six EU countries to create a Digital Academy for older adults. Scholars have also conducted a series of empirical studies on the cultivation of digital literacy among older adults, with programs providing support for older adults in a variety of ways, including technology instruction, learning resources, and teaching platforms. There is growing evidence that skills-based training programs are effective in improving older adults' digital literacy [32–34]. In addition to ubiquitous ICT use training, a particular focus has recently been on digital literacy in the eHealth domain for older adults [35, 36]. For example, Xie [37] used the National Institute on Aging (NIA) training toolkit as a tutorial dedicated to improving the ability to search for, understand, and assess health information for older adults.

3 A Value Co-creation Perspective on Digital Literacy Training

Based on previous studies [13, 22], digital literacy training is a multidimensional, multi-actor participatory, multi-stage, and multi-contextual concept. Although existing studies have reached a consensus on the umbrella conceptual framework of digital literacy, there is still a lack of in-depth investigation into the synergistic relationships and value networks among different actors in digital literacy cultivation. In general, promoting digital literacy is more focused on practical exploration and thus has a strong sense of practice-turn. For a long time, the introduction and borrowing of theory have not been dominant on this topic. Although some studies have emphasized a community-led perspective to analyze the multi-actor influences on digital literacy and construct a corresponding conceptual framework [38], further exploration is needed regarding the mechanism of the role of actor networks in this process and the coupling and evolution of value co-creation. This paper argues that digital literacy research for older adults urgently needs to explore phenomenon-focused problematization [39]. In other words, to break through the limitations of theoretical absence in traditional practice-oriented research, we must systematically explore the antecedents and processes of digital literacy cultivation actions and design the related open and reflective digital literacy training program.

In summary, the factors influencing the digital literacy of older adults can be summarized into four aspects: individual characteristics of older adults, technology affordances, family support, and community engagement. The actors involved in promoting digital literacy among older adults are diverse, including non-profit organizations, elderly care institutions, GLAM institutions, research institutions, and government agencies in addition to older adults [40, 41]. The promotion of digital literacy among older adults is not simply digital empowerment [42], but the participation of multiple actors to co-create a lifelong learning environment for older adults [15, 19]. This includes the provision of resources, technical support, and the development of information services that are both universal and personalized. For example, the spatial value of libraries and information professionals effectively promotes digital literacy formation among older adults, providing core support for digital literacy programs such as recruiting members, training venues, and online teaching resources [43, 44]. Another example is motivating college students to engage in digital literacy training for older adults to guide them through intergenerational learning to adopt new technologies and better adapt to a digital society [35, 45, 46]. However, current research still lacks an in-depth analysis of the value played by the relevant actors in the digital literacy cultivation program for the elderly. It focuses more on the training effect than on the mechanism of each participating actor's synergy and value generation.

Actor identification and resource interaction are essential elements of the value co-creation process, and resource co-design among multiple actors is key to decomposing the value co-creation process [47, 48]. Therefore, this paper calls for exploring models and best practices of digital literacy training for older people in family-led, technology-enabled, and community-engaged scenarios based on the theoretical perspective of value co-creation. This exploration will be conducted through value chain networks that emerge from the linkage, deduction, and transformation of actor-networks, from intergenerational, organizational, and societal perspectives.

4   The Need for Action Research

At the action level, several intervention studies have been conducted on digital literacy training for older adults. Common methods include pre- and post-test surveys, randomized controlled trials, and participatory designs. Early studies mainly used pre- and post-test surveys or cognitive tests to examine the effectiveness of digital literacy training. However, this approach has substantial endogeneity issues [36], and it is challenging to exclude the influence of contextual variables such as sociocultural factors. In recent years, digital literacy intervention studies have been conducted using randomized controlled trials [29, 49], which are better at mitigating endogeneity at the methodological level. However, there is an overall lack of explicit assessment of what older adults learn, as well as a lack of clarity about whether intervention effects change over time [45]. This paper argues that because digital literacy training for older adults involves different actors and is highly practical, there is an urgent need for a longitudinal interventional study of digital literacy programs for older adults in real-life scenarios [18]. Action research can undoubtedly meet this requirement.

Action research (AR) closely examines meso-level organizational change, community development, and the design and implementation of information systems and services [50]. The use of action research can bridge the gap between theory and practice, design practical programs based on theory, and further reflect on and refine theory in practice. To date, there have been relatively few action research studies conducted on digital literacy training [41, 51, 52], and although some relevant participatory design studies have been conducted (e.g., [31, 53]), there is no clear emphasis on the action research paradigm and following the normative process of action research in these studies.

Cultivating digital literacy among seniors does not happen overnight; one must be prepared for a long-term campaign. Due to the decline in physiological and cognitive functions of older adults, digital literacy training for seniors needs to be approached with special educational techniques, effective assistive technologies, and targeted incentives. More social experiments in real-life scenarios are required to fully integrate teaching resources, interactive technologies, and age-appropriate environments to make digital skills learning fun and educational for older adults. Therefore, action research is undoubtedly a possible solution to this problem.

The open, reflective, and iterative nature of action research helps to improve the effectiveness of digital literacy training and bring a more humanistic approach to older adults. Today, digital literacy training for older adults is not simply about exposing them to new technologies and teaching digital skills [54]. It's about improving their ability to access, create, share, store, utilize, and differentiate digital information, with the adoption and use of technology as the means rather than the ultimate goal. Therefore, the cultivation of digital literacy among older adults is a social practice that requires the intervention of multiple stakeholders and exploration of the socio-material properties of this social practice in shaping actor networks. Action research can greatly facilitate the phenomenon-focused problematization inquiry, distilling theoretical insights from digital literacy information practices, and conducting canonical action research based on theoretical foundations. At the same time, action research can effectively place different stakeholders in digital literacy training for older adults in a multi-stage, dynamically evolving action framework for exploration, especially the value propositions of different actors, the synergistic information behaviors among actors, and the value conflicts and tensions that arise in practice. Therefore, action research has the potential to bring out the best of value co-creation in digital literacy training for older adults. Meanwhile, some theoretical foundations in the value co-creation perspective, such as actor-network theory and affordance lens, can also better contribute to the design and implementation of action research.

5 Research Agenda

My reflections on the need and potential of action research in digital literacy training for older adults have led me to the following three recommendations. It is worth noting that these recommendations only serve as a primer, with the expectation that more rigorous and relevant findings will emerge from action research in digital literacy training for older adults.

5.1 Action Research on Digital Literacy Training for Older Adults in Developing Countries and Regions

Due to uneven national and regional development, older people in less developed regions face a more severe digital divide [55]. Therefore, digital literacy training for these older adults is even more urgent. This paper argues that action research on digital literacy training for older adults in developing countries and regions should pay attention to the following three issues. First, researchers should fully consider the local digital infrastructure status and conduct a necessary survey on the digital literacy level of older adults to adapt an action research program suitable for the local context. Second, the action research should continuously reflect on the negative impact of digital ageism on digital literacy training and target the digital skills readiness of older adults. Third, more critical reflections should be conducted in action research to be alert to the disruption of older adults' lives by technological colonialism, and to pay close attention to the impact of related actions on older adults' long-term digital survival.

5.2 Action Research for Specific Digital Literacy Goals for Older Adults

Due to the umbrella structure of the digital literacy concept [56], digital literacy training needs to be conducted with a targeted focus, which requires action research geared towards the specific information needs of older adults. For instance, digital literacy training for older adults has evolved from simply searching for information to screening it, given the early years of difficulty in accessing information and the current issue of overwhelming misinformation. Therefore, it is both urgent and timely to conduct action research on assessing the credibility of information for older adults. Another example is the growing use of social media among older adults to create and share information [57]. To meet such higher-order digital literacy needs, researchers can consider promoting older adults' creative digital literacy through intergenerational and vicarious learning modes, which can help them adapt and integrate better into the digital society.

5.3 Participatory Design Based on the Action Research Paradigm

Although several participatory design studies are currently underway in digital literacy training for older adults [58, 59], these efforts are more focused on exploring best practices and lack sufficient theoretical insights. An effective way to address this limitation is to conduct participatory design research based on an action research paradigm or, in other words, to promote digital literacy training for older adults based on a participatory action design approach. Specifically, researchers can consider participatory action design in three aspects: curriculum/syllabus, digital nudges, and informal learning environments. It is worth noting that in recent years, there has been an increased emphasis on both gamification and value-sensitive design in digital literacy training [60, 61], and by nature, these participatory designs are iterative and reflexive. The action research paradigm for integrating theory and practice can help improve the effectiveness and sustainability of digital literacy training for older adults in a fun and educational way.

Acknowledgment. This work was funded by the Key Projects of the National Social Science Foundation of China under Grant (No. 22&ZD327) and the National Science Foundation of China under Grant (No. 72074112).

References

1. Ihm, J., Hsieh, Y.P.: The implications of information and communication technology use for the social well-being of older adults. Inf. Commun. Soc. **18**, 1123–1138 (2015)
2. Sum, S., Mathews, M.R., Pourghasem, M., Hughes, I.: Internet technology and social capital: How the Internet affects seniors' social capital and wellbeing. J. Comput.-Mediat. Commun. **14**, 202–220 (2008)
3. Heart, T., Kalderon, E.: Older adults: are they ready to adopt health-related ICT? Int. J. Med. Inform. **82**, e209–e231 (2013)
4. Neves, B.B., Amaro, F., Fonseca, J.R.: Coming of (old) age in the digital age: ICT usage and non-usage among older adults. Sociol. Res. Online **18**, 22–35 (2013)
5. Delello, J.A., McWhorter, R.R.: Reducing the digital divide: connecting older adults to iPad technology. J. Appl. Gerontol. **36**, 3–28 (2017)
6. Friemel, T.N.: The digital divide has grown old: determinants of a digital divide among seniors. New Media Soc. **18**, 313–331 (2016)
7. Arthanat, S., Vroman, K.G., Lysack, C., Grizzetti, J.: Multi-stakeholder perspectives on information communication technology training for older adults: implications for teaching and learning. Disabil. Rehabil. Assist. Technol. **14**, 453–461 (2019)
8. Barrie, H., La Rose, T., Detlor, B., Julien, H., Serenko, A.: "Because I'm old": The role of ageism in older adults' experiences of digital literacy training in public libraries. J. Technol. Hum. Serv. **39**, 379–404 (2021)
9. Choi, E.Y., Kim, Y., Chipalo, E., Lee, H.Y.: Does perceived ageism widen the digital divide? And does it vary by gender? Gerontologist **60**, 1213–1223 (2020)
10. Chu, C.H., et al.: Digital ageism: challenges and opportunities in artificial intelligence for older adults. Gerontologist **62**, 947–955 (2022)
11. Charness, N., Boot, W.R.: Aging and information technology use: potential and barriers. Curr. Dir. Psychol. Sci. **18**, 253–258 (2009)
12. Xie, B., Charness, N., Fingerman, K., Kaye, J., Kim, M.T., Khurshid, A.: When going digital becomes a necessity: ensuring older adults' needs for information, services, and social inclusion during COVID-19. J. Aging Soc. Policy **32**, 460–470 (2020)
13. Julien, H.: Digital literacy in theory and practice. advanced methodologies and technologies in library science, Information Management, and Scholarly Inquiry, pp. 22–32. IGI Global (2019)
14. Oh, S.S., Kim, K.-A., Kim, M., Oh, J., Chu, S.H., Choi, J.: Measurement of digital literacy among older adults: systematic review. J. Med. Internet Res. **23**, e26145 (2021)
15. Schreurs, K., Quan-Haase, A., Martin, K.: Problematizing the digital literacy paradox in the context of older adults' ICT use: Aging, media discourse, and self-determination. Can. J. Commun. **42**, 359–377 (2017)

16. Tsai, H.-y.S., Shillair, R., Cotten, S.R.: Social support and "playing around" an examination of how older adults acquire digital literacy with tablet computers. Journal of Applied Gerontology 36, 29–55 (2017)

17. Alkali, Y.E., Amichai-Hamburger, Y.: Experiments in digital literacy. Cyberpsychol. Behav. **7**, 421–429 (2004)

18. Schirmer, W., Geerts, N., Vercruyssen, A., Glorieux, I., Consortium, D.A.: Digital skills training for older people: The importance of the 'lifeworld.' Arch. Gerontol. Geriatr. **101**, 104695 (2022)

19. Park, S.: Dimensions of digital media literacy and the relationship with social exclusion. Media Int. Aust. **142**, 87–100 (2012)

20. Davison, R.M., Martinsons, M.G., Malaurent, J.: Research perspectives: improving action research by integrating methods. J. Assoc. Inf. Syst. **22**, 851–873 (2021)

21. Bawden, D.: Information and digital literacies: a review of concepts. J. Document. **57**, 218–259 (2001)

22. Bawden, D.: Origins and concepts of digital literacy. Digit. Liter. Concepts Policies Pract. **30**, 17–32 (2008)

23. Koltay, T.: The media and the literacies: Media literacy, information literacy, digital literacy. Media Cult. Soc. **33**, 211–221 (2011)

24. Hunsaker, A., Hargittai, E.: A review of Internet use among older adults. New Media Soc. **20**, 3937–3954 (2018)

25. Zhao, Y.C., Zhao, M., Song, S.: Online health information seeking behaviors among older adults: systematic scoping review. J. Med. Internet Res. **24**, e34790 (2022)

26. Poynton, T.A.: Computer literacy across the lifespan: a review with implications for educators. Comput. Hum. Behav. **21**, 861–872 (2005)

27. Rasi, P., Vuojärvi, H., Rivinen, S.: Promoting media literacy among older people: a systematic review. Adult Educ. Q. **71**, 37–54 (2021)

28. Calvani, A., Cartelli, A., Fini, A., Ranieri, M.: Models and instruments for assessing digital competence at school. J. E-Learn. Knowl. Soc. **4**, 183–193 (2008)

29. Moore, R.C., Hancock, J.T.: A digital media literacy intervention for older adults improves resilience to fake news. Sci. Rep. **12**, 6008 (2022)

30. Seo, H., Blomberg, M., Altschwager, D., Vu, H.T.: Vulnerable populations and misinformation: A mixed-methods approach to underserved older adults' online information assessment. New Media Soc. **23**, 2012–2033 (2021)

31. Davis, N., Shiroma, K., Xie, B., Yeh, T., Han, X., De Main, A.: Designing eHealth tutorials with and for older adults. Proc. Assoc. Inf. Sci. Technol. **58**, 92–103 (2021)

32. Chang, S.J., Jang, S.J., Lee, H., Kim, H.: Building on evidence to improve ehealth literacy in older adults: a systematic review. CIN: Computers, Informatics, Nursing 39, 241–247 (2021)

33. Seo, H., Erba, J., Altschwager, D., Geana, M.: Evidence-based digital literacy class for older, low-income African-American adults. J. Appl. Commun. Res. **47**, 130–152 (2019)

34. Wang, X., Luan, W.: Research progress on digital health literacy of older adults: a scoping review. Front. Public Health **10**, 906089 (2022)

35. Caballero, J., Jacobs, R.J., Ownby, R.L.: Development of a computerized intervention to improve health literacy in older Hispanics with type 2 diabetes using a pharmacist supervised comprehensive medication management. PLoS ONE **17**, e0263264 (2022)

36. Fink, A., Beck, J.C.: Developing and evaluating a website to guide older adults in their health information searches: a mixed-methods approach. J. Appl. Gerontol. **34**, 633–651 (2015)

37. Xie, B.: Improving older adults' e-health literacy through computer training using NIH online resources. Libr. Inf. Sci. Res. **34**, 63–71 (2012)

38. Detlor, B., Julien, H., La Rose, T., Serenko, A.: Community-led digital literacy training: toward a conceptual framework. J. Am. Soc. Inf. Sci. **73**, 1387–1400 (2022)

39. Monteiro, E., Constantinides, P., Scott, S., Shaikh, M., Burton-Jones, A.: Editor's Comments: qualitative methods in is research: a call for phenomenon-focused problematization. MIS Q. **46**, iii–xix (2022)
40. Shapira, S., Yeshua-Katz, D., Goren, G., Aharonson-Daniel, L., Clarfield, A.M., Sarid, O.: Evaluation of a short-term digital group intervention to relieve mental distress and promote well-being among community-dwelling older individuals during the COVID-19 outbreak: a study protocol. Front. Public Health **9**, 577079 (2021)
41. Zhang, Y., Zheng, G., Yan, H.: Bridging information and communication technology and older adults by social network: An action research in Sichuan, China. Journal of the Association for Information Science and Technology (2022)
42. Hill, R., Betts, L.R., Gardner, S.E.: Older adults' experiences and perceptions of digital technology:(Dis)empowerment, wellbeing, and inclusion. Comput. Hum. Behav. **48**, 415–423 (2015)
43. Arthanat, S.: Promoting information communication technology adoption and acceptance for aging-in-place: a randomized controlled trial. J. Appl. Gerontol. **40**, 471–480 (2021)
44. Campbell, R.J.: Consumer informatics: elderly persons and the internet. Perspectives in health information management/AHIMA, American Health Information Management Association **2**, (2005)
45. Lee, O.E.-K., Kim, D.-H.: Bridging the digital divide for older adults via intergenerational mentor-up. Res. Soc. Work. Pract. **29**, 786–795 (2019)
46. McGinty, J.M.: Developing a training program for digital literacy coaches for older adults: lessons learned from the train-the-trainer program. J. Educ. Train. Stud. **8**, 62–69 (2020)
47. Ozcan, P., Eisenhardt, K.M.: Origin of alliance portfolios: entrepreneurs, network strategies, and firm performance. Acad. Manag. J. **52**, 246–279 (2009)
48. Vargo, S.L., Lusch, R.F.: Service-dominant logic: continuing the evolution. J. Acad. Mark. Sci. **36**, 1–10 (2008)
49. Ngiam, N.H.W., et al.: Building digital literacy in older adults of low socioeconomic status in Singapore (project wire up): nonrandomized controlled trial. J. Med. Internet Res. **24**, e40341 (2022)
50. Wilson, T.D.: Recent trends in user studies: action research and qualitative methods. Information Research 5, paper76 (2000)
51. McDougall, J., Readman, M., Wilkinson, P.: The uses of (digital) literacy. Learn. Media Technol. **43**, 263–279 (2018)
52. Ogbonnaya-Ogburu, I.F., Toyama, K., Dillahunt, T.R.: Towards an effective digital literacy intervention to assist returning citizens with job search. In: Proceedings of the 2019 CHI Conference on Human Factors in Computing Systems, pp. 1–12. (Year)
53. Darley, A., Carroll, Á.: Conducting co-design with older people in a digital setting: methodological reflections and recommendations. Int. J. Integr. Care **22**, 18 (2022)
54. Bhattacharjee, P., Baker, S., Waycott, J.: Older adults and their acquisition of digital skills: A review of current research evidence. Proceedings of the 32nd Australian Conference on Human-Computer Interaction, pp. 437–443 (2020)
55. Choudhary, H., Bansal, N.: Addressing Digital Divide through Digital Literacy Training Programs: A Systematic Literature Review. Digital Education Review 224–248 (2022)
56. Park, H., Kim, H.S., Park, H.W.: A scientometric study of digital literacy, ICT literacy, information literacy, and media literacy. J. Data Inform. Sci. **6**, 116–138 (2020)
57. Terp, R., Kayser, L., Lindhardt, T.: Older patients' competence, preferences, and attitudes toward digital technology use: explorative study. JMIR Hum. Factors **8**, e27005 (2021)
58. Cerna, K., Müller, C., Randall, D., Hunker, M.: Situated scaffolding for sustainable participatory design: learning online with older adults. Proc. ACM Hum. Comput. Interact. **6**, 1–25 (2022)

59. LaMonica, H.M., Davenport, T.A., Roberts, A.E., Hickie, I.B.: Understanding technology preferences and requirements for health information technologies designed to improve and maintain the mental health and well-being of older adults: participatory design study. JMIR Aging **4**, e21461 (2021)
60. Mesko, B., Győrffy, Z., Kollár, J.: Digital literacy in the medical curriculum: a course with social media tools and gamification. JMIR Med. Educ. **1**, e4411 (2015)
61. Weibert, A., Randall, D., Wulf, V.: Extending value sensitive design to off-the-shelf technology: lessons learned from a local intercultural computer club. Interact. Comput. **29**, 715–736 (2017)

Author Index

Printed in the United States
by Baker & Taylor Publisher Services